CANADIAN SPORT
Sociological Perspectives

CANADIAN SPORT
Sociological Perspectives

Richard S. Gruneau
John G. Albinson

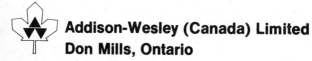

Addison-Wesley (Canada) Limited
Don Mills, Ontario

READING, MASS.: LONDON: AMSTERDAM: SYDNEY: TOKYO

Canadian Cataloguing in Publication Data

Main entry under title:

Canadian sport

English or French.
Includes bibliographies.

ISBN 0-201-02629-5 pa.

1. Sports – Canada. 2. Sports – Social aspects –
Canada. I. Gruneau, Richard S., 1948-
II. Albinson, John G., 1940-

GV585.C35   796'.0971   C76-017068-1

Copyright © 1976 by Addison-Wesley (Canada) Limited.
Published simultaneously in the United States.

ABCDEFGH   81079876

Printed in Canada

Acknowledgments

Les Canadiens Francais et Les Grands Jeux Internationaux first appeared in *Mouvement*, 7(1-2): 81-91, 1972. The original authors were Fernand Landry, Roger Boileau, and Yves Trempe. M. Boileau was responsible for the revised version which is included in the present book.

Ascription and Position: A Comparative Analysis of "Stacking" in Professional Football (Donald W. Ball) is reprinted from *The Canadian Review of Sociology and Anthropology*, Volume 10, 1973, by permission of the author and publisher.

The Economics of the National Hockey League (J.C.H. Jones) is reprinted from *The Canadian Journal of Economics*, February 1969.

Sports and Recreation in Communities of Single Industry is reprinted from *Minetown, Milltown, Railtown* by Rex Lucas by permission of University of Toronto Press.

Sports and the Career in Crestwood Heights is reprinted from *Crestwood Heights* by John R. Seeley, R. Alexander Sim, and Elizabeth W. Loosley by permission of University of Toronto Press.

Academic-athletic-popularity syndrome in the Canadian High School society (David Friesen) is reprinted from *Adolescence* Volume III (1) 39-52, by permission of the author.

The Legitimation of Violence: Hockey Players' Perceptions of their Reference Group's Sanctions for Assault (Michael D. Smith) is reprinted from *The Canadian Review of Sociology and Anthropology* Volume 12 (1), 1975, by permission of the author and publisher.

Legitimate Deviance and Social Class:Bar Behaviour during Grey Cup Week (Alan Listiak) is reprinted from *Sociological Focus* Volume 7 (3) Summer 1974, 13-44, by permission of the author.

CONTENTS

Preface

Despite its rather striking social and cultural importance, sport has been virtually ignored by the mainstream of Canadian sociology. At this writing, not one of the current spate of texts and readers on the sociology of Canadian society contains so much as a single chapter or article where sport is discussed in any detail. One can only presume that established Canadian sociologists have viewed sport as being too trivial to contribute to the "higher earnestness" of their professional calling. It is encouraging to note however, that within the last few years, growing numbers of researchers have suddenly recognized the social significance of sport as a legitimate area of scholarly concern. Indeed, the surge of interest in the nature and functions of sport as an institution in Canadian society is presently stimulating a good deal of research, and has led to the development of a surprisingly large number of university courses which specifically focus on the sociology of sport in Canada and other western industrial socieities.

Motivated by such developments, we started work on this book with the vague intention of compiling a series of articles which might serve as a general introduction to the social dimensions of sport in Canadian society. However, it was not until we confronted the problem of just how to put such a book together that we began to realize how disjointed such a collection could easily turn out to be. Like the numerous American "sociology of sport" readers, a comprehensive but introductory collection threatened to be little more than a potpourri of popular journalism, social psychology, macro-sociological analyses, and highly specific empirical studies. Since we have always found the utility of such books to be limited by their disjointed and inevitably a-theoretical posture, our alternative was to create a book which was deliberately narrower in focus, but which emphasized articles containing data which might serve as a foundation for empirically grounded theorizing, and as stimuli for further research. In other words, rather than attempt to compile a reader consisting solely of previously published general literature in the area, we sought to create a book which could serve both as a text for sociology of sport courses, and as a general sourcebook for more in-depth data on sporting activities in Canada. In this task, we were fortunate enough to enlist the aid of several young, outstanding social scientists who either wrote original papers for the book, or else revised previously published works so that they fit in better with our editorial plans. The result is a book that is far less a diffuse overview of sport's social dimensions than it is a series of conceptually related sections containing research articles that are variations on closely connected sociological themes.

Not everyone will be satisfied with either our selection of material or the distinctly sociological perspective utilized throughout the book. Similarly, there may be some disagreement with the specific character of the interpretive stance that is frequently employed. We make no bones about stating that our perspective is fundamentally a critical one which views sport in the context of such public issues of social structure as unequal life chances, problems of rationalization and bureaucratization, and basic crises in human values. However, we feel confident that our depiction of sport as an institution largely conditioned by the material foundations of social life, and existing in a society that is far less perfect and consensually based than most Canadians conceive it, will prove to have considerable explanatory power. The plan for this approach is as follows:

In *Part One* we present two papers which provide an introduction to sport as an area of sociological study, and which map out many of the themes and perspectives that are developed throughout the book. These papers not only include attempts to suggest some of the main characteristics of sport in both a definitional and sociocultural fashion, but in them, the authors reveal a sensitivity to the complex relationships between sport and ideology. Many of the key points developed in this section are linked to a concern for basic problems of development and change in sports which are greatly contingent upon the manner in which sport has become institutionalized in modern life.

The papers in *Part Two* of the book outline specific examples of the growth and institutionalization of sport in nineteenth century Canada. Themes discussed in this section include considerations of the related processes of urbanization, industrialization and technological development, formal organization, and democratization, all of which are at varying times, prerequisites for, and conditions of, the transformation of sport from a "folk" and "elite" recreational activity to an important component of the contemporary institutional structure.

One of these processes—the democratization of sport—continues to be a major theme in *Part Three* of the book. Here the authors discuss sport vis à vis its relationships to basic elements of social differentiation in Canada, like social class, ethnicity and gender. Each author is concerned, in some way, with the degree to which the equality of opportunity for participation and achievement is a bona fide feature of the current sporting scene.

Formal organization provides the unifying theme for the papers presented in *Part Four*. With the institutionalization of sport, formal organizations have developed which attempt to bring order, continuity and rational purpose to certain sport forms. A major type of formal organization in sports has been closely tied to the market-place. That is, the transformation of sport into a commodity in modern times, has provided both a vast product market for sports consumers, and a labour market for athletes, which tend to be regulated by profit-maximizing organizations. Given such developments, the papers included in this section deal with various aspects of such organizations, including their goals and the manner in which their goal requirements condition the career lines of the employees who work within them.

If most Canadians are affected by economically oriented sports organizations in the realm of entertainment and sports consumption, their active participation in sport and recreational pastimes is likely to be organized around patterns of voluntary participation in non-profit organizations. Generally considered, voluntary participation refers to the widespread involvement of Canadians in activities at the national or community level through public facilities, social agencies, sporting associations, clubs, minor leagues and school programs. The papers in *Part Five* of the book all deal in some way with selected correlates of organized and unorganized voluntary participation in sports and recreational activities both in Canada generally and in different community settings.

Finally, in *Part Six* of the book, we turn to a consideration of the values which underlie the "moral order" of certain forms of competitive sport. While the approach in Part Five focusses on the degree of involvement of Canadians in sport and recreational activities and on the factors influencing socialization *into* varying forms of direct involvement, *Part Six* concentrates on the values that are reflected and possibly developed *through* involvement in certain activities. The implications of these values impinge on the consideration of a wide range of public issues that are of frequent concern to Canadians.

It will be apparent that all of the issues discussed in this book are highly complex and deserve much more extended treatment than we have been able to give them. Nonetheless we believe that the assembled contributions combine a useful collection of empirical data with a range of highly interesting theoretical interpretations.

We have benefited in this project from the help of a substantial number of people. Our contributors were continually helpful and understanding. John Loy provided initial and constant encouragement. Many people at Addison-Wesley Canada helped the project at varying stages, and put up with missed deadlines and our inexperience with manuscript preparation. Don Macintosh provided us with both moral support and the funds for badly needed secretarial assistance. John and Monica Preston and Dave and Paula Neice made their homes available for last minute editorial changes. Betty Schieck, Carol Boyle, Glenna Stevens, and Ann Jones typed sections of the invariably illegible manuscript. Alan Ingham, Marion Meyer, Richard Ossenberg, and Rick Helmes all contributed ideas, or commented on parts of certain papers, and Rob Beamish wrote parts of the introductions to sections four and five. We are grateful to them all. Finally, we want to pay special thanks to Lee Wetherall and Shirley Albinson who patiently listened to innumerable drafts and tolerated the time we spent working on the book with (moderate) good humour.

Kingston,   Richard S. Gruneau
February, 1976.   John G. Albinson

CANADIAN SPORT
Sociological
Perspectives

PART ONE

The Sociological Analysis of Sport

Introduction

There are few dimensions of Canadian society that are more myth-shrouded than sport. Stereotyped assertions about sport building "character", or representing the "democracy of ability" (to use de Coubertin's famous expression), or functioning to relieve social tensions, are basic tenets of conventional wisdom which sometimes bear only a fleeting resemblance to social reality. Unravelling such myths in an attempt to arrive at an empirically grounded interpretation of the nature and functions of sport in modern life is a key task of sociological analysis. But this task in itself demands even broader considerations: for there is little point in identifying the nature and functions of sport unless an attempt is made to assess the *meaning* of sport for the current historical period, and its relationship to the inner lives and broader life chances of a variety of individuals. By these definitional standards, it can be argued that the sociology of sport contains three basic orienting features: it is *critical* in that taken-for-granted assertions in the sport world are "tested" against factual evidence[1]; it is *contextual* in that sport is depicted as reflecting, and occasionally influencing, the social conditions which surround it (cf., Page, 1973:16)[2]; and it is *evaluative* in that some attempt is made to infer the meaning of the role that sport plays in defining the quality of modern life. A sensitivity to all of these features is reflected in the two papers which make up this introductory section. Together, the contributors—Richard Gruneau and Roger Levasseur—provide an introduction to the main characteristics of the sociological perspective, a review of basic definitions, and a thematic overview of some of the major theoretical problems in the sociology of sport.

In the first paper, Gruneau argues that most of the literature in the sociology of sport confronts three constellations of issues: (a) those surrounding the definition of sport; (b) those surrounding problems of development and change in sport; and (c) those surrounding divergent theories of sport's nature and functions in modern life and the realtionship of these theories to personal values and the research process.

Gruneau points out that sports are multi-sided characteristics of life which serve many and diverse interests of individuals and groups, and which take on a wide variety of individual and collective representations. In an attempt to make some sense of this variability, sport is defined as falling on a continuum which runs from unstructured "play" to more regulated and institutionally established "sports". Specifically, he concludes that *play* can be thought of as a voluntary non-utilitarian activity characterized by the freedom to innovate, by spontaneity and by a lack of (externally imposed) regulation; *games* are more rule-bound and formalized, take on collective representations and are based on combinations of elements including competition, skill, pretense, chance, and vertigo; and *sport* is at once a range of activities (including many game forms) which are instrumental, somewhat utilitarian, highly regulated, institutionalized and which feature some demonstration of physical exertion or skill.

Of course, there is a problem here in that any effort to define sport is invariably imprecise. While Gruneau's attempt at concept clarification is necessary for research purposes, the definitional statements presented should not be interpreted as always matching the complexity of the existing reality. For example, Carlton (1975) has recently emphasized that abstract definitions are not adequate to sufficiently weight the differing levels of "artistry" or "expressivity" which may surface in even the most highly rationalized and regulated forms of sport. At the same time, there may be considerable difficulty in establishing the degree to which such things as physical games (i.e., British bull-dog or free-the-jail) or certain forms of "leisure sports" can be accommodated to the definitional continuum which is presented (cf., Page, 1973:46).

One thing that Gruneau makes very clear however, is that any attempt at definition which ignores the characteristics which have surrounded sport's transformation from an elite and folk recreational activity, into a major institutional component of modern life, will be seriously deficient. In fact, he argues that the institutionalization of sport, and a range of related sub-processes, comprise the major historical themes which sociologists encounter in their efforts to comprehend the nature and functions of sport. These sub-processes include the *rationalization* of sport, and its reflection in sport's *commercialization*, increasing *technical orientation*, *bureaucratization*, and *democratization*.

Consider for example, the theoretical implications of only one of these sub-processes—the tendency for organizational structures and abstract standards in sport to become somewhat fixed and enduring, and thereby "external" to the player. As organizations develop and set rigid bureaucratic standards for performance and involvement, individual athletes tend to lose their autonomy and capacity to innovate. This is not to suggest that such structures and established patterns are monolithic and unchanging. In fact, as Page (1973:34) argues:

> A sociologically and socially significant feature of organized sport indeed, is the *combination* of the disciplined rationality of bureaucracy, rivalling at times that of the army, and the opportunity for display of individual talent, manifesting the quality of individual play.

Yet, what Page neglects to point out, is that there is some debate among sociologists over the degree to which this "other face" of bureaucratic structures can continue to exist, given what appears to be the increasing concern for technology, efficiency and rational production in sports organizations. Some sociologists (Magnane, 1964; Brohm, 1972; Roszak, 1972; Ingham, 1975) have argued that the bureaucratic structures are already so rigid as to produce highly alienating conditions in nearly all areas of the sporting world. Gruneau suggests that such an assumption is one of the characteristics of those sociological theories which are subsumed by what sociologists call the *conflict* perspective. From this perspective the loss of individual autonomy and the rationalization of sport must be seen as a serious problem. On the other hand, those sociological theories which are subsumed by what sociologists refer to as the *order* perspective, are less likely to accentuate the rigidities of sport's organizational structures or to see great crises in personal autonomy emanating from them. From the order perspective the *evaluation* of autonomy is less important than the *description and explanation* of the social and cultural functions that are fulfilled by sport when it is viewed as an institution in modern life.[3]

The distinction between order and conflict perspectives is a complex one that we will not discuss beyond the above example. It should be emphasized however, that assumptions from each of these perspectives are common features of a large number of sociological analyses of sport. This book is no exception, and it will become increasingly evident in the introductions to the remaining sections that many of our own editorial sympathies tend to lie with the "domain assumptions" of the conflict perspective.

In his attempt to explore the key structural, ideological and symbolic features of modern sport, Roger Levasseur also appears to be somewhat sympathetic to the conflict frame of reference. Levasseur notes that the definition of sport can be variously conceived as accentuating leisure, work, and educational components which may not be affected by the same social conditions. However, when specifically examined, sport can be seen to include five significant dimensions: body action; competition; the pursuit of excellence; regulation (the respect for rules); and institutionalization.

Body action simply refers to the accent that sport puts on the potentialities and efficiency of the human body. *Competition* refers to the basic framework within which relationships in sport occur. It involves the affirmation of individual or group superiority, and as a hierarchical concept demands organization and measurement. *The pursuit of excellence* manifests itself in a concern for technique and specialization. For example, Levasseur points out that the "skier" of old is now a "slalom" or some other specialist, or that the all-round sprinter is now a "100 meter man" (cf., Brohm, 1972:29). He goes on to note how the several "levels" of competition lead to professionalization and to the development of an athletic "elite" of skilled competitors. He suggests that this tendency is problematic for "fun" in sport, because "fun" is usually inimical to the notions of measured results, invidious comparisons and the ethic of progress and competition. Sport is, of course, also regulated by *rules* which define action within sporting situations. In fact, sport is not only regulated, but can be seen to possess the characteristics of an *institution*. In a manner similar to Gruneau's discussion, Levasseur points out that as an institution, sport has symbolic meaning for collectivities, a history, traditions and records, and organizations which regulate it and give it some degree of institutional permanence.

Levasseur concludes that sport as "leisure" and sport as "work" share certain structural features, but are distinguished by the levels of performance obtained in each. Nonetheless, he suggests that what usually happens in industrial societies is that the "professional" model of sport imposes its logic on *all* sporting activities. As an example he notes that the organization and style of the N.H.L. is the dominant model for hockey in Quebec.

The next part of Levasseur's analysis concentrates on the attempt to identify the principal ideological representations and symbolic significance of sport in Canadian life. To begin, he notes that sport is commonly believed to instill socially accepted values, increase health, develop character, and function for catharsis and cohesiveness. Yet he emphasizes that, in most cases, the ideological discourses of sports promoters and organizers which influence such beliefs, bear little resemblance to the existing reality. This does not mean that peoples' beliefs about such things are not real or that these beliefs do not have tangible implications. For example, Levasseur asserts that the widespread belief in the value of "fair play" and in the mobility potential of sport (the rags to riches phenomenon) lead to passivity and reduce the possibility of conflict between social classes. Moreover, by producing an "elite" of skilled athletes whose position is justified by "ability," meritocratic[4] standards come to serve as general models for mass involvement.

Finally, Levasseur attempts to assess the symbolic significance of the athletic "elite" in its broadest context. He suggests that the system which leads to the creation of such an elite is intimately connected with the standards of production and consumption that condition such a large part of life in modern times. Elite athletes are used to endorse products and mold the buying habits of the public. At the same time this process creates "authority" figures. As individuals come to believe that the system of rewards in sport is legitimate, and as they come to view prominent figures in sport as authority figures, the hierarchical structure of sport correspondingly serves to solidify the existing pattern of social and political arrangements. It may be that Levasseur overstates the ideological and symbolic impact of sport in certain cases. His interpretations are impressionistic and are not backed by any systematic data. Yet, whether one agrees with all of his conclusions, Levasseur's discussion will be of considerable use for anyone who is interested in the relationships between sport, ideology and contemporary life.

NOTES

1. In fact, a good deal of research in the sociology of sport has been initiated as a specific response to certain "taken-for-granted" assumptions about sport's social and cultural characteristics. Reviews of literature specifically relating to some of the more common of these assumptions are provided by Edwards (1973:317-330) and Snyder and Spreitzer (1975).

2. At the same time, there has always been a group of social scientists and philosophers who emphasize that sport stands "outside" ordinary life as some vague metaphysical "form" or as an expressive reality. Simmel (cf., Wolff, 1950) came close to adopting this position in his recognition that the "forms" of play become "independent contents", and similar depictions of an "unreality" thesis can be found in Huizinga (1955) and McIntosh (1960). However it should be recognized that this position has always faced certain problems. In the first place, definitions of sport's autonomous and independent elements have tended to be evasive rather than concrete. Second, the *emphasis* on sport's "forms", or aesthetic components, runs the danger of trivializing the importance of the social structures and cultures within which such forms develop. This is not meant to suggest that sport is merely a *passive* reflection of social life, but only that its autonomy can easily be exaggerated. An interesting overview of the conceptual problems involved with this issue can be found in Dunning (1971).

3. Order and conflict perspectives tend to include assumptions that are associated with dominant and counter ideologies in Canadian life. A highly readable introduction to the "image" of Canadian society that these ideologies variously portray can be found in Marchak (1975).

4. A definition of the term "meritocracy" and a discussion of some issues related to the term can be found in Gruneau's paper in Part Three of this volume (see footnote 1).

REFERENCES

Brohm, Jean-Marie
1972   "Sociologie politique du sport." In Ginette Berthaud et al. (eds.), *Sport, culture et répression*. Paris: petite maspero.

Carlton, Richard
1975   "Sport as Art: Some Reflections on Definitional Problems in the Sociology of Sport." Paper presented at the first annual meeting of the Association for the Anthropological study of Play. Detroit.

Dunning, Eric
1971　　"Some Conceptual Dilemmas in the Sociology of Sport." In R. Albonico and K. Pfister-Binz (eds.), *Sociology of Sport*. Birkhäuser Verlag, Basel.

Edwards, Harry
1973　　*Sociology of Sport*. Homewood: Dorsey Press.

Huizinga, Johan
1955　　*Homo Ludens*. Boston: Beacon Press.

Ingham, Alan
1975　　"Occupational Subcultures in the Work World of Sport." In D. Ball and J. W. Loy (eds.), *Sport and Social Order*, Reading: Addison-Wesley.

Magnane, Georges
1964　　*Sociologie du Sport*. Paris: N. R. F. Gallimard.

Marchak, Patricia
1975　　*Ideological Perspectives on Canada*. Toronto: McGraw-Hill Ryerson.

McIntosh, P. C.
1960　　*Sport in Society*. London: C. A. Watts.

Page, Charles H.
1973　　"The World of Sport and its Study." In J. Talamini and Charles H. Page (eds.), *Sport and Society*. Boston: Little Brown.

Roszak, Theodore
1972　　"Forbidden Games." In M. Marie Hart (ed.), *Sport in the Sociocultural Process*. Dubuque: Wm. C. Brown.

Snyder, Eldon and Elmer Spreitzer
1975　　"Basic Assumptions in the World of Sport." *Quest*, (XXIV) Summer.

Wolff, K. H.
1950　　*The Sociology of Georg Simmel*. New York: The Free Press.

SPORT AS AN AREA OF SOCIOLOGICAL STUDY:
An Introduction to Major Themes and Perspectives[1]

Richard S. Gruneau

Sport, as Eric Dunning (1972) has recently reminded us, is something that most people in western industrial societies take for granted. They live in a world where exposure to sport in one form or another is inescapable, but they rarely question sport's existence or see it posing problems which require anything more than superficial explanations. Sport is something that may be enjoyed, played, worked at, discussed or even disliked, but it is not something that is systematically analyzed, criticized or understood in its broader context.

Yet for some people, superficial explanations are no longer satisfactory. Their indifference has been replaced by an uneasiness about the kind of institution that modern sport has become, and by a desire to understand the causal forces underlying its development. Attendant to this, they have begun to suspect that many of the commonly-accepted "truths" in the world of sport are less fact than rhetoric, and that the authoritative pronouncements made by sports organizers, journalists and political figures, frequently amount to little more than a mystification of the existing reality. This combination of uneasiness, inquisitiveness, and scepticism, has stimulated their tendency to ask distinctly sociological questions about the nature, functions, and "problems" of modern sport.

The Sociological Perspective

Sociological questions are motivated by an interest in looking some distance beyond the commonly accepted, or officially defined, descriptions and explanations of human action. As Peter Berger (1963:29) has argued, the sociological perspective presupposes an awareness that human events have different levels of meaning, some of which are hidden from the consciousness of everyday life. For example, when the sociologist is told that sport builds "character" he or she will seek to understand exactly *what* character traits are developed in sport, and just how *ideal* they really are. Similarly, if told that recruitment into most sports transcends ethnic or class stratification, the sociologist would seek to "test" the accuracy of the claim by probing the degree to which equality of opportunity actually does exist in the sporting world. In other words, there is a prominant debunking motif inherent in the sociological consciousness (cf., Berger, 1963:25-53).

Sociology also includes the basic recognition that the *personal troubles* individuals experience in various and specific milieux, are often caused by social structural changes[2] (Mills, 1970:14-20). These changes in themselves frequently reflect important *public issues* that must be considered in their broader context. Personal troubles are private matters; they have to do with those limited areas of life which fall within the scope of individual milieux. Public issues on the other hand, have to do with matters that transcend local environments and suggest an importance for the overall quality of social life. Consider some examples from sport.[3] A young hockey player may experience personal troubles by getting involved in a brawl while playing, but when brawling becomes a normal and inevitable occurrence in minor hockey, then this may be an indication of a structural issue having to do with the institution of sport itself, and other institutions that interact with it. To use another example, if a housewife does not seem to be able to find opportunities for physical recreation pastimes, it may be little more than a personal trouble, but if the majority, or even one special group of housewives, cannot develop healthy recreational pastimes, and if this adversely affects their physical and mental states of being, then we may be dealing with an issue whose solution does not lie in the range of opportunities open to any one individual. Solutions must be sought in the very structure of opportunities in the society and in the nature of the differential role requirements husband and wife are required to satisfy in the traditional marital situation.

Examples like the ones above are useful, because they underscore key elements of the sociological perspective and suggest how they can be applied to sport. The *promise* of the sociology of sport as a legitimate subdiscipline can be expressed in a simple two-pronged assertion. First, that sociology can somehow play a role in *clarifying* the nature and functions of modern sport itself, and second, that through such analyses, our *overall insights* into the dynamics of human life and social organization will be simultaneously enhanced.

That there is no single path to achieving the kinds of insights in question here, is revealed by the notable differences in the scope and focus of recent sociological studies. As Page (1973) points out, studies have varied in *scope* from small group analyses of the internal workings of sports teams, to the "large and complex social patterns" found in such sports as basketball and football, and they have varied in *focus* from the functions of sport in agrarian and industrial societies, to the role of sport in human development. But, nearly all of the studies share a significant common denominator in their tendency to be "contextually" based. The "sporting scene as a whole or some aspect of it is viewed in the context of the larger historical, social and cultural setting, and the linkages (or functional interrelations) between this setting and sport are given special attention" (Page, 1973:16). What differentiates the sociological examination of sport from purely descriptive expositions, is the attention the former pays to relationships, especially between sport and other institutions like the economy or political system. Thus, the main thrust of the sociology of sport is not the attempt to make isolated remarks about "what sport is like" (although these are both important and necessary), rather it is the continuous effort to relate sport to general features of social organization in order to gain a more coherent and comprehensive understanding of institutional arrangements in the whole society and the place of sporting activities within them.

It would be misleading however, to claim that this definition of the "focus" for sociological analyses of sport exhausts the diversity of perspectives characteristic of the subdiscipline. For example, Ball (see his paper in this volume) has suggested that there are really *two* approaches to the sociological study of sport; one which uses "sport data" to address more general sociological questions—*sociology through sport*—and the other, which views sport as a social reality "sui generis"—*the sociology of sport*.[4] On the surface, this distinction appears a credible one precisely because it recognizes that sport is both socially relevant and inherently interesting, and therefore worthy of study for its own sake. But at the same time, it is a potentially misleading construction. First, the argument that sport can be studied as a reality "sui generis" might be taken as a denial of the role that "outside" material forces play in conditioning sport's internal structure and logic. Second, such a distinction can all too easily become a rationalization for the implementation of isolated empirical studies of sport without regard to their more general sociological consequences.[5]

In contrast to Ball's distinction, it can be credibly argued that, for all its specializations, sociology remains a discipline whose *prime focus is the overall understanding of social organization*. As Berger (1963:25-26) suggests, the term "society" refers to the object "par excellance" of the discipline. Along similar lines, C. W. Mills (1970) identifies the "sociological imagination" as the comprehension of history and personal biography "and the relations between the two within society." By this standard, when one seeks to examine a particular aspect of social life like sport, it is necessary to pose one's questions with specific reference to the broad nature of social organization and the human condition. When one asks what the current nature of sport is, then it becomes also necessary to ask about its relationships to social structure. When one asks how sport has changed over time, then one should also ask how it has been affected by the historical period in which it moves. When one asks what varieties of men and women are involved in the varying features of sport, then it is only logical to ask what the relationship is between these people and the general conduct and character we observe in the society at this period in time. In other words, the sociology *of* sport and sociology *through* sport are merely two sides to the same coin. *Both* are a necessary foundation for any attempt to grasp the totality of sport's relationships to, and relevance for, the structure and processes of modern life.

What kinds of writing have most clearly exemplified the exercise of the sociological imagination in the study of sport? Many of the best examples can be found in the writings of some of the "classical" figures in the social sciences. A sense of the sociological imagination underlay the cutting edge of Thorstein Veblen's (1899) satirical depiction of the role of sport in the life styles of the "leisure class"; it was the factor that enabled George Herbert Mead (1934), to recognize the relevance of baseball as a forum for exposure to the organizing principles of community life; it stood firmly at the core of Max Weber's[6] ability to see the relationship between the structure of games in feudal society and the maintenance of "traditional domination"; it has been clearly evident in Johan Huizinga's (1955) thoughtfully speculative insights into "Man the Player"; and more recently, it has been displayed in works like Clifford Geertz's penetrating analysis of the cultural meaning of the Balinese cockfight (1972), or David Riesman and Reuel Denney's (1969) graceful essay on football and cultural diffusion.

To be sure, this list is far from exhaustive, but all of the authors included have revealed in some way both the promise that the analysis of sport holds for sociological study, and the utility of sociological analysis in helping to understand more about sport itself. From these and other writings, it is possible to begin to identify a range of sociological themes and issues which describe the major problems and perspectives of contemporary "sport sociologists." The passages which follow provide a brief overview of some of these themes and issues as well as the theoretical debates which often surround them. The discussion is organized under three headings: (a) problems of definition; (b) socio-historical concerns; (c) divergent theoretical perspectives. In the first section I attempt to suggest what sport is—its relevant dimensions and components; the second section is devoted to a discussion of the major themes underlying the assessment of how sport has changed and is changing historically; and the third provides a cursory review of divergent theoretical approaches to the meaning of socio-historical changes, the current functions of sport, and the role of personal values in structuring our interpretations of them.

Problems of Definition

As Page (1973:3) has suggested, most conventional definitions of sport are misleading, if only because one of sport's most striking characteristics is its "multi-sideness." Sport encompasses a range of behaviour that runs anywhere from high art and human drama, to the journeyman tasks of athletic labourers; it can accommodate a deadly seriousness with the frivolity of unstructured play; and it sometimes combines situations of great symbolic significance with situations having little "meaning" whatsoever outside of the personal experiences of the participants. Nonetheless, for purposes of analysis, it is necessary to have relatively clear definitions for the various concepts utilized in the description of sport-related activities.

Concepts refer to the shorthand representations that are utilized in categorizing particular classes of objects, events and processes.[7] The clarification of these concepts, facilitates communication between writers by providing a common ground for the construction of explanatory theory. If concepts are overly ambiguous, it is virtually impossible to achieve effective communication and understanding. Because of sport's multi-sided character, and its association with a broad range of human activities, one of the most basic problems in sport sociology is the problem of definition. For example, it is commonly suggested (cf., Weiss, 1971; Edwards, 1973) that the terms *play, games,* and *sport,* represent "core" concepts which define the major characteristics of human physical activity. But what particular characteristics of human action does each specifically refer to? What are their differences and similarities (for example, are there any differences between the "play" of young children and the so-called "play" of highly-skilled athletes)? Is the cultural significance and meaning of play any different from that of games or sport? Attempts to answer such questions have contributed to a substantial body of definitional literature.

(a) Play

Nearly all theories of play fall into two categories. In the first, play is seen as behaviour that serves some important biological or psychological function like "the reduction of surplus energy" (Schiller, 1875), "preparation for life (Groos, 1901), or "recapitulating" the evolutionary legacy of the past (Hall, 1920).[8] In the second case, the dominant and defining characteristics of play are simply its freedom, non-purposiveness, and capacity to "liberate" individuals from the constraints of reality. In a sociological sense, both approaches are important, but their emphases suggest different issues and problems. Consider for example, the work of George Herbert Mead and Jean Piaget (see Mead, 1964:209-216 and Piaget, 1962). While the methods and assumptions of these writers varied greatly, each sought to explore the role of play in the process of personality development and childhood socialization. In their work, play is depicted as a psychologically and sociologically relevant feature of human life by virtue of its functional and symbolic consequences for the genesis of personality, and the "self." But, neither Mead nor Piaget attempted to define the broader socio-cultural characteristics of play, or suggest the interconnections between different forms of play and their historical settings. Moreover, given their social-psychological concerns, neither author attempted to reveal the degree to which "play" is an evident feature of institutionalized games or sport itself.

Writers who have focused on the liberating aspects of play, have necessarily committed themselves to broader conceptualizations in order to clarify exactly what it is that play liberates people from. Immanuel Kant (1960:68) for one, contrasted unmotivated play which is "pleasant in itself," with work which "is undertaken for the sake of the end in view." Yet, the liberation thesis, in expanded and somewhat modified form, has been given its most graphic expression in Johan Huizinga's remarkable book *Homo Ludens: A Study of the Play Element in Culture*. Writing in the 1940's, Huizinga was critical of previous theories of play for their concentration on biological and psychological functions. He emphasized that previous theories had actually tended to leave unstated what play was, what it meant for the player, and its vital significance as a basis for culture (cf. McIntosh, 1960:116-122).[9]

In common with the "liberation thesis," Huizinga noted that all play was "first and foremost . . . voluntary activity" (Huizinga, 1955:7). He not only saw play as "free" but also as standing "outside ordinary life, and being "not serious"[10] even though it absorbed the player completely. Further dimensions of play included the following:

> It is an activity connected with no material interest, and no profit can be gained by it. It proceeds within its own proper boundaries of time and space according to fixed rules and in an orderly manner. It promotes the formation of social groupings which tend to surround themselves with secrecy and to stress their differences from the common world by disguise or other means. (Huizinga, 1955:13)

But, despite Huizinga's recognition that play consists of several dimensions, it should be emphasized that he saw the major characteristic of play behaviour as *freedom from restraint* (cf., Dunning, 1972:4).[11] Accompanying freedom from restraint is the freedom to innovate, and Huizinga saw innovation as a cornerstone of culture. Implicit in this, and in contradistinction to other "liberation" theorists, is the assertion that the play impulse is not restricted to game-like activities, but as a mainstay of civilization, has always been manifest in *creative* work. Paradoxically, Huizinga emphasized how most forms of organized sport had to be seen as *the antithesis of play*. As life in modern societies became increasingly regulated and routinized, and as play forms became "serious" and almost completely oriented to production, Huizinga felt that the capacity for innovation was reduced and that sports could no longer be depicted as truly representing the human play-impulse. He concluded that: "In the case of sport we have an activity nominally known as play but raised to such a pitch of technical organization and scientific thoroughness that the real play-spirit is threatened with extinction" (Huizinga, 1955:199).[12]

Whatever may be said about Huizinga's conclusions, there can be no contesting that the imagination and sense of historical vision which underlay *Homo Ludens* has few parallels. At the same time, it is important to note that not all of Huizinga's definitional assertions about play have been universally accepted. Weiss (1971) for one, has argued that play need not proceed according to rules, and that play can often be far more "serious" than Huizinga was willing to admit. In another case, Roger Caillois (1969:45) has argued that Huizinga's definition is both too broad and too narrow. It is too broad, because Huizinga implies that all play has an element of secrecy and mystery, when in fact, play is often ostentatious. It is too narrow, because by suggesting that play contains no material interest, Huizinga cannot explain betting and "games" of chance (cf., McIntosh, 1960). However, such criticisms do not attack Huizinga's basic thesis (i.e. that play is free from restraint) and Caillois retained much from Huizinga's basic position when he came to define play himself. Caillois defined play as "free, separate, uncertain, unproductive, and governed by both make believe and rules" (Caillois, cited in Edwards, 1973).

(b) Games

The real virtue of Caillois' work is that he goes beyond the notion of play and specifically attempts to define and classify the components of games. Unlike play (although the play element may be present in all games), games are more formally rulebound and structured.[13] Mead (1964:216-228) for example, argued that games differed from play by virtue of their level of organization. A child plays at specific roles like being a mother, a teacher, or a policeman, and attempts to understand and mimic the expected behaviours in each individual case, but in a game it is necessary to internalize the broader patterns of expectation concerning the roles of every other player. Thus, through the necessity of learning the formal and informal rules of games, and the tasks associated with particular roles (e.g. catcher or quarterback), game involvement features the onset of social responsibility (cf., Henricks, 1974). In a fashion similar to this, Caillois saw all game forms as being organized along a continuum running from the spontaneous activities of children to the organized play of adults, or as he put it, from *Paida* to *Ludus* (cf., Caillois, 1961; 1969). Furthermore, he broke the components of games down to include games of chance (alea), competition (agôn), mimicry and those which stress vertigo (illinx). As Table 1 reveals, games of competition include such things as races and athletics; games of chance include gambling; games where mimicry is the main component feature pretense; and games where vertigo is central, feature the disorientation of height or rapid movement.

TABLE I

CAILLOIS' CLASSIFICATION OF GAMES

	AGÔN (COMPETITION)		ALEA (CHANCE)	MIMICRY (PRETENSE)	ILINX (VERTIGO)

PAIDIA ↑
 noise
 agitation
 laughter
 dance
 hoop
 solitaire
 games of patience
 crossword puzzles
	races
	 combats
	 etc.
	 athletics
	 boxing
	 fencing
	 football
	 checkers
	 chess
		} not regulated	*comptines*
			 heads or tails
			
			 betting
			 roulette
			 lotteries
			    compounded
			    or parlayed
				childish
				 imitation
				 masks
				 costumes
				
				 theatre
					children's
					 swings
					 merry-go-round
					 teeter-totter
					 waltz
					 outdoor sports
					 skiing
					 mountain-climbing

↓ LUDUS					

The limitations of Caillois' scheme are rather obvious. For one thing, it is somewhat difficult to place particular game forms at any one point in the taxonomy because of intra-game variability. For example, football is a competitive game that can be played in a spontaneous and totally unorganized fashion, or as a highly organized and serious form of work. Thus, when utilizing Caillois' scheme, one must always be aware that most games can in themselves be organized on a spontaneity-regulation continuum. A more serious problem lies in the difficulty of classifying games on the basis of external evaluations of their dominant components. The use of taxonomies may seriously limit an understanding of both the personal "meaning" that game forms have for the participants, and the symbolic "meaning" that games have for collectivities. Finally, as McIntosh (1960) has suggested, there is some difficulty in establishing how certain activities fall into the various categories. Games emphasizing vertigo for example, may subdivide within Caillois' classifications of competition and chance depending on whether resourcefulness or resignation is the dominant factor. Can we argue that ski-racing is more vertiginous than competitive or vice-versa? Similarly, what percentage of boxing is chance, competition or, (in the case of Muhammed Ali especially), even mimicry? Moreover, at what point may we refer to particular game activities as sports?

(c) Sport

Attempts to clarify the conceptual elements of the term sport are complicated by the fact that sport appears to subsume certain elements of both play *and* games. However, as a general rule, when social scientists use the term sport they are referring to an activity which demands the demonstration in competition (whether against human competitors, the clock or such impersonal foes as mountain peaks, (cf., Talamini and Page, 1973:43), of some kind of physical exertion and skill. Additionally, their discussion is often framed in the context of the play-sport polarity that was detailed by Huizinga in *Homo Ludens*. Thus, sport as distinct from play, refers to competitive activities involving physical skills which are *oriented to specific ends, more instrumental than expressive, highly rational and subject to the influence of recorded histories and traditions* (refer to the discussion of institutionalization in the next section of this essay). For instance, Lüschen (1970:85) has argued that:

> Sport is a rational, playful activity in interaction, which is extrinsically rewarded. The more it is rewarded, the more it tends to be work; the less, the more it tends to be play.

By referring to work, Lüschen introduces an additional concept. Implicit in his suggestion is that the line between sport and work (or sport *as* work) is sometimes difficult to draw. But for purposes of clarity, I want to ignore the issue of work for this discussion, and arrange play and sport as the polar extremities of the continuum. Alan Ingham (in personal communication) has recently outlined a scheme which accentuates the progressive regulation, formalization and rationality that underlies movement along the continuum running from play to sport (see Figure 1). As Ingham and Loy have noted (1973), play forms become more formalized games through habituation, and specific game forms then become institutionalized as sports.

FIGURE 1

PLAY, GAMES AND SPORT: A DEFINITIONAL CONTINUUM

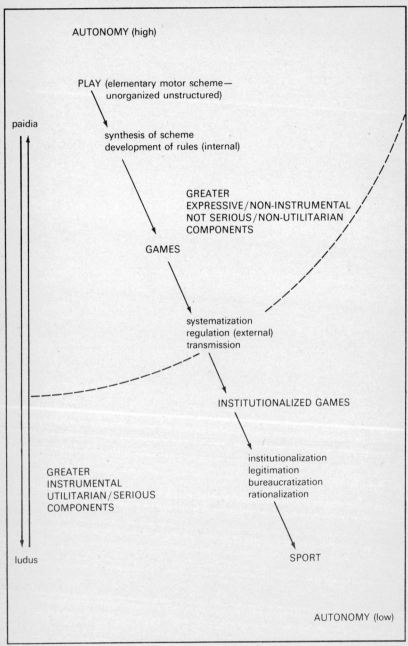

In summary, it must be admitted that there are some ambiguities in clarifying the definitions of play, games and sport. But, at the same time, it does seem that there is sufficient consensus in the literature to allow the sociologist to get on with the business of empirical research. *Play* is generally thought of as a voluntary, non-utilitarian activity characterized by the freedom to innovate, by spontaneity and by a lack of (externally imposed) regulation. *Games* are more rule-bound and formalized, take on collective representations, and are based on combinations of elements, including competition, skill, pretense, chance and vertigo. *Sport* is at once a range of activities (including many game forms) which are instrumental, somewhat utilitarian,[14] highly regulated, institutionalized, and which feature some demonstration of physical exertion or skill. One final note on conceptual clarification, concerns differences in *types* of sport that periodically occur in sociological literature. "Leisure-sports" refer to those activities like recreational fishing, snow-mobiling, swimming or tennis, which are not necessarily oriented to outcome or production as their prime function. Specifically "competitive sports" on the other hand are always oriented toward outcomes and production (i.e. skill mastery or winning) as a prime function. While the categories are not mutually exclusive, there do seem to be important variations in their degrees of regulation, organization, and purposes.[15]

Socio-historical Concerns

Much of modern sport continues to retain a strong play element, but in many ways the history of sport in the western industrial societies has been a history of its association with the changing social conditions of the capitalist industrial complex, and with the increasing values placed on organization, achievement, performance, and the mastery of technique. As suggested earlier in this essay, Huizinga was perceptive enough to recognize this transformation, and he built a concern for historical changes into his conceptual distinctions between play and sport as each existed in specific historical periods. Such an approach, although historically based, is certainly not at odds with the general scope and methods of sociological analysis. In fact, an interest in the identification of the dominant organizing principles of particular historical periods, and the analysis of their effects on institutional arrangements in those periods, is central to what C. Wright Mills (1960) has called the "classical" tradition in sociology.

There is some credibility in the assertion that most "classical" problems in sociology are intimately connected to one basic historical transformation: the transition of the social and cultural dimensions of life in feudal society to those which have come to characterize the rise of the modern industrial state (Mills, 1970). It was a concern for this transformation that dominated the thoughts and writings of sociologists like Karl Marx, Emile Durkheim and Max Weber, and it permeates such typological distinctions as Durkheim's *mechanical and organic solidarity*; Weber's *traditional and rational* modes of social and economic organization; Ferdinand Toennies' *Gemeinschaft and Gesellschaft*; and Robert MacIver's *communal and associational* relationships.[16] All of these ideal-typical conceptions of social change emphasize a shift from intimate, communally based, non-utilitarian sets of social structural relations, to more contractually based, individualistic and utilitarian patterns of social organization. Commenting on the differences between Gemeinschaft and Gesellschaft as typical of such transformations, Ingham (1975:345) notes that:

> *Gemeinschaft* is used to describe a form of social organization which is backward looking (based upon tradition), intimate (blood-linked), communal (actions are performed for the collectivity), relatively homogeneous (little division of labour), and in which work is viewed as life-activity. On the other hand, *gesellschaft* is used to describe a form of social organization which is forward looking (suffers from an illusion of progress, to use an idea of Sorel), loose (the most intimate bonding being the nuclear family), personal (actions are performed for one's own status or pecuniary enhancement), relatively heterogeneous (specialization has engendered an increasing division of labour), and in which work has become a means to an end (the acquisition of abstracted commodities which have universal exchange value, e.g. money).

The degree which social changes in sport have paralleled the transformation suggested by the above distinctions, is an issue which encompasses some of the most basic questions that must be asked about the current relationship of sport to social organization. Perhaps the most important of these questions concerns the very processes whereby sport has become *institutionalized* in the form that we now experience it.

Institutions in society, are distinctive patterns of social action which act as regulatory agencies shaping the contours of human choices and behaviours, and providing recognized, established, and legitimated ways of pursuing some activity (MacIver and Page, 1949; Gerth and Mills, 1964; Berger, 1963; Bierstedt, 1970). The process of institutionalization, as Blau (1964) notes, is usually initiated when basic patterns of action and associated values become so important to people that they seek their preservation in formalized arrangements that can be passed on to successive generations. In sport, the process of institutionalization has involved:

(a) the establishment of rules to be consistently followed so that *particularistic* game forms could become codified, formalized and more *universalistic* in character; and (b) the establishment of *formal organizations* which could regulate the shape of sporting activities and keep official records and histories. In accordance to this process, sport has become increasingly systematized, regulated and separated from spontaneous individual action (cf., Ingham and Loy, 1973). Hockey is not played with just any stick, but with a stick of specified material and dimensions. Players do not skate randomly, but as parts of a formalized division of labour. In other words, sports are not merely played (sic) but must be played "correctly." The structure of the game becomes increasingly "external" to the players.[17]

Another aspect of the process of institutionalization involves the necessity for existing patterns to be *legitimated* as they are passed on, through socialization, to children. For it is only through such a process that an institution can derive its historical reality. In literate societies like our own, this "reality" is transmitted and legitimated through the formal educational system, written records, literary works, and documents which embody the basic history of the institution, and the traditions and values often associated with it.

All of this is interesting enough, but the real issue here—or at least the one that frequently concerns people interested in sociological questions—involves an assessment of the *content* of the legitimated patterns, a concern over the degree to which the processes attendant to institutionalization actually do reflect changes from past situations, and the degree to which the changes that have occurred can be subsumed within the sociological typologies so commonly used to describe the transition from "traditional" to "modern" society. At first sight, it seems that the current dimensions of modern sport fit such models quite well. As Kando argues (1975:231):

> What both laymen and serious students of sport have in common is an awareness that words like professionalization, specialization, rationalization, bureaucratization, commercialization, organization and institutionalization, grasp well some of sport's most central tendencies.

But, one should keep in mind that this is not an exact statement of specific cases so much as a broad historical generalization. It is appealing because it encapsulates some of the most distinguishable features of sport and because it is compatible with generally accepted typologies suggesting how modern sport differs significantly from the less organized and less regulated play, game, and sport forms associated with the past. While there is certainly more than a small element of truth in this latter assumption, there is some danger in forgetting that typological distinctions between Gemeinschaft and Gesellschaft are simplified ideal types whose usage can obscure an understanding of key issues, unless the usage is guided by certain caveats.[18] For example, Huizinga's argument that medieval societies were "brimful of play" is largely based on the assumption that these societies worked on a system of mutual obligation (as opposed to a contractual system) and were somewhat free from the degree of regulation that we experience today. However, this idyllic depiction of feudal life should not be taken to suggest that brutally exploitative relationships between feudal lord and vassal did not co-exist with the system of mutual obligation, or that highly serious or nationalized sporting activities (often in the shape of paramilitary training) did not exist as well. Similarly, while we might agree with the basic principle of Huizinga's (1955:197) assertion that: "Now with the increasing systematization and regimentation of sport, something of the pure play quality is lost"—the assertion does not necessarily suggest that the Gesellschaft model is universally applicable to the modern scene.

The point is, that despite their utility, such models, and the processes which they represent, should not be reified. In fact, they often take the manner in which sport has been affected by the variety of sub-processes thought to be associated with its institutionalization as *given*, when this should really be seen as *problematic*. On the other hand, what models like Gemeinschaft and Gesellschaft help us to do, is identify those sub-processes which reflect the most striking characteristics of specific historical periods, and which have contributed, in some degree, to the structure and logic of sport as an institutional component of modern life. Of these sub-processes, one of the most influential has been the *rationalization* of sport (cf., Ingham, 1975).

Generally considered, the term rationalization refers to a process whereby action pursued in an affective manner as an end in itself and guided by traditional values or sentiment, becomes transformed into action that is oriented to particular ends in a secular atmosphere of efficiency and production.[19] As Gerth and Mills (1958) note, rationalization refers to a demystification of the world embodied in the move from *subjectivist* states and explanations, to calculating *objective* ones. Thus, Karl Marx saw the development of rational thought as a precondition for the rise of capitalist industrialism, and Max Weber detailed its later dominance in economic and political life as the cornerstone of bureaucratic organization.

It is not relevant for present purposes to engage in an extended analysis of the concept of rationalization and the various ways it has been understood in the writings of social scientists; it will perhaps suffice to recognize that in its broadest sense, modern sport appears as an increasingly rationalized activity that seems greatly caught up in the bureaucratic principles of economic production and political organiza- tion. To the degree that sport has been affected by the bureaucratized, rational calculation of big business and big government, it has become more structured and less play-like than in the past. Specifically, this change appears to have manifested itself in four ways which define the contours of sport as a modern institution: (a) the *commercialization* of sport and its increasing orientation to production and patterns of con- sumption; (b) the dominance of *technical efficiency* as a standard for "enjoyment" and achievement in sport (the Howie Meeker syndrome?); (c) the *bureaucratization* of sport, in order that universalistic standards can be maintained, and organized programs can be efficiently adminis- tered; and (d) at least some *democratization*, as sport has become organ- ized more on achievement criteria than ascriptive ones.

These rationalistic dimensions of the institutionalization of sport all represent key socio-historical themes. The shape of modern sport is largely a reflection of these themes but it is a reflection that people interpret in different ways. Debates over the current level of commer- cialization, about the degree to which sport has become democratized, and about the problems of bureaucratization, or the hegemony of techn- ocratic values, continue to define much of the literature in sport sociol- ogy (cf., Ingham and Loy, 1973; Page, 1973: 14-37; Kando, 1975:230-243; Gruneau, 1975; Ingham, 1975).

Divergent Theoretical Perspectives and the Problem of Values

The specific implications of the socio-historical themes discussed above, are frequently understood from the standpoint of sociological theory.[20] *Sociological theory* defines one's efforts to make sense out of factual information by suggesting ways in which research findings of one type can be related to findings of other types in a fashion which can be empirically examined. Theory guides research by suggesting patterns of relationships that may not be immediately obvious, but can be derived from factual information that is already collected, and it provides frame- works which are useful in interpreting the wider implication of specific data. However, there is some debate in sociology about exactly *what* may be considered legitimately as theory, and about the role that theory should play both in personal life and in the sociological enterprise. With the development of substantial sociological interest in sport over the last two decades, it has been only natural that aspects of such a debate have been reflected, on a smaller scale, by conflicts within the sociology of sport as well (cf., Loy and Kenyon, 1969; Scott, 1972; Hoch, 1972; Kenyon, 1974; Loy and Seagrave, 1974; and Melnick, 1975). An accurate understanding of these conflicts, demands at least some discussion of the broader debates they represent.

Sociologists tend to approach their subject matter and research in two ways. One group takes the position that sociology should try to be as much like the natural sciences as possible. They suggest that social phenomena can be considered as *positive measurable data* which can be subjected to objective "scientific" procedures, including the creation of deductive theoretical systems whose predictions can be empirically falsified. The other group, does not deny that theorizing should be empirically grounded, but they argue that the attempt to treat behavioural or cultural data as "social facts" obscures the important notion that "reality" is socially constructed and that interpretations of it (even social theories) are subject to the social and ideological configurations characteristic of particular historical periods. Thus, the degree to which the standard for sociological theorizing can, or should be cast in the model of the natural sciences is seen to be highly problematic.[21]

Yet, when taken in their extremes, both of these positions face definite problems. In the first case, the natural scientific model may lead to an overly mechanistic view of social structure. As John Rex (1974) has recently suggested, Emile Durkheim's argument in *The Rules of Sociological Method* that the notion of "value" in economics can be treated like any other "thing" in the universe and subjected to a series of "scientific" procedures, or George Lundberg's (1939) assertion that all social and cultural phenomena are merely physical, appear to elevate the spirit of mechanical scientism to an intellectual power. Similarly, the quest for social scientific "laws" of a manner similar to the laws of the natural sciences, has been dismissed by most knowledgeable writers as an impossible attempt to impose scientific rigor on a discipline whose methodological problems may differ considerably from the natural sciences. By the same token, the standard of "falsification" does little to develop an empathetic "understanding" of social phenomena, although it may be that this "understanding" is a perfectly legitimate and necessary component of sociological analysis.

In the second case, sociologists who have reacted to the "positivist" position in a strictly negative fashion have generally done so in one or a combination of two ways: (a) they argue that human behaviour cannot be analyzed in any form other than through an understanding of the processes by which individuals arrive at the "meanings" with which they evaluate society and structure their personal interpretive expressions of everyday life;[22] or (b) they argue that sociologists must at all costs make deliberate value judgements so as not to be merely the passive "scientific" technicians of the forces seeking to maintain the status quo. The first of these is an essentially methodological critique of the natural scientific approach to sociological explanation, and the second is an ideological criticism that has become central in the rationale for the desirability of a "radical" sociology. The former emphasizes that social data cannot be handled meaningfully (if at all) in a strictly "objective" manner, and the latter takes issue with the value-neutrality that ostensibly characterizes objective analysis.

But beyond certain levels, these alternatives to the natural scientific model can also be easily criticized. The first, through its concentration on the construction of the meanings surrounding the trivia of everyday life, runs the danger of rationalizing a withdrawal from the concern for the relationship between individual milieux and social structure. The second, through its deliberate attempt to be "radical" runs the danger of theoretical closure. Thus, where one reaction may become so a-political as to be meaningless, the other may become so deliberately political that research information is made to "fit" the orthodoxy being advocated. As I suggest later in this essay, the degree to which this latter phenomenon is completely unavoidable, is a rather difficult question, but it is certainly the case that the debunking motif in sociology should apply to all orthodoxies—even personally appealing ones. Otherwise, as Rex (1974) has emphasized, sociologists might as well wear uniforms and join churches.

There has been a great deal of confusion over these issues, and they have been stated and re-stated so many times that the original viewpoints of the "classical" sociologists whose positions are supposedly being represented have often been lost from sight. It is especially ironic, that if the positivist tradition in sociology owes much of its popularity to Emile Durkheim, the view that sociology must be "value free" has been usually attributed to Max Weber, a sociologist who continually emphasized the necessity of buttressing "objective" analyses of social conditions with more "subjective" attempts to "understand" their significance. Moreover, Weber came nowhere near advocating ethical or moral neutrality on the part of sociologists. He merely wanted sociologists to strive for the degree of objectivity necessary to resist the claim that personal value judgements can have some special claim to validity when given the trappings of "social science." Nonetheless, Weber did leave guidelines for action at the personal level somewhat unclear. Assume for instance that one's analysis of a phenomenon, some element of modern sport perhaps, uncovers a dimension that is obviously exploitative, or otherwise personally reprehensible. What then as a researcher is one obligated to do? Weber correctly saw the elevation of such questions to the realm of inquiry as highly problematic, and as easily leading to a level of ethical relativism that would make sociology nothing more than a branch of philosophy. But, he recognized that such questions remain, and we cannot wish them away by withdrawing into the comfortable world of "neutrality."

To a considerable degree, Marxism has offered more direct answers to the dilemmas posed above, for Marx always emphasized the *union* of thought and personal action as constituting the proper dimensions of inquiry. But as Giddens (1973:14) has noted, Marxism has also encountered rather obvious difficulties in seeking to sustain the claim to be *both* an empirically verified body of theory and a moral guide for political action.[23] Yet out of a combination of Marxist theory, Weber's methodological writings and the development of the sociology of knowledge, at least comes an important corrective to the dogma of a narrowly conceived empirical-analytic science. This simply is the recognition of the role that ideologies and vested interests play in contouring the kinds of questions and problems generally studied by sociologists, the categories by which they are studied, and the "domain assumptions" (cf., Gouldner, 1970) which underly them. From this, it can be argued that if decisions about what problems of modern life are worth investigating, the manner in which they are investigated, and the course of action to be taken, remain personal ones, the sociologist at least has the obligation to base interpretations on available evidence and to recognize both the normative assumptions and empirical limitations of specific theories. As Weber concludes (1949:81-82):

All knowledge of cultural reality, as may be seen, is always knowledge from particular points of view. When we require from the historian and social research worker as an elementary presupposition that they distinguish the important from the trivial and that they should have the necessary 'point of view' for this distinction, we mean that they must understand how to relate the events of the real world consciously or unconsciously to universal 'cultural values' and to select out those relationships that are significant for us.

In contrast to either Weber's sophisticated position or the methodological subtleties of classical Marxism, an influential body of early writing in the sociology of sport area defined the frames of reference for the subdiscipline in the context of a simplified natural science model of inquiry. Accompanying these definitional statements was an explicitly stated concern for the "problem" of value freedom in research (cf., Kane and Murray, 1966; Loy and Kenyon, 1969; Kenyon, 1974). In a few of these early writings, the concern for value freedom seems over-stated, but this is partially explicable by the historical conditions which have led to the "institutionalization" of the sociology of sport as a subdiscipline.

It is important to recognize that a large portion of the literature in the sociology of sport has come from the recently re-vamped field of physical education (cf., McPherson, 1975). Over the last two decades, the transformation of physical education from a profession, to a loose coalition of subdisciplines unified under such general titles as human kinetics, human movement studies, kinesiology or sport science, has included a widespread recognition of the necessity to *explain accurately* both the physiological and socio-cultural bases of sport. However, it became clear to many of the figures caught up in this transformation that accurate explanations of sport's social dimensions were greatly dependent upon the separation of research from the spirit of Rotarianism that had infused the traditional physical educator's approach to sport for over a century. Thus, when Gerald Kenyon and John Loy wrote their influential article "Toward a Sociology of Sport" in 1965, they emphasized that sociological analyses of sport should differ from traditional physical education by virtue of being "value free." As they put it:

> The sport sociologist is neither a spreader of gospel nor an evangelist for exercise. His function is not to shape attitudes but to describe and explain them.

Kenyon and Loy did not mean to suggest that researchers should not have personal values and opinions. Indeed, in a later essay Kenyon (1974) allowed that the "sport sociologist" may even be involved in "ideologically based social movements." However, Kenyon (1974:25) concluded that the degree to which research is fruitful depends upon the extent to which individual values can be held in check, and that this "non-normative" goal could only be attained through commitment to "the scientific method."

One might conclude then, that all Kenyon and Loy were really trying to suggest by their early guidelines can be summarized in two statements: (a) that individuals should try to control *a priori* assumptions about sport when doing sociological research; and (b) that science provides the "best" method for doing so. This seems fair enough, and it is certainly not incompatible with a main thrust of Weber's position, but it is also clear that Kenyon and Loy did not present their case as well as they might have. For instance, their failure to outline the various strengths, and especially, the *limitations* of the natural science model has resulted in their early guidelines being attacked as demonstrative of a narrow form of positivism rather than an accurate depiction of science (Scott, 1972; Melnick, 1975).[24] Moreover, their unfortunate tendency to use the terms "objectivity" and "value neutrality" in an interchangeable fashion, confuses different concepts and fails to distinguish between the necessity for maintaining discipline in problem-formation and research, and the issue of personal commitment. "Objectivity" and "neutrality" are not synonymous, as Weber recognized so well, and Kenyon and Loy's treatment of these concepts as such opened the door for so-called "radical" sport sociologists to criticize them for their lack of commitment to social problems and progressive change (cf., Scott, 1972; Hoch, 1972). Thus, Scott (1972) has emphasized that science is nothing more than a means to improve the human condition and that "value neutrality" in science necessarily commits one to the preservation of the status quo.

However, one cannot help but suspect that far too much has been made of this latter argument. The real danger of the uncritical acceptance of Kenyon and Loy's early guidelines is not the latent political implications that may or may not be directly involved with an imputed value neutrality, but rather it is the assumption that the "scientific method" and a specific set of research techniques themselves are a guarentor of objectivity—thus passing off research findings or theory which likely have a strong normative component as "objective" sociology. Of course, the same type of criticism can be applied to many of the deliberately "radical" analyses of sport in North America. Moral indignation and a commitment to progressive change are hardly guarantees of objective reasoning or even of factual accuracy, and the victimization of Marxist scholarship by a facile polemic like Paul Hoch's *Rip Off the Big Game* (1972) testifies to the dangers of commitment without content.

The point that is most often overlooked in discussions of the degree to which sociological study can and should be "value free" is that *any* action taken as a social scientist usually suggests some sort of ideological role. That is, a belief in, and the practice of, science itself can have ideological consequences.[25] In sport, as Ingham and Singh (1974) have so insightfully noted, the subjegation of sporting situations to "scientific" analysis imposes rational categories on the activity that are part of the broader processes affecting the development of modern life. The growth of physiological, psychological and sociological analyses of sport is but another symptom of sports rationalization. At the same time, the conventional and narrow interpretation of the scientific method as the necessity to identify all minute causal dimensions of behaviour in sport settings, carries with it an element of "liberal practicality."[26] Such an interpretation has led to an emphasis on scattered a historical studies, surveys and a religious-like belief that "all facts are created equal" which have all been compatible with the prevailing bureaucratic ethos (Mills, 1970).

On this point, consider the following personal example. While attending a recent meeting of a "Provincial Task Force on Sport and Recreation" I was informed that funded research in the Province should be geared toward the provision of "large blocks of machine readable data" which can be utilized in planning procedures. What is clear, is that such data and the usually accompanying belief that the causes of events are so infinitely complex that they can be best handled in a static quantitative fashion, is especially suited to the liberal ideal of piecemeal reform. It also carries with it a latent guide for political action. Not a conservative guide as Hoch (1972) and Scott (1972) would imply, but rather a liberal one. The liberal standard is committed to change but recognizes that if reality is infinitely complex, then we had best be careful about any action we plan to take. Presumably, if one is to be on the safe side, it makes sense from this perspective to change only one small detail at a time rather than advocate any major structural changes.

Even if the actual collection of those "large blocks of machine readable data" referred to above, were handled in a purely "objective" fashion, the process of research itself carries implications for personal values. This is especially true in the case of "applied" or "problem oriented research." The goal of "scientific" research as Kenyon (1974) describes it, is prediction and control. But for what purpose? It seems absurd to suggest that one can achieve a widespread consensus on what particular aspects of sport are problematic—for, as Mills states (1970) we cannot state a problem until we know "whose" problem it is. Thus, in one of his more reasonable works, Jack Scott (1971) has been critical of sport psychologists for their concern over how to "handle" problem athletes without asking whether or not the current structure and values of sport are problematic in themselves.

Along similar lines, it should be noted that the concern shown by some recreational specialists for the "rehabilitative" effects of sports participation on "deviant groups" rarely includes critical assessments of the social and legal structures within which the "deviant" labels are applied. To what degree can such programs be seen as "rehabilitative" or as unabashed agencies of social control?

The point is, that human beings do not approach the study of any aspect of society with a blank slate. In the course of his or her biography, each person develops a perspective which organizes his or her awareness, and which involves fundamental assumptions about the "normal" or correct operation of societal institutions (Connolly, 1973:13). These perspectives provide the frames of reference for our interests, personal and occupational moralities, and interpretations of problem issues, and it is likely that unless we are aware of their existence, our belief in science probably does as much to reinforce these frames of reference as transcend them.

If it is recognized that sociologists are not blessed with any special guarantee of objectivity in the course of their analyses, it becomes necessary to examine the kinds of assumptions that intrude on attempts to describe and theorize about particular phenomena. What happens for example, when empirical data seem compatible with more than one explanatory theory? As Connolly points out (1973:8), under conditions where more than one explanatory theory is compatible with the available evidence, "the investigator lacks secure and neutral ground from which to assess his moral commitments." It then becomes especially contestable "whether his theoretical posture reflects more the constraints of evidence, or his previous attachment to normative priorities congruent with that posture." But, what are some of the normative dimensions which impinge on different explanatory theories? Sociologists (cf., Horton, 1966; Lenski, 1966; Connolly, 1973; Marchak, 1975) have often argued that most of these dimensions can be classified into two distinct vocabularies of explanation whose underlying assumptions are rooted to dominant and counter-ideological positions in Western industrial societies.

The first of these, which John Horton (1966) has called the *order* vocabulary, is generally associated with most forms of political conservatism as well as modern liberalism. It emphasizes the primacy of *social systems* as the unit of analysis, and works from the assumption that socieites are natural, boundary-maintaining systems of action characterized by high levels of consensus on basic values. The order vocabulary places its emphasis on the problem of social and cultural integration, and it defines the study of system stability and departures from stability as the central problem for sociological analysis. From this perspective, consensus is to be expected as a "normal" state while dissensus is seen as dysfunctional for stability, and conflict and coercion need to be explained as "abnormal" features of social life. Stratification and social inequality are seen to arise out of the functional *needs* of social systems and are depicted as a reflection of the value system in those systems. The idea is that differential rewards in systems are a function of the degree to which men's abilities and performances measure up to the standards set by the society. The competition for rewards will supposedly guarantee that those with the most ability will rise to the top. Moreover, it is argued that since men differ in their innate abilities widespread inequality is inevitable.

The foci and normative underpinnings of the second vocabulary emphasize *conflict* rather than social order. From this perspective, the system is not seen as a reified entity based on consensual value levels, so much as a contested struggle for goods, services, power and privilege. Society is seen as nothing more than the creation of its members, and its social structure is only seen to be legitimate so long as it is adequately meeting the needs of all individuals. Stratification and social inequality are depicted as running contrary to human needs and to the maximization of human potential and as representing the "needs" of the upper classes more than the "needs" of the society. Thus, where the order vocabulary emphasizes cultural explanations of certain phenomena, the conflict vocabulary emphasizes material ones. Where the order vocabulary depicts system "health" as a major concern, the conflict vocabulary emphasizes that individual human needs surpass those of the "system." Finally, where the order vocabularly tends to view action as a derivative of the system, the conflict vocabulary tends to view the system as derivative of action. In Table II, some of the main assumptions of these perspectives are outlined in conjunction with a classification of their implications for studying sport.[27]

The analytical distinctions posed in Table II are necessarily simplified, and I certainly do not mean to imply that *all* theories in sociology can be classified within them. Yet, the assumptions of each, reflect major ideological positions that underly much of the writing in sociology, and generally contour popular *and* scholarly views of the key issues in modern life. As indicated in the Table, sport is no exception. For example, in the case of assumptions which can be variously related to certain elements of the order vocabulary, Kando (1975:233) has recently noted that three of five "major" approaches in the sociology of sport, are in some way, "functionalist" in focus[28]. That is, they concentrate on such areas as: (a) the role that sport plays in the process of socialization and the learning of culturally "appropriate" values; (b) the functional relationship between sport and work; (c) how sport might contribute to the functional "requirements" of social systems (cf., Kando, 1975: 233 for a brief review of literature associated with each of these approaches).

TABLE II ASSUMPTIONS OF ORDER AND CONFLICT VOCABULARIES AND THEIR APPLICATION TO SPORT

Order Perspective	Conflict Perspective
Image of Social Organization **(appropriateness)**	
1. The society is depicted as a natural boundary-maintaining system of action wherein individuals are shaped to existing patterns by virtue of the roles they are expected to play.	1. Society is seen ideally not as a creation separate from man, but only as a human construction. It is a contested struggle between groups with opposed aims and perspectives.
Analytic Focus	
2. As parts of a system each unit of society is analyzed vis-à-vis its relationships to the *whole*.	2. Focus tends to concentrate on individual human needs rather than those of the "system."
Major Problems	
3. The central problem of societies is system stability, thus transforming a concern for the *functions* and *dysfunctions* of particular units in the society into the major problem of sociological study.	3. The central problem in social life is the necessity for individuals to control the constraints that their creation (society) imposes on them. When the system is unresponsive to meeting human needs it must be changed.
How Order Is Achieved	
4. System stability (order) is a result of widespread consensus on individual role requirements and on the necessity for the maintenance of stability. Individuals learn appropriate values through socialization.	4. System stability in most cases is based on coercion and false consciousness.
Image of Deviance and Control	
5. System "health" is equated with existing values. When individuals act in a manner that runs contrary to the dominant value patterns it is usually an indication of system disorganization or "anomie."	5. "Health" is equated with unrealized standards. Society can become a structure whose dominant organizing principles separate, or "alienate" people from the "human" conditions of their existence.
6. *Social Control* refers to the mechanisms by which individual members who are anomic can be integrated back into the mainstream of social life.	6. *Social Control* refers to the mechanisms whereby individuals can organize to make those in positions of power in the society more responsive to the needs of the citizens.
Image of Social Inequality	
7. Some measure of inequality of condition is necessary to maintain the system as a going concern. The reason for this is that a hierarchy of rewards is seen as necessary to motivate the people with the most ability to get to positions of influence in the society.	7. Some inequality is inevitable but widespread inequalities in condition are inimical to satisfying human needs. Equality of condition and the equality of opportunity are not separate since unequal conditions become structured across genera-

TABLE II ASSUMPTIONS OF ORDER AND CONFLICT VOCABULARIES AND THEIR APPLICATION TO SPORT

Order Perspective	Conflict Perspective
The competition for scarce rewards ensures that this occurs. Thus there should be equal opportunity to compete for system rewards.	tions into social classes which limit the degree of equality of opportunity that can ever be achieved.

Dominant Values

8. The social good: balance, authority, order, quantitative growth.	8. Freedom as autonomy, change, action, qualitative growth.

Key Modes of Analysis

9. Natural science or empirical-analytic models: quest for general laws and repeated patterns gleaned through systematic empiricism; structural-functional analysis as organizing framework for data. Concern with objectivity and multiple causality.	9. Historical models, critical theories: quest for understanding through historical analysis and qualitative analysis; use of ideal-types; union of theory and practice; tolerance for unicausality, but generally assume dialectical causal processes.

Images of Sport in Society

10. Nominalistic interpretations (sport an abstraction cf., Dunning 1971), or sport as an "element of culture."	10. Sport is seen as a passive reflection of material foundations of social life (Vulgar Marxism), or as dialectically related to these foundations (Orthodox and Neo-Marxism).
11. Sport provides environment for learning important social roles and legitimate values.	11. Sport as play is inherently liberating, but is debased in its present form to reinforce values that are socially pathological.
12. Sport should be meritocratic. It has transcended class stratification through its democratization. Remaining differences in recruitment can be explained by "cultural" factors.	12. Sport should be more egalitarian. Democratization has yet to transcend class position. Differences in recruitment can therefore be explained by "structural" factors.
13. The logic of sport is depicted as stressing achievement and good character.	13. The logic of sport is depicted as stressing domination and elitism.
14. Sport is functional for social stability and order with some "dysfunctions." Some functions include its relationship to learning values and rules; social mobility; political solidarity; and catharsis. Dysfunctions may include such things as hyper-competitiveness, violence, etc.	14. Sport legitimates existing structure of social and political arrangements. It is a contributor to false consciousness (ie. an "opiate") and may reinforce conservative and/or liberal views. At minimum it encourages an a-political mentality.
15. Problems among athletes (ie. "problem athletes and how to handle them") are seen as anomic.	15. Problems among athletes are seen as reflections of alienation.
16. Standards for involvement include mastery of skill, achievement success and fitness.	16. Standards for involvement include joy of physical expression, fun and fitness.

The latter, macrosociological approach has been given its most graphic expression in the various writings of Günther Lüschen (1969;1970). Lüschen argues that sport can best be studied as a cultural subsystem of society which serves specific functions. He notes that the existence of widely agreed upon rules in sport suggests a large measure of normative consensus in social life. Because sport ostensibly reflects cultural values, it functions for *pattern maintenance* and *integration* at the level of the social system, and *goal attainment* at the level of the political system. That is, sport integrates members into the society through collective representations such as community teams and voluntary participation, and functions as a cohesive political force through a similar identification with international teams. Moreover, sport reinforces the learning of achievement orientations, aids in the learning of social roles and can serve as a *valuable* agency of social control. An obvious extension of Lüschen's perspective also suggests that conflicts, or "problems" in the sport world are often *dysfunctional* and need to be eradicated if system stability is to be guaranteed. If, for example, sport does not appear to be recruiting equally from all groups in a population, the order vocabulary would be critical of barriers that impede mobility and free completion for scarce rewards; its critical focus emphasizes the "equality of opportunity" rather than the "equality of condition." Similarly if "problems" develop in sport or are related to sport, they are likely viewed as the result of peoples' reactions to *anomic* social conditions. In this case the people need to be re-integrated into the prevailing system of values.

As a dimension of the order vocabulary, *structural-functional analysis* has occasionally been viewed as the "dominant paradigm" in sociological studies of sport (cf., Hoch, 1972; Melnick, 1975). Of course, structural-functional analysis does not exhaust the kinds of theories which might be subsumed by the order vocabulary, but it typifies many of the most striking features of the "order" frame of reference. However, to argue that structural-functional analysis itself has been the "dominant paradigm" seems to completely overlook the substantial literature devoted to the analysis of the "meanings" surrounding athletes' constructions of social reality (cf., Scott, 1968; Faulkner, 1974). At the same time, such an argument greatly underplays the rich tradition of Eastern and Western European Marxist scholarship which has continually provided major critiques of institutionalized sport in capitalist societies (cf., Brohm, 1972; Laguillaumie, 1972; Rigauer, 1969). These analyses, in common with some of the less rigorous writings of North American "radical" sport sociologists, popular writers and physical educators reflect many of the background assumptions of the conflict vocabulary.

The conflict vocabulary subsumes theories that depict sport as a reflection of the material rather than the cultural foundations of social life. As Pierre Laguillaumie (1972:32) argues:

> Le sport n'est pas un phénomène abstrait, un fait de culture en général, un acquis de l'humanité. Le sport n'est pas une entité supra-historique parcourant le cours des siècles. Comme toute réalité sociale, le sport s'inscrit dans le cadre de *rapports de production* qui déterminent fondamentalement sa structure interne, sa nature profonde.

Attendant to this assumption is the belief that sport is an *ideally* egalitarian institution that has been corrupted by the current structure of social and political arrangements. In its present form, the structure and logic of sport is viewed as creating the conditions for *alienation* among sports participants (Ingham, 1975)[29]; as epitomizing contemporary liberal ideology (Webb, 1969; Edwards, 1973; see also the papers in Part 6 of this volume); as retarding the political consciousness of individual citizens (Hoch, 1972; Brohm, 1972; Laguillaumie, 1972) and as reinforcing or legitimating the dominant value system. Fixed firmly in the institutional structure, sport is seen to be increasingly "external" to human action and needs, reflecting instead the basic categories of production and consumption which define life in western societies (cf., Brohm, 1972; Laguillaumie, 1972; Hoch, 1972; Vinnai, 1973 and Levasseur's paper in this volume). From this perspective, conflicts or problems in the sport world are not seen to lie with individuals, but in the very nature of the socio-political system that sport exists within. Thus, if sport does not appear to be recruiting equally from all groups in the population, the conflict vocabulary does not focus its criticism on the question of unequal recruitment, rather it concentrates on the problematic status of the widespread differences in reward associated with positions in the reward structure. These differences in reward are inevitably depicted as becoming structured across generations so that they always limit the degree of equality of opportunity that can ever be achieved.

Each of these sketches of the "domain assumptions" of order and conflict vocabularies is far from exhaustive. I have sought only to identify some of the main issues which allow one to differentiate between them, and have not attempted to suggest which represents the more "accurate" or empirically viable vocabulary.[30] On this question it will perhaps suffice to point out that theories associated with each vocabulary tend to address different issues and thereby have credibility within the framework of their own assumptions and in so far as they conform to particular ideological assumptions (like the "value" of equality, or the image of society as based on conflict or consensus). Our task is to be able to recognize our own moral commitments to the normative components of each, and then, through disciplined inquiry, test the evidence against the assumptions to reform our beliefs as best we can.

Summary and Concluding Comments

In this paper I have attempted to introduce some of the major themes and divergent perspectives central to the sociological study of sport. The discussion has been organized around three areas: (a) problems of defining sport and its sociologically relevant components; (b) the identification of key sociohistorical themes; and (c) the presentation of divergent perspectives on the nature of sociological theory, the relationship of theory to personal values and the implications of this relationship for analyses of sport.

In the first case, it was noted that there are basic ambiguities in any attempt to define sport, especially in the context of its relationship to the conceptual domains of play and games. However, for purposes of research, there appears to be a sufficient consensus on characteristics which can be utilized to differentiate sport from other areas of human endeavour.

In the second case, I suggested that the key historical themes surrounding sport's transformation from an "elite" and "folk" recreational activity to its more modern forms, can be located in its institutionalization and in the accompanying process of rationalization. Discussion and debate over the "stage" of these processes or their implications for the organization and character of modern sport make up much of the literature in the sociology of sport (for example see the papers by Levasseur, Gruneau, Curtis and Milton, and Albinson in this volume).

Finally, I argued that while sociologists can never be "value-free" (much less, value neutral), it is possible to develop theoretical frameworks from which to understand the nature, functions and problematic elements of sport in contemporary life. However, such theoretical constructions often carry important normative assumptions. Thus, it is important to be aware not only of the empirical limitations of social theories but also of the manner in which dominant and counter-ideological positions are being represented in a manner that may be fundamentally irreconcilable. This is not to imply that there are two competing *but equally legitimate* ideologically based realities rather than one empirically validated one. I have only suggested that writers carry domain assumptions into their analyses of social phenomena which generally contour their theorizing about what reality is like. The path to an accurate understanding of sport in modern life and the union of this understanding with personal action involves an encounter with just this point. Out of the encounter should come the realization that achieving the understanding necessary to precede action does not lie in either the mechanistic application of the natural scientific model of inquiry to sporting situations or in the attempt to construct a deliberately "radical" sociology of sport. Understanding lies in the identification of the linkage between personal values and the interpretation of evidence by viewing the several dimensions of one theory from the vantage point of another and then arriving at a conclusion. Simply stated, it lies in the reflexivity and critical "consciousness" of the sociological perspective.

NOTES

1. There are several good introductions to sport as an area of sociological study (cf., Loy and Kenyon, 1969; Dunning, 1972; Sage, 1974; McPherson, 1975; and Snyder and Spreitzer, 1975), however, with the exception of Page's (1973) graceful overview of the field, these tend to deal more with the historical development of the subdiscipline and with recent literature, than with the definition of basic concepts and the identification of major themes and theoretical perspectives. In this essay, I specifically focus on these latter concerns, especially where I feel they are relevent for thematically integrating the other material included in this volume. I am especially indebted to Alan Ingham for our many conversations over the years—people who are familiar with his work will recognize that much of the material I have included in the definitional and socio-historical sections, are issues that he has discussed in great depth on several occasions. The paper has also benefitted from the critical comments of John Albinson, Rob Beamish, Rick Helmes, Richard Ossenberg, and Lee Wetherall. Their constant reminders that this paper was being written at the introductory level prevented it from becoming another of my idiosyncratic exercises in self-clarification.

2. Social organization is made up of a variety of institutional orders organized around some particular function like political, economic, kinship and education systems. As Mills (1970:149) notes: "If we understand how these institutional orders are related to one another, we understand the social structure of a society. For 'social structure', as the conception is most commonly used, refers to just that—to the combination of institutions classified according to the functions each performs" (cf., Gerth and Mills, 1964).

3. The idea for the structure and style of these examples comes from Mills (1970:14-17).

4. This distinction is a common one in the sociology of sport literature. Loy and Seagrave (1974) have recently added a third approach which they refer to as "action oriented sociology of sport".

5. This is not to suggest that these problems occur in Ball's work. In fact, as his essay in this volume indicates, Ball is sensitive to the fact that the sociological perspective involves consideration of *both* the sociology *of* sport and sociology *through* sport.

6. See Weber (1968). Weber suggested that sporting activities played an important function in helping to create and sustain a system of ranks having a "traditional" ethos which helped to "bar the door to all forms of utilitarian rationality" (Bendix, 1962:364).

7. Background reading on *concepts* can be obtained in most of the research methods textbooks commonly used in sociology courses. In-depth discussions can be found in Selltiz et al. (1959) and Kaplan (1964).

8. For an overview of play theories see Millar (1968); Kraus (1971) and Ellis (1973).
9. Moreover, Huizinga did not see play as being a manifestation of culture but rather as a creator of culture. Play, Huizinga argues, is a "totality" (1955:3) that does not have "its foundation in any rational nexus". It is "older" than culture, and is not limited to the human species.
10. On the surface, this statement seems at odds with Huizinga's later recognition that play can be quite "serious" on occasion. The ambiguity lies in Huizinga's failure to define the term "serious". However, the key points that Huizinga seems to be trying to make are as follows: (a) play is "not serious" in essence because it is non-purposive; the act of playing is its own reward; (b) yet, because one type of play involves the *contest*, a winner and loser result, and rewards may accrue to the winner; (c) if the rewards and status resulting from play become more important than the act of playing itself, play has become "too serious".
11. I agree with Dunning completely on this point. McIntosh (1960) gets so caught up in the taxonomic and definitional elements of Huizinga's argument that he appears to lose track of the over-riding significance of "freedom from restraint" as the most sociologically relevant characteristic of play.
12. By way of background, it should be noted that Huizinga was a great student of feudal society (see his *The Waning of the Middle Ages*). In fact, his writing suggests a rather nostalgic view of the destruction of the system of mutual obligation which ostensibly characterized feudal times. Accordingly, there may be some credibility in interpreting his assessment of modern sport as a conservative reaction to the forces of industrialization and technology that grew out of the decline of feudal society and the rise of the modern industrial state.
13. Edwards (1973:55) defines the game as: "an activity manifest in physical and/or mental effort, governed by formal or informal rules, and having as participants opposing actors who are part of, or who represent collectivities that want to achieve a specific goal that has value beyond the context of the game situation that is, prestige, recognition, influence and so forth."
14. In a narrow functional sense, sports are decidedly non-utilitarian. The competitive swimmer is not swimming to a purposeful destination, the cyclist is doing more than using the bicycle for transportation. However, I mean "utility" here in a broader sense. To the degree that *sports* are defined in terms of status, rewards, and measured outcomes, they have a strong utilitarian component.
15. There are a myriad of related terms here like "contest", "recreation", and "athletics", but I feel that these tend to be peripheral to the terms I have chosen to discuss. For a review of some of these alternative terms see Edwards (1973) and Kraus (1971). Overviews of the definitional literature that are more in-depth than the brief discussion presented here, can be found in the philosophical discussions contained in Weiss (1971) and Osterhoudt (1973). A definition of sport which emphasizes sport's sociocultural elements can be found in Loy (1969).
16. Many sociologists have made a point of listing these distinctions in a manner similar to the way they are presented here. For some examples see Mills (1970) and Ingham (1975).
17. A discussion of this process can be found in Ingham and Loy (1973). The authors note that, as a result of the process of institutionalization, *a* way of doing things in sport, often becomes *the* way of doing things.
18. An excellent discussion of Weber's notion of "ideal type" can be found in Giddens (1971: 141-144).
19. "Rationalization" is a far more complex concept than this brief definition suggests. See for example, Marcuse (1964) and Habermas (1970). To date, the best attempt to examine the "rationalization" of sport can be found in Ingham (1975). For other examples see Rigauer (1969); Brohm (1972); Laguillaumie (1972).
20. For background reading on a wide range of approaches to the nature of sociological theory, see Rex (1961); Bottomore (1962); Kaplan (1964); Zetterberg (1965); Cohen (1968) and Nettler (1970).

21. For a more in-depth discussion of these issues from *both* sides, see Winch (1958); Popper (1959); Toulmin (1961) and Lakatos and Musgrave (1970).

22. In order to keep highly specific jargon to a minimum, I have used "personal interpretive experiences" as a substitute for the term "phenomenal". However, in this passage, I really mean "phenomenal" expression of everyday life, as discussed by Schutz (1962) and more colloquially, by Berger and Luckmann (1967).

23. And, as a result, Marxism has always tended to degenerate into straightforward positivism or alternatively, ethical relativism.

24. This is a somewhat unfair criticism given the fact that Loy and Kenyon's guidelines were aimed at an introductory audience. Indeed, the flexibility of Loy's position is suggested by his later work with Ingham (1973) and Seagrave (1974).

25. See for example, Habermas' (1970) discussion in Chapter 6 of *Toward a Rational Society*.

26. "Liberal practicality" is Mills' term (1970:87-112). My discussion of this element of sports policy has been greatly influenced by Mills' more general analysis.

27. This discussion of "order" and "conflict" perspectives has been greatly influenced by Horton (1966) and Connolly (1973). I am also grateful to Elizabeth Comack for suggestions on clarifying the distinctions between the two perspectives.

28. As an example of how assumptions may intrude on inquiry, even at the definitional level, witness Kenyon and Loy's early (1965) definition of the sociology of sport: "If sociology is the study of social order—the underlying regularity of human social behaviour—including efforts to attain it and departures from it, then the sociology of sport becomes the study of the regularity, and departures from it, of human social behaviour in a sports context."

29. For an excellent discussion of "alienation" and its differences from, and similarities to, "anomie", see Lukes (1974).

30. My position on the comparative efficacy of certain aspects of these approaches is detailed at some length in Gruneau (1975).

REFERENCES

Bendix, R.
1962   *Max Weber: An Intellectual Portrait.* New York: Doubleday.

Berger, Peter
1963   *Invitation to Sociology.* New York: Anchor Books.

and Thomas Luckmann
1967   *The Social Construction of Reality.* New York: Anchor Books.

Bierstedt, Robert
1970   *The Social Order* (3rd edition). New York: McGraw-Hill.

Blau, Peter
1964   *Exchange and Power in Social Life.* New York: John Wiley.

Bottomore, T. B.
1962   *Sociology: A Guide to Problems and Literature.* London: George Allen and Unwin.

Brohm, Jean-Marie
1972   "Sociologie politique du sport." In Ginette Berthaud et al (eds.), *Sport culture et répression.* Paris: petite muspero.

Caillois, Roger
1961   *Man, Play and Games.* New York: Free Press.

1969   "The Structure and Classification of Games." In J. Loy and G. Kenyon (eds.), *Sport Culture and Society.* Toronto: Macmillan.

Cohen, Percy
1968   *Modern Social Theory*. London: Heinemann Books.

Connolly, William E.
1973   "Theoretical Self-Consciousness." *Polity*, VI (1), Fall.

Dunning, Eric
1971   "Some Conceptual Dilemmas in the Sociology of Sport." In R. Albonico and K. Pfister-Binz (eds.), *Sociology of Sport*. Birkhäuser, Verlag, Basel.
1972   *Sport: Readings From a Sociological Perspective*. Toronto: University of Toronto Press.

Edwards, Harry
1973   *Sociology of Sport*. Homewood: The Dorsey Press.

Ellis, Mike
1973   *Why People Play?* Englewood Cliffs: Prentice-Hall.

Faulkner, Robert
1974   "Making Violence by Doing Work." *Sociology of Work and Occupations*. I(3).

Gerth, H. H. and C. Wright Mills
1958   *From Max Weber: Essays in Sociology*. New York: Oxford University Press.
1964   *Character and Social Structure*. New York: Harbinger Books.

Geertz, Clifford
1972   "Deep Play: Notes on the Balinese Cockfight." *Daedalus*, Winter.

Giddens, Anthony
1971   *Capitalism and Modern Social Theory*. London: Cambridge Press.
1973   *The Class Structure of the Advanced Societies*. London: Hutchinson.

Gouldner, Alvin
1970   *The Coming Crisis of Western Sociology*. New York: Basic Books.

Groos, Karl
1901   *The Play of Man*. New York: Appleton-Century.

Gruneau, Richard
1975   "Sport, Social Differentiation and Social Inequality." In D. Ball and J. W. Loy (eds.), *Sport and Social Order*. Reading: Addison-Wesley.

Habermas, Jürgen
1970   *Toward a Rational Society*. Boston: Beacon Press.

Hall, G. Stanley
1920   *Youth*. New York: Appleton-Century.

Henricks, Thomas
1974   "Professional Wrestling as Moral Order." *Sociological Inquiry*, 44(33).

Hoch, Paul
1972   *Rip Off The Big Game*. New York: Doubleday.

Horton, John
1966   "Order and Conflict Theories of Social Problems as Competing Ideologies." *American Journal of Sociology*, 71.

Huizinga, Johan
1955   *Homo Ludens: A Study of the Play Element in Culture*. Boston: Beacon Press.

Ingham, Alan G.
1975   "Occupational Subcultures in the Work World of Sport." In D. Ball and J. W. Loy (eds.), *Sport and Social Order*. Reading: Addison-Wesley.

and John Loy
1973   "The Social System of Sport: A Humanistic Perspective." *Quest* XIX, Fall.

and G. Singh

1974 "The Rationalization of Sport." A paper presented at the Annual Meetings of the Canadian Sociology and Anthropology Association, (Toronto).

Kando, Thomas
1975 Leisure and Popular Culture in Transition. St. Louis: C. V. Mosby.

Kane, J. E. and C. Murray
1966 "Suggestions for the Sociological Study of Sport." In J. E. Kane and C. Murray (eds.), Readings in Physical Education. London: Physical Education Association.

Kaplan, A.
1964 The Conduct of Inquiry. San Francisco: Chandler.

Kant, Immanuel
1960 Education. Ann Arbor: University of Michigan Press.

Kenyon, Gerald
1974 "A Sociology of Sport: On Becoming a Sub-Discipline." In George H. Sage (ed.), Sport and American Society. (2nd edition) Reading: Addison-Wesley.

and John Loy
1965 "Toward a Sociology of Sport." J.O.P.H.E.R. 36.

Kraus, Richard
1971 Recreation and Leisure in Modern Society. New York: Appleton-Century Crofts.

Laguillaumie, Pierre
1972 "Pour une critique fondamentale du sport." In Sport, culture et répression. Paris: petite maspero.

Lakatos, Imre and Alan Musgrave
1970 Criticism and the Growth of Knowledge. London: Cambridge Press.

Lenski, Gerhard
1966 Power and Privilege. New York: McGraw-Hill.

Loy, John
1969 "The Nature of Sport: A Definitional Effort." In J. Loy and G. Kenyon (eds.), Sport, Culture and Society Toronto: Macmillan.

and Gerald Kenyon
1969 "The Sociology of Sport as a Discipline." In J. Loy and G. Kenyon (eds.), Sport, Culture and Society. Toronto: Macmillan.

and J. O. Seagrave
1974 "Research Methodology in the Sociology of Sport." In J. Wilmore (ed.), Exercise and Sport Sciences Review. Vol. II. New York: Academic Press.

Lukes, Steven
1974 "Alienation and Anomie." In W. Connolly and Glen Gordon (eds.), Social Structure and Political Theory. Lexington: D. C. Heath.

Lundberg, George
1939 Foundations of Sociology. New York: Macmillan.

Lüschen, Günther
1969 "Social Stratification and Social Mobility Among Young Sportsmen. In J. Loy and G. Kenyon (eds.), Sport, Culture and Society. Toronto: Macmillan.

1970 "The Interdependence of Sport and Culture." In G. Lüschen (ed.), The Cross-Cultural Analysis of Sport and Games. Champagne: Stipes Publishing.

MacIver, Robert and Charles Page
1949 Society: An Introductory Analysis. New York: Rinehart.

Marchak, Patricia
1975 Ideological Perspectives on Canada. Toronto: McGraw-Hill Ryerson.

Marcuse, Herbert
1964 One-Dimensional Man. Boston: Beacon Press.

McIntosh, P. C.
1960   Sport in Society. London: C. A. Watts.

McPherson, Barry
1975   "Past, Present and Future Perspectives For Research in Sport Sociology." International Review of Sport Sociology 9.

Mead, G. H.
1934   Mind, Self and Society. Chicago: University of Chicago Press.
1964   On Social Psychology. Anselm Strauss (ed.), Chicago: University of Chicago Press.

Melnick, Merrill
1975   "A Critical Look at the Sociology of Sport." Quest, 24 (Summer).

Millar, Susanna
1968   The Psychology of Play. London: Penguin Books.

Mills, C. Wright
1960   "The Classic Tradition." In C. W. Mills (ed.), Images of Man. New York: George Brazillier.
1970   The Sociological Imagination. Middlesex: Penguin Books.

Nettler, Gwynn
1970   Explanations. Toronto: McGraw-Hill.

Osterhoudt, Robert
1973   The Philosophy of Sport. Springfield: Charles Thomas.

Page, Charles H.
1973   "The World of Sport and its Study." In John Talamini and Charles H. Page (eds.), Sport and Society. Boston: Little Brown.

Piaget, Jean
1962   Play, Dreams and Imitation in Childhood. New York: W. W. Norton and Co.

Popper, Karl
1959   The Logic of Scientific Discovery. New York: Basic Books.

Rex, John
1961   Key Problems of Sociological Theory. London: Routledge and Kegan Paul.
1974   Sociology and the Demystification of the Modern World. London: Routledge and Kegan.

Riesman, David and Reuel Denney
1969   "Football in America: A Study of Cultural Diffusion." In J. Loy and G. Kenyon (eds.), Sport, Culture and Society. Toronto: Macmillan.

Rigauer, B.
1969   Sport und Arbeit. Frankfurt: Suhrkamp.

Sage, George H.
1974   Sport and American Society. Reading: Addison-Wesley.

Schiller, Friedrich Von
1875   Essays, Aesthetical and Philosophical. London: George Bell.

Schutz, Alfred
1962   Collected Papers. Vol. I. The Hague: Nijhoff.

Scott, Jack
1971   "The Sport Psychologist-Friend or Foe." The Athletic Revoltuion. New York: The Free Press.
1972   "Introduction." In Paul Hoch, Rip Off The Big Game. Garden City: Anchor Books.

Scott, Marvin
1968   The Racing Game. Chicago: Aldine.

Selltiz, C., M. Jahoda, M. Deutsch, and S. W. Cook
1959   Research Methods in Social Relations. New York: Holt.

Snyder, Eldon and Elmer Spreitzer
1975   "Sociology of Sport: An Overveiw." In D. Ball and J. Loy (eds.), *Sport and Social Order*. Reading: Addison-Wesley.

Talamini, John and Charles Page
1973   *Sport and Society*. Boston: Little Brown.

Toulmin, Stephen
1961   *Foresight and Understanding*. New York: Harper and Row.

Veblen, Thorstein
1899   *The Theory of the Leisure Class*, New York: The Viking Press.

Vinnai, Gerhard
1973   *Football Mania*. London: Ocean Books.

Webb, Harry
1969   "Professionalization of Attitudes Toward Play Among Adolescents." In G. S. Kenyon (ed.), *Aspects of Contemporary Sport Sociology*. Chicago: The Athletic Institute.

Weber, Max
1949   *The Methodology of the Social Sciences*. New York: The Free Press.

1968   *Economy and Society*. 3 Vols. Totowa New Jersey: Bedminster Press.

Weiss, Paul
1971   *Sport: A Philosophical Inquiry*. Carbondale: Southern Illinois Press.

Winch, Peter
1958   *The Idea of a Social Science*. New York: Humanities Press.

Zetterberg, Hans
1965   *On Theory and Verification in Sociology*. Totowa New Jersey: Bedminster Press.

SPORT:
Structure, Représentations idéologiques et symboliques

Roger Levasseur

Introduction

Cet article vise essentiellement à susciter l'intérêt de la sociologie québécoise pour le sport, phénomène moderne négligé pour ne pas dire ignoré des sociologues d'ici, tant au niveau de la recherche empirique qu'au niveau de la théorie sociologique. Cette ignorance est d'autant moins acceptable que le sport prend dans notre société ainsi que dans les sociétés industrielles avancées une importance de plus en plus grande, tant sur le plan économique, politique, social que sur le plan idéologique. L'impact et les conséquences multiples des Jeux olympiques de Montréal de 1976, par exemple, sur la structure sociale de la société québécoise, mettent en lumière les grands enjeux de notre collectivité, les acteurs sociaux en présence, les objectifs et finalités poursuivis par ces acteurs.

L'intérêt quotidien manifesté par des centaines de milliers de Québécois pour les événements sportifs et leurs héros constitue une autre illustration de l'importance du fait sportif chez nous. Ainsi la contribution de la sociologie québécoise à la compréhension et à l'interprétation de ce phénomène majeur des temps modernes s'avère une tâche indispensable et urgente. Cet article se veut un apport à la fois modeste et partiel ainsi qu'un amorce d'échanges entre les sociologues intéressés par ce phénomène.

Essai de définition

Le sport, tel que nous le connaissons dans les sociétés industrielles modernes, pénètre plusieurs secteurs de l'activité humaine: le loisir, le travail et l'éducation. En effet, le sport peut s'exercer, dans un premier temps, d'une façon volontaire pendant les moments de loisir, où le coefficient de contrainte est à son minimum. Il peut également devenir un travail, c'est-à-dire une profession en mesure d'assurer, pour celui qui l'exerce, le moyen de "gagner sa vie". C'est le cas de l'athlète professionnel, ainsi que de tous ceux qui participent au processus de production de l'athlète: entraîneurs, instructeurs, professeurs, journalistes, etc. Enfin, l'éducation physique, qui se limite le plus souvent à l'apprentissage d'un ou de plusieurs sports, devient progressivement dans le système scolaire, tant du Québec que des autres sociétés industrielles, une matière obligatoire. Le sport est jugé non seulement dans nos écoles comme le moyen privilégié d'éducation physique, mais il s'identifie de plus en plus à l'éducation physique. Ces deux phénomènes, autrefois distincts, tendent à devenir dans nos sociétés modernes une seule et même chose.

Au-delà de la diversité des champs d'application du sport, retrouve-t-on la même logique, la même structure dans le sport? En d'autres termes, le sport-loisir, le sport-profession et le sport-éducation procèdent-ils d'une structure fondamentalement identique? Pour répondre à cette question, tentons de dégager les principaux éléments constitutifs du sport moderne.

La plupart des auteurs qui se sont penchés sur le sport, lui reconnaissent une spécificité propre, qui le distingue des autres phénomènes sociaux. Certains insistent davantage sur la compétition, d'autres sur les règles du jeu, d'autres sur la performance, etc. Pour les fins de cet article, nous retiendrons les éléments qui sont habituellement reconnus comme faisant partie inhérente de la pratique sportive. Le sport comporte d'une façon simultanée et complémentaire la présence de certains éléments qui le structurent. L'absence d'une ou de plusieurs de ces éléments réfèrent à un ou à des univers différents de celui du sport. Pour qualifier ces univers, certains parlent d'"activités de plein air", d'autres de "culture physique", de "condition physique", d'autres, enfin, de "gymnastique", mais en aucun cas il ne s'agit de sport.

Le sport exige la présence simultanée et interreliée des cinq éléments suivants:

1. *L'action du corps*: le sport implique que le corps soit au centre même de l'action. Il constitue avant tout une activité corporelle manifeste où l'accent est mis sur les potentialités et l'efficacité du corps humain. Tout sport comporte un minimum d'habileté physique de la part du participant.

2. *La compétition*: la compétition est la "forme spécifique, selon M. Bouet (1968), du rapport inter-humain dans le sport"; elle est un comportement de comparaison inter-humaine en vue de l'affirmation de la supériorité d'un individu ou d'une équipe par rapport aux autres, à partir d'instruments de mesure et de règles préétablis et unanimement acceptés. La compétition, en tant que telle, entraîne un double processus: un processus de hiérarchisation et un processus de mesure. Par le truchement des épreuves compétitives, les individus et les équipes sont hiérarchisés selon leur niveau de compétence et de rendement (faible, moyen, supérieur). L'organisation mondiale du sport constitue le modèle hiérarchique parfait: compétitions locales, régionales, nationales et internationales. Le niveau de compétence et de performance est d'autant plus élevé que les compétitions se déroulent au plan international et inversement. Quant au processus de mesure, le rapport compétitif implique, pour reprendre l'expression de M. Bouet (1968), "une opération où chacun se mesurant à l'autre fait office à la fois de mesureur et de mesuré."

3. *La recherche de la performance*: dans la confrontation sportive chacun des participants cherche à imposer sa supériorité en donnant le meilleur de lui-même, en visant la performance maximale. Cette visée de la performance se manifeste d'abord par une propension à une utilisation de plus en plus rationelle du corps par le truchement

d'un entraînement méthodique et systématique ainsi que par l'emploi de techniques de plus en plus raffinées. Elle se manifeste en second lieu par une tendance à la spécialisation sportive. Le skieur se spécialise dans le slalom ou la descente, le sprinter dans le 100 ou 200 mètres, etc. Un même sport a donc tendance à se décomposer en plusieurs épreuves en vue de l'obtention de résultats toujours meilleurs. Le sport "en miettes" devient de plus en plus une réalité moderne. La recherche de la performance favorise également la formation et le développement d'une élite sportive et du professionnalisme de même que le développement de l'industrie du spectacle sportif. Les hauts niveaux de performance et les exploits deviennent rapidement objets de spectacle. Enfin, la visée de la performance manifeste une propension à valoriser davantage les résultats que la participation à une épreuve sportive. Les résultats sont trop souvent la fin ultime de l'activité sportive. Dans le sport le plaisir est différé, il n'est pas inhérent à l'activité elle-même. La notion même d'"épreuve sportive" exprime bien cette réalité sociale du sport. L'enquête récente de Bouet et Orlick (1974) auprès de jeunes étudiants soit en éducation physique, soit impliqués dans des activités sportives, révèle qu'une fraction relativement importante de l'échantillon n'associe pas le sport à une activité procurant du *fun*. L'enquête confirme l'idée que le plaisir (*fun*) est à l'opposé d'une échelle de valeurs basée sur la comparaison objective, sur les résultats mesurés et sur l'éthique du progrès, de la compétition et du rendement.

4.   *Le respect des règles:* le sport n'est pas une activité improvisée, laissée à la fantaisie et à l'initiative de chacun des participants. Bien au contraire, le sport est une activité réglée, c'est-à-dire qu'elle est soumise à un ensemble de règles, de conventions, formant une véritable législation et définissant dans les moindres détails les façons de jouer "sportivement", de régir le rapport compétitif qu'implique tout sport. Cette législation sportive est une législation parallèle, de second degré par rapport à celle prévalant dans la vie de tous les jours. Elle est dite de second degré parce qu'elle permet à l'intérieur de normes et de règles préétablies l'expression de comportements et gestes violents (v.g. la boxe, le football), qui seraient normalement réprimés dans la vie quotidienne. La législation sportive "sublimise" la transgression des règles et des normes de la vie quotidienne et fait en sorte que la "mort soit jouée" et non réelle, pour reprendre l'heureuse expression de Bernard Jeu (1972).

5.   *L'institutionnalisation de l'activité:* le sport est non seulement une activité réglée, mais aussi une activité institutionnalisée, c'est-à-dire

qu'il possède les principales caractéristiques de l'institution sociale. En effet, les individus impliqués dans un sport représentent des groupes ou des collectivités plus larges qu'eux-mêmes. Tout sportif fait partie d'un club ou d'une association ou fédération quelconque, dont il porte les "couleurs". Il représente soit son club, soit sa collectivité immédiate (par exemple, sa paroisse, ou sa région) soit son pays (par exemple, les rencontres Canada-Russie au hockey). Chacune de ces instances, club, collectivité immédiate, nation, formule des attentes à l'égard des individus ou des "joueurs". C'est en autant que les individus satisfont ou non à ces attentes qu'ils seront évalués socialement (argent, honneur, prestige, pouvoir, etc.)

En plus de conférer à celui qui l'exerce un rôle social, le sport possède, comme toute institution sociale, une histoire, des traditions, des records, etc. socialement reconnus. Cette histoire et ces traditions au sens large du terme prennent corps dans une organisation structurée (associations locales, nationales et internationales) qui régit la pratique du sport et assure le caractère permanent de l'institution. En d'autres termes, le sport constitue une institution sociale d'une part en autant qu'il demeure un fait extérieur aux consciences individuelles, pour reprendre l'expression de Dürkheim, c'est-à-dire que tout sport et les règles qui le régissent existent en dehors de l'individu, qu'elles se transmettent de génération en génération; il est une institution d'autre part en autant que les règles, les rôles et attentes sont intériorisés par les individus. Du point de vue sociologique, l'individu pratique le tennis, par exemple, lorsqu'il se soumet aux règlements, traditions énoncées par la Fédération internationale de tennis. Sinon, l'individu joue, prend de l'exercice, mais ne fait pas de sport.

Peut-on maintenant conclure, après l'analyse des caractéristiques spécifiques du sport, que le sport-loisir et le sport-profession procèdent de la même structure? Fondamentalement, la même structure joue dans les deux cas. Ce qui distingue essentiellement ces deux secteurs du sport, c'est le niveau de performance atteint. Le sport-loisir se contente, de par sa nature, de performances moyennes ou faibles, tandis que le sport-profession exige des performances supérieures, Toutefois, c'est le sport-travail (entendons ici autant le professionnalisme que l'amateurisme marron) qui impose son modèle structurel au sport-loisir. Au Québec, par exemple, on joue au hockey dans les clubs de paroisses, tant chez les enfants que chez les adultes, suivant le modèle de jeu défini par la Ligue nationale de hockey. L'analyse marxiste, postulant la détermination en dernière instance de l'économique, pourrait, semble-t-il, trouver d'heureuses applications dans le phénomène sportif. Mais la question que l'on doit se poser à ce moment-ci est la suivante: est-il normal de procéder d'une structure identique, quand nous avons affaire à deux secteurs de l'activité humaine (le travail et le loisir) qui diffèrent essentiellement, tant en termes de nature que de fonction au sein des sociétés industrielles avancées? Cette question ne se posait pas, il y a un siècle, puisque la dichotomie sport-loisir et sport-profession n'existait pas! Le sport était le fait de la nouvelle bourgeoisie aristocratique qui pouvait s'adonner, sans se soucier de travailler, à ses activités favorites. Aujourd'hui, le sport est devenu pour un groupe encore relativement restreint d'individus un métier, une profession, tandis qu'il est pour la grande majorité des pratiquants, provenant de milieux plus diversifiés qu'il y a un siècle, un loisir. Le sport doit-il être conçu de la même façon pour ces deux groupes? Voilà la même question que précédemment, mais posée en termes différents. Ces interrogations doivent également porter sur les relations entre sport-travail et sport-éducation, sport-éducation et sport-loisir.

Enfin, terminons cette section sur la structure du sport en insistant sur l'importance de définir d'une façon opératoire le concept de sport, afin de permettre de cerner d'une façon suffisamment précise la réalité sociale du sport et d'éviter ainsi de confondre ce phénomène avec d'autres réalités. Dans le langage courant de même que dans plusieurs enquêtes scientifiques, des activités nombreuses, variées et très différentes les unes des autres, telles la marche, la raquette, la randonnée en bicyclette, le hockey, le ski, le tennis, la baignade, la pêche, la chasse, les échecs, etc. sont identifées à des activités sportives. Sans un minimum de définition opérationnelle et de rigueur logique, tout est sport et tout devient sport. Les cinq éléments (l'action du corps, la compétition, la recherche de la performance, le respect des règles et l'institutionnalisation) que nous avons identifiés comme participant à la structure du sport constituent les cinq grandes dimensions susceptibles de définir d'une façon opératoire le concept de sport et de jauger son importance empirique dans nos sociétés industrielles avancées.

Représentations idéologiques et symboliques

Le sport, comme toute institution sociale, développe un ensemble plus ou moins cohérent d'idées, d'images, de symboles, de représentations, de valeurs, de croyances, le diffuse auprès d'un public plus ou moins large et fait l'objet de conflits idéologiques entre ses différents définisseurs. Dans ce texte, nous présenterons succinctement dans un premier temps les principales images et représentations du sport qui sont présentes dans les sociétés industrielles avancées. Dans un second temps, nous examinerons quelques éléments idéologiques du discours des promoteurs du sport, tant des pouvoirs publics et privés que des associations et fédérations sportives. Enfin, nous terminerons cette section en montrant que l'élite sportive constitue une élite symbolique qui condense en elle une partie importante du discours idéologique sur le sport.

a)   Sport et représentations

Il s'agit ici de cerner les principales "valeurs-fins", attribuées socialement à la pratique sportive dans les sociétés industrielles modernes. Ces valeurs sont en quelque sorte les *représentations idéalisées* que les individus d'une collectivité se font concernant le sport. Si nous tentons de dégager les représentations globales de l'activité sportive présentes dans de larges secteurs de la population des sociétés occidentales, nous pouvons les ramener à cinq principales que nous présenterons maintenant[1].

Le sport est d'abord valorisé dans nos sociétés industrielles parce qu'on lui attribue la faculté de contribuer à l'amélioration de la santé et du bien-être corporel de la population. Des expressions populaires, telles que "le sport met en forme", "tient en condition", illustrent cette association spontanée que les gens font entre sport et santé, sport et bien-être corporel. Au Canada, cette association s'institutionnalise par l'intégration de l'organisme chargé de la promotion et du développement du sport au sein du Ministère de la Santé et Bien-être social. Pour l'État canadien, le sport est un moyen privilégié pour prévenir les maladies inhérentes à une mauvaise condition physique et pour garantir d'une façon permanente le bien-être physique des Canadiens. Donc, au Canada, comme dans d'autres pays occidentaux, le gouvernement ainsi que la population qu'il représente, associent en partie le sport à la santé et au bien-être physique.

Des secteurs encore nombreux de la population dans nos sociétés industrielles valorisent le sport pour son aspect ascétique. Le sport est identifié ici à la capacité de différer le plaisir immédiat et d'endurer de longues et pénibles périodes d'entraînement afin d'atteindre les plus hauts niveaux de réussite et de succès, de rendement et de performance. Cet ascétisme sportif semble participer à l'univers moral du protestantisme, tel que décrit et analysé par Max Weber dans sa thèse remarquable: *L'Ethique protestante et l'esprit du capitalisme*. C'est également dans cette optique qu'on présente le sport comme l'école par excellence pour la formation du caractère. En effet, le sport, en mettant l'accent sur l'effort physique, la performance, la réussite et non sur le plaisir et la jouissance, contribue à produire de "vrais hommes" et non des êtres dégénérés physiquement et moralement. Ainsi le sport contribue à la formation morale en développant chez l'individu le sens de la discipline, c'est-à-dire en favorisant la maîtrise de soi et le respect des valeurs sociales dominantes.

On attribue également à la compétition sportive la faculté de développer d'une façon spécifique, chez les individus qui s'y adonnent, certaines caractéristiques, certaines qualités particulières. Selon cette représentation collective, le sport favorise d'une façon automatique, par le truchement de la compétition, le développement du courage, de la persévérance, de la ténacité, etc. Le sport devient dans cette perspective une institution privilégiée de préparation à la vie, c'est-à-dire qu'il fournit aux jeunes les qualités et aptitudes nécessaires pour surmonter avec succès les défis (*challenges*) de la vie adulte, qu'il les prépare à occuper adéquatement leurs rôles dans une société qui repose essentiellement sur la compétition libre et ouverte entre les individus et les groupes sociaux. La croyance dans les bienfaits de la compétition demeure encore très vive même si dans la plupart des secteurs des sociétés industrielles avancées nous sommes plus près d'une situation de monopole que d'une situation de concurrence parfaite. Dans ce sens nous pouvons faire l'hypothèse que le sport demeure probablement le dernier secteur où les principes de la compétition s'appliquent d'une façon intégrale, contribuant ainsi à entretenir le mythe des mérites de la concurrence et de la compétition libres.

Le sport est également perçu chez une fraction plus ou moins large de la population comme un moyen privilégié de libération de l'agressivité, des tensions et frustrations engendrées par le mode de vie moderne. Le sport constitue une soupape idéale qui permet aux énergies réprimées dans la vie quotidienne de s'exprimer librement à l'intérieur de certaines normes et règles partagées par les participants eux-mêmes. Ces règles balisent l'instinct d'agressivité et les manifestations de violence et de brutalité dans un cadre bien circonscrit (arène de boxe, terrain de football). Dans cette perspective, le sport remplit des fonctions sociales diverses: 1) une fonction de catharsis, c'est-à-dire qu'il purifie le corps et l'esprit permettant ainsi à l'individu de reprendre normalement et plus efficacement son rôle social de producteur; 2) une fonction d'exutoire, c'est-à-dire qu'il favorise la libre expression de l'agressivité, de la violence et de la brutalité selon un cadre et des règles bien définies et acceptées de tous; 3) une fonction d'équilibre systémique, c'est-à-dire qu'il continue à maintenir le système social en équilibre, en permettant au plan social l'expression de l'agressivité et de la violence qui pourraient autrement s'attaquer au fondement même du système.

Enfin, le sport est perçu comme étant une activité qui favorise d'une façon toute particulière les relations et les échanges entre les individus et les groupes sociaux. Par le truchement de l'activité sportive, les individus peuvent, soit faire de nouvelles connaissances appartenant à leur propre groupe social ou à un groupe social différent, soit perpétuer et approfondir les relations existantes. Les expressions populaires, telles que "le sport permet de rencontrer les copains, les amis", "il permet de se faire de nouveaux amis", etc. illustrent la valeur de socialité et sociabilité que les gens attribuent d'une façon spontanée au sport.

Signalons en terminant que ces représentations idéalisées du sport ne sont pas exclusives et ne sont pas non plus hiérarchisées selon leur degré d'importance. Nous postulons seulement qu'elles existent d'une façon plus ou moins étendue dans les sociétés industrielles occidentales et au Québec. Seule une enquête systématique auprès de la population québécoise nous permettrait d'évaluer et d'hiérarchiser l'importance que les Québécois accordent à ces représentations. Notons enfin que ces représentations, tout comme les idéologies, dont nous allons maintenant traiter, ne correspondent pas nécessairement à la réalité sportive. Dans bien des cas, nous assistons à un décalage important entre les représentations et la situation; nous avons plutôt affaire à une réalité inversée qu'à un phénomène d'identité ou de correspondance.

b) Sport et idéologies

Les promoteurs et les producteurs du sport, c'est-à-dire tous ceux qui sont directement reliés à un niveau ou l'autre de son organisation et de son développement non seulement reprennent à leur compte les représentations idéalisées plus ou moins répandues chez les divers groupes sociaux, mais développent également un discours idéologique spécifique qui, au plan social, sert à la fois à expliquer et justifier la pratique sportive ainsi qu'à occulter ou masquer les aspects de la réalité sportive qui pourraient nuire à leurs intérêts directement liés au développement du sport. Examinons brièvement quelques éléments de ce discours idéologique.

La notion de *fair play*, "d'esprit sportif", constitue un des éléments majeurs de ce discours sur le sport. Par le truchement de la compétition à la fois franche et loyale, le sport posséderait *in se* la faculté, selon cette idéologie, de favoriser et de développer le respect mutuel entre adversaires, la détente, l'entente et même la coopération entre les individus et les peuples. De là à lier le *fair play* a l'apprentissage des vertus civiques, il n'y a qu'un pas, qui est facilement franchi par les idéologues du sport. Par ailleurs les rencontres sportives, au plan international, contribueraient à dégeler les relations entre les nations, à établir la "coexistence pacifique" entre les pays et à mettre entre parenthèses les divergences idéologiques, politiques et économiques pour fraterniser. Mais les derniers Jeux olympiques de Mexico et de Munich illustrent, entre autres, le décalage et le "déphasage" entre l'idéologie olympique et sportive et les réalités nationales et internationales.

Dans cette même ligne de pensée, les idéologues du sport tentent d'évacuer, d'éliminer, par leur discours, la réalité de la stratification sociale qu'on retrouve dans tous les secteurs d'activités de nos sociétés industrielles avancées. Le sport serait à l'abri des luttes des classes; tous les individus et les classes ou strates sociales seraient égaux devant le sport. Ce dernier est présenté principalement comme une rencontre compétitive entre deux ou plusieurs individus ou équipes, faisant face aux mêmes règles et aux mêmes obstacles objectifs, peu importe leur appartenance ou origine sociale. C'est l'individu ou l'équipe obtenant les meilleurs résultats, la meilleure performance qui l'emporte et non le fait d'appartenir à tel groupe, strate ou classe sociale. Toutefois on oublie souvent de mentionner que certains groupes ou certaines strates sociales sont plus égales que d'autres au point de départ. Et on conclut le tout en indiquant les origines souvent modestes de nos quelques héros nationaux: les Richard (hockey) les Béliveau (hockey), les Bourassa (golf), etc. De plus, le sport, toujours selon ce discours idéologique, favorise non seulement l'égalité objective des chances de réussite entre les individus et les strates sociales, mais encore il permet la rencontre entre des individus appartenant à des strates différentes. Autrement dit, il favorise le brassage social, le rapprochement entre des individus qui semblaient posséder au point de départ des intérêts et objectifs divergents, pour ne pas dire conflictuels. La confrontation de ce discours idéologique avec les études empiriques sur la participation sportive[2] nous révèle un écart sensible entre la réalité observée et le discours idéologique.

Enfin, l'organisation et le développement du sport, tel que nous l'avons défini antérieurement, appelle nécessairement la production d'une élite sportive. Et partant, les idéologues du sport élaborent un système de rationalisation et de justification de cette élite qu'on pourrait facilement ramener à la proposition suivante: le sport d'élite entraîne le sport de "masse" et inversement. La formation d'une élite sportive exercerait un effet d'entraînement positif auprès d'une population relativement amorphe au plan de l'activité sportive. L'élite propose un modèle que la "masse" pourrait imiter, dont elle pourrait s'inspirer. D'autre part, selon la même logique de pensée, le raisonnement inverse est également utilisé. La participation de "masse" au sport favorise la sélection d'une élite sportive de premier choix. Ainsi s'élabore une dialectique serrée entre le sport d'élite et le sport de "masse". Bref, l'important, c'est la production d'une élite sportive: on adoptera la justification aux circonstances et selon les "publics".

c) Sport et élites symboliques

A la suite de Caillois (1958), qui retenait comme l'une des caractéristiques fondamentales du jeu son improductivité matérielle, on a souvent appliqué cette qualité au sport. S'il apparaît juste que le sport n'est pas une activité proprement productive de biens et de services, on ne peut pas en dire autant au plan de la production symbolique. Il n'est pas exagéré d'affirmer que l'élite sportive est devenue dans les sociétés industrielles axées sur la consommation de masse, une véritable élite symbolique. Par élite symbolique, nous entendons des individus ou groupes qui se présentent ou qu'on présente comme les prototypes de certaines manières d'être, d'agir et de penser et qui incarnent certaines qualités, certaines valeurs (Rocher, 1969). Il suffit de parcourir les informations de la presse écrite et parlée au sujet de la vie "privée" des athlètes amateurs ou professionnels, de leur entraînement, de leur performance pour se rendre compte de la fonction éminemment symbolique et mythologique de l'élite sportive moderne. On les présente comme des modèles de courage, de persévérance, de ténacité, d'adresse, d'intelligence... bref, des "dieux" modernes. Ils deviennent des exemples à suivre, à imiter qui exigent l'identification. Le processus identification-imitation joue à plein dans la symbolique de l'élite sportive.

Une telle symbolique ne s'est pas développée en vase clos. Bien au contraire, elle a entretenu très tôt des relations étroites avec les autres instances de la réalité sociale ou de la formation sociale. Les appareils politiques et économiques ont récupéré cette symbolique pour promouvoir et défendre les fins propres du système économique et politique.

Au niveau de l'instance économique, l'élite sportive a été utilisée d'une façon de plus en plus intensive à mesure que s'est développée la consommation de masse. Les sociétés industrielles ont mis sur pied un ensemble d'instruments en vue de planifier non seulement la production massive de biens et leur distribution, mais également une consommation appropriée de ces biens. Pour maintenir cet équilibre instable entre la production et la consommation, les sociétés industrielles ont inventé un instrument des plus efficaces: le "système publicitaire." Vu que les biens produits sont définis de moins en moins par l'usager mais de plus en plus par les exigences du système industriel ou de l'"état industriel" pour reprendre l'expression de Galbraith (1967), le producteur a besoin dans ce nouveau contexte d'un appareil définissant pour le consommateur ce qui lui est nécessaire.

C'est au niveau du système publicitaire qu'intervient l'élite sportive. Par sa fonction symbolique, l'élite sportive contribue, en partie, à modeler, par le processus d'identification-imitation, les comportements de consommation de larges secteurs de la population, tout particulièrement les jeunes (Szpakowska, 1970), les secteurs les plus démunis, bref ceux qui sont en situation de "participation dépendante", selon l'expression de Touraine (1969). En d'autres termes, cette élite symbolique remplit le rôle de figure d'autorité, telle qu'entendue par M. Rokeach (1960), c'est-à-dire que les gens achètent tel ou tel produit, non à cause de la valeur intrinsèque du produit lui-même, mais parce que telle vedette sportive est associée à ce produit. Ces figures d'autorité que sont les athlètes modernes produisent des effets non négligeables sur la structure sociale. Ils contribuent, entre autres, à amenuiser l'esprit critique des gens et amènent ces derniers à remettre aux autres, c'est-à-dire aux figures d'autorité et ultimement au système industriel le soin de définir ce qui est bon, utile et nécessaire pour eux. Cette dépendance de secteurs relativement nombreux de la population vis-à-vis les figures d'autorité constitue une forme importante d'aliénation dans nos sociétés industrielles.

De ce qui précède on peut donc faire l'hypothèse que les sociétés avancées ont produit de nouvelles élites symboliques exerçant des fonctions conformes et cohérentes avec le nouveau système industriel. Nous faisons l'hypothèse que le rôle des élites symboliques, à la naissance des sociétés industrielles, consistait principalement à stimuler l'accumulation du capital nécessaire à la production. Cette fonction était remplie à l'époque par certaines élites religieuses (v. g. clergé protestant). Le rôle des élites symboliques dans les sociétés industrielles avancées consiste maintenant à stimuler la consommation dans un système où le maintien d'un taux de production élevé demeure l'objectif principal. Cette fonction est remplie présentement par les vedettes de tout acabit (vedettes de cinéma, vedettes de la télévision, de la chanson, du disque, etc.) parmi lesquelles les vedettes du sport occupent une place de premier plan.

En ce qui concerne l'instance politique, l'État, en tant que principal agent de l'appareil politique, utilise à des fins multiples la symbolique sportive. Il se sert en premier lieu de l'élite sportive comme élément d'affirmation du prestige national. Les victoires remportées par les athlètes nationaux dans les compétitions internationales deviennent facilement un critère par lequel on juge de la valeur respective des différents régimes politico-économiques. Ils ne sont plus de simples athlètes, ils deviennent des "ambassadeurs" de leur pays. Tout comme le diplomate-ambassadeur, l'athlète n'est pas neutre, il représente et défend les "couleurs" de son pays, lesquelles couleurs possèdent inévitablement une connotation politique.

Certain États peuvent également utiliser l'élite sportive comme élément d'affirmation d'une conscience nationale. Le Canada, de même que les jeunes nations qui ont accédé récemment à leur indépendance, demeurent des exemples typiques de cette forme d'utilisation de l'élite sportive à des fins spécifiquement politiques. L'État canadien, par exemple, consacre depuis plusieurs années des efforts considérables pour la formation d'une élite nationale représentative en vue de renforcer et de développer une plus forte cohésion sociale ainsi qu'une conscience nationale plus vive. Cette dernière est relativement faible au Canada, vu la diversité et les disparités très grandes entre les régions canadiennes ainsi que les velléités d'indépendance et d'autonomie légendaires du Québec en tant que province à forte dominante française (80%) à l'intérieur d'un Canada maissivement anglais.

Enfin, signalons que les élites sportives sont récupérées implicitement ou explicitement par les gouvernements comme un élément de plus en plus important de stabilité socio-politique. Pendant qu'une fraction importante de la population (se recrutant surtout parmi les secteurs les plus démunis, ceux détenant un potentiel inutilisé de revendications sociales) suit de près à la télévision ou au stade les exploits des vedettes sportives, les politiciens et les groupes dont ils représentent les intérêts peuvent vaquer tranquillement aux affaires de l'État. Pélé au Brésil de même que Maurice Richard au Québec ont dû jouer un rôle de cet ordre, c'est-à-dire "amuser le peuple" pendant que les élites politiques et économiques s'occupaient de la direction de la nation sans la Nation.

Conclusion

Nous nous sommes limités dans cet article à l'examen partiel de deux aspects du sport: 1) le sport en tant que phénomène social spécifique et structuré; 2) le sport en tant qu'objet de représentations collectives, de discours idéologique et d'utilisation symbolique. Nous nous proposons ultérieurement d'évaluer à partir des enquêtes empiriques disponibles, l'importance de la pratique sportive dans les sociétés industrielles avancées et au Québec en particulier. Cette analyse de la pratique sportive devra tenir des éléments suivants: 1) la fréquence et l'intensité de la pratique sportive; 2) les variables socio-démographiques et socio-économiques qui la déterminent; 3) l'importance de la participation des Québécois aux sports organisés (participation aux associations sportives, aux Jeux olympiques, etc.) par rapport aux autres sociétés industrielles. Cet examen nous permettra de mesurer d'une façon plus précise la distance entre l'instance des représentations et celle de la pratique.

Enfin soulignons l'urgence d'analyses et d'études de l'ascendant déterminant des appareils politiques et économiques sur le sport. Il importe de plus en plus, devant les interventions massives de ces deux appareils sur le sport, de définir la nature et la fonction de ces acteurs sociaux dans le développement du sport dans nos sociétés industrielles avancées.

NOTES

1. Voir à ce sujet, Edwards (1973).
2. Voir pour exemples Lüschen (1972); Comité d'Études sur la condition physique des Québécois (1974); et Kirsh et co. (1973). Consulter aussi l'article de Gruneau "Class Or Mass" dans ce livre.

OUVRAGES CITÉS

Bouet, Michel
1968   Signification du Sport. Paris: Éditions Universitaires.
et Orlick T.D.
1974   "The Meaning and Significance of Fun in Industrial Society and Competitive Sport." Communication présentée au Congrès de l'Association Internationale de Sociologie, Toronto, août.
Caillois, Roger
1958   Les jeux et les hommes. Gallimard, Coll. Idées, No 125.
Comité d'études sur la condition physique des Québécois
1974   Annexe sur les Rapports des Enquêtes. ronéo, Gouv. du Québec, Éditeur Officiel.
Edwards, Harry
1973   Sociology of Sport. Homewood: Dorsey Press.
Galbraith, John Kenneth
        Le nouvel état industriel. Paris: Éd. Gallimard.

Jeu, Bernard
1972   *Le sport, la mort et la violence.* Paris: Éditions Universitaires.

Kirsh, Carol; Dixon, Brian; Bond, Michael
1973   *Les loisirs du Canada 1972.* Direction Arts et Culture, Secrétariat d'État, Gouvernement Fédéral, Ed. Culturcan.

Lüschen, Günther
1972   "Social Stratification and Mobility Among German Sportsmen". In Eric Dunning (ed.), *Sport: Readings From a Sociological Perspective.* Toronto: U. of Toronto Press.

Rocher, Guy
1969   *Sociologie générale.* Tome III, Montréal: Editions H.M.H.

Rokeach, Milton
1960   *The Open and Closed Mind.* New York: Basic Books.

Szpakowska, Janina-Klara
1970   *Profils culturels des jeunes montréalais.* Publ. de l'Ecole de bibliothéconomie, No 3, Univ. de Montréal, Faculté des Lettres.

Touraine, Alain
1969   *La société post-industrielle.* Paris. Éd. Denoël.

PART TWO

The Growth and Institutionalization of Sport

Introduction

The roots of Canadian sport can be found in two areas. First, in the recreational activities of the frontier and farming districts of the late eighteenth and nineteenth centuries (cf., Howell and Howell, 1969; Wise and Fisher, 1975), and secondly in the sporting clubs of the urban elite and military garrisons (Lindsay, 1969; Wise and Fisher, 1975).[1] During these times, sport was not the highly visible and organized phenomenon that it is today, rather, sporting activities tended to be *periodic, ascriptive* and *unorganized.* The transformation of sport from this latter state, into the highly organized, regulated and competitive activities of the present and into a major component of "mass" culture, has occured in conjunction with basic changes in the structure and organizing principles of Canadian society itself. Understanding this transformation requires an elaboration of the unorganized and class-bound character of Canadian sport in the early nineteenth century.[2]

Pre-confederation Canada was an agricultural and primary resource based society whose mode of economic production was shaped by the mercantilist practices of the British colonial system (cf., Naylor, 1972; Teeple, 1972; Clement, 1975). At the risk of over-simplifying the class structure, the society could be classified into three distinct groups: (a) a colonial and merchant elite;[3] (b) a class of (primarily rural) independent commodity producers; and (c) a class of propertyless labourers (largely the result of restrictive colonial land granting policies and heavy immigration). Under these conditions, the comparative involvement of each group in varying kinds of sporting activites was influenced not only by the ascriptive character of the class system, but also by the amount of free time and resources to which the different groups had access. The dominant merchant and colonial elite participated in equestrian events or such "gentlemanly" games as cricket and generally looked to Britain for the standards and styles which came to define participation (cf., Mallea, 1975; Wise and Fisher, 1974).[4] Given the time, the independent commodity producers of the Canadian rural areas occasionally participated in "gymnastics, trials of strength, running and jumping and other popular pastimes as throwing the hammer and putting the stone" (Strickland, cited in Wise and Fisher, 1974:8), and the expanding labouring class shared in some of these activities and as well maintained an interest in footracing, and no-holds-barred wrestling and boxing. But, it would be misleading to assume that the rate and kind of participation in these various activities was similar for each of the class groupings described, or even that the overall level of involvement in sport was particularly high. This was especially true in the case of community sports and recreational activities. As Wise and Fisher, (1974:8) have indicated:

> ... most settlers did not have much time for sports and other amusements. Most men and women lived out their lives in their own communities whether in the fishing villages of the Atlantic colonies or in the seigneuries of the St. Lawrence valley, on the backwoods farms of Upper Canada, or around the trading posts of the Hudson's Bay Company in the West. When time permitted they played the games known to them but certainly not in any organized way.

Not only did the *objective* conditions of social existence define participation to a large extent, but participation was also affected by "non-rational" ideologies. Nowhere was this traditional non-rational sentiment expressed more graphically, than in the prominent position held by the church. Clergical ideology limited participation in games and sports by stressing that the body was always inferior to the spirit. Thus, sporting activities might well be pursued as a means to an end, but they could not be regarded as ends in themselves. In some of the more fundamentalist churches, this meant the repudiation of all forms of recreation and "frivolous" activities (Metcalfe, 1974).[5]

Yet if it can be argued that the potential for the growth of sport in early nineteenth century Canada was greatly retarded by class-bound opportunities and values, and by a disapproving church, how did sport's role in social life change? We would argue that much of the answer lies in three broad sets of changes associated with Canada's productive base.

First, the commercial sector of the Canadian upper class continued to develop and solidify. The needs of Canadian financial groups to expand to new resource markets in the Canadian hinterland, and to centralize their economic and political power in the metropolitan centres of Upper and Lower Canada led to a great emphasis on transportation and the development of related communicative technology. As transportation developed, the conditions were provided for urban expansion and the inter-urban transfer of commodities and people. Related to this, the success of Canadian merchant capital stimulated the expansion of middle class commercial occupations in the urban centres.

Second, in conjunction with transportation and technological developments (and occasionally in conflict with mercantile interests) industrial development began to occur in or near the urban areas. The rational process of industrialization had three major effects: (a) it created the necessary conditions for the mass production of manufactured goods; (b) it "rationalized" the concept of time; and (c) it added a group of industrial capitalists to the developing Canadian bourgeoisie.

Finally, the massive immigration throughout the nineteenth century provided a glut of urban labourers from the 1820's on. These immigrants introduced new ideas and competing ideologies which frequently conflicted with the dominant institutional patterns of the society.

Examining sport in the context of such developments, Ian Jobling notes how urbanization, transportation and changing technology provided the pre-requisites for the growth and institutionalization of sport in the latter half of the nineteenth century. Improved transportation facilitated inter and intra-urban competition, and technological developments in the media allowed for the stimulation of a broad interest in the results of competitions. Factory production of equipment and the establishment of designated hours for work and leisure, changed the nature of sport itself and provided increased accessibility.[6] Jobling's most important point however, is simply that the urban areas created conditions where an active commercial middle class could readily establish clubs and associations which could define the rules for participation in certain sport forms. This class came to dominate the organizational development of sport throughout the century.

A more in-depth discussion of the changing relationship of sport to social class is contained in Alan Metcalfe's examination of nineteenth century Montreal sporting clubs. Metcalfe analyzes the social backgrounds of the players and administrators of Montreal sporting clubs and compares them to the overall occupational, ethnic and religious composition of Montreal during specific periods. Montreal's earliest sporting clubs were organized by the city's colonial and merchant elite, but after the 1850's, the patterns of recruitment appear to change somewhat. Metcalfe points out that what occured, was a kind of *restricted democratization*. The organizational force in the Montreal sporting scene shifted from the colonial elite, to the city's commercial and professional groups,[7] but there continued to be a few club executives and members from the industrial working class. Moreover, francophone members were almost nonexistant, and the geographical location of events and facilities remained centred in the upper-middle and middle class districts of St. Antoine and Westmount throughout the latter third of the century.

It is apparent, that while sports in Montreal experienced some democratization during the period Metcalfe describes, the major "growth" of sport came through the increased accessibility of traditionally elite pastimes to the city's expanding commercial groups. The marked underrepresentation of blue collar workers in Metcalfe's samples of club members, suggests that the degree to which democratization automatically accompanied the early growth and development of institutionalized sport in Canada must be viewed with considerable caution.

To conclude this introduction, it should be noted that sport did indeed grow and flourish during the latter part of the nineteenth century. In conjunction with technological developments and the increasingly rational and secular nature of Canadian society, sports became a commercial enterprise (witness Jobling's brief comment about Ned Hanlan); the values of achievement and competitive success as ends in themselves began to develop as legitimate standards for participation (although this attitude was in constant conflict with the Victorian sporting legacy); consistent rules were established and sports became administered by governing bodies (the beginnings of bureaucratization); and aristocratic conceptions of sport became democratized in the face of the expansion of the upper-middle and middle class.

Yet, while the *beginnings* of sport's transformation into the kind of activity we experience today, lie in the developments of the nineteenth century, we should recognize that even by the turn of the century, sport for most Canadians was not a dominant feature of social life. Participation in most forms of sporting activity tended to remain the prerogative of the upper and middle classes. Moreover, a rejection of the casual professionalism which characterized many of the community-based sporting events of the period continued to be reflected in amateur sports policy well into the twentieth century. While organized amateur sports and games were defined as an integral part of the training of young "gentlemen" and were vigorously supported in clubs and private schools, the average Canadian experienced sport only as an occasional recreational activity or in the form of the dull military-like physical training (P.T.) of the public school system.[8]

NOTES

1. There are several "histories" of Canadian sport (ie. Bull, 1934; Roxborough, 1966; Howell and Howell, 1969), however one of the most lively, informative and accurate books available is Wise and Fisher (1974). Detailed reportorial discussions of specific periods can be found in Lindsay (1970); Cox (1970); and Jones (1970).

2. Two excellent historical discussions of social class and sport can be found in Weber (1971) and Mallea (1975).

3. Naylor (1972:6) suggests that the elite consisted of a merchant class and rich Loyalists, aligned with the colonial ruling class, the church and large land owners.

4. See S. F. Wise (1974) for an excellent overview of the games played by different sections of Canadian society.

5. Many of the issues covered in this introduction deal with social-structural changes. Readers should consult Metcalfe's (1974) interesting examination of the competing *ideologies* which were reflected in sport throughout the nineteenth century.

6. The changing concept of time is an especially important issue. Prior to the rise of industrialism, time was dominated by the natural rhythms of the day and season. Work began at daylight, concluded at dusk, and varied with the demands of the

season. With the factory system there developed a concept of time whereby time was measured as a discrete entity and therefore attained value in and of itself. There was a progressive delineation of time into generally recognized divisions of employers' time and free time. This delineation was important to the growth of modern sport because it gave the majority of the people the basic prerequisites of regular, organized sporting competitions—free time at regular intervals. It was only when man gained time off at predictable intervals that it was possible to schedule matches weeks, months, and years ahead. Therefore, the modern system of organization of leagues is a direct outgrowth of the changing concept of time. This changing attitude towards time also affected the form of the games. For instance, the outcome of a lacrosse match in the early years, 1870-1890, was determined by the best three out of five games which meant that a match was of indeterminate length lasting anything from five minutes to x hours. It was during the 1890's that the outcome of lacrosse games was decided within a defined time period. The impositions of time limits in football, lacrosse, and hockey was, therefore a further outgrowth of this changing concept of time. (The above note comes from Alan Metcalfe, in personal communication).

7. An overview of these issues in the context of basic developments in the political economy of Canada is currently in progress (cf., Gruneau, 1976).

8. For a discussion of the basic principles of this system see Cosentino and Howell (1971) and Metcalfe (1974).

REFERENCES

Bull, William Perkins
1934   From Rattlesnake Hunt to Hockey. Toronto: George McLeod.

Clement, Wallace
1975   The Canadian Corporate Elite. Toronto: McClelland Stewart.

Cosentino, Frank and Max Howell
1971   A History of Physical Education in Canada. Don Mills: General Publishing.

Cox, A.
1970   "Sport in Canada, 1968-1900." In Proceedings of the First-Canadian Symposium on the History of Sport. Edmonton: Fitness and Amateur Sport Directorate.

Gruneau, R. S.
1976   Elites, Class and Corporate Power in Canadian Sport." Doctoral dissertation in preparation; University of Massachusetts.

Howell, Nancy and Maxwell
1969   Sports and Games in Canadian Life. Toronto: MacMillan.

Jones, K.
1970   "Sport in Canada, 1968-1900." In Proceedings of the First-Canadian Symposium on the History of Sport. Edmonton: Fitness and Amateur Sport Directorate.

Lindsay, Peter
1969   "A History of Sport in Canada: 1807-1867." Unpublished doctoral dissertation, University of Alberta.
1970   "Sport in Canada; 1807-1867." In Proceedings of the First Canadian Symposium on the History of Sport. Edmonton: Fitness and Amateur Sport Directorate.

Mallea, John
1975   "The Victorian Sporting Legacy." McGill Journal of Education, 10(2).

Metcalfe, Alan
1974   "Some Background Influences on Nineteenth Century Canadian Sport and Physical Education." C.J.H.S.P.E., 5 (1).

Naylor, R. T.
1972   "The Rise and Fall of the Third Commercial Empire of the St. Lawrence." In G.
        Teeple (ed.), *Capitalism and the National Question in Canada*. Toronto: U. of To-
        ronto Press.

Roxborough, Henry
1966   *One Hundred—Not Out: The Story of Nineteenth Century Canadian Sport*. To-
        ronto: Ryerson.

Teeple, Gary
1972   "Land, Labour and Capital in pre-Confederation Canada." In G. Teeple (ed.),,
        Capitalism and the National Question in Canada. Toronto: U. of Toronto Press.

Wise, S. F.
1974   "Sport and Class Values in Nineteenth Century Canada." Paper presented at An-
        nual Meetings of North American Association for Sport History, London, Ontario.
        Ontario.

Wise, S. F. and Douglas Fisher
1974   *Canada's Sporting Heroes*. Toronto: General Publishers.

Weber, Eugen
1971   "Gymnastics and Sports in fin-de-siècle France: Opium of the Classes." *American
        Historical Review*, 76 (1).

URBANIZATION AND SPORT IN CANADA, 1867—1900

Ian F. Jobling

In the latter third of the nineteenth century, urbanization, a process by which urban areas emerge and develop out of the interaction of economic, technological and sociocultural influences (Meadows, 1957: 143), was a distinct phenomenon which influenced the development of sport in Canada. In 1867, when the population of the new Dominion of Canada was approximately three and a half million, less than twenty per cent lived in towns or cities (Stone, 1967: 29). The 1871 census of Canada indicated that there were twenty cities and towns with over five thousand inhabitants; the largest urban areas were Montreal (115,000), Quebec (56,999), Toronto (59,000), St. John (41,325) and Halifax (29,582). The only other urban areas with more than ten thousand were Hamilton (26,880), Ottawa (24,141), London (18,000) and Kingston (12,407). By

1901, not only had the number of cities and towns with more than five thousand residents risen to sixty-two, but twenty-four of them had a population of more than ten thousand (*Canada Census*, 1901, 1:22). The urban population had risen to thirty-five per cent by the turn of the century. In this paper I attempt to trace some of the effects of this urbanization on the growth and development of Canadian sport.

Transportation

An important factor in the development of urban areas was transportation between and within towns and cities. Although transport along the lakes and rivers had predominated through most of the century, it was the advent of the railway which had the greatest impact. A varied network of more than two thousand miles of rail linked the major cities and towns of Ontario, Quebec and the Maritimes by 1867 (Glazebrook, 1964, 2:94). The amount of track serving Canada from sea to sea had increased to nearly eighteen thousand by the end of the century.

Participants in most sports took advantage of the opportunities the railway companies offered in promoting passenger travel for special groups. The Canadian Pacific Railway company had a special interest in the Montreal Baseball Club and offered full exemption for team-managers, and special half-fare rates to teams willing to play the club (*The Globe*, March 1, 1900). On the prairies, the railway facilitated inter-town baseball games and tournaments; in 1888, Medicine Hat hosted the first baseball tournament on record in the Territory, with teams from Medicine Hat, Calgary, Lethbridge, and the mountain community of Donald participating (*Lethbridge News*, October 5, 1888). The Canadian Wheelmen's Association were frequently granted special concessions from the railway companies for their meetings, and in many parts of the Dominion hundreds of keen cyclists and fans travelled on special trains (*Winnipeg Free Press*, May 18, 1886; June 28, 1898; *The Globe*, May 20, 1890).

Train travel enabled teams to visit more than one town on a weekend trip and play a series of matches. In 1880, Fredericton curlers travelled to St. John to play against the Thistle Curling Club, and then continued on to St. Andrews the next morning for further competition (*Reporter*, Fredericton, February 11, 1880). Even in the formation year of the Edmonton Curling Club a rink travelled to a bonspiel in Winnipeg via the Canadian Pacific Railway from Calgary for a special return rate of twenty-five dollars (Reid, 1969: 65). Weekend trips for sport between Montreal and Quebec were popular, and the Royal Montreal Golf Club was one sporting group which received railway concessions from the North Shore Railway. Return tickets to Quebec cost three dollars each, and the secretary secured a Pullman sleeping car so as to accommodate the whole party for sixteen dollars (Royal Montreal Golf Club, 1923: 13-14). Travel to and from cities and towns took less time by train and thereby cut down the cost of tours. In 1894, an American college hockey team played in Montreal on a Friday night, spent all day Saturday on the train, and reached Toronto in time to play that night (*The Globe*, December 31, 1891).

The clubs which played in the National Lacrosse Association in 1899 included Toronto, Ottawa, Cornwall, Shamrock and Montreal. A detailed account of travelling expenses to be deducted from the gate receipts and given to the visiting teams was introduced. The amounts varied according to the distance: Montreal to Toronto and vice-versa was $250; Montreal-Ottawa, $100; Montreal-Cornwall, $80; Toronto-Ottawa, $200; Cornwall-Toronto, $200; Ottawa-Cornwall, $130 (*The Globe*, April 29, 1889). Although the comforts of train travel had improved, the Toronto Lacrosse Club were rather reluctant to play three games of the four to be played in Montreal during the 1886 season:

(The Montreal Club) . . . have had the great benefit of calm slumber and rest in their own beds on the evening previous to the contests, while our men have been jogging to and fro in broken rest over the wheels of a railway carriage all night (*The Globe*, November 27, 1886).

The popularity of rowing was encouraged by the railways as there were many generous concessions granted to rowing enthusiasts. For the regatta at Ottawa in 1867, the Ottawa and Prescott Railway offered return tickets at single fare rates, and free conveyance of boats as well (*Ottawa Times*, September 26, 1867). Citizens of smaller towns also benefited from this mode of travel as it enabled them to see popular sportsmen in person:

This afternoon Edward Hanlan, Wallace Ross, Edward Ross, David Ward . . . and other friends of the scullers, took the Northern Railway at Toronto for this town (Barrie). A parlour car had been kindly provided by Mr. Cumberland for the use of the party, who enjoyed the trip over the road immensely. At nearly every station along the line large crowds were assembled, all anxious to catch a glimpse of the champion and his rival from New Brunswick. (*The Globe*, August 10, 1878).

The railway companies knew that Edward ("Ned") Hanlan's popularity as a rowing champion would bring revenue from passenger traffic, so commissions were paid to the Hanlan Club (a group of businessmen who managed Hanlan's rowing commitments), which subsequently gave Hanlan his share. The total rail commission for Hanlan's appearance at the Barrie regatta was fourteen hundred dollars, and up to and including the Barrie regatta in 1878, the Hanlan Club received $3,900 from railroad companies as commissions for four regattas (*The Globe*, October 15, 1878).

Apart from their importance in promoting inter-urban competition in many sports and encouraging support from spectators, the employees of the railway companies often formed their own teams and clubs. The Great Western Railway Club (*Hamilton Times*, July 27, 1861) and the Montreal Grand Trunk Boat Club (Lindsay, 1969: 163) took part in rowing regattas. The Grand Trunk also had employees who participated in snowshoeing (Becket, 1882: 176, 185; *Montreal Gazette*, February 22, 1867). In 1897, the Grand Trunk company in Toronto converted one of their buildings on Spadina Avenue for Y.M.C.A. work. The facilities included a dormitory, restaurant, baths, small gymnasium and an outside playing area (Ross, 1951: 234). Basketball flourished within such railway organizations:

> At a meeting which was held in the railway Y.M.C.A. last evening a basketball league was organized composed of the following shops: — machine, blacksmith, car, and erecting shops. (*The Globe*, December 20, 1898).

The impact of railway transportation on the social activities of urban residents was considerable as the speed and comfort of this mode of travel encouraged inter-urban competition. Whereas in the early part of the nineteenth century the steamboat had been the important factor in promoting such competition (Lindsay, 1969), its degree of influence had been altered by the advent of the railways in 1856. However, the steamboats still played a prominent part in the period 1867-1900, especially during aquatic regattas. The popularity of rowing and sailing can largely be attributed to the part played by steamboats in making the regattas so enjoyable to the spectators enabling them to be amidst the activity.

Urban Transportation

Transport within towns and cities was becoming increasingly important as the urban areas spread. A horse-drawn omnibus service had served Toronto from 1849, but in 1861 the first horse-car street railway was introduced by the Toronto Street Railway Company (Toronto Transit Commission, 1967). By 1891, the city of Toronto covered an area of seventeen square miles, through which 68 miles of horse-car railway track ran to serve fifty-five thousand passengers daily. Most large cities had street railways by the turn of the century, and some railway systems were powered by electricity (Lavallee, 1961). By 1900, the amount of electric railway track was nearly seven hundred miles (*Canada*, 1900: 390).

Since the street railway companies had to maintain rolling stock to cope with the traffic demand at peak periods, efforts were made to utilize this stock at other times as well in order to spread the maintenance and overhead costs over more passenger miles. Special concessions and frequent services were provided for sporting occasions. For the opening of the new grounds of the Toronto Baseball Club in 1886, it was announced that the Metropolitan team from New York would play, and that "the Street Car Company signify their intention of granting transfer tickets and doing their best to accommodate the public" (*The Globe*, January 25, 1886). In cities which were not large enough to warrant a rail streetcar service, the main railroad was sometimes used to convey the sporting public. A new race track of the Winnipeg Turf Club was located along the C.P.R. South-western route, and arrangements were made with that company to carry passengers at reduced rates at half-hour intervals during turf meetings (*Winnipeg Free Press*, August 5, September 22, 1882). In response to the building of a new race track in Toronto in 1886, the Metropolitan railway, which connected with the Yonge Street cars of the city railway, was extended as far as the entrance of the Glen Grove Park so as to provide public transport to and from the park (*The Globe*, August 5, 1886). In Vancouver and New Westminster electric urban trains were running to Queen's Park in the 1890's, and multiple trains were required on the days in September when provincial or national lacrosse finals were played. Crowds of fifteen and twenty thousand people were reported to have thronged to these matches (Mather and McDonald, 1958: 136-137).

The Bicycle

Apart from the service in providing efficient transport to sporting events, bicyclists found that the introduction of the street-car railways gave them the opportunity of a "smooth ride" on the asphalted strip between the rails. The introduction of the "safety" bicycle in the late 1880's not only resulted in a large number of organized cycling clubs, but it also increased the mobility of town-folk—a factor which subsequently positively affected participation in other sports.

The contrast between "safety" cycling in the last decade of the century with "velocipedomania" which prevailed immediately following Confederation, was considerable not only in terms of equipment, but also in its influence on general urban social life. An editorial in *The Globe* of April 17, 1869, stated:

Velocipedomania is spreading to an inordinate extent. So long as their use was confined to the rinks, it was well enough, but now that they are making their appearance in scores on the sidewalks, they have got to be a nuisance. Complaints are heard on all sides, of the narrow escapes made daily by women and children . . . . If our city authorities could lay aside their petty quarrels for the nonce, and pass a little by-law on the subject, they would be doing good service.

In contrast to the above, cyclists of the 1890's were so numerous that they exerted a considerable amount of influence in the affairs of the towns. Cyclists everywhere were demanding improved roads and even special cycling paths (*Winnipeg Free Press*, May 13, 14, 1898). The Canadian Wheelmen's Association, formed in 1882, often attempted to exert pressure. In Toronto it was reported in *The Globe* of December 20, 1898, that "Aldermen who have affronted the board will have their 'Council aspirations punctured' if the wheelmen are strong enough to sway the vote." The C.W.A. members offered their support in the municipal elections to those civic representatives willing to take a certain position with respect to the construction and maintenance of roads, bridges and cycle-paths, as well as the enforcement of city by-laws related to cyclists.

As an additional effect, new commercial enterprises in the urban areas resulted from the popularity of the bicycle: Riding arenas and schools flourished (*The Globe*, February 10, 1896; "The Women's Pages", *Athletic Life*, 3: 169), but of far greater economic and commercial impact was the bicycle manufacturing, retailing and repairing industry. In 1899 there were over thirty bicycle manufacturers in Toronto alone, and in Weston the C.C.M. company was producing nearly forty thousand bicycles annually (*The Globe*, November 10, 1899). Timothy Eaton's store, which had produced its first catalogue in 1884 (Glazebrook, *et. al.* 1969: iv), was only one of many retail enterprises which produced detailed and specific catalogues on bicycles (Eaton's Catalogue, 1892-93).

The bicycle was one of the instruments of change in the attitude of women towards sport, and hastened many of the social changes the women's suffragette movements had been trying to introduce. Within a few years of the introduction of the bicycle there were changes in the fashion of women's dress that reformers had been seeking for generations (Aronson, 1965: 62). Women cyclists found that long skirts became entangled in the chain, sprockets and rear wheels of the bicycles, so they adapted their clothing to suit this new recreation. Soon after this emancipation, women's participation in other social sports such as tennis, croquet and golf increased, and the participation of women in sport became more socially acceptable.

Communication

The technological improvements in the communication of ideas and information were also factors which influenced the social life of urban citizens. Faster and cheaper typesetting methods and printing presses, and the decline in the cost of newsprint (Stevens, 1965: 132) made newspaper production more efficient, while widespread usage of the telegraph for transmitting and receiving information gave the reader more current news. Other innovations such as the Atlantic and Pacific cables, the typewriter, camera and telephone all contributed to making the impact of the newspaper on the daily lives of those whom the media reached greater.

Whereas there were less than five hundred periodicals published in Canada in 1874, there were more than twelve hundred by 1900 (Kesterton, 1967: 39). Increasingly throughout the period the daily newspaper devoted more columns to the reporting of sporting events, thereby promoting this activity in the social life of urban Canadians. In Toronto *The Globe*, gave excellent coverage under such headings as "Sporting Amusement Notes", "Sports and Amusements", "Sporting Intelligence", and "Sporting News". Most of the larger newspapers reported sporting events by the 1880's, and some even had regular columns which gave coverage of local, provincial and international (especially American) sport.

Sporting photographs began to appear regularly in periodicals in the latter decades of the century and were a feature which helped to make sport more popular. A prospectus of a new weekly sporting journal, *Canadian Cricket Field*, which was to be devoted "exclusively to the interests of cricket" was announced in *The Globe* on April 1, 1882. The first issue of *Athletic Life* appeared in 1895 stated the objectives of the journal:

> Our aim is to have a complete record of all games and pleasures, authenticated and under their proper heading, and to assist and encourage their development. In this we have been fortunate enough to secure the cooperation of recognized authorities in the different branches of sport, and with their assistance we shall seek to encourage all correspondence, under its own heading, as will serve to develop the different pastimes, and to discuss various modes of procedure or suggested improvements.

Urbanization and Industrialization

Although urbanization and industrialization can be independently variable (Moore, 1965: 334) they are associated in so many ways that the two processes supplement each other. At the time of Confederation most manufacturing in Canada was of a local handicraft nature requiring very little capital, and most of the country's trade was based on farm, fishing and timber products (Fullerton and Hampson, 1957: 11; *Royal Commission on Dominion-Provincial Relations* 1939: 26). From 1870 on, Canadian manufacturing received an impetus from the "second industrial revolution of steel and railroads" and "more advanced technology, corporate organization, and low-cost transport combined to foster a unified market and a factory-based system of specialized mass production to serve it" (Fullerton and Hampson, 1957: 12). Towards the end of the century many of the urban centres in Canada could provide the principal factors which determined the success of manufacturing industries and which were to greatly contour the shape of Canadian sport. These factors included the growth of an active commercial middle class; an efficient transportation system for the movement of raw materials to the urban market and for the distribution of manufactured products; a source of energy and power; and an adequate supply of skilled and unskilled labour (cf., Scott, 1926: 25).

Certainly, a ready labour force was available for industrial production in the urban centres. The presence of a dominant mercantile class and the monopolization of land by 1800, both combined with heavy immigration to allow for a surplus of propertyless labourers from the 1820's on.[1] While few of the members of this working class had ready access to most forms of sporting activities, a desire for recreational involvement frequently became a labour demand that was incorporated into the push for better working conditions and shorter working hours.[2]

Consider, for example, the movements for "early closing" which were in operation in the post-Confederation era (cf., *Daily Colonist*, Victoria, Sept. 26, 1888; *The Globe*, August 25, 1868; February 27, 1872; *Winnipeg Free Press*, July 4, 1900; Glazebrook, 1968: 188). A letter written from "An Employer" to the editor of the Quebec *Morning Chronicle* and published on January 15, 1867 included the following:

> Although from the nature of their business the large retail stores cannot join in the Saturday half holiday movement, there would, I think, be no difficulty in doing what is done in other cities, and in several stores in Quebec, i.e. let half the young men leave on Saturdays at noon, in their turn, thus enabling them to take daylight exercise in skating, snowshoeing or rifle-shooting, a boon they would have thankfully appreciated during the winter months.

Whether or not such requests were positively answered in *both* white and blue collar work settings is a rather problematic question, but by 1875 (June 29) the editor of the *Halifax Citizen* apparently had cause to report that "the Saturday half-holiday has become an institution, and no one adopting the system has yet had cause to regret it."

Sporting Facilities

As at least some urban residents acquired more leisure time to participate in many different social activities, sporting facilities were in great demand. When facilities were lacking the sporting enthusiasts often improvised or devised their own until the town authorities or, as was more likely, an enterprising citizen with a keen business sense, provided suitable arenas or venues. Sports equipment was also in great demand and many items and articles became cheaper and standardized as manufacturing developed.

Baseball was exceptionally popular in Toronto in the 1880's. After the opening international league game of the 1888 season the following comments appeared in *The Globe* of May 14:

> What a baseball town Toronto has come to be! Four years ago the promoters of the game in this city were glad to get an opportunity of using the Jarvis Street lacrosse grounds when the Canadian game was not on, and the interest in the game was very limited. But on Saturday the attendance on the Toronto Baseball Club's own grounds, unsurpassed by any of the International ball fields, was larger by 4,000 people than the attendance at the opening game in any other International city. And Toronto floats the championship flag.

Indoor curling rinks were also popular (*Montreal Gazette*, June 12, 1867; Reed, 1944: 18), and despite the fact that many cities required a licensing fee, they usually proved to be a profitable venture (*Toronto By-Laws*, 1870: 100). Indoor rinks made curling a more appealing sport and some excellent facilities were financed and erected by curling club members. In 1867 a new facility was built in Ottawa at the cost of one thousand dollars, and it included two curling lanes, archery galleries, bowling alleys and changing facilities (*Ottawa Times*, December 14, 1867). The Granite Curling Club of Toronto erected a new building in 1886, and in addition to curling facilities there were reading, billiard and card rooms, and lawn tennis courts (*The Globe*, December 1, 1886). The oldest curling club in North America, the Montreal Curling Club, moved to their own rink on St. Catherine Street, and in 1892 moved to St. Luke Street where there were "three sheets of superb ice, and lounging rooms with every comfort" (Montreal Curling Club, 1907: 36). Towards the end of the century lights powered by electricity made the conditions at night as good as during the day (*Calgary Herald*, October 1, 1890; *Lethbridge News*; June 9, 1895; Kerr, 1904: 367).

Skating rinks were built or leased by enterprising gentlemen, and there were many elegant rinks by the end of the century. The pride and joy of Montrealers was the Victoria Rink which, although built in 1862, was still the "largest and best skating rink in Europe or America" (Murray, 1892: 25). The arch-like roof was fifty-two feet above the two hundred feet by eighty feet expanse of ice. There was a platform around the wall for spectators, a podium for the band, and, before the advent of electricity, five hundred gas lanterns illuminated this magnificent structure (Jenkins, 1966: 406).

Hockey enthusiasts began to use the existing skating and curling rinks for their games but after the Amateur Hockey Association was formed in 1886, rinks designed specifically for that sport were soon built. (*The Globe*, December 9, 1895).

Although there were few golf courses available in urban areas, several golfing clubs were formed and members played on the commons. By the turn of the century, however, most of the large urban centres had at least one golf course (Cox 1969: 129-131). The Toronto *Globe* of November 17, 1896 reported that the Toronto Golf Club had "lockers containing the playing outfits of members, a number of whom are now exchanging morning coats and patent leathers for the businesslike golfing suits".

Lacrosse matches in eastern Canada attracted very large crowds so it was necessary for clubs to use arenas which could accommodate them. However, when Ottawa played Montreal in 1889, even the new grounds in Montreal could not accommodate the vast throng:

> To count it was impossible, but taking into consideration that the immense and commodious grand stand was crowded to its utmost capacity; that the cheap spectator's side could not accommodate any more; that parts of the fence were laden with enthusiastic supporters and that even the telegraph poles looked like trees laden with fruit, an estimate of 9,000 is perhaps too low. (*Ottawa Citizen*, August 19, 1889).

Swimming and bathing facilities were another undertaking which municipal councils often left to private enterprise. This recreational activity was the subject of many council debates which resulted in the areas and hours of bathing being carefully stipulated in by-laws. The penalty for illegal bathing in Halifax was between one and twenty dollars, or jail for up to ten days should a person "swim or bathe in the waters of the harbor near to any open wharf, slip or dock, or to any street or road in the city, or otherwise in such a situation as to be exposed to the view of spectators" (Halifax Council Laws, 1876: 208). When swimming areas were provided, swimming clubs were often formed. A swimming club was formed in Montreal in 1876; by 1879 there were over eight hundred members (*Le Nouveau Monde*, July 26, 1877; July 5, 1880).

Schools and the "Club" system

The schools and universities which were almost always located in the urban areas also served to promote the spread of sport within the communities. Games and sports were popular in the schools, and when students left to become a part of the urban labour force, or continued on to university, they maintained their interest in physical activity. Although there were few high schools during this period (Johnson, 1968: 87), institutions such as Upper Canada College, the University of Toronto, McGill University, Queen's University, University of Ottawa, Royal Military College, Victoria College, Acadia University, Dalhousie University and Manitoba College fostered recreational activities and sporting competition within their programmes of learning (Dickson and Adam, 1893; Johnson, 1968; Reed, 1944).

The origin of the "club " system of sport was a phenomenon of urbanization resulting from an uprooting of the traditional rural approach to recreation. Urban living imposed different restrictions on individuals and yet, concomitantly, it also offered more opportunities for individuals with common interests to assemble together and organize competition amongst themselves. Whereas the leisure activities of rural life were of an informal, loosely structured nature, the restrictions of space and time imposed upon the urban dweller caused him to adapt his sporting pursuits to fit in with this different mode of living. Harrison has stated that urbanization demanded economy of time which could be utilized by codifying the rules of sports, and by abandoning sports of uncertain duration. Many sports became codified in the latter third of the nineteenth century and were played according to stringent regulations and within a specific duration of time. Lacrosse was an example of this development.

In 1867 the rules of lacrosse stipulated that "a match will be decided by winning three games out of five" and a "game" occurred each time a goal was scored (*Montreal Gazette*, July 17, 1867). Consequently, the actual duration of a game could have been short, which did not suit the spectators, or as occurred on some occasions, have to be postponed because of darkness (Howell and Howell, 1969: 72). In 1888 the National Amateur Lacrosse Association fixed a time limit for matches, and in 1894 that same body changed all the association matches to the majority of games in two hours (*The Globe*, April 14, 1894).

Conclusion

What was the relationship between urbanization and sport in Canada in the period 1867-1900? As the number and size of towns and cities grew, so organized sport grew. Although the origins of many sports were in the rural settings, it was along with the processes of urbanization that pastimes and games developed into sports in order to provide regular competitive physical activity governed by established rules. It was in the latter years of the nineteenth century that local clubs, and town, city, regional, provincial and national leagues and associations began to emerge and govern sport. Sports which had regional, provincial or national associations by 1900 included baseball, cricket, lacrosse, English rugby, soccer, Canadian rugby, lawn bowling, lawn tennis, cycling, canoeing, rowing, curling, skating and hockey. Other associations which fostered and incorporated several sports had also been formed; these included the Montreal Amateur Athletic Association, the Toronto Athletic Club, and the Amateur Athletic Association of Canada.

Urban centres fostered and encouraged organized sport through better transportation, designated hours for leisure and recreational pursuits, the availability of sporting equipment and facilities, and perhaps of most importance, the personnel in the form of those urban dwellers who had both the opportunity and the desire to participate in sporting activities.

NOTES

1. (Editor's Note) See, for example, Gary Teeple, "Land, Labour, and Capital in Pre-Confederation Canada", (1972).

2. For a broader discussion of the issues surrounding work conditions see the *Royal Commission on the Relations of Labour and Capital in Canada, 1889*. (Editor's note) A history of Unionism in Canada can be found in Lipton, (1967).

REFERENCES

Aronson, S. H.
1965   "The Sociology of the Bicycle." T. E. Lasswell, et. al. (eds.), *Life in Society*. Chicago: Scott, Foresman.
Athletic Life
1895-1896   Selected issues. Vols. 1 and 3. Toronto.
Brett, K. B. and J. McErvel
1969   *A Shopper's View of Canada's Past—Pages from Eaton's Catalogues, 1886—1930*. Toronto: University of Toronto Press.
Canada
1902   *Census of Canada, 1901*. Vols. 1-4. Ottawa: King's Printer.
1939   *Royal Commission on Dominion-Provincial Relations*, Books 1 and 2. Ottawa: King's Printer.
1889   *Royal Commission on the Relations of Labour and Capital in Canada*. Ottawa: Queen's Printer.
1900   *Statistical Year Book of Canada for 1900*. Ottawa: Government Printing Bureau.

Cox, A. E.
1969   "A History of Sports in Canada, 1868-1900." Unpublished Ph.D. dissertation, The University of Alberta, Edmonton.

Dickson, G. and G. Adam
1893   A History of Upper Canada College, 1829-1892. Toronto: Rowsell and Hutchinson.

T. Eaton and Company Limited, Toronto
1892-1900   Sales Catalogues.

Fullerton, D. H. and H. A. Hampson
1957   Canadian Secondary Manufacturing Industry. The Royal Commission on Canada's Economics Prospects Ottawa: Queen's Printer.

Glazebook, G. P. de T.
1964   A History of Transportation in Canada, Vols. 1 and 2. Toronto: McClelland and Stewart.
1968   Life in Ontario—A Social History. Toronto: The University of Toronto Press.

Halifax City Council
1876   Laws and Ordinances relating to the City of Halifax. Halifax: James Bowes and Sons.

Howell, Nancy and M. L. Howell
1969   Sports and Games in Canadian Life, 1770 to the Present. Toronto: MacMillan.

Jenkins, K.
1966   Montreal, Island City of the St. Lawrence. New York: Doubleday.

Johnson, F. H.
1968   A Brief History of Canadian Education. Toronto: McGraw Hill.

Kerr, J.
1904   Curling in Canada and the United States. Toronto: Toronto News Co.

Kesterton, W. H.
1967   A History of Journalism in Canada. Toronto: McClelland and Stewart.

Lavallee, O.S.A.
1961   The Montreal City Passenger Railway Company. Montreal: Canadian Railroad Historical Association.

Lindsay, P. L.
1969   "A History of Sport in Canada, 1807-1867". Unpublished Ph.D. dissertation, The University of Alberta, Edmonton.

Lipton, Charles
1967   The Trade Union Movement of Canada, 1827-1959. Toronto: New Canada Press.

Mather, B. and M. McDonald
1958   New Westminster: The Royal City. Toronto: Dent.

Meadows, P.
1957   "The City, Technology, and History." Social Forces, 36.

Montreal Curling Club
1907   The Montreal Curling Club, 1807-1907 Montreal: A booklet published by the Club.

Moore, W. E.
1965   The Impact of Industry. Englewood Cliffs, New Jersey: Prentice-Hall.

Murray, N.
1892   Murray's Illustrated Guide to Montreal and Vicinity. Montreal: Norman Murray.

Reed, T. A.
1944   The Blue and White—A Record of Fifty Years of Athletic Endeavour at the University of Toronto. Toronto: University of Toronto Press.

Reid, J. E.
1969   "Sports and Games in Alberta Before 1900." Unpublished Master of Arts thesis, the University of Alberta.

Ross, M. G.
1951   The Y.M.C.A. in Canada. Toronto: The Ryerson Press.

Royal Montreal Golf Club
1923   The Royal Montreal Golf Club, 1873-1923. Montreal: A booklet published by the Club.

Scott, B. S.
1926   "Industrial History of London Since 1850." Unpublished Master of Arts thesis, University of Western Ontario, London

Stevens, G. R.
1965   The Incomplete Canadian—An Approach to a Social History. Canada: G. R. Stevens.

Stone, L. O.
1967   Urban Development in Canada. Ottawa: Dominion Bureau of Statistics.

Teeple, Gary
1972   "Land, Labour and Capital in Pre-Confederation Canada." In G. Teeple (ed.), Capitalism and the National Question in Canada. University of Toronto Press.

Toronto Transit Commission
1967   Transit in Toronto, 1849-1967. Toronto: A booklet published by the Commission.

Toronto Municipal Council
1870   By-Laws of the City of Toronto. Toronto: Henry Rowsell.

ORGANIZED SPORT AND SOCIAL STRATIFICATION IN MONTREAL: 1840-1901

Alan Metcalfe

Introduction

Both sport and social stratification have received scant attention from Canadian historians. Few systematic, in depth analyses of social stratification have been attempted,[1] and there have been even fewer inquiries into the changing relationship of systems of social stratification to sport. The recent work by Wise and Fisher (1974) stands as somewhat of an exception to this pattern, but even they have emphasized the influence of leading individuals on the growth and development of sport, rather than analyzing the impact of social stratifications itself.[2] In fact, sport gives the historian an ideal medium for examining systems of stratification in that it is in their free time that men and women are free to choose with whom they will associate. In such voluntary associations the basic underlying patterns of a society can be observed. The function of this paper is, therefore, twofold. First, to examine the growth of organized sport in Montreal with a focus on who played, administered and organized it.[3] Secondly, to examine the social characteristics of these individuals and groups in terms of ethnicity, occupation and religion. This examination should serve to give both a description of the growth of organized sport in late nineteenth century Canada and some insights into the composition of Montreal society.

The choice of Montreal as a focus for the analysis at hand was not fortuitous; it presents an ideal case study of Canadian sport and society. Throughout the nineteenth century it was the commercial centre of British North America and was the first city in terms of population and industry. Added to this was the fact that in some ways, organized sport in Canada, and perhaps North America, was a creation of Montrealers (cf., Wise and Fisher, 1974:13). Finally, it was in Montreal that we see most clearly a basic reality of Canadian life, the clash between the French and English speaking communities.

The Growth of Elite Sporting Clubs, 1840-1860

On Saturday afternoons, during the winter of 1840, a group of twelve Montrealers embarked on "constitutional tramps" into the wilds around the city. This was the inauspicious beginning of the prestigious and influential Montreal Snow Shoe Club (M.S.S.C.).[4] These excursions heralded the beginning of a flurry of interest in sport which culminated in the organization of curling, tandem, racquet, cricket, snow shoe and athletic clubs, to join the Montreal Curling (1807), and Hunt (1829) Clubs in providing recreation for the elite of Montreal society. In 1842, 241 leading French and British citizens formed the Montreal Olympic Athletic Club.[5] They also sponsored the snow shoe and racquet clubs, promoted the racquet court (1842), and played in the white versus Indian lacrosse game in 1843. The membership included officers from the military garrison, Scottish merchants, and a variety of professional and political figures, both French and British. The M.S.S.C. elected as its first president Col. Ermantinger, a fur trader and magistrate, and included as members his brother, the chief of police; E. Lamontagne, in later years a wine merchant in New York; C. J. Coursol, judge, major and M.P.; E. Goff Penny, later M.P. for Montreal; bank managers, lawyers, aides-de-camp to the governor general; and a future Under Secretary of State (cf., *Montreal Star*, July 7, 1885). Except for Nicholas "Evergreen" Hughes, the "father" of snow shoeing, lacrosse and athletics, who remained throughout his life a government clerk, the members were drawn from the highest social strata of Montreal society.

Although their primary function was *social*, these clubs did sponsor periodic competitions. Members of the Snow Shoe Club organized the first snow shoe races on the St. Pierre race course in 1843, and in the same year played in the first recorded white versus Indian lacrosse game.[6] The Olympic Athletic Club organized a regatta between Montreal and Quebec and in 1844 ran the Montreal Olympic Games, (Becket: 1877-1880). In these competitions, club members competed against men from all walks of life. The first snow shoe race was won by Deroche, a northwest Voyageur, in competition with Nicholas Hughes and five Indians. The major races in the Olympic Games were won by Sgt. McGillvary of the garrison; Tarisonkwan, an Indian; E. Burroughs, a lawyer; and "Evergreen" Hughes (Becket: 1877-1880). In the 1840's a Montreal boat pulled against one manned by Quebec watermen. This utopian view of friendly competition between the different strata of society should not be overdrawn. Such open competitions were few and social differences between competitors were still evident. The provision of a choice of prizes, medals or money was an explicit recognition of social differences while the refusal of a Quebec crew to row against Montreal because of the alleged inclusion of a working man, indicates that the differences were very real. In fact, the clubs as opposed to the competitions, were the exclusive preserve of the social elite.

The establishment of mills on the Lachine Canal in 1847 signalled the beginning of a new period in the history of Montreal—the era of industrialization. This, in conjunction with the opening of the Montreal Telegraph Company in 1847, the commencement of the Grand Trunk Railway in 1852, and the establishment of a rail link with Toronto in 1856, resulted in a change in the established patterns of work and leisure. No longer did the onset of winter herald the "cessation of the active bustle which characterizes the mercantile portion of our city" (*Montreal Transcript*, December 23, 1847); instead, commerce continued on a year-round basis. While the railway served to break down the seasonal differences of work and leisure, industrialization destroyed the daily rhythm, creating new concepts of time, symbolized by the pervasive presence of the factory whistle. Organized sport was largely a creation of this process.

The effects of industrialization were not felt immediately; sport was still organized spasmodically—a few snow shoe tramps, irregular competitions involving officers and men of the garrison, and infrequent regattas. Only one sport was played on a regular, organized basis—curling. By 1850, Montreal could claim three curling clubs; the Montreal (1807); the Thistle (1843) and the Caledonia (1850). Although there were references to curling on the river, these clubs were the only ones to be formally constituted; own private, covered rinks; and have a continuous existence to 1901. Their membership was drawn exclusively from the Scottish and native Canadian mercantile, professional class of St. Antoine and St. Laurent wards. The democratizing claims made by some for curling, were certainly not evident in Montreal—these clubs remained among the most exclusive throughout the nineteenth century.

Organizational Development and Democratization, 1860-1901

The birth of the Montreal Lacrosse Club (M.L.C.) in 1856 signalled a new era in the development of organized sport. Within four years there were six lacrosse teams, ten snow shoe and five cricket clubs. However, the main focus was *social* rather than *competitive*; there is little evidence of any regular competition, play being restricted to intra club practices. The existence of at least sixteen clubs implies a widening of the base of participation. In fact, the number of clubs obscures the common social origins of the lacrossists and snow shoers. Several of the new clubs were formed by dissatisfied members of the M.L.C. and the M.S.S.C. The lacrossists of summer became the snow shoers in winter; for instance, the executives of the Beaver Lacrosse and Snow Shoe Clubs for 1859-60 contained nine out of fifteen members in common. Added to this was the fact that there was little or no differentiation between executives and players; in 1860 seven of nine executives of the Beaver Lacrosse Club and six of nine of the M.L.C. were active players. In other words, the players, administrators and officials of the lacrosse and snow shoe clubs tended to be drawn from the same social group. Membership to these select clubs was further restricted by a system to control entry of undesireables. Aspiring members had to be nominated by two of the membership, investigated by a committee, and finally voted for by the membership of the club. Even at this stage most clubs included a system whereby 'one black ball in ten votes could exclude an applicant'.[7] This discriminatory system remained in operation throughout the nineteenth century.

The partial results of such exclusionary practices are revealed in Table I. The executives and players among membership of the sixteen clubs were drawn from 42% of the male population—the commercial and professional groups. In fact, selection was much more restricted—only a small percentage of the commercial group were from the lower levels of the commercial ladder; clerks, cashiers, bookkeepers; the majority of the others included partners in thriving firms and a variety of merchants, brokers and store owners. This was, indeed, the developing bourgeois elite of Montreal society.[8]

TABLE I

OCCUPATIONS OF A SAMPLE OF CLUB EXECUTIVES AND PLAYERS IN 1860, COMPARED TO MONTREAL LABOUR FORCE OF THE PERIOD

Occupation	Club Executives[a] & Players (%) (N=40)	Montreal Labour[b] Force (%)
Professional	20	4
Commercial		
(a) Businessmen, merchants and store owners	65 ⎫	22
(b) Bookkeepers, clerks and salesmen	8 ⎭	
Domestic	0	16
Industrial	0	41
Agriculture	0	1
Not Classified	7	16

a. Data from *Mackay's Montreal Directory, 1860-61*. (Montreal, 1860).
b. From *Census, 1861*.

The early 1860's were a period of slow growth for organized sport, yet significant changes were occurring which indicated a changing focus of sport.[9] In 1861-62 the snow shoe clubs inaugurated the yearly championship races, each club sponsoring races during the month of February. This led in the late 1860's to the growth of racing clubs; e.g., Alexandra 1869, Dominion 1868-1870, as opposed to the more socially oriented tramping clubs. Paralleling this was an increasing differentiation in competition between club members and non members—no longer did Voyageurs, Indians and NCO's from the garrison compete against club members, but rather in separate races. At the M.S.S.C. races in March, 1862, there were, an Indian race for $20, four open races, one club race and a garrison race for NCO's and privates for prizes of $6, $4, and $2.[10] Although this systematic discrimination was by no means general, there was an increasing differentiation between competitors in terms of the prizes offered; medals and trophies being offered to members and money to Indians, NCO's and later various tradesmen within the industrial establishments. This was the beginning of the amateur/professional conflict which plagued organized sport throughout the nineteenth century.[11]

In September, 1867, forty-two delegates from Ontario and Quebec met at Kingston, Ontario, to establish a National Lacrosse Association (N.L.A.). This meeting, called by a group of Montreal lacrossists led by Dr. W. G. Beers, was the first attempt to establish a "national" organization to control and administer the competitive team sport, and reflected a change in focus in which the *outcome* of the game assumed an increasingly important role.[12] The leadership of these English speaking Montreal merchants and professional men was central to the growth of sport organization in Montreal and Canada (cf Wise and Fisher, 1974:20). Many belonged to the M.L.C. and M.S.S.C. who, in 1877, joined forces to rent club rooms to provide for the social needs of the members.

In 1881, the M.L.C. and M.S.S.C. analgamated with the Montreal Bicycle Club (M.B.C.) to form the Montreal Amateur Athletic Association (M.A.A.A.). During the next two decades the M.A.A.A. expanded to include the Montreal Football Club, the Montreal Skating and Tobogganing Club, the Montreal Hockey Club and a lawn tennis club. This organization became the most important single body influencing the growth of organized sport in Montreal and Canada. On December 10, 1883, W. L. Maltby, H. W. Becket and Thomas L. Paton, all of the M.A.A.A., distributed a circular to clubs in Montreal pertaining to the formation of an amateur athletic association in Canada. The result was a meeting on December 13, 1883, which led to the creation of the Canadian Amateur Athletic Association (C.A.A.A.) on April 12, 1884.[13]

During the early years of the C.A.A.A. members of the M.A.A.A. played a significant role in the executive of the national organization; four presidents and thirty of 103 members of the executive between 1883 and 1890 were members of the M.A.A.A.[14] The M.A.A.A. was also involved in various other early national groups; A. T. Lane, Horace Tibbs, and Louis Rubinstein held executive positions in the Canadian Wheelmen's Association (1883) (C.W.A.) and were recognized as early as 1884 as having contributed significantly to the growth of "wheeling" in Canada.

In December, 1886, in conjunction with representatives from the Victoria, McGill, Crystal and Ottawa hockey clubs, representatives of the M.A.A.A. met to form an amateur hockey association of Canada. Louis

Rubinstein, the great Canadian figure skater, was officially recognized at the second annual meeting of the Canadian Amateur Skating Association (C.A.S.A.) for his contributions to the organization and development of the C.A.S.A. (Becket: 1886-1890). Throughout the nineteenth century the members of the M.A.A.A. were at the forefront in organizing and developing national organizations, in the promotion and hosting of national championships, and in the growth of Canadian sport per se.

The membership of the M.A.A.A. reveals the basic social characteristics of this powerful group. The predominance of white collar workers associated with the commercial activity of the city (87%) is clearly demonstrated in Table II. Certain segments of Montreal society were noticeable by their absence in the M.A.A.A.—particularly the upper and lower strata. There was for example, a complete absence of industrial workers. But perhaps more noteworthy was a lack of representation from the political, industrial and educational power elite; by 1901 the Molsons, Redpaths, and Allans were conspicuous by their absence; few professors from McGill were members and no reference could be found to the local and provincial political leaders.[15] Much of the organization of sport had shifted from the social elites of the first half of the nineteenth century, to the solid mercantile middle class of 1901. It was this group who was essential to the growth of organized sport throughout the late nineteenth century.

TABLE II

OCCUPATION OF EXECUTIVES AND PLAYERS OF M.A.A.A. AND AFFILIATED CLUBS IN 1901 COMPARED TO THE 1860 SAMPLE OF CLUB EXECUTIVES AND PLAYERS

Occupation	1860 Sample of Club Executives & Players (%) (cf., Table I) (N=40)	Executive & Players of M.A.A.A. & Affiliated Clubs in 1901[a] (%) (N=54)
Professional	20	13
Commercial		
(a) Businessmen, merchants and store owners	65	33
(b) Bookkeepers, clerks & sales personnel	8	47
(c) Managers & assistant managers of companies	0	7

[a]Data compiled from *Report of Directors of M.A.A.A., 1902; Lovell's Montreal Directory, 1900-1901 (Montreal: 1901).*

Yet, it would be misleading to imply that the growth and dominance of the mercantile middle class was the only force affecting the sporting activities of the period. The decade of the 1860's witnessed the emergence of new social patterns in the organization and playing of sports; clubs sprang up based on ethnicity, occupation, geographical location and even religion. In 1860, the Erina Lacrosse and Snow Shoe Clubs were formed by a group of Irish citizens. These clubs lived a brief life and then expired. More permanent was the Shamrock Lacrosse Club (1868) comprised of working class, Irish Catholics. The Shamrocks were the earliest working class organization and became the most successful lacrosse team in Canada between 1868 and 1885. These "horny handed sons of toil" were, for the most part, mechanics from the working class St. Anne's ward.[16] However, an analysis of the executives of this club illustrates a basic attribute of all successful Montreal clubs—the predominance of white collar workers. Of twenty-four executives of the S.L.C. in 1871, 1881, 1891 and 1901, only six were industrial workers—three machinists, a molder, a cattle foreman and a house painter—the remainder were clerks, bookkeepers, owners of businesses, a Q.C. and an M.D.[17] It would appear that although the players included working men, the organization was run by individuals with backgrounds that included some education and/or administrative experience.

In 1863, the Grand Trunk Railway Snow Shoe Club, located in Pointe St. Charles, was formed.[18] This was the first of many sporting clubs to bear the name of the G.T.R. Although there were G.T.R. clubs throughout the century, there were none who could claim a continuous existence. At the executive level, they exhibited the same characteristics as all the other clubs—dominance by white collar workers. If the trainmen, machinists, and workshop workers were involved in organized sport at all, it was at the playing level and certainly not in the administrative positions. These findings confirm the assertion that throughout the late nineteenth century much of organized sport continued to be dominated by the middle class.

By 1867, although organized sport existed on a more regular and widespread basis, it still lacked the regularity of league competition and formally organized structure. In fact, it had changed significantly since the 1840's when lawyers competed against Indians and Voyageurs. There was evidence of an increased social differentiation between players; no longer were the Indians admitted as equals to the snow shoe competitions; competitions between whites, and Indians were noticeable by their absence, except in lacrosse where the Indians of Caughnawaga and St. Regis still provided the best competition. At the same time, there was an increasing concern over the amateur/professional question which was, in part, an issue of social discrimination. Sport had entered an era of prolific growth and expansion, but parallel to the expansion was the beginning of the introduction of new standards of social exclusion.

Expansion in all aspects of sport continued between 1867 and 1885; 46 baseball clubs, 63 snow shoe and 78 lacrosse clubs competed for honours within the city.[19] Attempts to organize into local and national organizations were initiated by Montrealers; the Canadian Football Association (1873), the C.W.A. (1883) and the C.A.A.A. (1884) all owed their existence in some way to the efforts of Montreal sportsmen. New forms of competition developed; the Montreal Golf Club was founded in 1874, the Swimming Club in 1876, and Hockey in 1875. Mr. A. T. Lane claimed to be the first bicycle rider in North America (1873) and was responsible for the establishment of the first bicycle club in 1878.[20] Notwithstanding these significant changes, competition remained pre-industrial in nature—there were no regularly scheduled competitions; clubs still argued over the appropriate form of football; rules and regulations had not been standardized; and the uncertainty as to the length of the contest detracted from sport as a paying spectacle. Sport organization was in an embryonic state struggling towards the standardization necessary for large scale interclub, intercity competition.

The existence of 187 baseball, snow shoe and lacrosse clubs, in addition to the rash of competitions between employees of different organizations, churches and schools, indicates that the pool of players was expanding rapidly. New segments of society were represented in the new clubs; the first mechanics' lacrosse club (1872) and Le Canadien Snow Shoe Club (1878) were drawn from strata which previously had not been involved in organized sport. However as Table III indicates, there is little evidence of change in the basic composition of club members (nearly all of which were either executives or active sports participants). By 1881, 87% of the club members whose occupation could be identified, still belonged to the commercial and professional groups.

Table III fails to measure the increasing differentiation between players and executives that occurred between 1860 and the latter half of the century. For example in 1881, 37% of the executives of eight clubs were active players as opposed to the 80% of two clubs in 1861. In other words, by failing to differentiate between players and nonplayers in the membership, the data pattern revealed in Table III may obscure changes in the social positions of the players themselves. Nonetheless, all active players were club members by necessity, and Table III suggests that little democratization occurred in club membership between 1861 and 1901. The middle class continued to dominate, and few industrial workers were actually involved.

TABLE III

OCCUPATIONS OF SPORTING CLUB MEMBERS, 1861-1901[a] (PERCENTAGES)

Occupation	1861[b] (N=55)	1871 (N=86)	1881 (N=154)	1891 (N=159)	1901 (N=467)
Professional	20	16	16	8	13
Commercial	74	65	71	86	80
Domestic	0	0	0	0	0
Industrial	0	14	7	3	4
Agricultural	0	0	0	0	0
Not Classified	6	5	6	3	3

[a] Includes executives, players, and non-players.

[b] Data collected from *Mackay's Montreal Directory*,1860-61 (Montreal, 1860) and *Lovell's Montreal Directory*; 1871, 1881, 1891, 1901.

The marked growth of sports clubs in late nineteenth century Montreal must not be taken to imply that *all* of the new clubs were permanent or influential fixtures to the Montreal sporting environment. Indeed, the majority often "lived a feeble life and died a natural death".[21] These will-o'-the-wisp clubs exemplified a growing interest in sport but played a minor role in the codification of rules, promotion of competition, and the organization of local and national bodies. This may be the reason why baseball failed to make an impact upon Montreal; only thirteen clubs lasted for more than two years and none for the whole period. Of the sixty-three snow shoe clubs, only one, the M.S.S.C., thrived throughout the fifteen years and only six lived on into the 1890's. In addition to this, most of the clubs were concerned with the social aspects of snow shoeing and were not interested in organizing locally or nationally for the sake of competition. There were fifteen lacrosse clubs that maintained some degree of continuity throughout the nineteenth century, but only four or five of these were involved in a systematic way in the growth of the N.L.A.

Table IV illustrates clearly the central importance of a small group of sixteen clubs in the growth and development of six different sports on both a local and national level.[22]

In actuality, the social group from which the membership was drawn was even smaller than the figures would indicate; in the first place, four of the most important clubs—the Montreal Lacrosse, Snow Shoe, Hockey, and Football Clubs—were affiliated members of the M.A.A.A. Secondly, an examination of the executives of the other clubs reveals that many of their members also held membership in the M.A.A.A. In 1887, a newspaper stated of the M.A.A.A.:

A large proportion of the leading members of the other athletic clubs of the city owe it allegiance. The Montreal Yacht Club, the Montreal Golf Club, curling clubs and swimming clubs have in their membership so many members of the M.A.A.A. that we may be regarded as near relatives—the crew of the Lachine Rowing Club who hold the amateur four oar championship of the Dominion are members of the Association. The principle officers of the St. George Snow Shoe Club owe allegiance as members. More remarkable, still nearly all the members of the Britannia Football Club, the staunch rivals for the supremacy of the Dominion of the Montreal Club, are attached by membership to the same association which their rivals belong to by affiliation. (Becket, 1886-1891:19).

TABLE IV

CLUBS IN EXISTENCE FOR MORE THAN TEN YEARS, 1840-1901

Sport	Club	Founding Date
Lacrosse	Montreal (MAAA)	1856
	Shamrocks	1868
Snow Shoe	Montreal (MAAA)	1843
	St. George	1874
	Le Canadien	1878
	Argyle	1885
Cricket	Montreal	1840
Football	Montreal (MAAA)	1868
	Britannia	1874
	McGill	1873
Curling	Montreal	1807
	Thistle	1843
	Caledonia	1850
Hockey	Montreal (MAAA)	1884
	Victoria	1880
	McGill	1887

By 1901, the M.A.A.A. membership had grown to 2,331, but the majority were not involved in the administration and development of organized sport.[23] The power within the M.A.A.A. increasingly lay with the Board of Directors which was comprised of representatives from each of the affiliated clubs. Even though the lacrosse, snow shoe and other clubs maintained their independence, the composition of the M.A.A.A. executive from 1883-1897 clearly illustrates that the men who held the reins of the M.A.A.A. were the same individuals who were involved in the C.A.A.A., C.W.A., N.A.L.A., C.A.H.L. and C.A.S.A.[24] Of the seventy-one men who served on the executive during the fourteen year period, only nineteen were involved for more than three years. It was this small group of business owners and professional men who were actively involved in the local and national organizations. At least twelve of the nineteen were presidents, vice-presidents, secretary-treasurers, or committee members of the C.A.A.A., C.W.A., C.A.S.A. and N.A.L.A. The M.A.A.A. occupied a position of prestige and power in the organization of Canadian sport out of all proportion to its size.

When attention is focused on the totality of clubs and competitions which sprung up during the 70's and 80's, basic social patterns begin to emerge. Three different strata of society were involved in different types of sport: (a) a group comprised of the political and economic power elite; (b) some younger members of the elite and a mixture of commercial and professional men; and (c) an expanding group of socially heterogeneous individuals.

Representing the first group, the tandem and hunt clubs were exclusive in every sense of the word. Their membership included only the highest levels of society—the Molsons, Crawfords and Allans.[25] These clubs differed from the others in that *their major function was social and not competitive*. Throughout the century they remained the exclusive preserve of high "society".

At a different level, open to a wider but still exclusive base, were golf, hockey, football, lawn tennis and bicycling. Football was played by schoolboys, university students, graduates, and young men involved in the commercial life of the city. The members of both the Britannia and Montreal Football Clubs were drawn heavily from university graduates. Even in 1901 there were only four Canadian rule football teams in Montreal; these were the exclusive preserve of a small segment of society. There were three golf clubs in 1901—the Montreal, the Metropolitan, and Westmount—all highly selective and basically British, drawing heavily from the commercial and professional circles. All these clubs remained exclusive throughout the century; this is illustrated most clearly by the severely restricted number of teams. They were not democratized during this era. Bicycling started out as an elitist sport but by the 1890's had become embroiled in an amateur/professional conflict which was, in part, due to the entry of representatives from a different segment of society. This democratization of bicycling was parallelled by the gradual withdrawal of the M.B.C. from involvement in the affairs of the C.W.A.

It was in more competitive team sports that there was the greatest evidence of democratization. Although the white collar groups provided the leadership in organization and administration, different groups were involved in playing the game, albeit in a spasmodic and non-continuous capacity. Baseball was popular with French Canadian and working class groups. The rash of lacrosse games in 1881 prompted the Montreal Lacrosse Club to report in their Annual Review of 1881 that:

> "The closing weeks of the season were noticeable for the epidemic of lacrosse fever that attacked the youth of the city not immediately connected with any organized clubs and matches and return matches between the various trades, the printers, reporters and telegraph operators, caused quite an excitement among the contestants and their various supporters, and the grounds were in great demand."[26]

However, few of these groups organized themselves into clubs, and if they did, it was only for a brief moment in time. This should not obscure the fact that sport was being played by an increasingly large segment of the population although there is no evidence of a wider involvement in the organization and administration levels.

Democratization Reconsidered: Stratification and Ethnicity

A basic question underlying Canadian history pertains to the relationship between different ethnic groups, particularly between the French and the English. As suggested earlier in this paper, it was primarily in the 1870's and 1880's that teams with strong ethnic affiliations emerged: in the east end the French Canadian teams; in St. Anne's ward the Irish; and in St. Antoine's the English and Scots. From the outset of this period, teams from different ethnic groups competed together on the lacrosse fields and in the snow shoe races. This was clearly illustrated in the rivalry between the Montreal and Shamrock Lacrosse Clubs who contended for the championship of the Dominion between 1868 and 1885. Drawn from different social strata, they competed regularly but rarely interacted socially. As soon as French Canadian snow shoe and lacrosse clubs were formed they competed with the British clubs. In this instance, there was also social interaction as well as competitive contact. Accounts of the annual dinners of Le Canadien, Le Trappeur and Jacques Cartier Snow Shoe Clubs included toasts from representatives of the leading English speaking clubs. In the late 1880's, members of the snow shoe clubs in Montreal, both English and French, journeyed together to New York and paraded down Fifth Avenue.

In certain activities there were clubs that crossed ethnic boundaries. This was the case with the Montreal Swimming Club, formed in 1876; the membership included both French and English speaking members and at the annual meetings the reports were given in both languages. Added to this was the fact that the predominantly English St. George Snow Shoe Club included amongst its membership a number of French

Canadians. This fragmentary evidence does suggest that in certain instances members from both communities joined in both competition and socialization. It is interesting to observe that the clubs in which there was cross-ethnic interaction were those which tended to emphasize *social activities* as opposed to the *competitive activities*.

But, it would be a mistake to overemphasize the role that French Canadians played in the organized sporting activities of the period. Despite the inclusion of a few prominent French Canadian citizens, and notwithstanding the prolific expansion of clubs, the birth of new sports and the emergence of ethnic teams, organized sport in Montreal was largely dominated by the British middle class.

Relating to the above assertion of British dominance, Figure 1 illustrates the centrality of the St. Antoines ward as the place of residence of club members.[27] Comparing the data pattern displayed in Figure 1 to ethnic composition of Montreal (see Figure 2) it is possible to see that members from the predominantly French wards like St. Mary's are virtually non-existent. In other words, it seems that French Canadians (who at the time comprised 53% of Montreal's population) may have been virtually excluded from the mainstream of sports participation.[28] This contention is supported by the complete lack of French names among club members in the sample, and as Figure 3 reveals, by the dearth of recreational facilities in the eastern (largely French) portions of the city.

In summary, it can be argued that sport remained largely British, and was generally played and administrated by the men involved in the commercial life of the city who lived in St. Antoine's ward. This ward not only contained most club members and most of the available facilities, but also 67% of the club executives. Moreover, 63% of the organized games played in Montreal between 1870-1885 were played within its boundaries (see Table V).[29]

TABLE V
LOCATION OF GAMES PLAYED IN MONTREAL, 1870-1885[a]

Location	Number of Games Reported	%
St. Antoine's Ward	315	63
Pointe St. Charles Cote St. Paul Cote St. Henri	23	5
East Side	29	6
St. Laurent Ward	27	6
Not Identified	103	20

[a] Abstracted from *Montreal Star*, 1880-1885.

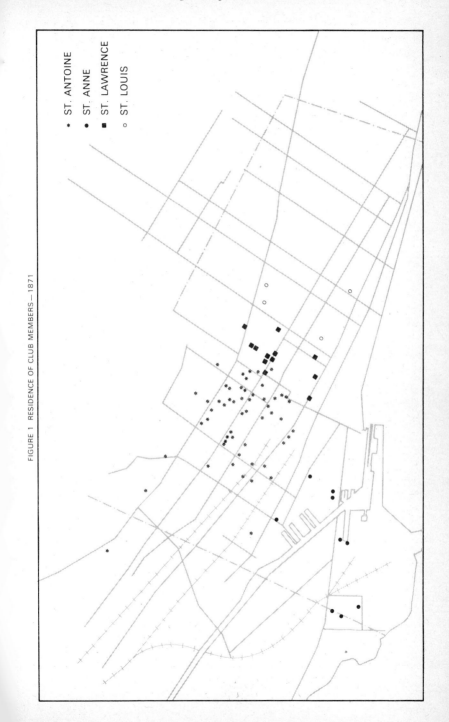

FIGURE 1 RESIDENCE OF CLUB MEMBERS — 1871

* ST. ANTOINE
• ST. ANNE
■ ST. LAWRENCE
○ ST. LOUIS

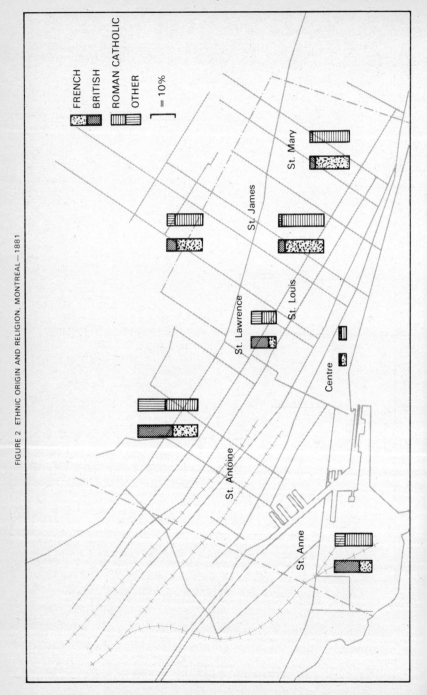

FIGURE 2 ETHNIC ORIGIN AND RELIGION, MONTREAL—1881

FRENCH
BRITISH
ROMAN CATHOLIC
OTHER

= 10%

St. Mary

St. James

St. Lawrence

St. Louis

Centre

St. Antoine

St. Anne

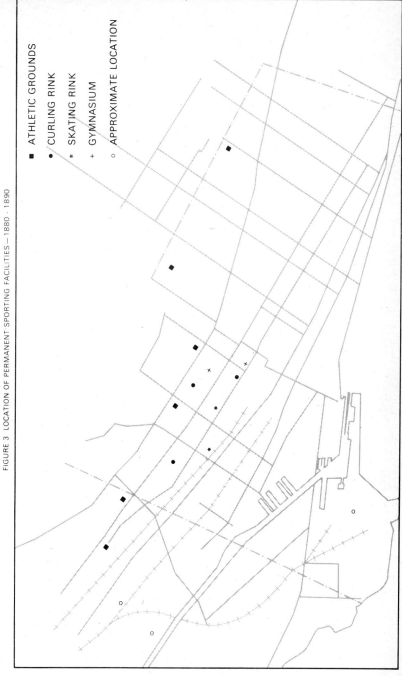

FIGURE 3 LOCATION OF PERMANENT SPORTING FACILITIES — 1880 - 1890

■ ATHLETIC GROUNDS

● CURLING RINK

✳ SKATING RINK

+ GYMNASIUM

○ APPROXIMATE LOCATION

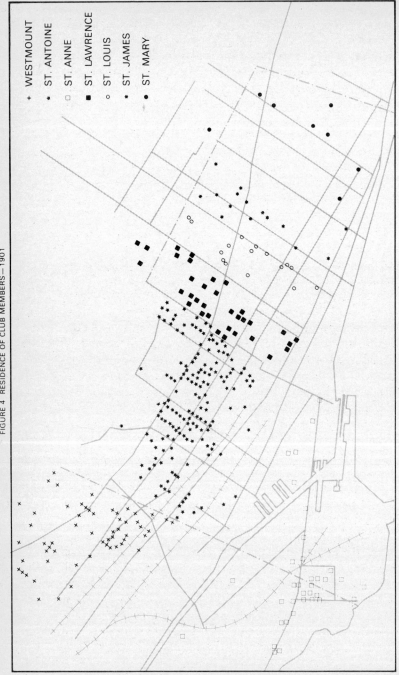

FIGURE 4 RESIDENCE OF CLUB MEMBERS—1901

+ WESTMOUNT
★ ST. ANTOINE
□ ST. ANNE
■ ST. LAWRENCE
○ ST. LOUIS
✳ ST. JAMES
● ST. MARY

In 1885 at the Annual Meeting of the National Amateur Lacrosse Association, the old championship system was abolished and replaced by a series system; in effect, a league; involving four teams, two each from Montreal and Toronto. Instead of spasmodic games, a regular schedule of games was developed. By 1901 there were at least twenty-two leagues involving 153 teams in eight sports. Sport was organized by schools, churches, YMCA and various work sponsored groups. Further to this, local amateur athletic associations had sprung up to meet the needs of different geographical locations; the M.A.A.A. served St. Antoine's ward and Westmount, the Montagnard A.A.A. the east end, the Argyle A.A.A. the periphery of St. Anne's and St. Antoine's wards, and Pointe St. Charles A.A.A. Organized sport was no longer the exclusive preserve of the British in the St. Antoine ward, and there was increased evidence suggesting that sport had truly become democratized.

However, a number of indices do not support this contention. Club membership at the turn of the century was still dominated by white collar workers (80%), over half of which continued to live in St. Antoine's ward. (See Figure 4). Add to this, the fact that 16% of club members were now living in Westmount (the nearly exclusive enclave of Protestant British) and a picture emerges which shows how organized sport continued to be a predominantly English affair even though French Canadians comprised 55% of Montreal's population. This concentration of clubs and players in the west end of the city is supported by the location of clubs and facilities (refer back to Figure 3)—50% of the membership of seventy-seven clubs was situated in St. Antoine and Westmount. Ninety-three per cent of the executives of fifteen hockey clubs also lived in this area. It would appear, therefore, that although organized sport had permeated throughout the whole city, the growth and concentration remained greater in the predominantly middle-class British areas.

It is evident from Figure 4 that there also continued to be a noticeable lack of participants from the working class areas of the city. The "city below the hill" which Ames (1897) described, contained only ten of the 459 identified executives and players in 1901 and none of these lived within the two ghetto areas of Griffin Town and the Swamp. Indeed, as was shown in Table III, only 4% of the sample of club members in 1901 were industrial workers. This lack of working class involvement in sport is given further support by the lack of facilities in St. Anne's ward, a predominantly labouring class area (see Figure 3).[30] However, there were signs that industrial groups were beginning to become involved in sport; the fathers of the secretaries of the Imperials and Strathcona Hockey

Clubs and the Beaver baseball clubs, all juvenile clubs, were two labourers and a train driver. Secretaries of a few clubs did live in working class areas. This should not be overemphasized however, since their involvement was peripheral and not related to the organization and administration of provincial and national organizations.

The involvement of the schools in organized sport with the inauguration of the School Athletic Association (1897) suggested a possible means of promoting competition amongst a wider segment of society. Once again, the reality reveals a different picture; at this time, high school education was reserved for a very small segment of society. Elementary education was neither general nor compulsory and there is little evidence that organized sport was played at any level except secondary. Therefore, the participants in high school sport were drawn from the sons and daughters of middle class Montrealers.

On the other hand, there were some indications that significant changes were taking place in the nature of sport, if not in the social composition of the executives and players. The M.A.A.A. was gradually losing its power to control affairs in amateur sports and was beginning to withdraw from involvement in the major amateur associations. Any real evidence of democratization, however, lies in the highly competitive sport of lacrosse. Lacrosse was moving rapidly towards professionalization and the players in the major lacrosse league were undoubtedly drawn from a different segment of society than the early lacrosse players. The involvement of working men, men from different ethnic groups, was evident. As the focus of sport switched to competition, there was an increased emphasis upon winning. This in itself meant a decreased importance being placed on *social origins* and an increased emphasis upon *ability*. The French Montagnard Lacrosse Club, competing in the National Amateur Lacrosse Union, included Irish and English Canadians on the team. It was at this level that the social barriers began to disintegrate and the real beginnings of democratization could be observed.

Conclusion

What conclusions can be drawn from the above analysis as to the relationship between sport and social stratification in Montreal during the second half of the nineteenth century? In the first place, the predominant position of the British, white collar middle class, *first as participants and always as organizers is striking*. There is no evidence to suggest that the working classes were ever successful in organizing and developing teams which had any degree of permanence. Although it is likely that the lower income and occupation groups did develop clubs, they were short-lived. It was the upper middle class who acted as the stimulus to the growth and development of sport, both on a local, provincial and national level and it was the men with organizational and commercial background who had the expertise necessary for the long-term development of an organization who provided the leadership. This leadership was provided first by the upper levels of white collar workers and increasingly as the century progressed by the clerks, bookkeepers, bank clerks, and cashiers.[31] Increasingly, these were the men who first as participants and later as organizers provided the necessary guidance for the growth and institutionalization of sport.

The second major feature was the predominance of the British of the St. Antoine's ward. Sport in Montreal during the nineteenth century was the history of the English, Irish and Scottish Canadians. French involvement came late and was never a powerful influence on the development of organized games. This was reflected in the location of clubs, the development of facilities and the home location of the executives. These all focused very heavily upon the predominantly Protestant British St. Antoine's ward and later Westmount.

Thirdly, if there was any democratization of sport, it was at the playing level only and never at the administrative or social levels. There were various methods of social discrimination which varied from sport to sport; the golf, hunt and tandem clubs were the exclusive preserve of the monied commercial and political elite. It was in the competitive team sports that any degree of democratization was to be found and even in this instance there was continued discrimination by ethnicity, occupation, religion and geographical location. It would appear that there was an increasing differentiation between players and executives as the century progressed. This, of course, lead or could lead to a difference of opinion as to the meaning of sport between different levels of the same organization. This was certainly evident in the difference between the objectives of the Montreal Lacrosse Club early in the twentieth century and the focus of the parent organization, the M.A.A.A. Finally, there was certainly rigid discrimination in the essentially *social* clubs in which the boundaries were strictly maintained.

In terms of the social structure of Montreal, the history of organized sport provides the foundation for some interesting hypotheses. It seems clear that there was a relatively rigid social system based heavily on occupation and ethnicity. However, the evidence does allow for the tentative suggestion that the barriers of occupational differentiation may have been greater than those of ethnicity. Where sports participation was concerned, French and English often communicated horizontally between groups of a similar social status rather than vertically with groups of a similar ethnic background. The involvement of the M.A.A.A. and the leading French Canadian clubs in exclusive bowling and billiard leagues in the late nineteenth century is concrete evidence of this. If this is the case, it was not language or ethnic background that was the major stumbling block to mass participation but rather that of social class.

NOTES

1. For some important exceptions see Katz (1971:209-244). (Editor's note): see also Teeple (1972); Johnson (1974); Ryerson (1968); Myers (1972) and Acheson (1972).
2. See Wise and Fisher (1974:13-25). The basic findings of this paper support many of the conclusions Wise and Fisher arrive at. However, this study which was completed independent of their work, details the issues in much greater depth
3. Organized sport is simply defined as formally constituted sporting clubs that promoted intra and inter club competition. This eliminates from consideration the mass recreational activities participated in at picnics and spasmodically throughout the year.
4. For a history of the M.S.S.C. see Becket (1882).
5. A list of names is given in the Montreal Daily Star, July 7, 1885.
6. For an in-depth description, see H. W. Becket, Scrapbook, Montreal A.A.A., 1877-1880 (page 71).
7. See Becket (1882). This system of black balling was general throughout many of the nineteenth century clubs. It was, of course, one of the most effective mechanisms to ensure social homogeneity.
8. A major problem facing scholars analyzing concepts such as social class and social stratification is one of definition. This problem is accentuated by the time difference; e.g. nineteenth century. It is dangerous to use modern measurement systems. A preliminary attempt to define nineteenth century social stratification has been undertaken by Katz (1971). This, however, is still in the early stages. Because of these problems no attempt has been made, in this paper, to define social stratification in a completely objective manner. The approach taken here has been to accept the differentiation systems used by nineteenth century Montrealers—the census occupational categories and subjective names such as "elite". The result is that certain well-defined strata do emerge from the findings of this study.
9. This changing focus is from social activities dominated by expressive dimensions of "play" or "recreation" to more instrumental "sport" forms such as athletics. Increasingly competition becomes the central focus of these clubs rather than the social activities associated with participation. See also Metcalfe (1975) for a case study of this process in lacrosse.
10. See the Minute Book of Montreal Snow Shoe Club, 1861-1870.
11. The amateur/professional conflict can, therefore, be seen as a confrontation between different social strata. There is evidence to support the hypothesis that it was, in fact, class conflict.
12. The term "national" should be approached with caution. Many of these organizations were "national" in name only, representing, for the most part, clubs or individuals in Montreal or Toronto. However, this in no way diminishes the role of Montreal in the growth of organized sport.
13. See the Minute Book of the A.A.A. of C., 1883, 1884.
14. Data from Annual Reports of Amateur Athletic Association of Canada, 1887-1889; and the Minute Book of the A.A.A. of C., 1883-1888.
15. A notable exception to this was Ald. Jas. McShane, Mayor of Montreal in 1891. He

was associated with many Irish clubs as Honourary President. However, there is no evidence that he ever took an active role in the affairs of any sporting clubs.

16. Evidence of the working class background of the Shamrocks can be found in *Montreal Star*, October 9, 1874; H. W. Becket, *Scrapbook of the M.A.A.A., 1877-1880*, (315-324). The Shamrocks are a fascinating group, obviously working class, who prospered in the midst of clubs comprised of the upper socio-economics groups.

17. The names of executives were taken from the *Montreal* Star, occupations from *Lovell's Montreal Directory, 1871, 1881, 1891, 1901*. The problem of sampling will be discussed later (see footnote 27); however, the sample was neither random nor unbiased. It is possible that more machinists, mechanics, etc. were involved at the administrative level but there is no doubt that the men who served for a prolonged period of time were for the most part white-collar workers.

18. The nature of the relationship of these clubs to the G.T.R. is unknown. They did play some games on G. T. property and most of the executives and players who could be identified were G.T. employees.

19. These clubs were extracted from the *Montreal Star, 1869-1885*, Becket, *Scrapbook M.A.A.A., 1872-76*; Becket, *Scrapbook M.A.A.A., 1877-1880*; Becket, *The Montreal Snow Shoe Club, Its History and Record*; H. W. Becket, *Record of Winter Sports, 1883-1884* (Montreal: 1884); *Minute Books of the Montreal Snow Shoe Club, 1861-1885*; *Minute Book of the Montreal Football Club, 1872-1885; Minute Book, Montreal Bicycle Club, 1878-1882*.

20. See the *Minute Book, Montreal Bicycle Club, 1872-1882*.

21. Cited in the *Minute Book, Montreal Snow Shoe Club, 1877*, November 14, 1877.

22. See *Montreal Star, 1868-1901*; Becket (1882); and Becket (1872-76), (1877-80), (1886-91).

23. See the *Report of Directors of M.A.A.A., 1902*.

24. C.A.H.L. refers to Canadian Amateur Hockey League Cf., *Report of Directors of M.A.A.A., 1902*.

25. The members of these clubs were drawn from the pinnacle of Montreal society. The membership of many older members of the M.A.A.A. is an indirect measure of the social status of the M.A.A.A.

26. Cited from *Minute Book, Montreal Lacrosse Club, 1882*.

27. Data from *Lovell's Montreal Directory, 1871-72*. The validity and reliability of the data presented in Figures 2 and 4 and Tables I, II, III is central to this paper. The identification of individual club members as living at a certain address is critical because this also gives the occupation. There was no clear-cut, simple method of identification but rather a complex set of criteria for identifying addresses, occupation, and ethnicity. In the first place, no name was identified if there was any doubt; this, in fact, led to the disregarding of much valuable data. The procedures followed for 1871 were followed for 1881, 1891, 1901. For 1870, 22 clubs and 197 players and executives were identified. Of these, only 86 were finally used.

Methods

1) Exact name and initials must be present; e.g., E. M. Ermatinger was omitted because the directory identified E. Ermatinger.

2) Addresses and/or occupations often given in newspapers. This often spread over 20 years; therefore, knowledge of individuals was accumulated over time.

3) Certain clubs were work affiliated; e.g., G.T.R. clubs. The occupations were thus used to identify addresses; e.g., Clerk in G.T.R. Audit Office—See G.T.R. Audit Office Hockey Club.

4) Information on address and/or occupation in the records of the M.A.A.A. Scrapbooks, Annual Reports of M.A.A.A. and affiliated clubs.

5) Secretaries' addresses frequently given in newspapers.

6) Location of clubs.

28. Data from *Census, 1871*. For the purpose of making generalizations 1871 was taken as representative since the distribution of population on the variables of religion and ethnic origin did not change significantly from 1861-1901.

29. The location of games and facilities (Table V and Figure 3) were abstracted from the *Montreal Star, 1880-1885.*
30. This contention is given concrete support in Terry Copp (1974:18).
31. There is little evidence at this stage to suggest that working men ever became involved in the growing provincial and national organizations. These remained the exclusive preserve of businessmen, university professors, and professional men.

REFERENCES

Acheson, T. W.
1972   "The Social Origins of the Canadian Industrial Elite, 1880-1885." In D. S. Mac-Millan (ed.), *Canadian Business History Selected Studies*, 1897-1971. Toronto: McClelland and Stewart.

Amateur Athletic Association of Canada
1883-1888   *Minute Book of the Amateur Athletic Association of Canada*
1887-1889   *Annual Reports of Amateur Athletic Association of Canada.*

Ames, H. B.
1897   *The City Below the Hill.* Montreal.

Beckett, Hugh W.
           Scrapbook, Montreal A.A.A., 1872-1876, 1877-1880, 1886-1890. Montreal.
1882   *The Montreal Snow Shoe Club: Its History and Record.* Montreal.
1884   *Record of Winter Sports, 1883-1884.* Montreal.

Copp, Terry
1974   *The Anatomy of Poverty: The Condition of the Working Class in Montreal, 1897-1929.* Toronto: McClelland and Stewart.

Johnson, Leo
1974   *Poverty in Wealth.* Toronto: New Hogtown Press.

Katz, Michael B.
1971   "Social Structure in Hamilton, Ontario." In E. S. Thernstrom and R. Sennett (eds.), *Nineteenth Century Cities: Essays in the New Urban History.* New Haven: Yale Press.

Metcalfe, Alan
1975   "Sport and Athletics: A Case Study of Lacrosse, 1860-1890." *Journal of Sport History, 3(1).*

Montreal Amateur Athletic Association
1902   *Report of Directors of M.A.A.A.*

Montreal Bicycle Club
1872-1882   *Minute Book Montreal Bicycle Club.*

Montreal Football Club
1872-1885   *Minute Book of the Montreal Football Club.*

Montreal Lacrosse Club
1881   *Montreal Lacrosse Club Annual Review.*
1882   *Minute Book Montreal Lacrosse Club.*

Montreal Snow Shoe Club
1861-1885   *Minute Books of the Montreal Snow Shoe Club.*

Myers, G.
1972   *A History of Canadian Wealth.* Toronto: James, Lewis and Samuel.

Ryerson, Stanley
1968   *Unequal Union*. Toronto: Progress Books.

Teeple, Gary (ed.)
1972   *Capitalism and the National Question in Canada*. Toronto: University of Toronto Press.

Wise, S. F. and Fisher, Douglas
1974   *Canada's Sporting Heroes*. Toronto: General Publishing.

PART THREE

Sport and Social Differentiation

Introduction

Like all areas of social life, sport has been greatly influenced by the institutionalized divisions that characterize modern societies. The most basic of these divisions occur between social classes, ethnic groups, the sexes, and different races (cf., Gruneau, 1975). However, these categories not only reflect important social *differences* in western industrial societies, they often incorporate social *distances* as well. Whereas the idea of social differentiation itself does not imply any rank or value among the differentiated elements, people frequently make invidious comparisons between themselves and others on the basis of social and biological characteristics (cf., Dahrendorf, 1969). The ensuing evaluations and rankings tend to become integrated into structured systems of inequality that put limitations on individual life chances (cf., Weber, 1958; Tumin, 1967).

We suggested in the last section, that structured social inequality was clearly reflected in the organization and development of sport in nineteenth century Canada. However, while it is often recognized that nineteenth century Canadian sport was contoured by class and status distinctions, most Canadians seem confident that structural barriers have "decomposed" over the last seventy-five years, thereby allowing upper class pastimes to trickle down to the "masses." Indeed, it is popularly believed that the transformation of "class sport" into "mass sport" has liberated sport's inherently democratic elements to the point where "ability" counts most and rewards accrue only to the most highly skilled. In recreational activities, Canadians often think of themselves as a "leisure society" where all people have equal opportunities for participation, and at the same time, with the development of professional sports over the last half century, sport has become the backdrop for innumerable rags-to-riches tales. All of these developments appear to suggest the non-discriminatory character of sport in modern Canadian life. In this section however, each of the contributors focuses on an aspect of social differentiation and inequality in modern sport, and calls some of these commonly-accepted beliefs into question.

In the first paper, Richard Gruneau picks up on the "democratization" theme previously discussed by Metcalfe in "Organized Sports and Social Stratification in Montreal" (Part Two of this volume). Gruneau suggests that the term "democratization" in sport can actually encompass *two* divergent interpretations. One approach depicts sport as a fully democratized part of "mass" society and the other depicts it as a "bourgeois" component of liberal democracy.[1]

In an attempt to suggest which perspective appears to have the greatest explanatory power, data are presented which indicate the class and status group backgrounds of a national sample of amateur athletes. Athletes are shown to come from middle annd upper-middle class families, although differences by "type" of sport participated in, and geographic region occur. Gruneau argues that the class differences that are revealed cannot be satisfactorily explained by reference to the value differences between classes, or to differences in childhood socialization, without recognizing that these phenomena are anchored to the structure of unequal social condition which characterizes Canadian society. He concludes that "until the situation occurs when well placed families are no longer in a position to confer differential advantages and a broader range of life chances to their children, a high degree of social self-recruitment into preferred activities will continue freely from one generation to the next, broadly based athletic recruitment will be an improbability, and the equality of opportunity to participate and achieve in organized recreational and competitive programs will be higher within classes than between them."[2]

In common with the under-representation of lower class children in Gruneau's study, was a parallel under-representation of children from francophone families (even on the team sample from Quebec). This finding is highly compatible with the data presented by Roger Boileau, Fernand Landry and Yves Trempe in "Les Canadiens francais et les Grands Jeux internationaux." Boileau et al. collected data on the ethnic composition of over 60 years of Canadian international sports teams in an attempt to evaluate the comparative participation of francophones. Their data are rather striking—with the exception of weightlifters (haltérophilie), francophone athletes have been consistently under-represented when compared to the percentage of francophones in the Canadian population.

Why do these patterns occur? Boileau and his colleagues opt for an explanation which stresses cultural factors.[3] They note that Quebec was largely a rural and "traditional" society until the early 1960's. Intensely competitive urges and a need for achievement in sport were not a part of the dominant value system. At the same time, Boileau et al. argue that the lack of involvement in sports was also contingent upon a rejection of the personal values of anglophones—many of which were thought to be reflected in the structure and organization of sport. Admittedly, there is credibility in this argument, but we suspect that Boileau et al. may underplay the issues of French dependence and the degree to which certain activities were in fact, nothing more than the restricted pastimes of upper-middle class anglophones. As Metcalfe has noted previously (in this volume) even in the distinctly *rational* environment of urban Montreal, francophones could scarcely be found in organized sports.[4]

In the third paper in this section Ann Hall examines "minority group"[5] involvement of a different sort by focusing on the leisure pastimes of Canadian women. Hall notes that sociologists actually know very little about the factors which account for, and impede, the involvement of women in sports and physical activities. In an effort to suggest an explanation of what factors are relevant, she builds a causal model based on background data collected from a sample of 552 Canadian women. The model suggests that early socialization and early involvement, and present situational factors, account for nearly all of the variance. Attitudes and dispositional factors exert little influence.

As a concluding section, Hall points out the constraints that women's roles in the traditional marital situation exert on the opportunities for physical activity. Because the institution of marriage does not endorse shared roles, women are less likely (especially at specific stages of their life cycle) to participate in physical recreation than men. The degree to which this occurs is attenuated somewhat by the effects of high socio-economic status and overall level of *family* involvement in sports activities.

In the final paper in this section, Don Ball attempts to assess the ascriptive effects of selected status variables in the highly specific organizational setting of the Canadian Football League. Recently, it has been argued (cf., Edwards, 1972; Loy and McElvogue, 1972) that black athletes continue to experience discriminatory practices in professional football by being "stacked" at certain positions. Motivated by such allegations, Ball sets out to analyze the degree to which "stacking" on the basis of both race *and* national origins is a reality in the C.F.L.

Studies of this type have commonly used a centrality model, whereby the significance of particular positions is evaluated by their degree of centrality to game action (cf., Grusky, 1969).[6] However in addition to this model, Ball utilizes a model which defines positions as "primary" and "supporting" based on their importance to the direct achievement of team goals. In the case of the centrality model Ball infers that blacks are stacked in certain positions in the C.F.L. and that a similar (but less striking) pattern can be observed for Canadians versus imports. In the case of the primary and supporting player model, Canadians are noticeably absent from the primary positions—more so even than blacks (who tend to be American).

Are Canadians discriminated against in the C.F.L.? Ball's data do not really allow one to infer that discrimination does or does not exist, and his analysis is slightly dated,[7] but his research does suggest that Canadian players have been "stacked" by position. They are less likely to occupy central positions, tend to make lower salaries than imports, and are less likely to perform at primary positions. Whether such patterns are caused by discrimination or some other factor, is a matter for personal interpretation. The point is, that the pattern exists, and as Ball concludes, it may be just "one more tile in the mosaic of the branch plant economy."

NOTES

1. For excellent discussion and review of the meaning of "liberal democracy" see Macpherson (1965).
2. It is ironic that Gruneau details patterns of sport involvement that are less democratized and pluralistic than one might suspect. Such patterns stand in direct contradiction to Canadian "cultural" policy. Addressing the Canadian Conference on the Arts in September of 1970, the Secretary of State outlined the orientation of present government policy toward the arts. Policy is designed to meet three objectives (cf., Canada, 1974:28):

    (a) *Cultural Pluralism*—"cultural pluralism recognizes the interest and absolute value of all cultural expression and does not set up opposition between various forms of culture such as high or popular." In the minister's words "we will work to reduce budgeting inequalities which tend to give privileges to one cultural group at the expense of others."

    (b) *Democratization*—the necessity to democratize culture rests upon the principle that tax monies obtained from all tax payers should not be spent for the benefit of one group. Furthermore, "to democratize culture is to ensure the propagation of our heritage and to encourage cultural expression at all levels of our society."

    (c) *Decentralization*—the policy of decentralization recognizes the regional inequalities in the government's support for culture and has been described as an equalizations program. It seeks the diffusion of culture not only among all classes but throughout the various regions of the country.

3. "Cultural" explanations of the comparative positions of francophones are typified by Gérin's analysis of the family (1964). However an alternative "structural" argument is provided by Dofny and Rioux (1964) (cf., Rocher, 1975). Also, compare "cultural" explanations, to the class analysis provided by Bergeron (1971). (cf., Gruneau's discussion of "cultural explanations" in the first paper in this section).

4. However, there is no reason to believe that the under-representation of francophones that are described by Gruneau and Boileau et al. is likely to continue. The Quebec government's commitment to amateur sport since the "Quiet Revolution" has increased markedly—from well under a million dollars per year in the early 1960's to over 38 million in 1974-75 (cf., Quebec *Public Accounts*, 1960-1974; we want to thank Barb Whitehead for bringing these data to our attention). For some background reading on the "Quiet Revolution" see Rioux and Martin (1964); Bergeron (1971) and Ossenberg (1974) as well as many articles in *Recherche Sociographiques*.

5. As Vallee notes (1975:173), "minority" is a term which is used in more than one sense. "On the one hand it is used to mean a group which is smaller in number than another group. On the other hand it is used to mean subordinate or inferior status." It is in this latter sense that we use the term here.

6. For a brief critique of centrality models, see Kando (1975).

7. For example, in the last two years, as the Canadian college draft has developed, the C.F.L. has been playing more and more Canadians in "primary positions." This is not to suggest however, that the changes have been sufficient to invalidate Ball's conclusions.

REFERENCES

Bergeron, Léandre
1971   A History of Quebec: A Patriote's Handbook. Toronto: New Canada Press.

Canada
1974   Citizen Participation in Non-Work Time Activities. Vol. 1, Ottawa: Secretary of State.

Dahrendorf, Ralf
1969   "On the Origin of Inequality Among Men." In André Béteille (ed.), Social Inequality. Baltimore: Penguin Books.

Dofny, Jacques and Marcel Rioux
1964   "Social Class in French Canada." In Marcel Rioux and Yves Martin (eds.) French-Canadian Society. Toronto: McClelland Stewart.

Edwards, Harry
1973   The Sociology of Sport. Homewood: Dorsey Press.

Gérin Leon
1964   "The French-Canadian Family." In Marcel Rioux and Yves Martin (eds.), French-Canadian Society. Toronto: McClelland Stewart.

Gruneau, Richard
1975   "Sport, Social Differentiation and Social Inequality." In D. Ball and J. W. Loy (eds.), Sport and Social Order. Reading: Addison Wesley.

Grusky, Oscar
1969   "The Effects of Formal Structure on Managerial Recruitment" In J. W. Loy and Gerald S. Kenyon (eds.), Sport, Culture and Society. Toronto: Macmillan.

Kando, Thomas
1975   Leisure and Popular culture in Transition. St. Louis: C. V. Mosby.

Loy, John and J. McElvogue
1972   "Racial Segregation in American sport." In M. Marie Hart (ed.), Sport in the Socio-cultural Process.

Macpherson, C. B.
1965   The Real World of Democracy. Toronto: C.B.C.

Ossenberg, Richard
1974   "The Conquest Revisited: Another Look at Canadian Dualism." In R. Breton (ed.), Perspectives on Canadian Society. Toronto: C.S.A.A. Monograph.

Rioux, Marcel and Yves Martin
1964   French Canadian Society. Toronto: McClelland Stewart.

Rocher, Guy
1975   "Formal Education: The Issue of Opportunity." In Dennis Forcese and Stephen Richer (eds)., Issues in Canadian Society. Toronto: Prentice-Hall.

Tumin, Melvin
1967   Social Stratification. Englewood Cliffs: Prentice-Hall.

Vallee, Frank
1975   "Multi-Ethnic Soceieties: The Issues of Identity and Inequality." In Dennis Forcese and Stephen Richer (eds.), Issues in Canadian Society. Toronto: Prentice-Hall.

Weber, Max
1958   "Class, Status, Party." In H. Gerth and C. W. Mills (eds.), From Max Weber: Essays in Sociology. New York: Oxford Press.

CLASS OR MASS:
Notes on the Democratization of Canadian Amateur Sport

Richard S. Gruneau

Sport has long been regarded as a graphic symbol of meritocracy[1] in the western industrial societies. On the playing field it has traditionally been taken-for-granted that all compete equally under conditions whereby available rewards accrue to the most highly skilled. However, the extent to which sport has always reflected this situation in either the process of athletic recruitment, or the allocation of subsequent rewards, is a rather problematic question. For clearly, the history of western sport has been characterized by overt discrimination and rigid socioeconomic bias.[2] Thus, the popular image of sport as an unequivocal "democracy of ability" has usually represented a somewhat exaggerated and perhaps even mythical view. But within the last few decades, many writers have emphasized how sport is much less affected by structured social ranking than in the past. Page (1973) for one, has noted that a major characteristic of sport's transition from a rigidly defined nineteenth century "elite" and "folk"[3] activity to its more modern forms, has been its "democratization". In this paper I examine two contrasting perspectives on this democratization, and data which may be of some use in evaluating which of the perspectives has the greatest relevance for explaining the current socioeconomic dimensions of Canadian amateur sport.

Perspectives on Democratization

Generally considered, the term democratization implies the widening availability of, and diminishing separatism in, varying forms of sport involvement.[4] However, this definition, like many in sociology, is analytically imprecise. It resonates better as a shorthand expression of social changes than as a sociological understanding of these changes, and therefore allows considerable disagreement over its contours and limitations. Yet, for most sociologists and popular writers, the democratization of sport has been narrowly understood. Its primary focus has concerned the declining relevance of social class and status barriers as factors affecting both the differential accessibility of various aspects of sport involvement and athletic achievement, and the stimulation of mass, or broadly based, athletic participation.

Apparently, the expansion of opportunities in sport over the last century corresponds with a shift from traditionally aristocratic and bourgeois class inequality in western industrial societies, to a situation where structured inequality has been largely vitiated through broad patterns of social mobility, and through actual changes in social condition,[5] brought on by the contingencies of mass leisure, mass consumption and mass entertainment (cf. Barber, 1957; Kaplan, 1960; Betts, 1974).[6] Of course, not all sociologists have necessarily viewed all the consequences of such changes in a completely positive manner (cf., Stone, 1973; Kando, 1975),[7] but for the majority, the growth of a generally democratized "mass sport," has been heralded as a testament to the inherently classless and nondiscriminatory character of modern life. The image of the "affluent democracies" where class and other barriers have decomposed, stands as one of the most powerful and persistent themes in the writings of modern sociologists, and sport has recurrently been suggested as both a graphic reflection and symbolic initiator of these changes.[8]

Unfortunately, the popularity of such a perspective does not necessarily make it correct. For example, much of the recent sociological literature on social class and other aspects of structured inequality in western industrial societies, emphasizes that the decomposition of particularistic barriers in social institutions has not been achieved to the degree that is popularly believed (cf., Bottomore, 1966; Parker, 1972; Giddens, 1973; Johnson, 1972; 1974; and Clement, 1975).[9] Moreover, recent empirical studies of active sports participation in the United States and Europe have generally indicated that as an institution, sport appears to have offered little exception to this pattern. Although it is somewhat of an oversimplification, the findings here can be classified under two broad headings: (a) those studies dealing with "leisure-sport" involvement, and (b) those studies dealing with more organized competitive forms. Most of the former have indicated considerable differences in the significance of selected correlates of active participation,[10] but as a general pattern it appears that the lower fifths of the income and occupational ranges tend to be substantially under-represented in the majority of activities (cf., Clarke, 1956; Stone, 1957; Boston, 1968; Emmett, 1971; Kraus, 1971; Burdge, 1974). This relationship is emphasized even more clearly by data on participation in competitive amateur sports. Despite some recruitment differences among sports, nearly all studies have indicated that active involvement is positively related to middle and upper-middle class and income levels[11] (cf., Loy, 1969; Lüschen, 1969; Webb, 1969; Collins, 1972).[12] Furthermore, a somewhat enduring consistency between the rank ordering of certain competitive sports and the classes and status groups from which they draw their membership, seems to hold in a variety of different countries and across a range of differentially selected sample groups.

While such findings may allow for the assertion that the "leisure class" (see Veblen, 1953) has been somewhat transformed by the changing social conditions of modern life, it seems premature to assert as Stone (1973) does, that the "leisure class" has become a "leisure mass." Such an assertion completely overlooks the consistency of results which suggest how sports participation continues to remain less universalistic than particularistic. In fact, given the consistency of particularistic findings on a range of types of *active* sport involvement, it may make some sense to develop and argue a contrary perspective on sport's democratization; one that depicts the reduction of barriers to athletic recruitment less as the harbinger of the classless society, than the result of the appropriation of "folk" and "elite" traditions in sport by the ascendant middle classes of the last century. The implication here is not that the broad-scale erosion of such things as social class differences in sport testifies to the "success" of contemporary liberal democracy as a "levelling" form of political economic organization,[13] but rather that the traditional class legacies have not entirely disappeared, and that where they have, they have often been replaced by new forms of social distinction.[14] For example, over the last century, market position and increasing tendencies to assess personal worth in terms of exchange value[15] appear to have increasingly made inroads into the legacies of property, lineage, or racial and ethnic status as the dominant conditions for involvement and the allocation of subsequent rewards. These changes, in the context of their association with the rationalistic[16] forces of the contemporary productive process, conceivably reflect the "bourgeoisification" of sport far more than they demonstrate its association with "massification", or "class decomposition." Such a view does not imply that socioeconomic changes in sport have *totally* excluded the opportunity for the underprivileged to develop their physical capacities; nor does it deny that considerable democratization has occurred—it only asserts that the locus of sport's democratization can be found in the bourgeoisie[17] and that this change has not necessarily been a levelling force or a linear progression toward equality so much as a basic extension and consolidation of middle class privilege in and through the sporting world.

The Canadian Case

Which of these perspectives on democratization offers a more accurate interpretation of the development of sport in Canada? It must be conceded that there have been great changes in the degree of exclusivity of various sport forms over the last two centuries. As Metcalfe (see his paper in Part Two of this volume) and others (cf., Wise and Fisher, 1974) have argued, sport in early nineteenth century Canada was greatly affected by class divisions. That is, despite the existence of comparatively egalitarian "folk" recreational activities among frontier Canadians or the urban working classes, the roots of *organized* sports participation can be traced to the leisure pastimes of the "soldier-gentlemen" of the early British military garrisons (Lindsay, 1969); the sporting clubs of the urban elite and developing entrepreneurial classes of the late eighteenth and early nineteenth century (Metcalfe, 1972; Wise and Fisher, 1974); and the private school and university backgrounds of Canada's anglophonic charter group. Such circles of influence reflected British upperclass traditions in a "Victorian Legacy" (cf., Mallea, 1975) that ingrained a distinctive aristocratic bias to the earliest organization and administration of Canadian sport. This bias manifested itself in the rather clearly defined (and often legally sanctioned) rules of class, racial and ethnic exclusion that guided the organized activities of the period,[18] but the bias was given its general expression in simple conditions of scarcity. Most people had neither the time, money, nor opportunity to participate in an organized fashion, and when they were involved, it was often only through the then "vulgar" alternative of professionalism.

The contemporary scene, of course, appears vastly different. Extreme class and status-linked barriers to sports participation appear to have been greatly challenged by the changing social conditions of Canadian society. At one level, such factors as technological changes in industry and communications, the expansion of economic surplus, shifts in religious values, the historical concern of the military over fitness, the expansion of the educational system, and the rise of industrial and community-based sports programs, have all been important in broadening the exposure of sport to diverse groups in the population.[19] At another level, given the quantitative growth of the Canadian bourgeoisie and the gradual institutionalization of the rational meritocratic values of liberal democracy, achievement, success, and a concern over the *outcome* of sporting events have all been instrumental in re-assessing both the *utility* and the *desirability* of ascriptive barriers to participation[20] and achievement. Finally, in the shape of state intervention in sport, universal access and the equal opportunity for achievement have come to be increasingly defined as "social rights' of citizenship rather than "privileges" of class or status. As T. H. Marshall (1950) has argued, governments in most of the modern liberal democracies have developed commitments to move in the direction of the equality of citizen rights, not just in a civil and political sense, but also in the guarantee of comparable degrees of health and welfare for their citizens. Since the early 1960's Canada's expanding federally and provincially supported sports and recreational programs have been designed (in theory) to broaden at least partially the base of athletic participation in Canadian society.[21] In the face of all of these indices of massification and increased opportunity, it appears difficult to argue with the assertion made in the Canadian government's 1969 *Report of the Task Force on Sport for Canadians* that: "The aristocratic conception of sport has democratized; a whole new world of human activity has been born in which millions take part. . . . "

But it is important to reaffirm here that the decline of the "aristocratic" conception of sport does not necessarily mean that *all* "class" standards for participation have entirely eroded or that new standards have failed to develop. A concentration on the social structural and cultural changes in Canadian society which appear to have been so instrumental in democratizing sport, virtually predisposes one to underplay the persistence and possible emergence of factors which continue to guarantee some measure of continuity in the advantaged positions of certain groups. Especially problematic in this regard, is the fact that most Canadians *want* to believe not only that their sports are freely meritocratic, but that they "mirror" a democratic and classless society. As Marchak (1975:15) aptly puts it:

> Canadians may not quite believe that all people have equality of opportunity, that birth has no effect on rank, or that anyone may rise to the top. But they see these as defects or imperfections in a classless and mobile society, to be reformed or acknowledged perhaps, but not to be interpreted as evidence of a class structure. Golf, appliances, deodorants and Beethoven are equally available to all, and the lack of class distinctions is nowhere more apparent than in the market place.

The prevalence of such beliefs, frequently buttressed by the importation of American stereotypes, reinforces the image of Canada as an affluent leisure society where the problems of inequality are best thought of as "personal troubles of milieu" rather than "issues" of social structure.[22] For, the argument runs, if there is still some measure of inequality today, the existence of an expanded opportunity structure implies that differences between individuals and groups can be explained on the basis of individual achievement rather than on the basis of commonly shared social characteristics.

As attempts to speculate on the legitimacy of such beliefs in the context of sport involvement, empirical studies of the current socioeconomic dimensions of sports participation in Canada have been only of limited value. The few studies of sporting pastimes in this country have tended to concentrate on "leisure-sport" involvement, and have generally emphasized a range of background factors like age, sex, and socialization influences, without attempting to integrate these constellations of variables into general statements on the relationship of sport to the class structure (cf., Kenyon and McPherson, 1973; Hobart, 1974; White, 1975). Moreover, as these studies have differentially defined independent and dependent variables, and have utilized divergent research strategies and sample populations, it is difficult to summarize coherently their findings for an understanding of the complex relationship between sport and structured social inequality in Canada. Despite these limitations, most of the studies are unanimous in their suggestion that specific forms of active sports participation in Canada remain conditioned by socioeconomic factors that seem generally linked to class position. Typical of such findings are those documented in Curtis and Milton's ambitious secondary analysis of Canadian "leisure-sports" participation (see Part Five of this volume).[23] Their findings revealed socioeconomic differences in both active and passive participation, and showed that sports tended to *recruit from high social participators in general*. Although the authors advise "caution" in generalizing about differences or lack of differences, and about the strength of socioeconomic correlates across different types and dimensions of sporting activity, their data, in common with those of other studies, go some way toward suggesting that the open "leisure society" has yet to materialize in Canada.

But, sociologists' concern with dimensions of "leisure-sports" participation in Canada has not been matched by a parallel concern for the dimensions of more organized competitive forms. This inattention is striking because it is frequently the competitive forms of sport which are invoked as having especially revealed the changes in condition and opportunity that have characterized the recent development of the modern liberal democracies. For instance, at one point in his analysis of the club life of "Philadelphia Gentlemen," American sociologist E. Digby Baltzell (1958:360) notes how "Changing sporting mores and the changing social origins of sportsmen are often sensitive seismographs of social upheaval." Thus, they can be particularly relevant as foundations on which to make general inferences about the equality of life chances in societies where sporting activities appear important. Even more significant, however, is that the socioeconomic contours of competitive sport can be (and frequently are) interpreted as a *symbolic* statement of the effectiveness and meritocratic character of the distribution of rewards in a market society. As such, competitive sport should receive special attention in any analysis of the comparative explanatory power of divergent perspectives on the "democratization" of sport in Canadian Society. In the passages which follow, data on the social origins of competitors at the 1971 Canada Winter Games are viewed with these issues in mind. Given that the information presented is "cross-sectional" rather than "longitudinal" it would be hazardous to speak directly to the actual question of trends as *specific properties of the data*, but a snapshot of patterns at a fixed point in time does suggest *current* degrees of "class" or "mass" participation.

Some Methodological Considerations

The Canada Winter and Summer Games are alternating national events which provide inter-provincial competition for junior (and some senior) provincial champions in selected sports. The information presented here is taken from a stratified sample survey (n = 877) of the competitors at the 1971 Winter Games in Saskatoon that was administered by DuWors and Gruneau (1972).[24] For the presentation at hand, the focus is on possible correlates of social inequality as reflected through occupation of athletes' fathers, parent's education, reported family income, ethnicity and religion. All of these correlates have frequently been referred to as empirically relevant dimensions of social inequality in Canada (see for example, Porter, 1966), but they are organized here into two conceptually distinct categories: (a) class backgrounds, and (b) status-group association. Class backgrounds are indexed by income and education correlates, and *especially* father's occupation. As Parkin (1972) points out, the occupational order in all of the capitalist industrial societies is generally the "backbone" of the reward structure, and as such it must be seen as the foundation of modern class inequality.[25] "Other sources of economic and symbolic advantage do exist alongside the occupational order" but these generally seem to be secondary to those deriving from position in the marketplace (Parkin, 1972:18).[26] Occupational data for this study were coded on a six category occupational ranking index which combines prestige rankings with the comparative weight of education and income for occupational incumbents (Blishen, 1958:1971).[27]

Status-group association includes such factors as ethnicity and religion. Literature on social stratification and inequality in Canadian society affirms that these factors nearly always intrude on the issue of class position (cf., Porter, 1966; Dofny and Rioux, 1964; Kelner, 1973; Cuneo and Curtis, 1975; Forcese, 1975; Vallee, 1975; and Clement, 1975), but as Weber (1958) once remarked about status-groups generally, sometimes the loyalties and emotional identifications involved in them rival and surpass those of class, and sometimes they cut across class lines. The ethnicity of Canada Games athletes was determined by their parents' places of birth and the reported national origin of their family name (self-designated ethnicity).

Backgrounds of Canada Games Athletes

(a) Social Class Correlates

Occupational data presented in Table 1 immediately reveal that the fathers of competitors at the 1971 Canada Games came from a wide range of occupational backgrounds. However, when compared to national male labour force percentages, athletes' fathers were over-represented in the professional and white collar occupational categories

TABLE I

OCCUPATION OF ATHLETES' FATHERS COMPARED TO CANADIAN MALE LABOUR FORCE (CMLF) PERCENTAGES

Fathers Occupation by Blishen Category	CMLF as Calculated by Blishen (1961 figures) [d]	CMLF using 1971 Figures[e] (approximate)	Male Athletes' Fathers (N=509)	Female Athletes' Fathers (N = 368)	Total (all Athletes) (N = 877)
1 (70.00+)	4		12	19	15
2 (60.00-69.99) [a]	4	25	9	11	10
3 (50.00-59.99)	9		10	14	12
4 (40.00-49.99) [b]	20	20	23	21	22
5 (30.00-39.99)	32		16	16	16
6 (below 30.00)	31	55	16	9	13
Other	-	-	6	6	6
Did not Answer	-	-	7	4	6

[a] includes professional, managerial, financial and technical occupations;
[b] includes clerical, sales, white collar and service occupations;
[c] includes production and primary industry, crafts, transport skilled and unskilled labour;
[d] Bernard Blishen, "A Socioeconomic Index for Occupations in Canada" in Canadian Society: Sociological Perspectives, Toronto: Macmillan, 1971.
[e] Ministry of Industry, Trade and Commerce, Perspective Canada (1974:123)

(especially Blishen categories 1, 2 and 3) and under-represented in those categories primarily reflecting blue collar and primary industry occupations.

Establishing the "degree" of over- or under-representation from Table 1 is complicated by the fact that the only complete classification of the Canadian male labour force by Blishen's categories is based on 1961 figures. Blishen's top three categories roughly include professional, managerial, technical and finance occupations, which in 1961, made up 17% of the male labour force, white collar sales, clerical and service occupations (category 4 approximately) made up 20% of the 1961 male labour force, and the remaining 63% included a range of prodution occupations, primary industries and skilled, semi or unskilled labour (categories 5 and 6). Using Blishen's figures as a reference, the 37% of athletes' fathers who were classified in the upper three Blishen categories contrasts starkly with the 17% of the male labour force who ostensibly engaged in such activities. Similarly the 29% of athletes' fathers coming from the lower two Blishen categories contrasts even more glaringly with the 63% of the labour force which Blishen suggested could be classified at this level.

It would be a study in itself to up-date Blishen's index, thus the comparisons presented above are somewhat tied to 1961 male labour force averages. Yet, (taking a certain degree of methodological license) it is possible to make approximate estimates of how occupational data from the latest Canada census (1971) align with the general occupational groups subsumed under Blishen's categories. "Statistics Canada" figures[28] on the 1971 *male* labour force indicate that professional managerial and technical occupations now include 25% of the male labour force; clerical, sales and service occupations 20%: and production and primary industries, skilled and unskilled labour 55%. Comparing athletes' fathers' occupations to these data makes the pattern of over and under-representation less striking perhaps, but still reveals a distinct association with professional and commercial activities.

One additional feature of Table 1 that seems worth noting, is the difference in occupational percentages between the fathers of male and female athletes. Whereas 31% of the fathers of male athletes had upper-middle and middle class category 1, 2 or 3 occupations, 44% of the fathers of the female athletes were ranked at this level. At the same time, fewer of the fathers of female athletes appeared to be working at occupations that could be classified as lower class. These findings are somewhat compatible with those of Lüschen's (1969) study of athletes in German sports clubs. Commenting on marked class differences between male and female competitors, Lüschen suggested that there are strong

TABLE II

PROVINCIAL RANKINGS ON BASIS OF MEAN OCCUPATIONAL INDEX SCORES (BLISHEN) FOR ATHLETES' FATHERS (PROVINCIAL MALE LABOUR FORCE AVERAGES, AS CALCULATED BY BLISHEN, INCLUDED IN BRACKETS)[d]

Rank on Mean Blishen Score for Athletes' Fathers	Subsample sizes (N)	Percentage of Athletes' Fathers in top 3 Blishen categories[a]	Percentage of Athletes' Fathers in Blishen Category 4[b]	Percentage of Athletes' Fathers in Blishen Categories 5 and 6[c]	Other and Did not Answer
1) Alberta	(85)	52(19)	19(20)	24(62)	5
2) Manitoba	(88)	43(17)	17(22)	28(62)	12
3) Ontario	(84)	38(19)	29(20)	21(61)	12
4) Saskatchewan	(91)	44(17)	20(19)	31(64)	5
5) Nova Scotia	(71)	37(12)	16(25)	35(63)	12
6) Newfoundland	(81)	33(11)	21(16)	30(73)	16
7) New Brunswick	(75)	30(13)	21(20)	25(68)	24
8) P.E.I.	(50)	30(10)	44(18)	18(72)	8
9) Quebec	(98)	31(17)	27(19)	37(65)	5
10) Yukon	(43)	25	19	40	16
11) British Columbia	(74)	28(17)	22(19)	43(64)	7
12) North West Territories	(37)	25	14	41	20

[a] Includes professional, managerial and finance occupations:
[b] Includes clerical, sales and service occupations:
[c] Includes production and primary industry, skilled and unskilled labour occupations.
[d] See Blishen, (1971).

social barriers for lower class women who are interested in participating, and achieving rewards, in competitive sport.

The information detailed in Table 1 is aggregate data containing the occupations of all athletes' fathers. Since economic disparities between Canada's provinces tend to be significant, provincial variations in the occupational characteristics of athletes' fathers are detailed in Table II.

In the face of disparities in wealth and employment opportunities, and the different market characteristics of regional labour forces, provincial differences in athletes' fathers' occupations were to be expected. However, in *all* provinces (even the generally disadvantaged Maritimes) athletes' fathers were substantially over-represented in middle class occupations, and substantially under-represented in lower-ranking ones. Particularly noticeable is Alberta, where athletes' fathers on over *half* the provincial team sample were employed in high-ranking professional and white collar occupations. By contrast, athletes' fathers from British Columbia appear to approximate more closely general male labour force percentages. The near proportional pattern of the occupations of athletes' fathers from the British Columbia team also contrasts with the middle class over-representation of athletes' fathers from the Maritime teams. It may be that in those provinces where class and status-group inequalities are most graphic, competitive sport tends to over-recruit from the highest strata in the middle class. This hypothesis receives some support in Table III, which compares Blishen's ranking of provincial male labour forces (1971:507) on the basis of their average index scores, with the mean occupational index scores of athletes' fathers. Table III indicates that athletes' fathers from the "poorest" provinces did not necessarily have the lowest mean occupational index scores.

Aggregate data on athletes' parents' education are presented in Table IV. The data pattern generally supports the upper middle and middle class bias displayed in the distribution of athletes' fathers' occupations. Twenty nine percent of athletes' fathers, and 20% of athletes' mothers, had some university experience whereas the national (1971) percentage for the Canadian population over the age of 35 is approximately 16%. The pattern of over-representation also occurs at the level of high-school graduates. Table IV also reveals that 40% of middle-aged Canadians had elementary school or less in 1971, but only 17% of the athletes' fathers and 16% of the athletes' mothers are classified on this basis.

The reported incomes of athletes' families are generally consistent with the findings on athletes' fathers' occupations and parents' educations.[29] In Table V the 1970 Canadian family income range is divided into quartiles (each contains one quarter of all family income recipients)

TABLE III

COMPARISON OF RANKS BASED ON MEAN BLISHEN SOCIOECONOMIC INDEX SCORES FOR PROVINCIAL
LABOUR FORCES (MALE) AND ATHLETES' FATHERS IN PROVINCIAL TEAM SAMPLES

Rank on Mean Socioeconomic Index Scores for Provincial Labour Force (male) (Blishen, 1971:507)	Rank on Mean Socioeconomic Index Scores for Athletes' Fathers in Provincial Team Samples
1 Ontario	1 Alberta
2 Alberta	2 Manitoba
3 Manitoba	3 Ontario
4 British Columbia	4 Saskatchewan
5 Quebec	5 Nova Scotia
6 Saskatchewan	6 Newfoundland
7 Nova Scotia	7 New Brunswick
8 New Brunswick	8 Prince Edward Island
9 Prince Edward Island	9 Quebec
10 Newfoundland	10 British Columbia
	11 Yukon
Data for Yukon and North West Territories not presented by Blishen	12 North West Territories

TABLE IV

HIGHEST LEVEL OF SCHOOL ATTENDED BY ATHLETES' PARENTS COMPARED TO NATIONAL AVERAGES FOR
CANADIAN ADULTS (IN PERCENT)[a]
(N=877)

Educational Level	Athletes' Father	Athletes' Mother	Approximate National Averages (1972) (Men and Women 35 and over)
Elementary School or less	17	16	40
Completed Some High School	23	28	27
Finished High School	23	28	17
Completed Some University	10	9	5
Finished University	19	11	11
Other (i.e., vocational training)	6	7	-
Did Not Answer	2	1	-

[a] Percentages for civilian non-institutional population 35 and over calculated from data presented in Statistics Canada, *The Labour Force* Feb. 1973, Vol. 29 #2.

TABLE V

PERCENTAGE OF CANADA GAMES ATHLETES' PARENTS LOCATED BY QUARTILES[a] OF THE 1970 CANADIAN FAMILY INCOME RANGE[b]

Lowest Quartile	Second Quartile	Third Quartile	Highest Quartile	No Answer [c]
9	19	23	26	23

[a] Each quartile contains one quarter of all family income recipients; for example, the lowest quartile contains the quarter of Canadian families with the lowest incomes.

[b] Data calculated from *Statistics Canada Daily*, Wednesday, June 23, 1974.

[c] 23% non-response consisted of 201 respondents. Of this group 33% had fathers whose occupations were classified in the top three Blishen categories whereas only 20% of the group had fathers in the bottom two Blishen categories.

and then compared to the distribution for athletes' families. Most noticeable is that only 9% of athletes' reported family incomes fall in the bottom quartile of Canadian family income earners. But, the income data are undoubtedly skewed somewhat by the large non-response (23%). However, an examination of the occupations of the fathers of those who failed to respond to the income probe suggests that the majority of non-responses would generally tend to fall in the top half of the range. For example, only about 25% of the 201 athletes who failed to report a family income, had fathers whose occupations were classified in the bottom two Blishen categories; 21% of them had fathers whose occupations fell in Blishen category 4; and 33% had fathers whose occupations fell into the top three Blishen categories.

One problem with viewing general social class correlates of any group of athletes has to do with the fact that critical subsample variations become submerged in the aggregate. *Sport per se*, is so wide a category, that to assess its relationship to class inequality without examining specific sport differences can be misleading, and tends to neglect the "folk" and "elite" traditions of specific activities. Thus, in Table VI it is relevant to observe that those sports like boxing, weightlifting and wrestling which demand a less expensive venue, or tend to be stereotypically linked up with "folk" and underclass traditions and lifestyles, appear to recruit their participants from families where the fathers' occupation actually does have a lower ranking than sports like synchronized swimming, badminton, gymnastics or skiing.[30] Such findings are not surprising, and they are somewhat consistent with the kinds of rankings detailed in studies of amateur and school sport in other societies (Loy, 1969; Webb, 1969; Lüschen, 1969). But it would be misleading to suggest that sports like boxing are necessarily underclass sports simply because they rank *lower* than upper-middle class on the basis of the

TABLE VI
TYPE OF SPORT RANKED BY MEAN OCCUPATIONAL INDEX SCORES FOR ATHLETES' FATHERS

Blishen Category into which mean score falls	Rank on Mean Occupational Index Scores for Athletes' Fathers	Subsample Sizes (N)	Percentage of Athletes' Fathers in top 3 Blishen Categories	Percentage of Athletes' Fathers in Blishen Category 4	Percentage of Athletes' Fathers in Blishen Cagegories 5 and 6	Other	Did Not Answer
(60.00-69.99)	Synchronized Swimming	(42)	72	12	12	2	2
	Badminton	(44)	54	16	9	16	4
(50.00-59.99)	Gymnastics	(46)	48	28	15	2	6
	Alpine Skiing	(62)	48	31	16	2	3
	Speed Skating	(52)	43	31	20	2	6
	Figure Skating	(46)	41	33	22	4	—
	Nordic Skiing	(41)	37	12	27	13	12
	Table Tennis	(38)	35	21	34	2	8
	Basketball	(96)	39	19	29	10	3
	Volleyball	(109)	39	21	32	5	4
	Curling	(64)	30	28	37	—	5
	Fencing	(21)	29	10	29	19	14
(40.00-49.99)	Hockey	(84)	22	29	39	4	7
	Wrestling	(43)	21	12	45	12	10
	Judo	(25)	16	12	48	20	4
	Weightlifting	(36)	9	19	59	11	3
	Boxing	(28)	4	21	50	4	22
1961 CMLF Averages (Blishen)			17	20	63	—	—
1971 CMLF Averages (Approximate)			25	20	55	—	—

occupations of the athletes' fathers. Samples of sports participants must be compared to national or regional labour force percentages. When this is done for the sample at hand, it becomes apparent that the percentages of athletes' fathers in blue collar, production and primary industry occupations is barely equal to, or does not exceed, the proportion of the Canadian male labour force involved in these activities. Thus, even though fathers from the highest ranking occupations are under-represented in these activities, the pattern of representation tends more to lower-middle class and upper status blue collar recruitment,[31] than a clear reflection of underclass dominance.[32] Other sports however, tend to be much more dominated by the middle and upper-middle class. The mean occupational score for athletes' fathers in all but five sports falls consistently within the range of the top three Blishen categories. Synchronized swimming and badminton are rather startling in this regard, but in at least six activities, the percentage of athletes' fathers whose occupations fall in the top three Blishen categories exceeds 40%.

(b) Status Group Correlates

In conjunction with the view that sport has been a significant aspect of class decomposition and "massification" in Canadian society, is the idea that sport simultaneously reduces the social distance between ethnic and religious groups by promoting harmony and friendship between them. Along these lines, I should mention that the particular theme of the 1971 Canada Winter Games was "Unity Through Sport."[33] While this theme distinctly referred to anglophonic and francophonic "unity," it presumably was meant to encompass the range of groups making up the Canadian "mosaic." Used in the above sense, the term "mosaic" has gained popularity among Canadians partly as a result of a generalized tendency to view Canada in a socially pluralist fashion. The current "official" version[34] of Canadian society suggests that Canada is a federated mosaic of distinct but equal cultural groupings, each sharing in the rewards that their union brings. Under this arrangement differences are bound to arise, but, given the equal involvement of all in national events, it is argued that the difficulties can be assuaged in the pursuit of collective goals. Unfortunately, the comparative equality of groups in the mosaic seems to have remained convoluted by the invidious ranking of these groups in the current system of structured inequality. As Porter (1966) described so clearly in *The Vertical Mosaic*, Canada's cultural groupings—its status groups—are arranged hierarchically such that some groups are far more equal than others. To what degree are any of these cleavages revealed among Canada Games athletes?

TABLE VII

BIRTHPLACE OF ATHLETES' PARENTS[a]

Place of Birth	Fathers		Mothers	
	(N)	(%)	(N)	(%)
Canada	691	78.8	714	81.4
British Isles	59	6.8	54	6.1
German and Scandinavian	38	4.3	46	5.1
"Other"	72	9.3	58	6.8
No Answer	7	0.8	5	0.6

[a] Percentages of Countries counting at least 1% of the total.

Note: Required citizenship is not a contaminating variable here since any landed immigrant who had been a resident for two years or more was eligible.

Table VII presents data on the country of origin of athletes' parents. What is immediately obvious is that the overwhelming majority of the athletes who competed at the Games were second generation Canadians. Over 80% of the parents of the athletes were born in Canada, and when parents born in the British Isles are included, the percentage climbs to over 85%. In other words, perhaps we might question the degree to which high level amateur sport in Canada appears to be heavily recruiting from the Canadian immigrant populations of the last thirty years.

In the sense that country of origin of parents does not really index all possible ethnic or religious differences, athletes were asked to designate their own ethnicity to the best of their ability. This is a particularly crude index of active cultural differences in lifestyle or viewpoint between athletes, but it does appear to have some value in providing an overview of general patterns of status group association. These data are outlined in Table VIII, although their presentation must be guided by a further caveat. Simply, many athletes either refused to answer or felt that they could not accurately designate their ethnicity. Thus, the "unknown" category in some of the provincial subsamples is substantial enough to make the patterns displayed of dubious reliability. Yet, in spite of the problems of making overly specific conclusions here, the data patterns described in Table VIII are highly compatible with other studies of differential status group involvement in Canadian life (cf., Vallee, 1975). For example, the under-representation of athletes from French backgrounds even on the provincial teams of Quebec and New Brunswick is striking. This finding corroborates those of Boileau et al. (see their paper in this volume), who have documented the continued

TABLE VIII

ETHNIC COMPOSITION OF PROVINCIAL TEAMS (PERCENT REPORTED AFFILIATION) COMPARED TO PROVINCIAL AND NATIONAL AVERAGES (1971) (PROVINCIAL AVERAGES DISPLAYED IN BRACKETS) [a]

Provincial Team	Subsample Size (N)	British Isles	French	German and Scandinavian	Other European	All Others	Unknown
Newfoundland	(81)	54(94)	6(3)	3(1)	6(.5)	5(.5)	26(1)
P.E.I.	(50)	48(83)	12(14)	8(2)	6(.5)	6(.5)	20(-)
Nova Scotia	(71)	56(78)	10(1)	10(7)	3(2)	1(2)	20(1)
New Brunswick	(75)	39(58)	20(37)	9(2)	1(1)	6(1)	25(1)
Quebec	(98)	16(11)	40(79)	6(1)	6(7)	20(2)[b]	12(-)
Ontario	(84)	41(59)	4(10)	8(10)	19(16)	7(4)	21(1)
Manitoba	(88)	47(42)	10(9)	15(20)	12(21)	6(7)	10(1)
Saskatchewan	(91)	46(42)	2(6)	24(28)	9(17)	6(6)	13(1)
Alberta	(85)	41(47)	1(6)	23(25)	10(17)	6(3)	19(2)
British Columbia	(74)	45(58)	4(4)	8(18)	17(12)	4(6)	22(2)
Yukon	(43)	42(49)	2(7)	11(17)	5(10)	5(15)	35(2)
North West Territories	(37)	27(25)	5(7)	22(7)	- (5)	11(54)[c]	35(2)
Total all Athletes	(877)[d]	41(45)	10(29)	13(10)	9(12)	7(3)	20(1)

[a] Data compiled from Ministry of Industry, Trade and Commerce; *Perspective Canada*, (1974:264-265).

[b] 17% of Quebec team listed ethnicity as "Canadian"

[c] Large percentage for "all others" here due to substantial Indian and Inuit population

[d] Averages may not work out exactly due to rounding

under-representation of francophones on Canadian international sports teams. Moreover, in the sense that studies have suggested that franco-phones tend to have underclass status more than anglophones, their comparatively small percentages in this sample seem compatible with the data presented on class correlates of involvement. A final observation from Table VIII, is that athletes from German and Scandinavian back-grounds are represented in greater proportion than either the French or "other European" categories.[35]

TABLE IX

RELIGIOUS AFFILIATIONS OF ATHLETES AND ATHLETES' PARENTS COMPARED TO NATIONAL AVERAGES (IN PERCENT)

Religious Affiliation	Athletes' Father	Athletes' Mother	Athlete	Canadian Population (1971) [a]
Catholic	33	34	31	46
Protestant	32	32	26	18
Anglican	12	14	12	12
Reformed Bodies[c]	5	5	5	7
Lutheran	4	4	3	3
Other	4	4	4	10
No Religion	2	2	9	4
No Answer	7[b]	6	11	—

[a] Data compiled from Ministry of Industry, Trade and Commerce; *Perspective Canada* (1974:281)

[b] Numbers do not add up to 100% because of rounding

[c] Includes Presbyterians and Baptists

Because ethnicity and religion are relatively consistent dimensions of status group association, it is not surprising to find that the under-representation of predominantly Catholic groups like francophones or Italians is partially reflected in the religious affiliations of athletes and their parents. Table IX shows that athletes and athletes' parents were over-represented in the Protestant denominations, and under-represented in the Catholic ones. Again, this finding is somewhat compatible with those of other studies. Lüschen (1972:27) has noted that: "Max Weber's findings about the relationship between the Protestant ethic and the spirit of capitalism may thus well be extended to the "spirit of sport:" Lüschen sampled over 1800 members of German sports clubs and found that just under two-third of the total sample, and three-quarters of the "*high achievers*" were Protestant. By contrast, the religious data were less strik-ing in the Canada Games sample. While Protestants were over-represented when compared to national percentages, they comprised less than a third of all athletes. Moreover the class correlates of involvement detailed earlier, appear to suggest that socioeconomic level might well be a far better predictor of high level competitive involvement than religious affiliation.

Finally, given the myriad of cultural stereotypes about sports participation ranging from skiers named Hans or Stein to francophone weightlifters—possible relationships that might exist between ethnicity and type of sport participated in are examined in Table X. Again, the previously suggested caveats apply, especially in the case of those sports where the percentage of "unknown" responses is excessive. Within these limitations however, some interesting data patterns are displayed in Table X. Somewhat striking for instance, is that synchronized swimming and badminton, the two highest ranking sports on the basis of fathers' occupation, are greatly over-represented in the British Isles category. Among athletes

TABLE X

TYPE OF SPORT PARTICIPATED IN BY ETHNIC GROUPS (PERCENT REPORTED AFFILIATION)

Sport	Subsample sizes (N)	British Isles	French	Highest Percentage in addition to British Isles or French		All Others	Unknown
Badminton	(44)	64	2	7	(Canadian)[a]	11	16
Basketball	(96)	46	12	12	(Germanic)	18	12
Boxing	(28)	32	21	7	(Germanic)	4	36
Curling	(64)	53	3	14	(Germanic)	18	12
Fencing	(21)	56	14	20	(Germanic)	6	4
Figure-Skating	(46)	35	17	13	(Other European)	13	22
Gymnastics	(46)	35	9	11	(Canadian)	15	30
Hockey	(84)	32	16	12	(Germanic)	9	31
Judo	(25)	44	8	16	(Germanic)	8	24
Alpine Skiing	(62)	37	14	14	(Germanic)	14	21
Nordic Skiing	(41)	44	5	27	(Germanic)	4	20
Speed Skating	(52)	33	6	13	(Germanic)	19	29
Synchronized Swimming	(42)	71	2	10	(Germanic)	12	5
Table Tennis	(38)	37	5	24	(Asian and Other European)	8	26
Volleyball	(109)	38	11	19	(Germanic)	21[b]	11
Weight Lifting	(36)	28	31	8	(Germanic)	5	28
Wrestling	(45)	42	5	16	(Other European)	18	19
National Averages		45	29	10	(Germanic)	15 (others)	1

[a] Athletes listed ethnicity as "Canadian"

[b] High percentages "in Others" column refer primarily to "Other European".

from French backgrounds, the only sports that appear to be represented in or near proportion are weightlifting and boxing. Interestingly Boileau et al. (in this volume) have reported a higher than usual percentage of Francophones in these particular sports over the last seventy years. Turning to other groups, one can observe (not surprisingly) that Germans and Scandinavian backgrounds are prominent in nordic skiing. Thus, it seems clear that athletes from various sections of the Canadian "mosaic" find themselves in nearly all sports, but at the same time, it is noticeable that some groups appear to cluster around particular types of activities.

Explaining the Differences

The data on Canada Games athletes indicate noticeable differences in condition between athlete's families and those of Canadian families generally. More important is that the differences are not randomly distributed, reflecting differences of *individual* abilities, but appear to be affected both by class position and (somewhat more equivocally) status group association. Such findings hardly corroborate an image of Canadian sport which features patterns of mass participation and universal access. Yet, the question might still be legitimately raised as to whether the differences in social condition presented above are simply the result of different choices, or differential ambition and effort which is being rewarded in a classless and generally meritocratic system, or whether they represent crystallized social structural barriers which limit both the rate and quality of participation in preferred activities. Such questions easily transcend the limited explanatory power of the descriptive findings of the Canada Games study, and an attempt to respond to them in even a conjectural fashion demands some reference to the broader sociological literature on sport, social inequality, and the changing character of Canadian society.

Central to this problem is the nature of the relationship between differences in social condition and the existence of a true "equality of opportunity" to surpass these differences. To argue that the "democratization" of sport in Canada has yet to transcend the effects of class position and status-group association, is to argue that differences in social condition continue to remain structured in such a way as to put significant limits on the degree of "equality of opportunity" that can ever be achieved. By contrast, the idealized vision of liberal democracy, features the decomposition of structured differences in social condition (like social class) to the point where they eventually become mere quantitative differences between strata and no longer pose any problems for free movement in the reward structure. In the shape of implied explanations of inequality, a belief in the limited democratization of our institutions (sport included) emphasizes the continuance of at least some forms of overt discrimination and unconscious structural barriers to the equality of access and achievement, and the image of a "mass" or a fully democratized society, emphasizes sub-cultural differences in socialization which affect attitudes to achievement, success and preferred activities.

Undoubtedly, both of these constellations of influence have effects on such things as involvement and achievement in sporting activities of different kinds, but the question of the manner in which they are related to one another is largely dependent upon the degree to which one concludes that the contingencies of class and status no longer exert an ascriptive effect. I would like to re-emphasize at this point, that the image of a thoroughly democratized, if not a completely "mass" society, has dominated much of a recent sociology (especially in the United States), and for many, has become a crucial "domain assumption"[38] in the literature on the sociology of sport. Attendant to this, has been the elevation of "socialization" or "value" explanations of differential involvement and achievement to the apparent level of conventional wisdom. While there are a wide range of specific details believed to be most significant for understanding differential sport preferences and levels of aspiration, the majority of the explanations are organized around some combination of three variants.

The first variant emphasizes differences in skills and information in conjunction with the lifestyles of disadvantaged individuals. A corollary to this is the assertion that the socialization patterns of the poor, or of minority status-groups, are not adequate to sufficiently affirm the "positive" values of such things as fitness, physical recreation and competitive athletics. Thus, some have argued (see Kraus, 1965) that the poor not only lack a "constructive concept of leisure" but they also reject sporting possibilities in favour of more pathological pursuits.

The second variant to "cultural" explanations of under-representation is derived from the work of John Roberts, Brian Sutton-Smith and their co-researchers, (see for example Roberts and Sutton-Smith, 1969; Sutton-Smith et al., 1969) and develops the argument that sport and game preferences are a reflection of cultural differences in child-rearing. As "institutionalized games" (Loy, 1969), sports apparently provide expressive models which provide settings wherein the conflicts engendered in child-rearing are assuaged. Through the "buffered learning" that different game forms provide, children ostensibly make "enculturative" step-by-step progress toward adult behaviour. Sutton-Smith et al. (1969) argue that because individuals from the upper strata supposedly emphasize values of achievement in child-rearing, their children tend to become pre-disposed toward games of "physical skill" or combinations of "skill and strategy." Alternatively, lower status groups who emphasize responsibility training, predispose their children to prefer activities where the "chance" element is high (for example, as Weinberg and Arond (1969) point out where the prospect of a "lucky" punch exists).

The third and final variant of cultural explanations focuses on the broader milieu of different strata and is specifically concerned with the issues of atmosphere and ambition—atmosphere, because it is commonly believed that part of the subculture of the lower strata is a concern for toughness and physical dominance which tends to involve the children from these families in sports emphasizing muscular and combative elements; ambition, because it is argued that the values supporting *success* in sport, school or the career are not appropriately developed. Here the argument is that the kinds of values associated with "success" in any aspect of life in the western industrial societies—individualism, competitiveness and a willingness to delay immediate gratification in order to insure future goals—are more characteristics of middle status rather than lower status "culture," of Protestantism rather than Catholicism; and in Canada, of anglophones rather than francophones.

All of these assertions appear to have some basis in act, but they become problematic when, given a belief in an expanded opportunity structure, they are treated as *independent* causes. How independent are they really? In the case of the first variant, the rejection of available opportunities for the poor, or lack of awareness argument, assumes that the facilities and programs actually do exist and are both geographically and financially accessible. At present we lack clear cut empirical evidence concerning the degree to which the availability is as ubiquitous as many seem to feel. In the case of the second variant, there does appear to be support (Davis, 1951; Davis and Havighurst, 1946; and Erickson, 1947) for some of the assumptions being made about class differences in child-rearing, but the assignment of sport and game activities to rigid taxonomic categories (skill, strategy and chance) is highly arbitrary and may show little resemblance to the phenomenological meaning that certain activities have for the participants. Moreover, Roberts and Sutton-Smith and their co-researchers emphasize cultural differences between strata without attempting to discuss the mutually interactive role between them and the class structure. Finally, it can be argued that the third variant, which finds its broadest base of support in the writings of Herbert Hyman (1953), simply overstates the case for differential levels of ambition. As Porter (1968) has noted, the acceptance of differential attitudes to achievement is based on "questionable" assumptions. The disadvantaged classes and status groups may place a lower emphasis on "success" defined in conventional terms, but this may be because they are aware of, and have a fatalistic view of existing structures of inequality (cf., Scanzoni, 1967). Parkin (1972:67) for example, notes that "ambition does not flourish in an atmosphere thick with warning against the danger of getting big ideas." Yet, the question of ambition, as Turner (1964) suggests, may really be more related to where one "starts" in the reward structure and the nature of the structural impediments which must be overcome (see Keller and Zavaloni, 1964). The amount of ambition required by an underclass child to reach the same goal as a child from a middle or upper class family must be greater because they have a relatively greater distance to go to attain it. Given problems of cost, access and coaching, it may take more ambition for a child from a poor family to aspire to a regional championship than it does a middle class child who aspires to be a Canada Games medalist or a national champion. Correspondingly, the involvement of the poor and of certain status groups in sports like boxing or weightlifting must surely be a partial function of their comparitively low costs and even that they are "left" as less preferred activities by the middle classes.

My point here is simply that one should be aware of the limitations of cultural or "value" explanations of differences in social condition whereby the culture and life styles of the underclasses and minority status groups, are seen as the prime contributor to their disadvantaged positions. These "explanations" may in fact explain little unless they are viewed in the context of the structured nature of inequality that appears to remain a fact of life in the western industrial societies. Structural factors intrude on the culture and life styles of different groups in a variety of ways which may significantly contour both the objective opportunity for, and the subjective attitudes to, participation and achievement. Consider for example, the obvious prevalence of economic barriers. True, more sporting equipment, facilities and programs exist now than any time in Canada' past, but this is not to say that the *proportional* participation of Canadians in sporting activities is any higher than it was 75 years ago, or that all have access to these facilities and programs. In fact it is clear that for most Canadians, sporting activities continue to be subordinated to the contingencies of everyday economic life. According to the 1969 Senate Committee Report on Poverty and the Economic Council of Canada, anywhere from 25 to 30% of Canadians live at or below conditions that can only be described as impoverished. Moreover, census figures (see *Perspective Canada*, 1974) and longitudinal studies of economic change indicate not only that economic differences between groups are failing to dissolve, but that the gap between the upper and the lower levels of the

Canadian income range is increasing rather than decreasing. Leo Johnson (1974:7) for example, outlines how over the last 25 years, the highest two deciles of Canadian income earners received about half of all new income, whereas the bottom half of the income range only increased their percentage by 20.

Concurrent with such changes, it seems to have been necessary for more members of Canadian families to obtain additional employment in order to cling tenaciously to the economic position presently in hand. This fact, in the context of the effects of additional family responsibilities, the necessity to provide further income, and the possibility of missing opportunities after school because of employment, necessarily precludes regular involvement in organized programs by large numbers of young Canadians. For, while evidence suggests that it is the family environment which represents the *first influence* directing children into sport and specific types of sporting activity, it is likely the school environment where children get their greatest exposure to low cost recreational, athletic and coaching programs.

Under present conditions however, the school itself may be less an agency of democratization than a factor which serves to further crystallize existing differences. While discussing the role of education in fostering occupational mobility and related life chances, Rocher, (1975) and Pike (1975) have pointed out how Canada's educational systems have tended to legitimate existing status differences and confer new ones rather than working toward the demise of invidious comparisons based on commonly shared social characteristics. Upper and middle class children are usually more involved and successful in most aspects of school life and tend to be more attuned to the values which guide educational expectations and goals (Pike, 1975:7). By contrast, underclass children often suffer by a poorer academic performance and a lack of understanding and reverence for the school's demands. This lack of understanding and distance from the *formal* dimensions of education itself is also reflected in the "*informal*" ones as well. Moreover, the necessity for, and the perceived possibility of, immediate gratifications in the work world combine with this distance from educational objectives to terminate many educational careers prematurely, turning them, as Pike argues (1975:8), into poorly paid low status employment. As individuals leave an environment where the cost and availability of sports facilities and programs are partially controlled for, it seems reasonable to assume that their active participation is largely curtailed and generally transformed into more passive forms of sports consumption. All of this is not to suggest that the educational system and achievement in its curricular and extra-curricular programs is impervious to the ambitions and abilities of underclass children who come to understand the schools' demands and the formal system of rewards and statuses in it; it only suggests that the image of the school as a necessary guarantor of democratization in any form is perhaps rather facile.

In summary, the implications of the contingencies stated above, and the related character of unequal condition and unequal opportunity in Canada, clearly intrude on the question of sport's democratization—both as an aspect of individual life chances and as a related dimension of social mobility. If we concentrate on changes in social condition that appear to have characterized Canadian society, we might well argue that the aristocratic standard for participation has been democratized. But to interpret this as any index of classlessness in Canadian sporting activities would be misleading. In both leisure-sport, as Curtis and Milton have pointed out (see Part 5 of this volume), and high level competitive sport involvement as I have attempted to show here, it seems that the effects of sport's democratization have been largely limited to the middle class and at best to those skilled manual workers who may use the middle class as a reference group. Presumably, there might be somewhat different patterns in the case of recruitment into professional sport (Kidd and MacFarlane [1972] for example, argue that "Hockey is everyone's sport no matter what their class"), and if viewed in a purely cognitive sense, sport may be truly mass-like. But, if one focusses on most forms of amateur sport, the following conclusion may be warranted. Until the situation occurs when well-placed families are no longer in a position to confer differential advantages and a broader range of life chances to their children, a high degree of social self-recruitment into preferred activities will continue freely from one generation to the next, broadly based athletic recruitment will be an improbability, and the equality of opportunity to participate and achieve in organized recreational *and* competitive programs will be higher within classes than between them.

NOTES

1. A "meritocracy" is simply a system where the distribution of rewards is based exclusively on an individual's abilities. In recent years, there has been a great debate among social scientists and philosophers over the degree to which social justice in modern life should be based exclusively on meritocratic principles. Some (cf., Davis and Moore, 1945) argue that a system of unequal rewards based on meritocratic standards is necessary to insure quality in leadership and performance in modern life as long as there is open and unrestricted competition, or opportunity, for the highest positions. Others (cf., Spitz, 1974) argue that: (a) as long as a system of highly unequal rewards persists, those who achieve in it will always be in a position to pass on at least some of the advantages associated with their achievements to children or personal associates thereby vitiating true equality of opportunity in future competition;

(b) standards set by the meritocratic "elite" at any time may be subconsciously (or even consciously) discriminating; (c) the existence of a meritocracy does not substantially affect the problem of *inequality* itself. In this latter case, it is argued that, while specific *individuals* may ascend to elite positions, a great percentage of the population will remain substantially neglected or underprivileged. Consider, for example, the full application of meritocratic standards to sport. To emphasize these to their logical limits would imply that programs only be designed for those who showed the most ability—progressively culling out those who could not compete. This then would be a programme designed in principle and in theory, to develop an athletic *elite*. On the other hand, consider an *egalitarian* programme designed to meet the play-urges and recreational needs of human beings regardless of their abilities. This would be a programme designed for *all* individuals. In the former programme, rewards would be based on *achievement*; in the latter they would be based on *participation*. The obvious dilemma here is how to balance the moral recognition that *all* men and women have equal rights and social needs, with a desire to develop outstanding performances by the creation of structural systems which guarantee inequalities in result. This dilemma stands at the core of contemporary political philosophy, and as suggested, it also manifests itself in the world of sport. For a more in-depth discussion of these issues as they relate to sport see Gruneau (1975). A broader analysis of the egalitarian-meritocracy debate can be found in Bell (1972); Schaar (1967); Spitz (1974); Jencks et al. (1972) and Simon (1974). An entertaining satire of structured meritocracy can be found in Young (1961).

2. This bias is described in a variety of sources. For a review of sport and racial discrimination see McPherson (1974). The best overview of gender-based discrimination (although restricted to the American context) is Gerber et al. (1974).

3. Elite sports of course, refer to such activities in history as manorial hunting, early tennis and organized equestrian events ("the hounds" or polo). (This list is hardly exhaustive.) Folk sports refer to wrestling, some early forms of ball games (of the inflated bladder variety), cockfighting (and other "blood" sports) and footracing. A discussion of such activities in Elizabethan England can be found in Brailsford (1969).

4. See the discussion by Page (1973:25-32).

5. Throughout this paper I use the terms "equality of condition" and "equality of opportunity." Differences in "condition" refer to variations in factors like income, education, occupation, exposure to health care services, amount of leisure time, and overall quality of life, all of which are contained within the general organizing framework of a society and often manifest themselves as dimensions of structured social ranking (cf., Clement, 1974;3-4, Gilbert and McRoberts, 1975). Conversely the issue of "opportunity" focuses at the individual rather than the social structural level, and is concerned with the degree of freedom that persons have in moving within the restrictions frequently imposed by the reward structure. The main thrust of my concluding argument in this paper is based on a recognition that inequalities in conditions are "ordered" in such a way that they put confining limits on opportunity (Clement, 1974).

6. Typical of this perspective is Kaplan's (1960) comment that in "no area of American life more than its leisure activity is the outdated concept of class made apparent." Hodges (1964:167) is more guarded when he suggests that class differences in sports and leisure are still often of "transcendent" consequence, but he concludes by suggesting that the barriers are "diminishing in importance as we become an ever more homogeneous people." (Note that Hodges is referring to American society here).

7. While "mass sport" implies democratization, both Stone (1973) and Kando (1975) argue that the price has been high. Each depicts an increasing tendency for "mass spectacle" and the debasement of many of sport's "nobler" elements as adjuncts to massification. In fact, Kando goes as far as to compare the current state of American sport to that period of decadent Roman history where the colliseum and gladitorial combat were elevated to a moral equivalent of life in the society. Additionally there have been numerous criticisms of "mass leisure," usually in the context of polemics

against the supposed decline of the work ethic, or in the case of neo-Marxists, against the substitution of "trivialized leisure" for a lack of meaningful work (cf., Aronowitz, 1973; and Rinehart, 1975).

8. See the section on theoretical issues in Gruneau's paper in Part One of this volume. The comparative approaches to sport as an *abstraction*, as a *cultural* phenomenon and as a *material* phenomenon are discussed vis-à-vis their relationship to order and conflict theories. The first of these approaches emphasizes sport's transcendental character, the second its supposed ability to *cause* change by virute of its symbolic meaning, and the third, the image of it as a reflection of social conditions.

9. There is a substantial amount of literature supporting this point but for an excellent overview of the main issues see Westergaard (1972).

10. An example of these correlates would be age, sex, educational level, income level and occupation. For a review of some of the different impacts of such variables on "leisure sport" participation, see Curtis and Milton (Part 5 of this volume) and Hall (her paper in this section).

11. We might note here that this finding is even more significant when the differences in sample groups are compared. For example, Collins' (1972) data are based on Olympic athletes, Lüschen's (1969) are from a sample of members of German sports clubs and Webb's (1969) and Loy's (1969) data involve athletes from two prominent American universities.

12. For socio-economic data on a limited population of Japanese athletes, see Sugawara (1972). Some tentative findings on class and sport in Australia are detailed in Pavia (1973; 1974).

13. Betts (1974) takes this position when he argues that the relationship of sport to capitalism has been "productive" by virtue of its role in facilitating the proliferation of athletic facilities and the growth of "mass" sport.

14. A broader discussion of this point can be found in Gruneau (1975).

15. As personal relationships become contractually based in the labour market, Marx saw a growing tendency for individuals to be seen less as ends in themselves and more as means—through their labour power—to particular ends (notably production). The contours of the relationships then could be seen as ones which featured an *exchange*. The labourer was paid for work but at a rate which was not commensurate to the real value of the labour in the productive process. The "surplus" value remaining then manifested itself as profits for the entrepreneur.

16. While the term rationalization can have a variety of meanings (cf., Mannheim, 1960; Gerth and Mills, 1958), my usage of it throughout this paper has primarily been influenced by the interpretations of its meaning and significance that can be found in the writings of Karl Marx and Max Weber. In a general sense, "rationality" refers simply to a "disenchantment" or demystification of the world. Logic, and reason other than ideational factors, underlie its development. In an applied economic sense, it becomes the driving force of utilitarian productive process and, in a bureaucratic sense, it refers particularly to "rational efficiency, continuity of operation, speed, precision, and calculation of results" (Gerth and Mills, 1958:49).

17. "Bourgeoisie" is a broadly based term referring to the dominant class in the western industrial societies. Moreover as a conception of the occupational order it encompasses a large number of the positions associated with the productive process. Generally, the "bourgeoisie" can best be thought of as "stratified" into two components. The upper group refers to those who largely own or control the process of production itself through shares, and board memberships and the lower group is categorized by a range of "middle class" occupations surrounding independent commodity production, professional activities, and the commercial world of business and its administration.

18. For example, as Mallea (1975) notes, early rules of the British A.A.U. included the fact that anyone who was "by trade or employment for wages a mechanic, artisan or labourer" was ineligible to enter its competitions. Also, in Canada, as late as the late 1920's, blacks were not allowed to compete in some major Canadian boxing events. In 1913 the Canadian Amateur Athletic Union announced that "no coloured boxer will

be allowed to compete in the Canadian championships . . . competition of whites and coloured men is not working out to the increased growth of the sport" (cited in Wise and Fisher, 1974:129).

19. See Jobling's paper in this volume for a brief discussion of urbanization and technology. Various articles detailing other influences on the development of sport can be found in selected issues of the *Canadian Journal of History of Sport and Physical Education.*

20. These values, as Page (1973:27) notes, are particularly emphasized by the "professionalization" of sports wherein ascriptive barriers to recruitment have been "weakened by the rational calculation of big business." For a broader discussion of such themes see Gruneau (1975) and Ingham (1975).

21. Commenting on Canadian sports policy in 1974, Health Minister Marc Lalonde stated that: "We have a double purpose: We want to help the best Canadian athletes in their pursuit of excellence, but at the same time we are equally concerned with the general fitness and recreation of Canadians" (*Toronto Star*: Wednesday, January 2, 1974). Yet, such programs as *Participaction* notwithstanding, funding seems overwhelmingly directed to sporting associations, the majority of which are especially concerned with the production of quality athletes. For example, in 1972-73 according to a pamphlet detailing the membership and functions of the "Canadian Sports Federation" *Sport Canada* was to receive 6.5 million in grants and *Recreation Canada* 2.3 million. Most of Sport Canada's money was earmarked for sporting associations and for such agencies as the "Canadian Olympic Association" and "Canadian Coaching Association." Moreover, given that the period from 1970 to the present has involved a major push for Olympic success—*production* has clearly superceded *participation* as *the* major goal for sports policy.

22. See Mills' distinction between "personal troubles" and "public issues" in *The Sociological Imagination* (1970;14-16).

23. Refer also to Hall's discussion of these data in Part III of this volume.

24. A broader discussion of the sample and methods of the Canada Games project can be found in Gruneau (1972).

25. In *The Canadian Class Structure*, Forcese (1975) lists Parkin as an author who disagrees with the use of occupations as the proper focus for class analysis. This is certainly an error, since Parkin specifically goes to some lengths to praise Max Weber's recognition that market position rather than property ownership is the major distributive characteristic of class stratification.

26. "Position" however does not imply that the occupational order is a continuum having no "breaks." Parkin (1972:25) notes for instance, that despite a measure of affluence on the part of some skilled labourers, the line of cleavage between "classes" still falls between manual and non-manual occupational categories. The latter group lack comparable long term advantages and fringe benefits, whereas the former's advantages include: "better promotion and career opportunities; greater long-term economic security and, for many, guaranteed annual salary increases on an incremental scale; a cleaner, less noisy, less dangerous, and generally more comfortable work environment; greater freedom of movement, and less supervision . . . ".

27. Examples of occupations classified by Blishen's categories include:
   Category 1 (index number 70:00-79.99); chemical engineers, professors and teachers, selected business owners and managers.
   Category 2 (60.00-69.99); accountants, auditors, owners and managers, health services.
   Category 3 (50.00-59.99); security salesmen and brokers, technicians.
   Category 4 (40.00-49.99); real estate salesmen, technicians, telephone operators, foremen in selected industries.
   Category 5 (30.00-39.99); postmasters, typists, foreman, plumbers, millmen.
   Category 6 (below 30.00); labourers, textile occupations, lumbermen.
   The "break" between manual and non-manual work primarily occurs in the fourth and fifth categories. Solid upper-middle and middle class occupations fall in categories

1, 2 and 3; category 4 and some occupations in 5 include lower-middle class white and sometimes blue collar occupations. The remainder of categories 5 and 6 reflect occupations generally held by lower class individuals. In the analysis at hand, I have made breaks between categories 1, 2, 3 and category 4 and between 4 and categories 5 and 6.

28. See *Perspective Canada*, 1974, a compendium of social statistics released by Ministry of Industry, Trade and Commerce.

29. Measuring association here, gamma for education correlated with occupation was .786; gamma for income and occupation was .732.

30. However, this table does mask gender differences that may change rankings somewhat. For example, male and female table tennis players came from much different family backgrounds and this fact cannot be observed in Table VI as it now stands. Male and female data are not presented separately because of small subsample sizes. I felt that sport-group differences could best be presented without controlling for gender. It should be recognized that this variable is likely affecting the rankings somewhat. Rankings of participation by sport where gender is controlled for can be found in Gruneau (1972). A modification of Table VI which uses slightly different occupational breakdowns, but which controls for gender, can be found in Gruneau (1975:164).

31. Upper status blue collar occupations might include such things as foremen in craft industries or *highly*-skilled labourers. See Mackenzie's *The Aristocracy of Labour* (1973).

32. The mean socio-economic index scores for boxing and weightlifting come very close to falling into the category 5 occupational range. But even this category does not reflect the lower orders of the occupational hierarchy.

33. It is somewhat revealing that this theme "Unity Through Sport" was chosen to symbolize the "Games." The "Games" followed barely three months after the events of October, 1970 and the accompanying controversy over the War Measures Act. Thus the theme undoubtedly carries distinct political overtones.

34. Witness Prime Minister Trudeau's comment that in Canada: "there is no official culture, nor does any ethnic group take precedence over any other" (cited in Pike, 1975:2).

35. Note that German and Scandinavian representation was high in most sports rather than just those like skiing or others which conventional stereotypes might suggest.

36. As Porter has suggested, (1966:101-102) Protestantism in Canada (the numerically superior British charter group is mostly Protestant and Anglican) is certainly more associated with higher socio-economic status than Catholicism. However, it is suggested that this relationship is "attributed to historical and social causes rather than to doctrinal differences in religious orientations to the world." (Porter, 1966:100). Thus, the argument is that Weber's thesis regarding the doctrinal incompatibility of Catholicism with a fully developed industrial order is not necessarily being supported by data such as those referred to above. S. D. Clark claims that "Essentially the religious influence exerted through Protestantism in Canada has been no more favourable to the promotion of economic enterprise than the religious influence exerted through Roman Catholicism ... Where the Protestant religious organization has been strong the Protestant population has tended to be as economically unprogressive as the Roman Catholic population." (Clark, 1968:175).

37. However, this rather neat relationship does not hold beyond these two sports. While much of the Canadian upper-middle class is made up of people with British-Isles family histories, not all British-Isles immigrants have necessarily been located at this level. This seems to have been especially true for Irish Catholics for example. The point is, that while a British-Isles family history has frequently been a *characteristic* of those with advantaged status in Canadian society, ethnicity in itself has not always been a *guarantor* of class position.

38. Simply stated, "domain assumptions" refer to underlying beliefs about particular patterns of relationships that structure inquiry and explanation in a specific manner.

See Gouldner's description in *The Coming Crisis of Western Sociology* (1970). It is frequently the "domain assumptions" that writers have which comprise the ideological and normative dimensions of their "theories" (see my discussions in Part One of this volume).

39. See also his essay on "The development of class in Canada" in G. Teeple ed. *Capitalism and the National Question in Canada* (1972).

REFERENCES

Aronowitz, Stanley
1973   *False Promises*. New York: McGraw Hill.

Baltzell, E. Digby
1958.   *Philadelphia Gentlemen*. New York: Free Press.

Barber, Bernard
1957   *Social Stratification: A Comparative Analysis of Structure and Process*. New York: Harcourt Brace and World.

Bell, Daniel
1972   "On Meritocracy and Equality." *The Public Interest*, 29, Fall.

Betts, John R.
1974   *America's Sporting Heritage 1850-1950*. Reading: Addison-Wesley.

Blishen, Bernard
1958   "The Construction and Use of an Occupational Class Scale." *Canadian Journal of Economics and Political Science*, XXIV, November.
1971   "A Socio-Economic Index for Occupations." In Bernard Blishen, Frank Jones, Kaspar Naegele, John Porter, (eds.), *Canadian Society, Sociological Perspectives*. Toronto: Macmillan.

Boston, R.
1968   "What Leisure?." *New Society*, 26, December.

Bottomore, T. B.
1966   *Classes in Modern Society*. New York: Vintage Books.

Brailsford, Dennis
1969   *Sport and Society: Elizabeth to Anne*. Toronto: University of Toronto Press.

Burdge, Rabel J.
1974   "Levels of Occupational Prestige and Leisure Activity." In George H. Sage (ed.), *Sport and American Society*. Reading: Addison-Wesley.

Clarke, A. C.
1956   "The Use of Leisure and its Relation to Levels of Occupational Prestige." *American Sociological Review*, 21, June.

Clark, S. D.
1968   *The Developing Canadian Community*. Toronto: University of Toronto Press.

Clement, Wallace
1975   *The Canadian Corporate Elite*. Toronto: McClelland and Stewart.

Collins, L. J.
1972   "Social Class and the Olympic Athlete." *British Journal of Physical Education* 3 (4). (4).

Cuneo, Carl and James Curtis
1975   "Social Ascription in the Educational and Occupational Status Attainment of Urban Canadians." *Canadian Review of Sociology and Anthropology*, 12 (1).

Davis, Alison
1951   *Social Class Influences Upon Learning.* Cambridge: Harvard University Press and
and R. J. Havighurst
1946   "Social Class and Color Differences in Childrearing." *American Sociological
Review.* 11, December.

Davis, Kingsley and Wilbert Moore
1945   "Some Principles of Stratification." *American Sociological Review,* 10, April.

Dofny, Jacques and Marcel Rioux
1964   "Social Class in French Canada." In Marcel Rioux and Yves Martin (eds.), *French
Canadian Society.* Toronto: McClelland and Stewart.

Du Wors, Richard E. and Richard S. Gruneau
1972   "Facts Toward a Foundation for Canadian Programmes in Amateur Sports." Research Report presented to the Canadian Fitness and Amateur Sport Directorate,
Ottawa.

Emmett, Isabel
1971   *Youth and Leisure in an Urban Sprawl.* Manchester: Manchester University Press.

Erickson, M. C.
1947   "Social Status and Child-Rearing Practices." In T. Newcomb and E. L. Hartley,
Readings in Social Psychology. New York: Holt, Rinehart and Winston.

Forcese, Dennis
1975   *The Canadian Class Structure.* Toronto: McGraw-Hill Ryerson.

Gerber, Ellen, et al.
1974   *The American Women in Sport.* Reading: Addison-Wesley.

Gerth, H. H. and C. Wright Mills
1958   *From Max Weber: Essays in Sociology.* New York: Oxford University Press.

Giddens, Anthony
1973   *The Class Structure of the Advanced Socieities.* London: Hutchinson.

Gilbert, Sid and Hugh McRoberts
1975   "Differentiation and Stratification: The Issue of Inequality." In Dennis Forcese and
Stephen Richer (eds.), *Issues in Canadian Society.* Toronto: Prentice-Hall.

Gouldner, Alvin
1970   *The Coming Crisis of Western Sociology.* New York: Basic Books.

Gruneau, Richard S.
1972   "A Socio-economic Analysis of the Competitors at the 1971 Canada Winter
Games." Unpublished Master's thesis, Department of Sociology, University of
Calgary, Alberta.
1975   "Sport, Social Differentiation and Social Inequality." In D. Ball and John W. Loy
(eds.), *Sport and Social Order.* Reading: Addison-Wesley.

Hodges, H. M.
1964   *Social Stratification.* Cambridge Mass: Schenkman.

Hobart, Charles
1974   "Active Sports Participation Among the Young, The Middle-Aged and the Eld-
erly." Paper presented at the C.S.A.A. meeting, Toronto.

Hyman, Herbert
1953   "The Value Systems of Different Classes." In R. Bendix and S. M. Lipset (eds.),
Class, Status and Power. Glencoe, Illinois: The Free Press.

Ingham, Alan G.
1975   "Occupational Subcultures in the Work World of Sport." In D. Ball and J. W. Loy
(eds.), *Sport and Social Order.* Reading: Addison-Wesley.

Jencks, Christopher, et al.
1972   *Inequality: A Reassessment of the Effect of Family and Schooling in America.*
New York: Basic Books.

Johnson, Leo
1972   "The Development of Class in Canada" In G. Teeple (ed.), *Capitalism and the National Question in Canada*. Toronto: University of Toronto Press.

1974   *Poverty in Wealth*. Toronto: New Hogtown Press.

Kando, Thomas
1975   *Leisure and Popular Culture in Transition*. St. Louis: C. V. Mosby.

Kaplan, Max
1960   *Leisure in America*. New York: John Wiley.

Keller, Suzanne and Marisa Zavalloni
1964   "Ambition and Social Class: A Respectification." *Social Forces*, 43, October.

Kelner, Merijoy
1973   "Ethnic Penetration into Toronto's Elite Structure." In James E. Curtis and William G. Scott (eds.), *Social Stratification: Canada*. Toronto: Prentice-Hall.

Kenyon, Gerald S. and Barry McPherson
1973   "Becoming Involved in Physical Activity and Sport: A Process of Socialization." In G. Lawrence Rarick (ed.), *Physical Activity: Human Growth and Development*. New York: Academic Press.

Kidd, Bruce and John MacFarlane
1972   *The Death of Hockey*. Toronto: New Press.

Kraus, Richard
1971   *Recreation and Leisure in Modern Society*. New York: Appleton-Century Crofts.

1965   "Recreation for the Rich and Poor: A Contrast." *Quest*, 5.

Lindsay, Peter
1969   "A History of Sport in Canada: 1807-1867." Unpublished doctoral dissertation, University of Alberta.

Loy, John
1969   "The Study of Sport and Social Mobility." In G. Kenyon (ed.), *Aspects of Contemporary Sport Sociology*. Chicago: The Athletic Institute.

Lüschen, Günther
1969   "Social Stratification and Social Mobility Among Young Sportsmen." In J. W. Loy and Gerald Kenyon (eds.), *Sport Culture and Society*. Toronto: Macmillan.

1972   "The Interdependence of Sport and Culture." In Marie Hart (ed.), *Sport in the Socio-Cultural Process*. Dubuque: William C. Brown.

Mackenzie, Gavin
1973   *The Aristocracy of Labour*. London: Cambridge University Press.

Mallea, John
1975   "The Victorian Sporting Legacy." *McGill Journal of Education*, 10(2).

Mannheim, Karl
1960   "Types of Rationality and Organized Insecurity." In C. Wright Mills (ed.), *Images of Man*. New York: George Braziller.

Marchak, Patricia
1975   *Ideological Perspectives on Canada*. Toronto: McGraw-Hill.

Marshall, T. H.
1950   *Citizenship and Social Class*. Cambridge University Press.

McPherson, Barry D.
1974   "Minority Group Involvement in Sport: The Black Athlete." In J. Wilmore (ed.), *Exercise and Sport Sciences Reviews, Volume II*, New York: Academic Press.

Metcalfe, Alan
1972   "Sport and Class Concepts in Nineteenth Century Canada." Paper presented at the Annual Meeting of the American Sociological Association, New Orleans.

Page, Charles H.
1973   "The World of Sport and its Study." In John Talamini and Charles H. Page (eds.), *Sport and Society*. Boston: Little Brown.

Parker, Richard
1972   *The Myth of the Middle Class.* New York: Harper Colophon.

Parkin, Frank
1972   *Class Inequality and Political Order.* London: Paladin.

Pavia, Grant
1974   "An Investigation into the Sociological Background of Successful South Australian Footballers." *The Australian Journal of Physical Education*, 63, March.

1973   "An Analysis of the Social Class of the 1972 Olympic Team". *The Australian Journal of Physical Education*, 61, September.

Pike, Robert
1975   "Introduction and Overview." In Robert Pike and Elia Zureik (eds.), *Socialization and Values in Canadian Society, Vol. II.* Toronto: McClelland and Stewart.

Porter, John
1966   *The Vertical Mosaic.* Toronto: University of Toronto Press.

1968   "The Future of Upward Mobility." *American Sociological Review*, 33, (1).

Report Of The Special Senate Committee On Poverty
1971   *Poverty in Canada.* Ottawa: Information Canada

Rinehart, James
1975   *The Tyranny of Work.* Toronto: Longmans

Roberts, John M. and Brian Sutton-Smith
1969   "Child Training and Game Involvement." In J. W. Loy and Gerald J. Kenyon (eds.), *Sport, Culture and Society.* Toronto: Macmillan.

Rocher, Guy
1975   "Formal Education: The Issue of Opportunity." In Dennis Forcese and Stephen Richer (eds.), *Issues in Canadian Society.* Toronto: Prentice-Hall.

Scanzoni, J.
1967   "Socialization, Achievement, and Achievement Values." *American Sociological Review*, 32(3).

Schaar, John
1967   "Equality of Opportunity and Beyond" In *Nomos IX: Equality.* New York: Atherton Press.

Simon, Robert
1974   "Equality, Merit and the Determination of our Gifts." *Social Research*, 41(3).

Spitz, David
1974   "A Grammar of Equality." *Dissent*, Winter.

Stone, Gregory P.
1957   "Some Meanings of American Sport." Proceedings of the 60th Annual College Physical Education Association Meetings, Columbus, Ohio.

1973   "American Sport: Play and Display." In John Talamini and Charles H. Page (eds.), *Sport and Society.* Boston: Little, Brown.

Sugawara, Ray
1972   "The Study of Top Sportsmen in Japan." *International Review of Sport Sociology.*

Sutton-Smith, Brian, John Roberts and Robert M. Kozelka
1969   "Game Involvement in Adults." In J. W. Loy and Gerald S. Kenyon (eds.), *Sport, Culture and Society.* Toronto: Macmillan.

Turner, Ralph
1964   *The Social Context of Ambition.* San Francisco: Chandler.

Vallee, Frank G.
1975   "Multi-Ethnic Societies: The Issues of Identity and Inequality." In Dennis Forcese and Stephen Richer (eds.), *Issues in Canadian Society.* Toronto: Prentice-Hall.

Veblen, Thorstein
1953   The Theory of the Leisure Class. New York: Mentor.

Webb, Harry
1969   "Reaction to Loy's Paper." In Gerald S. Kenyon (ed.), Aspects of Contemporary Sport Sociology. Chicago: The Athletic Institute.

Weber, Max
1958   Class, Status, Party" In H. H. Gerth and C. W. Mills From Max Weber: Essays in Sociology. New York: Oxford University Press.

Weinberg, S. Kirkson and Henry Arond
1969   "The Occupational Culture of the Boxer." In J. W. Loy and Gerald S. Kenyon (eds.), Sport, Culture and Society. Toronto: Macmillan.

Westergaard, J. H.
1972   "The Withering Away of Class: A Contemporary Myth." In Paul Blumberg (ed.), The Impact of Social Class. New York: Thomas Crowell.

White, T. H.
1975   "The Relative Importance of Education and Income as Predictors in Outdoor Recreation Participation." Journal of Leisure Research, 7(3).

Wise, S. F. and Douglas Fisher
1974   Canada's Sporting Heroes. Toronto: General Publishing.

Young, Michael
1961   The Rise of the Meritocracy. London: Penguin.

LES CANADIENS FRANÇAIS ET LES GRANDS JEUX INTERNATIONAUX (1908 - 1974)

Roger Boileau
Fernand Landry
Yves Trempe

Introduction

La question est d'importance, car elle contient le passé et touche l'avenir d'une bonne part de l'activité sportive du pays à laquelle les Canadiens francais ne sont certes plus étrangers ou indifférents et aux relations entre les groupes ethniques au Québec.

Nous croyons qu'à l'aube de la célébration de la XXIe Olympiade de Montréal, ce thème apparaît opportun pour les éducateurs et la gent sportive du Québec. Dans l'état actuel des bouleversements d'ordre social, économique et politique que connaît le Québec, les transformations rapides du système d'éducation ainsi que de la pensée et les habitudes de vie de la population prennent, entre autres, une importance sans précédent et jouent un rôle fécondateur marquant dans la mutation du système de valeurs. Au Québec comme dans le reste de l'Amérique du Nord, force nous est de constater le sens et la fonction sociale de plus en plus marqués que prend et occupe le sport dans la vie contemporaine. Le sport professionel par son emprise monopolisante de l'intérêt général a joué jusqu'à maintenant un rôle d'importance qui a canalisé, en raison de l'anémie de l'organisation du sport amateur, la majeure partie de l'intérêt populaire. Pour le Canadien francais aussi le sport n'est plus un luxe; s'il n'est pas encore et partout activité de masse, du moins est-il occupation ou préoccupation croissante tant sa présence devient envahissante. Témoins les nombreux organismes surgis depuis quelques années, l'apport plus considérable de gouvernements, l'engagement plus diversifié des professionnels de l'activité physique et l'éveil des mass-media à cette réalité nouvelle.

Au Québec comme ailleurs, les formes du sport n'ont pas toujours été celles que nous connaissons aujourd'hui. Influencées par la nature changeante d'une société traditionelle en évolution tardive par rapport à l'ensemble de l'Amérique du Nord, ces formes se sont chargées, au cours des dernières décades, de perspectives d'intention et de caractères d'organisation propres à la société québécoise qui expliquent bien l'importance prise par certains sports en nos milieux et l'ignorance de certains autres.

L'engouement actuel des masses pour le sport de grand spectacle ne prouve pas nécessairement qu'elles en aient compris la signification réelle. Tous, en effet, n'apprécient pas au même point le sens véritable de la haute compétition et les jugements ne sont pas toujours des plus nuancés sur la valeur éducative, récréative ou culturelle de la haute performance, surtout dans les sports qui ignorent les classements traditionnels et les bruyants championnats.

Un reflet, non l'unique, de la place réelle que le sport de compétition occupe dans la vie et dans la pensée d'un peuple nous paraît être l'observation, sur une période de plusieurs années, de la variété et de la qualité de la haute performance comme mode d'expression naturelle de l'élite sportive. Ces manifestations particulières de la chose sportive, directement mesurables, sont peu discutables, les critères d'excellence étant les mêmes de par le monde; seules leur nécessité et leur utilité sont loin d'être reconnues de tous.

Malgré les querelles du sport amateur national et international l'histoire, la tradition et la prestige des grands jeux internationaux semblent continuer d'imposer universellement un idéal de promotion de valeurs humaines fondamentales. L'esprit olympique, par les jeunes qui en sont animés tour à tour depuis le début du siècle, a su construire, malgré les dangers qui y sont inhérents, les plus prestigieuses manifestations sportives de l'histoire et sans doute les plus ouvertes et les plus pacifiques des compétitions entre les nations.

La vocation internationale du sport telle que manifestée entre autres aux Jeux olympiques, aux Jeux du Commonwealth et aux Jeux panaméricains continue donc de se vouloir avant tout celle d'un langage pacifique qui permette aux hommes de se rencontrer, de se connaître et de se comprendre.

L'expérience montre bien qu'il y a une relation entre le genre, le nombre et la qualité de l'élite sportive, l'intérêt des jeunes pour le sport et la sympathie des adultes pour sa cause sur les plans local, national et international. La participation canadienne actuelle aux championnats amateurs et aux Jeux internationaux reflète indubitablement un ensemble de facteurs historiques, ethniques et socio-économiques propres au Canada.

Le début du XXe siècle n'avait vu se produire que de bien lents changements dans la condition humaine des Canadiens d'expression française; l'empire du machinisme, la montée de l'automation et de la cybernétique ainsi que les bouleversements sociaux n'ont eu que tardivement chez eux, par rapport à l'ensemble des États-Unis et de nombreuses nations du monde occidental, des effets profonds et suffisamment marquants pour modifier les modes de vie et de pensée. Alors qu'en Angleterre, en France et aux États-Unis, Arnold, de Coubertin et Sloane préparaient déjà les voies de la réconciliation définitive entre la culture et le sport et jetaient les bases d'une transformation radicale de l'éducation de la jeunesse, on se disputait encore au coeur du Canada français, sous l'influence d'un jansénisme vieilli, sur la valeur humanisante du sport, et on retardait gravement son implantation sous sa forme moderne et dynamique.

Au tournant du siècle, un immense élan avait déjà emporté vers le sport les Canadiens anglophones et nos voisins américains. Peu à peu, la compétition internationale ou la haute performance en était venue à conditionner en quelque sorte chez eux le développement du sport et son organisation même. Nous croyons qu'il n'en fut pas de même chez les Canadiens d'expression française. De Coubertin (1890) avait su d'ailleurs remarquer avec regret, lors de son voyage au Canada en 1889, que les institutions canadiennes anglaises virilisaient leur jeunesse avec les sports, cependant qu'il n'était pas question, pour les Canadiens français de l'époque, de s'adonner à des distractions aussi puériles:

> Les élèves du collège de Montréal sortaient en promenade au moment où notre "calèche" s'arrêtait devant le perron. Ils portaient d'atroces redingotes râpées et une ceinture de serge verte enroulée autour de la taille. Rien ne peut rendre l'air piteux et incomplet que leur donnait ce costume; on eût dit un cortège de ratés. L'intérieur du collège me parut assez en rapport avec les êtres qu'il renferme; la propreté la plus élémentaire en est absente; dans les dortoirs, quatre rangées de lits à peine espacés et des cuvettes microscopiques mises là comme à regret, par une concession maussade aux idées du jour. Ils sont 350 élèves dans cette boîte et ils ne payent que 80 dollars (400 francs) par an. Mais la congrégation des Sulpiciens est si riche! Ne pourrait-elle faire quelque chose pour ses élèves? Et que deviennent les revenus de la moitié de Montréal qu'elle possède sans avoir à payer? . . . Quelle révolution ils sont en train de se préparer là-bas!
>
> J'ai visité encore des "High schools", L'École polytechnique, l'Académie commerciale, puis des écoles anglaises: partout le même contraste. Ici, des muscles, de l'activité, de la hardiesse, des regards bien francs: là, des membres maladroits, des attitudes gauches, aucune indépendance, rien de viril. Leur rude climat leur rend la santé malgré tout, mais le caractère ne germe pas, qui pourrait ensuite le créer de toute pièce? Nous sommes entrés en passant dans un gymnase où beaucoup d'écoliers se livraient à des exercices de force et d'agilité . . . tous anglais!

Une étude attentive des délégations canadiennes aux Jeux internationaux depuis leur instauration nous laisse voir qu'il y a chez les deux groupes ethniques principaux du Canada, des différences profondes dans les niveaux de participation et de performances atteints. Cet état de choses reflète, selon nous, des différences d'intérêts et d'attitudes qui ont jusqu'à récemment menacé l'évolution, chez les Canadiens français, des principales spécialités du sport amateur international contemporain.

Sport et Ethnicité

La question des relations ethniques et raciales dans l'univers sportif a été examinée depuis quelques années par un nombre accru de chercheurs qui ont surtout essayé de cerner la réalité de la présence des athlètes noirs américains au sein d'équipes professionnelles (baseball, football, basketball). De ces recherches se dégage une certaine unanimité pour reconnaître qu'une discrimination ouverte et systématique s'est produite aux États-Unis jusqu'à la deuxième guerre mondiale. Mais même si les nécessités d'un marché accru et l'excellence des performances des noirs, associé à une certaine ouverture d'esprit du public leur ont permis de pénétrer petit à petit quelques sports plus facilement accessibles, une discrimination plus subtile n'en continue pas moins de subsister encore aujourd'hui, limitant et contenant leur présence dans des proportions arbitraires et dans des rôles particuliers.

Smith et Grindstaff (1970) ont identifié pour le football, quatre de ces pratiques discriminatoires:

a)   le système de quota qui détermine le nombre limite d'athlètes noirs dans une équipe;

b)   la compétition forcée (*stacking*) entre athlètes de couleur pour certaines positions (par exemple demi offensif au football);

c)   la concentration des athlètes de couleur à des positions non centrales;

d)   l'accès bloqué ou fort limité à des postes de commande dans la structure du pouvoir (entraîneur, administrateur, etc.)

Une explication alternative à l'approche basée sur la discrimination a été proposée récemment par McPherson (1973). Il suggère en effet que les positions occupées par les athlètes noirs au sein d'une équipe ne sont pas déterminées par des pratiques discriminatoires mais plutôt par l'expérimentation d'une socialisation des rôles différente par leur propre milieu dès le jeune âge, qui valorise certaines activités sportives, fonctions et rôles au détriment d'autres.

Y a-t-il discrimination envers les athlètes canadiens-français au Canada? Il n'est guère possible, compte tenu de l'absence d'étude, de répondre objectivement à cette question ou de donner foi à l'une ou l'autre de ces approches théoriques, les quelques travaux sur les athlètes canadiens-français n'y étant qu'indirectement liés.

C'est ainsi que dans son étude de la relation entre la centralité et la mobilité sociale des joueurs de hockey de la Ligue nationale de hockey, Roy (1974) constata qu'en dépit d'une représentation égale aux athlètes anglophones aux positions centrales d'où émergent habituellement les administrateurs de la ligue, les joueurs francophones étaient nettement sous-représentés dans ces fonctions. Toutefois lorsqu'il fut demandé aux joueurs à la retraite (1949-1973) si, durant leur carrière, ils avaient songé à occuper une fonction administrative quelconque dans la LNH, 11.1% seulement des joueurs francophones, contre 52.1% des joueurs anglophones répondirent positivement. S'agit-il d'un refus de travailler dans un environnement linguistique différent? de la fausse perception d'un refus presque assuré de la part des autorites? d'un simple et véritable manque d'ambition? La question reste ouverte.

Dans un récent article, Marple (1975) a mis en évidence le paradoxe de la performance des joueurs de hockey professionnels (LNH et LMH) canadiens-français et le traitement qui leur serait donné par les équipes de ces deux ligues (à l'exception des Canadiens de Montréal). L'auteur constate d'abord que leur présence est passée de 14% durant la période de 1910-1939 à 28.5% durant les saisons 1960-1963. Se basant ensuite sur des rapports de journalistes qui avaient noté que les joueurs francophones sont moins bien traités, qu'ils se tiennent à l'écart et que dans certains clubs l'usage de la langue française est interdit en tout temps, l'auteur conclut à l'existence de pratiques discriminatoires à leur égard puisque leurs performances sportives se révèlent supérieures à celles de tout autre groupe ethnique et ne justifient pas un tel traitement.

> Les joueurs francophones au sein d'équipes comptant une proportion de francophones au-dessus de la moyenne (21.4%), même s'ils jouent dans moins de matches, comptent plus de buts et plus de passes et occupent un rang beaucoup plus élevé chez les compteurs que les autres groupes. Dans des équipes à prédominance française au Québec ou près de ses frontières, les francophones dominent partout et de façon très évidente.

Aussi attirante qu'elle paraisse, la conclusion de Marple ne prouve en rien l'existence de pratiques discriminatoires envers les Canadiens français. Bien qu'il ait démontré la supériorité de leurs performances, la démonstration de discrimination ne repose que sur des observations non systématisées de journalistes et non sur une véritable opérationalisation du concept.

Considérations méthodologiques

Nous ne considérons dans ce travail que la présence de représentants francophones au sein des missions canadiennes aux Jeux olympiques, aux Jeux du Commonwealth et aux Jeux pan-américains. Nous entendons par "représentants" les athlètes et le personnel de soutien, soit les entraîneurs, gérants et assistants, à l'exception des chefs de délégation, du personnel médical ainsi que des arbitres et juges. Un représentant canadien-français ou francophone est défini comme une personne de nom à consonance française et/ou de langue maternelle française qui a pu être identifiée dans les rapports officiels. Cette approche méthodologique peut apparaître discutable au lecteur étranger à la réalité québécoise. Elle fut utilisée antérieurement dans le domaine sportif par Landry et al. (1966) et Marple (1975). Bien que sa validité n'ait pas encore été vérifiée, nous croyons que les caractéristiques de la population québécoise contemporaine se prête encore à ce type d'analyse. En effet, cette dernière est issue d'un bassin original réduit (environ 60,000 habitants lors de la conquête) qui s'est perpétué grâce à un taux spectaculaire de fécondité[1] plutôt qu'à l'apport d'immigrants (Charbonneau: 1973). De plus, les mouvements d'assimilation culturelle chez les deux principaux groupes linguistiques du

Québec ont été de faible importance, compte tenu du long repli des Canadiens français. Lorsqu'ils eurent lieu, il s'agissait surtout de francophones qui changeaient d'allégeance, si bien que les pourcentages exprimés dans ce texte représentent des maxima. Si quelques erreurs se sont glissées dans l'interprétation des noms, elles ont eu l'effet d'exagérer légèrement la participation des francophones, et non le contraire. Finalement, les anglophones québécois se sont assimilés massivement à la culture anglophone, ne laissant en présence que deux groupes linguistiques.

A cette immobilité relative des deux groupes dominants, les facteurs suivants ont contribué à réduire les risques d'erreur inhérents à une telle approche méthodologique: (a) des entrevues et vérifications avec des représentants de divers organismes[2], (b) des vérifications de documents et (c) l'implication et la connaissance du milieu sportif québécois par les auteurs.

Participation des Francophones aux Jeux internationaux

Les dernières statistiques démographiques officielles (recensement du Canada: 1971) nous montrent que la population totale du pays n'est plus formée que d'un peu plus d'un quart de Canadiens d'expression française[3]. Dans la province de Québec[4], la proportion des Canadiens français atteignait cependant 80.7% au même recensement, alors que celle des anglophones se situait à environ 13.0%. Ces proportions, pour une gamme de raisons complexes sur lesquelles nous allons revenir, ne se retrouvent pas lorsque l'on observe la part qu'a occupée le Canada français dans l'ensemble de la participation aux grands Jeux internationaux.

Dans un travail antérieur (Landry et al.: 1966), nous avons fait ressortir le fait que les provinces canadiennes les plus populeuses étaient celles qui, comme l'on devait s'y attendre, fournissaient la plus forte proportion des délégations canadiennes internationales. Nous avons démontré qu'il se trouvait cependant un trompe-l'oeil dans la contribution élevée de la province de Québec à ces délégations, la part des Canadiens français se montrant, à l'analyse, inversement proportionnelle à leur supériorité démographique dans le cadre géographique. A titre d'exemple, pour les Jeux olympiques d'été et d'hiver qui ont eu lieu entre 1948 et 1964, il n'y eut que 60 francophones sur un nombre total de 214 représentants de la province de Québec qui ont fait partie des diverses délégations canadiennes. Ainsi donc, alors que la population francophone du Québec gravitait à cette époque, comme aujourd'hui encore, autour de 80%, il n'y eut, par contraste durant cette période que 28% de francophones dans le contingentement québécois aux délégations canadiennes.

Les Francophones aux Jeux olympiques d'été

Le tableau I fait ressortir les rapports ethniques des délégations qui ont participé aux Jeux olympiques d'été. Les francophones qui forment près d'un tiers de la population canadienne, n'ont que très rarement fourni plus de 10% de la représentation totale à ces Jeux. Avant la deuxième guerre mondiale la participation des francophones avait atteint 8.3% aux Jeux de Stockholm (1912) mais était retombée à moins de 3% à ceux de Los Angeles (1932) et à ceux de Berlin (1936). Le sursaut de 15% des premiers Jeux d'après-guerre tenus à Londres (1948), a été suivi d'une baisse progressive: Helsinki (1952), 7.5%; Melbourne (1956), 6.1%: Rome (1960), 4.2%; Tokyo (1964), 3.7%. Aux Jeux tenus à Mexico en 1968, la participation des francophones allait se situer, mais pour une deuxième fois seulement, à près de 10%. Il ne s'agissait toutefois pas d'une véritable relance de l'élite sportive francophone au niveau international, puisqu'aux derniers Jeux de Munich en 1972, les Canadiens français ne composaient à nouveau que 5.7% de la délégation canadienne.

Les auteurs désirent attirer l'attention sur la distribution de la représentation dans certaines des spécialités individuelles les plus prestigieuses des Jeux olympiques, entre autres sur l'athlétisme, la natation et la gymnastique. On constatera avec aisance que dans les deux premières spécialités, la participation des francophones a été on ne peut plus marginale alors qu'au contraire, dans la troisième discipline, elle a été un peu plus significative depuis 1956.

Globalement, depuis le début du siècle, la participation des francophones aux Jeux olympiques d'été s'est avérée bien en deçà de leur proportion démographique dans l'ensemble du Canada. Leur participation maximale s'est produite en 1948 à Londres, alors qu'ils composaient 14.9% de la délégation canadienne. Mais cette poussée subite qui coïncidait avec l'apparition de la Palestre nationale sur la scène du sport amateur québécois de niveau international n'a pas été maintenue. Le tableau de leur participation pourrait se résumer par l'image de trois poussées timides (1912 avec 8.3%; 1948 avec 14.9%; et 1968 avec 9.4%) entrecoupées de longs déclins progressifs.

Pour l'ensemble des 19 autres activités qui ont figuré au programme de ces Jeux, seules quelques activités sportives individuelles ont vu une participation francophone de quelque importance. Il s'agit de:

—l'escrime en 1932 (20%), en 1948 et 1952 (50%), en 1956 (100%) et en 1968 (20%);

—l'haltérophilie en 1948 et 1952 (50%), en 1956 (60%), en 1960 (25%), en 1964 (50%), en 1968 (28%) et en 1972 (20%);

—le cyclisme en 1948 (57%), en 1956 (25%), en 1968 (50%) et en 1972 (20%);
—la boxe en 1948 (25%) et en 1960 (40%);
—la lutte en 1952 seulement (40%).

Les Francophones aux Jeux olympiques d'hiver

L'histoire des Jeux olympiques d'hiver ne remonte qu'à 1924. Au tableau II, on peut constater une première présence francophone aux Jeux de 1928 tenus à St-Moritz, c.-à-d. un représentant sur une délégation totale de 25 personnes. Aux Jeux de Lake Placid (1932), la participation francophone allait dépasser légèrement 10%, niveau où, après un seuil inférieur de 4% aux Jeux de Garmisch-Partenkirchen en 1936 suivi d'un niveau record de 15% en 1948, elle demeurera relativement bien stabilisée aux Jeux de Oslo (1952), ainsi qu'à ceux de Cortina (1956) et de Squaw Valley (1960). Aux Jeux de 1964, célébrés à Innsbruck, et à ceux de Grenoble tenus en 1968, et aux récents Jeux de Sapporo en 1972, l'indice allait cependant vite décliner au niveau où il se trouvait avant la dernière guerre mondiale, soit à environ 5%. Le lecteur peut aisément remarquer que dans certaines des spécialités les plus prestigieuses des Jeux d'hiver, à savoir le patinage artistique, le hockey et le ski, ce n'est qu'à cette dernière spécialité que la participation francophone a atteint quelque importance, soit 5 participants sur une équipe de 16 concurrents, aux Jeux de 1952.

En résumé, depuis le début des Jeux olympiques d'hiver, la participation des francophones s'est avérée bien en deçà de leur proportion démographique dans l'ensemble du Canada. A l'instar des Jeux d'été, leur participation maximale s'est produite en 1948 et dans des proportions similaires (14.6%), mais contrairement aux Jeux d'été ce sommet a pu être maintenu au niveau d'une participation de 10% au cours des trois Olympiades subséquentes.

Synthèse de la Participation francophone aux Jeux olympiques d'été et d'hiver

Si l'on accepte le fait que les Jeux d'été et d'hiver célèbrent la même Olympiade, l'on peut, en faisant la somme des participants à chaque Jeux, obtenir ainsi une image globale qui illustre encore mieux les tendances. Le tableau III se veut un illustration de l'ensemble.

TABLEAU I
PARTICIPATION DES FRANCOPHONES AUX JEUX OLYMPIQUES D'ÉTÉ

Activités	1908* Part. Totale	1908* Part. Franco.	1912 Part. Totale	1912 Part. Franco.	1924 Part. Totale	1924 Part. Franco.	1928 Part. Totale	1928 Part. Franco.	1932 Part. Totale	1932 Part. Franco.	1936 Part. Totale	1936 Part. Franco.
Athlétisme	25	0	18	3	27	2	42	0	38	0	35	0
Aviron	0	0	10	0	18	0	13	0	21	0	13	0
Basket-ball	0	0	0	0	0	0	0	0	0	0	20	1
Boxe	0	0	0	0	11	1	11	1	9	1	9	0
Canoë	5	0	0	0	4	0	0	0	0	0	8	0
Cyclisme	0	0	2	0	1	1	8	1	9	0	7	0
Equitation	1	0	0	0	0	0	0	0	0	0	0	0
Escrime	2	0	0	0	0	0	0	0	5	1	10	1
Gymnastique	0	0	0	0	0	0	0	0	0	0	0	0
Haltérophilie	0	0	0	0	0	0	0	0	0	0	0	0
Hockey sur gazon	0	0	0	0	0	0	0	0	0	0	0	0
Judo	—**	—	—	—	—	—	—	—	—	—	—	—
Lacrosse	15	0	—	—	—	—	—	—	—	—	—	—
Lutte	1	1	0	0	5	0	7	0	8	0	7	1
Natation et plongeon	1	0	3	0	5	2	10	1	24	1	27	0
Pentathlon moderne	—	—	—	—	—	—	—	—	—	—	—	—
Tennis	3	0	0	0	0	0	—	—	—	—	—	—
Tir a l'arc	—	—	—	—	—	—	—	—	—	—	—	—
Tir a la cible	17	0	3	0	7	0	0	0	0	0	0	0
Water polo	—	—	—	—	1	0	0	0	16	0	1	0
Yachting	0	0	—	—	0	0	0	0	0	0	0	0
Total	70	1	36	3	79	6	91	3	130	3	137	3
% de la participation francophone	1.4		8.3		7.6		3.3		2.3		2.2	

*Au moment de la rédaction du présent travail, des données officielles n'avaient pu être obtenues pour les Jeux de 1904 (St. Louis) et pour ceux de Paris (1900) auxquels le Canada a pris part.

TABLEAU I (suite) PARTICIPATION DES FRANCOPHONES AUX JEUX OLYMPIQUES D'ÉTÉ

Activités	1948 Part. Totale	1948 Part. Franco.	1952 Part. Totale	1952 Part. Franco.	1956 Part. Totale	1956 Part. Franco.	1960 Part. Totale	1960 Part. Franco.	1964 Part. Totale	1964 Part. Franco.	1968 Part. Totale	1968 Part. Franco.	1972 Part. Totale	1972 Part. Franco.
Athlétisme	37	4	27	0	20	0	17	0	17	0	31	1	37	1
Aviron	14	1	18	0	17	0	18	0	18	1	15	0	19	0
Basket-ball	17	0	15	0	14	0	14	0	13	0	0	0	0	0
Boxe	12	3	10	1	7	0	5	2	5	0	6	1	7	1
Canoë	8	1	14	0	7	0	8	0	8	1	12	1	17	3
Cyclisme	7	4	3	0	4	1	3	0	0	0	8	4	15	3
Equitation	0	0	6	0	8	0	8	0	2	0	14	0	17	0
Escrime	6	3	2	1	1	1	1	0	4	0	5	1	8	0
Gymnastique	1	0	0	0	3	1	4	1	5	1	12	3	14	2
Haltérophilie	6	3	6	3	5	3	4	1	4	2	7	2	5	1
Hockey sur gazon	0	0	0	0	0	0	0	0	17	0	0	0	0	0
Judo	—	—	—	—	—	—	—	—	—	—	—	—	6	0
Lacrosse	—	—	—	—	—	—	—	—	—	—	—	—	—	—
Lutte	6	1	5	2	3	0	4	0	5	0	10	1	11	1
Natation et plongeon	13	0	12	2	12	0	12	0	17	0	23	0	50	0
Pentathlon moderne	—	—	—	—	—	—	—	—	—	—	—	—	5	0
Tennis	—	—	—	—	—	—	—	—	—	—	—	—	—	—
Tir a l'arc	—	—	—	—	—	—	—	—	—	—	—	—	8	0
Tir a la cible	0	0	4	1	5	1	8	0	7	0	11	1	12	0
Water polo	—	—	—	—	—	—	—	—	—	—	—	—	13	2
Yachting	7	0	12	1	8	0	12	1	12	0	16	1	21	1
Total	134	20	134	10	114	7	118	5	134	5	170	16	265	15
% de la participation francophone	14.9		7.5		6.1		4.2		3.7		9.4		5.6	

*Au moment de la rédaction du présent travail, des données officielles n'avaient pu être obtenues pour les Jeux de 1904 (St. Louis) et pour ceux de Paris (1900) auxquels le Canada a pris part.
Le trait indique que l'épreuve n'était pas au programme officiel des jeux en question

TABLEAU II PARTICIPATION DES FRANCOPHONES AUX JEUX OLYMPIQUES D'HIVER

Activités	1924		1928		1932		1936		1948	
	Part. Totale	Franco. Phone	Part. Totale	Franco- phone	Part. Totale	Franco- phone	Part. Totale	Franco- phone	Part. Totale	Franco- phone
Biathlon	-	-	-	-	0	0	0	0	0	0
Bobsleigh et luge	-	-	-	-	0	0	0	0	-	-
Curling	-	-	-	-	16	0	-	-	-	-
Dog derby	-	-	-	-	5	2	-	-	-	-
Hockey	9	0	13	0	14	0	15	1	21	4
Patinage artistique	2	0	5	0	10	1	7	0	7	0
Patinage de vitesse	1	0	3	0	11	1	1	0	5	0
Ski	-	-	4	1	23	5	1	0	15	3
Total	12	0	25	1	79	9	24	1	48	7
% de la participation francophone	0.0		4.0		11.4		4.1		14.6	

TABLEAU II (suite) PARTICIPATION DES FRANCOPHONES AUX JEUX OLYMPIQUES D'HIVER

Activités	1952		1956		1960		1964		1968		1972	
	Part. Totale	Franco- phone	Part. Totale	Franco- phone	Part. Totale	Franco- phone	Part. Totale	Franco- phone	Part. Totale	Franco- phone	Part. Totale	Franco- phone
Biathlon	-	-	-	-	-	-	-	-	5	0	0	0
Bobsleigh et luge	0	0	0	0	0	0	10	0	18	1	15	0
Curling	-	-	-	-	-	-	-	-	-	-	-	-
Dog derby	-	-	-	-	-	-	-	-	-	-	-	-
Hockey	21	0	20	2	20	2	24	2	22	2	0	0
Patinage artistique	7	0	9	0	10	0	14	0	12	0	10	0
Patinage de vitesse	4	0	4	0	6	0	5	0	8	1	12	2
Ski	16	5	13	3	18	4	23	1	24	1	27	2
Total	48	5	46	5	54	6	76	3	89	5	64	4
% de la participation francophone	10.4		10.9		11.1		3.9		5.6		6.2	

* Le trait indique que l'épreuve n'était pas au programme officiel des jeux en question

TABLEAU III   SYNTHÈSE DE LA PARTICIPATION FRANCOPHONE AUX JEUX OLYMPIQUES D'ÉTÉ ET D'HIVER D'AVANT-GUERRE

	1908		1912		1924*		1928		1932		1936	
	Part. Totale	Part. Franco	Part. Totale	Part. Franco	Part. Totale	Part. Franco	Part. Totale	Part. Franco	Part. Totale	Part. Franco	Part. Totale	Part. Franco
Sous-Total Jeux d'été % francophone	70	1 / 1.4	36	3 / 8.3	79	6 / 7.6	91	3 / 3.3	130	3 / 2.3	137	3 / 2.2
Sous-total Jeux d'hiver % francophone					12	0 / 0.0	25	1 / 4.0	79	9 / 11.4	24	1 / 4.1
Total	70	1	36	3	91	6	116	4	209	12	161	4
Total du % de la participation francophone		1.4		8.3		6.6		3.4		5.7		2.5

TABLEAU III (suite) SYNTHÈSE DE LA PARTICIPATION FRANCOPHONE AUX JEUX OLYMPIQUES D'ÉTÉ ET D'HIVER

	1948		1952		1956		1960		1964		1968		1972	
	Part. Totale	Part. Franco	Part. Totale	Part. Franco	Part. Totale	Part. Franco	Part. Totale	Part. Franco	Part. Totale	Part. Franco	Part. Totale	Part. Franco	Part. Totale	Part. Franco Phone
Sous-Total Jeux d'été % francophone	134	20 / 14.9	134	10 / 7.5	114	7 / 6.1	118	5 / 4.2	134	5 / 3.7	170	16 / 9.4	265	15 / 5.6
Sous-total Jeux d'hiver % francophone	48	7 / 14.6	48	5 / 10.4	46	5 / 10.9	54	6 / 11.1	76	3 / 3.9	89	5 / 5.6	64	4 / 6.2
Total	182	27	182	15	160	12	172	11	210	8	259	21	329	19
Total du % de la participation francophone		14.8		8.2		7.5		6.4		3.9		8.1		5.7

*1924 marque l'année des premiers Jeux d'hiver.

Avant l'avènement de la deuxième guerre mondiale, (tableau III, partie 1) la participation totale des francophones aux Jeux d'une olympiade, même avec l'addition des Jeux d'hiver en 1924, n'a jamais pu dépasser le niveau de 8.3% qui a été atteint en 1912. Après la deuxième guerre mondiale, il est intéressant de noter (tableau III, partie 2) que le seuil supérieur de 14.8% aux Jeux de Londres en 1948 n'a été que bien éphémère puisque l'indice de participation des francophones allait retomber à environ 8% dès l'Olympiade suivante célébrée à Helsinki (1952), s'y maintenir en 1956 (7.5%) et même tomber encore plus bas à celle de Rome en 1960 (6.4%) et à celle de Tokyo en 1964 (3.9%).

En résumé, la participation des francophones aux Jeux olympiques d'été et d'hiver s'est révélée constamment inférieure à leur représentation démographique au Canada. Alors que les Canadiens français représentent en moyenne 30% de la population canadienne depuis le début du siècle, leurs performances sportives ne leur ont permis de constituer qu'une seule fois plus de 10% des délégations canadiennes aux Jeux d'une olympiade.

Participation des Francophones aux Jeux du Commonwealth

La situation que veut illustrer le tableau IV est sensiblement parallèle à celle des Jeux olympiques. La participation des francophones dans l'ensemble des six derniers Jeux (Vancouver, Cardiff, Perth, Kingston, Edinburgh et Christchurch) n'a pas dépassé 12%. Le haut de 19.4% que l'on peut observer pour les Jeux de Auckland (1950) constitue l'indice collectif de participation le plus élevé qu'ait atteint la représentation francophone à tous les grands Jeux internationaux auxquels le Canada ait participé. Fait à remarquer, les moyennes de participation par Jeux ont diminué de façon presque systématique entre 1950 et 1970, passant de 19.4% à 4.3%, et il est impossible de dire si la hausse récente à 10.2% est l'aboutissement d'un plan d'action concerté pour hausser leur nombre ou le fruit du hasard.

En résumé, la participation des Canadiens français aux Jeux du Commonwealth révèle une présence constamment en deçà de leur proportion démographique au Canada. Tout comme pour les Jeux olympiques d'été et d'hiver, leur participation maximale se situe à la même période (1950) et à un niveau assez similaire (19.4%). De plus, à l'image des Jeux olympiques d'hiver, le sommet de 1950 a été suivi d'un plateau d'environ 10% qui s'est maintenu durant les quatre Jeux subséquents.

A l'instar des Jeux olympiques d'été, leur présence dans les spécialités traditionnellement prestigieuses de l'athlétisme et de la natation s'est avérée à peu près nulle. Pour l'ensemble des neuf autres activités sportives qui ont figuré aux programmes de ces Jeux, les francophones se sont distingués avec des pourcentages un peu plus élevés dans les mêmes spécialités individuelles qu'aux Jeux olympiques d'été:

—l'haltérophilie en 1950 (80%), en 1954 (44%), en 1958 (62%), en 1966 (50%) et en 1974 (71%);
—le cyclisme en 1958 (28%), en 1962 (60%) et en 1966 (57);
—l'escrime en 1950 (50%) et en 1954 (41%);
—la lutte en 1950 seulement (42%);
—la boxe en 1958 (27%) et en 1974 (25%);

Les Francophones aux Jeux pan-américains

Le tableau V illustre à nouveau la situation des francophones pour ces Jeux. Sur un total de 368 représentants canadiens qui ont participé en juillet 1971 aux Jeux de Cali, il n'y avait que 38 francophones, soit 10.4% de la délégation. Ce pourcentage dépasse légèrement celui des Jeux de 1967 tenus en sol canadien à Winnipeg où la participation des francophones ne s'est élevée qu'à 8.3%. Aux Jeux de 1963 tenus à São Paolo, la participation des francophones avait atteint un haut de 11.8% tandis qu'à l'instar de la situation aux Jeux olympiques, elle avait été inférieure de 10% aux Jeux précédents, soit ceux de Chicago en 1959, (8.9%) et ceux de Mexico en 1955, (5.6%). Les pourcentages reflétant la participation des francophones se situent donc, dans l'ensemble des Jeux pan-américains, à un niveau très inférieur à la moyenne optimum que donnerait une participation proportionnelle au rapport de la population canadienne.

Des spécialités considérées prestigieuses comme l'athlétisme, la natation et la gymnastique, seule cette dernière a vu une participation francophone substantielle. Depuis 1959 où ils ont composé 28% des représentants canadiens de cette discipline, leur participation est passée tour à tour à 42% (1963), à 33% (1967) et à 53% (1971). Parmi les 19 autres spécialités qui ont composé les programmes de ces Jeux, on retrouve essentiellement les mêmes spécialités individuelles qu'aux autres Jeux, où la participation des francophones s'est quelque peu distinguée:

—l'haltérophilie en 1959 (50%), en 1963 (60%), en 1967 (33%) et en 1971 (30%);
—l'escrime en 1955 (50%) et en 1967 (20%);
—la boxe en 1959 (42%), en 1963 (25%) et en 1971 (33%);
—le tennis en 1959 (40%) et en 1967 (28%);
—le cyclisme en 1959 (25%), en 1963 (33%), en 1967 (36%) et en 1971 (23%);

TABLEAU IV PARTICIPATION DES FRANCOPHONES AUX JEUX DU COMMONWEALTH

Activités	1950**		1954		1958	
	Part. Totale	Franco-Phone	Part Totale	Franco. Phone	Part. Totale	Franco. Phone
Athlétisme	29	2	80	2	26	1
Aviron	0	0	22	0	20	1
Badminton	—	—	—	--	—	—
Boxe	7	0	16	3	11	3
Cyclisme	5	0	13	2	7	2
Escrime	4	2	12	5	7	1
Haltérophilie	5	4	9	4	8	5
Lawnbowling	1	0	8	0	8	0
Lutte	7	3	16	3	8	0
Natation, plongeon	14	3	34	3	16	0
Tir a la cible	—	—	—	—	—	—
Total	72	14	210	22	111	13
% de la participation francophone		19.4		10.5		11.7

TABLEAU IV (suite) PARTICIPATION DES FRANCOPHONES AUX JEUX DU COMMONWEALTH

Activités	1962		1966		1970		1974	
	Part. Totale	Franco-phone	Part. Totale	Franco-phone	Part. Totale	Franco-phone	Part. Totale	Franco phone
Athlétisme	19	0	38	1	64	0	36	2
Aviron	18	1	*	—	0	0	—	—
Badminton	—	—	9	1	12	2	12	0
Boxe	7	1	10	1	10	0	8	2
Cyclisme	5	3	7	4	10	1	4	0
Escrime	5	0	10	1	14	2	—	—
Haltérophilie	6	2	10	5	11	2	7	5
Lawnbowling	5	0	—	—	8	0	8	1
Lutte	6	0	11	1	12	1	12	2
Natation, plongeon	14	1	24	0	46	0	40	1
Tir a la cible	—	—	9	0	—	—	10	1
Total	85	8	128	14	187	8	137	14
% de la participation francophone		9.4		9.1		4.3		10.2

*Le trait indique que l'épreuve n'était pas au programme officiel des jeux en question.

**Les données obtenues ne sont pas officielles pour les jeux qui se sont déroulés en 1930 (Hamilton), en 1934 (London) et en 1938 (Sidney)

TABLEAU V PARTICIPATION DES FRANCOPHONES AUX JEUX PAN-AMERICAINS

Activités	1955* Part. Totale	1955* Franco-phone	1959 Part. Totale	1959 Franco-phone	1963 Part. Totale	1963 Franco-phone	1967 Part. Totale	1967 Franco-phone	1971 Part. Totale	1971 Franco-phone
Athlétisme	14	1	33	0	19	1	59	2	51	1
Aviron	0	0	21	2	13	1	32	0	21	1
Baseball	—	—	—	—	—	—	21	1	20	2
Basket-ball	12	0	30	0	26	0	28	1	26	0
Boxe	0	0	7	3	4	1	10	1	9	3
Canotage	—	—	—	—	—	—	20	2	—	—
Cyclisme	0	0	8	2	3	1	14	5	13	3
Équitation	2	0	6	0	0	0	16	0	13	1
Escrime	2	1	7	0	5	0	15	3	15	2
Gymnastique	0	0	14	4	12	5	18	6	15	8
Haltérophilie	0	0	5	1	5	3	9	3	10	3
Hockey sur gazon	—	—	—	—	—	—	—	—	18	0
Judo	—	—	—	—	—	—	6	0	—	—
Lutte	1	0	8	0	7	0	10	2	12	1
Natation, plong. n. synch	40	2	26	1	16	2	37	0	56	5
Soccer	—	—	—	—	—	—	20	0	20	2
Tennis	0	0	5	2	2	0	7	2	—	—
Tir à la cible	0	0	11	2	13	2	26	2	20	0
Volley-ball	0	0	10	0	11	0	27	1	26	5
Water polo	0	0	0	0	10	0	11	2	14	1
Yachting	0	0	11	1	7	2	10	0	9	0
Total	71	4	202	18	153	18	396	33	368	38
% de la participation francophone	5.6		8.9		11.8		8.3		10.4	

*Les Jeux pan-américains débutèrent officiellement en 1951 (Buenos Aires). Le Canada participa pour la première fois en 1955 (Mexico).

TABLEAU VI   DISTRIBUTION PAR ACTIVITE DE LA PARTICIPATION FRANCOPHONE AUX GRANDS JEUX INTERNATIONAUX

Activités	Jeux olympiques			Commonwealth			Pan-americans			Partici-pation Totale	Part. Franco-phone	Pourcentage du Total
	Part. Totale	Part. Franco	% Franco.	Part. Totale	Part. Franco	% Franco	Part. Totale	Part. Franco	% Franco			
Athlétisme	371	11	3.0	292	8	2.7	176	5	2.8	839	24	2.9
Aviron	194	2	1.0	60	2	3.3	87	4	4.6	341	8	2.3
Badminton	—	—	—	33	3	9.1	—	—	—	33	3	9.1
Baseball	—	—	—	—	—	—	41	3	7.3	41	3	7.3
Basket-ball	93	1	1.1	—	—	—	122	1	0.8	215	2	1.0
Biathlon	5	0	0.0	—	—	—	—	—	—	5	0	0.0
Bobsleigh et luge	43	1	2.3	—	—	—	—	—	—	43	1	2.3
Boxe	92	11	12.0	69	10	14.5	30	8	26.7	191	29	15.2
Canoe	86	6	7.0	—	—	—	20	2	10.0	106	8	7.5
Curling	16	0	0.0	—	—	—	—	—	—	16	0	0.0
Cyclisme	72	14	19.4	51	12	23.5	38	11	28.9	161	37	23.0
Dog derby	5	2	40.0	—	—	—	—	—	—	5	2	40.0
Equitation	55	0	0.0	—	—	—	37	1	2.7	92	1	2.2
Escrime	43	8	18.6	52	11	21.2	44	6	13.6	139	25	18.0
Gymnastique	41	8	19.5	—	—	—	59	23	39.0	100	31	31.0
Haltérophilie	37	15	40.5	56	27	48.2	29	10	34.5	122	52	42.6
Hockey sur gazon	17	0	0.0	—	—	—	18	0	0.0	34	0	0.0
Hockey sur glace	179	13	7.3	—	—	—	—	—	—	179	13	7.3
Judo	6	0	0.0	—	—	—	6	0	0.0	12	0	0.0
La crosse	5	0	0.0	—	—	—	—	—	—	15	0	0.0
Lawnbowling	—	—	—	38	1	2.6	—	—	—	38	1	2.6
Lutte	72	6	8.3	72	10	14.0	38	3	7.9	182	19	10.4
Natation-plongeon-nage synchronisée	209	7	3.3	188	8	4.2	175	10	5.8	573	25	4.4
Patinage artistique	93	1	1.1	—	—	—	—	—	—	93	1	1.1
Patinage de vitesse	60	4	6.7	—	—	—	—	—	—	60	4	6.7
Pentathlon moderne	5	0	0.0	—	—	—	—	—	—	5	0	0.0
Ski	164	25	15.2	—	—	—	—	—	—	164	25	15.2
Soccer	3	0	0.0	—	—	—	40	2	5.0	40	2	5.0
Tennis	8	0	0.0	—	—	—	14	4	28.6	17	4	23.5
Tir a l'arc	8	0	0.0	—	—	—	—	—	—	8	0	0.0
Tir a la cible	74	3	4.0	19	1	5.3	70	6	8.6	163	10	6.1
Volleyball	0	0	0.0	—	—	—	74	6	8.1	74	6	8.1
Water polo	13	2	15.4	—	—	—	35	3	8.6	48	5	10.4
Yachting	106	3	2.8	—	—	—	37	3	8.1	143	6	4.2
Total	2177	143	6.6	930	93	10.0	1190	111	9.3	4297	347	8.1

Distribution relative par specialité de la Participation totale des Francophones aux Jeux internationaux

Le tableau VI favorise une vue d'ensemble, et par spécialité, de la participation des Canadiens français aux différents Jeux internationaux. La moyenne générale pour tous les Jeux se situe à 8.1%, soit un total de 347 représentants francophones sur un ensemble de délégations se chiffrant à 4297 personnes. Les deux seules moyennes générales de participation francophone[5] qui soient supérieures au rapport proportionnel de la population canadienne-française du pays (26.9%: recensement de 1971) sont celle de l'haltérophilie avec 43% et celle de la gymnastique sportive avec 31%. De l'éventail des spécialités qui se trouvent à la fois au programme des Jeux olympiques, des Jeux du Commonwealth et des Jeux pan-américains, les moyennes les plus élevées se voient, dans l'ordre, au cyclisme (23%), à l'escrime (18%), à la boxe (15.2%) et à la lutte (10.4%). Dans les spécialités qui par leur caractère saisonnier ne se retrouvent pas à tous les grands Jeux internationaux, les moyennes les plus élevées se voient au tennis (23.5%: Jeux pan-américains actuels et anciennement aux Jeux olympiques), au ski (15.2%: Jeux olympiques d'hiver seulement), au water-polo (10.4%: Jeux olympiques d'été et pan-américains), et au badminton (9.1%: Jeux du Commonwealth seulement). Exception faite de la gymnastique sportive où la participation des Canadiens français est bien à la hauteur, on ne retrouve pas dans les autres spécialités reconnues comme les plus prestigieuses des grands Jeux internationaux, de participation francophone qui ait quelque importance numérique; en athlétisme, elle est de 2.9%; à l'aviron, 2.3%; à la natation, au plongeon et à la nage synchronisée, 4.4%; au patinage artistique, 1.1%; au hockey sur glace, 7.3%. Enfin, au cours des Jeux d'hiver, il n'y a jamais eu, à notre connaissance, de participant francophone dans les spécialités du biathlon et du curling, ni aux spécialités du hockey sur gazon et du judo traditionnellement au programme des Jeux d'été.

Commentaires

Il ne fait pas de doute que le nombre total de participants aux délégations internationales, considérées les unes par rapport aux autres, tend à fluctuer selon l'influence de facteurs qui incluent entre autres l'importance relative des Jeux concernés, l'éloignement du lieu où ils se déroulent, le temps de l'année où ils se tiennent, l'état de développement de l'infrastructure humaine et matérielle relative à la chose sportive et enfin, à la base pour le peuple et ses athlètes, l'état de notoriété et de diffusion

FIGURE 1

PARTICIPATION FRANCOPHONE AUX DELEGATIONS TOTALES CANADIENNES AUX JEUX OLYMPIQUES (ETE ET HIVER)

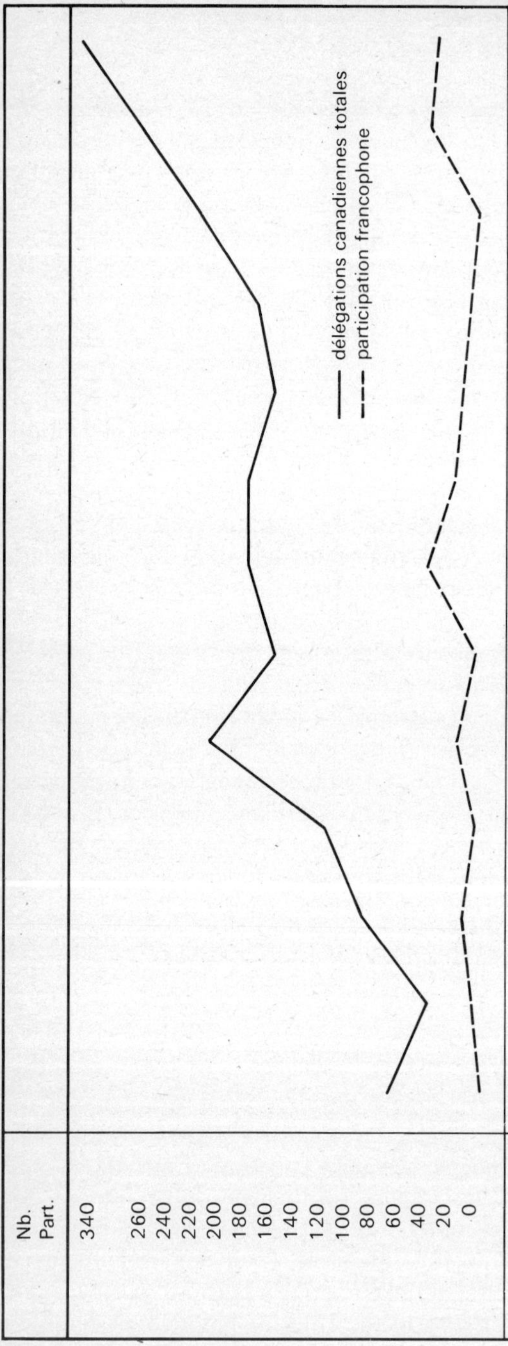

Légende : —— délégations canadiennes totales ; - - - participation francophone

Nb. Part.	1908	1912	1924	1928	1932	1936	1948	1952	1956	1960	1964	1968	1972
Participation totale	70	36	91	116	209	161	182	182	160	172	210	259	329
Participation francophone	1	3	6	4	12	4	27	15	12	11	8	21	19

des disciplines sportives retenues au programme des Jeux en question. L'évolution des indices de participation des Canadiens français aux Jeux internationaux ne semble cependant pas, dans l'ensemble, suivre la somme algébrique des facteurs ci-haut mentionnés. Par exemple, d'un nombre total de représentants déjà peu impressionnant aux Jeux olympiques d'été et d'hiver célébrés en 1948 (27: cf. figure 1) nous avons vu le nombre baisser progressivement à 15 (1952), puis à 12 (1956), puis à 11 (1960) et enfin à 8 en 1964, et la hausse subite de 21 représentants en 1968 ne s'est pas poursuivie, la délégation de 1972 (Munich et Sapporo) ne comptant que 19 francophones, alors que, exception faite du chiffre total des délégations de 1956 (Melbourne et Squaw Valley), le nombre total des représentants canadiens à l'étranger tendait sensiblement à augmenter et que le cadre du programme des Jeux demeurait plutôt stable. Il semble donc qu'en ce qui concerne les Jeux olympiques, l'écart entre le nombre de représentants francophones et les autres ne tende qu'à augmenter avec le temps.

Les fluctuations des courbes aux Jeux du Commonwealth (figure 2) sont fort différentes. Alors qu'elles épousaient un certain parallélisme de 1950 à 1966, elles manifestent depuis des tendances à la fois centrifuges (1970) et centripètes (1974).

FIGURE 2

PARTICIPATION FRANCOPHONE AUX DÉLÉGATIONS TOTALES CANADIENNES AUX JEUX DU COMMONWEALTH

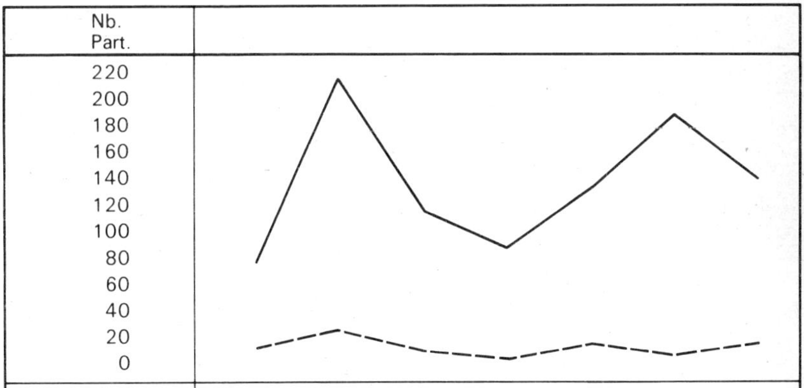

	1950	1954	1958	1962	1966	1970	1974
Participation totale	72	210	111	85	128	187	137
Participation francophone	14	22	13	8	14	8	14

—— délégations canadiennes totales
-- participation francophone

FIGURE 3

PARTICIPATION FRANCOPHONE AUX DELEGATIONS TOTALES CANADIENNES AUX JEUX PAN-AMERICAINS

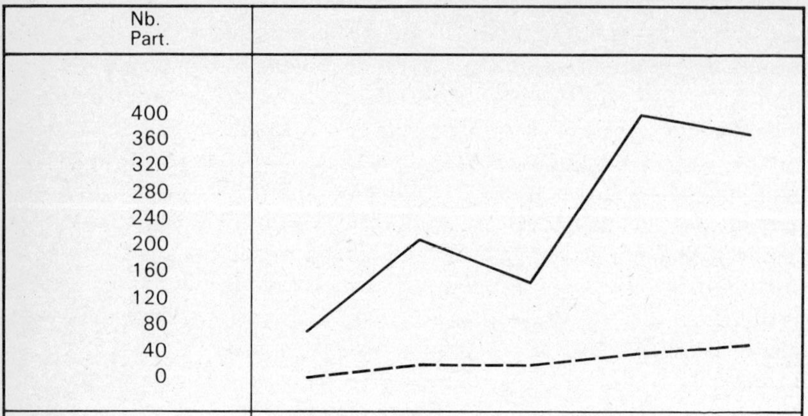

Nb. Part.					
400 360 320 280 240 200 160 120 80 40 0					
	1955	1959	1963	1967	1971
Participation Totale	71	202	153	396	368
Participation Francophone	4	18	18	33	38

——— délégations canadiennes totales
——— participation francophone

Aux Jeux pan-américains (figure 3), on observe une tendance à nouveau différente des autres Jeux. Pendant que les délégations canadiennes fluctuaient considérablement en nombre d'un Jeux à l'autre, le nombre de représentants francophones n'a pas cessé d'augmenter entre 1955 et 1971.

Nous passons ici sous silence le fait qu'il n'y a eu, jusqu'à maintenant, qu'une infime partie de représentants francophones dans les personnages officiels[6] des délégations. Ce fait ne peut à notre avis que refléter, du moins en partie, la place qu'ont occupée dans le passé les Canadiens français dans les affaires des organismes nationaux et provinciaux de régie du sport amateur.

Cet état de choses ne nous semble pas l'effet du hasard mais plutôt la conséquence de la situation particulière dans laquelle évolue la nation canadienne-française d'une part, et d'autre part, la rançon d'un manque d'engagement et d'une absence de planification et d'enthousiasme collectif dans la cause du sport amateur à caractère international.

L'octroi des Jeux olympiques d'été à la ville de Montréal lors de la session d'Amsterdam en 1970 n'apparaît donc pas comme l'aboutissement logique de la croissance et du développement planifié du phénomène sportif chez les Canadiens français, mais plutôt le couronnement des efforts habiles et patients d'un petit groupe d'hommes sous la direction du maire de Montréal.[7] Cette responsabilité nouvelle qui incombe particulièrement aux Montréalais et aux Québécois met en lumière le paradoxe de la faible participation de la majorité francophone au niveau international du sport amateur et le rôle administratif de premier plan qu'ils jouent depuis de début de l'actuelle Olympiade.

Si l'on récapitule l'ensemble de la participation des Canadiens français aux délégations canadiennes des grands Jeux internationaux, on constate que leurs moyennes de participation, depuis 1908, sont toutes bien en deçà de leur représentation démographique dans l'ensemble du Canada: 6.6% aux Jeux olympiques d'été et d'hiver (1908-1972), 9.3% aux Jeux pan-américains (1955-1971) et 10% aux Jeux du Commonwealth (1950-1974). Quant à leurs participations maximales pour ces mêmes périodes, elles révèlent des percées fort timides: 11.8% en 1963 pour les Jeux pan-américains, 14.6% en 1948 pour les Jeux olympiques d'hiver, 14.9% en 1948 pour les Jeux olympiques d'été et 19.4% en 1950 pour les Jeux du Commonwealth.

Conclusion

Depuis le début du siècle, le Québec où vit la très grande majorité des Canadiens français est passé graduellement, comme les autres provinces d'ailleurs, de l'état de société traditionnelle à celui de société industrielle avancée; cependant, les transformations de l'univers des valeurs et de la mentalité du Canadien français ne se sont pas faites au même rythme. Sans trop simplifier la réalité, qu'il nous soit permis de dire avec Guy Rocher (1969b: 11) que les Canadiens français sont entrés dans l'âge industriel avec "un esprit, des attitudes, des catégories mentales qui appartiennent encore à l'état traditionnel pré-industriel." Chez les Canadiens français dont la mentalité traditionnelle a longtemps reposé sur une idéologie agriculturaliste et une vision du monde essentiellement religieuse et vénératrice du passé, les notions d'éducation, de compétence, de travail, de pouvoir et de finalité humaine et sociale n'ont connu qu'une lente maturation jusqu'à ce que les secousses d'après-guerre viennent consacrer un nouvel élan où sont mis en question les projets de valeurs humaines, depuis leurs fondements jusqu'aux options politiques où elles débouchent maintenant. Il n'est donc pas étonnant que dans le passé, l'activité sportive comme moyen de formation, la compétition et l'excellence sportive prises comme moyen de relations interpersonnelles et de réalisation personnelle, n'aient pas occupé une place importante dans l'univers de valeurs des Canadiens français. Sous cet aspect, et à la dérobée de la plupart des Canadiens français, il s'était opéré un divorce entre la mentalité de ces derniers, celle des Canadiens anglophones et celle des jeunes de nombreuses autres nations du monde occidental.

Dans un document antérieur (Boileau et al.: 1972), nous avions noté qu'à l'époque où les Jeux olympiques renaissent et orientent les peuples vers la promotion du sport amateur, il y a chez la nation canadienne-française une forte imperméabilité aux idéologies et aux valeurs que ces dernières véhiculent. On craint à la fois la déculturation et la néocultura-tion. On se méfie de tout ce qui est étranger à sa culture traditionnelle et aux valeurs qu'elle privilégie. Selon Hagen (1962), une telle manière de penser, de sentir et d'agir découle, chez les peuples minoritaires, d'événements clefs qui, dans le temps et l'espace, ont orienté et façonné le développement et le comportement de leur collectivité. Parmi ces événements, le plus marquant nous apparaît être la succession du régime anglais au régime français et l'influence marquante du régime américain avec tout ce que ces événements comportent de tendances et d'influences colonisatrices et néo-colonisatrices. Ces dernières signifient pour Rocher (1969a: 478-483): (a) L'exploitation économique étrangère, (b) la dépendance politique, (c) les barrières raciales et sociales, (d) l'atomisa-tion sociale, (e) l'établissement d'un système de justification et (f) les attitudes correspondantes. L'ensemble de ces facteurs produisant "une société économiquement peu avancée, dont le développement écono-mique, politique, culturel et social est soumis à l'ensemble des rapports de dépendance dans lesquels elle se trouve obligatoirement engagée, avec une ou plusieurs sociétés économiquement plus avancées." Hagen (Harvey, 1971: 121) nous fournit une partie de l'explication de l'appari-tion de ce comportement chez les peuples "traumatisés" lorsqu'il affirme que "les réactions de défense d'un groupe colonisé amènent celui-ci à nier le système de valeur du conquérant d'abord ... ainsi que le système auquel il identifie l'autre." Il poursuit en ces termes:

> Tout groupe qui est soumis au traumatisme d'une colonisation ou d'une con-quête réagit spontanément contre le conquérant ou le colonisateur pour sauver sa propre identité vis-à-vis de l'autre ... Cette réaction de défense prend la forme (a) d'une négation (rejet) du système de valeur de l'autre et (b) d'une retraite sur soi; à ce moment le conquis ou le colonisé tend à surévaluer ce qui le distingue de l'autre et s'enferme dans une vision autoritaire du monde ... ce qui constitue un système de protection.

Au moment où les Jeux olympiques modernes apparaissent (1896), les intérêts premiers de la collectivité canadienne-française sont concentrés autour de quelques aspects particuliers (la foi, la langue, la famille) de leur survivance et de leur devenir collectif. Le fait de s'adonner à la pratique des sports de façon systématique et soutenue représente alors un investissement irrationnel, compte tenu des défis à relever sur les plans social, politique, économique et culturel; d'autant plus que l'on sait le statut privilégié dont bénéficie le sport chez "l'autre".

De telles conditions associées à la présence longtemps restreinte de classes sociales moyennes chez les Canadiens français justifient en partie la venue tardive des programmes d'éducation physique et de sport scolaire chez eux, la carence des installations servant à ces fins, l'ignorance ou l'indifférence collective générale devant les exigences du sport amateur et de ses relations avec l'éducation et la vie du peuple. Ces lacunes rendent encore plus méritoires les succès de ceux qui, par les efforts les plus grands et dans des conditions de milieu très peu favorables, ont su se hisser et souvent se maintenir au rang des athlètes internationaux dans leur spécialité. Le fait que le plus fort degré de participation des Canadiens français aux délégations internationales se découvre dans les spécialités sportives individuelles et bien particulières de l'haltérophilie, de la gymnastique et du cyclisme, ne nous apparaît pas étranger à l'ensemble du contexte evolutif et de réalisation bien particulier que nous avons tenté de décrire.

Et demain . . .

La faiblesse continue de l'indice de participation des Canadiens français aux Jeux internationaux de la dernière décade, bien que témoignant des efforts collectifs des années qui les ont précédés, ne peuvent malheureusement pas refléter les indices d'une mutation profonde qui s'est faite depuis 1960 chez les Canadiens français relativement à la chose sportive (Pinard, 1975: 301-316).

En l'espace de quelques années seulement et pour ainsi dire d'un seul bond, les Canadiens français se sont lancés sur la route de la poursuite de l'excellence dans les spécialités à caractère amateur traditionnel et international.

Le travail de pionnier des professeurs d'éducation physique aux différents paliers de l'enseignement, la montée et l'expansion du sport scolaire et universitaire, la multiplication des compétitions locales, régionales et provinciales, ont rapidement accentué l'enthousiasme collectif et ont donné des objectifs nouveaux et précis à l'effort des sportifs canadiens-français et de leurs entraîneurs. Avec fermeté, on s'est attaqué à la fois à la préparation à la haute performance et à la relève pour demain. Témoins et agents de cette mutation, les Canadiens français se sont donnés à la fois des objectifs de rattrapage, de développement et d'excellence. Le présent marque déjà un changement du meilleur augure. Les efforts patients et obscurs de tous ceux qui dans la première partie des années 60 ont fourni la preuve non équivoque de leur engagement total à l'égard de la cause du sport amateur—présence, participation, animation—se voient maintenant encouragés et soutenus par de nouveaux organismes. Qu'il nous suffise de citer la cristallisation tardive et subite mais non moins importante de corps intéressés et impliqués dans la chose sportive:

—à la suite de la création du Ministère de l'Éducation (1964), celle d'une division de l'éducation physique au même ministère (1965);

—l'action gouvernementale par le truchement de son organisme présentement identifié comme un Haut-Commissariat à la jeunesse, aux loisirs et aux sports (1968);

—la venue de la Fédération d'éducation physique du Québec, regroupant en une association professionnelle les professeurs d'éducation physique de la province (1965), et transformée (1972) en l'Association des professionnels de l'activité physique du Québec (APAPQ);

—sur le plan scolaire, la création des associations sportives intercollégiales des régions de Montréal (ASIRM: 1967) et de l'est du Québec (ASIEQ: 1968), celle de la Fédération du sport scolaire du Québec (1968), et enfin celle de l'Association sportive universitaire du Québec (ASUQ: 1971);

—sur le plan civil, la structuration en un temps incroyablement court de la Confédération des sports du Québec (CSQ: 1968) regroupant la majorité des fédérations sportives provinciales avec tout ce que cela implique de ramifications en associations sportives régionales ainsi que son équivalent dans le monde du loisir, la Conférence des organismes régionaux de loisir du Québec (CORLQ: 1969);

—sur le plan du sport amateur d'élite, la participation des athlètes canadiens-français comme groupe, aux Jeux d'été et d'hiver canadiens depuis 1967, à laquelle s'ajoute le véritable grand banc d'essai des Jeux d'été et d'hiver du Québec depuis 1971; l'attribution, depuis 1973, de crédits spéciaux et importants aux athlètes du Québec par "Mission 76" dont l'objectif est précisément de hausser la participation des Québécois à 30% des délégations canadiennes; enfin, l'acceptation récente (1974) du Haut-Commissariat à la jeunesse aux loisirs et aux sports de créer un organisme permanent (Institut national des sports) voué exclusivement au développement du sport amateur d'élite, en remplacement de "Mission 76".

Voilà donc des dispositions et des mesures concrètes susceptibles d'encourager chez les francophones un réveil d'énergie nouvelle et de leur assurer une présence plus dynamique sur la scène du sport amateur canadien. Conséquemment il est réaliste de penser que l'indice de participation des Canadiens français aux délégations internationales ne saurait tarder maintenant à s'infléchir vers le haut.

NOTES

1. De 1760 à 1960, la population du monde s'est multipliée par quatre; la population de souche européenne par cinq ou six; les Canadiens d'origine française par 80 (Le Maclean, Oct. 1973, p. 4).
2. Entrevues avec: Colonel John W. Davies, ex-président de l'A.A.U. of Canada et ex-président de la British Empire and Commonwealth Games Association of Canada; E. Howard Radford, ex-secrétaire de l'Association olympique canadienne; P. Meunier et P. Labelle du Service des relations publiques de l'AOC.
3. Pourcentages de francophones dans la population du pays aux recensements officiels décennaux: 1901, 30.8%; 1911, 28.7%; 1921, 28.1%; 1931, 35.1%; 1941, 31.9%; 1951, 32.2%; 1961, 30.4%; 1971, 26.9%. Population totale du pays au recensement de 1971: 21 568 311; canadiens d'expression française, 5 793 650.
4. Province de Québec (1971): population totale de 6 027 764 dont 80.7% de Canadiens français, 13.0% d'anglophones et 6.2% des autres ethnies.
5. Nous ne considérons pas comme ayant quelque signification la moyenne brute de 40% du Dog Derby, cette spécialité n'ayant paru qu'une seule fois au programme des Jeux d'hiver, soit en 1932.
6. Nous entendons par personnages officiels les responsables et le personnel administratif des délégations. Les entraîneurs et les soigneurs ont été comptés au nombre des participants.
7. A plusieurs reprises, la ville de Montréal a posé sa candidature pour l'organisation des Jeux olympiques: 1929 et 1939 pour les Jeux d'hiver et 1966 et 1970 pour les Jeux d'été, les deux dernières tentatives étant sous l'administration Drapeau (COJO: 1973).

JEUX OLYMPIQUES

Report of the First Canadian Olympic Athletic Team
1908.   London, Eng., July 13th to July 25th.
Canada at the Olympic Games
1912   The Vth Olympiad: Stockholm, Sweden, June 29th to July 22nd.
Canada at the Olympic Games
1924   The VIIIth Olympiad: Paris France, May 3rd to July 27th. The 1st Winter Olympic Games: Chamonix France, January 25th to February 4th. Official report of the Canadian Olympic Association—1920 to 1924.
Canada at the Olympic Games
1928   The IXth Olympiad: Amsterdam, Holland, July 28th to August 12th. The 2nd Winter Olympic Games: St-Moritz, Switzerland, February 11th to February 19th. Official report of the Canadian Olympic Association—1924 to 1928.
Canada at the Olympic Games
1932   The Xth Olympiad: Los Angeles, U.S.A., July 30th to August 7th. The 3rd Winter Olympic Games: Lake Placid, U.S.A., February 4th to February 15th. Official Report of the Canadian Olympic Association—1928 to 1932.
Canada at the Olympic Games
1936   The XIth Olympiad: Berlin, Germany, August 1st to August 16th. The 4th Winter Olympic Games, Garmisch-Partenkirchen, February 6th to February 16th. Official report of the Canadian Olympic Association—1932 to 1936.
Canada at the Olympic Games
1948   The XIVth Olympiad: London, Eng. July 31st to August 14th. The Vth Winter Olympic Games: St-Moritz, Switzerland, January 30th to February 8th. Official report of the Canadian Olympic Association—1938 to 1948.

Canada at the Olympic Games
1952   The XVth Olympiad: Helsinki, Finland, July 19th to August 3rd. The VIth Winter
         Olympic Games: Oslo, Norway, February 15th to February 25th. Official report of
         the Canadian Olympic Association—1948 to 1952.

Canada at the Olympic Games
1956   The XVIth Olympiad: Melbourne, Australia, November 22nd to December 8th.
         The VIIth Winter Olympic Games: Cortina d'Ampezzo, Italy, January 26th to Feb-
         ruary 5th. Official report of the Canadian Olympic Association—1952 to 1956.

Canada at the Olympic Games
1960   The XVIIth Olympiad: Rome, Italy, August 25th to September 11th. The VIIIth
         Winter Olympic Games: Squaw Valley, U.S.A. February 11th to February 22nd.
         Official report of the Canadian Olympic Association—1957 to 1960.

Canada at the Olympic Games
1964   The XVIIIth Olympiad: Tokyo, Japan, October 10th to October 24th. The IXth
         Winter Olympic Games: Innsbruck, Austria, January 29th to February 9th. Official
         report of the Canadian Olympic Association—1961 to 1964.

Canada at the Olympic Games
1968   The XIXth Olympiad: Mexico City, October 12th to October 27th. The Xth Win-
         ter Olympic Games: Grenoble, France, February 6th to February 18th. Official
         report of the Canadian Olympic Association—1965 to 1968.

Canada at the Olympic Games
1972   The XXth Olympiad: Munich, Germany, August 26th to September 10th. The XIth
         Winter Olympic Games: Sapporo, Japan.

JEUX DU COMMONWEALTH

Canada at the British Empire Games
1950   Auckland, New Zealand, February 4th to February 11th. Official report of the
         British Empire Games Association of Canada—1938-1950.

Canada at the Vth British Empire and Commonwealth Games
1954   Vancouver, British Columbia, July 30th to August 7th. Official report of the British
         Empire and Commonwealth Games Association of Canada—1950-1954.

Canada at the VIth British Empire and Commonwealth Games
1958   Cardiff, Glamorgan, Wales, July 18th to July 26th. Official report of the British
         Empire and Commonwealth Games Association of Canada—1954-1958.

Canada at the VIIth British Empire and Commonwealth Games
1962   Perth, Western Australia, November 22nd to December 1st. Official report of the
         British Empire and Commonwealth Games Association of Canada—1958-1962.

Canada at the VIIIth British Empire and Commonwealth Games
1966   Kingston, Jamaica, August 4th to August 13th. Official report of the British Empire
         and Commonwealth Games Association of Canada—1962-1966.

Canada at the IXth British Commonwealth Games
1970   Edinburgh, Scotland, July 16th to July 25th. Official report of the British Empir
         and Commonwealth Games Association of Canada—1966-1970.

Canada at the Xth British Commonwealth Games
1974   Christchurch, New Zealand, January 24th to February 2nd. Official report of th
         British Commonwealth Games Association of Canada—1970-1974.

JEUX PAN-AMERICAINS

Official Report of Canada's Participation in the 2nd Pan-American Games
1955   Mexico City, Mexico.

Official Report of Canada's Participation in the 3rd Pan-American Games
1959   Chicago, USA, August 27th to September 7th.

Official Report of Canada's Participation in the 4th Pan-American Games
1963   São Paolo, Brazil, April 20th to May 5th.

Official Report of Canada's Participation in the 5th Pan-American Games
1967   Winnipeg, Canada, July 23rd to August 6th.

Canada: VI Juegos Panamericanos
1971   Cali, Colombie, 30 juillet au 13 août.

OUVRAGES CITÉS

Boileau, R., Larouche, R., Landry, F.
1972   "Les Canadiens français et les Grands Jeux internationaux: Analyse conjecturelle".
         Congrés international des sciences en sport, Munich, août.

Charbonneau, H.
1973   *La Population du Québec: Etudes rétrospectives.* Trois-Rivières. Les éditions Boréal
         Express.

Comité d'organisation des Jeux olympiques de Montréal,
1973   "Apothéose d'une longue tradition". *Rendez-vous 76 Montréal* 1:5, (août).

De Coubertin, P. F.
1890   *Universités transatlantiques.* Paris: Hachette.

Hagen, E. E.
1962   *On the Theory of Social Change.* Homewood: Dorsey Press.

Harvey, P.
1971   "Pourquoi le Québec et les Canadiens français occupent-ils une place inférieure sur
         le plan économique?" *Le Retard du Québec et l'Infériorité économique des Cana-
         diens français.* R. Durocher et P.A. Linteau (éditeurs). Trois-Rivières: Les éditions
         Boréal Express.

Landry, F., Turgeon, C., St-Denis, C.
1966   "Les Canadiens français et les Grands Jeux internationaux." *Mouvement* 1 (mars).

Marple, D. P.
1975   "Analyse de la discrimination que subissent les Canadiens francais au hockey pro-
         fessionnel". *Mouvement.* 10: 7-13, (mars).

McPherson, B. D.
1973   "Minority Group Involvement in Sport: The Black Athlete". In J. D. Wilmore (ed.),
         Exercise and Sport Science Review. New York: Academic Press.

Pinard, G.
1975   "Le sport s'organise". *Une certaine révolution tranquille* La Presse (ed.), Montréal:
         Editions La Presse.

Rocher, G.
1969a   *Sociologie générale.* Tome III (Le changement social), Montréal: Éditions Hurtu-
         bise, HMH Ltée.

Rocher, G.
1969b   "La crise des valeurs au Quebec." *Le nouveau défi des valeurs.* Collection Con-
         stantes, Volume 20, Montréal.

Roy, Gilles.
1974   "The Relationship between Centrality and Mobility: The Case of the National
         Hockey League".M.Sc. thesis, Faculty of Human Kinetics and Leisure Studies,
         University of Waterloo, Waterloo.

Smith, G. et Grindsdaff, C. F.
1970   "Race and Sport in Canada". Congrès annuel de l'Association canadienne des
         sciences du sport, Québec, octobre.

SPORT AND PHYSICAL ACTIVITY IN THE LIVES OF CANADIAN WOMEN

M. Ann Hall

Girls and women have traditionally engaged in athletic activities to a more limited extent than boys and men. This has been so both in terms of their rate of participation and in terms of the number of sports in which they take part. We believe this should no longer be accepted as a matter of course.

Report of the Royal Commission on the Status of Women in Canada (1970)

Introduction

In dealing with sport within the context of social differentiation Gruneau (1975:21) points out that "like all areas of social life, sport has been greatly influenced by the institutionalized divisions and inequalities that serve to differentiate society." To understand the nature of sport one must come to grips with the various social distinctions that exist primarily between social classes, between ethnic and racial groups, and more important to the discussion in this paper, *between the sexes*.

Sexual differentiation manifests itself in many ways but it is most conspicuous in the gender roles and status alternatives which are available to men and women.[1] As one author succinctly put it: "both men and women are in boxes, [but] the men's box is more attractive, more desirable, more variable vocationally, and economically richer than the women's box" (Gerber, 1973). Generally when we speak of gender roles, we mean the rules that must be followed in order to fulfill the social prescriptions of one's sex, in other words, the ideal expectations of proper behaviour attributed to one sex or the other. As far as status is concerned, there is little doubt that women possess a lower social standing than men in general and that their roles in society are less highly valued (Henshel, 1973). There are fewer status alternatives available to women, hence far fewer rewards and considerably less access to prestige and power.[2]

Sport as a societal microcosm cannot help but reflect the sex structure inherent in society itself. Granted the "second sex status" accorded to women's sport, to use Page's (1973) phrase, is slowly disappearing, but more often than not the imputation of female inferiority pervades the sporting world. It stems mostly from the invidious comparison of men's and women's sport which often seeks to belittle and denigrate female performances rather than considering them *sui generis*. In part this explains the wide and probably unclosable gap between the sexes in the psychological and material rewards obtainable through sport (Page, 1973).

Sociological Analyses of the Female in Sport

Even though the volume of sociological literature both on sport and on sex roles is increasing rapidly, the social significance of women's participation in sport has remained a much neglected area of research and scholarly discussion. That women have been studied at all seems more a commentary on the anomalous nature of women's sport, than a recognition that sportswomen and their sport constitute a worthy and fruitful area of scholarly investigation.[3]

One would expect, however, that the ever increasing volume of literature and studies subsumed under the rubric of the sociology of sex roles or the sociology of women must inevitably examine the subject if only from the perspective of leisure. Strangely enough, women's leisure, and more specifically sport, has been virtually ignored by the editors of anthologies on women, although less so by the authors of books about gender roles. Either the authors and editors of these volumes feel unqualified to write about sport and leisure, or they dismiss it as irrelevant and unimportant to the real issues underlying gender-based social differentiation and inequality. For instance, Janeway (1971:265) suggests that just as women's skills, once necessary for feeding and clothing mankind, have *deteriorated* into hobbies, crafts and the like, so too have men's skills and prowess, such as hunting, *degenerated* into sport. For Janeway, sports are adult play, leisure-time activities which imitate the realities of work and as such are a substitute for living.[4]

By far the most scholarly and perhaps the only theoretical analyses of women in sport from a sociological perspective are Felshin (1974) and Willis (1973). Both these discussions are very important contributions to the sociological literature on female sport involvement because they are theoretical analyses concerned with meaning, values, and social explanation. Both Felshin and Willis attempt to merge a theoretical explanation of the cultural meaning of sport with a broader understanding of the dynamics of gender-based differences in participation. As Willis explains:

> The approach accepts the obvious differences in sports performance between men and women, accepts that cultural factors may well enlarge this gap, but is

most interested in the manner in which this gap is understood and taken up into the popular consciousness of our society. In this perspective the fact of the gap is incontrovertible, but it is an *'inert fact'*, socially speaking, until we have explained the colossal *social* interest in it.

The articles by Felshin and Willis are also important because they are written from two quite different perspectives and yet in many ways support similar conclusions. Felshin writes from the feminist position suggesting that the participation by women in sport is viewed as either "rational and desirable or as a fairly ubiquitous social problem" thus creating an interactive dimension between women on the one hand and sport on the other, more concisely called a dialectic. Felshin argues that in reality the woman in sport is a social anomaly both because her behaviour runs counter to the acceptable norms of feminine demeanour, and because, according to men, her very participation tends to downgrade and denigrate the sport itself. The feminist position wishes to change all this arguing that the woman in sport does not need to apologize for her participation because, as Felshin puts it, "the normative stereotypes are oppressive and antithetical to the development of human actualization."

Willis' thesis, written from an essentially Marxist viewpoint, is that "sport reflects a crucial, central feature of our culture; anxiety about sex roles." Accordingly, this sex role anxiety manifests itself in social differentiation between the sexes with male domination the most prevalent, a belief that is vital to the functioning of the capitalist economy. One ideology which pervades the capitalist system is that women are different and inferior; therefore, women in sport, because they cannot participate equally with men, merely reinforce the existing ideologies.

Given that the articles by Felshin (1974) and Willis (1973) stand as exceptions to the virtual absence of sociological analyses of women in sport, there still remains an ever-increasing number of journalistic social commentaries on the subject. Yet, much of this literature is strictly reportorial, being concerned more with facts and examples illustrating discrimination and sexism, than with an objective analysis of the conditions which underlie them.[5] Moreover the journalistic literature is overwhelmingly slanted toward discussion of the female in competitive sport, with little commentary reserved for women's recreational participation. Even the few sociological accounts that address the issue of women's participation in sporting activities generally, underplay the significance of the physical activities of ordinary women. In other words, the role that sport and physical activity play in the average women's life, particularly with attention to the institutions of marriage and the family, the assumptions on which they are based, and the restricting roles that women play within them, has rarely been discussed from either a journalistic or a sociological perspective. The discussion in this paper is an attempt to redress the balance by examining the question of why some women, particularly in the Canadian context, make sport and physical activity a significant aspect of their lifestyle while others do not. The discussion will also focus on male-female differences in sport participation in an effort to comprehend more fully the reasons for the obvious and marked social differentiation by gender in "mass" sport.[6]

Overview

The remainder of the paper is divided into three major sections. The first examines sport and physical activity patterns among Canadian women on the basis of information obtained from a national survey of leisure time activities. The second attempts to explain sport involvement, or rather the lack of it, among Canadian women using as a basis the information obtained through an extensive survey conducted by the author. Since the major purpose of the study was to test the efficacy of a theoretical model, the evaluation required the use of multivariate analysis. Although I have attempted to explain the procedures in non-mathematical terms, the techniques employed do require a general understanding of basic statistics. Following from the findings of the Canadian survey, and that of similar studies on the correlates of female sport involvement in Britain and the U.S.A., the third section examines the constraints which marriage and family impose upon a woman in relation to her leisure time.

Sport and Physical Activity Patterns Among Canadian Women[7]

Inherent in the majority of promotional campaigns, government recreation programs and literature on the subject is the assumption that sport or physical activity is an unimportant element in the lifestyle of Canadians since their pattern of living is dominated essentially by sedentary activities. In the spring of 1972 a national Canadian survey of leisure time activities was conducted by the Secretary of State in cooperation with Statistics Canada (Kirsh, *et al.*, 1973). Among the types of leisure time activities investigated were *sports*, such as bowling, curling, hockey, badminton, and the like as opposed to *physical activities* which included, for example, jogging, cycling, and exercise programs. The findings were specific and detailed, but in general the evidence was that during a three month winter period, 33 percent of the Canadian population took part in either sport or physical activities or both for at least one to three hours per week. However, since two-thirds of the sports and physical activities participants were under 35 years of age (almost half of these being between 14 and 19), this means that *approximately 22 percent of the adult population engaged in some form of sport or physical activity at least once a week* during the three month period under investigation. It should also be noted that the percentage of adults who devoted more than seven hours per week to sport or physical activity was very small indeed (approximately 5 to 6 percent).

The quality of lifestyle among Canadians comes more clearly into focus when you consider that of the same people surveyed regarding their active leisure pursuits, 40 percent indicated that they spend more than fifteen hours per week watching television. Viewed from this perspective, for every hour spent in sport or physical activity, the average Canadian who participates probably spends anywhere from five to eight hours watching television.

Unfortunately, the 1972 Canadian leisure survey did not provide a breakdown by sex (see however, the analysis by Curtis and Milton in Part 5 of this volume), except to point out that housewives were the most under-represented group on the basis of their participation in sports activities (although frequent participants in "physical activities" included a considerably larger proportion of housewives than did the sports participants). Further information provided by Statistics Canada showed, however, that although sex differences in sports participants do exist, they are not marked. For instance, 17.7 percent of the male population between 20 and 44 years engage in sport activities at least one to three hours per week in contrast to 13.9 percent of the female population in the same age category. The differences become more marked as the number of hours per week involvement increases, since in the same age category, 4.1 percent of the males participated in sport from eight to fourteen hours per week as compared to 1.6 percent of the females. Finally, the differences between sexes are minimal as age increases. In the 45 to 54 age group, 88.4 percent of the females reported that they engaged in no sport activity as opposed to 82.4 percent of the males. There were virtually no sex differences in physical activity participation.[8]

For any woman, it is possible to define her situation in terms of the combination or constellation of roles she plays at any particular point in time, and hence to examine the relationship between her role constellation and her leisure patterns. A woman's life-cycle stage with its related constellation of roles is both a facilitator and deterrent to the amount and type of sport or physical activity in which she can become involved. Indeed it may well be much more of an inhibiting factor for women than for men. Sillitoe's (1969) massive survey of British recreation patterns showed very clearly that marriage for many women represents an almost immediate cessation of active involvement in sport, whereas the decline is much more gradual for men although marriage does have an influence.[9] With the coming of children, the mother withdraws from this type of activity to an even greater extent with sometimes very little chance of ever coming back to it. There would appear to be no reason why the same would not be true for Canadian women, and in fact, there is some evidence which supports this pattern (cf. Murphy, 1969; and Hall, 1974).

As the 1972 Canadian leisure study pointed out, women, and in particular housewives, are somewhat over-represented in physical activities and under-represented in sports activities. By far the most popular activities among Canadian women are walking, swimming, skating, bicycling and bowling since at least 10 percent of the female sample participated in each with almost 50 percent stating that walking was their favorite physical activity.[10] In general, women in contrast to men participate less frequently and in fewer numbers in a smaller number of sport and physical activities.

Explaining Sport Involvement Among Canadian Women

CORRELATES OF INVOLVEMENT

The material presented in this section stems from one study alone, that of Hall (1974), and is part of a larger social survey involving over 1200 British and Canadian women from all walks of life. The purpose of the study was twofold: first, to specify the optimal environmental conditions in which individual characteristics predictive of athletic potential are most likely to be nurtured, and second, to identify the environmental and cultural conditions which must remain present in order that sport or physical activity continue to be a significant aspect of a woman's life style. Its scope was all women, not just those already committed to sport, but more importantly those women who for one reason or another are neither interested nor probably even suited to the consuming demands of high level sport involvement. It focussed in part on the many women who experience the sheer joy of movement in some form or other; for the purposes of the study, it was inconsequential whether this movement took the form of sport.

The Governing Conceptual Scheme: In their classic work on the American occupational structure, Blau and Duncan (1967) refer to their analysis framework as a 'governing conceptual scheme' stating that it is quite a commonplace one. Much the same could be said about the conceptual

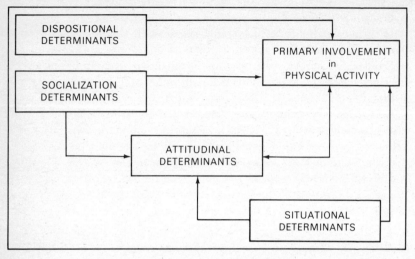

framework (see Figure 1) used in the Hall (1974) study since it posited four major determinants of primary involvement in sport and physical activity among females: (1) socialization determinants, (2) dispositional determinants, (3) attitudinal determinants, and (4) situational determinants. The relationship among the factors is such that primary involvement is thought to be determined directly by all four determinant categories as well as indirectly by socialization factors mediated by attitudes. Moreover, attitudes themselves will be directly influenced by socialization and situational determinants as well as primary involvement.

The inclusion of variables within each of the determinant categories was based largely on the intuition of the researcher since at that time no empirical studies designed specifically to investigate a range of possible correlates of female sport involvement had been completed. Furthermore, in view of the nature of the study as a tentative step in the development of sport involvement theory, it was deemed essential to include as many factors as could justifiably be related to the complex phenomenon under investigation.[11] This does not mean that there are not many as yet unidentified variables which may well have greater significance in accounting for differences in the extent of female participation in sport.

The unique variables and variable combinations within the four determinant categories were as follows:

Situational Determinants
1) Age
2) Educational background
3) Marital status°
4) Ages of children°
5) Employment status°
6) Socio-economic status
7) Religious preference
8) Recreation related situational variables
   a) General leisure index
   b) Activity level of husband
   c) Present family involvement
   d) Secondary involvement
° Combined to form one variable (Role Constellation)

Socialization Determinants
1) Activity involvement of previous significant others
2) Respondent's activity level when younger
3) Enjoyment of school physical education
4) Sibling status
5) Past family economic status

Attitudinal Determinants
1) Attitudes towards women's participation in physical activity
   a) as a social experience
   b) for health and fitness
   c) as the pursuit of vertigo
   d) as an aesthetic experience
   e) as a cathartic experience
   f) as an ascetic experience
2) Attitude towards the traditional role of women in society
3) Attitude towards the concept 'Feminine Woman'
4) Attitude towards the concept 'Athletic Woman'
5) Congruency between a feminine and athletic woman
6) Professional orientation of attitudes towards play

Dispositional Determinants
1) Body esteem
2) Self esteem
3) Need to achieve success
4) Need to avoid failure

The operationalization of the dependent variable, degree of primary involvement in sport and physical activity, was based on the dimensions of involvement suggested by Loy (1969). By taking into account the breadth and depth of participation it was possible to generate an index of involvement that had sufficient discriminatory power to allow for comparisons among groups classified by position on the involvement continuum.[12]

The Sample: The sample consisted of 552 Canadian women approximately half of whom participated at least regularly if not extensively in sport and physical activity with the remaining half participating marginally or not at all. Primarily they were city dwellers, usually between 18 and 30, better educated than average, and in general had an advantaged socio-economic status. They were evenly split between married and single, about half of them worked full or part-time and those in the labour force were usually single or married but without children.

Data Collection: Data were obtained by means of a mail questionnaire during a three-month winter period in 1973. Although there was some variance among the sixteen groups comprising the sample, the overall percentage of returned and completed questionnaires was 60.2 percent.[13] There was no evidence of response bias between groups thought to be likely sports participants and those for which participation was considered unlikely, but of course this does not preclude the possibility of bias within groups, especially the low participant ones.

The Analysis: Although the analysis in the original study began simply at the level of accepting or rejecting the numerous theoretical propositions which defined the linkages between individual variables, followed by bivariate and multiple regression analysis, we begin the discussion here with the multiple regression analysis.

The first step in the analysis concerns only one block of the governing conceptual scheme (Figure 1), that of the socialization determinants. Since the data are essentially ordinal, Kendall's rank-order correlation coefficients were calculated and later transformed into estimates of the product-moment correlation coefficients.[14] Table I presents the results of a correlational analysis of the socialization variables.

The dependent variable in this case was the respondent's activity level when younger after leaving the school environment; there are four independent variables: activity involvement of previous significant others, enjoyment of school physical education, sibling status, and past family socio-economic status. The results of the step-wise regression whereby variables enter the regression equation one at a time on the basis of their contribution to the unexplained variance are summarized in Table II.

TABLE I

CORRELATION MATRIX OF SOCIALIZATION DETERMINANTS FOR 552 CANADIAN WOMEN

	A	B	C	D	Y
A: Activity involvement of previous significant others	——	.215	.039	.249	.513
B: Enjoyment of school P.E.		——.	.005	.066	.536
C: Sibling status			——.	.003	.072
D: Past family socio-economic status				——	.086
Y: Activity level when younger					——

TABLE II

BETA COEFFICIENTS AND COEFFICIENTS OF DETERMINATION FOR SPECIFIED COMBINATIONS OF VARIABLES
(N = 552 Canadian Women)

Dependent Variable	Beta Coefficients for Independent Variables				Coefficient of Determination (R^2)
	A	B	C	D	
Y	.417	.443	.064	.011	.457
A	——	.249	.040	.249	.066
B	——	——	.065	-.128	.064

Y: Activity level when younger
A: Involvement of previous significant others
B: Enjoyment of school physical education
C: Sibling status
D: Past family socio-economic status

From the relative size of the normalized regression co-efficients or beta co-efficients, it is clear that past family socio-economic status and sibling status add very little to the amount of variance explained in the dependent variable, activity level when younger. In fact both of these variables can be dropped from the equation with only a negligible decrease in the amount of explained variance.[15] It should be recognized however that the effects of socio-economic variables (even inter-generationally) are being largely controlled for by the homogeneity of the sample. Nonetheless, socio-economic distinctions were retained in order to illustrate the usefulness of path analysis as a final step in the analysis of the socialization determinants.

Path analysis involves theoretical assumptions not required by multiple regression, but the statistical basis is essentially the same. The prime theoretical assumption required of path analysis is that there be a causal or temporal ordering of the variables which is external or à priori to the

FIGURE 2: PATH MODEL OF SPORT SOCIALIZATION DETERMINANTS
(N = 552 Canadian Women)

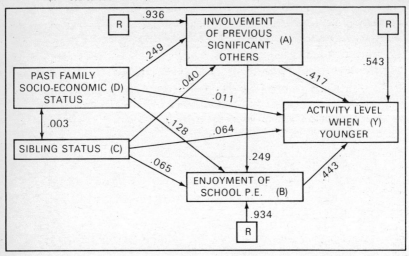

observed correlations between the variables. Moreover, the causal sequencing is assumed to be complete since unknown or unmeasured causes can be represented by a residual factor presumably uncorrelated with the others in the system (Duncan, 1966; Land, 1969).

It is assumed that two variables, past family socio-economic status and sibling status are contemporaneous from the respondent's point of view and that they precede the involvement of previous significant others. This is not to say, however, that delayed effects from past family socio-economic status and sibling status to activity level when younger are not present. Similarly, although the enjoyment of school physical education is probably contemporaneous with the involvement of previous significant others, we assume that significant other involvement will precede it in time. Therefore, not only will the socio-economic status of the respondent's family, as well as her sibling status, directly affect enjoyment of school physical education, the effect will be mediated through the sport involvement of significant others. Finally, each of these variables will directly influence the involvement when younger *after* leaving the school environment, and naturally they will precede it in time. We also assume that an earlier variable (for instance, past family socio-economic status) may affect a later one not only directly but also through an intervening variable (in this case, involvement of previous significant others). A convenient way to represent the system of relationships among the socialization variables is shown in the path model of Figure 2.[16]

Theoretically the path model should reflect the causal ordering of the observed variables and empirically it should account for the observed correlations among the measured variables. For example, let us see if the observed correlation between activity level when younger (Y) and past family socio-economic status (D) is equal to the correlation implicit in the path diagram of Figure 2. We will use the accepted notion for path coefficients, that is P_{YD} where the first subscript is the variable at the head of the path, the effect variable, and the second is the causal variable. According to a fundamental theorem of path analysis (Duncan, 1966), the the following holds true:

$$r_{YD} = P_{YD} + P_{YA} r_{AD} + P_{YB} r_{BD} + P_{YC} r_{CD}$$

Since $r_{AD} = P_{AD} + P_{AC} r_{CD}$

and $r_{BD} = P_{BD} + P_{BC} r_{CD}$

thus $r_{YD} = P_{YD} + P_{YA} P_{AD} + P_{YA} P_{AC} r_{CD} + P_{YB} P_{BD} + P_{YB} P_{BC} r_{CD} + P_{YC} r_{CD}$

$$= (.011) + (.417)(.249) + (.417)(-.040)(.003) + (.443)(-.128) +$$
$$(.443)(.065)(.003) + (.064)(.003)$$
$$= .058$$

Although there is some discrepancy with the observed correlation (.072), the value calculated does compare favourably. Each correlation could be traced back in this way in order to test the validity of the model; suffice it to say that although minor discrepancies were found, the magnitudes were not large enough to invalidate the model.

It is also instructive to examine the magnitudes of the direct and indirect influences on the three *effect* variables in the path diagram (Y, A and B). Another of the fundamental theorems of path analysis states that the sum of all indirect effects is given by the difference between the simple correlation and the path co-efficient connecting the two variables (Land, 1969). For example, since r_{YB} is .536 and p_{YB} is .443, the aggregate of indirect effects is .093. These indirect effects are accounted for by common causes of Y (activity level when younger) and B (enjoyment of school physical education) which in this case only slightly inflate the correlation between them. Similarly, the aggregate of the indirect effects between Y and A (involvement of previous significant others) is .096. Even though the aggregate of the indirect effects relative to the direct is not substantial, these variables do have common antecedent causes and the path model is lacking in the sense that it does not make these causes explicit.[17]

TABLE III
BETA COEFFICIENTS AND COEFFICIENTS OF DETERMINATION FOR SPECIFIED COMBINATIONS OF VARIABLES (N = 552 Canadian Women)

Dependent Variable	1	2	3	4	5	6	7	8	9	10	11	12	13	14	15	Coefficient of Determination (R^2)
1		.390			.111	-.110	.111	-.449	.355		.023	.021	.221	-.066	.023	.660
2			.342					-.237	.393	.365	-.043	.034	.104			.396
3				.378	-.071	-.071	-.045								-.021	.413
4										.433						.187
5		.085						-.180	.016		.144	.202	-.147			.087
6		.199						-.432				.391	.022			.260
7		.114						-.065	.149		-.015	.026	-.144			.077

1: Active participation
2: Activity level when younger
3: Secondary involvement
4: Enjoyment of school physical education
5: WPA (Pursuit of Vertigo) attitude
6: WPA (Ascetic Experience) attitude
7: WPA (Health and Fitness) attitude

8: Age
9: Present family involvement
10: Involvement of previous significant others
11: Role constellation
12: Socioeconomic status
13: General leisure index
14: Self-esteem
15: Need to avoid failure

Thus far, our analysis has shown that two major determinants of activity level when younger are enjoyment of school physical education experiences and involvement of previous significant others. Furthermore, for the population under study, the analysis rather obviously provides little justification for considering past family socio-economic status and sibling status as determinants. Inclusion of a comparable number of women from lower socio-economic levels may conceivably have altered the pattern of determinants but this remains a question for further research. In any case, our main interest lies not in the level of participation when younger but in the present degree of active involvement in sport and physical activity.

Table III shows the beta coefficients and coefficients of determination for specified combinations of variables which were chosen on the basis of an initial factor analysis and regression analysis of the total correlation matrix.[18] Two variables, activity level of the husband and respondent's educational level, were eliminated from the start since they correlated highly with two others (present family involvement and socio-economic status respectively). A path model is not presented because it is impossible to sequence logically a series of contemporaneous variables such as those which represent situational factors; moreover, there is no justification for assuming that behavioural dispositions, such as the need to achieve success and one's self-esteem, precede the attitude formation process and vice versa. In addition, postulated in the governing conceptual scheme (Figure 1) was a reciprocal influence path from involvement back to attitude. Since measures of both variables were taken at the same point in time, it is illogical to use one variable as an explanation of the other without reckoning with the reciprocal influence of one upon the other. Therefore the two dependent variables are simultaneously determined and the methodology required to estimate the parameters of a simultaneous equation model is beyond the scope of this study.[19]

From the beta coefficients in Table III, we see that along with age, an extremely important determinant of active participation is the present involvement of one's current family. For married women without children, there is a need for a highly supportive husband who himself is an active sports participant and who encourages his wife in this form of recreation. If the woman has a family, then it seems likely that her children are both a reason and a stimulus for greater involvement in physical recreation.

The results also point out the importance of active involvement when younger. In fact, in a further regression, present family involvement, an observed measure on married women only, was removed from the analysis; consequently, activity level when younger became the most important determinant of present involvement. This is not to suggest that for single women the level of involvement when younger is more important than the influence of present significant others, especially those who are supportive toward physical recreational pursuits. Unfortunately, no attempt was made to measure the influence of these significant others in the present study.

All but seven percent of the active participation coefficient of determination (.660) in the regression analysis was accounted for by only three independent variables: present family involvement, activity level when younger, and age. This means that the high degree of association between, for instance, present involvement and past involvement is misleading simply because both variables have common causes which the causal scheme has failed to make explicit. These unknown and unmeasured causes could be any number of things, such as the extent and quality of school physical education experiences, the influence and sports participation of one's childhood and adolescent peer group, or the general availability of sporting opportunities in one's past, and perhaps the most important of all, one's physical and psychological predisposition for athletic activity, some of which is most certainly biological in origin.

Among the remaining variables in the regression analysis, it is clear that they are relatively unimportant in accounting for much variation in any of the dependent variables. In this respect, it would seem reasonable to assert that attitudes believed relevant to female athleticism are unimportant determinants of female sport involvement when placed in a system which also considers socialization and present situational factors since the latter are by far the best predictors. Furthermore, the low coefficients of determination associated with each of the attitudinal variables gives little credence to the assumption implicit in the governing scheme that situational factors directly influence attitudes.

Summary: The findings of this study do not provide a great deal of support for an overall acceptance of the hypothesized causal scheme, Attitudes and behavioural dispositions at least so far as they were defined and operationalized, are unimportant determinants of sport involvement among Canadian women. Certainly, past experiences and to a greater extent present situational factors account for virtually all the explained variance in present sport involvement. Moreover, this explained variance among individuals is due to the explanatory power of a very small number of variables, primarily the activity level when younger, the complexity of a woman's life-cycle stage, and if she is married, the interest and participation of her family. The fact that involvement when younger accounts for much of the variance in present participation is not only misleading but also disturbing, since both the dependent and independent variable have common causes which are not made explicit by the causal scheme. Nonetheless, it seems certain that these unknown and unmeasured causes have their roots in vastly disparate sport socialization experiences among individuals, and until a good deal more is known and understood about this process of socialization into sport roles, it is pointless to continue seeking the explanation for differential participation among females in attitudinal and dispositional factors.

THE CROSS-CULTURAL EVIDENCE

Theoretical models are valid only for the population in which they are tested and their generality can only be examined through comparative testing of different populations. Although the data presented in the preceding section concerned Canadian women, the study from which the data were drawn (Hall, 1974) utilized two sample populations, the other being a group of British women. In so far as it was possible, the Canadian and British samples were compatible in all respects.[20]

Generally, and on the basis of this study alone, Canadian women were found to be more active in sport and physical activity than their British counterparts. The difference lies in the use that Canadians are able to make of the out-of-doors, and the fact that there is more opportunity for what could be called casual involvement in activities such as skating, skiing, swimming, boating, hunting, and fishing. These activities are rarely accessible to the average British woman, unless of course she goes on a special holiday.

With respect to the socialization determinants, it was clear that in the Canadian sample less importance was attached to school physical education experiences as a determinant of past involvement whereas the involvement of previous significant others was of slightly greater significance. The reverse was true for the British sample and the degree of importance between the two variables was more marked with enjoyment of school physical education being by far the most important correlate. This would suggest that the school in British society is more of a support system for sports participation among girls than is true in Canada, a finding which makes a good deal of sense in view of the number of single sex schools in England where sports are usually an important aspect of school life. Thus, in Canada, where school sport for girls is not accorded the same prestige as seems to be the case in England, the family then becomes a very necessary support system for athletic involvement. This is not to suggest, however, that the family in British culture does not provide a supportive environment for sports participation which influences later involvement. There was a high degree of inter-correlation in the British sample between present involvement, activity level when younger, and involvement of previous significant others which suggests that women who from an early age make physical recreation an important part of their life style also seek a supportive environment later in order to pursue their interests.

In terms of attitude, there were two interesting cross-national differences. First, the relationship between attitude toward an 'athletic woman' and active participation was much stronger in the British sample than it was in the Canadian. However, despite the stronger relationship, this particular attitude remained an unimportant determinant of involvement given the importance of other factors. Similarly, the Canadians showed a more favourable attitude toward the health and fitness aspect of physical activity, but again the difference was unimportant in view of the larger scheme.

As was true for the Canadian sample, all but a small percentage of the variance in active participation among British women could be explained by the same three variables (present family involvement, activity level when younger, and age) in addition to a fourth, complexity of the role constellation. It should be noted that a woman's age and complexity of her role constellation are closely correlated, especially for married women with children. A woman's role constellation is probably most constraining in the early years of marriage when she may have to contend with small children and possible part-time employment outside the home. Therefore in both cultures there is a need for a highly positive support system, since a women's previous commitment to sport and physical activity is often forgotten given the constraints of marriage and a family.

The need for a positive support system was illustrated clearly in a similar study undertaken by Richardson (1974) among American college graduates. The study involved 386 college educated women residing mostly in a southern United States city, and utilized similar if not identical measuring instruments and analysis techniques to the Hall study. In discussing the result of a step-wise multiple regression, Richardson (1974: 187-7) reported:

From the beta weights it would seem then that age, influence of the mother when younger as a sport participant model, influence of the most frequent sports partner, and activity level of the respondent soon after graduating from college, (in that order) were the major determinants of present primary involvement in physical activity. Apparently, when taken alone, age did not directly affect participation but, in conjunction with other variables, it demonstrated a clear, inverse effect.

... It would appear then, that once the role model has been provided and assuming an opportunity set conducive to continued activity on a voluntary basis after graduation, the continued support of significant others sustains and encourages the degree of involvement in physical activity on the part of these women until the effects of age reduce their participation.

Finally, in a study which utilized the original data of the Richardson study and a portion of the data from the Hall study, Richardson and Hall (1974) were able to test the efficacy of the conceptual model (Figure 1) in explaining variations in degree of primary involvement among English, Canadian, and American women. Although many similarities were present, there were some obvious differences:

> Beyond activity level when younger and present family interest (including the husband's) there are no relatively powerful predictors of participation since none of the remaining variables in each cultural group account for more than 8 percent of the variance with most of them accounting for 1 to 3 percent. However, it is noteworthy that more similarities exist between the British and Canadian women than with the American women. Aside from activity level when younger in the British group and present family involvement in the Canadian sample, three of the best four predictors are essentially the same: attitude towards women's participation as a social experience, older brother in the family and self esteem. This pattern does not occur among the American women where the activity level of the mother and an unfavourable attitude towards women's participation as the pursuit of vertigo are most important predictors (Richardson and Hall, 1974:19).

The cross-cultural studies of female sport and physical activity involvement conducted thus far suggest several conclusions. *First*, women are becoming increasingly less passive in their leisure pursuits although married women in particular tend to select recreational activities in which all members of the family can participate or which do not necessarily require a partner (e.g. walking, swimming, and bicycling). *Second*, there is a high degree of association between present and past involvement which unfortunately can only be due to common causes as yet unknown and unmeasured. *Third*, attitudes and motivational dispositions play a minimal role in determining the degree of primary involvement since situational and socialization determinants are by far the most important. Given the right conditions, socialization and situational factors apparently provide the initial impetus, the continued support, and the present opportunity to be involved to a greater extent than is otherwise possible.[21] *Fourth*, married women often look to their husbands as a source of support, companionship, and instruction in physical activities. If the support and encouragement is absent, or the contingencies of running a household take precedence, married women with families simply do not participate. A fuller discussion concerning the constraints which marriage and the family impose on a woman is presented in the next section.

The Constraints of Marriage and Family

> *I married young and had five children in rather quick succession and that plus working left very little time for anything except sheer survival until the last four or five years. In these last years I have gradually become aware of myself as a person something a little more than "right-hand man" to a family. This kind of experience and up-bringing must be very common to women of my age (40 years) and probably even more pronounced in groups where education and income do not provide any opportunities at all.*
>
> A Canadian mother

The woman who made this statement was explaining why she had not been involved in any form of sport or physical activity since before her marriage. Others have expressed similar sentiments as one woman indicated rather indignantly: "It's nearly impossible to enter into any physical sport when you've worked all day and then cooked supper, done the cleaning and washing, etc." Another lamented: "Only men can pop out for a couple of hours in the evening for a mid-week training session.". The reason, suggested others, why some married women have the time to participate is that they are fortunate enough to afford household help. Therefore the constraints imposed by marriage, the family, and possibly work, are very real to those women who obviously place *their* interests and leisure pursuits far behind, if not to the point of total exclusion, their commitments to the maintenance of a household. For some, it is only a temporary denial and they expect to resume past interests as their children grow older and become less dependent. "I have chosen the wife-mother route," commented one young mother, "and for the very early years of one's family, physical recreation becomes difficult at best . . . ." Unfortunately, very few of these women do pick up where they left off so to speak, since it is only the exceptional woman who will return to an activity of her youth, such as sport, when she sees no evidence of her friends doing the same. Unless she has maintained a pattern of physical activity throughout her nurturing years, rarely will she resume an active interest in sport nor will she seek out new opportunities and skills to pursue this form of leisure.

For men, marriage has substantially less effect on their sport involvement especially in the early years of sharing.[22] Whatever decline in sports participation there is among males in their twenties is probably due more to their entrance into the labour force or their embarkation on a career than to the constraints of a marital relationship, be it official or otherwise.[23]

Jessie Bernard, an American sociologist who has spent a lifetime study-ing family organization, has stated: "There are two marriages ... in every marital union, his and hers. And his ... is better than hers" (Bernard, 1972:15). As Bernard goes on to point out, there is unequivocal evidence that first, marriage is good for men; second, men need marriage more than women do; and third, once men have experienced marriage, they can hardly do without it.[24] On the other hand, marriage for women is often not what it is for men. Numerous research studies show that more married women as compared to married men experience severe psycho-logical problems. When comparing single men and women, the average single woman shows up better on every index—education, occupation, income, and mental health.[25]

There is also substantial evidence to support the contention that wives do more of the adjusting in marriage than do husbands. As Bernard (1972:44) points out: "The husband upon marriage maintains his old life routines, with no thought, or expectation of changing them to suit his wife's wishes." The wife *has* to adjust because she generally has more at stake than the husband; if she doesn't, she may lose everything. Thus it should come as no surprise to find that even among happily married couples, fewer wives than husbands report agreement in such areas as finances, religion, sex, inlaws, friends, and even recreation.[26]

There is another dimension of marriage in which women take on more than their share since in most cases they are entrusted with the child-care and housekeeping. In contrast to work performed outside the home, work done in the home, characterized by Bernard (1974) as *motherwork* and *housework*, although extremely time-and-energy-consuming is also routine, monotonous, and devoid of prestige, giving little status to those who do it (Henshel, 1973). Hannah Gavron, who has written an excellent little book entitled *The Captive Wife: Conflicts of Housebound Mothers*, succinctly describes the dilemma facing mothers when she says: "In fact the advent of children brings with it isolation, confusion, and insecurity."

What I have been discussing here are the often constraining roles which women play within the marriage bond as we know it today. It is important to note that although *both* husbands and wives are constrained within marriage, there is far less release for the wife, especially if she must cope with the added responsibility of being a mother. Others have defined this inequity in much stronger terms. For instance, Edward Ryan, a young Canadian lawyer concerned about the current legal con-cept of marriage, has put forth the thesis that whatever assumptions govern the family and marriage also determine "who has what opportun-ities, what rights and what responsibilities not only in the matrimonial home, but also in that large world that lies beyond it" (Ryan, 1975:2).

Family law, according to Ryan, legalizes the provider-dependent relationship between men and women which by itself means that women are excluded, on the basis of their sex alone, from the meaningful opportunities and status alternatives I spoke about at the beginning of this paper. For Ryan, "marriage is the primary relationship between the sexes, and as such, is the primarly source and primary justification for sexually-based discrimination in society."

Participation in sport and physical activity as a leisure time pursuit is but *one* of the opportunities often denied women, especially those whose responsibilities include motherhood and the maintenance of a household. The fact that women participate in athletic activities on a more limited basis than men is merely symptomatic of a more pervasive injustice in society. Edward Ryan claims that "Canadian society is a caste system based on sex" (Ryan, 1975:1). Perhaps this is too condeming, but until the institution of marriage encompasses a shared-role pattern whereby women achieve some relief from the entire responsibility for childcare and housekeeping, they will continue to be denied the same opportunities as men in all spheres of human existenc .²⁷

At this point, let us return briefly to the concrete evidence about female leisure patterns in an effort to illuminate further the contentions which have been made throughout this section. We know that regardless of sex, participation in sport and physical activity is a function of age, education and socio-economic status (cf., Burton, 1971; Elliot, *et. al.*, 1970; Kenyon, 1966; Kirsh, *et al.*, 1973; Murphy, 1969; Robinson, 1967; Sillitoe, 1969). Although it was underplayed in the data analysis presented, we know from other studies that socio-economic level is probably more of a determining factor for women than it is for men. The recreational activities of working-class women are essentially home-centred (usually watching T.V.); these women are isolated during the day and the exigencies of children and finance often preclude leisure activities outside the home during the evenings (Gavron, 1966; Komarovsky, 1962). Television is the main form of entertainment for working-class families and sometimes a source of discontent between husband and wife in their choice of leisure activity. As one woman in Gavron's (1966:111) study of British working-class mothers complained: "The trouble is when he comes home in the evenings all he wants to do is watch television, he's tired you see. Whereas for me, well I've been home all day and I'd like to go out." Komarovsky (1962) in her classic study of American blue-collar marriage found that less educated husbands spend more of their leisure with male friends than did the more educated men. In essence, this meant that the wife stayed at home for her leisure unless of course she had her night out also.

Among husbands and wives, shared leisure activities are far more common among the middle class than they are among the lower socio-economic groups. Gavron (1966), whose study also included middle-class mothers, found that over half of the husbands would r   t in the evenings without their wives, and those who did tended to stay home on set evenings so that their wives could pursue their own activities.

Not only does socio-economic status, particularly in the case of lower-income wives, greatly affect their recreational pursuits, it also seems likely that the relationship between participation and life-cycle stage (or role constellation) among women varies with their socio-economic status. Murphy (1969), in her study of Canadian urban women found no relationship between degree of participation and life-cycle stage for women in the upper socio-economic level, but there was a significant relationship for those in the middle and lower strata. Similarly, Angrist (1967) found that among a large sample of American college-educated women in various stages of the life-cycle there were no differences in the degree of leisure activity.[28] There was a noticeable decline, however, in active leisure such as sport at the life-cycle stage where the mother was most involved with pre-school children; consequently, her leisure activites were restricted to those easily pursued at or near the home such as watching television, hobbies and informal visiting. As the children grew older, mothers in the Angrist study were able to increase their community, recreational and self-enrichment pursuits.

Therefore, homemakers in the middle, and more so the upper, strata of society are usually able to retain a degree of free time for themselves. No doubt the advantages of their situation make available household help, day-care facilities, and the necessary transportation to enjoy the activities of their choice.

The general pattern for a great many Canadian women today is to work until marriage, continue for a short period after marriage, stop temporarily when the children are young, and return again to the labour force sometime after the children are less dependent.[29] Although there are numerous studies which examine the role of women in the labour force, there is a dearth of research pertaining to the working mother and her leisure patterns. Assuming that employed mothers would not deprive themselves entirely of recreational activities, Nye (1963) argued that the type of social life which entailed, for example, informal visiting would obviously be sharply curtailed with a concomitant rise in recreational activity requiring no advance planning, little expenditure of time and energy, but some expenditure of funds (such as commercial spectator recreation). The data collected from some 2000 women in three urban-American centres did not entirely support his hypothesis since the employed mothers were found to participate less in recreational activities involving advance planning and continuing commitments, but they also participated in commercial recreation in equal proportions to the non-employed mothers. Moreover, the mothers employed only part-time closely followed the recreation patterns of those not in the labour force at all. Finally, family recreational activities such as visiting relatives, organized games at home, family picnics, and vacations appeared not to be affected by the employment status of the mother. The researchers concluded that although the employment of mothers results in a decline of recreation involving social relationships outside the family, intra-family and commercial recreation were not appreciably affected. However, one cannot assume that the differences found were a result of employment, nor can the similarities be taken as evidence that employment makes no difference, since no attempt was made to compare the levels of recreational participation, before and after employment, nor were any other variables taken into consideration. Nevertheless Nye's conclusions were tenuously supported by Murphy (1969) who found that work outside the home was not a significant factor influencing commercial spectator recreation but that it did affect active involvement in physical recreation.

On the other hand, in an extensive study of dual-career families (families characterized by both the husband and wife having a high degree of commitment and aspiration in the world of work), it was found that leisure and recreation activities were often sacrificed very early on in the marriage. Many were able, however, to cope with the resultant strain by deliberately "working" at leisure, delegating many of the less desirable chores to others, essentially housekeepers and *au pair* girls, and modifying their work commitments to make them as compatible as possible with the other's (Fogarty, Rapoport and Rapoport, 1971).

It has not been the intent of this section to present a picture of the housewife, particularly one who is employed outside the home, as so overburdened with responsibilities that she is denied any form of leisure or recreation. Rather the purpose has been to illustrate that married women with families simply do not have the same opportunities as men to participate in recreational activities because the institution of marriage as we know it today does not endorse completely shared roles. In general, husbands are the major breadwinners and wives are entrusted with the prime responsibility of childcare and housekeeping. Certainly husbands whose wives are not employed outside the home and whose children are of school age, will say they envy their wife's leisured role while they are under constant pressure to ensure that such leisure will continue. I would argue that although husbands claim they have little leisure due to the pressures of work, their situation is self-imposed and it does not deny them the opportunity. For wives, even the opportunity is often denied.

Summary and Concluding Comment

In this paper I have attempted to describe the role that sport and physical activity play in the lives of Canadian women. We saw that women in our society participate less frequently and in smaller numbers in fewer sports and physical activities than do men. Married women are noticeably absent from sports participation and if they do participate it is primarily in the less structured physical activities such as walking, swimming, skating, and so on. Although studies concerning the correlates of sport involvement among adult women are scarce, an exploratory cross-cultural study conducted by the author suggested that involvement in the past is a major determining factor of present participation which unfortunately tells us little about the common causes of past and present involvement. We do know, however, that in order for a woman to have become involved in sport in the first place, and for her to continue, she has continually been in an environment which is highly supportive of her activities—family, school, peer group, and husband. Where this support is lacking, and particularly in the case of married women with children, the exigencies of their situation often take precedence over their own leisure time.

Although attitudes are important facilitators of behaviour, the fact is that most women possess highly positive attitudes towards aspects of female athleticism, and yet many do not actively participate in sport. There are some who would claim that the pejorative images we suspect women to hold of sport and of women athletes are deterrents to female participation, but the evidence shows that the lack of involvement by women, or men for that matter, cannot be a function of negative attitudes.

Rather, we must turn elsewhere for an explanation. Certainly a good deal of variance in activity patterns both within and between sexes can be explained by socialization factors. But despite the research, we still do not have a definitive answer to the following question: Do boys and girls become differentially involved in sport because they are treated differently, or do boys and girls receive different encouragement to take part in sport because they demonstrate a contrasting predisposition to become involved from the beginning?

Not only do we need to look to the socialization process for our answers, we must also re-examine our methodology. Longitudinal studies with larger, more representative, samples would contribute a good deal more to our understanding of why some females choose to engage in sport and physical activity and why some do not. This is not to say that *ex posto facto* survey studies should be discontinued, although taken collectively they provide no clear evidence of the antecedents of female sport involvement. On the contrary, they are especially useful for *theory trimming*, and providing they maintain a high methodological sophistication and rigour, they should generate hypotheses which could be tested more thoroughly through in-depth, longitudinal, and case studies.

Finally, it must not be forgotten that one of the real barriers to participation, specifically for married women, is the fact that they, and not their husbands, are entrusted with the responsibility of childcare and housekeeping while in some cases working, albeit quite willingly, on a full-time basis outside the home. Their lack of participation is the result of an injustice in the realm of marriage and family. Until responsibilities within the household are more equitably shared, married women with families will always be under-represented in sport involvement surveys. To some this may seem of little importance, but the implications can hardly be ignored. At least one study (Elliott, *et al.*, 1970) has demonstrated that participation in sports is a significant factor in the mental health of a large sample of urban, Canadian women.

NOTES

1. The term *gender* roles is being used here rather than the more common *sex* roles. In doing so, I am taking the lead from Tresemer (1975:308-9) who points out quite correctly that "sex" refers to the dichotomous distinctions between male and female based on physiological characteristics whereas "gender" refers to the psychological and cultural definitions of the dimensions of *masculine* and *feminine*. Therefore, when speaking of a learned role, the proper term is gender role.

2. For information concerning status differentials among men and women in Canadian society see: *Report of the Royal Commission on the Status of Women in Canada* (1970) particularly Chapters 2, 3 and 7; various working papers which available from the federal Advisory Council on the Status of Women, and Chapter 4 in Henshel (1973).

3. In fact, of ten sport sociology texts and anthologies published between 1969 and 1975, only *three* have a separate chapter or section devoted to an examination of female sport involvement. Only one text contains a special section on the female role in sport within a chapter dealing with racism and discrimination. This material is a mere 2.4 percent of the total content. The percentage of "fringe articles", that is, those which either allude to the role of women in sport or report studies which included females in the sample, is also negligible. Of more significance is that only *one* of the ten texts was edited by a woman, and of some 200 unique articles in the anthologies, a mere *eight* percent were authored or co-authored by women. Unfortunately, the editors of sport sociology texts were and often still are at a loss to locate suitable material on women for inclusion in their volumes since there has been very little original research

or scholarly writing done in that area. The reader who is familiar with Jan Felshin's section entitled "The Social View" in E. W. Gerber, et al., *The American Woman in Sport* (1974); the section on "Sociological Considerations" in D. V. Harris (ed.), *Women and Sport: A National Research Conference* (1972), or the relevant sections in Volumes I (1971) and II (1973) of the *DGWS Research Reports: Women in Sports* has fairly well covered the available literature with the exception of several master's and doctoral theses, unpublished papers, and a few published articles.

4. Anthologies such as Safilios-Rothschild's *Toward a Sociology of Women* (1972), Huber's *Changing Women in a Changing Society* (1973), or Stephenson's *Women in Canada* (1973), which are fairly typical of readers used in an increasing number of women's studies courses, do not discuss aspects of women's leisure nor the involvement of women in sport. Original works on women are few, and although books such as Stoll's *Female and Male* (1974), or Chafetz's *Masculine/Feminine or Human?* (1974), which examine male-female differences from the perspective of socialization and social structure, contain passing references to sport, there are no scholarly analyses of the female role in sport contained within the sociological literature on women.

5. Within the Canadian context this approach is best represented in articles by Batten (1973), Gauthier (1973), Hoffman (1975), Howell (1974), Mallovy (1975), Tyrwhitt (1975).

6. The term "mass sport" is being used here in a simplistic sense to mean the participation in sport by all sectors of society and not just those of the elite classes, a phenomenon which occurred in the post-industrialism of western society. For an excellent discussion on the problems of an oversimplification such as this, see Gruneau (1975:158-168).

7. Some of the material in this section has also appeared in a June, 1975 working paper entitled "Motivating Canadians to Become Physically Active", researched and written by the author for the Recreation Committee of the National Advisory Council on Fitness and Amateur Sport.

8. It is virtually impossible to make comparisons with other countries on the basis of these statistics because rarely in national leisure-time surveys is the concept of 'participant' comparable. Until such time that sophisticated cross-national studies are conducted on the leisure-time activities of similar and disparate cultures, we can make no assumptions as to whether the Canadian participation level is substantially different to that of other nations.

9. In Sillitoe's sample, 23 percent of the single men between 23 and 30 years were active participants, and 28 percent of the single women. At marriage, the drop-off for men was to 20 percent, whereas for women it went to 10 percent. With the coming of children, the men precipitated to 10 percent and the women to 2 percent active participants.

10. The most popular activities for men were walking (37.9%), swimming (30.2%), hunting and fishing (30.8%), skating (16.9%), snowmobiling (14.7%), hockey (13.9%), bowling (12.4%), bicycling (11.9%) and golf (11.4%). This information was obtained directly from Statistics Canada.

11. For an elaboration of the governing conceptual scheme and a full explanation of the theoretical rationale underlying the determinant categories, see Chapter 2 (pp. 14-41) in Hall (1974). For a detailed explanation of the measuring instruments, the reader should refer to Chapter 3 (pp. 42-103).

12. For a description of how the Participation Index was computed in the Hall (1974) study, see pp. 100-101.

13. The sixteen sample groups consisted of the following: Canadian Olympic team, Canadian national basketball team, Canadian national field hockey team, fencers, basketball league players, fastball league players, field hockey league players, squash players, university students, curling club members, library staff, hair-dressers, apartment dwellers, university graduates, keep-fit class members, and bank employees. The highest response rates were among the Canadian national teams (90.0% and 80.0%), the basketball and fastball league players (83.3% and 72.7%), and fencers (78.0%). The lowest

responses came from the bank employees (30.0%), hairdressers (38.3%), library staff (56.0%), and university graduates (56.7%).

14. For an explanation of this procedure see Hall (1974:134-6).

15. The usual criterion for determining the significance of a regression coefficient is that the regular regression coefficient be at least twice the size of its standard error (this would correspond roughly to the .05 level of significance for a normally distributed variable in the sample).

16. In the path model or diagram, the straight lines connecting one variable to another represent *direct* influences whereas the curvilinear line with an arrow at both ends is intended to sum up the correlation between two variables. Therefore the number beside this line in Figure 2 is the correlation coefficient (.003) between variables D and C for this particular population. The other numbers entered on the diagram are *path coefficients* which are in fact the normalized regression coefficients or beta coefficients from the regression analysis. These path coefficients indicate the direction and magnitude of the direct effect of an independent variable on the dependent variable when two or more independent variables are considered simultaneously in the regression analysis. Finally, the lines indicating 'R' as their source represent residual paths which stand for "all other influences on the variable in question, including causes not recognized or measured, and departures of the true relationships from additivity and linearity, properties that are assumed throughout the analysis" (Blau and Duncan, 1967:171). In other words, the residual path coefficient is a convenient representation of the extent to which the variables in the system fail to account for the variation in the dependent variable. The residual path coefficient is calculated as $\sqrt{1 - R^2}$, where R^2 is the coefficient of determination. It should be noted that the size of a residual is no guide whatever to the validity of the causal interpretation. Since the residual represents unobserved causal factors presumable *uncorrelated* with the others in the system, it is important to ask whether the unmeasured variables it stands for are in fact uncorrelated with the causes depicted in the path model.

17. Mapes and Allan (1973) and Allan (1974) recommend the use of a factor analysis prior to path analysis to determine the number of immediate causes of any dependent variable. Their assumption is that the overall rank (number of factors) in a principal-factor solution is equal to the number of true causes. Therefore a path analytic model with four independent variables should have four factors, otherwise there is conceptual redundancy. This was, in fact, done and the interested reader should consult Hall, 1974:149-151.

18. See Hall, 1974: 140-153.

19. See Duncan (1971) and Land (1971) for excellent expositions of the proper methodology.

20. See Hall, 1974: 110-124, 213-222.

21. However, if demographic factors such as education, socio-economic status, age and role constellation are partially controlled by virtue of the homogeneity of the sample, then attitudinal factors become much more significant as predictors of primary involvement.

22. Refer again to Note 9.

23. To the best of my knowledge, there are no studies which have examined the active leisure patterns of males in the context of marriage and family, nor have there been any which have *specifically* investigated the effects of work and career on adult male sports participation.

24. See Bernard (1972), Chapter Two, pp. 16-27.

25. See Bernard (1972), Chapter three, pp. 28-58 in addition to the extensive tables beginning on p. 331.

26. See Harvey J. Locke, *Predicting Adjustments in Marriage: A Comparison of a Divorced and Happily Married Group.* New York: Holt, 1951:68-69 quoted in Bernard (1972).

27. For an excellent discussion of the possibilities of a shared-role pattern within marriage, see Bernard (1972), Chapter Eleven, p. 277-297.

28. As already noted, a similar pattern was found in the Richardson (1974) study, and to a certain extent in the Richardson and Hall (1974) data.
29. In 1971, Canadian women comprised almost 33 percent of the labour force and of these 57 percent were married. The highest female labour participation rate is in the 20 to 24 age group; it peaks again in the 35 year category and again but less so in the 45 to 49 age group (Labour Canada, 1971).

REFERENCES

Allan, G. J. Boris
1974   "Simplicity in path analysis." *Sociology*, 8(2).

Angrist, Shirley S.
1967   "Role constellation as a variable in women's leisure activities." *Social Forces*, 45.

Batten, Jack
1973   "Something to cheer about." *Homemaker's Magazine*, 8 (5).

Bernard, Jessie
1972   *The Future of Marriage.* New York: Bantam.
1974   *The Future of Motherhood.* New York: The Dial Press.

Blau, Peter and Otis D. Duncan
1967   *The American Occupational Structure.* New York: John Wiley.

Burton, Thomas L.
1971   *Experiments in Recreation Research.* London: George Allen and Unwin.

Chafetz, Janet S.
1974   *Masculine/Feminine or Human?* Itasca, Illinois: F. E. Peacock.

Duncan, Otis D.
1966   "Path analysis: sociological examples." *American Journal of Sociology*, 72.
1971   "Peer influences on aspirations: a reinterpretation." In H. M. Blalock (ed.), *Causal Models in the Social Sciences*, New York: Macmillan.

Elliott, David H.
1970   "Causes and consequences of differential leisure participation among females in Halifax, Nova Scotia." Paper presented at the CASS/ACSS Conference.

Felshin, Jan
1974   "The social view." In E. W. Gerber, *et al.*, *The American Woman in Sport.* Reading, Mass.: Addison-Wesley.

Fogarty, Michael P., Rhona Rapoport and Robert N. Rapoport
1971   *Sex, Career and Family.* London: George Allen and Unwin.

Gauthier, Linda
1973   "The second sex fights back." *Amateur Sport*, 4(3).

Gavron, Hannah
1966   *The Captive Wife.* London: Penguin.

Gerber, Ellen W.
1973   "The unimportance of sex-role identification or why all roses are roses." Paper presented at the 49th Annual Conference of the Western Society for Physical Education of College Women, Salisham, Oregon.

Gruneau, Richard
1975   "Sport, social differentiation and social inequality." In D. W. Ball and J. W. Loy, *Sport and Social Order: Contributions to the Sociology of Sport.* Reading, Mass.: Addison-Wesley.

Hall, M. Ann
1974   "Women and physical recreation: a causal analysis." Unpublished doctoral dissertation, University of Birmingham, England.

Harris, Dorothy V.
1972   Women and Sport: A National Research Conference. University Park, Pa.: The Pennsylvania State University.
1971   D.G.W.S. Research Reports: Women in Sports, Vol. I, AAHPER Press

Henshel, Anne-Marrie
1973   Sex Structure. Toronto.: Longmans.

Hoffman, Abigail
1975   "Running for Gold." Macleans, 88(2).

Howell, Reet
1974   "Women's sport: the awakening." CAHPER Journal, 41(2).

Huber, Joan (ed.)
1973   Changing Women in a Changing Society. Chicago: The University of Chicago Press.

Janeway, Elizabeth
1971   Man's World, Woman's Place: A Study in Social Mythology. London: Michael Joseph.

Kenyon, Gerald S.
1966   "The significance of physical activity as a function of age, sex, education and socio-economic status of Northern United States adults." International Review of Sport Sociology, 1.

Kirsh, Carol, et. al.
1973   A Lesiure Study—Canada 1972. Arts and Culture Branch, Department of Secretary of State, Government of Canada.

Komarovsky, Mirra
1962   Blue-Collar Marriage. New York: Vintage.

Labour Canada
1971   Women in the Labour Force 1971 Facts and Figures. Women's Bureau.

Land, Kenneth C.
1969   "Principles of path analysis." In Sociological Methodology 1969. San Francisco: Jossey Bass.
1971   "Significant others, the self-reflexive act and the attitude formation process: a reinterpretation." American Sociological Review, 36.

Loy, John W.
1969   "The nature of sport: a definitional effort." In J. W. Loy and G. S. Kenyon (eds.), Sport, Culture and Society. New York: Macmillan.

Mallovy, Naomi
1975   "Women in Sports." Homemaker's Magazine, 10(7).

Mapes, Roy and G. F. Boris Allan
1973   "Path analysis—a cautionary note." The Sociological Review, 21.

Murphy, Barbara
1969   "Participation of married women in physical recreational activities as a function of socio-economic status and family life cycle stage." Unpublished M.A. thesis, The University of Alberta, Edmonton.

Nye, F. Ivan
1963   "Recreation and Community." In F. I. Nye and L. W. Hoffman, The Employed Mother in America. Chicago: Rand McNally.

Page, Charles H.
1973   "Pervasive sociological themes in the study of sport." In J. T. Talamini and C. H. Page, Sport and Society: An Anthology. Boston: Little, Brown.

Recreation Committee
1975   "Motivating Canadians to Become Physically Active, A Working Paper." Ottawa: National Advisory Council on Fitness and Amateur Sport.

Report of the Royal Commission of the Status of Women in Canada
1970   Ottawa: Information Canada.

Richardson, Dorothy A.
1974   "*Women and physical activity: A sociocultural investigation of primary involvement.*" Unpublished doctoral dissertation, University of Georgia.

and M. Ann Hall
1974   "Women and physical activity: A cross-national perspective." Paper presented at the Canadian Association of Sport Sciences Meetings, Edmonton, Alberta.

Robinson, John P.
1967   "Time expenditure on sports across ten countries." *International Review of Sport Sociology*, 2.

Ryan, Edward F.
1975   "Maintenance obligations in a new legal concept of marriage." Address to the National Meeting, Canadian Status of Women Councils, Saskatoon.

Safilios-Rothschild, Constantina
1972   *Towards a Sociology of Women.* Lexington, Mass.: Xerox College Publishing.

Sillitoe, K.
1969   *Planning for Leisure.* Government Social Survey, London: H.M.S.O.

Stephenson, Marylee (ed.)
1973   *Women in Canada.* Toronto: New Press.

Stoll, Clarice S.
1974   *Female and Male.* Dubuque, Iowa: Wm. C. Brown.

Tresemer, David
1975   "Assumpions made about gender roles." In M. Millman and R. M. Louter (eds.), *Another voice: Feminist Perspectives on Social Life and Social Science.* Anchor Press/Doubleday.

Tyrwhitt, Janice
1975   "Women in Sport: Winners or Losers?" *Reader's Digest,* 107(642).

Willis, Paul
1973   "Performance and meaning: A socio-cultural view of women in sport." Paper presented at the Women and Sport Symposium, University of Birmingham, England.

ASCRIPTION AND POSITION:
A Comparative Analysis of "Stacking" in Professional Football[*]

Donald W. Ball

One of the emergent characteristics of the sociology of the sixties was the development of a substantive focus on sport. Among the major reasons for this development were the increasingly large number of persons and volume of resources involved in sport and the recognition of the pre-eminently social nature of sport as a form of conduct.

Sport as a social activity is particularly amenable to general sociological scrutiny because sports *qua* games may be heuristically treated as closed systems, with explicit and codified normative regulations, for example, rulebooks, and precise and public measures of outcomes, performances, efficiency, and the like. Such an approach is basically one of a "sociology *through* sport," using sport data to address more general sociological questions.

Although sport may be treated "as if" it is a bounded system, empirically it is embedded in the larger society—acting and reacting and mirroring that broader societal context. Sport is neither trivial nor merely a laboratory for the sociologist, but an important dimension of human experience and concern. This perspective is one that focuses on "sport and society" or the "sociology *of* sport," viewing sport as a social reality *sui generis*.

The following discussion will be concerned with patterns of differential treatment of professional football players in Canada and the United States. Such differences will be considered both with regard to (i) the variables of race and national origins, that is, a sociology of sport; and (ii) in terms of which of two theoretical models can best account for any differences found; that is, a sociology *through* sport.

[*] I am indebted to Cameron Ball, Neil Ball, and Philip Pollard for their help in procuring some of the data on players in the Canadian Football League used in this article. This project was partially supported by a University of Victoria Faculty Research Grant (08 518). Helpful comments were received from colleagues when earlier versions of this material were presented in seminars at the University of Alberta and the University of Calgary; from Brian Currie of the University of Victoria, and John Loy of the University of Massachusetts. A more extensive formulation was presented to the symposium on Man; Sport, and Contemporary Society, Queens College of the City University of New York, March 1972.

Approaching the Problem

In considering the differential treatment of professional athletes on the basis of race, there are two broad approaches. One, "the Jackie Robinson story" basically says (regarding blacks), "you never had it so good" (Boyle, 1963; Olsen, 1968). This view emphasizes the opportunities for mobility made available to minority group members by professional sport. Thus, professional sport is seen as an accessible "legitimate opportunity structure" (Cloward and Ohlin, 1960).

The other view might be called "the Harry Edwards corrective" (Edwards, 1969). This perspective acknowledges the availability of entrance into sport for minority members, but points to continued discriminatory practices within the context of the structure of sport. Of special attention by this school have been their allegations of "stacking."

Stacking, the practice of positioning athletes in team sports on the basis of particularistic rather than universalistic characteristics has been alleged and described by Edwards (1969), Meggysey (1970), and Olsen (1968); and empirically demonstrated by Loy and McElvogue (1970), along with confirmatory research by Brower (1972). Essentially, *stacking in sports involves assignment to a playing position, an achieved status, on the basis of an ascribed status* (Davis, 1949;96—117). A focal concern by sociologists of sport has been the stacking of team members on the ascriptive basis of race, (for example, Loy and McElvogue, 1970; Brower, 1972; and Edwards, 1969). As is the case with much material of a sociological perspective, the works cited above are primarily or exclusively referring to situations in the United States.

In the following discussion, the theoretical formulation and empirical investigation begun on US professional football by Loy and McElvogue (1970) will be applied to Canadian sport, replicated on race (also see Smith and Grindstaff, 1970; Barnes, 1971), and *extended to national origins* with comparative data drawn from professional football in the US and in Canada from the Canadian Football League (CFL). Additionally, an alternative theory will be proposed as of equal or greater power in explaining Canadian patterns.

The Centrality Theory

Drawing upon Grusky's theory of organization structure (1963) and Blalock's propositions regarding occupational discrimination (1962), Loy and McElvogue (1970;5—7) have formulated a theory to explain the disproportionate presence—stacking—of blacks in some positions, and their practical absence from others in professional football and baseball. In doing so, they conceive of teams as work organizations, and the positions within them as analogous to occupations.

Employing baseball teams *qua* formal organizations for his empirical examples, Grusky has asserted that the formal structure of an organization systematically patterns the behaviours associated with its constituent positions along three interdependent dimensions: spatial location, nature of organizational tasks, and frequency of interaction. The major theoretical thrust of Grusky's organizational model is contained in the statement that "all else being equal, the more central one's spatial location: (1) the greater the likelihood dependent or coordinative tasks will be performed and (2) the greater the rate of interaction with occupants of other positions. Also, the performance of dependent tasks is positively related to frequency of interaction" (1963:346).

Centrality, then refers to (i) spatial location and (ii) the attendant kinds of tasks and interaction rates. From a structural standpoint it is best operationalized, at least in the case of fixed-position team sports taken-as-formal-organizations (for example, football or baseball), by spatial location.

Like Grusky, Blalock's consideration of interaction, task dependency, and occupational discrimination turned to baseball for empirical examples to bolster the theoretical propositions. Blalock's propositions can be readily synthesized with Gruksy's model. As Loy and McElvogue put it, "since the dimensions of interaction and task dependency treated by Blalock are included in the concept of centrality, we integrated his propositions under a more general one, stating that *discrimination is positively related to centrality*" (1970:7; emphasis added).

Centrality and Professional Team Sports

In professional team sports a specific variant of occupational discrimination is *stacking*: the arbitrary inclusion or exclusion of persons vis-à-vis a playing position on the basis of ascriptive status, for example, race. Thus, Loy and McElvogue predicted as their specific theoretical proposition that stacking, a form of "racial segregation in professional team sports is positively related to centrality" (1970:7).

The Original Test of the Proposition

For their first test of the prediction, Loy and McElvogue turned to major league baseball in the United States. Using 1967 data and treating catchers and infield positions as central, the outfield as non-central (and excluding pitchers as unique and neither), they found that 7 out of 10 white players ($N = 132$) occupied central positions, while only 1 out of 3 blacks ($N = 55$) were so located (1970:8−10; also see 15−24). Statistically significant beyond the .0005 level, the baseball data were strongly supportive of their model and the stacking prediction it generated. They next turned their attention to US professional football.

The Case of Professional Football

Although there are differences between the rules and positions regarding professional football in Canada and the United States, these are increasingly more historical than actually differentiating (on the convergence between the two games, see Cosentino, 1969). Table I indicates the central and non-central positions which characterize both offensive defensive formations, and subsumes the minor differences between the two sets of procedures in force on each side of the border.

TABLE I

CENTRAL AND NON-CENTRAL POSITIONS ON OFFENCE AND DEFENCE[a]

	Offence	Defence
Central:	centre quarterback guards	linebackers
Non-central	tackles ends flankers, wide receivers running backs	tackles ends backs, safeties

[a]Adapted from Loy and McElvogue (1970:10 − 12).

Data

Loy and McElvogue's American football data (1970:11−13) were drawn from yearbooks for the 1968 seasons of the American Football League and the National Football League and classified all starting players (except specialty teams) by offensive or defensive position, along with race, black or white. All data on American professional football employed in the following is taken from their study.

The data on the Canadian Football League personnel presented here is for the 1971 season. It is drawn from the *Canadian Football League Player Photos, Official 1971 Collection*, a widely distributed promotional device, and checked where possible against other and similar sources (on the rationale for using such mass-circulation-based data see Ball, 1967;452−453). These materials provide a 75 per cent sample of the

32-man roster allowed each of the nine teams in the league, and like the Loy and McElvogue data, are based upon pre-season, but accurate, forecasts. For each player information is available on position, on race (from a photograph), and usually on national origin and on prior education and playing experience. Although a 75 per cent sample should yield an $N=216$, due to missing information it is reduced slightly here to $N=209$. On the whole, visual inspection suggests the sample is representative. However, it is slightly biased toward imports in terms of national origins.

Although this attribute, national origin, is an important independent variable, its bias is neutralized by percentaging against the unbalanced marginal totals. However, because of the limitations of the sample, the following is claimed to be no more than a "demonstration" (Garfinkel, 1964), rather than a more rigorous "investigation." (On the methodological problems of using rosters, for example the lack of stability within seasons, see Smith and Grindstaff, 1970:60 – 62). Finally, though the data cover only one season in each case, other research has shown aggregate sport data to be quite stable over time (on international figure skating, see Ball, 1971; on baseball, see Loy and McElvogue, 1970:15– 22).

Centrality, Stacking, and Race: A Comparison

According to the Loy-McElvogue hypothesis, blacks in professional football will be stacked at non-central positions and excluded from central ones. Comparing their data on the American NFL (columns B and D of Table II) with data on the CFL (columns A and C) indicates a similar pattern in each case: blacks are virtually excluded from central positions in professional football on either side of the border. The similarity of the patterns is as striking as the moral implications, are obvious; neither virtues nor vices are respecters of national borders (also see Smith and Grindstaff, 1970:47–66; and more generally, Cosentino, 1969, on the "Americanization" of Canadian football).

Centrality, National Origins, and Stacking

Unlike professional football in the United States, Canadian football has been historically cross-cut by another ascriptive status of its players; national origin, Canadians and imports (for the latter, read Americans). Americans have been playing football in Canada at least since 1912 in the forerunners of the CFL and the rugby unions (Cosentino, 1969:48–49).

TABLE II

RACE OF PLAYERS BY CENTRALITY OF POSITION
FOR CANADIAN AND US PROFESSIONAL LEAGUES
(adjusted percentages)[a]

Position	Percentage of whites		Percentage of blacks	
	(A) Cdn.	(B) US[b]	(C) Cdn.	(D) US[b]
Offence				
Central	47	45	06	02
Non-Central	53	55	94	98
Total percentage	100	100	100	100
N	97[a]	220	19[a]	66
Defence				
Central	28	37	—	06
Non-Central	72	63	100	94
Total percentage	100	100	100	100
N	83[a]	192	12	94

[a] Percentage adjusted to compensate for the additional position in Canadian football. This position is non-central; thus the non-central raw number is multiplied by .875 (7/8) to equalize with US formations. Adjusted base numbers, upon which percentages are calculated are: 97 = 90; 83 = 75; and 19 = 17. This procedure is not necessary in subsequent tables where comparisons are limited to CFL players only.
[b] US data for 1968 from Loy and McElvogue (1970:10—12).

It should be understood that the categorization of national origins to be used here, Canadians and imports, is not the same as that used by the CFL itself. The League's definition emphasizes prior experience as well as citizenship and nativity, the criterion herein employed. Thus, an American player without US high school or college experience becomes a non-import under League definitions. Put another way, national origins are ascriptive, while League definitions may be achieved. Consistency suggests the utility of opting for the former as an analytical variable.

Canadians and Imports: The Data

When nativity is considered, the null form of the stacking hypothesis predicts no differences between the proportion of centrally located Canadians and imports. In other words, the relationship should be one of parity.

TABLE III

NATIONAL ORIGINS OF CFL PLAYERS AND CENTRALITY OF POSITION

Position	Percentage of Canadians	Percentage of Imports
Central, all	27	35
Non-Central, all	73	65
Total	100	100
N	94	110
Offence		
Central	34	41
Non-central	66	59
Total	100	100
N	50	64
Defence		
Central	18	26
Non-Central	82	74
Total	100	100
N	44	46

Following Loy and McElvogue (1970), Table III presents the distribution of imports (Americans) and Canadians in the CFL in terms of the centrality model. It is clear that whether one looks at over-all patterns, or at offensive or defensive alignments separately, imports predominate over Canadian players in terms of the proportion of central positions they occupy. The difference on offence is particularly interesting, since almost half of the central Canadians are at one position only ($N=8$), that of centre. Smith and Grindstaff (1970:36) have described the centre as a position usually manned by Canadians and "generally acknowledged to require less skill." Thus, if central positions are assumed to be in some ways more "difficult" as well as more "desirable," Canadians predominate at only the least of these. Additionally, because of the restrictive quota on imports (maximum of 14 out of 32 players *per* team in 1971), quantitative differences are actually more extreme than their apparent magnitude.[1]

To demonstrate that Canadians and imports are differentially distributed is not to demonstrate "stacking" *per se*, however. It is frequently alleged that imports are the more skilled players by virtue of their superior training rather than their ability; especially in terms of their college and university football experience (see former import Hardimon Curetan, quoted in Barnes, 1971:43—54). At the same time, although perhaps not widely recognized, the fact is that approximately half of the Canadians in the Canadian Football League played football while attending college or university in the United States. Such "crash courses" have often been the instigation of CFL teams themselves (Barnes, 1971).

TABLE IV

PRIOR BACKGROUND EXPERIENCE OF CFL PLAYERS AND CENTRALITY OF POSITION

Position	Percentage US college	Percentage Other
Central, all	31	20
Non-Central, all	69	80
Total	100	100
N	45	44
Offense		
Central	37	21
Non-Central	62	79
Total	100	100
N	32	14
Defence		
Central	15	20
Non-Central	85	80
Total	100	100
N	13	30
Central Positions		
Offence	86	33
Defence	14	67
Total	100	100
N	14	9

Thus, examining Canadian players in terms of prior playing experience would allow for an assessment of a *training* versus *stacking* hypothesis. Table IV presents data on Canadian players in terms of centrality and whether or not they played collegiate football in the United States or had some other form of prior experience, for example, Canadian university, junior football, or high school participation.

If training accounts for the differential positioning of imports and Canadians, it should virtually disappear in the cases of Canadians with US collegiate experience. From these data can be seen: (i) over-all, American collegiate experience is associated with centrality; (ii) that this association is especially marked on offence; but (iii) slightly reversed for the defensive unit. However, recalling Table III, neither the over-all nor the offensive proportions of US trained Canadians at central positions reaches the percentage of such positions occupied by imports. Although these data do not compel the acceptance of a stacking hypothesis, they do argue the rejection of one based upon training alone.

The reversal of the association between US training and centrality when the defence is considered is somewhat anomalous. However, upon closer examination it appears to be at least partly artificial. Few US-trained Canadians play defence: less than half as many as the "others" without such experience (13 to 20). Further, most Canadians *cum* American collegians in central positions are on offensive units, while the reverse is true for those without such experience.

TABLE V

OFFENSIVE AND DEFENSIVE PLAYERS IN THE CFL
BY NATIONAL ORIGIN AND PRIOR BACKGROUND EXPERIENCE

Position	Percentage by national origin		Percentage by background, Canadians only	
	Imports	Canadians	US College	Others
Offence	58	53	71	26
Defence	42	47	29	74
Total	100	100	100	100
N	110	94	45	44

This last is part of a more general pattern. "Most teams play more of their imports on offense rather than defense because coaches feel that normally it takes more talent and experience to play offense, and that it is possible to train Canadian players with less experience to do an adequate job of defense" (Smith and Grindstaff, 1970:60). The data in Table V substantiate this statement. Imports predominate over Canadians on offence, but US-trained Canadians do so especially compared to those without such experience.

Centrality: An Overview

In general, the ascriptive statuses of Canadians and imports do appear to be differentially positioned in terms of the centrality model. Assuming, for whatever reasons, that central positions are more desirable or more rewarding, the ascribed status of imports is associated with such location, and that of Canadian with the alternative of non-centrality. When Canadians are categorized as those with US collegiate football experience, or those without it, the deficit position is explained and reduced, but not removed.

Still, the differences are not of sufficient magnitude to warrant an exclusive employment of the centrality model as an explanatory tool in the case of differential positioning by national origins in the CFL. In sum, centrality shows more power as regards stacking and the ascriptive criterion of race than it does regarding nativity.

Primary and Supporting Players: An Alternative Model

As does the Loy and McElvogue model, this model looks at football teams as a set of positions constituting a formal work organization.

However, where the centrality model looks to spatial location, the primary-supporting model looks to organizational goals and the nature of organizationally defined tasks.

The overreaching goal of a football team is to win games. To accomplish this, teams are divided into subunits or separate organizations within organizations: the offensive and defensive units.

Within each of these organizations, offence and defence, positions can be differentiated on the basis of task-orientation into primary and supporting positions. The former, the *primary positions* are those within the organization charged with the basic achievement and realization of the organization's goals. *Supporting positions*, on the other hand, are defined as those responsible for assisting the primary positions in their efforts toward goal-achievement, but not ordinarily directly involved in such accomplishment. Put grossly, primary positions (and thus their occupants, the players) are doers: supporting positions are helpers (for a more generalized and abstract, but similar approach, see Etzioni, 1961; 93–96).

When the offensive unit of a football team is considered in terms of the primary-supporting model, with its goal of moving the ball and scoring points, the primary positions are the quarterback, the running backs, and the pass catchers, that is, the ends, flankers, and wide receivers. These are the positions sometimes called by the coaches the "skill positions" (see, for instance, Oates, 1972). The supporting positions, whose task is to assist the goal-directed activities of the primary positions, are the offensive guards, the offensive tackles, and the centre. These are the basic positions charged with blocking so that others may advance the ball. Although the centre handles the ball on every play, it is only to deliver it to the quarterback (except in kicking situations), at the quarterback's initiative, and from a symbolically subordinate posture. It may be noted that although the offensive guards and centre are central in terms of spatial location their tasks are supporting rather than primary.

A further refinement within the primary offensive positions is the distinction between those that are *proactive* and initiate goal-directed activity and/or carry it out independently, and those that are *reactive* or dependent upon the activities of other primary positions for participation. Quarterbacks initiate activity and act independently, and running backs act independently once in possession of the ball: these positions are proactive. Ends, flankers, and wide receivers must wait for a pass to realize their primary, goal-related tasks: they are reactive.

The language of football points to the primary-supporting distinction within the defensive alignment. The common collective term for the defensive backs and safeties is the "secondary." By implication other defensive positions are primary—and so they are. In combination or alone it is the task of the defensive tackles and ends, the "front four," along with the linebackers, to stop running plays before the ball carrier can get past them, and/or get to the quarterback before he can throw a pass. Only if these positions fail to do so does the secondary formally come into play to stop a runner who has progressed downfield or to break up or intercept a pass or to stop a successful receiver from making further progress. Thus, on defence the primary positions are the defensive tackles and ends and the linebackers. The supporting positions are the defensive backs and safeties of the secondary. (Table VI summarizes the above six paragraphs.)

TABLE VI

PRIMARY AND SUPPORTING POSITIONS ON OFFENCE AND DEFENCE

	Offence	Defence
Primary	quarterback[a]	tackles
	running backs[a]	ends
	flankers, wide receivers[b]	linebackers
	ends[b]	
Supporting	centre	backs
	guards	safeties
	tackles	

[a]   Proactive
[b]   Reactive

Nationality and Experience: the Data

The data in Table VII array the same information in terms of the primary-supporting model which were shown in Tables III and IV with the centrality model.

As the data show, in all cases imports are more likely to occupy primary rather than supporting positions, while in only one case, offence, do Canadians reach the parity of a 50—50 split. This despite the fact that over half (56 per cent in 1971) of each roster must be Canadian. The difference between imports and Canadians is most dramatic in the case of the initiating, independent proactive offence positions and the dependent reactors: where imports are proactors in almost three out of every four cases, Canadians are reactors two out of three times. The effect of US collegiate experience is mixed and relatively slight except in

TABLE VII

PRIMARY AND SUPPORTING PLAYERS IN THE CFL
BY NATIONAL ORIGIN AND PRIOR BACKGROUND EXPERIENCE

Position	Percentage by national origin		Percentage by background, Canadians only	
	Imports	Canadians	US College	Others
Primary, all	68	49	47	50
Supporting, all	32	51	53	50
Total	100	100	100	100
N	110	94	45	44
Offence:				
Primary	73	50	47	57
Supporting	27	50	53	43
Total	100	100	100	100
N	64	50	32	14
Defence:				
Primary	61	48	46	47
Supporting	39	52	54	53
Total	100	100	100	100
N	46	44	13	30
Offence, Primary Only:				
Proactive	72	36	47	25
Reactive	28	64	53	75
Total	100	100	100	100
N	47	25	15	8

the case of the proactive-reactive distinction, where US collegiate experience is almost twice as likely to be associated with the occupancy of
proactive positions compared to a lack of such experience. But never
does this former group equal the proportion of imports at primary
positions in general.

Comparison with the Loy-McElvogue centrality model (Tables III and
IV) indicates that the primary-supporting model shows much greater
differentiation with regard to national origins of CFL players. However,
the centrality scheme was originally developed to explain racial differentiation in professional team sports. Thus, Table VIII compares Canadians
and imports while controlling for race.

As Table VIII shows, we might speak, none too figuratively it seems,
about the "white niggers of the CFL" (after Vallières, 1971). If the
assumption is again made that, like central positions, primary positions
are the more desirable and rewarding—then only in the case of defence
where Canadians are stacked (see Table V and accompanying discussion)
does the proportion of Canadians exceed that of blacks in primary
positions. Further, blacks themselves are traditionally stacked in the
supporting defensive secondary (Loy and McElvogue, 1970:13).

TABLE VIII

PRIMARY AND SUPPORTING PLAYERS IN THE CFL
BY NATIONAL ORIGIN AND RACE OF IMPORTS

	Percentage of imports		
Position	whites	blacks	Percentage of Canadians
Primary, all	71	60	49
Supporting, all	29	40	51
Total	100	100	100
N	80	30	94
Offence			
Primary	71	79	50
Supporting	29	21	50
Total	100	100	100
N	45	19	50
Defence			
Primary	71	27	48[a]
Supporting	29	73	52
Total	100	100	100
N	35	11	44
Offence, primary only			
Proactive	75	67	36
Reactive	25	33	64
Total	100	100	100
N	32	15	25

[a]   Includes one black.

Salary

The assumption that central and/or primary positions are somehow more
rewarding and more desirable has been invoked several times in the
preceding pages (also see Homans, 1950:140–144). If the assumption is
valid, the question becomes one of measurement: what data might be
brought to bear to compare (i) the differential rewards of central and
non-central along with primary and secondary positions in terms of
national origins of the players; and (ii) the magnitude of these differences
when it is the two models that are compared.

Salary provides just such a measure. Barnes (1971:144–145) lists average salaries by position for each team and for the CFL as a whole for the
1967 season. Table IX presents this salary information. In interpreting
these figures, a *caveat* should be kept in mind. Barnes's definitions of
Canadians and imports are those of the League, not the criterion of
national origin used here. Thus, some Canadians as *per* League classification may be imports or Americans in terms of actual nativity. Therefore,
salary differentials are, if anything, conservative, since some high-salaried
Americans could be classified as Canadians by the League's standards.

TABLE IX
DIFFERENCES IN AVERAGE SALARIES: CENTRALITY AND PRIMARY-SUPPORTING MODELS BY NATIONAL ORIGINS [a]

	Centrality Model				Primary-Supporting Model		
	Imports	Canadians	Difference		Imports	Canadians	Difference
Offence				*Offence*			
Central	$13,300	$13,200	$ 100	Primary	$13,612	$12,295	$1,317
Non-Central	13,087	8,958	4,129	Supporting	12,783	8,516	5,267
			X=2,114				X=3,483
Defence				*Defence*			
Central	11,375	8,625	2,750	Primary	12,191	8,708	3,483
Non-Central	12,783	8,516	4,267	Supporting	13,750	8,050	5,700
			X=3,508				X=4,591
Combined average			2,811				3,941

[a]Calculated from Barnes, 1971:144—145

The findings emerging from Table IX are of several kinds. First, in all comparisons imports are rewarded more highly than Canadians. Vallières has described "white niggers" as "the cheap labor that the predators of industry, commerce, and high finance are so fond off" (1971:19). Originally applied to Francophones vis-à-vis Anglophones, "white nigger" also fits the salary situation of Canadians in the Canadian Football League.

Secondly, in the case of imports on defence, the expected salary differential is reversed for both models. Since blacks are traditionally stacked here the finding is all the more surprising. In all other cases (six out of eight), however, differences are as expected, with central and primary players, whether Canadians or imports, reported as more highly rewarded.

Thirdly, when the two models are compared, the magnitude of differential rewards is greater for the primary-supporting model compared to that based upon centrality—in effect, validating the greater utility of the former over the latter, at least in the case of Canadian football.

Discussion

The purpose of this paper has been twofold: (i) from the standpoint of the sociology *of* sport, to investigate patterns of stacking of imports and Canadians in the Canadian Football League, using the basic ascriptive difference of nativity rather than race; and (ii) from the perspective of sociology *through* sport to compare two models of ascription-based organizational-occupational differentiation.

Are Canadians discriminated against in the CFL? The data are relatively clear-cut. They are less likely to occupy central positions than imports, and still less likely to perform at primary positions compared to secondary ones. Further, their average salaries are lower than those of imports, especially within the context of the primary-supporting model. At the same time, Canadian players with US collegiate football experience are more likely than other Canadians to be located at central or primary positions, though never to the same extent as imports. Thus, while US collegiate experience reduces the differences between imports and Canadians, these differences do not disappear. Is this discrimination? Unless discrimination is operationally defined it remains a moral meaning, subject to the relativization of all such terms. However, a majority of roster positions coupled with a minority of primary or central positions does demonstrate a *prima facie* case worthy of further consideration.

Both Loy and McElvogue (1970:18) and Smith and Grindstaff (1970), although referring to race, argue that stacking is a function of team management rather than of the players themselves. In 1969 in the CFL all 9 head coaches were Americans, as were 31 of the 32 assistant coaches, and 6 of the 9 general managers (the most recent year for which data were readily available (Smith and Grindstaff, 1970:4).

In effect what seems to happen is this: when Americans coaching in the CFL have a first-year prospect from the United States, they also have a set of expectations about his abilities based upon their knowledge of the calibre of football characteristic of the rookie's school, the level of competition, the coaching he likely received, etc. Alternatively, a new American prospect may have had professional experience in the States to generate such expectations among the coaches. For the Canadian collegiate football player (or one up from junior football) no such expectations exist. In a word, the American coaches know a lot about American football. They know little about football in Canada outside of the CFL. Thus, they are more likely to (i) go with the American import, who if not a proven quantity is likely to generate great expectations; and (ii) assume that Canadians, especially those without US collegiate experience, are simply less skilled or talented since they haven't been measured on the recognized testing grounds of the US playing fields.

If discrimination is too strong a word, *benign neglect* is not. These same coaches are, after all, responsible for the similar distribution of blacks at central and non-central positions in both American and Canadian professional football.

The question can also be raised as to why the centrality model is most powerful with regard to stacking and race and works best in the United States, and the primary-supporting model is more useful in accounting for stacking by national origin in the CFL.

First of all, though both models are concerned with ascription, there is a vast difference between race and nativity. And although there are many stereotypical assumptions about black athletes, especially in the US (see for instance, Edwards and Russell, 1971; Brower, 1972), it is not clear that there are similarly extensive attributions about Canadians, and by Americans concering the former's athletic ability (however, see Barnes, 1971).

Secondly, the centrality model was first (and most thoroughly) tested with regard to baseball, while the primary-supporting model was formulated specifically with regard to Canadian football, thus helping to account for its greater power regarding the CFL.

Thirdly, the centrality scheme emphasizes ascriptive differentiation on the basis of extra-organizational social characteristics, for example, race and interaction patterns. The primary-supporting model starts with organizational characteristics and then looks for ascriptive differentiation among members—and in the case of American-controlled but quota-bound Canadian football it finds them.

In the US situation there are no formal rules which require blacks to be on team rosters. In Canada, a fixed proportion of each roster must be Canadian. The primary-supporting model points to where those least talented or skilled will, in effect, be likely to do the least damage. Thus, blacks in the US (and US imports in Canada) play strictly on the basis of ability—in fact they may have to be better than their white counterparts (Rosenblatt, 1967)—but Canadians in the CFL are guaranteed their quota. Therefore, a task-based model should be more useful in predicting where they may be stacked, as the primary-supporting scheme in fact is.

In sum, Canadians in the CFL are stacked: on defence, in supporting and reactive positions; and even with US collegiate experience they are excluded from the more rewarding and desirable positions: This differential treatment is also reflected in the lower salaries they receive compared to those of imports. Whether caused by discrimination or benign neglect is a matter of definition—even if functionally equivalent in terms of consequences.

Needless to say, the usual *caveats* concerning further research apply here. The explanation of stacking which postulates a lack of expectations about Canadian players is speculative, but worthy of further interest. If valid, it is just one more tile in the mosaic of the branch plant economy. Finally, as will be obvious to many, this is not a "fan's-eye" view, but a sociological one. The fan may look for, and to, exceptions such as high-salaried, Canadian-trained quarterback Russ Jackson; the sociologist points instead to patterns. And, as has often been the case, the exposition of deviant-case analysis by laymen often functions to bolster the state of things as they are.

NOTES

1.   Unfortunately, sample data do not allow for this factor to be weighted or otherwise controlled. Its effect is to minimise actual differences, and to make apparent differences more conservative.

REFERENCES

Ball, Donald W.
1967   "Toward a sociology of toys: inanimate objects, socialization and the demography of the doll world." *Sociological Quarterly*, 8:447—458.

1971   "The cold war on ice: the politics of international figure skating." Paper presented to the third Canadian Symposium on Sport Psychology, Vancouver.

Barnes, LaVerne
1971   *The Plastic Orgasm*. Toronto: McClelland and Stewart.

Blalock, Hubert M., Jr.
1962   "Occupational discrimination: some theoretical propositions." *Social Problems*, 9:240—247.

Boyle, Robert H.
1963   *Sport—Mirror of American Life*. Boston: Little, Brown.

Brower, Jonathon J.
1972   "The racial basis of the division of labor among players in the National Football League as a function of racial stereotypes." Presented to the Pacific Sociological Association, Portland, April 13—15.

Cloward, Richard A., and Lloyd E. Ohlin
1960   *Delinquency and Opportunity*. Glencoe: The Free Press.

Cosentino, Frank
1969   *Canadian Football: The Grey Cup Years*. Toronto: Musson.

Davis, Kingsley
1949   *Human Society*. New York: Macmillan.

Edwards, Harry
1969   *The Revolt of the Black Athlete*. New York: The Free Press.

Edwards, Harry, and Bill Russell
1971   "Racism: a prime factor in the determination of black athletic superiority." Presented to the American Sociological Association, Denver, September.

Etzioni, Amitai
1961   *A Comparative Analysis of Complex Organizations*. Glencoe: The Free Press.

Garfinkel, Harold
1964   "Studies of the routine grounds of everyday activities." *Social Problems*, 11:255—250.

Grusky, Oscar
1963   "The effects of formal structure on managerial recruitment: a study of baseball organization." *Sociometry*, 26:345—353.

Homans, George C.
1950   *The Human Group*. New York: Harcourt, Brace and World.

Loy, John W., and Joseph F. McElvogue
1970   "Racial segregation in American sport." *International Review of Sport Sociology*, 5:5—24.

Meggysey, Dave
1970   *Out of Their League*. Berkeley: Ramparts Press.

Oates, Bob
1972   Column on the 1971 National Football League all-star team. *The Sporting News*, 173 (January 15):17.

Olsen, Jack
1968   *The Black Athlete—A Shameful Story*. New York, Time.

Rosenblatt, Aaron
1967   "The failure of success." *Trans-action*, 4:51-53.

Smith, Gary, and Carl F. Grindstaff
1970   "Race and sport in Canada." London: University of Western Ontario (mimeo).

Vallières, Pierre
1971   *White Niggers of America*. (Trans. by Joan Pinkham). New York and London: Monthly Review Press.

PART FOUR

The Formal Organization of Sport

Introduction*

A theme presented throughout this volume has been that sport develops as an institutionalized form of physical activity within a particular set of socio-historical conditions. It has been argued that all institutionalized aspects of sport, including its rules, ideologies, values and formal organizational structure emanate from its social (and especially material) context. From this perspective, the papers included in this section all illustrate some of the dynamics of the formal organization of sport in Canadian society.

To begin, we want to emphasize that one of the most striking manifestations of sport's institutionalization in twentieth-century Canadian life has been its transformation into a marketable commodity. As various organizations developed in an attempt to bring order, continuity and rational purpose to certain sport forms, it was inevitable in our capitalist economy that some of these organizations would tie sport into the marketplace. Subsequently, sport increasingly became structured into the dominant patterns of production and consumption in Canadian society, developing on the one hand a vast product market, and on the other a highly specialized labour market. What has followed, has simply been the progressive development of profit-maximizing organizations in the sport world which are designed to exploit these markets and regulate the manner in which "competition" occurs within them. In so doing, the purposes and goals of profit-maximization have come to define much of the organizational behaviour in the sport world, thereby conditioning the career lines of those who work within the constraints that such goals impose. [1]

The manner in which the principles of profit-maximization are reflected in the structure and policies of sports organizations is made clear in Colin Jones' (1969) study of the National Hockey League. Jones begins by emphasizing that the economics of the N.H.L. can best be understood by the application of basic microtheory based on a profit-maximizing hypothesis. The assumption is that the owners of each *club* want to maximize *personal profits*, but in order to do so, they must maximize *joint profits*. The maximization of joint profits necessitates organization into a *league of clubs* which can dictate subsequent intra and inter-league relationships. In other words, the owners of the individual clubs attempt to form a *cartel*, with the purpose of restricting competition and dividing markets among firms in the industry (cf., Noll, 1974(a).

---
*
 Co-authored by Rob Beamish

Jones examines two aspects of the N.H.L.'s late 1960's organizational structure—the output (or revenue) side, and the input (or player) side. Regarding revenue, Jones notes that profits in the N.H.L. have always been affected by four criteria (three of which were unaffected by the emergence of the W.H.A.): (a) sources of revenue; (b) interdependence of clubs; (c) the uncertainty of game outcomes; and (d) the monopoly of the product being marketed. As an axiom, revenue is dependent upon attracting people to watch games, and the greater the degree of uncertainty over the outcome, the more likely it is that people will attend. In order to maintain a high degree of uncertainty, the players (or supply variables) must be distributed as evenly as possible, and the distribution must be maintained. Finally, until the W.H.A. developed, the monopoly position of the N.H.L. influenced revenue by allowing the league to market a unique product without major competition cutting into the profits.

On the supply side, Jones discusses several factors which have helped the N.H.L. to maintain a relationship with players compatible with league goals. Some of the most important of these considerations include: (a) the *monopsony*[2] position of the N.H.L. which, until just recently, allowed the league to pay players as close to the *opportunity cost*[3] as possible; (b) the inter-league relationships between the N.H.L. and other professional and amateur leagues which served to "evenly" distribute talent through draft and firm agreements; and (c) the use of reserve caluses, options and "compensation" practice to restrict the free movement of players within the organizational structure.

It should be noted that Jones' paper was written during the late 1960's, and recent events have created a somewhat different set of circumstances. He attempts to account for some of these events in an updated postscript which considers the emergence of the W.H.A. and related legal issues of competitive policy. In the postscript Jones suggests that his early model continues to have a good deal of explanatory power.[4] The combined original paper and updated postscript present the reader with an excellent portrayal of how the dynamics of profit-maximizing organizations control the free movement of organizational personnel.[5]

In the next paper Barry McPherson examines the personnel turnover and organizational effectiveness of N.H.L. teams. McPherson sets out to test the hypothesis that personnel turnover enhances organizational effectiveness. This hypothesis is based on the premise that professional sports teams have always promoted, demoted, traded or drafted players in an attempt to develop a winning team. After a comparison of player performance data and won-lost records with rates of turnover, McPherson concludes that (in an aggregate sense) there does *not* appear to be a relationship between the entrance of new personnel at the management or labour level, and changes in group success.

McPherson's analysis is particularly interesting because it presents data challenging the widely-held belief that trades are necessary to build a "winner." But it should be seen that by the logic of Jones' profit-maximization thesis, the development of lopsided and consistent winning is impossible in an organizational structure that limits inter and intra-league personnel exchange patterns. This has implications for McPherson's study because it suggests that the most accurate definition of organizational "effectiveness" may be based less on "winning games" than it is on generating profit. Indeed, some personnel turnover undoubtedly exists to create either balanced competition or to attract a "crowd pleaser" (like Eddie Shack), rather than being geared toward the provision of "winning combinations." As Jones points out, "complete collusion" in the N.H.L. does not exist, but it is clear that the over-arching goal of the league has always been individual and joint profits. Thus, it may well be that personnel turnover bears little relationship to success when defined in terms of won-loss records, but it may have more congruence to success if success is defined in economic terms.

The final paper in this section is Mike Smith and Fred Diamond's study of career mobility among players in the National Hockey League. Smith and Diamond examined data on player's careers, and present findings to illustrate comparative patterns of mobility for both pre and post-N.H.L. expansion periods. While most of the players played ten years or more, and almost 60% played more than fifteen years, only a third of all players actually spent more than 10 years in the N.H.L. itself. In addition, many of the players failed to play the five years necessary for full pension benefits.

League expansion is often thought to have extended the careers of many players, but Smith and Diamond argue that expansion appears to have had little effect on extending the occupational tenure of the "marginal" player. While the "longevity" of "established" or "star" players increased slightly with expansion, the number of players who played "four years or less" differed only slightly from the pre-expansion period. It appears then, that the formal organizational structure of the N.H.L. (and of all professional team sports) creates an environment where careers are of short duration. Smith and Diamond suggest that the environment also leads to a high degree of involuntary career movement through trades, promotions and demotions. One out of every three professional hockey players in the post-expansion era has experienced four or more downward moves (demotions), and another third has experienced two or three downward moves. In fact, Smith and Diamond emphasize that 70% of all players in the professional game have terminated their careers in the minors. Using qualitative examples they conclude their discussion by indicating the impact that such moves have on the players themselves.

As a final part of this introduction we want to add a brief note about players' salaries, their working conditions, and some of the generally perceived "problems" in modern professional sport. There are two popular images of modern professional athletes: (a) the athlete as alienated labourer and (b) the athlete as over-paid elite entertainer. In the first case, as Smith and Diamond point out, the degree to which personal autonomy can flourish in profit-maximizing organizational structures is a questionable one. Professional athletes working in such settings are easily alienated, since the organizing principles involved, allow athletes to become nothing more than "objects" that have commercial value (cf., Ingham, 1975).[6] The problem however is that in our present sociopolitical system *all* wage-earners become commodities to some extent. As a result the term alienation has become "one of the chief cant phrases of our time, lumping together the mildest of dyspepsias with some of our deepest metaphysical fears" Jay, 1973:XV).   Perhaps the great irony of professional athletics is that the "players" (read workers) are doing something that they claim to love and which ideally should be highly liberating; but they are only doing it in an environment where they have little control over their actions and where the goal is simple production. To compete and be paid for it, is all that some ask. For others, no price is high enough. Nonetheless, if we move our analysis from the problems of autonomy and powerlessness to the basic facts of income, we note that despite the potentially alienating conditions of the framework within which sports careers are pursued, there is indeed a good deal of money to be made. Obviously, the "athlete as proletarian" thesis is challenged by the comparatively advantaged positions that many professional athletes hold in the societal reward structure.

Yet, while professional athletes are hardly "working class" in the traditional blue collar sense, there is some danger in elevating them to a status that transcends their actual social position. The "athlete as over-paid elite entertainer" is as narrow an interpretation as the "athlete as proletarian." Consider salaries. In 1973, as economist Gerald Scully (1974) points out, the average income in the N.H.L. was 40,000 dollars[7] (Jones estimates the 1974 N.H.L. average to be in excess of 60,000 dollars)—high perhaps, but in these inflationary times not completely out of line with the highest ranking salaries of other bourgeois professional occupations. When this figure is coupled with the occupational tenure data presented by Smith and Diamond, the image one gets is not so much the champagne life of the sports star but rather of the career lines of athletic-journeymen whose ascent into the income brackets of the upper-middle class *rarely* transforms itself into lasting social or economic privilege. However, the popular image of today's professional athletes is that they are all "making it big" and that their inflated salaries are making professional sport unprofitable, driving up ticket prices and indeed threatening the very structure of professional sport itself. While it is certainly true that the salaries of some athletes seem excessive, to blame the financial problems in professional sports on athletes' salaries exclusively, is not only faulty logic; it is bad economics. Ticket prices for example, are *not* determined in the *labour market*, they are determined in the *product market* (cf., Noll 1974 (b); Scully, 1974).

> What is being divided among the players and the owners is monopoly rents accruing from the monopoly franchise rights of the team. The division of these rents between players and owners depends on institutional rules but it does not affect the price. The optimal price that a team will charge is the same whether players salaries are high or low . . . (Noll, 1974(b):13-14).

In summary, we want to stress that basic "problems" in the world of professional sport do not lie with players' unionization, with their salaries or with such things as over-expansion, diluted leagues, and teams which jump from city to city. These are, after all, only manifestations of the contradictions that are inherent in profit-maximization itself. It is here that the problem lies, and as long as professional sport is based on this principle, it will be unrealistic to suggest that social or community needs will be a factor affecting "policy" in the athletic marketplace.

NOTES

1. There are several good reviews of sports organizations as profit-maximizers. Two of the most comprehensive are Noll (1974(a)) and Burman (1974).
2. Monopsony is a one buyer market, as opposed to monopoly which is a one seller market. The players have only one buyer to whom they may sell their labour power. Thus, competition for employment positions depresses the bargaining power of the player. Jones states that "although the clubs may fail to minimize player costs in line with their monopsony power, this is not due to any benevolent use of their power, but rather to the fact that such power is not absolute." It should be noted that while monopsony power is not "absolute" to "key" players on a team—it is virtually absolute to marginal players. As Brian Conacher (1970:56-59) indicates, when a player goes to training camp, it is not 85 players trying out for 20 positions, but 70 players trying out for two or three (See Barnes 1970:145-63) and Meggyesy (1971: 134-138) for some critical views on contract negotiations.)

3. Opportunity cost is a comparison of actual cost and the cost that would have been involved in deploying resources in a manner other than the one selected. Jones points out that an owner has the opportunity to employ various combinations of player personnel to field a competitive team. The owner has the opportunity to weigh the cost of a "star studded" line up of high-priced players with one of marginal, low cost players, or some combination of the two. Because of a monopsony position, owners can play off these variables to force down opportunity cost.

4. Economic theory cannot exist by itself as a predictive model, because to do so, it must assume that man acts like a commodity in a non-voluntaristic fashion. Thus in the postscript Jones can only infer rather than accurately *deduce* what will happen to hockey in the future. The attitude of players like Robin Sadler (cf., Globe and Mail, *Weekend Magazine*, Jan. 24, 1976) who turn down 250,000 dollar contracts because the game is not enjoyable, the unpredictable nature of government action and the prospects for increasingly militant "labour" action by players, all serve to emphasize the role played by subjectively motivated human action which cannot be accounted for in purely economic models (cf., Anspach, 1974; Foley, 1975).

5. The N.H.L.'s board of governors has always contended that such restrictions on competition in business practice is necessary in order to promote competition on the ice. We want to emphasize that the validity of this contention has been increasingly challenged in recent years (Canes, 1974; Noll, 1974(a); 1974(b); Scully 1974; Scoville, 1974). Its acceptance or rejection stands at the heart of the debate over the social justification for restrictive business practices in professional sport.

6. The "alienation" issue is a complex one that we cannot detail in the introduction at hand. An excellent (but challenging) discussion of alienation in sport can be found in Ingham (1975). For some journalistic discussions of the effects of alienation, see Terkel (1974: 499; the section on Eric Nesterenko) and Shaw (1972).

7. Scully points out that 1973 averages for football and basketball were 27,500 and 90,000 dollars respectively. The average N.H.L. salary the year prior to the development of the W.H.A. was 25,000 dollars. It rose to 40,000 with a year of the W.H.A.'s development. Of course, salaries have continued to rise since 1973 (some journalists "estimate" that the 1976 average may go as high as 80,000 dollars), however, it should be pointed out, that averages are often misleading statistics where income is concerned, because they tend to inflate given the existance of a few very high salaries. We suggest that the *median* income (the point at which 50% of the cases fall above or below) of athletes would be much lower.

REFERENCES

Anspach, Ralph
1974   "The Inconsistency of Current Micro-and Macro- theories and the Conception of Man as a Factor of Production." *Review of Social Economy*, 32, April.

Barnes, Laverne
1971   *The Plastic Orgasm.* Toronto: Simon and Schuster.

Burman, George (ed.)
1974   *Proceedings of the Conference on the Economics of Professional Sports.* Washington: National Football League Players Association.

Canes, Michael
1974   "The Social Benefits of Restrictions on Team Quality." In Roger Noll (ed.), *Government and the Sports Business.* Washington: The Brookings Institute.

Conacher, Brian
1970   *Hockey in Canada: The Way It Is.* Toronto: Gateway Press.

Foley, Duncan
1975   "Problems vs. Conflicts: Economics Theory and Ideology." *The American Economic Review*, 65, May.

Ingham, Alan
1975   "Occupational Subcultures in the Work World of Sport." In D. Ball and John W. Loy (eds.), *Sport and Social Order*. Reading: Addison-Wesley.

Jay, Martin
1973   *The Dialectical Imagination*. Boston: Little Brown.

Meggyesy, Dave
1971   *Out of Their League*. New York: Ramparts Press.

Noll, Roger
1974(a)   "The U.S. Team Sports Industry: An Introduction." In Roger Noll (ed.), *Government and the Sports Business*. Washington: The Brookings Institute.
1974(b)   "The Product Market in Sport." In George Burman (ed.), *Proceedings of the Conference on the Economics of Professional Sports*. Washington: National Football League Players Association.

Scully Gerald
1974   "Player Salaries." In George Burman (ed.), *Proceedings of the Conference on the Economics of Professional Sports*. Washington: National Football League Players Association.

Scoville, James
1974   "Labour Relations in Sports." In Roger Noll (ed.), *Government and the Sports Business*. Washington: The Brookings Institute.

Shaw, Gary
1972   *Meat on the Hoof*. New York: Dell Books

Terkel, Studs
1975   *Working*. New York: Avon Books.

THE ECONOMICS OF THE NATIONAL HOCKEY LEAGUE*[1]

J. C. H. Jones

Recently there have been attempts to bring the NHL under the Combines Act.[2] These resulted from the NHL's failure to grant Vancouver and Quebec City franchises in the expanded league, and from the refusal

* Thanks are extended to: Professors J. R. Gould, London School of Economics, W. R. D. Sewel, G. R. Elliott, L. Laudadio, and L. I. Bakony, University of Victoria, who made many helpful suggestions; and Dick Beddoes, Ernie Fedoruk, Ivan Temple, Scott Young, and the NHL and its member clubs who provided invaluable background information.

to allow a former player to "retire" to join the Canadian National (amateur) Team. Consequently, on the assumption that such actions demonstrate that the NHL is a business like any other business and thus, presumably, should be treated like any other business, it must fall under the Act.[3] Alternatively, it has long been argued by team owners that their prime interest is in "love of the game"[4] and not in a purely business venture. It is the purpose of this paper to show that, given the unique features of professional sport, the conduct of the NHL can be explained without any behavioural assumption of "love", by the application of basic microtheory based on a profit maximizing hypothesis. This is done by constructing a theoretical model of the NHL and testing the implications of the model against its actual conduct.

The Theoretical Framework

The unique feature of professional sport is that in the sporting production function no club[5] in and of itself produces a saleable output (a game), only an input (the arena and/or the team). Therefore, each club must form a coalition with another club to produce a revenue-generating output. Total revenue is the product of number of games, number of seats sold, and average price per seat. Given that a coalition between at least two clubs if necessary, when the number of clubs exceeds two, a super coalition of clubs (a formal organization, the league) is more effective and efficient in performing certain joint functions, for instance, distributing the group product (scheduling), and dealing with the relationships between clubs and between the group and other groups.

Given mutual dependence, let us assume the following. First, the optimum goal of each club is to maximize profits. Second, the league desires to maximize the material welfare of its member clubs and therefore its optimum goal is that the clubs act so as to maximize joint profits. In an oligopoly situation neither optimum will be attained. Instead, because of the opposing forces which simultaneously move the clubs between the two optima, a qualified joint profit maximizing position will be achieved (Fellner, 1965). In this case the position will be one which is compatible with maintaining the viability—that is, the survival—of the league. [6] Given mutual dependence, a club cannot survive if all other clubs do not survive. Hence, the actions of each club must be constrained by the operational necessity of maintaining the league. Thus, the "equilibrium" position for the group is one in which the clubs are earning profits that are sufficient to keep them in the league and so preserve the viability of that organization.

Subject to the constraints that the league remain viable and that the institutional framework is given and does not change throughout the analysis,[7] let us assume that each club wishes to maximize profits. So, with output given, each club attempts to maximize revenue and minimize costs. In these circumstances we would expect the following.

On the revenue side, though the demand for the output is a function of the usual variables[8] (tastes, prices, incomes, quality, substitutes, etc.) the most interesting feature of the sporting demand function is *competition* between teams. Thus, other things being equal, the greater the degree of competition the larger the crowds and, hence, the greater the revenue. The degree of competition can be measured by the degree of uncertainty over the outcome of the game, so that the greater the uncertainty the larger the "gate." However, when uncertainty disappears and the result can be predicted with a high probability of success, attendance suffers. Consequently, mutual dependence is not confined solely to producing a game but also to producing a crowd, because the revenue of every club depends on the performance of *both* teams. Clear superiority or inferiority affects the gate of both teams because it reduces uncertainty. Therefore, for the league as a whole the greater the uncertainty of the outcome (the closer the teams are in rank standing, the "better balanced" the league), the greater the aggregate attendance. Hence, the aim being to maximize revenue we would expect that, in contrast to most oligopolistic situations, the group wishes to promote competitive equality between clubs.

However, for each club to accept unequivocally joint profit maximization as furthering its own aim of profit maximization it must be assumed that collusion is complete (Fellner, 1965:131-2) and that no club has any incentive for winning continually. If these two latter requirements are not met, the desire to maximize uncertainty will no longer be paramount. If for instance the incentive to win exists, clubs will desire to increase the certainty of winning the game, rather than the uncertainty of its outcome.

This gives rise to two conflicts—first, between optimum group and club objectives and the means by which they may be achieved; and second, between clubs. If there are consistent winners and losers, the non-attainment of goals by losers will result in pressure to improve their positions. This inter-club conflict could result in warfare which might destroy the league as a viable organization, so worsening the position of every club. Therefore we would expect a solution compatible with preserving the viability of the league. Although it will not be one which results either in joint profit maximization for the group or attempted profit maximization for each club, it will ensure group "equilibrium."

On the supply side, the single most important input is the human one —the players. This is the major element promoting uncertainty over the outcome of the game. Hence we would expect that most moves by the group to improve inter-club competition would involve some means of redistributing or equalizing this element. In addition, the players distinguish NHL hockey on a quality basis from all other hockey. That is, NHL hockey is superior to all other hockey because its inputs are superior. Therefore, one would expect the NHL to attempt to obtain the best players available, vis-à-vis other competitive leagues. Finally, in the cause of minimizing the cost of this input we would expect the group to minimize inter-club competition for factors.

Consequently, if the foregoing is correct we would expect that: (1) the league attempts to promote competitive equality between clubs primarily through the redistribution of players; (2) should collusion be incomplete then solutions other than (1) will be adopted in order to maintain group stability; (3) the group will attempt to employ the best players available so as to differentiate their product from other similar products; (4) they will attempt to accomplish (3) at minimum cost. In order to see if these predictions are borne out by the actual behaviour of the NHL the remainder of the paper is divided into: a brief outline of the pertinent organizational characteristics of the NHL and testing propositions (1) and (2); an examination of (3) and (4); and application of the theory to those 1966 issues which gave rise to the policy questions—the NHL expansion and the new professional-amateur hockey agreement.

Demand and Revenue (Pre-Expansion)

The organization of the NHL (1966) is defined by the following structural characteristics. The National Hockey League is made up of six clubs (in Canada, Toronto and Montreal, and in the United States, Boston, Chicago, Detroit, and New York), each of which holds a franchise which allows commercial exploitation of NHL hockey in a defined spatial area (the city in which the club is located plus a radius of 50 miles of the corporate limit). This monopoly right is marketable as the franchise may be sold and/or moved subject to the agreement of three-quarters of the remaining league clubs. Each club is selling a highly differentiated product (NHL hockey) and entry is completely blocked unless the group decides to admit new clubs. The league itself is governed by one representative from each club (Board of Governors) and a president who supervises its day-to-day operations. Its function, aside from providing a formal channel of communication, is chiefly administrative; the president is merely the agent of the owners having nothing more than control over the "morals of the game."[9] The intra-league relationships are explicitly defined by the league constitution and by-laws, although a considerable degree of latitude is allowed each club in its own spatial market area. For instance, each club is allowed to set its own admission prices, and negotiate TV and radio contracts; each team participates in 70 games, 35 at home and the same number "on the road"; the revenue from any game goes entirely to the home club and, assuming no TV receipts, depends on the number of paid admissions; and, any game is sold at a variety of different prices which, depending on one's view of the relationship between the seat and the view of the game, can be considered either product differentiation or price discrimination.

PROPOSITION 1. PLAYER REDISTRIBUTION AND COMPETITIVE EQUALITY

The data necessary to test statistically the relationship between attendance and uncertainty as specified by the model are unfortunately unavailable.[10] However, it seems that, in order to attempt to ensure a degree of uncertainty the NHL clubs have adopted a system of what could be called co-operative "handicapping," the object of which is to try and ensure that individual clubs do not accumulate all the best players and so destroy inter-club competition. The more obvious examples are as follows: (1) each club is allowed a maximum number of players under contract—a "reserve list" of 30 players plus 3 goal keepers —and out of these 33 an NHL "protected list" of 18 plus 2 goal keepers. Any player not on a "protected list" but on a reserve list who is under contract to an NHL club can be drafted (claimed) by another NHL club for a fixed draft price of $30,000 (1967); (2) any NHL draft is based on the *last* club in the league having first pick of all non-protected players. Then it is the turn of the fifth club and so on in inverse order of league standing; (3) during the course of a season a club may wish to assign a player to a club outside the NHL. This the club cannot do unless all clubs in the league agree, in effect "waiving" him through the league. If any other league club wants the player on waivers it may claim him at the predetermined waiver price. Again, the team ranked last in the league at the time waivers were asked has first choice.

Such handicapping is necessary because complete collusion does not exist. Although the clubs have solved many of the problems which distrupt typical oligopolistic arrangements—particularly, each club sets its own prices in its own monopolistic spatial area—collusion is still incomplete because playing talent is distributed unequally and there is incentive to win.

TABLE I

PAID ATTENDANCE AS A PERCENTAGE OF MAXIMUM SEATING CAPACITY AND FINAL RANK IN LEAGUE FOR
CHICAGO BLACK HAWKS, 1949-47 to 1966-67

Season	Final rank in League	Paid attendance as a percentage of maximum seating capacity[a]
1946 − 47	6	85
1947 − 48	6	84
1948 − 49	5	81
1949 − 50	6	67
1950 − 51	6	44
1951 − 52	6	26
1952 − 53	4	47
1953 − 54	6	24
1954 − 55	6	23
1955 − 56	6	26
1956 − 57	6	22
1957 − 58	5	35
1958 − 59	3	44
1959 − 60	3	49
1960 − 61	3	60
1961 − 62	3	70
1962 − 63	2	92
1963 − 64	2	99
1964 − 65	3	100
1965 − 66	2	105
1966 − 67	1	103

SOURCE: Estimated from figures supplied by the NHL.

[a]Where the figures exceed 100 this means that all seats were sold and the remainder of
the crowd utilized standing room.

PROPOSITION 2. COMPETITIVE EQUALITY AND GROUP STABILITY

If playing talent were not unequally distributed we would expect every
game to end in a tie, or each team to win exactly half its games, or each
club to win the league championship one-sixth of the time (preferably
once every six years). None of these hypotheses is supported by the facts.
For instance, in the twenty seasons from 1946-47 to 1965-66, Montreal
finished first nine times and second seven; Detroit finished first nine
times, second twice, and from 1948-49 to 1956-57 finished first every
year except one, when they finished second. At the other end of the
scale, during the same time span, Boston finished last five times, and
fifth four times, the highest finish being scored in 1948-49 and 1958-59;
Chicago finished last nine times and fifth twice; New York finished last
four times and fifth ten times; Toronto finished first twice, second five
times and last only once. Thus, given the unequal distribution of ability,
maximum uncertainty cannot result.

At the same time there is an incentive to *win*. The first four ranked teams in the league compete for the Stanley Cup, a post-regular season finale which increases the revenue of these clubs. In addition, given the degree of uncertainty, a winning club draws larger crowds than a losing one. This latter point has been frequently noted (Deacon, 1952), and Chicago is often cited as the prime example. Despite the lack of data necessary to estimate accurately the demand function, there does appear to be a correlation between Chicago's performance (winning or losing) and attendance. This is shown in Table I. Following the Second World War attendance was high but fell consistently as the club's record of futility continued (1946-47 to 1951-52). In 1952-53 the club made the "play-offs" and attendance rose but fell again as the club reverted to last place. In 1957-58 the team finally escaped last place and attendance increased. By 1958-59 they reached the play-offs and since then have never finished lower than third—a situation reflected in the club's attendance figures.

The upshot of incomplete collusion is conflict between optimum group goals and club goals, and between club goals. These conflicts could destroy the league so there must be some solution other than maximizing uncertainty. If we assume that the game results are not rigged in advance, two solutions (or some combination of the two) suggest themselves.

First, there must be a system of side payments whereby winners compensate losers. This could take the form either of profit redistribution or redistribution of that element which primarily promotes the uncertainty —the players. For instance, at the end of each season profits could be redistributed or the best players from the winning clubs could be transferred to the losing clubs. If a financial side payment were adopted the object would be to attempt to retain the club goal and achieve a form of joint profit maximization without maximizing uncertainty. Yet this would only ensure a more or less equal profit distribution because, unless it is assumed that the demand curve facing the individual club is quite inelastic, group revenue would fall as the degree of certainty increased. This, however, ignores all the difficulties which arise in practice when group revenue is shared.[11] With player redistribution, the objective would be to maximize uncertainty by moving closer to the optimum group goal. In effect, this would completely subordinate club objectives to the group which, as long as there is ony incentive to win at all, would be alien to the club. However, the draft and waiver system is a "human" side payment which goes part way towards solving the conflict problem by moving closer to the group goal of maximizing uncertainty. Nevertheless, it does not go all the way.[12]

Second, the objectives of the clubs must undergo some reassessment because they are unattainable simultaneously, and joint profit maximization requires complete adherence to group objectives. Consequently, there must be recourse to a second-best solution which ensures group stability even though it represents a non-optimum situation from the point of view of each club. To deny this is to ignore the implications of the fact that each club is mutually dependent on another club. Thus, although the best of all worlds for the club is the certainty of victory, because of mutual dependence such victory may be a pyrrhic one at the gate. Hence, for every club, the minimum of all possible acceptable solutions is not to be a consistent loser; but the minimum of all possible maximum solutions is to qualify for the Stanley Cup play-offs. In other words, in the NHL a "winning club" is one which makes the Stanley Cup play-offs which means finishing ranked in the first four in the league. From this point of view, the league championship is nothing more than a 210 game elimination contest to decide which clubs have the distinction of playing off for "The World's Hockey Championship." (This should not be confused with the World Championships sponsored by the International Amateur Hockey Association.)

The fact that there are *four* winners resolves much inter-club conflict by increasing the chance that each club has of "winning." However, the clubs are not totally indifferent about their position in the first four rankings because the first-and-second-place clubs play off against the third-and-fourth-place clubs and have the home ice advantage for four out of the seven games. Thus, we have competition for "league standing." This tends to spread the degree of competition among more teams in the league.

At the same time, although the probability of winning the Stanley Cup is a positive function of league standing—between 1946-47 and 1968-69, the league winner has won the trophy ten times, the runner-up six times, the third-place team three times, and the fourth twice—the league winner has in fact only won it less than 50 per cent of the time. Hency the degree of uncertainty over which is the superior team increases with the addition of the play-offs.

If this argument is correct one would expect to see the influence of striving to reach the play-offs reflected in attendance figures. Again, although total statistical information is imperfect, this would appear to be the case. For example, between 1948-49 and 1968-69, Montreal never played to less than 100 per cent of seating capacity. But during that time it was never out of the play-offs and won eight Stanley Cups—five in a row.[13] During the same period, Toronto never played to less than 100 percent of seating capacity. However, it failed to make the play-offs only twice and won seven Stanley Cups. Similarly, Detroit has only missed the play-offs once and although it only reached 100 per cent of seating capacity in 1966-67, attendance has been very stable, never falling below 72 per cent of capacity.

When a club does not achieve its minimum objectives it will create pressure to change more fundamentally the rules of conduct which govern intra-league relationships. For instance, some clubs may not make the play-offs for a long period of time. Or again, the waiver rule may not fulfil its purpose because, as waivers can be withdrawn, they may be a search for market information as a prelude to trading. Then, if the league is to remain viable more drastic changes will have to be made. The two most notable examples concern the introduction of: (1) the original intra-league draft in 1954 and (2) the universal amateur (Junior) draft in 1962.

(1) In the late forties and early fifties there were in effect two divisions in the NHL: Detroit, Montreal, and Toronto—whose successes were reflected at the gate; and Boston, New York, and Chicago who had difficulty winning and drawing crowds. Chicago was about to drop out of the league. However, James D. Norris was "urged" to buy the club by the Board of Governors of the NHL even though he already had an interest in the New York Rangers (and holding an interest in more than one club was illegal under the NHL constitution). Norris agreed to buy the franchise, (United States, 1957:2972-77) but the problem was the quality of the players. Norris attempted to buy players from the "have" clubs but their owners would not co-operate. The upshot was that in 1954 a draft rule was adopted by the NHL clubs over the protests of Montreal against whose highly productive farm system it was directed (Selke, 1962:137).

Under this system each club was only permitted to "protect" a maximum of 18 players and two goalkeepers. Beyond this number a player under contract to any NHL club could be drafted for $15,000. This innovation assured the league as a whole of a pool of professional talent no matter how unproductive the individual farm systems might be, and went some way towards satisfying the weaker teams.

(2) The introduction of the amateur draft arose out of the Shock incident. In the early sixties Boston was consistently last in the league. To try to rectify the situation Boston attempted to buy the best Junior prospect in Ontario and Quebec. This involved Boston in a price war with other NHL clubs over Ron Shock. Boston apparently won out with a bonus of $10,000 and signified their willingness to repeat the process with other Juniors (Beddoes, 1966). Such financial competition was averted when the clubs agreed to establish the universal amateur draft

whereby weaker teams could draft two players from their competitiors' sponsored teams at a fixed price ($3,000). Once again, there was a pronounced shift in league policy to counteract the pressure placed on it by one club.

Both these examples illustrate two striking facts. First, both moves were in the direction of increasing the competitiveness of all clubs. Secondly, despite potential and actual conflict the inter-club agreement is stable over time. Although most of the conditions for stable collusion are present—small numbers and a formal organization make policing easier, markets are spatially separated, there is no unilateral price policy, and there is group control over new innovations and entrants—the factor which distinguishes the professional sporting leagues from other oligopolistic coteries is *mutual dependence*. Once the implications of this are grasped the only factors that can destroy the group are: shifts in the demand for the product which forces withdrawal of the league or clubs; ignoring mutual dependence so that one or two teams become so superior as to reduce uncertainty to zero; the wish of members of the group to dissolve the league;[14] or competition from some other group which sells a generically similar product.

Thus, on the revenue side the model appears to explain the activities of the NHL quite well.

Supply and Cost

On the supply side the model implied that the NHL would attempt to employ the best players available vis-à-vis other leagues so as to differentiate their product, and that they would do so at the minimum possible costs. The league largely succeeds in the former through its monopsonistic power in the labour market, the result being that the NHL sells a superior product and simultaneously keeps out potential entrants. However, although inter-club competition for players is reduced almost to zero, it is not certain that clubs maximize rent by forcing wages to opportunity costs because the lack of information allows only a highly speculative conclusion.

PROPOSITION 3. LABOUR MARKET CONTROL AND INTER-CLUB COMPETITION (1966)

The monopsonistic position of the NHL and its clubs is based on the standard player's contract and the protected list, on ownership of and affiliation agreements with, minor professional league clubs, and on the

CAHA-NHL agreement which gives the NHL control of amateur hockey. The result is that the hockey labour market can be considered to be vertically integrated (see Figure 1). It may be roughly divided into three stages pyramidically:[15] at the apex stands the NHL; one stage further back, the minor professional leagues; finally at the base the amateur leagues which are themselves vertically integrated on an age basis (see Figure 1, n. 2). Each of these stages may be thought of as adding *quality* to the input so that the NHL ultimately ends up with the superior player. Thus, in contrast to vertical integration in product markets, the NHL is not interested in the minor league outputs as inputs in the NHL, but only in the fact that by producing outputs the minor leagues add quality (seasoning) to their inputs which in turn become NHL inputs. Nevertheless, control over outputs does give the NHL clubs direct control over inputs.

FIGURE 1

VERTICAL INTEGRATION IN THE HOCKEY MARKET

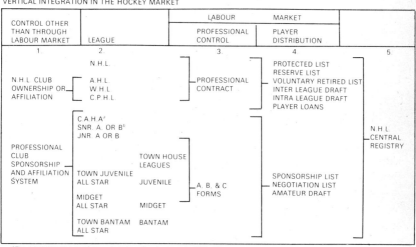

[a] The administrative breakdown into branches is shown in Table III.

[b] The age limits for the competitive categories are Senior and Intermediate (no limit). Junior (under 20), Juvenile (under 18), Midget (under 16), Bantam (under 14), Pee Wee (not shown, under 12).

Broadly, the vertical system works as follows: NHL clubs own and control clubs in the minor professional leagues and, through the "sponsorship" and "affiliation" system, amateur clubs (Figure 1, col. (1)). At the amateur level, in order to play in Juvenile or Junior clubs players have signed "option" agreements (col. (3)), which gives the professional club ownership of amateur playing rights and the right to require the players to sign a professional contract when requested to do so. All professional players are tied to the NHL club by the contract (col. (3)), and are distributed among teams and leagues according to distribution lists (col. (4)). The whole distribution system is run by the NHL Central Registry (col. (5)), an arm of the league charged with keeping track of and co-ordinating all changes in player distribution.

The major bases of monopsony power and their influence on inter-club competition for players are as follows.

(i) *Standard professional contract.*[16] Although the club that signs a player has prior monopsonistic claim to his services (up to the limit imposed by the protected list), in effect he becomes part of the professional hockey player pool because he can be traded, drafted, or assigned to another club (United States 1957:2988). The monopsonistic status of the club is determined by the "assignment,"[17] and "option" clauses of the contract. The former clearly spells out that the player has no control over where and for whom he plays professional hockey. Failure to report to the club to which he may be sold or transferred, means suspension. This in turn means, not only that he cannot play for any other professional club, but that, as the CAHA recognizes all professional suspensions, he cannot play amateur hockey. Thus there is no way he can earn a living by playing hockey other than with an NHL sponsored club. Indeed, once a contract has been signed there are only two ways he can escape the NHL and still play hockey. First, he may no longer have the ability to remain in professional hockey so that, after asking waivers, the club concerned can terminate the contract. Second, he may retire from professional hockey by placing his name on the club's "voluntary retired list" and with the club's *permission* be reinstated by the CAHA.[18]

Complementing the assignment clauses is the "option" or "reserve" clause (clause 17) the burden of which is to put the onus of contract renewal solely on the club. The player cannot break the contract by refusing to sign and still continue to play hockey, and although provision is made for compulsory arbitration, it turns out that the arbitrator is the league president.

The "reserve clause" in conjunction with the "protected list" produces a system which, according to the league president, is the most effective and efficient for producing competitive equality (United States 1958: 506). The argument usually advanced to support this contention is that because the league is made up of rich and poor clubs, if the market were free rich teams would bid away all the choice talent. The outcome would presumably be a diminution of the necessary uncertainty. However, this argument ignores the mutual dependence which must exist, the fact that there has not been competitive equality in the NHL for the last 20 years, and that the cost of entry ensures that there are no rich and poor clubs. Moreover, the equality of competition can be brought about equally well by the free market.[19] But the reserve rule makes it cheaper. Clearly, the reserve clause is an element of market control which stops the player from selling his services to the highest bidder. This is perfectly consistent with the club wishing to minimize cost.

(ii) *The minor professional leagues* In their organizational set-up, distribution lists, and in the rules governing inter-club conduct, the minors are almost exact replicas of the NHL. The single most pertinent fact is that they operate as a farm system for developing NHL players. They are dominated by the NHL either through direct NHL club ownership, affiliation agreements with NHL clubs, or the "joint affiliation agreement"[20] between the NHL and the minor leagues.

The degree of ownership integration varies with each NHL club—on the one hand, each owns a CPHL team, on the other, in 1966 only Toronto was fully integrated by ownership of Rochester, Victoria, and Tulsa.[21] But every NHL club either through ownership or affiliation is represented in each league (see Table II). Broadly speaking "affiliation" defines a relationship between a minor and major club whereby the NHL club loans players to the minor club (or provides other financial assistance), and the minor clubs allow the NHL clubs to use spaces on their lists.[22] From the point of view of control, the key element in the agreement is that, in contrast to NHL clubs, minor clubs can transfer players directly to the NHL without first obtaining waivers from clubs in their own league. In addition, should the farm system of a particular NHL club fail to produce sufficient talent, minor league players may be drafted (for inter-league draft, see Figure 1, col. (4)).

These relationships ensure that the distribution of professional playing talent is in the hands of the NHL and so automatically precludes the minor leagues from challenging the position of the NHL.

(iii) *The amateur leagues* The main factors giving the NHL effective control of amateur hockey are the following three points from the CAHA-NHL agreement.[23]

First, the CAHA recognizes the NHL as the sole and exclusive governing body and bargaining authority for professional hockey.

Second, the NHL obtains direct access to the labour market through the sponsorship system. Sponsorship means the exclusive right of *a professional* team to direct the affairs of any two amateur teams (United

TABLE II

THE OWNERSHIP AND AFFILIATE RELATIONSHIP BETWEEN THE PROFESSIONAL
LEAGUES AND CLUBS, AND THEIR JUNIOR SPONSORED CLUBS
(as of January 1967)

Leagues	Professional and Junior Clubs								
NHL JUNIOR[a]	Boston Estevan Niagara Falls	Chicago St. Catharines Dixie Beehive	Detroit Weyburn Hamilton	Montreal Montreal Peterboro	New York Kitchener Burlington	Toronto Marlboros Ottawa			
CPHL[b] JUNIOR[a]	Oklahoma Winnipeg Braves Winnipeg Warriors	St. Louis Sudbury Moose Jaw	Memphis Edmonton Oil Kings Edmonton Canadians	Houston Chatham Lachine Maroons	Omaha Brandon North Bay	Tulsa Markham London			
AHL[c] JUNIOR[a]	Hershey Oshawa Winnipeg Monarchs	Buffalo Sarnia	Pittsburgh Stratford (& minor assoc.) St. Jerome (& minor assoc.)	Quebec Regina Pats Quebec	Baltimore Kitchener	Rochester Cornwall Trois Rivières	Providence Nationale Maisonneuve	Cleveland Kirkland Verdun Maple Leafs	Springfield
WHL[c] JUNIOR[a]	San Francisco Shawinigan Waterloo	Portland Flin Flon Fredericton (& whole assoc.)	Los Angeles Saskatoon Sorel Hawks	Seattle Ft. William Hull	Vancouver Winnipeg Rangers Kingston Frontenacs	Victoria Calgary Buffalos Melville (Sask.)			

[a] Junior A and B.

[b] Each club is owned by the NHL club vertically above it.

[c] The clubs in this league have working agreements with more than one NHL club.

States, 1957: 3054-58). However, due to ownership and affiliation at the minor professional level, the NHL club really directs eight or more amateur clubs. Taking Toronto as an example, this can be illustrated by Table II. Toronto directly sponsors two Junior teams, the Marlboros and Ottawa. But in 1966 through its ownership of Tulsa, Rochester, and Victoria it sponsored Junior teams in Markham, London, Cornwall, Trois Rivières, Calgary, and Melville.

In addition to the NHL, two sponsored clubs rule. The CAHA definition of a *club* includes Senior, Intermediate, Junior or Juvenile, Midget and Bantam teams, so that sponsorship can give rise to a chain of affiliates which increase the degree of vertical integration (See Figure 1, col. (2)) (Canada, 1967: 13-14).

Table III, in conjunction with Table II, shows that there is geographical concentration of sponsorships in Ontario and Quebec, and in the large metropolitan centres throughout the country. This means that there has been considerable player mobility which has led to wholesale special exceptions to CAHA rules concerning inter- and intra-branch transfers.

TABLE III

NUMBER OF SPONSORED JUNIOR TEAMS AND ALL JUNIOR TEAMS IN EACH CAHA BRANCH
(as of January 1967)

Branch	Number of Junior A teams	Number of other Junior teams	Number of sponsored teams
British Columbia[a]	10	13	0
Alberta[a]	6	8	3
Saskatchewan[a]	6	6	6
Manitoba[a]	6	7	6
Thunder Bay[b]	8	0	1
Ontario Hockey Assoc.[c]	13	111	11A + 9B
Ottawa and District[d]	10	20	2
Quebec[e]	18	66	11
Maritimes[f]	12	0	1
Newfoundland[a]	7	0	0
Canada	96	231	50

[a] Branch covers the entire province.

[b] North-West Ontario, west of the 85th Meridian.

[c] Ontario (excluding Thunder Bay, and Ottawa and District) plus the counties of Temiscamingue, Rouyn, Noranda, Abitibi East, and Abitibi West in Quebec.

[d] That part of Ontario east of and including the counties of Leeds, Lanark, and Renfrew, plus the counties of Pontiac, Hull, Gatineau, and Papineau in Quebec.

[e] Quebec (excluding those parts of Quebec in Ontario Hockey Association and Ottawa and District).

[f] New Brunswick, Nova Scotia, and Prince Edward Island.

Third, control of individual players is extended by use of "try out" ("A" form) and "option" ("B" and "C" forms) agreements which attempt to bind amateurs to a particular professional club when they have reached sixteen years of age.[24] While the A form merely gives negotiation rights, the B and C forms give the club an exclusive continuing option on the player's services both amateur and professional. Indeed, when a C form has been signed the player is a professional. As it is in the signing of amateurs that the greatest competition occurs between NHL clubs, the sponsorship list, the universal amateur draft (see section II) and the negotiation list attempt to circumscribe this. The former is analagous to the protected list and the latter makes for orderly negotiation.

Finally, a series of minor points reinforce NHL control. These include the CAHA's adoption (with minor changes) of NHL playing rules, acceptance of the voluntary retired list, and agreement that no amateur club can bind a player with a reserve clause. The total outcome is that the amateur-professional relationship is the same as exists between professional leagues—domination by the NHL.

The total outcome is likely to be that, as the model forecasts, the NHL does employ the superior players vis-à-vis other competitive leagues.

PROPOSITION 4. MONOPSONY POWER AND PLAYER COSTS

Given the monopsony power of the NHL and its clubs, is it exercised so that player costs are minimized? Because there is no information available on wages, what follows must be regarded as highly speculative.

In general there are two extreme views on the subject of wages of professional athletes and their opportunity costs. One suggests that given the monopsony power of most major league clubs in any sport—football, baseball, or basketball—there is no reason for wages to be above opportunity cost. The other view points out that the large sums paid to professional athletes are bound to be above their opportunity cost—where else could Willie Mays make $125,000 or Wilt Chamberlain $250,000—which suggests that monopsony power is illusionary.

Hockey would appear to fall into the first category because there is no reason why wages should be above opportunity costs.[25] With NHL control over entry, competition from any other league which could increase factor cost (as the American Football League did for the National Football League) is absent. Thus, the only way wages could rise above opportunity costs would be through inter-club competition. But the option clause, protected list, and voluntary retired list, severely limit such rivalry. Competition is a factor in signing amateurs (e.g., the Shock incident) prior to option agreements, but again negotiation and sponsorship lists are confining factors.[26]

Nevertheless, the annual rash of prolonged barn painting and other assorted reasons for "holding out" suggests that the process of wage determination is more a matter of bilateral bargaining than the straight application of monopsony theory. The situation is indeed a bargaining one due to two factors. First, given that the demand for any input is wholly a derived demand, as the club desires to win, it is not completely indifferent over whether the player performs for the team or not. Thus if the club has to pay more for a winning team than a losing team it will do so. Second, if attendance is a function not only of the performance of the teams but also of individual stars (irrespective of the performance of the team) then once again the club would be willing to pay above opportunity cost. Of course both factors assume that the human inputs are heterogeneous and there is no possibility of substitution at a lower wage. The upshot is that monopsony power is not absolute. It is true that each club has the power to drive wages to opportunity costs and, coupled with the threat of suspension which automatically disbars a player from organized hockey, make this stick. But, given that winning is important and the "superstar" effect does exist, the player may be able to bargain his wage above pure opportunity cost.

The bargaining range is set by value product and opportunity cost. Where the wage actually falls within this range depends on the bargaining strength of the player and the extent to which the team is ready to enforce the rules and regulations. If the player is extremely valuable to the team in that there are no good substitutes, he may be able to bargain for a wage significantly above his opportunity cost. There is no doubt, for instance, that certain "superstars" make large salaries because of their ability to draw crowds, and therefore make important contributions to the gate. For example, although in the 1966-67 season Chicago finished first in the league for the first time ever, attendance was lower than in 1965-66 when the club finished second. Although we would have expected the reverse to be true, the statistics ignore one qualitative factor—in 1965-66 Bobby Hull broke the 50-goal record. Similarly, in 1965-66 Boston finished fifth rather than last and, as expected, attendance increased. In 1966-67 they reverted to last, but attendance increased. One of the major reasons was the play of Bobby Orr. Yet it is doubtful if either of the above players received his value product.[27]

However, what about the player whose ability is not unique and for whom there are reasonably good substitutes? His salary may be above his opportunity costs if there are substantial external benefits to winning or if there is group bargaining. In the first case, consider how much is a winning Montreal team worth to its (1966) owners, Molson Brewery? If the external benefits are strong then the club may give a player a substantial portion of his rent for a winning team.

In the second case, although group bargaining by players can be very effective because the game depends on the labour input, it requires that the players' group be sufficiently inclusive (the four professional leagues) so that substitution is impossible. Under these circumstances the players' union was effective in raising both salaries and fringe benefits for *all* players during the fifties. The same is apparently true of the new association formed in 1967.

However, given the NHL view of what constitutes arbitration, and the monopsonistic power of the clubs, it would be very strange if the wages of all players were too far above their opportunity costs. While the club may not push salaries to their lowest levels—even on the basis of wishing to maintain player morale (Rottenberg, 1956: 253)—there is certainly no reason to believe that the converse is true. Thus, although the clubs may fail to minimize player costs in line with their monopsony power, this is not due to any benevolent use of their power but rather to the fact that such power is not absolute. Consequently, if we take into account the need to win, the heterogeneity of inputs, strengths and weaknesses in the bargaining process, the need to ensure player morale, etc., we could conclude that the clubs are minimizing player costs. However, it must be stressed that as we have no data this conclusion is highly conjectural.

Nevertheless, on balance we are probably justified in saying that on the supply side the implications of the model have been largely borne out.

Expansion and the 1966 Agreement with the CAHA

The foregoing analysis dealt with the NHL as it existed prior to the 1967-68 season. In 1966 two events occurred which changed its character—the league expanded by granting franchises to Los Angeles, San Francisco, Philadelphia, Pittsburgh, Minneapolis, and St. Louis; and the NHL-CAHA agreement was rewritten. Do either of these changes invalidate the above analysis? The answer is no, and both changes can be explained by using the same hypothesis, that the clubs are interdependent profit maximizers.

Why did the league expand? The answer is primarily associated with the revenue which can be obtained from increasing the extent of the market through television.[28]

Over the period 1960-61 to 1965-66, all NHL clubs were consistently playing at or moving towards, capacity. By 1965-66, Chicago and Montreal were over 100 per cent of seating capacity. Toronto had dropped below capacity for the first time in memory, while Detroit, New York, and Boston were playing at 96, 80, and 85 per cent of seating capacity respectively.[29] When full capacity attendance is achieved, revenue can be increased by boosting the size of the arena, increasing the number of games, and/or increasing ticket prices. However, if we make the reasonable assumption that there is a ceiling on arena size, number of games and ticket prices, then there is a limit to the extent that the local market can be increased. This revenue ceiling can be removed by use of television at either a local or national level.

If there is positive excess demand in the local market it can be met either by closed circuit TV or local commercial stations. Commercial TV is probably the best way of attracting the marginal viewer, providing that the substitutability between "live" and TV hockey is relatively small. If it is not, the club runs the possibility of losing a large portion of its "live" audience, so that total net revenue may not increase. Indeed most clubs who have used TV to expand their local markets have gone to closed circuit television because it appears to offer less of the "substitutability" drawbacks associated with commercial TV.

On the other hand, when commercial TV is used the object is usually expansion in other than local markets. To reduce the danger for substitutability there are usually local blackouts when the local team plays at home. When there is no blackout, revenue may fall. For instance, in the 1956-57 season Boston had four out of ten games carried nationally by CBS, playing New York twice, Detroit once, and Montreal once. The average "live" gate from these four games was $14,892 compared with $24,910 per game "for non-televised engagements against the same clubs." For these games the Bruins received $10,000 from CBS, therefore ending with a revenue loss of $1,018 (Fin. Post, 1957). Yet Montreal and Toronto have never suffered the same fate and consistently play to over 100 per cent of seating capacity.

However, US national network TV does pay the most money for televising sport. Thus, if a team is playing to capacity crowds and is already utilizing closed circuit television, a national TV contract appears very profitable. But the prerequisite for a national contract is a national market. The expansion placed teams in the remaining major US television markets (excluding the south). The NHL did obtain a national TV contract from CBS.[30]

Thus, solely on the basis of television it is possible to explain the distribution of new franchises and why Vancouver and Quebec City were omitted. The Canadian TV hockey market is already dominated by Montreal and Toronto. What advantages would accrue to Toronto and Montreal if expansion took place in Vancouver and Quebec City? As it was predictable that new teams would be inferior to Montreal and Toronto, it is doubtful if either the CBC or CTV could have been persuaded to substantially increase their price to accommodate two new teams. At the same time the addition of the Canadian cities was not necessary to get an American TV contract.[31]

Given the expansion, the basic model can also help explain in more detail the "stocking" of the new teams, and the formation of the new NHL division.

With the degree of control over players it was obvious that the new clubs would have to stock their teams from the rosters of the existing clubs.[32] If the maximum amount of competition was the league objective, this could only be promoted by a draft which allowed no protection of any player by any club. However, given the incentive to win, such a move would obviously not appeal to the existing clubs. Hence, no open draft.

In 1966, following pressure from various sources to take amateur hockey out of professional hands, the CAHA-NHL agreement was rewritten. However, although the new agreement appears to be more palatable the NHL has in fact retained the same degree of monopsonistic control at possibly a cheaper price. The main provisions of the new agreement are as follows (Canada, 1967: 19-26, 65-68).

The NHL will terminate all sponsorship of amateur clubs. All amateurs will only be drafted when they reach 21 years of age and the "try-out" and "option" agreements will be discontinued. The NHL will pay a set amount to the CAHA for each player drafted. Finally, a player development fund will be set up, financed by the NHL, to develop hockey players.

What advantages does this arrangement have from the point of view of the NHL? First, although it appears to give control of amateur hockey back to the CAHA and so dispel most of the public outcry over professional control, it really only makes this control more indirect. For instance, despite the loss of sponsorships and A, B, and C forms, etc., the NHL has the *exclusive* right to draft all amateurs who will still (according to the agreement) be playing under NHL rules. The purpose of the option agreements, sponsorship lists, etc. was to reduce inter-club competition for players; this purpose is *retained* by the new universal draft. In fact, it is probably retained at a cheaper price than would otherwise have had to be paid. With six new clubs entering the league there would have been extreme competition for players. This would have resulted in increased prices for players and increased costs of setting up amateur farm systems. With the new agreement all such cost disappears.

Second, financial control still rests with the NHL through control of the Joint Development Committee, which approves all payments to the CAHA leagues. As there is no information on how much it cost the NHL clubs to run their amateur farm systems, one cannot judge how adequate the amount of money invested by the NHL under this new arrangement is. However, it is doubtful that even by doubling the size of the NHL the funds going to amateur hockey will be doubled. Thus, there is again a potential cost saving to every club.

Third, ultimate control still resides with the NHL because if it is not satisfied with the number of or calibre of players developed, the CAHA has agreed to implement a program of accelerated player development.

Thus, in any weighing of costs and benefits it appears as if the NHL has increased its benefits at a lower cost.

Conclusion

Given the fact that the evidence appears to accord with what the model predicts we can justifiably say that the conduct of the NHL can be explained by the model. However, whether the model provides any indelible guides to public policy is another matter. The NHL clearly possesses monopoly and monopsony power, and if the possession of market power is enough to warrant application of the Combines Act then the NHL is liable. But as the Act presently stands there is some doubt as to whether any liability exists, because professional sport is considered a *service*, and *services* are immune from prosecution under the Act.[33] Whether it is desirable that the NHL be placed under the Act (irrespective of its market power) is another matter. Perhaps there are wider questions of the public interest which are not represented by the Act. Nevertheless, what is clear is that a complete reappraisal of the Combines Act vis-à-vis professional sport should be undertaken.

NOTES

1. Public information on the operation of the NHL is extremely meagre. The best of what does exist is contained in two statements by Clarence Campbell, President of the NHL, made during U.S. Congress, Hearings before the Antitrust Subcommittee ... *On Organized Professional Team Sport*, 1957 (United States: 1957), and *On Organized Professional Team Sport*, 1958 (United States: 1958) (hereafter, referred to as *Celler Hearings* and *Kefauver Hearings*, respectively). The former also contains copies of the NHL Constitution and By-Laws.

2. See Bill C-132, first reading Feb. 25, 1966.

3. See, for example, remarks of Mr. Ron Basford, who introduced C-132, in Commons Debates, June 13, 1966, 6364.

4. See, for instance, statements by Mr. James D. Norris at *Celler Hearings*, (United States; 1957:2978) and more recently Clarence Campbell, quoted in Olsen (1965).

5. Throughout this paper the following definition holds: the club, is an input made up of human and physical capital; the team, the coach, and the management represent the human capital; the arena and equipment are the physical capital.

6. For a good discussion of the criterion of variability and survival and its implications for prediction and the explanation of economic behaviour see Alchian (1950).

7. Given are: the number of teams, the number of games, arena seating capacity, the production function and the techniques specifying how the inputs should be combined (i.e., game rules) including, number of players, size of ice surface, size of goal, etc.—in short all factors considered in the Constitution, By-Laws, and Playing Rules of the NHL.

8. Though no attempt is made to specify all the factors which could affect attendance, the following are mentioned because they are more or less unique to hockey (although analagous factors are found in other sports):
(1) the drawing power of a particular "super-star" (e.g. Richard, Howe, Hull) or team irrespective of the projected outcome of the game. It is interesting to note that when exhibitions are staged between NHL and minor league clubs (when the outcome of the game is not important), very often the ability of a particular star of the NHL team is heavily stressed in pre-game advertising; (2) the style of hockey played—defensive, offensive, the likelihood of fights, etc. Clarence Campbell, for instance, has said that offensive style hockey which increases scoring has a positive effect on attendance (see Deacon, 1952). Certainly over the years the rule changes have attempted to make hockey a faster, more wide open game, for example, the forward pass, the red line, etc; (3) the selling job that radio, T.V., and newspaper sports writers do for hockey, sometimes called the "fourth estate benefit"; (4) whether the game is played during the weekend or mid-week; (5) parking and the weather; (6) in Toronto and Montreal "conspicuous consumption," and when Toronto plays Montreal—ethnic considerations.

9. See statement of Clarence Campbell (United States, 1958: 504). This emphasizes that "franchises" in hockey are different from those granted to automobile or farm implement dealers, for example. Here the franchise controls the central organization.

10. However, the case has been succinctly stated by Conn Smythe, "New York and Boston keep drawing because there are only six teams in the league ... so you've always got an attraction coming in. But if you had two more teams that couldn't win games it would be different. If you had four rotten teams in the league you'd have a hell of a time getting people in the rink. They wouldn't buy season tickets for 35 games a year knowing that they had to take 15 or 20 lousy games" (Olsen, 1965: 66).

11. Financial side payments are practised with varying degress of complaint from the member clubs by the Canadian Football League.

12. Inter-club trades could be considered a form of side payment especially if they are motivated by the desire to strengthen weaker clubs. For instance, over the years there has been a noticeable tendency for winning teams to avoid trading with each other and to trade with losing teams.

13. The Montreal example is similar to that of Chicago except that in Chicago capacity has not changed, but in Montreal it has as follows: 1946, 9,600; 1949-50, 12,400; 1950-51, 13,201; 1951-52, 13,307; 1953-54, 13,488; 1954-55, 13,531; 1959-60, 13,708; 1960-61, 13,728; 1966-67, 14,097. Data supplied by the Montreal Club.

14. The NHL was formed when the National Hockey Association was dissolved to "freeze out ... Eddie Livingston whose team ... had somehow got under the skin of the boys from Ottawa and Montreal" (Selke, 1962: 56).

15. Throughout the paper "professional" hockey means those clubs whose players have signed a Standard Player's Contract and covers the NHL and the "minors," i.e., American Hockey League (AHL), Western Hockey League (WHL) and Central Profes-

sional Hockey League (CPHL). Any club whose players have not signed such a contract are considered "amateurs," nominally controlled by the Canadian Amateur Hockey Association (CAHA).

16. The author was unable to obtain an up-to-date Player's Contract, but current information suggests that it has changed very little for ten years (this applies both to content and numbering of the clauses). All references are to the 1958 version found following p. 790, *Kefauver Hearings* (United States, 1958).

17. See particularly clauses 11, 6, and 18.

18. NHL By-Laws Section 8 (5) and (6).

19. It should be noted that the parallels between baseball and hockey are very close, and in fact the rules and regulations governing the NHL "evolved out of the experience of baseball" (United States, 1957:2982). Also see Rottenberg (1956).

20. This agreement was drawn between the NHL, AHL, WHL, and the Quebec Hockey League. Since then the Quebec League has gone out of existence but available evidence suggests that things have not changed significantly with the addition of the CPHL, especially as all the clubs in this league are directly owned by NHL clubs (United States, 1957: 3112-3124).

21. During the 1965-66 fiscal year Toronto sold its interest in Rochester, and at the end of the 1966-67 season the Victoria franchise was moved to Phoenix and sold to local interests.

22. See the "Joint Affiliation Agreement," clause 4 (United States, 1957: 3114).

23. See C.A.H.A. Rules (1954; 67-70) which contains a synopsis of the CAHA-NHL agreement. Although a new agreement came into effect in 1958, the *Report on Amateur Hockey* (Canada, 1967) suggests that no major changes took place in 1958. It should be noted that the NHL acts for all professional hockey leagues when dealing with the CAHA (United States, 1957: 3121).

24. (United States, 1957: 3079-82) (CAHA, 1954: 71-77).

25. Although it would be interesting to compare the wages and working conditions of hockey players with other professional sports lack of data precludes this.

26. Signing amateurs can be expensive as the following shows. "Detroit, Chicago, New York, Montreal, Toronto scrambled for Frank Mahovlich when he was a 14-year-old playing for Schumacher Lions, Leafs got him. They paid him $1,000 to sign a Junior B certificate; $1,300 a year for tuition, laundry money, and three trips home each of the 5 years he was a St. Michael's College; $1,000 to the scout who signed him to a "C" form $10,000 bonus to the "Big M" to turn professional; $10,000 for his first years salary" (Mortimer, no date: 22).

27. Rottenberg (1956: 253) argues that the only circumstances in which a player would receive his full value is if all players on the team insisted on receiving theirs. Then the rents would be zero.

28. One additional reason for expansion can usually be found in the desire of the established clubs to blockade entry. For instance, the New York Mets received a franchise in the National Baseball League only after the formation of a third major baseball league was seriously mooted (Breslin, 1963: 47-9). However, considering NHL expansion, the formation of a major rival league was not considered a serious possibility at this time.

29. Calculated from figures supplied by the NHL.

30. CBS is to pay the NHL a total of $3.6 million over three years; $600,000 the first year (the old teams are to share this equally among themselves); $1,200,000 the second year and $1,800,000 the third (in the last two years the money is to be split 12 ways). Reported by the CP (Victoria Daily Times, 1966).

31. However, Vancouver could have had a franchise if the city had sold to Stafford Smythe (principal owner of Toronto Maple Leafs) and associates a downtown block for $1. Smythe would then have provided a team and an arena. Whatever one thinks of the move and no matter how sympathetic one is to Vancouver's drive for major league status, this proposal was a massive attempt at using full line forcing!

32. This was also an opportunity for the existing teams to reap a little extra reward. For

$2 million per club the new teams were allowed to draft 20 players each, owned by the old clubs.

33. See Commons Debates, Feb. 23, 1966: 1670; Report of the Director of Investigation and Research, March 1966: 7; Combines Investigation Act; and Henry (1967).

REFERENCES

Alchian, A.A.
1950   "Uncertainty, evaluation, and economic theory." *Journal of Political Economy*, 58.

Andrews, R. (ed)
1967   *National Hockey League Guide 1966-67*. Montreal.

Beddoes, Dick
1966   "N.H.L. brand on the young." Toronto: *The Globe and Mail*, April 26.

Breslin, Jimmy
1963   *Can't Anybody Here Play This Game*. New York: Viking Press.

C.A.H.A.
1954   *Hockey Rules 1954-55*. Toronto: Canadian Amateur Hockey Association.

Canada
1967   "Report on Amateur Hockey in Canada," Ottawa: Department of National Health and Welfare, National Advisory Council on Fitness and Amateur Sport Hockey Study Committee.

Deacon, P.
1952   "Thinner ice for pro hockey." Toronto: *Financial Post*, April 19.

Fellner, W.
1960   *Competition Among the Few*. New York: A. M. Kelley.

Financial Post
1957   "Big troubles ahead for the N.H.L." Toronto, November 20.

Henry, D. H. W.
1967   "Developments and proceedings under the Combines Investigations Act for the year ended March 31, 1967." *The Antitrust Bulletin*, 12.

Mortimore, G. E.
No Date "What happened to hockey." Toronto: *The Globe and Mail*.

Neale, W. C.
1964   "The peculiar economics of professional sport." *Quarterly Journal of Economics*, 78 (February).

Olsen, J.
1965   "Private game: no admittance." *Sports Illustrated*, April.

Rottenberg, S.
1956   "The baseball players' labor market." *Journal of Political Economy*, 64.

Selke, Frank J.
1962   *Behind the Cheering*. Toronto: McClelland and Stewart.

United States
1957   House of Representatives Committee on the Judiciary. Hearings before the Antitrust Subcommittee on Organized Professional Team Sport (Congressman Celler, chairman).

United States
1958   House of Representatives Committee on Judiciary. Hearings before the Antitrust Subcommittee on Organized Professional Team Sport (Congressman Kefauver, chairman).

THE ECONOMICS OF THE N.H.L. REVISITED:
A Postscript on Structural Change, Behaviour and Government Policy*

The article "The Economics of the National Hockey League" attempted to explain intra-league behaviour in terms of profit maximization assumptions and a quasi joint profit maximizing model. At that time inter-league behaviour was dominated by the fact that the N.H.L. was in a monopoly-monopsony position. Since then there have been a number of developments—continued N.H.L. expansion, the creation of a rival league, adverse antitrust rulings, threatened government regulation— which are potentially significant for both intra- and inter-league behaviour. Therefore, the purpose of this postscript is to attempt to explain these developments, the effect they have had on N.H.L. behaviours, and the future prospects for the league.

The major conclusion is that the main influence on both intra- and inter-league behaviour has been the birth of the rival World Hockey Association (W.H.A.) which has compromised the monopoly-monopsony position of the N.H.L. Whether these changes in behaviour are permanent or not depends on the survival of the W.H.A., and, failing that, the extent to which government is prepared to intervene in the market.

For ease of exposition this paper is organized into three parts: (1) the product market, (2) the labour market (although it should be stressed that these markets are interdependent insofar as successful entry in the product market necessitates breaking the monopsony power of the N.H.L.), and (3) future prospects and government policy.

Product Market

Since 1967 the two basic changes in the "major hockey league" product market have been: (a) a continuation of N.H.L. expansion with the addition of six teams;[1] and (b) the birth of the World Hockey Association (1972)[2] selling a product generically similar to N.H.L. hockey. What are the reasons for these structural changes and what impact would we expect them to have on N.H.L. league and club behaviour?

As far as the structural changes are concerned, if the model developed in the previous article is applicable, we would expect both the N.H.L.

---

* The author would like to thank W. D. Walsh for helpful discussions and comments.

expansion and the entry of the W.H.A. to be adequately explained by profit maximization motives. With regard to N.H.L. behaviour, while both structural changes potentially lead to changes in behaviour we expect the behaviour to differ depending on whether or not the monopoly-monopsony position of the N.H.L. remains intact. Since N.H.L. expansion does not disturb its monopoly-monopsony position, and therefore does not force any change in its player restrictions, we do not expect intra-league behaviour to differ significantly from that described by the quasi joint profit maximization model: retaining the restrictive player provisions only ensures that competitive equality will not be achieved and any changes in behaviour will be second best responses to the inevitable conflict between clubs and the league. But whatever form the responses take, they will be geared to ensuring the viability of the league.

On the other hand, because the W.H.A. challenges the monopoly-monopsony position of the N.H.L. the implication is that there will be substantive changes in both inter-and intra-league behaviour. That is, since the product differentiation advantage of the N.H.L. (its superiority over other existing leagues and potential entrants) rests on its superior players, if the W.H.A. is to be competitive then it must acquire N.H.L. calibre players either from existing N.H.L. teams and/or from amateur ranks. Therefore, the W.H.A. must successfully overcome the monopsony position of the N.H.L. by offering established N.H.L. players less restrictive player contracts and/or more money. If this ploy is successful then the N.H.L. will have to respond in kind. This in turn means that N.H.L. group behaviour in the labour market will change significantly from what it was under monopsony circumstances.

In addition, should these changes in group behaviour intensify conflicts between N.H.L. clubs—if, for example, the group response to W.H.A. competition is to remove the reserve clause and this leaves the way open for N.H.L. clubs who want to ensure victory to compete with each other for players—then we can also expect intra-league behaviour to change. Again, however, we would expect the league to adopt solutions to resolve these conflicts and maintain league viability.

To determine if these expected patterns of behaviour in fact follow from the structural changes we must examine N.H.L. behaviour since expansion took place and the W.H.A. went into operation.

The N.H.L. Expansion

The N.H.L. expansion can be adequately explained by the profit maximization motive. On the supply side, the established clubs found expansion profitable: as joint profit maximizers the established clubs shared equally in both expansion revenue (each new club was assessed an entrance fee of $6 million) and revenue from the national T.V. contract.[3] On the demand side, new franchisee's were entering a sport where the clubs were not only thought to be typically profitable[4] but where there was also the added inducements of a national T.V. contract, and the unique tax advantages associated with owning a sports franchise. This latter point is particularly important because, under U.S. tax laws, operating losses from a sports franchise can be written off against the owners' outside income, and team assets—principally the players—can be depreciated over a three to five year period (Okner, 1974).

If profit maximization can explain the expansion, what about intra-league behaviour? Here the quasi joint profit maximization model seems appropriate. Despite the protestations that "balanced competition"[5] is the goal of all sports, no special provisions were made to stock the new franchises with players beyond allowing each new team to draft first in the initial year. Since the restrictive labour market covenants were retained, the result is that competitive equality—no matter how it is measured[6]—has scarcely been a factor. This is hardly surprising although the league did its best to hide it.[7] Eventually, however, the major concession to the inevitable conflict between the club's desire to win and the league's desire for competitive equality led to the second best solution of creating more winners by sub-dividing the original two divisions (1966) into four (1974-75) and increasing the number of play-off teams from eight to twelve.[8]

In short, while the monopoly-monopsony position of the N.H.L. remained intact (1966-1972), intra-league behaviour followed a pattern very much as outlined by the quasi joint profit maximization model. However, the entry of the W.H.A. produced significant changes in inter-league behaviour.

The World Hockey Association

Again, profit maximization motives adequately explain the entry of the new league. The W.H.A. was created along the same lines, for the same reasons, by the same promoters who set up the American Basketball Association, and the now-defunct World Football League. The major short run reason for setting up the league was the profit possibilities associated with the U.S. tax laws described above (Business Week, 1974). In the longer term, the American Football League model was seemingly appropriate: a T.V. contract enables a new league to compete successfully for players with an established league (so compromising the established league's monopoly-monopsony position) and this eventually allows the new and established leagues to merge (and so re-establish a monopoly-monopsony position) and increases profits for all clubs.

In terms of behaviour, if the W.H.A. was to successfully challenge the N.H.L. then it must obtain N.H.L. calibre players. Therefore, the first moves by the W.H.A. had to take place in the labour market.

Labour Market

If we assume that the W.H.A. is willing to compete for players, then to break the monopsony power of the N.H.L. the W.H.A. must: (i) break the restrictions (particularly the reserve clause) of the N.H.L. (and minor league) players contract if it wishes to sign established N.H.L. players; (ii) sign amateur players who are not bound by a reserve clause. The W.H.A. attempted to do both.

The reserve clause was successfully challenged by the W.H.A. in *Philadelphia World Hockey Club* v. *Philadelphia Hockey Club* (1972), when the N.H.L. was enjoined from enforcing its reserve clause.[9] This allowed the W.H.A. to sign a number of established N.H.L. players (Hull, Sanderson, McKenzie, Parent) which was mandatory if the W.H.A. was to obtain a national T.V. contract (which for a short period of time it did).

What was the N.H.L. group reaction? We would expect the N.H.L. to be competitive not only in financial terms but also in terms of modifying the restrictive covenants of its own player contracts. In the former case this has been apparent insofar as the average N.H.L. salary (excluding fringe benefits and play-off money) went from $22,000 in 1967 to an apparent $60,528 in 1974 (Canada, 1974:20). In addition, the reserve clause was removed from the player's contract and replaced by a one-year option clause (Canada, 1974:20). Thus, the N.H.L. reacted to competition from another league by modifying its group rules of conduct.

However, the modified rules also provide some threat to N.H.L. stability because the option clause also affects intra-league behaviour. That is, the option clause means that a player could now move between N.H.L. clubs. Therefore, given the individual club's desire to win, competitive bidding for players who have played out their options could take place between N.H.L. clubs. This could affect the viability of the league.

This possibility was forestalled by instituting a "compensation rule" so that if a player plays out his option and moves to another N.H.L. club, that club must provide compensation in the form of players to the original employer club. If the two clubs cannot agree on compensation then the compensation decision is made by an impartial arbitrator (Canada, 1974:23). This is the N.H.L. version of the "Rozelle rule" the intent of which is to stop players moving between clubs. In the N.H.L. case there are few examples of players actually playing out their options and moving to other N.H.L. clubs (this may be partially due to the fact that the option rule has been operating for a short period of time), although if a player wished to move to another N.H.L. club and used the threat of jumping to the W.H.A. then presumably "compensation" will be arranged in the form of a trade, especially if the player is considered particularly valuable.[10]

However, the real significance of the "compensation rule" from the point of view of intra-league behaviour is that, although competitive pressure from the W.H.A. potentially affected group stability, the N.H.L. used the rule to resolve the conflict and so ensured group stability.

Since the C.A.H.A. and N.H.L. agreement of 1966 ended the amateur sponsorship system, the signing of amateurs by the W.H.A. was superficially easier. Although it was more profitable for the C.A.H.A. if their players signed with N.H.L. clubs (the N.H.L. paid compensation to the C.A.H.A. for every player signed, but no satisfactory long term agreement has been worked out with the W.H.A.) the C.A.H.A. could not control whether an amateur signed with the N.H.L. or W.H.A.

How did the N.H.L. react to W.H.A. incursion into the amateur market? There is some evidence from the W.H.A. that although a draft procedure is followed, if a draft selection could not be signed by the drafting team then another team in the league would be allowed access to the player rather than see the player go to the rival league (Alyluia, 1973:374). Whether or not the N.H.L. reacted by following a similar pattern is conjecture.[11] However, when the W.H.A. signed "under age" players (initially the W.H.A. was not very successful in signing draft age players so they attempted to sign amateurs who had not reached draft age) the N.H.L. countered with an "under age" draft of its own, although it was discontinued after one year.

Therefore, in summary, it is obvious that the competitive pressure of the W.H.A. forced the N.H.L. to modify its inter-league (group) rules of conduct. This primarily shows up in the removal of certain restrictions in the Players Contract and the increase in player salaries. In addition, the removal of the restrictions could have led to intra-league problems but these have been largely solved by the "compensation rule". Once again a quasi joint profit maximization position which is consistent with league viability has been achieved.

The Future Prospects

What are the future prospects for major league hockey? Although there are a number of soft financial spots, there seems little doubt that the N.H.L. will endure. But what form it will take depends largely on the existence of the W.H.A. and it is the continued existence of the W.H.A. which is problematical.

Although there is little hard financial data available, what little does exist suggests that the W.H.A. may be in some difficulty. The league has no national T.V. contract, it has failed to place teams in areas with lush local T.V. markets, and crowds necessary to support a major league operation have rarely been the rule.[12] Therefore, despite tax advantages, it is extremely doubtful whether the W.H.A. can continue to exist in its present form.

If it does not, any of four alternatives may be *à propos*: the league could retrench by reducing the number of clubs but still retain its major league status; the league could retrench and become a minor league;[13] the league could fold completely (the W.F.L. scenario); some of the existing clubs (if not the whole league) could merge with the N.H.L. (the A.F.L. scenario).[14]

In all but the first instance the monopoly-monopsony position of the N.H.L. would be restored. This has serious implications for both labour and product markets.

In the labour market the obvious implication is that the N.H.L. would once again be in a position to absorb the rents the players were receiving during the W.H.A.—N.H.L. competition for their services. However, given the absence of a competing league, the extent to which the N.H.L. can successfully absorb rents partially depends on how successfully the N.H.L. Players Association can transform the wage determination process into genuine bilateral bargaining.

Although the N.H.L. Players Association has been successful in negotiating a wide range of fringe benefits, whether it can successfully fill the gap left by the W.H.A. is conjecture. For example, can the Association bargain successfully over removal of the restrictive covenants in the Players Contract if a competitive alternative to the N.H.L. does not exist? As long as the Association is recognized under the U.S. Labor Management Relations Act and operates under the procedures of the National Labor Relations Board then all covenants can be negotiated as conditions of employment. But how successful will such negotiations be without the goad of a competitive alternative like the W.H.A.?

Perhaps the goad can be supplied by the antitrust laws. After all, it was the decision in *Philadelphia World Hockey Club* v. *Philadelphia Hockey Club* which eliminated the reserve clause and it is possible that parallels for hockey may be drawn from the recent decision in *Kapp* v. *National Football* League (United States, 1974). That is, whatever happens to the W.H.A. it is unlikely that the reserve clause will be reintroduced into the Players Contract. However, the present option clause plus the "compensation rule" have the same effect so that if the W.H.A. disappears the reserve clause is *de facto* resurrected. But in the *Kapp* case the court agreed that the "Rozelle rule" (and for that matter the "draft") was an "unreasonable"[15] restraint of trade despite the fact that it is generally recognized that the collective bargaining process immunizes employee agreements from the antitrust laws (United States, 1974: 83-87).

If this decision stands—and because it was made by a lower court, it will undoubtedly be appealed—then the U.S. antitrust laws may supply the necessary back-up muscle to force genuine collective bargaining.

In addition, recent proposed changes in the Canadian antitrust laws could also aid the Players Association in its bargaining efforts.[16] Briefly, the intent of the amendments to the Combines Act is to make league agreements covering the draft, and reserve and option clauses, etc., illegal unless it can be shown that they are "reasonable". The restrictions will be considered reasonable if they are necessary to maintain "reasonable balance" among teams, or if the league concerned is organized on an "international basis." Strictly speaking, since there has never been competitive equality in the N.H.L., the league should be automatically liable but the "international" defence probably means that the league is immune.[17] Therefore, the legislative back-up for the Players Association will probably have to come from the U.S.

If the monopoly-monopsony position of the N.H.L. is restored we can probably look forward to a period of militant labour action similar to that which has already begun in baseball and the National Football League. However, in the final analysis both sides will come to some accommodation although without the W.H.A. it appears as if the seller's market for the players will be a thing of the past.

With regard to the product market the demise of the W.H.A. as a competitive league allows the N.H.L. to reassert its monopoly poisition in "major league" hockey. This raises the usual questions about monopolists restricting output (in this case franchises) and increasing price. Given the furor that usually accompanies franchise expansion and franchise shifts, it is unlikely that the government can avoid intervention in some form or other. Therefore, the pertinent question is what direction will public policy take? Normally, where monopoly exists public policy attempts to rectify the situation either by promoting competition or by direct regulation.

Presumably, in the sports context, promoting competition involves encouraging the formation of new leagues. Among other things this entails easing entry conditions which in turn means ending most of the restrictive covenants in the labour market. These covenants do not lead to competitive equality in any league (indeed they are not designed to do so and may even positively retard competitive equality) but they allow the N.H.L. to exert monopsony power which is the major barrier to entry. Therefore, removing the restrictions would give a new league access to players.

However, the survival record of new leagues in most professional sports has not been good, even when they have had access to players.[18] This suggests that most professional sports leagues may fall into the category of "natural" monopolies and therefore any attempt to promote competition as an antidote to monopoly will be ineffective. The appropriate direction for public policy would therefore seem to be some form of regulation.

This would be more appropriate if the minimum unit of entry is somewhat less than a league. That is, if the minimum unit of entry is a team (and, as expansion demonstrates, teams do enter established leagues and survive), then the entry problem becomes more difficult because entry now requires players *plus someone to play*. Therefore, is the government prepared to set conditions under which new teams enter franchised leagues? Should public policy regulate expansion (and franchise shifts) or should we allow established leagues to operate as if they had a valid patent?

The answers to these questions are not easy and will certainly be controversial, but it is increasingly certain that legislators are going to be asked to provide answers in the near future. The question is not whether the government will interfere but the *extent* to which it will interfere.

NOTES

1. Buffalo and Vancouver (1970), New York (Islanders) and Atlanta (1972) and Kansas City and Washington, D.C. (1974).
2. Since its birth in 1972 the W.H.A. has gone through a number of team and location changes. At present (December 1975) teams are located in: Quebec City, Toronto, Winnipeg, Calgary, Edmonton, Hartford, Cleveland, Houston, Denver, Cincinnati, San Diego, Pheonix, Minneapolis, and Indianapolis.
3. In addition, the New York Rangers were compensated to the tune of $5 million when the Islanders infringed on the Rangers' territorial rights. The actual location of new

franchises can be partially explained by the desire of the league to appropriate major U.S. T.V. markets (Atlanta for example) although defensive (the wish to minimize the costs which could be imposed by a rival league, for example, N.Y. Islanders) and political (the attempt to minimize the costs of government interference, e.g. Washington, D.C.) reasons probably played some role.

4. There is little financial data on N.H.L. teams. However, the conclusion in the text is drawn from Noll (1974: 24-29). There are, however, some currently admitted soft sports in Oakland, Pittsburg, Washington, D.C., Kansas City, Atlanta and also possibly Detroit.

5. See the evidence of Clarence Campbell in the Senate of Canada, *Proceedings of the Standing Senate Committee on Banking, Trade and Commerce*, November 13, 1974, p. 22 (Canada, 1974). Hereafter all references to the Proceedings will be shortened to *Proceedings*.

6. There are a number of ways that competitive equality could be quantitatively measured. For example, if the labour market restrictions resulted in competitive equality we would expect: (a) the number of championships should tend towards equality over time; (b) the won-loss record of teams should tend towards equality over time; (c) championship teams should win by smaller margins over time; (d) the variance of won-lost distributions over time should be significantly reduced; (e) teams may switch positions over time (first one year, last the next, etc.). None of these tests indicated that competitive equality has improved over the period.

7. With the 1966 expansion there was no intention of promoting competitive equality. Clarence Campbell noted: "Our expansion was generated on the principle that the new teams should compete primarily among themselves. We realized at once that we could not run a separate league for them ... We had to adjust our concept so that we could have the benefit of competition among the new teams competing among themselves, but, at the same time, they would be sufficiently integrated to have the full aura of a major league (Canada, 1974:18).

8. The same sort of multidivision play off system has also been adopted in baseball and by the National Football League.

9. The court found that the N.H.L. possessed unreasonable monopoly power because it controlled (through its restrictive labour market covenants) almost all hockey players available for major league play and therefore made it impossible for a new league (the W.H.A.) to compete successfully (United States, 1972).

10. This appears to be the case in the recent "trade" of Marcel Dionne from Detroit to Los Angeles.

11. There are no obvious examples of N.H.L. clubs allowing other teams access to players they could not sign. However, it is possible that *prior* to the draft N.H.L. clubs would investigate the prospects of signing a player *if* they drafted him. If the N.H.L. club decided that a player cannot be signed then the club could either draft someone else or trade the draft rights to another N.H.L. club who felt that it could sign the player. The trading of first round draft choices between Montreal and Vancouver in 1972 and Atlanta in 1973 may be cases in point.

   If, on the other hand, N.H.L. clubs do not give other clubs access to players they cannot sign, and these players sign with W.H.A. clubs this probably indicates that in the N.H.L. the club goal is a stronger motivational factor than league goals. For the W.H.A., promoting the *league* is important therefore club goals would be subordinate to league goals so that it would be important for some club in the league to sign the player.

12. Accurate financial information on the operations of the W.H.A. is almost nonexistent. However, the Chairman of the W.H.A. is reported as stating that: W.H.A. clubs have lost $15 million in their first three years of operation (excluding the loss attributable to the defunct franchises in Michigan and Chicago); and a crowd of 9,000 fans a game is necessary for clubs to "even consider breaking even" but this figure is only approached by a small number of clubs. See *The Globe and Mail*, October 11, 1975, p. 43.

13. In some respects this may be an attractive proposition because the entry of the
    W.H.A. emasculated the American, Central and Western Hockey Leagues. Therefore,
    the W.H.A. could possibly retrench and become a "senior" minor league filling much
    the same role as the old American Hockey League.

14. This, of course, has been already mooted and in 1973 the N.H.L. Players Association
    announced that it was retaining counsel to challenge any such merger.

15. The judge found that "a rule imposing restrictions virtually unlimited in time and
    extent goes far beyond any possible need for fair protection of the interests of the club
    owners . . . " and that it imposes upon the player-employees such undue hardships as to
    be an unreasonable restraint (United States 1974: 82).

16. As of November 1975 the Bill was in the Senate of Canada and should be returned
    shortly to the Commons for final passage.

17. The Executive Director of the N.H.L. Players Association, R. A. Eagleson, did not
    believe that the legislation was "the most appropriate," but the players "require the
    advantage of the bill if nothing else is available" (Canada, 1974: 18).

18. The World Football League died after one season, the American Basketball Associa-
    tion is falling apart (some clubs have formerly applied to join the National Basketball
    Association) and there are rumours that several W.H.A. Clubs may fold before the end
    of the season.

REFERENCES

Alyluia, K.
1973   "Professional Sports Contracts and the Players Association," *Manitoba Law Jour-
         nal.*
Business Week
1974   "A Quarterback of Tax Shelters," January 12.
Canada
1974   Senate of, *Proceedings of the Standing Senate Committee on Banking, Trade and
         Commerce.* Ottawa: Government of Canada.
Noll, R. G. (ed.)
1974   *Government and the Sports Business.* Washington, D.C.: The Brookings Institute.
Okner, B. A.
1974   "Taxation and Sports Enterprizes." In R. G. Noll (ed.), *Government and the Sports
         Business.* Washington, D.C.: The Brookings Institute.
United States
1972   "Philadelphia World Hockey Club v. Philadelphia Hockey Club." 351, *Federal
         Supplement* 462 (Eastern District Pennsylvania).
United States
1974   "Kapp v. National Football League." 390, *Federal Supplement* 73.

INVOLUNTARY TURNOVER AND ORGANIZATION EFFECTIVENESS IN THE NATIONAL HOCKEY LEAGUE[1]

Barry D. McPherson

Introduction

In recent years there has been substantial interest in the study of processes that influence the structure and function of formal organizations (March and Simon, 1958; Etzioni, 1964; March, 1965; Prince, 1968; Grusky and Miller, 1970; Tausky, 1970; Maurer, 1971; Azumi and Hage, 1972; Perrow, 1972; and Price, 1973a, 1973b). Although many parameters of formal organizations have been studied, much of this interest has focused on the issue of organizational *effectiveness* (e.g., Price, 1968). For example, since the maintenance of a competent labour force is essential for the continued and successful existence of any organization, all organizations have replacement procedures whereby personnel are added or deleted at the management or worker level. Whatever form this replacement process takes (e.g., hiring, promotion, demotion, firing), it is usually the case that when a new member enters an organization, gains or losses in productivity occur (Caplow, 1964: 169). Thus, a fundamental question for organizational analysts is the degree to which turnover at various levels in the organizational structure has a positive or negative influence on its effectiveness.

Historically, professional sports organizations have promoted or demoted players to subsidiary units within the organizational set (i.e., farm teams), or traded or drafted players from other organizations within the industry in an attempt to develop a "winning" team. As McNeil and Thompson (1971:626) have noted, "organizations which place a premium on physical skills, such as sport teams, can be expected to have high attrition rates". In other words, since most sports organizations adhere to *achievement* rather than *ascriptive* criteria for membership, high turnover rates are likely to occur. Yet, few organizational studies have attempted to relate the high rate of turnover on sports teams to various indices of team success or failure.[2] This dearth is surprising because it would seem that by their very nature, sports organizations provide an excellent opportunity to study the phenomenon of involuntary turnover (cf., Price, 1973a). In addition to their high turnover rates, sports organizations are stable in size, have well-defined and easily recognizable roles and goals, and have a readily identified authority structure (Grusky, 1963b). Furthermore, in most cases they represent a closed social system and, as Ball (1974) has noted decisions concerning changes in personnel, except for early retirement, are made by the organization rather than by the individual.

Guided by the aforementioned rationale, this paper is an attempt to examine the relationship between turnover and team effectiveness in the National Hockey League for the period of 1950 to 1966. Specifically, the following questions are considered:

(1) Does player turnover have a positive or negative influence on team effectiveness?

(2) Does management turnover have a positive or negative influence on team effectiveness?

(3) Does the influence of personnel turnover on organizational effectiveness vary by playing position?

(4) Does a change in personnel have an immediate or a delayed impact on organizational effectiveness?

A review of the broader organizational literature dealing either directly or tangentially with such questions, leads to four basic hypotheses.

Hypothesis 1

Organizational effectiveness is negatively related to personnel turnover at both management and worker levels.

Whenever a new member enters a group, a socialization process is initiated. This process operates on both the task and social levels and, as Caplow (1964:169) has noted, involves losses as well as gains in productivity. More specifically, Evans (1963:436) stated that the socialization process tends to interfere with organizational effectiveness. For example, Gouldner (1954), Klein (1956), Argyle *et al.* (1958), Trow (1960), Evans (1963) and Caplow (1964) all found a negative relationship between member succession and effectiveness. To what extent does this negative relationship hold for sport organizations where involuntary turnover is the norm?

In the only attempt to date to determine the relationship between labor turnover and organizational effectiveness within sport organizations, Loy (1970) examined major league baseball between 1948 and

1968. He found a correlation of $-.54$ between the number of new players and the team won-lost percentage. Furthermore, he found that the five teams with the *highest* rate of turnover had a significantly lower team standing in the league than did the five teams with the *lowest* rates of turnover.

On the management level, Grusky (1963a) examined professional baseball teams from 1921 to 1941 and from 1951 to 1958 and found a correlation of $-.43$ between the rate of managerial turnover and team effectiveness. Gamson and Scotch (1964) rejected Grusky's explanation by presenting a "scapegoat" theory wherein they argued that the replacement of the manager of a losing team is a ritual designed to have a psychological effect on team performance but which, in reality, has little effect on team productivity. Their analysis of mid-season changes of managers suggested a trend which would offer some support for the scapegoating theory.

Loy (1970) noted that there was a moderate tendency for team performance to improve following a managerial change. In addition, he found no significant difference in team effectiveness whether the new manager was recruited from within or outside the organization. Eitzen and Yetman (1972) examined the coaching records of NCAA college basketball teams and found a correlation of $-.24$ between turnover rate of coaches and winning percentage during the period 1930 to 1970, and a correlation of $-.28$ during the period 1960 to 1969. In a comparison of high and low turnover teams they found a similar relationship ($r = -.21$), and noted that losing teams were more likely to be characterized by high turnover rates. A more interesting finding of this study appeared when they controlled for the winning percentage of the former coach and found that a coaching change made no difference in the performance of the team in the following year.

In summary, the results suggest that labor turnover has a negative effect on organizational effectiveness, whereas management turnover may have either a negative effect, a positive effect or no effect on group productivity. Since this inconsistent finding may be due to sport differences or to methodological differences, the present study examines the relationship at both the labor and management level for another sport, namely professional hockey.

Hypothesis 2

The influence of personnel turnover on organizational effectiveness varies by position.

The playing position which undergoes a change in role incumbent may also influence the success of the organization. For example, employing Grusky's (1963b) centrality model, there is some evidence to suggest that the more central the position in the social structure, the greater the probability that co-ordinated tasks will be required for success. If this proposition is viable, it can be argued that if personnel changes are made in certain roles, then organizational efficiency may be decreased more so than with changes in other positions. In addition, because certain positions (e.g., centers or wings) require greater interaction with others or vary by complexity and degree of specialization, the socialization process on both the task and social levels may require different lengths of time before skills are mastered. Therefore a change of personnel at one position may have a greater or lesser impact on the organization than a change at another position. Some support for this hypothesis was presented by Loy (1970) in his analysis of professional baseball. He found that player turnover in central positions (i.e., infield) was more highly correlated with team effectiveness ($r = -.35$). He suggested that the process for learning infield roles is more difficult, and therefore the effectiveness of the organization is adversely influenced by infield changes.

Because of the dynamic structure of professional hockey, it is more difficult to classify roles (functionally or structurally) as central or peripheral. However, the demands of the four playing positions (i.e., goal, defense, center, wing) are quite different, and therefore personnel changes at each position may have different effects on team productivity.

Hypothesis 3

The greater the differential improvement on performance measures between new and replaced members, the greater the organizational effectiveness.

Whenever a new individual enters the organization, his performance is evaluated in terms of the contribution he makes versus that which the replaced individual made in the previous year. Thus, if the new member(s) outperform(s) the departed member(s) on a number of performance measures, then the effectiveness of the organization should increase. Furthermore, if the performance of the new member is considerably above average (i.e., a star) or below average (i.e., a marginal player) then team success would be increased in the former situation and decreased in the latter situation.

Hypothesis 4

> *The influence of personnel turnover on organizational effectiveness varies with time: The greater the time from turnover, the more effective the organization.*

If changes in personnel have an initial detrimental effect on organizational effectiveness, this may disappear over time as the new member becomes fully socialized and integrated into the new social system. Although no longitudinal studies have been completed to examine this question, Eitzen and Yetman (1972) did study the impact of coaching stability on team success. They found that the record of coaches who remained at one institution for eight or nine years improved over the earlier years. Furthermore, of those who remained ten, eleven, or twelve years an almost equal number had better or worse records, while those who remained beyond twelve years experienced decreasing effectiveness in the later years. In summary, they noted that although a coaching change appears to have little initial impact upon team performance, the longer the tenure, the greater the possibility that an organization will become more successful (cf. Rose, 1969).

Since the longitudinal effect of labor turnover on organizational effectiveness has not been examined, this study sought to determine if changes in playing personnel would lead to increased team success (i.e., winning percentage), one, two, and three years following the initial change. It was argued that after a period of one to three years, players will have been totally integrated into the team at both the task and social levels, and therefore any initial losses in group productivity will have been overcome with time.

METHODS

Sample

The sample consisted of all players who played at least twenty games in a given year for one of the six National Hockey League teams between 1950-51 and 1965-66. During this sixteen year period, each team was permitted to have twenty players on the team, fifteen or sixteen of which (one goal-tender, four or five defensemen, and nine or ten forwards) played regularly and therefore contributed to team productivity. It was assumed that players who did not appear in at least twenty games made little or no contribution to team productivity and thus they were excluded from the analysis.

Although statistics were collected for individual players, the unit of analysis was the team. During the sixteen years covered by this study, there were 96 units of analysis (6 teams x 16 years) which had varying numbers of new players and varying degrees of success in a given year.

The period between 1950-51 and 1965-66 was chosen for analysis because the league at that time formed a closed system, especially with respect to recruiting personnel. That is, the six teams had monopsonistic power in the labor market (Jones, 1969:10). Furthermore, each team had a number of "farm teams" at a lower level of competition and through these a further chain of affiliates as far down as the "Bantam" (13-14 years old) classification (Jones, 1969:13).

Collection of Data

Data were based on a secondary analysis of statistics recorded in the National Hockey League Press and Radio Guide, 1950-51 to 1965-66 (McKenzie and Andrews, 1950-66).

1. *Dependent Variables.* For each unit of analysis the following measures of team effectiveness were recorded: Number of Games Won; Number of Games Lost; Number of Games Tied; Total Goals Scored; Total Goals Against; Total Team Standing in the League; Number of Stanley Cup Championships; Team Winning Percentage; Team Penalty Minutes; Team Winning Percentage one, two and three years after each given year; and, the difference in team performance from the previous year on goals for, goals against, league standing, and team points.

2. *Independent Variables.* For each of the 96 units of analysis the team roster in a given year was compared with the previous year. All players who played at least twenty games and who were not on the team the previous year were recorded as a new player and their playing position was noted. These players may have entered the new organization via the inter- or intra-league draft, via trades with other organizations within the league, or by being promoted from a minor league affiliate. Two further subsets of new players were identified as either "stars" (i.e., fifty or more scoring points), or "marginals" (wings and centers with less than ten points). If a new coach or general manager joined the organization, this was also recorded. Finally, the differential performance between the new and replaced players on the following measures was computed for each playing position: goals scored; assists; total points; penalty minutes; and for the goaltenders, goals against average.

Data Analysis

The average turnover rate per year was computed by dividing the total number of new personnel at each position by the number of years (i.e., 16). For the positions of defence and wing, the number of new personnel was divided by two since there were two possible openings at these positions.

RESULTS[3] AND DISCUSSION

Descriptive Statistics Related to the Dependent Variable: Organizational Effectiveness

Team effectiveness was measured by the direction of performance change on a number of team measures. Table I presents the mean performance and range for four measures of effectiveness, while Table II indicates the direction of change from the base year on seven organizational effectiveness variables. As can be seen in Table I the mean number of goals scored (offensive effectiveness) and the mean number of goals against (defensive effectiveness) in any one season tend to be similar for the 96 teams studied over the sixteen year period. Thus, while the range in any one season may vary greatly, in the long run the impact of virtually no difference between offensive and defensive performance is that approximately an equal number of games are won and lost (mean winning percentage = .499). This result is even more apparent in Table II when the direction of change on the seven effectiveness variables is considered over the sixteen year period. On all seven measures, there appears to be an almost equal probability that a team will experience an increment or decrement in performance in a given year. Specifically, it was found that of the sixty teams that changed their position in the league standing from the previous year, 37 moved either up or down one position, 18 changed two positions, while only 5 teams moved three positions in the following year. Furthermore, for those teams that scored more or fewer goals from one year to the next, the range of difference was from 1 to 54 goals. Thus, few significant changes in organizational effectiveness occur from one year to the next. This does not imply, however, that playing talent is distributed equally. As Jones (1969:5) noted, "if the talent was equally distributed we would expect every game to end in a tie, or each team to win one-half of its games, or each team to win the league championship one-sixth of the time." Quite obviously this has not occurred. Thus, while the winning percentage of all teams in the sixteen year period was .499, certain organizations tended to be more successful, specifically Montreal, Detroit and Toronto (Table III). For example, Montreal or Detroit finished in first place in 15 of the 16 years, Montreal was always in the play-offs, Detroit missed in 2 years and Toronto only missed the play-offs in 3 years (cf. Jones, 1969). Thus, the league at this time was somewhat dichotomized between the "haves" and the "have nots".

TABLE I

ORGANIZATIONAL EFFECTIVENESS

Indicator	Mean	S.D.	Range
Team Goals Scored Per Year	193.39	28.47	133-259
Team Goals Against Per Year	192.80	37.85	131-306
Total Team Points	70.10	16.49	31-101
Winning Percentage	.499	.14	.190-.771

TABLE II

PERCENTAGE OF TEAMS WHICH EXPERIENCED EITHER AN IMPROVEMENT, DECREMENT OR NO CHANGE IN ORGANIZATIONAL EFFECTIVENESS FROM THE PREVIOUS YEAR
(N = 96 teams)

Indicator	Improvement	Decrement	No Change
Total Goals Scored	52.1 (50)	47.9 (46)	—
Total Goals Against	40.6 (39)	55.2 (53)	4.2 (4)
League Standing	31.3 (30)	31.3 (30)	37.5 (36)
Total Team Points	43.8 (42)	51.0 (59)	5.2 (5)
Winning Percentage 1 Year After Base Year	46.9 (45)	52.1 (50)	1.0 (1)
Winning Percentage 2 Years After Base Year	53.1 (51)	46.9 (45)	—
Winning Percentage 3 Years After Base Year	49.0 (47)	49.0 (47)	2.1 (2)

TABLE III

TEAM STANDING, 1950-51 TO 1965-66

Team	League Standing						Stanley Cup Championships
	1	2	3	4	5	6	
Toronto	1	4	5	3	2	1	4
Montreal	8	6	2	—	—	—	8
Detroit	7	1	1	5	1	1	3
Boston	—	1	2	5	3	5	0
New York	—	1	1	2	9	3	0
Chicago	—	3	5	1	1	6	1

Descriptive Statistics Related to the Independent Variable: Personnel Turnover

Personnel turnover and the impact of this process was measured respectively, by the number of new individuals in six roles within professional hockey, and by the difference in performance in these roles between the new and replaced individuals. Table IV indicates the number of new personnel by team, year, role and status. Over the sixteen year period, there were an average of 35.25 player changes per year, 5.88 player changes per team per year, and 94 new players per organization. In short, professional hockey organizations initiate numerous player turnovers in an attempt to realize a higher level of group effectiveness.

TABLE IV

NUMBER OF NEW PERSONNEL BY TEAM, POSITION AND STATUS

| | Administration | | | Players | | | | Status | |
Team	Manager	Coach	Goal	Defense	Wing	Center	Total	Marginal [a]	Star [b]
1	3	5	6	17	28	19	70	15	2
2	1	1	5	14	29	9	57	8	2
3	1	2	4	28	53	22	107	23	2
4	1	4	12	33	41	24	110	11	3
5	1	10	8	26	46	22	102	21	4
6	1	6	5	33	44	36	118	20	2
	8	28	40	151	241	132	564	98	15

[a] Number of Wings and Centers with less than 10 points (goals and assists)
[b] Number of Players with 50 or more points during the 1st year on the team (goals and assists)

In order to determine the extent to which the new players made a greater or lesser contribution than the replaced players to team effectiveness, a comparison was made on a number of performance measures. These are illustrated in Table V. Although the new personnel outperformed the former players at most positions and in most categories, the proportion of times in which an improvement was noted was seldom beyond 55 percent, with no measure indicating more than a 59 percent improvement. The greatest disparity between those changes which led to an improvement and those which led to a decrement was in the category of assists. This held for all positions. Thus, although there was a great variation in the actual difference between the new and replaced players on most performance categories, the over-all effect was an almost equal probability of the change leading to an improvement or decrement in team performance.

TABLE V
DIRECTION OF DIFFERENTIAL PERFORMANCE BETWEEN
NEW AND REPLACED PLAYERS ON PERFORMANCE MEASURES BY POSITION

INDICATOR	IMPROVEMENT (%)	DECREMENT (%)	NO CHANGE (%)	RANGE (N)
A. ALL PLAYERS				
Goals Scored	51.0	42.7	5.2	1-65
Assists	59.4	37.5	2.1	1-78
Total Points	55.2	43.8	---	1-118
Penalty Minutes	41.7[a]	57.3	---	2-263
B. DEFENSEMEN				
Goals Scored	49.2	43.3	7.5	1-15
Assists	58.2	35.8	6.0	1-32
Total Points	59.7	37.4	2.9	1-41
Penalty Minutes	46.3[a]	52.2	1.5	2-195
C. WINGS				
Goals Scored	51.9	44.4	3.7	1-65
Assists	58.0	42.0	---	1-70
Total Points	56.8	43.2	---	1-172
Penalty Minutes	55.6[a]	44.2	---	2-264
D. CENTERS				
Goals Scored	47.5	49.2	3.3	1-40
Assists	57.6	42.4	---	1-61
Total Points	54.2	45.8	---	1-93
Penalty Minutes	49.2[a]	50.8	---	2-182
E. GOALTENDERS				
Goal Against	54.7	45.3	---	1-96

[a]An improvement represents fewer penalty minutes

Hypothesis 1

Organizational effectiveness is negatively related to personnel turnover at both management and worker levels.

In order to test this hypothesis nine indicators of personnel turnover were cross-tabulated with four measures of organizational effectiveness. It was found that none of the cross-tabulations were statistically significant at the .05 level. That is, there appeared to be no association between a coaching change; a general managerial change; the total number of new players; the number of new goaltenders, defensemen, wings or centers; the number of new "stars" or the number of new "marginals"; and, any of the following four dependent variables: direction of difference (improvement, decrement, or no change) in team performance from the previous year in league standing; total goals scored; total goals against; or total team points.

Since the influence of new personnel on team effectiveness may be different for either the successful or unsuccessful teams, similar analyses were run controlling for position in the league standing. Those teams which finished first, second or third at any time in the sixteen year period were compared with those who finished in fourth, fifth or sixth place. Again, even when position in the league standing was controlled, there was no significant association between any measure of personnel turnover and team effectiveness.

In summary, there appears to be no relationship between the entrance of new personnel at either the management or labourer level, and a significant change in group success. Thus, the results do not support those presented by Grusky (1963a), Loy (1970), and Eitzen and Yetman (1972) wherein personnel turnover had a detrimental influence on organizational effectiveness. The results of this analysis are not surprising in view of the almost equal probability of a team experiencing an improvement or decrement in performance in a given year. That is, there is a regression to the mean. This point has previously been discussed by Eitzen and Yetman (1972) who noted that after a change in personnel the poorer teams tended to improve the following year while the successful teams tended to deteriorate strictly as a matter of probability. They argued that success or failure results from chance factors operating in one direction or the other. Furthermore, they noted that it is virtually impossible for highly successful teams to improve to any great extent, and similarly, unsuccessful teams can only remain weak or improve slightly. Thus, in a zero sum situation such as the closed system of the National Hockey League, the changing of personnel appeared to have little influence on organizational success, especially since there were very few changes of position in the league standing.

A further explanation for the lack of relationship between turnover and effectiveness may be related to the implicit management policy suggested by Jones (1969:7) wherein there has been a tendency over the years for successful teams to avoid trading with each other, and to trade almot exclusively with the less successful teams. While this practice would appear to strengthen the weaker teams, it ensures that an organization's closest competitors are not given the opportunity to improve. If this practice actually exists, then many of the intra-league trades and drafts may be token attempts to improve weaker teams, or may be made for reasons emanating from the social domain. In Table VI the number of in-season changes in personnel which occured in the period 1950-1966 between and within teams in the upper or lower division are noted. As can be seen, most trades occured between teams in the upper ("haves") and lower ("have-nots") division, or between teams in the lower division. Thus, this trading pattern was unlikely to result in significant improvements since many of the upper-lower trades involved sending one or two marginal members to the lower division team in return for one average player.

TABLE VI
PATTERN OF IN-SEASON TRADES (1950-51 TO 1965-66)

Division	Number of Trades	Percent of Trades
Upper[a]Lower[b]	57	66.3
Lower-Lower	22	25.6
Upper-Upper	7	8.1
TOTAL	86	100.00

[a]Upper= Toronto, Montreal, Detroit
[b]Lower= New York, Chicago, Boston

A final factor that may account for the results is the nature of the system being studied. In contrast with investigations of professional baseball and college basketball, this study focused on a closed monopsonic system wherein the six organizations had exclusive access to, and control of, the labor force. Thus, once an organization gained control of a highly skilled labor pool (i.e., farm system) or was given exclusive rights to geographical regions which were high producers of potential laborers (cf. Rooney, 1974), then this organization obtained not only success, but power to control the labor force. In the National Hockey League this phenomenon occurred with three organizations who subsequently became the "haves" and tended to dominate the system until a more equitable and liberal policy of labor equalization (draft whereby the least successful team selects first) was initiated and until competition forced expansion and a new league. In conclusion, a longitudinal analysis of the impact of personnel changes suggests that there is an equal probability of a change in personnel having a positive or negative influence on organizational effectiveness.

Hypothesis 2

The influence of personnel turnover on organizational effectiveness varies by position.

As noted in the previous section there was no relationship between team effectiveness and the introduction of a new coach, general manager, goaltender, defenseman, wing or center into the organization. Thus, this hypothesis was not supported.

Hypothesis 3

The greater the differential improvement on performance measures between new and replaced members, the greater the organizational effectiveness.

A comparison of the new and replaced players on goals scored, assists, total points, penalty minutes, and goaltender's goals against average indicated that in most cases the new players slightly outperformed the replaced players and therefore one would expect that team effectiveness would increase. Yet, as indicated in Table II, there appears to be an almost equal probability of a team increasing or decreasing its effectiveness. Therefore, in order to determine whether an improvement in team effectiveness was related to a differential improvement in performance between the new and replaced players, cross-tabulations were computed. It was found that if the new players (wings, centers, defensemen) outscored the former players, there was a greater likelihood that a team would improve its league standing (Table VII). However, the only significant association for a specific position was that between direction of change in league standing and the direction of change in performance between the new and replaced goaltender's goals against average (Table VIII).

In summary, with two exceptions, the direction of performance differential between new and replaced players had little influence on team effectiveness.

TABLE VII

THE RELATIONSHIP BETWEEN DIRECTION OF DIFFERENTIAL PERFORMANCE BETWEEN NEW AND REPLACED PLAYERS IN GOALS SCORED AND THE DIRECTION OF DIFFERENCE IN LEAGUE STANDING FROM THE PREVIOUS YEAR

	League Standing		
Goals Scored	*Improved*	*No Change*	*Decreased*
Improved	14	23	12
No Change	4	1	0
Decreased	11	12	18

$X^2 = 10.87$, $df = 4 (p .05)$

Gamma = .18

TABLE VIII

THE RELATIONSHIP BETWEEN DIRECTION OF DIFFERENTIAL PERFORMANCE BETWEEN THE NEW AND
REPLACED GOAL TENDER'S GOALS AGAINST AVERAGE AND THE DIRECTION OF DIFFERENCE IN LEAGUE
STANDING FROM THE PREVIOUS YEAR

	League Standing		
Goals Against Average	Improved	No Change	Decreased
Improved	13	7	3
Decreased	0	8	11

$X^2 = 17.42$, $df = 2(p\ .01)$

Gamma $= .26$

Hypothesis 4

*The influence of personnel turnover on organizational effectiveness
varies with time: The greater the time from turnover, the more effective
the organization.*

In the rationale it was argued that even if a change in personnel was
initially disruptive to an organization, this would be reduced in time as
the new members became socialized in the task and social domains.
Since no relationship between turnover and effectiveness was obtained it
was not possible to test this hypothesis. Furthermore, when the turnover
variables were cross-tabulated with the direction of change in team
winning percentage one, two and three years after a change in personnel
was initiated, in no case was there a significant relationship or even a
pattern of increasing or decreasing effect for one variable over the three
year period. Thus, this hypothesis was not supported and remains to be
tested in other organizational settings.

Summary and Conclusions

In summary, an analysis of labor and management changes in the
National Hockey League from 1950-51 to 1965-66 indicated that while
many changes in personnel were made, and while the turnover rate
varied by position, there was no relationship between either the number
of turnovers or the position which underwent the turnover, and organizational effectiveness. Therefore, it can be concluded that the replacement of personnel by a sport organization will not guarantee greater

effectiveness in either the current year or in subsequent years. In fact, trading for "future considerations" and "future drafts" may be a more effective way to increase the success of a sport organization. That is, one or two new players are introduced as needed, while the pool of talent within the organization and the power of the organization is increased.

While this study has examined the impact of personnel turnover on organizational effectiveness, other organizational parameters also influence effectiveness and should be examined in sport systems. For example, individual and team morale; job satisfaction; the relationship between management and worker goals for the organization; the number of spectators attending the games; the amount of profit realized per annum; the quality of "farm" systems; the quality of administration; and the leadership style of coaches may also influence the immediate or future effectiveness of a sport organization.

In conclusion, it is recommended that future studies concerning turnover and organizational effectiveness should examine: (1) the effect of trading for future draft choices; (2) the impact of the mechanism of player turnover (i.e., draft, trade, promotion, or retirement); (3) the impact of personnel turnover on team effectiveness over a longer period of time; and, (4) the influence of adding inexperienced (i.e., rookies) or experienced (i.e., veterans) to the organization. In all of these studies, a comparative analysis with a variety of sport organizations should be initiated to control for sport specific phenomena (e.g., see Ball, 1974).

NOTES

1. This study was supported by a University of Waterloo Research Committee Grant, January, 1973.
2. For some rather notable exceptions see Grusky (1963a); Rose (1969); Loy and Sage (1970); Eitzen and Yetman (1972); Loy and Sage (1973); Ball (1974).
3. I would like to acknowledge the assistance of Ernie Fraser who coded and analyzed the data for this study.

REFERENCES

Argyle, M. et al.
1958   "Supervisory methods related to productivity, absenteeism, and labor turnover." *Human Relations,* 11.
Azumi, K. and J. Hage.
1972   *Organizational Systems.* Lexington, Massachusette: D. C. Heath.
Ball, D. W.
1974   "Replacement processes in work organizations: task evaluation and the case of professional football." *Sociology of Work and Occupation I.*

Caplow, T.
1964   *Principles of Organization*. New York: Harcourt, Brace and World.

Eitzen, D. S. and N. R. Yetman.
1972   "Managerial change, longevity, and organizational effectiveness." *Administrative Science Quarterly*, 17.

Etzioni, A.
1964   *Modern Organizations*. Englewood Cliffs: Prentice Hall.

Evans, W. M.
1963   "Peer-group interaction and organizational socialization: a study of employee turn-over." *American Sociological Review*, 28.

Gamson, W. A. and N. A. Scotch.
1964   "Scape-goating in baseball." *American Journal of Sociology*, 70.

Gouldner, W. A.
1954   *Patterns of Industrial Bureaucracy*. Glencoe, Illinois: Free Press.

Grusky, O.
1963a   "Managerial succession and organizational effectiveness." *American Journal of Sociology*, 69.

1963b   "The effects of formal structure on managerial recruitment." *Sociometry*, 26.

and G. A. Miller (eds.).
1970   *The Sociology of Organizations: Basic Studies*. New York: Free Press.

Jones, J. C. H.
1969   "The economics of the national hockey league." *Canadian Journal of Economics*, 11.

Klein, J.
1956   *The Study of Groups*. London: Routledge and Kejan Paul.

Loy, J. W.
1970   "Where the action is: a consideration of centrality in sport situations." Paper presented at the Second Canadian Psycho-Motor Learning and Sport Psychology Symposium, Windsor, Ontario.

1970   "The effects of formal structure on organizational leadership: an investigation of interscholastic baseball teams." In G. S. Kenyon (ed.), *Contemporary Psychology of Sport*. Chicago: The Athletic Institute.

1973   "Organizational prestige and coaching career patterns." Paper presented at the 36th Annual Meeting of the Southern Sociological Society, Atlanta, Georgia.

March, J. G.
1965   *Handbook of Organizations*. Chicago: Rand McNally.

and H. A. Simon.
1958   *Organizations*. New York: John Wiley.

Maurer, J. G.
1971   *Readings in Organization Theory*. New York: Random House.

McKenzie, K. and R. Andrews (eds.)
1950-60 *National Hockey League Press and Radio Guide*. Montreal: The National Hockey League.

McNeil, K. and J. D. Thompson.
1971   "The Regeneration of Social Organizations." *American Sociological Review*, 36.

Perrow, C. B.
1972   *Complex Organizations*. Chicago: Scott, Foresman.

Price, J. L.
1968   *Organizational Effectiveness: An Inventory of Propositions*. Homewood, Illinois: R. D. Irwin.

1973a   "Toward a theory of turnover." Presented at the Annual Meeting of the American Sociological Association, New York.

1973b   "The correlates of turnover". Mimeographed re-print, Sociology Working Paper
         Series, 73-1, University of Iowa.

Rooney, J. F.
1974   A Geography of American Sport: From Cabin Creek to Anaheim. Reading, Massa-
         chusetts: Addison-Wesley.

Rose, J. D.
1969   "Attribution of responsibility for organizational failure." Sociology of Social Re-
         search, 53.

Tausky, C.
1970   Work Organizations: Major Theoretical Perspectives. Illinois: F. E. Peacock.

Trow, D. B.
1960   "Membership succession and team performance." Human Relations, 13.

CAREER MOBILITY IN PROFESSIONAL HOCKEY*

Michael D. Smith and Frederic Diamond

In the mélange of case studies that seems to characterize the sociology of occupations are numerous investigations of the work world of professional athletes. Some have been partially or wholly concerned with career mobility (Andreano, 1965; Charnofsky, 1968; Gregory, 1965; Grusky, 1963; Haerle, 1975; Hare, 1973; Lever, 1969; Mihovilovic, 1968; Roy, 1974; Scott, 1968; Stone, 1971; Weinberg and Arond, 1952; Yetman and Eitzen, 1972): several are richly detailed; but few have as their basis a comprehensive set of quantitative data. A step in this direction was taken in the present research which is addressed to career lines in professional hockey.

* This is a greatly revised version of a paper presented at the Eighth World Congress of
  Sociology, Toronto, August 1974. We wish to thank Robert R. Faulkner for his criticisms
  of this paper and to absolve him from responsibility for its shortcomings. We are also
  grateful to Maurice Reid, Director of the Hockey Hall of Fame in Toronto, for his
  co-operation in making available to us the National Hockey League Guides.

The aims were, first, to prompt a realistic view of an occupation more loaded than most with a freight of myths, and, second, to uncover data and concepts needed for the generation of substantive theory in the sociology of sport.[1]

In this paper, we compare the career mobility of two cohorts of National Hockey League players. The focus is on horizontal and downward movement, scant attention being paid to upward mobility (the theme of innumerable "rags to riches" sport stories). Quantitative data are employed in describing patterns of career movement; qualitative data in examining the meaning of this movement from the standpoint of those who experienced it. Indeed, the concept of career seems particularly suited to linking the objective and subjective dimensions of social reality, for as Faulkner (1973:334) notes:

> On the one hand, careers are made up of systems of positions, their relation to one another, and typical sequences of movement within and through them. On the other hand, members acquire ways of thinking, feeling, and believing about these arrangements; they orient themselves, positively and negatively, emotionally and intellectually, toward the roles they are paid to perform and the routes they are constrained to pursue.

Management-Worker Relations in the National Hockey League

Hockey's pinnacle, the National League, was from its beginning in 1917 a model of economic enterprise, enjoying a monopoly of the hockey industry for a fifty-year span between the demise of two rival major professional leagues in 1926 and the appearance in 1972 of the World Hockey Association. NHL owners and managers established early the habit of squeezing out not only incipient competition but dissident workers in their own ranks—would-be players' representatives and the like. Yet during the turbulent pre-World War II years, as franchises collapsed and new ones arose, management in its efforts to built the game occasionally made money a secondary consideration. But the post-war bosses invariably put profits first, as professional hockey became big business. Owners became wealthy while players remained relatively in the same economic position. Players had no say in their work conditions or career chances; they were (and still are) arbitrarily drafted, sold, traded, loaned, released, put on waivers, and shunted up and down within the organizations, often with bewildering rapidity (Conacher, 1972: 7-16; Kidd and McFarlane, 1972; 99-121).[2]

It was shortly after the War, too, that the NHL achieved complete control over the careers of virtually all hockey aspirants in North America. The chief mechanisms of this accomplishment were the "reserve clause," which gave each of the six NHL members perpetual option on the services of all players signed, and the "chain system," an arrangement with the Canadian Amateur Hockey Association whereby each NHL club controlled a string of minor professional and amateur teams all the way down to "bantam"(thirteen to fourteen years old) level (Jones, 1969).

Beginning in 1967, however, events transpired that brought about dramatic changes in the work context and career opportunities of hockey personnel: a players' association was established, which has since wrested a measure of control and some of the profits from the owners; the NHL expanded to fourteen teams (and will have expanded to twenty by the 1975-76 season); and in 1972 the rival World Hockey Association was formed. This mushrooming of positions at the top not only has opened the door for greater numbers to enter major professional hockey, it appears to have prolonged the playing lives of those in the twilight of their careers and to have altered the structure of mobility in other ways. And now, as in the early 1920s, players can sell their services in the marketplace. Yet the "reserve clause" remains, and players under contract are still subject to frequent uprooting.[3]

Hockey in Canada: Mystique and Reality

It is difficult to understand fully the occupational career of the hockey player without taking into account the game's mystique in Canada. At least since 1931, when radio began to bring the NHL into Canadian homes coast-to-coast, hockey has commanded the attention of Canadians like no other public activity. As Kidd and McFarlane (1972:17) explain: hockey, "after all, was the only popular culture we did not import." Performers, like Brazil's footballers (Lever, 1969) or American baseball players in the game's heyday (Andreano, 1965), enjoy unflagging attention by the mass media, and the "stars" have been elevated to the status of national folk heroes. The symbolic significance of these "success stories," perhaps more than anything else, has obscured the reality of what it is to be a professional player.

Like other major professional sports, hockey differs significantly in several ways from most lines of work: big league performers now get high wages,[4] lavish fringe benefits, and public adulation—all at an early age. Over one hundred games and 100,000 miles air travel yearly, however, together with constant pressure to perform at maximum efficiency, probably blunts the glamour, as a former veteran player suggests (Nesterenko, 1974: 383):

Travelling in the big jets and going to and from hotels is very tough. We're in New York on a Wednesday, Philadelphia on a Thursday, Buffalo on a Saturday, Pittsburgh on a Sunday, and Detroit on a Tuesday. That's just a terrible way to live. (Laughs.) After the game on Sunday, I am tired—not only with my body, which is not a bad kind of tiredness, I'm tired emotionally, tired mentally. I'm not a very good companion after these games.

And unlike most occupations, careers are generally over by age thirty-five. (Ironically, professional sport has a longer socialization—usually beginning in early childhood—yet a shorter life than perhaps any other career.) But perhaps the most interesting aspect of hockey's "back region"—lost in a morass of Horatio Alger tales—is the horizontal and especially the downward mobility undergone by countless numbers of players during their careers. The sheer amount of this movement, not to mention its social and psychological consequences, has been almost ignored by those who write about the game.

Method

From the annual *National Hockey League Guides*, (McKenzie and Andrews, 1951-1972), biographical data were obtained on all players who performed in at least twenty-five NHL games and who retired from 1951 (the first year for which there are complete records) through 1972. Six cases had to be discarded, leaving a final sample of 313, or 98 per cent of the players of that period.

We computed players' year of retirement; then divided the sample into two cohorts: those who retired before and those who retired after the League expansion of 1967. The impact of this now dichotomous variable (in effect, a measure of organizational change) on player's career routes was determined by cross-tabulating it with the following variables, which were either coded directly from the biographical materials or subsequently computed: number of years in professional hockey (minor league and NHL), number of years in NHL, total number of moves (upward, downward, and horizontal), number of cities played in, number of horizontal moves (minor league to minor league or NHL to NHL), number of downward moves (NHL to minor league), first professional team (minor league or NHL), and last professional team (minor league or NHL).

Finally, although hockey has yet to produce a "participant-as-observer" of the calibre of baseball's Bouton (e.g., 1969) or an "observer-as-participant" as perceptive as Plimpton (e.g., 1966), we were able to obtain several journalistic and ethnographic accounts of how players subjectively encountered the career experiences catalogued above. Such an approach, if not allowing for the examination of *all* members' realities, at least allows for the examination of *some* members' realities (Ball, 1974).

Career Mobility in Professional Hockey

Table I gives descriptive statistics for selected variables before aggregation and regrouping. Tables II through X describe more fully patterns of occupational longevity, geographical, horizontal, and downward movement in professional hockey, and reveal that organizational expansion significantly affected the shape of players' career routes.

TABLE I

DESCRIPTIVE STATISTICS FOR SELECTED VARIABLES BEFORE REGROUPING

Variables	Mean	Median	Standard Deviation	Range
No. yrs. in pro. hockey	12.1	11.5	4.3	2-25
No. yrs. in NHL	6.3	4.9	4.9	1-20
Age at retirement	33.5	33.7	4.1	23-46
Total No. moves	7.4	7.0	4.3	0-23
No, different cities played in	6.1	5.9	2.8	1-15
No. downward moves	2.1	1.9	1.5	0-7
No. horizontal moves	5.3	4.9	3.2	0-18

Career longevity. Table II shows that almost three-quarters of the entire sample spent ten years or more in professional hockey and 28.8 per cent fifteen years or more. But when period of retirement is taken into account, it can be seen that post-expansion players who lasted at least fifteen years disproportionately contributed to the ranks of these performers.

TABLE II

PERIOD OF RETIREMENT BY NUMBER OF YEARS IN PROFESSIONAL HOCKEY

Period of Retirement	Number of Years in Professional Hockey									
	1-4 yrs.		5-9 yrs.		10-14 yrs.		15 yrs. or more		Totals	
	N	(%)	N	(%)	N	(%)	N	(%)	N	(%)
Pre-expansion	8	(3.7)	65	(30.1)	111	(51.4)	32	(14.8)	216	(69.0)
Post-expansion	1	(1.0)	11	(11.3)	27	(27.8)	58	(59.8)	97	(31.0)
Totals	9	(2.9)	76	(24.3)	138	(44.1)	90	(28.8)	313	(100)

These numbers are greatly deflated when NHL experience (Table III) is separated from total professional experience. Only 25.6 per cent played ten years or more in the NHL and 8 per cent fifteen years or more. Again the post-1967 veterans are greatly over-represented in the fifteen years category. The reverse holds in the other career length panels of both Tables II and III, where in every case the post-1967 retirees are out-proportioned by those who retired prior to that year. Put differently, in Table II, ten-year veterans outnumber three to one those who played fewer than ten seasons, while in Table III, ten-year men are outnumbered three to one. These findings suggest that the expansion of 1967, and subsequently, attenuated the playing-lives of many performers., probably marginals, in particular, who had spent a considerable part of their careers in the minor leagues (an argument to which we shall return).

TABLE III

PERIOD OF RETIREMENT BY NUMBER OF YEARS IN NHL

Period of Retirement	Number of Years in NHL								
	1-4 yrs.		5-9 yrs.		10-14 yrs.		15 yrs. or more		Totals
	N	(%)	N	(%)	N	(%)	N	(%)	N	(%)
Pre-expansion	104	(48.1)	65	(30.1)	14	(18.5)	7	(3.2)	216	(69.0)
Post-expansion	43	(44.3)	21	(21.6)	15	(15.5)	18	(18.6)	97	(31.0)
Totals	147	(47.0)	86	(27.5)	55	(17.6)	25	(8.0)	313	(100)

It may be, too, that organizational expansion has altered hockey's age-graded mobility criteria: the normative expectations as to what level ought to have been achieved by a certain age existing particularly in organizations that put a premium on physical skill. Faulkner's (1974) comparative analysis of careers in hockey and the symphony orchestra (which have an almost identical hierarchical structure) emphasizes age as a key variable in understanding mobility processes in these occupations. Although elite musicians enjoy much longer stays in the top stratum (the average is eighteen years) than do hockey players, the occupations have several similar age-situated mobility (or in this case immobility) norms; in both, for example, an aspirant who remains in the lower stratum too long as a smaller likelikhood of promotion. "I'd say that after 28," one hockey player states, "'the odds are against you.... My wife and I say we'll give it till 26 or 27 maybe, then I'll know if I'll be in the NHL. After that they give up on you" (Faulkner, 1974: 156). Career "timetables" are a way of structuring uncertainty. They emerge from information obtained from the experience of others who have gone, or are going, through a similar series of events (Roth, 1968), and they fluctuate with organizational size (Grusky, 1968), among other variables; thus one suspects that as aging hockey players have been given new lives in the seller's market created by expansion, the industry's socially constructed conceptions of age have shifted upwardly. Furthermore, longer occupancy of a cohort at one organizational level sets off reverberations, such as the slower incorporation of new recruits into that level. But this subject is explored in Faulkner's paper in much greater detail than can be done here.

The volume of mobility. Job precariousness, of course, has always been a hazard in professional sport. Table IV gives the combined horizontal and vertical mobility for the present sample (i.e., any move within the "organizational set").[5] About 75 per cent moved at least five times, and 28.8 per cent did so ten times or more. (Seven players moved not at all, and one uprooted twenty-three times.) Consistent with the data presented in Tables II and III, the post-1967 cohort outstripped its pre-expansion counterpart nearly two to one in the frequent (ten or more) moves category, whereas a greater percentage of the latter was likely to be moderately or infrequently mobile.

TABLE IV

PERIOD OF RETIREMENT BY TOTAL NUMBER OF MOVES

Period of Retirement	Total Number of Moves							
	0-4 moves		5-9 moves		10 moves or more		Totals	
	N	(%)	N	(%)	N	(%)	N	(%)
Pre-expansion	66	(30.6)	112	(51.9)	38	(17.6)	216	(69.0)
Post-expansion	17	(17.5)	28	(28.9)	52	(53.6)	97	(31.0)
Totals	83	(26.5)	140	(44.7)	90	(28.8)	313	(100)

Geographic mobility. In sport, unlike most other lines of work, occupational mobility, whether vertical or sideways, almost always involves geographic mobility (Table V). This means relocation not only for the worker but usually for his family, if he has one, although an alternative taken by many athletes is to commute seasonally to the new work-place. Players, however, may expect and accept frequent migration as part of the job, and the positive features of the new situation, of course, may outweigh the negative aspects of moving, as in the case of promotion. Nevertheless, one suspects that the frequent disruptions (one player was employed in fifteen *different* cities) have their costs: "These days are not good ones for boys aged fourteen and ten with an absentee father," declared a veteran goalkeeper several years ago explaining one of his several retirements (O'Brien, 1972: 119). (He has since returned to the game.) Says the wife of another much-travelled performer: "I haven't really enjoyed it...we were never anywhere longer than two years...I'm not a good hockey wife because it bothers me to have him away so long. But I'd also start to worry because it felt like each trade was a demotion" (Boulton, 1975: 13). Life in professional sport does not appear conducive to family stability, although some athletes are able successfully to "juggle" family and career (Glaser and Strauss, 1971: 159).

TABLE V

PERIOD OF RETIREMENT BY NUMBER OF DIFFERENT CITIES PLAYED IN

Period of Retirement	Number of Different Cities							
	0-4 Cities		5-9 Cities		10 Cities or more		Totals	
	N	(%)	N	(%)	N	(%)	N	(%)
Pre-expansion	75	(34.7)	131	(60.6)	10	(4.6)	216	(69.0)
Post-expansion	18	(18.6)	51	(52.6)	28	(28.9)	97	(31.0)
Totals	93	(29.7)	182	(58.1)	38	(12.1)	313	(100)

Horizontal mobility. Table VI shows that horizontal mobility was a fact of life for most hockey practitioners, especially those whose careers extended into the expansion era. 81.4 per cent of this group was laterally mobile on at least four occasions. The NHL expansion drafts of 1967 and later, in which the established teams stocked the new ones (with marginal players), alone must have contributed significantly to this number.

TABLE VI

PERIOD OF RETIREMENT BY NUMBER OF HORIZONTAL MOVES

Period of Retirement	Number of Horizontal Moves							
	0-1 moves		2-3 moves		4 moves or more		Totals	
	N	(%)	N	(%)	N	(%)	N	(%)
Pre-expansion	30	(13.9)	49	(22.7)	137	(63.4)	216	(69.0)
Post-expansion	7	(7.2)	11	(11.3)	79	(81.4)	97	(31.0)
Totals	37	(11.8)	60	(19.2)	216	(69.0)	313	(100)

But the sociologist's definition of horizontal movement does not always coincide with that of the mover; all organizations on one level of a hierarchical structure are not equally rewarding places to work. Being traded to Toronto from some other major league city, for instance, may be regarded as upward mobility because of increased opportunities for status conversion in a hockey conscious milieu, while news that one is going, say, to Kansas City may be met with dismay. In the minor professional system, Rochester, during the mid-1960s, was considered a good place to be sent because it was the player source most often tapped by its major league parent. Besides, the team travelled on an old chartered DC-3, while others in the American League went by bus (Conacher, 1972:73-74). Obviously, a variety of economic and status gains and losses, contingent upon the characteristics of the mover, his destination and former location, may accompany what ostensibly is horizontal mobility. Perhaps the only clear-cut success in the professional sport hierarchies is making the "big" leagues, which, according to most of Faulkner's (1974: 144) minor leaguers, is the "only place to be."

The career strivings of some professional athletes, like Becker's (1952) public school teachers, may consist entirely of movement within a stratum; but the majority of players have little control over this aspect of career (recent opportunities to "jump" to rival leagues notwithstanding). A hockey player may ask to be traded to another team but will be fortunate if management decides it is in its interest to arrange the transaction. When accomplished, though, calculated career moves are usually viewed positively, as one would suspect, and do not require the same psychological adjustments as involuntary moves (Glaser, 1968).

On the other hand, to be traded or sold involuntarily may involve self-definitions of failure since it is to be told symbolically that what is gained is at least equal to, or perhaps of greater value, than what is being lost (Ball, 1974). The ambiguity of the situation is put succinctly by an NHL defenseman traded for the second time in thirteen months:

> A trade is a hell of a shock.... Your first reaction, or at least mine, is disappointment that a club has decided it no longer needs you or that you somehow haven't been doing a job for them. That hurts.
> Then you look on the positive side. St. Louis was a challenger, a team that was rebuilding. Montreal was something else, a really strong team with a tradition of winning championships. Now the question arises: Could I stick? (Proudfoot, *Toronto Star* 13 February 1975a: B2).

The frequent suddenness of such moves is legendary. Writes Boulton (1975: 11-13) of Morley (Larry) Hillman, who has performed on sixteen

different professional teams: "How many times has he heard the foot-
steps in the hall and the chilling early-morning call from the other side
of the door: Hey Morley, wake up. The G.M. wants to see you." Hillman
describes his feelings on such occasions: "Brutal really brutal . . . it shocks
the hell out of me; it really does . . . I just can't believe its happening."
And later: "Let's face it . . . a player like me is not exactly in the driver's
seat." And then there is the indignity of not being able to fit into the new
team:

As soon as you get traded, you want to check one thing—the opposing team's
lineup. You've got to know where you fit in. When Boston traded for me, I
thought what do they want with me? I had roomed with Johnny Bucyk the
year before in Detroit so I called him. I said, 'How many defensemen you
guys got?' He said, 'Six.' I said, 'Where do I fit in?' Bucyk says, 'I dunno.' So I
said, 'Chrissakes, what are they trying to do to me?' (Boulton, 1975: 13).

Hillman's situation, of course, and that of the man he may or may not
have replaced on this occasion, is an outcome of the structure of the
organizational set, each team being allowed only a certain number of
players on its roster and, consequently, at each position. Contrary to the
entrepreneurial ethos, Faulkner (1974: 145) reminds us, mobility in
hockey is an *aggregate phenomenon* governed both by the availability of
positions into which entry is sought and the number of aspirants for
those positions.

Downward mobility. As for downward mobility (Table VII), in few
other jobs is it so common. Sixty-six per cent of the post-expansion
players were demoted at least twice;[6] and 33 per cent were downwardly
mobile four times or more—all in a brief span of time and at a young
age.

Why were the post-expansion players apparently more often downwardly mobile than their predecessors? The number of minor professional teams consistently supplying workers to the major leagues has
remained relatively unchanged for more than two decades (McKenzie
and Andrews, 1951-1972), while the NHL mushroomed after 1967, and
there would appear to have been a lesser, not a greater, likelihood of
demotion.[7]

But we have already suggested that frequently downward moving
marginal major leaguers, most of whose careers began in the 1950s, are
over-represented in the post-1967 cohort;[8] thus, it appears that frequent
demotions experienced by these players prior to 1967 contributed most
to the initially puzzling findings in Table VII and hence to the apparently diminishing ratio of horizontal to vertical mobility. To test this

TABLE VII

PERIOD OF RETIREMENT BY NUMBER OF DOWNWARD MOVES

Period of Retirement	Number of Downward Moves							
	0-1 moves		2-3 moves		4 moves or more		Totals	
	N	(%)	N	(%)	N	(%)	N	(%)
Pre-expansion	98	(45.4)	94	(43.5)	24	(11.1)	216	(69.0)
Post-expansion	33	(34.0)	32	(33.0)	32	(33.0)	97	(31.0)
Totals	131	(41.9)	126	(40.3)	56	(17.9)	313	(100)

TABLE VIII

PERIOD OF RETIREMENT BY NUMBER OF DOWNWARD MOVES CONTROLLING FOR NUMBER OF YEARS IN PROFESSIONAL HOCKEY

Number of Downward Moves Controlling for Number of Years in Professional Hockey											
0-1 Moves				2-3 Moves				4 Moves or more			
1-9 yrs.		10 yrs. or more		1-9 yrs.		10 yrs. or more		1-9 yrs.		10 yrs. or more	
N	(%)	N	(%)	N	(%)	N	(%)	N	(%)	N	(%)
a. 36	(36.1)	62	(63.9)	34	(36.2)	60	(63.8)	3	(12.5)	21	(87.5)
b. 5	(15.2)	28	(84.8)	5	(15.6)	27	(84.4)	2	(6.2)	30	(93.8)

Period of Retirement

a. Pre-expansion
b. Post-expansion

interpretation further, period of retirement was cross-tabulated by number of downward moves, controlling for number of years in professional hockey. The results, presented in Table VIII support the foregoing argument. In each cell, the veteran players outnumber those who skated fewer than ten seasons, a differential most pronounced among those who moved four or more times and who retired after 1967.

If such movement can be considered failure, then not only was failure endemic, most players terminated their careers on this note (Table IX). While it is common knowledge that many NHL players apprentice in professional hockey's lower ranks (Table X), the discovery *that 70 per cent finished there* (Table IX) was unexpected. We point out, finally, that a smaller portion (59.8 per cent) of the post-1967 cohort was in a state of downward mobility at career end than was the case in the earlier group (75.5 per cent). This will no doubt become increasingly typical as the balance between major and minor league positions continues to shift.

TABLE IX

PERIOD OF RETIREMENT BY LAST PROFESSIONAL TEAM

Period of Retirement	Last Professional Team					
	Minor Pro.		NHL		Totals	
	N	(%)	N	(%)	N	(%)
Pre-expansion	163	(75.5)	53	(24.5)	216	(69.0)
Post-expansion	58	(59.8)	39	(40.2)	97	(31.0)
Totals	221	(70.6)	92	(29.4)	313	(100)

TABLE X

PERIOD OF RETIREMENT BY FIRST PROFESSIONAL TEAM

Period of Retirement	First Professional Team					
	Minor Pro.		NHL		Totals	
	N	(%)	N	(%)	N	(%)
Pre-expansion	127	(58.8)	89	(41.2)	216	(69.0)
Post-expansion	71	(73.2)	26	(26.8)	97	(31.0)
Totals	198	(63.3)	115	(36.7)	313	(100)

Ball (1974) has provided a theoretical framework for the analysis of failure in sport in terms of (1) group reaction to the failed and (2) the latter's reaction to himself as a "self." Ball speculates, first, that the reactions of the failed's "others" tend to take the form of a "shutting out" process whereby the failed acquires the (transitional) status of "non-person" (Goffman, 1956, cited by Ball, 1974: 11): "physically of the setting, legitimately present, but lacking social acknowledgement of [his] others and thus interactionally absent." Bouton's (1971, cited by Ball, 1974: 12-13) account of baseball (similar to hockey with its major-minor league structure and movement back and forth) is illustrative: on being sent down to a minor league team: "as I started throwing stuff into my bag, I could feel a wall invisible but real, forming around me. I was suddenly an outsider, a different person, someone to be shunned, a leper." On another occasion: "You walk into the clubhouse and you see a guy packing his bag and you both try not to look at each other. Most guys won't pack until they know everybody is on the field." The failed's presence may be a disturbing reminder to others of their own mortality and, of course, gone is the status by which they knew him best.

For the failed, with the spoiling of his organizational identity goes a major anchorage of self. A friend of Derek Sanderson, a troublesome but talented one-time Boston performer once demoted to the American Hockey League, observes: "How Derek hates it in the AHL! It degrades him." Even when a player "goes down" temporarily to regain his playing legs after an injury, or for a "refresher course" of some sort, there is the realization that it is usually peripheral members, rarely the "stars," who suffer such indignities, (despite the case of Sanderson). A stint in the minor leagues, then, if not plainly failure tends to be a reminder of one's marginality, although some, like Hillman, appear resigned to their lot (Boulton, 1975:12-13):

> The reason Hillman submits to such embarrassments is simple: he likes to play hockey. He's from the old school; the game gets to him. So long as he's paid to play hockey, he can be insulted, disgraced, demoted, loaned out, placed on waivers, abused by management, have Clarence Campbell tell him how much he's worth, be cast aside to dreary outposts like Rochester like so many empty, sticky Cracker-Jack boxes; and it makes no difference. Hillman staggers off and comes back for more.

In his study of industrial managers, Goldner (1968) found that organizations attempted to soften the potentially disruptive features of demotions by cloaking them in ambiguity. One such technique was "zig-zag" mobility: combining a demotion with the prospect of subsequent promotion, thereby "cooling out" the demoted. It may be that a similar organizational adaptation has evolved in the hockey industry. There is always the hope among minor league players that they will get another "chance in the 'big tent'" (Conacher, 1972: 75), and, indeed, many do. A variation of this organizational strategy is the creation of positions to meet the ego-needs of failed "stars," as when an important ex-player is moved into a prestigious but relatively powerless "front office" job. The problem for the organization is to avoid both alienating the demoted and shattering the motivation of those immobile in the lower strata.

"Zig-zag" mobility notwithstanding, the accoutrements that validate one's definition of self-as-major league athlete vanish in the transformation to "minor leaguer," for there is a gulf between the two (Ball, 1974; Conacher, 1972:66-77). Former Toronto Maple Leaf, Jerry James, for instance, played out his career in Yorkton, Saskatchewan ("after I got cut . . . I was just another guy with five kids and no job") where " . . . everything comes hard. Meeting a payroll. Getting ice time for practice. Hot water for the showers. The Prairie League . . . even has a hard time getting a mention in the Hockey News. . . . " (Alderman, 1972:12). Conacher

(1972:75-76) describes life in the comparatively heady environment of the American Hockey League:

> Even on days when the team practiced, there was plenty of time with nothing to do. Players would idle it away in bars, or lounging in movies, all the time with the distant hope that they might be called up to the NHL. It was often lonely and degrading for a player during these times, sitting, waiting for the phone call that would never come or wishing he was at home with his family in another city.
>
> I imagined that most of the veteran pros like Bronco Horvath, Gerry Ehman, Dick Gamble and Eddie Litzenberger, had resigned themselves to making the best out of playing minor pro hockey. The road back to the NHL was just too steep [owing to career timetables, perhaps]. The middle group, consisting of players like Larry Hillman, Jim Pappin, and Duane Rupp, kept hope alive that a break would come and they might return. . . .

The bleakness of this scene is softened by the realization that individuals as well as organizations work out adaptations to failure. Conacher suggests as much in his reference to Horvath *et al.* in the above passage. The key, perhaps, to maintaining integrity of self in the face of demotion and subsequent lack of mobility lies in the process of self-redefinition — an adjustment that may begin in anticipation of failure and continue after it (Goldner, 1968). Like Goldner's managers, some of Faulkner's immobile American Hockey League players had come to terms with their situation by (1) making comments on the price one must pay to move upwards, (2) shifting attention from work to family or some other sphere, (3) emphasizing the good points of their present position, and so on.

> The National League is *not* the only league to play in. Believe me, I've given it a good shot but the going up and down like a yo yo, the moving of the family, and all that. We've paid the price, but it's a good life here. Even right here [in the minors] where else can you make this kind of money and meet the people you do? I enjoy my friends here, I have no complaints because not everyone gets the chance to have the life we've had. I want to play a few more years, and like I say, it's been good to us (Faulkner, 1974: 157-158).

Downward "skidding." It appears, however, that not only do a large number of professional hockey players finish their playing careers on a note of downward mobility, many continue to skid in this direction,[9] particularly, of course, those who have not "hedged their bets" against the inevitable economic and prestige losses that accompany retirement from sport. The trauma so inherent in this process is severe and widespread enough in North America to have inspired the United Athletes

Coalition, an organization begun in 1973 whose aim is to help ex-professional athletes cope with the abrupt transition from fame to relative obsurity (for as Stone [1973: 70] has observed: "Notoriety and fame are shortlived and differ radically from privilege and dignity"). In the words of one of the Coalition's rehabilitates, former Canadian Football League player, Boyd Carter (Proudfoot, *Toronto Star* 29 January 1975b:(C2):

> Believe me, the world is full of ex-athletes kidding themselves and each other about stuff that went by the boards 10-15-20 years ago—as if anybody cared any more, or could even remember. And those are the well-adjusted guys. The others are bums or lushes or addicts. I know. I've been down there pretty low. And the process starts the day you wake up and realize you can't play for anybody any more.
>
> One day people can't do enough for you because you're the big star of the Argos. Next day, you're not playing any more and hey, they can't remember your name. Boyd who was that again? I'll tell you, there aren't many guys properly prepared for that let-down—either emotionally or financially.

Post-Script

Since 1972 there has been continuing expansion of major professional hockey. In that year was established the twelve-team World Hockey Association which will reportedly grow to fifteen members by the 1975-76 season. And by 1975-76 the NHL will have tripled its pre-1967 membership. In short, the 120 major league positions of 1966 will have exploded to over 600 by 1975. This will undoubtedly result in more opportunities to enter the "big leagues," longer stays there, greater horizontal mobility, and, if the number of minor league positions remains static or shrinks, lessening likelihood of finishing in the lower echelons.

Roles related to the administration, promotion, and servicing of hockey have grown apace; indeed the occupational structure of the industry has the shape of an inverted pyramid (Stone, 1973). These opportunities, undoubtedly, are not a direct function of growth alone but also of the increasing complexity that usually accompanies organizational expansion (Grusky, 1968: 370). In any case it may be that the career trajectories of more players will extend into these secondary positions, but it is equally plausible that sport is becoming too bureaucratized to leave in the hands of only semi-qualified former practitioners.[10] Perceiving that "staying in the game" is problematic and realizing that their occupational experience generally does not qualify them for non-sport careers, journeymen and marginal players, especially, no doubt increasingly will acquire higher educations and other anticipatory adaptations against the day when their physical ability fails them, as it must do. And as long as there is a major-minor league hierarchy, and the latter do not become solely instructional leagues, downward mobility in mid-career will remain a fact of life for many hockey practitioners. A substantial number, too, will continue to end their careers on this note, staving off as long as possible the distress that accompanies retirement. To quote Eric Nesterenko (1974:384): "I don't have another vocation. I have a feeling unless I had one, my life might be a big anticlimax. I could get a job, but I don't want a job. I never had a job in the sense that I had to earn a living just for the sake of earning a living. I may have to do that, but I sure hope I don't."

NOTES

1. We have found instructive Glaser and Strauss' (1967; 1972) conception of "grounded theory," in which emphasis is put on the *process* of "discovering" theory from data. The chief strength of this approach is that it is "a way of arriving at theory suited to its supposed uses" (Glaser and Strauss, 1967: 3): grounded theory always "works," as opposed to "speculative" (logico-deductive) theory, based on *a priori* assumptions, in which the connection between theory and evidence must often be "forced."

2. Whether or not present-day professional athletes are exploited is a difficult question to answer, partly because it has more than one dimension. On solely economic grounds, however, Noll (1974: 124) demonstrates that star players generate much more revenue for their teams than they are paid in salary (Marx's "surplus value"). Another side of the issue is illuminated by Eric Nesterenko (1974: 383), a veteran performer of more than twenty NHL seasons:

   I became disillusioned with the game not being the pure thing it was earlier in my life. I began to see the exploitation of the players by the owners. You realize owners don't really care for you. You're a piece of property. They try to get as much out of you as they can. I remember once I had a torn shoulder. It was well in the process of healing. But I knew it wasn't right yet. They brought their doctor in. He said, "you can play." I played and ripped it completely. I was laid up. So I look at the owner. He shrugs his shoulders, walks away. He doesn't really hate me. He is impersonal.

3. A performer in his first three years can be demoted at the whim of management, but after this period he must consent to "go down"—a recent NHL Players' Association victory.

4. Scoville (1974: 198) reports that the average major league hockey salary rose from $24,000 in 1971-72 to $40,000 in 1972-73, primarily, of course, a function of the establishment of the World Hockey Association. The average for 1974-75 was over $50,000 according to the *Toronto Star*.

5. After Caplow (1964: 201-216), "organizational set" is defined as a stratification system made up of two or more settings.

6. Demotion may have been for one or more games. Sometimes a player may not subjectively define a short stay in the minors as demotion.

7. Blitz (1973) calculates that in 1972 there were about 420 major professional to 380 minor professional positions in hockey. (The latter refer to the American, Western, and Central Leagues—officially NHL-sponsored organizations. There are, of course, other "minor" minor leagues.) The number of minor professional teams has not changed much in the last decade, whereas major professional teams have gone from six in 1966 to about thirty in 1974.

8. Although Scoville (1974: 198) reports that sixty-six of the seventy-nine NHL players signed by the WHA in 1972 were "regulars," many of these may have been "marginals" prior to the initial NHL expansion in 1967.

9. Roy (1974) obtained completed questionnaires from 58.4% of all retired NHL players, 1950 to 1972. The data reveal that 65% have jobs ranking in the top three Blishen socioeconomic categories: 55 per cent in class three, 8.8 per cent in class two, 2.5 per cent in class one. Roy notes, however, an overrepresentation of "stars" and an underrepresentation of "journeymen" and "marginals" in the sample, a function of knowledge of the present whereabouts of the former and not of the latter. Hill and Lowe (1975) provide a melancholy catalogue of suicide, mental illness, and other misfortunes which have befallen retired athletes.

10. 73.9 per cent of management positions in hockey are filled by former players (80.4 per cent coaches, 58.5 per cent managers); still, these positions are few in number (Roy, 1974).

REFERENCES

Alderman, T.
1972   "The Yorkton Terriers Lost Again Last Night—But it was a Good Game, We only Broke Two Sticks." *Canadian Magazine*, January 29.

Andreano, R.
1965   *No Joy in Mudville*. Cambridge, Mass.: Schenkman.

Ball, D. W.
1974   "Failure and Sport." Paper presented at the VIII World Congress of Sociology, Toronto.

Becker, H. S.
1952   "The Career of the Chicago Public Schoolteacher." *American Journal of Sociology*, 57.

Blitz, H.
1973   "The Drive to Win: Careers in Professional Sports." *Occupational Outlook Quarterly*, Summer.

Boulton, R.
1975   "Hello! Goodbye!" *Canadian Magazine*, January 11.

Bouton, J.
1971   *Ball Four*. New York: World.

Caplow, T.
1964   *Principles of Organization*. New York: Harcourt, Brace and World.

Charnofsky, H.
1968   "The Major League Professional Baseball Player: Self-Conception Versus the Popular Image." *International Review of Sport Sociology*, 3.

Conacher, B.
1972   *Hockey in Canada: The Way It Is!* Richmond Hill, Ontario: Pocket Books.

Faulkner, R. R.
1973   "Career Concerns and Mobility Motivations of Orchestra Musicians." *The Sociological Quarterly*, 14.
1974   "Coming of Age in Organizations: A Comparative Study of Career Contingencies and Adult Socialization." *Sociology of Work and Occupations*, 1.

Glaser, B. G.
1968   "Moving Between Organizations." In B. Glaser (ed.), *Organizational Careers: A Sourcebook for Theory*. Chicago: Aldine.

Glaser, B. G. and A. L. Strauss
1967   *The Discovery of Grounded Theory.* Chicago: Aldine.
1971   *Status Passage.* Chicago: Aldine – Atherton.

Goffman, E.
1956   "Embarrassment and Social Organization." *American Journal of Sociology,* 62.
1959   *Presentation of Self in Everyday Life.* Garden City, New York: Doubleday Anchor.

Goldner, F.
1968   "Demotion in Industrial Management." In B. Glaser (ed.), *Organizational Careers: A Sourcebook for Theory.* Chicago: Aldine.

Gregory, P. M.
1965   *The Baseball Player: An Economic Study.* Washington, D.C.: Public Affairs Press.

Grusky, O.
1965   "The Effects of Formal Structure on Managerial Recruitment: A Study of Baseball Organization." *Sociometry,* 26.
1968   "The Effects of Succession: A Comparative Study of Military and Business Organization." In B. Glaser (ed.), *Organizational Careers: A Sourcebook for Theory.* Chicago: Aldine.

Haerle, R. K.
1975   "Career Patterns and Career Contingencies of Professional Baseball Players: An Occupational Analysis." In D. W. Ball and J. W. Loy (eds.), *Sport and Social Order.* Reading, Mass.: Addison-Wesley.

Hamilton, S.
1974   "Baseball Player." In S. Terkel (ed.), *Working.* New York: Pantheon.

Hare, N.
1973   "The Occupational Culture of the Black Fighter." In J. Talamini and C. Page (eds.), *Sport and Society: An Anthology.* Boston: Little; Brown.

Hill, P. and B. Lowe
1974   "The Inevitable Metathesis of the Retiring Athlete." *International Review of Sport Sociology,* 3-4.

Jones, J. C. H.
1969   "The Economics of the National Hockey League." *Canadian Journal of Economics,* February.

Jordan, P.
1974   "The Vita's Still Dolce, But. . . . " *Sports Illustrated,* January 27.

Kidd, B. and J. McFarlane
1972   *The Death of Hockey.* Toronto: New Press.

Lever, J.
1969   "Soccer: Opium of the Brazilian People." *Transaction,* December.

McKenzie K. and R. Andrews (eds.)
1950-1972   *National Hockey League Guides.* Montreal: The National Hockey League.

Mihovilovic, M.
1968   "The Status of Former Sportsmen." *International Review of Sport Sociology,* 8.

Nesterenko, E.
1974   "Hockey Player." In S. Terkel (ed.), *Working.* New York: Pantheon.

Noll, R.
1974   "Attendance and Price Setting." In R. Noll (ed.), *Government and the Sports Business.* Washington, D.C.: The Brookings Institution.

O'Brien, A. and J. Plante
1972   *The Jacques Plante Story.* Toronto: McGraw-Hill Ryerson.

Plimpton, G.
1966   *Paper Lion.* New York: Harper & Row.

Proudfoot, J.
1975a   "Awrey Performs Perilous Routine to Prevent Goals." *Toronto Star*, February 13.
1975b   "Tragedy of Ex-Argo: From Heights to Depths." *Toronto Star*, January 29.

Roth, J. A.
1968   "The Study of the Career Timetables." In B. Glaser (ed.), *Organizational Careers. A Sourcebook for Theory*. Chicago: Aldine.

Roy, G.
1974   "The Relationship Between Centrality and Mobility: The Case of the National Hockey League." Unpublished M.Sc. Thesis, University of Waterloo, Waterloo, Ontario.

Scott, M.
1968   *The Racing Game*. Chicago: Aldine.

Scoville, J. G.
1974   "Labor Relations in Sport." In R. Noll (ed.), *Government and the Sports Business*. Washington, D.C.: The Brookings Institution.

Shaw, G.
1972   *Meat on the Hoof*. New York: St. Martin's Press.

Stone, G.
1971   "Wrestling—The Great American Passion Play." In E. Dunning (ed.), *The Sociology of Sport*, London: Frank Cass.
1973   "American Sports: Play and Display." In J. Talamini and C. H. Page (eds.), *Sport and Society: An Anthology*. Boston and Toronto: Little; Brown.

Weinberg, S. K. and H. Arond.
1952   "The Occupational Culture of the Boxer." *American Journal of Sociology*, 57.

Yetman, N. R. and D. S. Eitzen.
1972   "Black Americans in Sports: Unequal Opportunity for Equal Ability." *Civil Rights Digest*, 5.

PART FIVE

Sports and Recreation in the Canadian Community

Introduction*

It is at the community level, that most Canadians get their first-hand contact with the sporting world. Public facilities, social agencies, clubs, minor leagues and school programs, provide environments for the voluntary use of "free time" to be devoted to varying dimensions of competitive or recreational physical activities.[1] But, Canadians seem to know very little about the overall "levels" of involvement in such activities, the features of community organization which influence involvement,[2] and the "meaning" of different types of involvement in specific community settings. The papers included in this section all concentrate on varying aspects of these issues, and provide a wide-ranging overview of the role of sport in the Canadian community.

In "Social Status and the Active Society", Jim Curtis and Brian Milton present data from a secondary analysis of a national study of leisure time use. Their discussion is based on an attempt to determine both how physically "active" or "sedentary" Canadian society actually is, and how selected correlates like age, sex, social class, and "centrality" influence participation in physical and sports activities. The authors note that much of the literature on "mass society" suggests how social class and other factors affecting participation are "homogenizing" in modern life. Sociologists have argued that over the last few decades the United States and Canada have been progressively transformed into middle class "leisure societies" where traditional social distinctions are no longer relevant. However, Curtis and Milton's data do not appear to support either the active "leisure society" thesis or the "homogenization" thesis to any great extent. Canadians are largely *sedentary* (although seasonal fluctuations occur) and *high social status* continues to be a major predictor of active involvement. Curtis and Milton conclude that the "typical" sports activist and spectator, is likely to be young, high in status, male, and actively involved in a wide range of community affairs.[3]

How might these findings be explained? Curtis and Milton indicate that both structural and social-psychological considerations are relevant. On the social-psychological side, sport may recruit from a class of people who simply get around more, like to socialize, have more energy, and tend to be interested in the affairs of the community. However, we suspect that structural explanations of voluntary participation may be even more meaningful. As Gruneau emphasizes in his paper in Part Three of this volume, it is likely that opportunities for participation, and the values surrounding a desire to maintain active community involvement,

*Co-authored by Rob Beamish

are directly related to the structure of opportunity and condition in Canadian society. Unequal social conditions, based on the differential access to rewards and privileges, put limitations on the range of opportunities available to certain groups. Thus, it is not surprising to note that class and status variables are consistently related to social participation in virtually all of the modern liberal democracies (cf; Gordon and Babchuk, 1959; Erbe, 1964; Hagedorn and Labovitz, 1968; Babchuk and Booth, 1969; Curtis, 1971; Tomeh, 1973; Frizzell and Zureik, 1974).

Social class in particular, appears to be the most clearly defined factor affecting differential involvement. This is not to say that status group factors like age, sex and ethnicity do not exert independent effects, but that these potential sources of advantage or disadvantage generally seem to be secondary to those derived from the division of labour, property ownership and position in the productive process. Because voluntary associations tend to reflect the normative order of middle class life (cf., Gordon and Babchuk, 1959; Tomeh, 1972), and because middle and upper-middle class individuals experience socialization conducive to a positive pre-disposition toward "participation" (cf., Lipset, 1968), people from these groups are more likely to be integrated into the "central" affairs of the community (cf., Sallach, 1973), including the participation in physical and sports activities.

Yet, there are a wide range of factors other than class and status which affect patterns of social participation in Canada. In the second paper included in this section, Rex Lucas examines how some of these factors affect recreational patterns in Canada's single industry towns. Because Lucas' discussion focusses on recreation in a particular context, the broad *generalized* structural explanations which we suggested were appropriate for defining involvement at the national level must be seen to be tempered by the interplay of *particular* factors emerging from the local context. In this regard Lucas points to three particular factors which positively influence participation.[4]

The first of these factors relates back to the notion of centrality and social integration. This factor is simply that the "size" of the community mediates the impact of broader structural factors affecting recreational involvement. Indeed, Lucas specifically notes that small towns best exemplify the "essence" of voluntary associations. Because the community is small there is greater opportunity for interaction close to its central core and subsequently there is greater social integration and accompanying recreational participation.

Most research into voluntary participation suggests that there are two broad categories of voluntary associations—*instrumental and expressive*.[5]

Instrumental associations recruit their members almost exclusively from the middle and upper-middle class, whereas expressive associations tend to be more democratized. This is important, because the second major factor affecting participation in communities of single industry is the degree to which voluntary associations tend to be of the expressive variety. In *Minetown*, of 175 club meetings in a year, over 90 percent were devoted to entertainment. Also, there were another 60 "open" events which might be defined as expressive endeavours.

Finally, Lucas points to the importance of the local "values" surrounding recreational involvement. To help man escape the basic eighteenth century "sins" of "pride, envy, sloth, intem'rance, av'rice, ire and lust", it is felt by some that work and "approved play" are essential components of life in small towns. Recreation takes on a moral dimension and becomes viewed as a necessary means of social control especially important in areas where "the winter nights are long". Consequently, there are some additional "ideological" incentives to encourage support for recreation which may not be deemed quite as "essential" in Canada's more cosmopolitan urban centres. [6]

While all these considerations favour high rates of recreational activity, Lucas notes that there are negative influences as well. The first concerns facilities. Private control of facilities can lead to the exclusion of entire segments of the town's population. In addition, facilities that are built must be financed by the community either directly (i.e. Community government), or indirectly (e.g. Church, clubs, unions). In a community where "permanency" is questionable, long term financial commitments are difficult to encourage. The issue is further complicated by differences in public opinion over the degree to which recreation should be organized. Moreover, single industry communities often lack the personnel who will undertake the instrumental roles of associations. As Lucas points out, "When the population is small, the range of interested and vital people is limited".

"Sports and the Career in Crestwood Heights" is taken from John Seeley, Alexander Sim and Elizabeth Loosley's "classic" 1950's study of an upper-middle class Toronto suburb. Life in *Crestwood Heights* itself has likely changed in the last twenty years, but we suggest that Seeley and his co-authors offer a description of the "meaning" of sport in upper middle-class suburban settings which continues to be highly informative.

By way of background, it should be noted that Crestwood Heights is a far more ethnically homogeneous and economically privileged community than those which Lucas describes. The standards which underlie participation in sports activities are not based so much on expressive pursuits as instrumental ones. For example, Seeley et al. point out that attitudes to almost all forms of activity in Crestwood Heights revolve around the *career* and a belief in the necessity for "success". To the people of Crestwood Heights, "the career is of all concerns the most momentous. It may be called 'success', or 'getting ahead', or 'doing well'. Whatever its name, it is thematic to the mythology of the western world." As a result, even in recreational activity, the youth of the community do not engage in sport or games as activities to be participated in for enjoyment only. Sport provides an enculturative milieux that prepares boys to become executives, or more broadly, upwardly mobile *career competitors*. The playing field mirrors the arena of aspirations which define the ultimate goals of Crestwood Heights' youth. The ideal is to compete, to be the "star", or the captain, but achievement must always be circumscribed by conventional liberal standards of "propriety". The achiever must acknowledge the assistance of his "teammates", and not over-react to "success" or "stardom".

In the final paper, David Friesen discusses the role of sport in the value systems of a sample of Canadian high school students during the mid-1960's. The school is a focus for community interest in sports, and the degree of interest that students show in sporting activities is frequently an excellent index of the "importance" given to these activities in the community itself. However, Friesen is especially interested in defining the students attitudes toward "valued" aspects of school life as features of the micro-system of the school's "subculture". Following the widely regarded work by James Coleman in the United States (1963), Friesen attempts to test the commonly-held assertion that adolescents value "athletics" over "academic achievement". Indeed, the beliefs that Canadian students are often too athletically motivated, see sport as a central value defining their high school experience, and denigrate academic work accordingly, have been prominent features of conventional wisdom for the last two decades.

Yet, Friesen's data suggest that surprisingly, the attitudes of Canadian high school students in the mid-sixties did not fit such conventional stereotypes. While students noted that athletics and popularity were important, the majority defined academic achievement as the most "enduring value" of the high school experience, and nearly all students saw the importance of academic achievement for obtaining future goals. Friesen also points out that students were far less active than one would expect—only half of them had ever been involved in any type of extracurricular activity.

Friesen's conclusions are interesting, but it should be noted that his presentation raises as many issues as it appears to resolve. In the first case, multiple categories like "scholar-athlete" or "athlete-scholar" may have been more discriminating methods of classifying the data and may have led to different findings. Second, the fact that none of the variables which Friesen presents are held constant, may imply that there are some as yet undiscovered relationships in the data. Finally, given the importance of class and status variables as factors which generally affect "participation" Friesen leaves us wondering "who" it is that is involved with sports. Do the attitudes of children from underclass families differ from those of middle class families (we suspect they do)? How important are age and "previous success" in either school or sports, as factors affecting attitudes to athletic and academic achievement? Questions like these should inform any attempt to update or follow-up on Friesen's groundbreaking effort to understand the "meaning" of sports in the subculture of Canadian high schools.

NOTES

1. Of the four papers in this section, the papers by Curtis and Milton, and by Lucas conform most readily to an analysis utilizing voluntary association considerations. While the presentations by Seeley et al. and Friesen do not reflect these considerations as directly, they nonetheless, describe important features of social participation. In addition, while some may wish to argue that these papers are not all dealing with group activities, and therefore fall outside the concerns of *voluntary association* literature, we agree with Curtis and Milton, who state; "Contrary to what may be conventional wisdom, we found nothing in the literature on sports and physical activity ... to suggest that they were particularly 'private' activities."

2. Factors which are commonly thought to influence socialization *into* varying types of sporting activity include class position of family, type of community, level of community interest in sport, family interest, the media, and the school. For a review of the comparative impact of social factors see Kenyon and McPherson (1974). An excellent overview of the process of socialization and its relationships to sport can be found in Ingham (1972) and Loy and Ingham (1972).

3. Additional data on "leisure" and sports participation in Canada can be found in Kirsh et al. (1973); Proceedings of the First Montmorency Conference on Leisure (Canada: 1973); *Citizen Participation in Non-Work Time Activities* (Canada: 1974(a)); and *Perspective Canada* (Canada: 1974(b)).

4. The "technical" expressions for these concerns are ideographic (particular) and *nomothetic* (generalizing or law-like). It is largely in the sociology of Max Weber that the polarization and mutual exclusiveness of these two modes of explanation is refuted. Weber argued that *both* were important. The nomothetic explanations help continuity of understanding and ideographic factors furnish the essential contextual variables that enable a complete *verstehen*, of understanding, to be obtained (cf., Aron, 1964: 64-75; Freund, 1968: 37-59; Weber, 1949).

5. *Instrumental* voluntary associations are generally concerned with the selection and implementation of long term goals and objectives. They do not, for the most part, offer immediate gratification as a direct outcome of participation. In addition, they are directed to policy conerning the community or public-at-large rather than the association itself. As a general rule, the greater the political power an instrumental association possesses, the more "exclusive" it becomes (Sallach, 1973). On the other hand, *expressive* voluntary associations are concerned with goals that are more immediate and

group or self directed. They provide opportunities for immediate gratification through the activity of the group (cf., Gordon and Babchuk, 1959; Jacoby and Babchuk, 1963; Simpson and Gulley, 1967; Booth, Babchuk and Knox, 1968; Ross, 1972).

6. While it is true that participation rates in small towns are high, the picture of involvement that Lucas constructs appears to underplay the degree to which social class factors actually are operating. A concentration on such traditionally non-blue collar activities as "cocktail parties", "bridge clubs", "tennis", and the "theatre" may skew interpretations in a middle-class direction. In one case for example, Lucas himself notes that miners are often marginal figures in community activities. The fact that Lucas does not provide a demographic analysis of his respondents makes it unclear exactly how *representative* his presentation actually is.

7. There have been many analyses of the role that sport plays in the school. Most of these analyses have been concerned with establishing the degree to which school athletes are superior or inferior students. Typical of such studies in the United States, are Schafer and Armer (1968); and Rehberg and Schafer (1968). A summary of the consequences of participation in interscholastic sports can be found in Phillips and Schafer (1971). Canadian data on these issues are provided by Jerome and Phillips (1971).

REFERENCES

Aron, Raymond
1964   *German Sociology*. New York: The Free Press of Glencoe.

Babchuck, Nicholas and A. N. Booth
1969   "Voluntary Association Membership: A Longitudinal Analysis." *American Sociological Review*, 34.

Betz, Michael and Bennett Judkins
1975   "The Impact of Voluntary Characteristics on Selective Attraction and Socialization." *Sociological Quarterly*, 16 (Spring).

Booth, A. N., N. Babchuck and A. Knox
1968   "Social Stratification and Membership in Instrumental-Expressive Voluntary Associations." *Sociological Quarterly*, 9.

Canada
1973   *Lesiure in Canada*. Proceedings of first Montermorancy Conference on Leisure (1969). Ottawa: Fitness and Amateur Sport Directorate.

1974(a) *Citizen Participation in Non-Work Activities*. Vol. I, Ottawa: Secretary of State.

1974b   *Perspective Canada*. Ottawa: Ministry of Industry, Trade and Commerce.

Curtis, James
1971   "Voluntary Association Joining: A Gross National Note." *American Sociological Review*, 36.

Erbe, W.
1964   "Social Involvement and Political Activity: A Replication and Elaboration." *American Sociological Review*, 29 (April).

Freund, Julien
1968   *The Sociology of Max Weber*. New York: Patheon Books.

Frizzell, Alan and Elia Zureik
1974   "Voluntary Participation: The Canadian Perspective." In D. H. Smith (ed.), *Voluntary Action Research*. Lexington: D. C. Heath.

Gordon, Wayne C. and Nicholas Babchuck
1959   "A Typology of Voluntary Associations." *American Sociological Review*, 24, (February).

Hagedorn, R. and S. Labovitz
1968   "Occupational Characteristics and Participation in Voluntary Associations." *Social Forces*, 47.

Ingham, Alan
1972   "Socialization, Dialectics and Sport." A paper prepared for the conference, *Women and Sport*, Pennsylvania State University, August 13-18.

Jacoby, A. and N. Babchuck
1963   "Instrumental and Expressive Associations." *Sociology and Social Research*, 47, (July).

Jerome, Wendy and John C. Phillips
1971   "The Relationship Between Academic Achievement and Interscholastic Participation: A Comparison of Canadian and American Schools." *CAHPER*, 37. (Ian/Feb).

Johnson, Graham
1975   "Voluntary Associations and Social Change: Some Theoretical Considerations." *International Journal of Comparative Sociology*, (Spring).

Kenyon, Gerald and Barry McPherson
1974   "Becoming Involved in Physical Activity and Sport: A Process of Socialization." *International Review of Sport Sociology*, 1, (9).

Kirsh, Carol, Brian Dixon and Mike Bond
1973   *A Leisure Time Survey*. Ottawa. Statistics Canada.

Lipset, Seymour
1968   "Social Stratification." *International Encyclopedia of the Social Sciences*. New York: Growell Collier and Macmillan.

Loy, John and Alan Ingham
1972   "Play Games and Sport in the Psychosocial Development of Children and Youth." In G. Lawrence Rarick (ed.), *Physical Activity: Human Growth and Development*. New York: Academic Press.

Phillips, John C. and Walter Schafer
1971   "Consequences of Participation in Interscholastic Sports: A Review." *Pacific-Sociological Review*. 14(3), July.

Rehberg, Richard and Walter Schafer
1968   Participation in Interscholastic Athletes and College Expectations." *American Journal of Sociology*, 73 (May).

Ross, Jack
1972   "Toward a Reconstruction of Voluntary Association Theory." *British Journal of Sociology*, 23 (March).

Sallach, David
1973   "Voluntary Associations and Power: A Reassessment." A paper presented at the annual meetings of the American Sociological Association. New York.

Schafer, Walter and Michael Armer
1968   "Athletes are Not Inferior Students." *Trans-Action*. November

Simpson, Robert L. and William Gulley
1967   "Goals, Environment Pressures and Organizational Characteristics." *American Sociological Review*, 27; (June).

Tomeh, Aida
1973   "Formal Voluntary Organizations: Participation Correlates and Interrelationships." *Sociological Inquiry*, 43 (3-4).

Weber, Max
1949   *On the Methodology of the Social Sciences*. Translated by E. A. Shills and H. A. Finch, Glencoe: The Free Press.

SOCIAL STATUS AND THE "ACTIVE SOCIETY":
National Data on Correlates of Leisure-Time Physical and Sport Activities[1]

James E. Curtis and Brian G. Milton

Participation in sports and physical activities is said to play a vital role in modern society. But, despite the possibility of wide-ranging social implications,[2] there has been a paucity of detailed empirical research into the sociology of sports and physical activity.[3] This has been especially true in Canadian society. As a beginning, in this country, there is a need for a basic, thorough appraisal of the characteristics of those who are involved in sports and physical activities. This descriptive task is our main concern here.

Social Status and Involvement in Sports and Physical Activities: Previous Literature

Works in social stratification and the emergent field of sociology of leisure are replete with contradictory assertions, impressions, and speculations about whether or not (or to what extent) post-industrial nations have moved (1) toward rather homogenetic leisure life styles and (2) towards either some form of "sedentary" or "spectator" populations as opposed to an "active leisure society" (cf., e.g., Hodges, 1964:149ff; Collins, 1958; Bergel, 1962:361ff; Boston, 1968; Roberts, 1970:86ff; Green, 1964:107-112; and Dumazedier and Guinchat, 1968). A common assertion in North America is that spectatorship is becoming a general social problem of the adult populations in advanced societies, that we have become soft and sedentary people who prefer to sit and watch the sports activities of a select few. One writer representative of this point of view has observed that "the seated figure of the 20th century is unmatched by any conventional posture in the past" (Collins, 1958:19). On the other hand, quite an opposite pattern, or social change, may be suggested by recent North American evidence of a "stay fit movement" as manifest in the new popularity of bicycling, jogging, hiking, camping, sports "house leagues" in work places, health club activities and so on, as leisure-time pursuits (e.g., Malcolm, 1972). In addition, government physical fitness committees and school fitness programmes have been actively organizing and using the media to promote physical activity in Canada (e.g., Particip-action) and various other nations.[4] Survey findings from limited previous studies in other countries do not clearly support either the sedentary society or active society views, and, of course, each may be somewhat of an oversimplification. Researches in the U.S. reveal differing findings on the extent of popularity of sports and physical activities, and on whether or not participating oneself or watching the physical activities of others is preferred (cf., e.g., Faunce, 1963; de Grazia, 1962; Kenyon, 1966; Robinson, 1967.)

Whatever general propensities there currently are to participate in or watch sports and physical activities in modern societies, there are likely to be important social sub-group differences in this regard—as there are for other forms of social activity. The previous literature has also contained discussions, hypotheses and some findings bearing on this point. However, again there are marked inconsistencies in these. For example, there is evidence that involvement as a participant in physical activities is inversely related to *age* among American adults (e.g., de Grazia, 1962:441ff; Kenyon, 1966; Stone, 1969), but findings on spectator involvement at sports events by age show contradictory patterns of both inverse relationships (de Grazia, 1962) and no relationship (e.g., Kenyon, 1966; Stone, 1969). There are a few detailed studies of adult *sex roles* for physical and sports activity, but in most of the work available female participation in sports, especially in competitive sports, has been found to be lower for American females than for males, as conventional wisdom might suggest (e.g., Lundberg *et al.*, 1934; Coffey, 1965; de Grazia, 1962). One regional study showed no adult sex role differences in involvement in physical activities broadly defined (Kenyon, 1966). In the same study, however, watching sports was significantly higher among males than among females.[5]

Alternative hypotheses and findings have also been presented for the relationship of physical activity and spectatorship to *socio-economic status* measured in terms of educational status, income categories and occupational levels. For example, Lundberg *et al.* (1934) reported over thirty years ago that participation in games and sports varied by type but not by overall activity level when different occupational strata were compared in a U.S. community. Other more recent U.S. works have indicated that there are educational status or occupational level differences in both physical and sports activity and live spectatorship. Direct relationships of occupation or education level to both variables have been reported (e.g., de Grazia, 1962; Kenyon, 1966; Ward, 1956; White, 1955). Others have suggested that, with some important exceptions, sports activity and live spectator activity are most characteristic of the middle and upper middle class levels with some curvilinearity in the relationships for persons in the highest occupational and income levels (e.g., Clarke, 1956; Stone, 1957). Still others have argued that the lower occupational class is more active in competitive sports while the middle class is more likely to be among spectators for such activities (Bergel, 1962:418ff).[6]

At the same time, several writers have contended that the "massification" of society which is said to have occurred over the years has resulted in a narrowing, if not complete leveling, of social class differences in the amount and type of sports involvement (cf., Barber, 1957:152ff; Bergel, 1962:403ff; James, 1963; and Hodges, 1964:165ff). Hodges, for one, has observed that "in participation sports as in other areas of life, it is apparent, social class differences . . . are diminishing in importance as we become an even more homogeneous people" (Hodges, 1964:167). And he further adds that "with spectator sports even more than with participation sports, whatever class linked relationships prevail today must—if the long run trend continues—dissolve to the point where they are all but invisible" (Hodges, 1964:168). Somewhat similar trends may also be occurring for selected sex and age-linked differences.[7]

Such differences in findings and interpretations of the extent and correlates of sports and physical activity may be partly a function of research conducted at different points in time (assuming change through time), but they probably also hinge heavily on the following issues. There has been a paucity of dependable and comparable evidence for various time periods on which to base interpretations. What studies there are in each nation have been characterized by differing research methods and differing definitions of such variables as social status and sports involvement. Detailed multivariate analyses with controls are scarce, and where controls have been made, these have differed across studies. We have spoken mostly of U.S. research here, but the limited work available has been conducted in different national settings—as well as in different types of communities and in different time periods. In North America and elsewhere, when representative samples have been employed, these have generally been applicable only to a limited universe such as a specific region, a local community, a particular population, one sex or a limited age range.[8] These factors, of course, make it difficult to synthesize conclusions from previous work into a coherent picture of the contemporary pattern of sports and physical activity involvement in the general population. The problem of obtaining reliable evidence is particularly acute in Canada because there have been few systematic studies conducted here.[9]

A logical starting point in beginning to remedy this situation would seem to be the provision of detailed contemporary information on sub-group differences in sports activity derived from multivariate analyses of representative samples in several nations. The present paper reports on national survey data that begin to meet this need for the Canadian case. Our data source does not allow us to speak to changes through time or cross-national differences, but we are able to provide detailed/controlled benchmark data on levels of activity across social sub-groups.

Working Hypotheses

Previous research on sports and physical activity involvement gave us the sometimes conflicting patterns of findings (and suggestions of alternative hypotheses) just mentioned. And there is very little in the way of a theory of sports involvement in the previous literature to provide a starting point. We decided therefore, to begin our analysis with "working" hypotheses which are derivable from the general idea that both rank and relative centrality of social status are directly related to sports and physical activity. These are propositions which are supported by considerable research on somewhat related dependent variables. Our reading of the broad literature on extra-family social participation suggested that these propositions apply to a range of voluntary types of extra-home social involvement (including various types of voluntary association activities, political behaviour, and youth cultural activities; cf., Hausknecht, 1962; Milbrath, 1965; Burnstein, 1972; Vaz, 1965; and Allardt *et al.*, 1958, among others). We suspected that these propositions would apply equally well to involvement in different categories of sports and physical activities. We assumed that overall involvement in leisure-time sports and physical activity would be directly related to different indices of (1) social rank and (2) integration into the community. Despite the strong "physical" component of our dependent variables, we saw forms of sports and physical activity as among many alternative forms of extra-home voluntary social activity. Contrary to what may be a conventional wisdom, we found nothing in the literature on sports and physical activity and in our own experiences (and other persons' reports of their experiences) with these activities to suggest that they generally were peculiarly *private* activities—i.e., generally not involving *social* activities outside the home, the awareness of one's activities by others and the presentation of self to others.

In general theoretical terms, our independent variables—measured here as differences in social class, sex, and community event involvement because these were the only appropriate characteristics on which we had available information—should be seen as measures of social status on either a high-low dimension (social class and sex) or a centre-periphery dimension (community event involvement). The centre-periphery dimension refers to a person's integration into the community through the number of ties he/she has to other persons and events in the wider society. Other things being equal, those who are relatively central in terms of a range of such ties should be more involved in sports and physically active leisure activities. Conversely, those who are lower in centrality should be less involved in sports and physically active leisure pursuits (see, in addition to the studies cited above, findings and interpretations discussed by Bavelas, 1960; Lerner, 1957; Eisenstadt, 1966; and London and Wenkert, 1969). We expected this pattern of findings, and greater sports and physical activity with higher social rank, because (1) we assumed that sports and physical activity involvement is generally valued and rewarding in today's society and, other things equal, will be pursued by persons in various sub-groups and (2) following the literature in other areas, persons higher in status and centrality are much more likely to have *greater participation "resources"* at their disposal. These resources may include, e.g., social contacts, communication on the normative status of sports activity, knowledge of sports and physical activities, access to facilities, past experience in organized sports and other organized activities, interaction skills, leisure time, and so on. The exigencies of the data source drawn on here leave something to be desired in that information was not afforded on such intervening variables, but we can test the basic hypotheses having to do with rank and centrality of statuses and involvement in physical and sports activities.

Our working hypotheses for involvement in sports and physical activity then, were as follows: (1) social class level (in this instance, educational status because that is the only s.e.s. variable available in our data source) is positively associated with participation; (2) men are more likely to participate than women; and (3) those who frequently attend community events (various measures) are higher in participation than those who are less involved in such community activities. We chose to control our analysis on two other variables, age level and marital status of respondents. We expected that there would be an inverse relationship between age, and sports and physical activity involvement and spectatorship, and our preliminary analyses showed this usually to be the case. This probably occurs because with increasing age there is a decrease in physical ability to do well some types of more active sports and physical activities. Perhaps there is also a concomitant decrease in interest in (and time spent on) sports, and sports involvement may progressively lose out to other types of "competing" leisure time pursuits learned over the years (cf., Glenn and Grimes, 1966). Marital status is a relative centrality variable of a different order than community involvement (cf., Hall's paper in this volume). For many, being married probably has the strong, but contradictory, effect of close ties to one specific adult individual and his or her immediate social networks (and sometimes to children's networks) *and a* reduction of the *range* of ties to others in the wider community who may be involved in and encourage involvement in physical activity or sports. In other words, this may, in many instances, be a focused rather than a diffuse type of structural integration. In addition, being married involves major and continuing commitments of time and energy to a sphere of activity—to family support and home-related activities. (There very likely are also sociologically significant sex differences in this respect with more of the responsibility being held by the female.) Other things equal, this would limit the time available for leisure activity of any sort, save as family and home-related activities. Following this latter line of argument, one might expect that married persons of both sexes, because of more work and family time responsibility, would be less involved in sports and physical activity than their single counterparts.

Method and Data

Our findings are from a supplemental set of questions appended to the Canadian government's monthly Labour Force Survey in March, 1972. The survey regularly involves a stratified, multi-stage national sample of some 65,000 individuals. The supplement yielded reports on selected leisure-time activities for respondents aged 14 and older. The study was not designed as a time-budget survey; i.e., there was no measurement of the amount of non-work time available to Canadians or the precise budgeting of time. Rather, respondents were asked about their participation in the arts, adult education, popular entertainment, hobbies, sports and physical activities. For the present, our focus is on information about the latter facets of leisure activity.[10]

The leisure time supplement information also included data on the respondent's age and sex. Data for each respondent in the supplement were then linked to information on the same respondent's marital status and educational status as reported in the main labour force survey questionnaire. We were provided with these linked sets of supplement/labour force survey records for secondary analysis. From these were selected, for present purposes, those cases where respondents were aged twenty or older. This yielded a working sample of 40,370 adult respondents after missing cases were excluded.[11]

Our independent and control variables are either self-explanatory or described below. The dependent variables were operationalized as follows:

(1) *Attendance at Sports Events* was defined as (a) the number of times the respondents had attended sports events for which no admission was charged since January 1, 1972 plus (b) the same information for sports events requiring paid admission.[12] We have defined *no spectating for the period as low activity* (coded = 0) and *attendance at one or more events as high activity* (coded = 1).

(2) *Physical and Sporting Activity* was measured in three ways: first, by the number of hours per week spent in *physical activity* – jogging, cycling, exercise programmes and so on (0 = less than 4 hrs.; 1 = 4 hrs. or more); secondly, by the number of hours per week spend in *sports activity*—bowling, curling, hockey and so on (0 = less than 4 hrs.; 1 = 4 hrs. or more); and thirdly, by the *number of sports* in which the respondent regularly participated—on the average at least once a week in season (0 = less than 2 sports; 1 = 2 or more sports).[13]

Our large N allowed us to run contingency control table analyses involving all independent variables simultaneously with sufficiently high cell frequencies for interpretation. We did these analyses especially to check on interaction, or the ways in which patterns of findings for a given predictor differed across sub-groups formed by cross-classifying categories of our other predictor variables. We discuss those interactions that were significant here.[14] As it turned out, however, there were few interactions and we chose to employ another multivariate procedure that had the added virtue of making for greater ease and economy in data presentation. This procedure, known as Multiple Classification Analysis or MCA (Andrews *et al.*, 1967), is a technique that can be used to examine the relationship between a single predictor (independent) variable and a dependent variable, or the relationship between each set of predictor variables and a dependent variable, holding the effects of the remaining predictors constant. To determine the relationship between an independent variable and a dependent variable, the computing routine gives the gross mean value of the dependent variable for the respondents in each category of the predictor variable. When multiple predictors are used, MCA yields an adjusted net score which is equivalent to the mean value of the dependent variable for each category of the predictor, after controlling statistically for the effects of the remaining predictors.[15] These are the scores presented in our Tables I-III. When dichotomized dependent variables, scored as "high" = 1, and "low" = 0, are used to generate these scores, as in the present case, the resulting scores may be interpreted as the proportions or the "adjusted proportions" (when there are controls involved) of those who reported "high" levels of activity. The programme also gives *eta* and *beta* coefficients which, when squared, roughly indicate the proportion of the total variance in the dependent variable accounted for by the effects of each predictor variable by itself (*eta*), and by the effects of each predictor variable after partialing out the effects of the other predictors (*beta*). A summary of *beta* coefficients is presented in Table IV.

Findings

Table I gives (1) the overall level of involvement on the four dependent variables and (2) the uncontrolled and controlled findings of levels of activity for each category of the two social status predictors and our two control variables. The first column under each dependent variable gives the uncontrolled involvement scores for each sub-group on a predictor variable, and the second column gives the adjusted (adjusted for the effect of the other three independent and control variables) involvement scores. Table II reports findings on the same types of analyses for the relationship between attendance at community events (5 different measures) and the 4 dependent variables. Here controls are made for education, sex, marital status, and age.

The Overall Extent of Sports and Physical Activity

Perhaps the most interesting aspect of the findings for the overall sample is the rather low proportion of Canadians who either watched or actively participated in sports and physical activity during the time period under consideration. Less than one in four respondents (23%) reported having attended one or more free or paid sports during the 2½ month period (cf. Table I). Roughly 8% reported having attended one or more free events, while approximately 16% said they had attended one or more paid events in the same period.[16] The difference here may reflect the relative frequency of the two types of events in Canadian communities, greater publicity attached to paid events, and the fact that free events often involve lower calibre and non-professional sports groups which tend to generate less public interest. Figures were more similar for higher attendance rates at free and paid events over the period, with 4% and 6% respectively attending 5 or more events in the 2½ month period. There seems to have been somewhat more time spent on actual sports and physical activity than in live sports spectatorship, assuming, say, 1-2 hours of involvement for each sport event attended. Twenty-seven percent of the overall population reported involvement of 1 hour or more per week in sports and or physical activity. Fifteen percent reported having been involved in leisure time physical activities for an average of 1 hour or more a week for the 2½ months, and 18% reported the same amount of time given over to sports activity. Five and 8% respectively, were involved in physical and sports activities for 4 hours or more per week on an average.

TABLE I

INVOLVEMENT IN SPORTS AND PHYSICAL ACTIVITIES BY EACH OF FOUR SOCIAL BACKGROUND VARIABLES WITHOUT CONTROLS AND WITH STATISTICAL CONTROLS (MCA), NATIONAL ADULT CANADIAN SAMPLE.

		Activities[a]							
Social Background Predictors		*Sports Spectating*		*Physical Activity*		*Sports Activity*		*No. of Sports*	
	(N)	N.C.[b]	W.C.[c]	N.C.	W.C.	N.C.	W.C.	N.C.	W.C.
Total	(40,370)	.234		.052		.076		.374	
Education Level									
Up to 8 Yrs.	(14,264)	.122	.154	.021	.027	.030	.041	.211	.259
Some H. School	(11,810)	.261	.251	.049	.048	.082	.081	.412	.397
H. S. Graduate	(6,919)	.300	.283	.074	.069	.105	.099	.474	.447
Non-U./Post-Sec.	(3,523)	.316	.298	.076	.070	.108	.101	.503	.475
Some Univ.	(1,942)	.375	.335	.104	.095	.135	.118	.553	.494
Univ. Degree	(1,912)	.364	.322	.116	.113	.154	.136	.583	.524
Sex									
Male	(19,769)	.286	.289	.052	.052	.103	.104	.439	.442
Female	(20,601)	.183	.180	.051	.051	.050	.049	.312	.309
Age									
20-24 Yrs.	(5,084)	.369	.337	.099	.086	.139	.121	.574	.536
25-34	(8,790)	.305	.286	.065	.058	.107	.099	.505	.474
35-44	(8,075)	.294	.290	.051	.051	.083	.083	.418	.410
45-54	(7,650)	.201	.209	.039	.042	.056	.061	.322	.331
55-64	(5,407)	.121	.138	.034	.041	.040	.047	.231	.256
65-69	(2,029)	.080	.114	.029	.040	.030	.044	.177	.229
70 Yrs. and Over	(3,335)	.043	.085	.020	.031	.013	.028	.092	.159
Marital Status									
Married	(31,395)	.236	.234	.049	.050	.073	.073	.382	.380
Other	(8,975)	.224	.233	.061	.056	.086	.086	.347	.353

[a]Coding for the four dependent variables was as follows: *Sports spectating*—0 equals no attendances since January 1st and 1 equals one or more attendances since that time; *physical activities* and *sports activities*—0 equals less than 4 hours in the activity per week and 1 equals 4 or more hours in the activity per week; *number of sports*—0 equals one or no sports in season and 1 equals 2 or more sports in season. See footnote #13 for the questions used.

[b]N.C. equals no controls used.

[c]W.C. equals with statistical controls for the other three variables (from among education, sex, age and marital status).

Thus it was only a small minority of Canadian adults who were involved in live spectatorship and sports and physical activity during the months referred to. These levels of involvement, because they seem low absolutely speaking, might be interpreted as providing some support for the "sedentary society" interpretation. Further limited support for the "sedentary" interpretation might also be found in the fact that in other data from the same survey (not reported here) 37% and 12% respectively, reported doing the comparatively sedentary activities of T.V. watching and radio listening for an average of 15 hours or more per week (8% were this heavily involved in leisure reading). Ninety-four percent, 71% and 71% respectively reported watching T.V., listening to radio and reading for more than 1 hour per week. These three activities alone were far more popular (or more frequent) than either sports spectatorship or sports and physical activity. Indeed, these three activities were the most frequently cited of all leisure-time uses asked about in the survey. First, some of this may be a function of the colder time of year to which our findings refer. This is suggested by other data that report numbers of sports participated in throughout the year (Table I, columns 7 and 8). Sixty-four percent of respondents reported participating in one or more sports "on a regular basis—on the average at least once a week in season"; 37% reported being this heavily involved in 2 or more sports in season; and 23% and 14% respectively reported participation in 3 or more and 4 or more sports in season. Unlike the data on recent weekly activity, these findings portray a much more physically active population—but *in season*. A majority of Canadians say they have a sport which they are regularly involved in and over one-third say they have multiple activities which are regularly pursued when season permits. Given the data on hourly activity over the three months of the study though, these sports must be focused at a different time of the year. In addition, an obvious point that should be kept in mind, is that any clear conclusion that Canadian society is "more" or "less" "sedentary" or "active" should be based on comparative data—either historically or cross nationally of a sort that we do not have available. Comparisons of activity levels across social groups at the point in time of our survey are possible, and we turn to this now.

Activity Differences by Social Background Characteristics

Educational Status and Sex Differences. As expected, consistent findings of direct relationships between educational level and our four indices of sports and physical activity were found, both without controls and in controlled comparisons. As Table I shows, with controls for age, sex and marital status, the adjusted percentages with spectatorship involvement (one or more attendances) increased from 15% for those with grade eight or less to 34% for those with some university education and 32% for those with university degrees. This decline of an adjusted 2 percentage points between the "some university" and "university degrees" groups was the only curvilinearity in the education relationships for any of the dependent variables. Differences between the "eight years of school or less" and "university degree" groups were adjusted percentages of 3% and 11%, 4% and 14%, and 26% and 52% for high physical activity (4 hours or more per week), high sports activity (4 hours or more per week) and high number of sports (two or more in season) respectively (see Table I). Our contingency control analysis for education, sex, age and marital status by the dependent variables (and for these independent variables with community event attendance added as a control) showed these direct relationships with education to hold across all sub-group comparisons. Education was also among the strongest and most consistent predictors of sports and phsyical activity across measures of dependent variables.

When we consider the relationship of sex and our activity measures we find some interesting differences. Without controls and in controlled comparisons, males were more involved than females on all three measures of sports involvement. Differences (controlled comparisons) in levels of high involvement for sports spectating, sports activity, and number of sports were 29% versus 18%, 10% versus 5% and 44% versus 31% respectively (see Table I). In the case of physical activity, however, the relationships by sex were less clear. Females were the same as males in high physical activity of 4 hours or more per week, both without controls and in controlled comparisons. Contingency control tables showed that males were generally very slightly higher in involvement than females, but among the younger, less educated sub-groups there were a couple of reversals in the relationship, with females being slightly more involved than males. None of these differences were very large (always being under 2 adjusted percentage points).

Differences by the Age and Marital Status Controls. Findings for the relationships between age and sports and physical activity were largely as expected, with inverse linear relationships between age and the four activity measures, both without and with controls for education level, sex and marital status. One minor exception to the generally linear pattern, appeared for sports spectating between the 25-34 years old and 35-44 years old groups. Among these groups, there was no decline in activity with age. Contingency control analysis also revealed a few reversals and changes in the general pattern for age among specific sub-groups. For example, age differences in high physical activity (4 hrs. per week or more) for both sexes, and in high sports activity (4 hrs. per week or more) for females, were negligible at the higher education level of "some university or more".[17] For these higher education older groups, involvement in sports and physical activity was higher than ever, for the lower education younger groups. These findings suggest that involvement more likely remains high with increasing age for those high in education. This interpretation must be made with caution, however, since longitudinal data are required to conclusively demonstrate that this pattern occurs.

Patterns of activity by marital status showed only very small and, in some instances, inconsistent differences without controls. Married persons were slightly more involved in sports spectatorship and multiple activities and less involved in physical and sports activity.[18] With controls on sex, age and education, these small married-non-married differences were further diminished for all activity dependent variables except sports activity, where the introduction of controls had no particular effect (Table I).

In the contingency control analysis however, modest but nevertheless significant patterns for the effects of marital status specified by age and, to a lesser extent, sex emerged. For males aged 35 or older, those who were married were somewhat more highly active on all four measures of physical and sports activity; 18 of 24 comparisons for the four activity measures showed higher involvement for married persons and in the six exceptions, differences were low (below 3%) in all but one case. Younger males (aged 20-34) showed a different pattern; for this group, at each education level, there tended to be somewhat more sports and physical activity for non-married persons than married persons. Eight of 12 comparisons showed no difference, and 2 comparisons showed slightly higher activity for married persons. Much the same pattern as just described obtained for females, the exception being among those with lower and middle education (secondary school graduate or less) where the younger, as well as middle-aged and older, females showed slightly more sports and physical activity involvement for married persons than for non-married persons.

Attendance at Community Events as a Correlate. Table II shows that there is a strong direct relationship between attendance at non-sports community special events[19] on the one hand, and the four measures of involvement in sports and physical activity on the other—and this relationship is maintained with participation in community events operationalized in five different ways.

TABLE II

INVOLVEMENT IN SPORTS AND PHYSICAL ACTIVITIES BY ALL COMMUNITY EVENTS ATTENDANCE (2 MEASURES) AND BY CULTURAL EVENT ATTENDANCE (3 MEASURES), WITHOUT CONTROLS AND WITH STATISTICAL CONTROLS (MCA) FOR EDUCATION, AGE, SEX, AND MARITAL STATUS

	Activities[a]											
	Sports Spectating			Physical Activity			Sports Activity			No. of Sports		
(N)	N.C.[b]	W.C.[c]	eta/beta	N.C.	W.C.	eta/beta	N.C.	W.C.	eta/beta	N.C.	W.C.	eta/beta
Total (40,370)	.234			.052			.076			.374		
Extent of Community[d] Event Attendance												
Level 1 (21,420)	.113	.138		.027	.035		.043	.057		.245	.293	
Level 2 (9,214)	.303	.281		.050	.045		.086	.077		.437	.397	
Level 3 (4,493)	.394	.361		.078	.068		.119	.101		.536	.475	
Level 4 (2,407)	.416	.384		.106	.092		.130	.110		.608	.543	
Level 5 (1,302)	.451	.414		.124	.107		.153	.128		.662	.587	
Level 6 (1,534)	.559	.522	.328/.267	.180	.160	.166/.130	.199	.170	.158/.104	.717	.638	.314/.213
Degree of Community[d] Event Attendance												
Level 1 (21,890)	.121	.146		.029	.037		.045	.058		.253	.299	
Level 2 (7,931)	.294	.274		.050	.046		.082	.074		.425	.389	
Level 3 (4,348)	.375	.344		.061	.053		.114	.099		.517	.460	
Level 4 (2,499)	.402	.365		.093	.080		.122	.100		.587	.518	
Level 5 (2,263)	.444	.403		.119	.103		.143	.118		.641	.563	
Level 6 (1,439)	.569	.522	.317/.253	.192	.170	.165/.129	.218	.185	.160/.107	.730	.639	.307/.204

INVOLVEMENT IN SPORTS AND PHYSICAL ACTIVITIES BY ALL COMMUNITY EVENTS ATTENDANCE (2 MEASURES) AND BY CULTURAL EVENT ATTENDANCE (3 MEASURES), WITHOUT CONTROLS AND WITH STATISTICAL CONTROLS (MCA) FOR EDUCATION, AGE, SEX, AND MARITAL STATUS

| | | Activities[a] | | | | | | | | | | | |
| | | Sports Spectating | | | Physical Activity | | | Sports Activity | | | No. of Sports | | |
	(N)	N.C.[b]	W.C.[c]	eta/beta	N.C.	W.C.	eta/beta	N.C.	W.C.	eta/beta	N.C.	W.C.	eta/beta
"High" Culture[d]													
Event Attendance													
Level 1	(34,995)	213	.220		044	.047		070	073		349	359	
Level 2	(4,151)	353	.313		087	.073		107	088		512	452	
Level 3	(983)	397	.351	.126	130	.107	.095	143	118	.060	612	544	.135
Level 4	(180)	411	.370	.089	139	.114	.067	133	108	.031	644	581	.086
Level 5	(61)	623	.567		279	.254		098	088		623	537	
"Information" Culture[d]													
Event Attendance													
Level 1	(35,769)	212	.219		042	.044		068	071		342	353	
Level 2	(2,971)	383	.328	.146	109	.093	.134	130	105	.091	600	520	.188
Level 3	(1,122)	418	.359	.097	155	.136	.106	149	121	.055	660	575	.126
Level 4	(508)	484	.413		191	.168		187	152		697	597	
"Mass" Culture[d]													
Event Attendance													
Level 1	(23,350)	121	.144		030	.038		045	057		258	303	
Level 2	(10,447)	321	.296		060	.053		093	081		470	421	
Level 3	(4,485)	439	.400	.348	097	.082	.149	137	114	.169	594	515	.306
Level 4	(1,640)	579	.533	.286	135	.117	.110	188	160	.117	705	613	.197
Level 5	(448)	737	.682		212	.187		277	240		799	688	

[a] See Table 1 for definitions of these variables.

[b] N.C. equals no controls introduced.

[c] W.C. equals with controls for education, sex, age and marital status.

[d] See footnote #19 for definitions of these variables.

TABLE III

INVOLVEMENT IN COMMUNITY EVENT ATTENDANCE BY PHYSICAL ACTIVITY AND SPORTS ACTIVITY WITHOUT CONTROLS AND WITH STATISTICAL CONTROLS FOR FOUR SOCIAL BACKGROUND VARIABLES. NATIONAL ADULT CANADIAN SAMPLE, 1972

| | | All Community Event Attendance | | | | | | Cultural Event Attendance[a] | | | | | | | | |
| | | Degree of | | | Extent of | | | "High" Cult. | | | "Infor." Cult. | | | "Mass" Cult. | | |
	(N)	N.C.[b]	W.C.[c]	eta/beta	N.C.	W.C.	eta/beta	N.C.	W.C.	eta/beta	N.C.	W.C.	eta/beta	N.C.	W.C.	eta/beta
Total	(40,370)	.261			.241			.133			.114			.422		
Physical Activity (hrs. per week)																
No hours	(34,394)	.218	.234		.196	.212		.110	.119		.086	.093		.377	.398	
1-3 hours	(3,892)	.518	.419	.238	.501	.403	.252	.269	.216	.161	.272	.227	.214	.689	.562	.218
4-7 hours	(1,445)	.501	.412	.147	.499	.413	.161	.253	.206	.099	.283	.243	.157	.662	.549	.115
8 hrs. or more (	639)	.504	.412		.499	.412		.263	.219		.293	.252		.665	.555	
Sports Activity (hrs. per week)																
No hours	(33,097)	.219	.237		.200	.217		.117	.124		.095	.102		.370	.395	
1-3 hours	(4,209)	.445	.363	.207	.421	.344	.207	.213	.180	.103	.196	.160	.131	.656	.542	.224
4-7 hours	(1,874)	.465	.384	.117	.439	.362	.120	.204	.170	.057	.211	.170	.076	.662	.553	.115
8 hrs. or more (	1,190)	.476	.379		.444	.354		.196	.158		.212	.170		.655	.528	

[a]See footnote = 19 for definitions of these variables.

[b]N.C. equals no controls introduced.

[c]W.C. equals with controls for education, sex, age, and marital status.

The more *extensive* the participation in community activities (i.e., the more different types of events attended in the 2½ month period) the higher the sports and physical activity involvement. At the same time, the more *intensive* the community event participation (i.e., the more overall attendances regardless of the type of event) the higher the sports and physical activity involvement. When community events were sub-divided into "mass culture events", "information-oriented culture events", and "high culture events" (see footnote #19), the same general pattern obtained for all four dependent variable measures with the relationships being particularly strong for mass culture participation, less strong for information-oriented culture activities, and least strong, but still in evidence, for the effects of high culture activities on at least two of the dependent variables. In the case of sports activity and number of sports pursued in season, the relationship of high culture was less clear with a curvilinear pattern appearing for sports activity, and a slight decline in sports involvement appearing in the uppermost two levels of the predictor for number of sports done in season. These latter findings suggest the need for caution in arguments that there is not something of a disjunction between sports participation and "highbrow" culture activity involvement in the population. Participation in most types of community events seems to be positively associated with involvement in sports and physical activity. However, the incremental effect of increased units of involvement in "high culture" events, is different than is the case for all other kinds of activity. But, even for these "highbrow" activities, there is a positive association between sports and physical activity involvement and attendance at community events at least at the lower levels of involvement.

We also checked on whether or not increased levels of involvement in sports and physical activities appeared to be associated with progressively more community event involvement. This would be expected, other things equal, if greater involvement in sports and physical activities led to other forms of community involvement. This would not be expected, for example, if sportsmen and women tended to "specialize" in their sports and physical activity at the expense of attention to community events, or if increased amounts of time spent in sports and physical activities interfere with community attachment time commitments. Data bearing on these issues are presented in Table III. Here we present findings for physical and sports activities (4 levels ranging from no hours per week to 8 hours or more per week) as a predictor of our five types of community event involvement with controls for the other four predictors (education, sex, age and marital status) discussed above. The pattern of findings shows that, for all types of community involvement, persons involved in sports and physical activities are more involved in community events than their non-active counterparts. But progressively greater levels of physical and sports activity are not associated with a change in community event involvement in a more frequent or less frequent direction. There can be several possible interpretations of these patterns, including the two just mentioned above. We would favour these.

Relative Effects of the Five Predictors and Controls. Table IV presents summary measures (*beta* coefficients) for the relative independent effect of each of the five predictor and control variables for each dependent variable. Since attendance at community events had an effect on all four dependent variable measures, and is highly correlated with our other predictors, controlling for it tends to depress the effects of each of the other four social background characteristics. In order to highlight the relative independent effects of these four variables, findings are also presented here for their effects with attendance at community events not included as a control variable (see figures in parentheses in Table IV).

TABLE IV

BETA COEFFICIENTS FOR THE EFFECTS OF FIVE VARIABLES ON PHYSICAL AND SPORTS ACTIVITIES

	Activities							
Predictors	Sports Spectating		Physical Activity		Sports Activity		No. of Sports	
Education (6 levels)	.081	(.149)[a]	.072	(.108)	.081	(.110)	.132	(.189)
Age (7 levels)	.135	(.190)	.050	(.069)	.085	(.105)	.191	(.234)
Sex	.127	(.128)	.002	(.003)[b]	.103	(.103)	.137	(.138)
Marital Status (2 levels)	.014	(.001)	.001	(.010)	.013	(.020)	.035	(.023)
Attendance at Community Events[c] (6 levels)	.253		.129		.107		.204	

[a] Parentheses indicate beta coefficients without controls for attendance at community events.

[b] Not significant at .01 level. All other patterns were statistically significant at .001.

[c] This variable is defined as the "all community event attendance (degree of)" measure in Table 11.

Spectatorship: For spectatorship as the dependent variable, involvement in community events had, by far, the strongest predictive import. With a beta coefficient of .253 it had almost twice as much effect as the next strongest predictor, age. Following age, with controls for community event involvement, sex had the next strongest predictive power followed by education level and the slight effect of marital status. Without such controls, the pattern for education and sex is reversed with education predicting next best after age (beta = .149) followed by sex (beta = .129). This change of order can be accounted for in terms of the respective relationships between sex and education level and involvement in community events (betas of .009 and .243).[20] With controls for involvement in community events then, much more of the effect of education level as compared to sex is factored out. Nevertheless, no one of these variables accounts for the apparent influence of the other; each of the four (excluding marital status) retains a strong independent effect when there are simultaneous controls for the other three.

Physical Activity: When we consider physical activity as the dependent variable, again involvement in community events has the most prominent impact, followed by education level and age. Excluding community involvement as a control variable, education level has a strong effect (beta = .108) and age a modest one (beta = .069). Controlling for the effects of involvement in community events, the independent effects of education and age are reduced considerably but the relative order remains unchanged. The effects of marital status and sex on physical activity are negligible.

Sport Activity: With the exception of marital status, all predictor and control variables had a fairly modest independent impact on sports activity. With attendance at community events included among the predictors, the beta coefficients ranged from a maximum of .107 (attendance at community events) to а minimum of .081 (education level). Without controls for community involvement the range was even narrower but the rank order was reversed. In this latter case, education level was the best predictor of sports activity, followed by age and sex in that order. The difference in magnitude of the betas concerned, however, was very slight indeed.

Number of Sports Involved in: The beta coefficients for participation in multiple sports were strong for all three predictor variables and age. The independent effect of marital status was again small but considerably larger than for any of the other three dependent variables. With attendance at community events excluded, age predicts "number of sports" best, followed by education level, sex, and a small effect for marital status. With controls for community involvement this order is changed somewhat with attendance at community events predicting best followed by age, sex, education level and marital status in that order.

Summary and Discussion

The following composite picture may be drawn from the findings on who is actively involved in live spectating and sports. Speaking first of findings without controls, the sports activist and spectator is more likely to be high in social status, male and young as we had hypothesized. Perhaps surprisingly though, females are about as involved in physical activities as males. Those involved in various community events are also more likely to be sports activists and spectators than those who are not involved in community events. Marital status did not show a clear relationship to the sports activity variables.

This picture is changed somewhat as follows, however, when findings from the controlled multivariate analyses are considered. First, for our two control variables: age differences in physical activity are negligible for higher education sub-groups. High social status seems to "cancel out" the effect of age. Age differences in sports activity between middle aged and older sub-groups generally diminished with controls. This is not surprising given that older persons are more likely to be female and lower in education and structural integration—all characteristics which are associated with lower activity. Age and sex also specify slight effects of marital status. Married males tended to be more active than their non-married counterparts, except among younger males where the opposite pattern tended to obtain. Females were generally more active if they were married rather than single. The exceptions to our predictions here may result from several factors that we alluded to as cautions earlier; integration into the family is a special case. For example, for younger males the time spent starting and getting ahead in a job and in starting a family may severely limit possibilities for sports and physical activity as compared to possibilities for unmarried males. Thus, for this group structural integration into adult life through marriage seems to lead to less involvement. Marriage perhaps means substantial disengagement from a sports-oriented male youth culture. Participation in sports and physical activity for middle aged and older married males may be more frequent because jobs, careers and families are under way (perhaps taking somewhat less time and attention) and because types of popular physical activity and sports involvement are changed to somewhat more work and family-related activities (e.g., spectating with children, spouse, co-workers or friends, bicycling, hiking, and sports with family or neighbourhood and working acquaintances). The findings for females suggest that women (especially those with lower education levels) may participate most "through" families or spouses. First of all, single working women may have less time for physical activities and sports than married females. Moreover, Canadian society probably provides limited opportunities for involvement by unattached females or groups of females (there are some exceptions in community organizations and exercise and keep-fit groups, for example). In addition, married females are likely encouraged to participate on a regular basis in sports and physical activity *with* their family and *by* their active children and spouses, while unmarried females may mostly participate in sports on social occasions with men. These interpretations are hunches which go well beyond our data here, but they may be qualifications that will have to be made in the relative centrality hypothesis in further research. Some of this further work must especially be directed to the theoretical significance of the types of interaction effects that we have described here.

Educational status was directly related to sports and physical activity and spectatorship. This finding differs from some previous reports, especially those describing curvilinearity in the relationship of social status to activity, but all such discussions have given more weight to occupation and income (at least in composite measures) as social status measures (e.g., Clarke, 1956; Stone, 1957; Bergel, 1962). Educational status and community involvement were consistently strong predictors of activity across the dependent variables. However, sex and age had a strong effect for some relationships as well. Compared to the other independent variables, sex (and age) are the best predictors of sports spectatorship and multiple sports involvement and they seem to have little effect on level of physical activity. For sports spectatorship and multiple sports activities especially, sex, education, community involvement and age, all had effects independent of the influence of each other. There are some very clear differences in overall activity levels between social sub-groups formed by these 4 independent variables. On the whole, there seemed to be little sports and physical activity involvement, but, for what involvement there was, important social status differences obtained. Homogenization (if it is taking place) for these dependent variables is not that complete.[21] Since social class differences have figured prominently in previous discussions of massification and homogenization trends, it is perhaps important to also note that for both spectatorship and multiple sports activity educational status was the poorest of the social status predictors of involvement. However, education did have a consistent independent effect across the several dependent variables. All this is to suggest the need for considerable caution in generalizations about differences (or lack of differences) and about the predictive strength of education and other social status correlates across different dimensions of sports activity.

In conclusion, we would emphasize that this analysis obviously provides only the very beginnings of several researches that require attention, granted the theoretical and practical import attending issues of active leisure-time use. Theoretically, the phenomena of changing voluntary time uses will come to provide an intriguing chapter in the sociological history of institutional change.[22] Practically there are potential policy implications flowing from any substantive demonstration of the sedentary society thesis,[23] either for Canada comparatively speaking or for large social sub-groups within Canada. The findings reported here offer both some reason for caution in sometimes overdrawn statements of the homogenization thesis, and they may provide some basis for concern with respect to the nature of the sedentary society. Our findings point especially to the following research and theoretical implications that go beyond the data that we have at hand.

First, there is the question of changes in involvement with seasons. Our findings should be replicated for other seasons in Canada and for other nations and climates; ideally, some research should be longitudinal in design. Our data patterns on current sports activity and numbers of sports regularly pursued in season may be seen as very tentative support for recent arguments on the rather extreme seasonal variability in forms of social participation in colder climates. "Some apparently like it hot" for many forms of social (including perhaps sports and physical) activities (see Michelson, 1972). If this is the case, there are important social planning implications flowing from this for societies in northern climates.

Secondly, still at issue is the question of leisure life styles, both in terms of specific types of activities that persons are involved in and in terms of "trade-offs" that take place in selecting activities from one or more general categories of leisure activity over activities from other categories. We have been able to show that "opposite" types of sub-groups (in terms of high-low status and relative centrality) tend to have quite different levels of physical and sport activity. But this should be seen as only the beginning of this type of analysis. One next step needed in leisure research is factor analytic work on the specific types of leisure time uses that run together as most popular for various social substrata of adults. This should include detailed work on *types* of sports as well. In addition, the precise relationship of these "leisure activity styles" to types of resources that come into play in pursuit of sports and other leisure time activities needs to be spelled out in detail in case study and survey research involving information on more variables than we have had available to us here. Studies involving time budget surveys are most appropriate for researching some of these issues. This is especially true for work on one issue involved here; *viz* the "limits" of the structural integration or relative centrality hypothesis. Other things equal, those who are more integrated into the community show a tendency to be more involved in sports and a range of other leisure-time activities than those who are less central. But given scarce time and resources for all individuals (though these resources may differ by social sub-strata) presumably this direct relationship is only up to some point of high involvement in a limited number of leisure activities or lesser involvement in a somewhat broader range of activities ("specialists" *vs.* "generalists"). As suggested for (1) the cases of young married males and females and (2) "high brow" culture and sports activities here, there are many situations where available participation resources on the one hand, and other work and family leisure time commitments on the other, are such that sports (and many other possible leisure activities) may lose out to the prior commitments or to more pressing or higher priority activities. Detailed analyses of such "trade-off" situations are needed for the further development of viable theories of physical activity and leisure styles.

Finally, a theoretical issue that deserves attention is the question of alternative interpretations or theories accounting for the relative centrality finding. A first alternative to our social structural level, "centrality" interpretation would be a "selection theory". Sports and physical activities may recruit selectively from a class of high social participators in general—with common social psychological characteristics. These people may simply get around more because they have more energy, wish to socialize more, or are more interested in other aspects of social life than those who tend not to attend community affairs.[24] Our emphasis in interpretation has been less social psychological—that centrality to participation resources, and socialization to them, accounts for variance in involvement in the social and physical activities. But the two processes, this and selection, doubtless occur simultaneously to some extent. Detailed longitudinal studies would be required to determine the relative importance of these two types of processes. Research dealing with such variables as differences in energy levels and extroversion could also shed light on this question.

NOTES

1. We thank members of the Cultural Information Section, Educational Division, Statistics Canada, for calling our attention to the national survey data drawn on in this

paper. Analyses of other findings from this survey, on adult leisure-time activities, are reported by Milton (1976). Selected other findings from the entire survey population (aged 14 and over) have been presented in Kirsh et al. (1973).

2. For example, such activities are said to help support the normative order, reinforce important shared values, provide settings in which to engage in expressive and socio-emotionally gratifying activities, provide feelings of accomplishment and self-worth for participants, offer opportunities for conspicuous consumption, serve as vehicles for social mobility for some, and help to maintain a high level of physical fitness (cf., e.g., Lüschen, 1967; Maheu, 1962; James, 1963; Weiss, 1969; Veblen, 1899; Loy, 1969).

3. A number of explanations have been offered for the fact that sociological theory and research on sports and physical activity has been selectively inattended to in the literature. Lundberg *et al.* argued some years ago that this was the case for the study of leisure behaviour in general because the use of leisure time was seen as, "subject to the relatively 'free' choices of individuals and therefore, supposedly largely unstandardized" (Lundberg *et al.*, 1934). Other reasons, for sports activities, could be that the behaviour may be seen as (1) less "serious", (2) less consequential for society (e.g., not involving individual and group life chances, such as in the marketplace) and (3) less "social" (largely physical and biological level dependent variables) than many other phenomena that sociologists might choose to study.

4. More consistent with the latter phenomena are other writers' observations through the years that people have "deserted the spectator sports in droves" (Larrabee, 1960:43) and that "the itch to do things rather than sit and watch has actually cut down spending at the box office during the nation's greatest prosperity" (Editors of *Fortune*, 1958:165; cf. Hodges, 1964:149ff and Kando, 1975:216ff).

5. Some observers have argued that changes in types of girls' games and sports activities in modern societies reflect the changing role of women in other spheres of social activity and that the physical activity interests of men and women may be coming to overlap more and more in modern societies (cf., e.g., Rosenberg and Sutton-Smith, 1960 and the different researches on sex differences cited in Lüschen, 1967).

6. There are also different data patterns and conclusions in writings on the amount and type of involvement in sports and games by children from different social classes (see, e.g., the studies reviewed in Lüschen, 1967).

7. In recent years, increasing spare-time, earlier retirement, better health, greater affluence, an equalitarian change in sex roles, "democratization" of one time higher class activities (e.g., skiing, golf and tennis), and the proliferation of public and commercial recreation facilities may all have worked to level various social sub-group differences in extent of sports involvement.

8. Cf. Lundberg, *et al.* (1934); White (1955); Clarke (1956); Stone (1957); de Grazia (1962); Faunce (1963); Kenyon (1966); and Stone (1969). Two major exceptions to this are the national studies conducted by the U.S. Outdoor Recreation Resources Review Commission and the twelve nation ISA study conducted by Alexander Szalai and others. A summary of findings from the former can be found in Cicchetti (1972). For the latter see Szalai *et al.* (1973). See also the following for reviews of studies of sports and other leisure time activities in various countries: Lüschen, 1967 and Dumazedier and Guinchat, 1968.

9. Gruneau's (1972) study of selected background characteristics of athletes participating in the 1971 Canada Winter Games is an exception for a limited universe of Canadian sportsmen and women. See his "Class or Mass" essay in Part Three of this volume.

10. More details on the sample and methodology are available from a Dominion Bureau of Statistics publication (1965). See also Kirsh *et al.* (1973) for the questionnaire and selected findings from the survey.

11. There was some unavoidable loss of N in the process of linking records. This loss was non-systematic and resulted because data from two month's (different) surveys had to be compared and part of the sample from the first month had been outrotated in the

second month. Procedures for this are discussed more fully in the D.B.S. publication (1965). N's for each comparison are provided in the tables.

12. Since the data were collected in the latter half of March, 1972 this represents a 2½ month *winter* period. This applies to all of our dependent variables except one dealing with the number of sports regularly participated in—*in season*. Cutting points for high and low activity were largely dictated by the not-so-detailed coding procedures used in the study. These tended to preclude the use of overall summative activity indices. Fortunately, what our data base lacked in detailed coding it more than made up for in large sample size, adequacy of sample, and the possibilities for rich multivariate analyses.

13. The questions asked were as follows:

"Please indicate by a check mark the number of times you attended a sports event since January 1, 1972. In Part A, report on those events for which an admission fee was paid by you or by someone else on your behalf; in Part B, report on events for which no admission was charged."

"On the average since January 1, 1972 about how many hours per week have you spent in the activities listed below?; physical activity (jogging, cycling, exercise programmes, etc.,), sports activity (bowling, curling, hockey, badminton, etc.,)."

"Do you participate on a regular basis (on the average at least once a week in season) in any of the following activities? Check Yes, or No for each activity; golf, tennis, bowling, curling, skating, snow skiing, snowmobiling, swimming, water skiing, jogging, walking for exercise, bicycling for exercise, fishing or hunting, recreational hockey, other sports or recreational activities (specify)."

14. Space limitations preclude presentation of the contingency control tables here. These may be obtained from the authors on request.

15. For further information on MCA see Andrews *et al.* (1967). A limitation of MCA is that the dependent variable must be either a normally distributed interval variable or a dichotomy. In the present analysis this requirement is met in our dichotomy of the dependent variable (as O vs. 1.). This means that the mean value of the dependent variable for each category of the predictor variable corresponds to and may be interpreted as the ("adjusted") proportion of respondents involved at the defined level.

16. These figures are taken from the contingency control table analysis alluded to above. Because the total sample N's between these analyses and the MCA analysis differ slightly the percentages given are slightly different than those that would be provided by the MCA analyses. The figures vary by less than 2 percentage points in either direction across the two forms of analysis.

17. This holds only until age 70 at which point there is a marked decline in activity despite the advantages that higher education apparently brings. This is probably because the physiological deterioration of the body reaches a point at which social factors can only minimally intervene.

18. With sports spectatorship sub-divided into free and paid events married persons were more involved in the former and less involved in the latter.

19. The question was as follows: "Please indicate by a check mark the number of times you attended each event listed below since January 1, 1972. In Part A, report on those events for which an admission fee was paid by you or by someone else on your behalf. In Part B, report on events for which no admission was charged; live theatre, opera or operetta, ballet, classical musical performance, other musical performance, other live performance, visit to a museum, visit to a public art gallery, visit to a historic site, fair, exhibition, carnival, or movie." The five predictors that appear in Table 2 represent various constructions of responses to this question. All community event attendance (extent of) refers to the sum of discrete events each respondent attended. Level 1 refers to no events, level 2 to one event and so on up to level 6 which represents five or more different events. All community event attendance (degree of) refers to the sum of attendances, regardless of the event, of each respondent. Level 1 refers to no attendance, level 2 represents attendance at any one of the events only

once, level 3 represents 2 attendances and so on up to level 6 which refers to 5 or more attendances at any event. High, Information, and Mass Cultural Event Attendance are coded in the same way as All Community Event Attendance and operationalized as follows: "high culture" = attendance at theatre, opera, ballet and classical music performances; "information culture" = visits to museums, art galleries or historical sites; and "mass culture" = movies, carnivals, fairs, musical or other similar live performances.

20. These findings come from the extended version of Table IV. A similar rationale probably accounts for several other reversals in the case of the other dependent variables.

21. However, whether or not there are more or less marked social status differences in sports activity as compared to involvement in other voluntary social behaviours (e.g., travel patterns, political participation, visiting patterns, and eating patterns, among many others) are open questions that require further attention. In short, there may be far more homogenization of this facet of leisure-time use than in other aspects of leisure social activity.

22. Contemporary German sociologists (notably Gehlen, Schelsky and Habermas) have argued that modern society is characterized by a fundamental institutional cleavage; a cleavage between the *public* and *private* spheres of social life. The institutions of the public sphere, in particular those of the economy and state, have been and continue to be fairly structured. It is argued that this has not been true of the private sphere. The most important relation of most individuals to the public sphere is through their work. Conversely, the private sphere is experienced (or inhabited) during the leisure-time. Major current changes in the private sphere are seen to be increased time allocation to this and a large scale development of new programmes, social agencies and other institutional arrangements for the *structuring* of use of time here. Gehlen (see, e.g., Berger, 1965) has referred to this as the development of *secondary institutions* and sees this as a major aspect of future change in the private sphere.

23. We will not list the practical issues here. These are dealt with elsewhere in the literature (cf., e.g., the references in footnote #2). Suffice it to say that, for example, there is the well documented relationship between physical activity and health and physical fitness.

24. The social determinants of these characteristics are other interesting empirical and theoretical questions.

REFERENCES

Allardt, E. et al.
1958   "On the cumulative nature of leisure activities." *Acta Sociologica*, 3.

Andrews, F., J. Morgan and J. Sonquist
1967   *Multiple Classification Analysis.* Ann Arbor: University of Michigan, Institute for Social Research.

Barber, B.
1957   *Social Stratification: A Comparative Analysis of Structure and Process.* New York: Harcourt, Brace and World.

Bavelas, A.
1960   "Communication patterns in task-oriented groups." In D. Cartwright and Alvin Zanders (eds.), *Group Dynamics.* New York: Harper and Row.

Bergel, E. E.
1962   *Social Stratification.* New York: McGraw-Hill.

Berger, P. L. and Kellner, H.
1965   "Arnold Gehlen and the theory of institutions." *Social Research*, 32 (Spring).

Boston, R.
1968   "What leisure?" *New Society*, 26 (December).

Burnstein, P.
1972   "Social structure and individual political participation in five countries." *American Journal of Sociology*, 77 (May).

Cicchetti, C. J.
1972   "A review of the empirical analyses that have been based upon the national recreation surveys." *Journal of Leisure Research*, 4 (Spring).

Clarke, A. C.
1956   "The use of leisure and its relation to levels of occupational prestige." *American Sociological Review*, 21 (June).

Coffey, M. A.
1965   "The sportswoman—then and now." *Journal of Health, Physical Education and Recreation*, 36 (February).

Collins, H.
1958   "The sedentary society." In Larrabee, E. and R. Meyersohn (eds.), *Mass Leisure*. Glencoe, Illinois: The Free Press.

de Grazia, S.
1962   *Of Time, Work and Leisure*. New York: 20th Century Fund.

Dominion Bureau of Statistics
1965   Canadian Labour Force Survey Methodology, 1965. Catalogue No. 71-504. Ottawa: Queen's Printer.

Dumazedier, J. and Guinchat, C.
1968   "La sociologie du loisir." Current Sociology, 16 (1).

Editors of Fortune
1958   "$30 billion for fun." In Larrabee, E. and R. Meyersohn (eds.), *Mass Leisure*. Glencoe, Illinois: The Free Press.

Eisenstadt, S. N.
1966   *Modernization: Protest & Change*. Englewood Cliffs, N.J.: Prentice Hall.

Faunce, W. A.
1963   "Automation and leisure." In Smigel, E. O. (ed.), *Work and Leisure*. New Haven: College and Univeristy Press.

Glenn, N. D. and M. Grimes
1966   "Aging, voting and public interest." *American Sociological Review*, 33 (August).

Green, A. W.
1964   *Recreation, Leisure and Politics*. New York: McGraw-Hill.

Gruneau, R. S.
1972   An Analysis of the Socio-economic Characteristics of the Athletes Who Competed in the 1971 Canada Winter Games. Unpublished M.A. thesis, U. of Calgary, Calgary, Alberta.

Hausknecht, M.
1962   *The Joiners*. New York: Bedminster Press.

Hodges, H. M. Jr.
1964   *Social Stratification*. Cambridge, Mass.: Schenkman.

James, C. L. R.
1963   "Cricket in West Indian culture." *New Society*, 36.

Kando, T. M.
1975   *Leisure and Popular Culture in Transition*. St. Louis: C. V. Mosby.

Kenyon, G. S.
1966   "The significance of physical activity as a function of age, sex, education and socio-economic status of northern United States adults." *International Review of Sport Sociology*, 1.

Kirsh, C. et al.
1973   A Leisure Study—Canada 1972. Ottawa: Dept. of Secretary of State.

Larrabee, E.
1960   The Self-Conscious Society. Garden City: Doubleday.

Lerner, D.
1957   "Communication systems and social systems." Behavioral Science, 2.

London, J. and R. Wenkert
1969   "Leisure styles and adult education." Adult Education Journal, 20.

Loy, J. W. Jr.
1969   "The study of sport and social mobility." In G. S. Kenyon, (ed.), Sociology of Sport.
         Chicago: The Athletic Institute.

Lundberg, G., Komarovsky, M. and M. A. McInerny
1934   Leisure: A Suburban Study. New York: Columbia University Press.

Lüschen, G.
1967   "The sociology of sport." Current Sociology, 15 (3).

Maheu, R.
1962   "Sport and culture." International Journal of Adult and Youth Education, 14.

Malcolm, A. H.
1972   "Cemeteries opening gates for recreation." New York Times, Sunday, Dec. 10, pp.
         1 & 76.

Michelson, W.
1971   "Some like it hot: social participation and environmental use as functions of the
         season." American Journal of Sociology, 76 (May).

Milbrath, L. W.
1965   Political Participation. Chicago: Rand McNally.

Milton, B.G.
1976   Social Status and Leisure-time Activities. Montreal: Canadian Sociology and
         Anthropology Assn. monograph—forthcoming.

Reissman, L.
1954   "Class, leisure and social participation." American Sociological Review, 19 (February).

Roberts, K.
1970   Leisure. London: Longmans.

Robinson, J.
1967   "Time expenditures on sports across ten countries." International Review of Sport
         Sociology, 1.

Rosenberg, B. G. and B. Sutton-Smith
1960   "A revised conception of masculine-feminine differences in play activities." Journal
         of Genetic Psychology, (March).

Stone, G. P.
1957   "Some meanings of American sport." 60th Proceedings, College Physical Education
         Association.
1969   "Some meanings of American sport: An extended view." In G. S. Kenyon, (ed.),
         Sociology of Sport. Chicago: The Athletic Institute.

Szalai, A. et al.
1973   The Use of Time. The Hague: Mouton.

Vaz, E.
1965   "Middle class adolescents, self reported delinquency and cultural activities." Cana-
         dian Review of Sociology and Anthropology, 2 (February).

Veblen, T.
1899   The Theory of the Leisure Class. New York: Macmillan.

Ward, J. A.
1956   A Study of the College Educated Women of America, New York, cited by S. de Grazia in Of Time, Work and Leisure. New York: 20th Century Fund, 1962.

Weiss, P.
1969   Sport: A Philosophical Inquiry. Carbondale; Illinois: Southern Illinois University Press.

White, R. C.
1955   "Social class differences in the uses of leisure." The American Journal of Sociology, 61 (September).

SPORTS AND RECREATION IN COMMUNITIES OF SINGLE INDUSTRY

Rex Lucas

People living in communities of single industry, like people everywhere, spend a major proportion of their day away from their place of employment; this part of the day is conventionally called leisure. Many participate in leisure time activities. Recreation had and still has a moral dimension. This is well illustrated in the common sense phrases so frequently heard in every day life. People are urged to use their leisure time constructively; others decry the increase in spectator activities rather than in participation. A busy round of activities is "a good thing"; drowsing in front of the television set with a bottle of beer is felt to be morally inferior to taking part in sports or hobbies. Courses are for "self-improvement". The shorter work week is alleged to introduce the "problem" of leisure time; some urge that people be educated for the use of leisure. The retired are advised to take up a hobby "for something to do".

Recreation as Social Control

Many of the post industrial revolution leisure time activities were explicitly set up so that young workingmen would be saved from the grog shops, taverns and beer parlours. Organizations were set up to benefit "mind, body, and spirit". All of this suggests that implicitly and explicitly leisure activities are to keep people from other pleasures or sins. And the seven deadly sins of 1711 are quite complete: "pride, envy, sloth, intemp'rance, av'rice, ire, and lust"; after those, what else is there? The basic "sins," sex, liquor, drugs and gambling have been around for a long while. S. D. Clark (1942) catalogues the moral indignation concerning drinking, gambling, fornicating and opium-smoking from the earliest settlement of Canada until World War I, from Louisburg on the east to the Yukon on the north and west. From the beginning, officials, churchmen and moralists were concerned in stopping "sin". In many ways sobriety and piety became connected: "Satan finds some mischief still for idle hands to do."

> Two contrary assumptions about sobriety and piety dwell comfortably side by side. On the one hand, they are considered, like thrift and industry, as characteristics of the country rather than the city. The freedom, diversity, anonymity, and excitement of urban life are thought to encourage hedonism, while the rural pattern of living, with its stress on hard work, strong informal social controls, and lack of opportunity for dissipation is believed conducive to self-denial and restraint. In Canada the surveys of the Canadian Institute of Public Opinion dealing with attitudes towards Sunday observance and the drinking of alcoholic beverages substantiate this view. On the other hand, qualities such as sobriety have been linked with the Protestant ethnic, and hence with urbanism and capitalism; their exercise in one's own calling and their imposition on others are considered to have played a part in providing the modern entrepreneur with a clear conscience and disciplined work-force (Burnet, 1961: 70)[1].

Perhaps the linking of leisure time and moral and religious commitment is responsible for the ideological fervour which underlies so many leisure time activities. To many it has become an obligation "All work and no play (approved play, that is) makes Jack a dull boy." In contemporary society some would add "apathy" to make an eighth deadly sin. The pace maintained by suburban families to taxi their children to their various activities connotes an implicit moral obligation. In any isolated northern community of single industry when asked about the large families in the community, many respondents reply "the winter nights are long up-here", with all of the implication of time on one's hands. Sports are seen as building "character" and participation in team sports is often required as a qualification for the work world, possibly because team athletes learn "sportsmanship—the art of cheating while pretending not to".

Army officers keep their men busy at basic training camps, councillors at summer camps fill the day with constant "activities". Some community members stated that it was important for the men to work long hours during construction so that they did not have time to talk. Parents "organize" birthday parties for six year-olds (otherwise they would fight —and have a nice time). Isolates, now, as in the days of Plymouth Colony, are suspect. All of this leads to the conclusion that social control is one of the functions of recreation.

Although social control is undoubtedly important, voluntary associations perform other functions, whether or not they are recognized by the participants. Some of the typologies developed suggest some of these functions. One classification, for instance, is in terms of "performance," "sociability", "symbolic-ideological", "productive"—each of these as seen by the participants (Warriner and Prather, 1965). Another classification distinguishes between "instrumental", "mixed", and "leisure" types (See Lundberg et al., 1934). Another is, "expressive groups," and "instrumental groups" (Rose, 1965). A still further typology is based upon "accessibility of membership, status defining capacity of the association, and the function of the organization for the participant defined as instrumental and expressive" (Gordon and Babchuk, 1959). Others have usefully distinguished between the influence of voluntary organization activity upon the integration of the personality system (social-psychological) and on the integration of the social system (sociological) (Babchuk and Edwards, 1965). One other author sees voluntary organizations in terms of "goal attainment", "social integration" in the criss-crossing of membership, "pattern maintenance" in the reaffirmation of shared values, and in the "facilitation" of other functions (Smith, 1966). Generally speaking, most authorities consider voluntary associations to be crucial to a "late liberal" philosophy; they are seen as best exemplified in the small town, and somewhat threatened in the city[2].

Nevertheless there is no agreement on what items or combination of items constitute the most desirable leisure time activities. The multitude of activities, active, inactive, group and individual, some requiring elaborate facilities and equipment, present great problems to any small town; few towns can maintain the range of activities necessary to please all tastes of all age groups.

An almost obsessive quality has been attributed to recreational activities, voluntary associations and formal organizations in communities of single industry by Derbyshire (1960) and Robinson (1962).[3]

A visitor to one of Canada's resource towns is immediately struck by the number and variety of recreational amenities available—swimming pools, artificial ice arenas, golf courses, recreation halls, parks and playgrounds, to mention but a few—and the high degree of participation in off-duty recreational programs, be they athletic, welfare, fraternal, church, youth, cultural, educational or social. Our four cases are no exceptions. The nature and extent of recreational facilities and of residents' participation in active clubs and organizations go far beyond what is found in ordinary communities of the same population size elsewhere (Robinson, 1962: 87-88).

If, however, one moves beyond the superficial view and asks towns-people about recreation—what recreation members of the family partici-pate in, facilities that are available and used, facilities that are missed—seemingly contradictory statements, often in the same interview, are consistently found. Respondents maintain: (i) there really is nothing to do in the community, (ii) the community is overorganized, (iii) they are very busy, and small-town life is most rewarding, and (iv) people are apa-thetic. In order to explore these statements, it is necessary to examine the complex field of recreation in more detail.

Numbers of Associations

One community studied maintained 125 organizations. Few people there have more than one or two club affiliations, and the entire population—men, women and children—numbers fewer than 1500 people. This means that there are about ten people per organization, assuming that every person joined one organization. In Minetown (adult population 3000), a count was made of the meetings and entertainments provided by clubs for adults during a six-month period (November to June). It was found that male fraternal lodges held 44 meetings, female fraternal (sic) lodges held 22 meetings, male church clubs held 16 meetings, female church clubs 20, men's service clubs 22, other female clubs 17, other male clubs 9, and miscellaneous clubs with mixed male and female membership held 40 meetings. This amounted to 175 meetings, and of these 157 were basi-cally devoted to entertainment. In addition, one fraternal lodge held 22 public bingo parties, another men's club held 20 public bingo parties, and there were eighteen public dances.

Railtown, a community of 3000 (total population), maintained 150 voluntary associations. Robinson (1962:88) notes that one of his commun-ities (then in a very early stage of its development) had "about 60 social cultural, recreational, political, ethnic and fraternal organizations . . groups"[4]. In still another community (less than ten thousand), there was a roster of 96 very active organizations. But this did not give any indication of the activities. (This community is hardly typical because the organization details were in the hands of a recreation director):

In an ordinary town you have about 14 percent participation in the recreation programme; here it is 95 percent. It takes about 400 volunteers, leaders, to keep this programme going. For example, the library requires 40 volunteers to operate it. The youngsters are looked after in their team sports, not by one team—we have 35 teams; and the coaches and leaders of these are changed every eighteen months—in other words, parents take turns.

It is difficult to interpret statements such as these, or, indeed, rates of participation because of the poverty of Canadian research material. Hausknecht (1962) has compiled material from two national studies in the United States (reputed to be a nation of joiners) and has come to the following conclusions which are relevant to our discussion: only about 35-55 per cent of Americans belong to voluntary organizations; membership correlates directly with income, education and occupation, and inversely with size of community; membership by age represents a normal curve slightly skewed toward the upper age ranges; married individuals are more likely to belong than single, widowed, and especially divorced and separated individuals; home-owners are more likely to be joiners than are renters; native versus foreign born seem not to be associated with membership in voluntary associations; Protestants have significantly higher membership rates than Roman Catholics even with religious commitment kept constant; sex, age, race, religion, political identification, size of community, home-owners versus renters, and socio-economic status all affect the type of association one is likely to belong to[5].

Social Dimensions of Apathy

The recreational association of Milltown distributed a "Recreation Interest Survey" asking the respondents to check the activities which interested them most. Of the 70 activities listed, 36 were printed in bold type, indicating that these 36 were already organized. This survey was first published in the company paper and later distributed to 2000 families who were water tax payers. From the company paper distribution eight replies were received, and from a later house-to-house distribution forty replies were returned.

The rate of reply was interpreted locally as an indication of a low level of interest (apathy), but a further consideration of the questionnaire probably clarifies the issue. It is doubtful if individuals who already participate fully in the activities of the town would submit their interests again: to them, there would be no need. This leaves the individuals who are interested in participating in an activity not currently organized (provided there are "enough" people interested to make it financially self-supporting). Many activities, such as boxing, ceramics, puppets, or weight-lifting, have such limited appeal that the basis for a club is questionable. Then, there are a series of activities which, although popular, are not usually performed in a group—bicycling, fly-casting, music instruction, sewing, etc. A third category of interests has a limited appeal and, to be meaningful, they require competition: volleyball, soccer, or rugby. Some sports have so little chance of finding an opposing team that the high expenditure in equipment is barely warranted.

Each organization has a small number of vital members. From time to time, some activity becomes popular, and for a brief time acquires a large active membership. Others, however, such as the chess club, the square dancing club, and other specialized activities seldom have more than a handful of ardent members. It is difficult for these organizations to be self-supporting, even if only a modest rent is asked for their premises. It is also obvious that no one club will have a permanent, large and enthusiastic following; it is impossible to have them all thriving. Hence, to each individual club president, the citizens may seem apathetic. Apathy, an over-used and misleading word, usually means "no one else is interested in what I want to promote."

But the accusation of "over-organization" is equally appropriate because those interested in specific organizations are actively recruiting new members; from the point of view of any one individual and potential recruit there are too many demands upon non-working time. A considerable amount of work is required to keep each organization operating.

From the point of view of the volunteer leaders, and those who attempt to participate in a wide range of activities, the community is over-organized because many calls are made upon the time of the keenest participators. A community can be characterized as over-organized or apathetic at the same time, depending upon the point of view. The busy people find the interpersonal contacts involved in these activities rewarding.

In what sense is there "nothing to do?" The short answer is that there is nothing *new* to do. The same old faces and the same old activities are fine, but there are occasions when it would be pleasant to "have a change of scene" or see a play, or perhaps, just for once, go to a night club. In other words, despite the high (some would claim, the frenetic) level of activity in the community, there are a number of activities that are not there and never will be. Each of the four statements about community apathy, over-organization, social reward and lack of things to do, is quite accurate in a certain sense.

A more detailed consideration of recreation may help to amplify these points. First, social leisure time is spent in two ways: in informal casual primary groups (a number of friends in for bridge for the evening), or within the more formal arrangements of the voluntary association (team sports, amateur theatre). The more formal voluntary organization will be considered first. Unlike the less formal, home-based social intercourse, the formal voluntary group has no ready-made facilities.

Recreation Facilities

A number of basic facilities are required for any elementary form of community recreation; these include some sort of hall for bridge parties, meetings, dances, teas, and some sort of sports area. Facilities may include this basic minimum or an elaborate set of plants providing a recreation centre, stadium, skating rink, playing fields and golf course augmented by restaurants, snack bars, taverns, bars, night clubs, bowling alleys, and billiard rooms.

The problems faced by a community of single industry, with a population of less than 30,000, involve the distribution of the costs of these facilities, and decisions on necessities, priorities, and the range of facilities. The building may be undertaken by the company, community, school, churches, unions, or the clubs. The agency that undertakes the capital and maintenance costs affects the use of the building. It makes a great difference socially, for instance, if the only available hall was built and maintained by the Orange Lodge, the town, the company, the union, the school, the Roman Catholic Church, or a business entrepreneur.

Usually a division of labour emerges, so that a variety of facilities under a number of sponsors is available. The people of many communities of single industry have fallen heir to some sort of facilities erected by the industry during the early stages of the town's development (often as a temporary expediency). One example is noted by this respondent in Milltown:

> The recreation centre has quite a long history. Originally, a number of people from the plant and from the office wanted some sort of recreation. Some wanted to wrestle, box, and so on. So they formed an Athletic Association. The company helped them out a little, and they thrived or languished from time to time according to the mood. Then, when wartime expansion came along, we were very crowded: people living in construction camps, boarding in town and so on. They had to have some sort of recreation. So the recreation centre was built as a temporary building. The Athletic Association and the company took over and the company decided to take over any deficit. The building is still there, [but] now the place is a little dead. It provides some recreation and does a good job. But part of it is going to be replaced.

Another respondent warns about the difficulties involved in this sort of arrangement:

> Handouts are not a part of the company's function. They are the worst thing you can give these people. The company should handle the initial investments like golf courses or gyms, etc., but for the use of these, people should pay. They should be made to realize that they must be part of the activities in the town and the only way to feel such a part is to make some of the burden theirs.

As we have previously seen, those companies that feel they must provide minimal facilities in early development are anxious that the community take over these responsibilities at later stages. This process of disengagement introduces friction and disquiet.

Robinson suggests that the characteristic social activities are due to the company policy:

> Much of the responsibility for this "busy, busy" free time must be ascribed to the sponsoring companies. The companies have felt that in order to have a stable and contented labour force in the industrial plant, the employees and especially their wives and children, must be happy in their leisure hours. An employee who is actively engaged in sports or hobbies, they reasoned, has no time or excuse to grumble, and is, therefore, likely to be happy at his work if he is happy at his play and home life. Hence, the companies encouraged organization of and participation in recreation activities, and in many instances provided such facilities themselves during the early stages of the town's growth (Robinson, 1962: 87).

Aside from ascribing a corporate motivation to a company, and over-generalizing, there is some truth in this statement, for employees do have leisure time and they require facilities outside their homes. One respondent noted the difference that a curling rink made to holding engineers in Milltown, a fairly isolated community of single industry:

> That is something that the company could have had here 20 years ago. It is something that would have kept many people here. Something as simple as that. We have about 100 playing. Perhaps 15 of those wouldn't have stayed in the last six years if they hadn't had something like curling to keep them occupied during the winter time. Fifteen may sound like a small number, but when you have a trained man and you multiply him by fifteen, then those fifteen saved, pay for the rink in no time. But the company hemmed and hawed and waited and produced grandiose schemes for stadiums seating 20,000 and other impractical ideas instead of doing something concrete about the situation. There was actually nothing fifteen years ago to stop them from putting up a sheet or two sheets as they have today. Ten or twenty thousand dollars spent that way will save the company one or two hundred thousand dollars in manpower in terms of qualified and experienced engineers.

Sponsorship and Restrictions

Another respondent described a community in which the company transferred the responsibilities for facilities which it built, very soon after their completion:

> A number of social and recreational activities of course are private—the skating rink is private, the golf club is about 18 miles from here, where grass will grow, and it was built by the company originally, at great cost, and is now given over to its private membership. There is no yacht club—there used to be one but it was a drinking club rather than a yacht club and it has gone into disuse. There is some talk of reorganizing it very soon. There is a swimming pool.

As noted above, however, the company is not the only or even chief culprit. Each sponsoring institution imposes some restrictions upon the use of facilities:

> As far as recreation is concerned, we really don't do enough about it. Kids are looked after to a large extent by the school which has playgrounds. We have organized playgrounds attached to the school. Unfortunately the School Board has taken down all the equipment for the summer, although we agreed to monitor the playgrounds for the children's entertainment. We contribute to the recreation centre, which is a separate organization and administered by the shareholders, or members, or the people who contributed to it. The recreation centre is free to all children but a charge of $15 per family is made for adults and [they are] encouraged to bring their children in on this family membership.

Each institution then imposes a distinctive type of restriction upon the use of the facilities. The effect does not stop there, however, because the programmes often come under the direct sponsorship of the owner of the building. The owner of the building provides a subsidy for the organization using it; rents, if any, are nominal. Thus a church auditorium may, on one hand, be restricted for the use of members of the denomination, thus segmenting the social activities of the town, or the church may exercise some control over the use to which the auditorium is put—some denominations do not permit the use of the hall for dancing or card parties, or bingo, or theatrical performances. Many schools have stringent regulations concerning their property. Catholics are unlikely to attend activities in the Masonic Temple. To the extent that the facilities and sponsorship restrict participation, leisure time activities inhibit social integration and enhance in-group values.

On the other hand, commercial enterprises are rare, particularly while the population is small or in the early stages of community development.

It is felt to be far too hazardous to open a first-class restaurant and bar, bowling alley or amusement park, not to mention a theatre for stage plays. As each sponsor has notions of appropriate facilities, most communities of single industry lack services such as night clubs which, though not necessarily essential to daily living, are accepted parts of the urban scene.

Hotel, Dining and Drinking Accommodation

In fact, many communities do not have a hotel; others would not have one if it had not been built or subsidized by the company. These hotels are curious institutions; originally built to accommodate important guests of the company, they are usually utilized to house new management personnel while they are getting settled, and at the same time they provide some services to the community they become expensive tangles of incompatible aims. One company hotel was attempting to provide simultaneously a "show place" for the district, living quarters for some of the young, unmarried management personnel, a luxury hotel for company executives and guests of distinction, a social centre for the community, a tourist resort, and a location for a plant, social and business functions.

It is easy to see that these various functions are incompatible. By making some functions feasible, the hotel immediately sets up conditions by which other functions are inconceivable. For instance, it is not possible to have the main part of the hotel taken over for a local dance while important guests are resting. It does not seem wise to foster easy informality among the permanent guests while entertaining world-renowned figures. The type of furniture and decorum expected by an ambassador may not be appropriate to a labourer. On-the-line workers often feel uncomfortable when a farewell smoker is held in a luxurious setting.

A recent newspaper story noted the closing of one such hotel which had been operated for forty years.

> . . . No buyer for [the] landmark has come forth and the citizens of [the town] are worried about the hotel's plight. One company official said high operating losses had made it impossible for [the company] to continue in the hotel business. The inn has always been a deficit operation for the company. The 120-room hotel employs 35 full-time workers. The inn is the town's most beautiful building. It stands on a hill that rises from the river and it overlooks groves of white birches, green elms and ash and green pines. Perhaps the inn's proudest occasion was when Queen Elizabeth and Prince Philip registered there in 1961. The inn was built in 1928 to provide accommodation for

company employees and visiting officials and customers. Very few guests register at the inn and there are few borders. On Saturday night, the plush bar is quiet. The [company] hopes the building will be bought and used, but high operating costs may scare off potential buyers.[6]

Interviews suggest that from time to time people become bored with the daily routine of work and the evening routine of amusing themselves with all the work and organizing that self-entertainment entails. This lack of break in the normal routine, even in the form of a visiting circus, is the most difficult thing that a young family faces: "It's tiresome for the wives also. There is no place for them to go. There is no shopping district to putter around. So that when you come home at night they want to go out. Where do you go? A movie perhaps, but it's no excuse for a theatre." Another respondent said:

We have nothing to fall back on here. There never has been a bar. We have tried to get one. There have been three referendums and the bar down below was built when we were fairly sure that it would come through—but it didn't. I think the company is quite anxious that it should. During construction they did not want it—because it would be very troublesome. But it would add revenue for us, and make the place much more pleasant—cocktails before dinner, and so on. It would cut down drinking in the rooms appreciably. But I do not know when it will come, if ever.

Officers of Voluntary Organizations

In a small, isolated community of single industry, the citizens become aware of the limitations of their human resources and talents. Participation in voluntary associations, clubs, hobby groups, sports, and so on rests to a considerable extent upon the abilities of fellow citizens to organize and administer; often the existence of the group depends upon someone's specialized skills. Lack of a wide range of activities is often spoken of as "apathy"; this term raises the interesting question of whether a "leader" organizes, sparks and "leads" a groups, or whether a number of enthusiasts band together to form a group and find a "leader." A number of respondents noted the upsurge in particular activities when, for instance, a new clergyman or teacher comes to the community; the clergyman might begin a young people's club, or revitalize women's activities in the church; the new teacher might be a soccer enthusiast, or reintroduce extra-curricular drama into the school.

But the main weight of responsibility for voluntary organizations falls upon the citizens of the community. It is well known that institutional office and voluntary association responsibilities are accepted by a comparatively small group of people in any community: "you get a few people, a good few, who spend a great deal of time and effort on various specialized activities. People here are rabid supporters of one thing or another. You cannot attend everything. Your time is not long enough. Then there are those that do not do anything. You find them everywhere." This activity and interest is usually cyclical, depending to some extent upon age and other related family responsibilities the individual maintains.[7] When the population is small, the range of interested and vital people is limited. In addition, the community of single industry is subject to a high level of mobility and feeling of impermanence among those at the apex of the single industry and the stratification hierarchy. The importance of this mobile group lies not only in their numbers and their position in the social structure, but also in their education, recreation and sports background, as well as experience and skills useful to the community.

Dependence on Specialized Skills

Respondents note the drastic effects when a voluntary leader with special skills moves out of the community or becomes ill. One respondent, for instance, discusses the absolute dependence upon local talent for some sorts of activities:

> We have a drama league—English and French. We provide facilities, actually we rent the church basement for them, give them guidance. We have music, choral and ballet, or rather, we have had it from time to time. Actually our programme is very low as far as the arts are concerned. This is partly because we have to go with the trends and fads and partly because we are restricted by the talent at hand. If we haven't got the people to teach ballet and haven't got the people to lead choral, then there is nothing very much that we can do about it. Most of the groups are fairly active, depending on the leadership. At the moment I would say about 25 per cent of our programme is very active and carries on with continuity. The Choral Society, for instance, is the one that is bogged down at the moment because their director is ill. She is pregnant and is going to be ill for some little time.

Another respondent made the same point about a different community:

> A good example of the sort of thing that happens—we had a very good theatrical group here, it went into a big boom and then it suddenly died. The people who were interested in directing moved out of town and the impetus just wasn't there. It has been recently revived because some of the people who have moved into the town are great enthusiasts and we have had three one-act plays running for three nights and getting 1200 people there. So it is on the

upswing. Badminton, on the other hand, was really thriving with 80 people, and now it is down to 30 and it will probably go down further, until another natural group leader turns up . . . The younger people have no interest in the town affairs. All they want to do is please themselves. Fishing, hunting and playing softball; they are all for that. But when it comes to meetings of any sort, you don't see them.

Or,

The merchants and railway officials, who are considered to be part of the upper social echelon of the community, as well as the "outsiders," for example, the teachers, are blamed as well: "The merchants and railway officials don't help the town out much. Even the teachers don't take part in any community activity. Their attitude is that they are only here for a short time, so the hell with the community. Most of these people who come in are just here to grab the money" (Andrews, 1967: 49-51).

Many activities of a very specialized nature cannot be supported by a small population. Often it is difficult to find enough active members for these activities, in a large urban area. This inability to find members and maintain a membership holds, whether the activity is subsidized or not:

As far as community spirit is concerned, the community is just what you make it. There is enough diversity here, enough people here, to be able to find a group with whom you are compatible, if you want to play bridge, if you want to play poker, go to a show [movie], golf, etc. It is all here. It depends on the individual and nothing else. My interests? Poker; summer: golf, garden; winter: read, magazines, radio library bridge, etc. As far as recreation is concerned, there is pretty well everything here. But I can't name a single organization in town that is really vital and that completely finances itself. They have all been subsidized. The golf club? Yes that is expensive, but most people feel that it is expensive anywhere. It is vital and it would be a great deal more expensive if it were not for the company. They looked after the construction—which was done at the time of plant construction, some charged to the government, and some to expense accounts and so on.

The Role of the Recreation Director

In those communities with a recreation director, no one is sure whether he should act as initiator or merely as an administrator. When he does act as initiator, the project does not always succeed, as noted in this account:

The recreation director has done a good job. He is a sincere man; I don't know how he is getting along. He pushes a great number of things—for instance the playgrounds—for supervised play. He thinks it is a good idea and so do I. That was done by public subscription. He came round to the house one year—I did not have any children at that time, but I thought that there was a good idea behind it, so I gave him $5. The next year I did the same. I understand that it has been abandoned this year, due to lack of interest and support. But that is something that he has pushed strongly.

Recreation directors based in a recreation centre, although few in number, do provide among other things continuity of leadership and facilities, a central source of information, and a focal point through which new programmes are initiated. They are able to co-ordinate and assist local leaders and coaches. With a full-time employee, it is possible to bridge gaps between the local fads and flurries of activity, and make it possible for a new organized activity to emerge when appropriate:

At the present time, as I said before, we are no longer promoting new activities and we do not encourage the perpetuation of old ones, in fact none of these clubs are inactive. As soon as they are inactive, they go out. We now ask, as we said before, that there be a need or concern about something before we will do very much about it. The non-joiner does all right for himself. You have a number of people who just don't do anything in group activities, yet they have beautiful gardens, or you have others who will go out and golf but will golf at dusk when there is no one around. These people are respected, they are fine, they want to choose it that way. We have one curler who goes down with his team and he will go down and curl for two hours with his team once a week and he will not say a word to anyone from the time he comes in until the time he leaves. I don't know what he is doing, he may be thinking chemistry problems all the way through this.

Fads and Fashion

Individual enthusiasms, collectively, pass almost unnoticed in the city. In the small community, however, disaffection or disinterest among a very few people soon makes itself felt and the activity is temporarily doomed:

Now get this! I was phoned to ask if I would help out in a plan to organize a ball team for the kids—that I would only have to turn out, with an assistant, every two weeks. I said "sure". It seemed to be well organized—pick up the balls and the bat from the recreation director's house, take them down, and the kids would be there; spend a couple of hours supervising and then return the equipment. I said "sure" and the two of us went down to the field at 7:00. There was one person there—a little girl. Where were the thirty to forty others?

Or:

> There is little that we can do as the crowd is very unpredictable and this place was hardly built to be a teen centre. In the same way I have tried to have table service in the grill, but one day two people go down and the next thirty. One lady tried very hard to get the young people together in the Anglican Church—an AYPA—but she got so far and the thing fell through. From time to time they have fads here. First it was square dancing. Everyone danced for a year, then it was reduced to 30, and now it is one yearly Klondike party. That is the way everything goes.

The Community Age Cycle

Shift work interferes with the services that the individual is able to contribute to the community. But other factors influence the interaction; the extent of the participation of adults in community services depends upon their age and stage of life. During pregnancies and when children are very young, the wife, and usually the husband too, retires from community activites. When the children enter school and take their part in recreational groups, the parents become involved. They are either shamed into it, or are in active competition with other parents, or they need the sheer assurance of supervising their own children when they are absent from home. Once parents become involved in kindergarten or Wolf Cubs, they seldom remain in this position, for ten years later the same parents may be found coaching hockey or chaperoning a high school dance. Parents are drawn into active community participation through their children:

> There is lots to do—there are clubs galore. I took my turn, and I did a lot in the Boy Scouts and so on—for years. I gave it up a few years ago. When I retired, I called a meeting of parents for the last meeting and said that a lot of boys were outgrowing the Scouts and anyway they needed a different type of recreation beside the scouts, and I suggested baseball. The first thing mentioned was—"Let's approach the company!" I said: "No. Either we look after it ourselves for our children or we will let it go." No one was interested.

This directing of adult activities toward their children is reflected in another phenomenon—the cycle of the community. The stages of the development of the community have been noted earlier; once the community has reached maturity, the cycle of retirement, employment of young people, the raising of families, and the lack of employment opportunities and forced migration for youngsters continues. Any child who is born and brought up out of phase, as it were, has fewer recreational activities. The children who grow up out of phase are those who "have nothing to do," because the majority of parents are preoccupied with the development of life of a different age groups. This problem may be illustrated by a letter to a newspaper editor written by a youth who left his community:

> In one part of your paper I see where a "great number of the town's young people are being deceived." That's too bad! It could, of course, be because the young people of the town have never had enough to do with town affairs—not been allowed to express their desires as to the needs of the town, enough for older, more sensible people to know whether they are capable of thought or not . . .
> Why can't the people get together, and if they want something to scrap about and insult each other about, make it something useful . . . like a new rink, a diving tower at the beach, rugby teams, etc. in the high school—along with boxing, wrestling, and other sports, in a well-equipped gymnasium— which is, needless to say, something I never saw until I left my home town . . .

In an urban setting this correspondent might have been able to carry out his interests more easily. The small single-industry community can seldom cater to minority interests.

Comparisons of Recreation:

Interests of Youth

That these are minority interests is indicated in a study of youth made in 1966. The sample involved 96 youths; 24 from an Ontario urban area; 24 from Ontario communities of single industry; an additional 24 respondents were from a Quebec urban area and 24 were from Quebec communities of single industry. Each group of 24, all superior students in grade 11, was made up of 12 girls and 12 boys. These students were given a list of leisure time activities and asked whether they participated regularly, occasionall, or never. Only three activities were participated in regularly by 50 per cent or more of the students: reading (61 per cent), sports (50 per cent), and cruising (promenade) (57 per cent).

There are interesting differences even among these leisure time patterns; for instance, reading is an urban phenomenon—almost twice as many urban students claim to read regularly than small town students. Sports, on the other hands, seem to be more popular in small towns, and

Ontario and Quebec girls cruise more regularly than boys: perhaps it is part of the female role to wander round to see and be seen!

As might be suspected, most activities fell into the "occasional" category: movies (78 per cent), hobbies (53 per cent), dancing (57 per cent), television (50 per cent), meeting friends in restaurants (42 per cent), parties (80 per cent), clubs (47 per cent), political clubs (39 per cent), and participation in the arts (42 per cent).

Almost 35 per cent of the students did not have a hobby; the replies suggested that urban students participated in hobbies more than small town students, and more Ontario students had hobbies than Quebec students. On the other hand, a disproportionately large number of urban students report that they had never danced—perhaps there are many more alternatives available. Television watching was selected almost as many times as a regular activity as an occasional one. All Quebec students reported that they went to restaurants to meet friends, but almost 20 per cent of the Ontario students claim never to have participated in this activity. In all, 11 per cent claim they had never gone to parties.

Social club activities were much more widely participated in by students from Ontario. Generally, team games were male preoccupations, but 42 per cent of all the students never participated; the proportion was even higher in Quebec. On the other hand, the arts seemed to be the preoccupation of urban females; 40 per cent of the students never participated. It is also clear that at the high school level the students were not actively preoccupied with political clubs (UN, Model Parliament, etc.): 40 per cent occasionally and 15 per cent regularly took part.

The students were not all active in executive work in various organizations: 40 per cent of the students were not serving on any executive (and this was evenly distributed in urban and small town student population, Quebec and Ontario). Among the 56 who were serving, 60 per cent were on the executive of one organization each; 4 students were on four or more executives of school, church or other types of clubs.

In general terms, the major leisure time activities of these young people were informal and social, including movies, parties, cruising, and meeting friends, or solitary activities such as reading and individual sports; there is less interest in organized activities. This small sample suggests that despite differences in available facilities and differences in the social setting in which they live, there are relatively few major differences between the leisure activities of small town youth and those of the urban areas.

Expectations of Citizens

Many citizens, who are able to, leave the community on every possible occasion, enjoy recreation "outside."

> There is still an exodus from town at the weekends although it is not as great as it used to be—now mainly the mobile single people go. But most of the professional staff do a lot of travelling in relation to their work. Of the other people some have summer cottages, but relatively few, as it is mainly the staff who want to get away from the telephone. They find it necessary to have a summer cottage somewhere where no one can reach them. Of the 5200 people in town, however, 375 are young, unmarried people. These included professional staff, young professional staff just out of college, and teachers. About 30 per cent of the teachers are unmarried.

Regardless of sponsorship, there are particular recreational facilities that are not found in small communities. In many ways, the citizens have more facilities and programmes within easy reach than many suburban families; but the local human resources and talents are limited; activities are high on participation and low on skill, appreciation, or spectator characteristics. Further, many of these activities, whether within voluntary associations or in informal cliques and friendship groups, rotate within the same orbit, with the same people working for the same company. There is no way to move to a new crowd, or to lose oneself in the anonymity of the Forum or Maple Leaf Gardens. This being given, the attitudes toward this type of life depend to a large extent upon the expectations of the individual.

Contrast the views of this young lady with those in the succeeding quotation! The native-born states:

> Yes, I was born here, and have lived here all my life. Oh yes, I love it. We have lots to do—it is quiet but we enjoy it very much. In the winter we skate and ski—it is very quiet in the winter. But in the summer there is swimming, tennis, parties and in the summer the students are all home.
>
> The tennis courts are not very good. We do play badminton in the winter, but it is not very good either. The ceiling is too low. Now the construction people are here, it is really lively. They like to come to our parties too—are you staying long?
>
> They have a dance in the neighbouring town in the Recreation Centre every two weeks or so, and guest can go. They have dances at the golf course too. Here we have had a few dances but they are not held very often because someone got tight once and they did not like it.

The recent arrival, however, notes:

> I like to live here for a short time, but I would not like to live here for the rest

of my life. I miss concerts, music, good reading, I miss a lot of things which I believe are necessary for a happy cultural life. This is helped by many things here—there are few concerts a year—three or four a year only; nevertheless they are important. The show [movie], well, we go fairly often; it is not too bad. We do resort to the radio, reading books and that sort of thing.

Other respondents are aware that those who grew up in small towns and are familiar with the patterns of life fit into life in a small community of single industry with more ease than does the individual born in a city.

Actually there is only a certain group who really likes this town. A lot of the young engineers hate it. This is because they have nothing to do—especially if they have been city dwellers. Newlyweds are not a good bet, they like a very gay life and are not happy, especially the wife who is alone all day. The wife is the important factor. No husband can stay, no matter how content he is, if the wife is nagging and discontented. It is no place for the wife who is a cultural enthusiast. If her life is symphony orchestras, ballet, etc., then she should not be here. I think that the best bet is a young, small town couple with a young family.

Contrariwise, the small town youth has difficulties in adjusting to urban life, as one respondent points out:

This is a good place to bring up kids. School is the best in the province. But this is true only to a certain age. They go as far as grade 11. Then for 12 they have to go out to some other place to get their last year before going to university. This is very expensive.

Another problem has arisen on this point. These kids have been brought up in isolation and they have never seen bright lights. And once they get away the experience is very difficult. They have been raised in a vacuum and the shock is very hard on their academic study. There are a number of examples of boys who did very well in school here and went away and failed miserably. The only way you can account for it is their discomfort and preoccupation with new, complicated surroundings.

But, according to one informant, it is all worth the price: "However, everyone seems to be very happy with the recreation. I think it is one of our great achievements. In fact the stores would like to use a lot of High School boys on the weekend for extra help, but they find it very difficult because the boys are all involved in leagues and recreation and teams and this sort of thing."

Informal Relationships

The great majority of relationships in the community are carried out within the family and small informal friendship groups.

Many of the wives congregate in small groups for afternoon tea and morning coffee. The most popular pastime is bridge—both in clubs [almost exclusively female] and in casual games [mixed]. Many of the husbands either bowl or curl in the winter or golf and play tennis in the summer. Both husband and wife attend the moving pictures when there is a good one, and usually they attend any special events such as a Gilbert and Sullivan operetta, or a play. Many of them claim that if they attended all the activities sponsored by the various clubs and associations, they would have more than they could possibly handle. The majority of married adults' activities take place in small circles of friends.

One respondent described the weekly and seasonal activities:

In our leisure time we have friends in to play bridge. There are a lot of bridge clubs, both afternoon and evening. Not many mixed clubs; my wife plays every second week and I play poker every second week. We alternate week about so there is someone home with children. We have a tremendous number of social evenings: Two nights curling, during the season, the odd show [cinema], whenever there is a concert or play, we go to that. Around Christmas there are a lot of cocktail parties and that sort of thing.

In summer, bridge drops off and people go to the tennis courts, play golf, swim, have picnics, do gardening and see less of their neighbours. There is a wonderful spirit here—but a clique spirit. You are in the group or you are not. Each has a fine time but it is restricted. Not much point trying to mix incompatible people.[8]

Another notes:

We have social life but not of the organized type like you'd find at the Rec. Centre or in sports. I've given up the golf club because I want to save some money this year. Most of our social life centres around three or four families, but even that has fallen off in the past three or four years. I think the main reason for that is that nobody can afford to. No one has the money to entertain, well, shall we say, royally. I hate to give a cocktail party because I think it's a cheap way of getting out of social obligations that have accrued. So what do I do? Don't entertain, don't go out. Oh, we have our own small group where there is no necessity to worry about returning parties, etc. Talk at these gatherings usually turns to company talk. It's almost inevitable.

Another more transient member of management notes:

We play a lot of bridge and enjoy it, and we go out to friends' houses and ask them back. This has recently been curtailed because my wife is expecting her first baby, and does not feel too well. Still I am not a part of the community, still a stranger, and I know that I am not going to remain here long—two years at the most—a short training programme. I find the isolation, both psychological and actual, very great. It would not be so bad if I had a car, but I haven't got one. I never expect to have one, or at least not for a long time.

A single male member of management who lives in the company staff house describes his activities:

> There are organizations which I belong to. There is a great amount of leth-argy. There are chronic gripers, cynics, and those who are perfectly happy to do nothing. I lay this down to personal differences. After an evening party at the staff house, several have said "that was fun, isn't it nice to *get together*." There are a lot of parties but these go from room to room. A lot of drinking is done. But I have made a great attempt to get some of the cynics to get out to participate.
>
> I have also been in the St. Mark's players, and there we have had a lot of fun. We put on two plays and the turnout for them was quite good. That takes up quite a bit of my time.
>
> Then I play badminton, which is quite good although the ceiling is far too low; but we have a lot of fun. I also play golf in the summer, play tennis, use my car a lot, and this year I also attended art classes.

One account gives much of the mood of the social life of this particular town:

> But I like living here—there is lots of good fishing. There are many who hate it. My wife likes it. As soon as I am off to work she will get on the telephone, and there are the other young wives who will talk to her for hours. Then everyone will scurry around and do their work and go out with the baby carriage and do their shopping—and walk two abreast, chatting again. She is very happy. I am very fond of music and I do miss that here. The radio reception is very poor and you cannot pick up anything during the day and at night very little.

Recreational Interests of Age Groups

Many respondents point out that the social and recreation requirements are quite different for differing age groups. This is so everywhere, but in a community of single industry the recreational patterns and emphasis tend to follow the age cycle. The next two accounts, for instance, talk about the plight of children who have been born and are living out of phase, as it were, with their contemporaries: "My children have found it extremely quiet and they get quite restless here. I think it is a shame that a city of this size can't provide any more in the line of recreation." And:

> They can't play tennis after five. They can't go to the recreation hall because they are too young. Take those two away and what have you got? There is talk among my daughter's crowd about leaving. The majority, if not all of them, talk about getting out of town. They feel tied down here. They find no means of working off excess energy, so that there is constant talk of leaving. Personally I'm not worried about her leaving. She may.

In contrast, another respondent admitted that his interests were modest, and certainly he was not very concerned about the recreational problems of youth. "Of course I am an older man and your interests and leisure and everything else is always changing. The preferences of an older person are different from those of a younger one. Perhaps some of the younger people are not as content as I am because when you get to my age, you are more interested in slippered ease."

Another respondent felt that times had changed and, although he did not understand the problems of youth, they gave him a feeling of virtue:

What was there to do when I was a child? Nothing. There was no recreational centre. We played a bit of hockey. Money was hard to come by. Our main recreation was fighting French kids. We had a very dull time. One thing which stands out in my mind was the work done by Mrs. X who organized a dancing class when we were 13 or 14. She charged 25 cents per month and donated her time. We did not have to have any money—she taught us social poise and how to dance . . . this went on for several years and among that group we had houseparties, which gave us something to do on Saturday night. That stood out as one of the brightest pictures of my childhood.

The younger generation—they have a different set-up. I have a kid brother 15, he plays tennis—much cheaper than it used to be; he plays golf, goes to the restaurant, sips cokes, etc. He always seems to have something to do, whereas I had less.

A female respondent said: "My observation of small towns was that they were much better for boys than for girls. Boys, through sports and so on, often got attached to the community. Girls had to get out." Other respondents noted that occupation of the invididual and age both made differences in the experienced recreation needs:

The miners themselves don't take a big part in our programme. They like to go to the lakes and fish, etc., because that gets them away from the mines and out of the whole area. Their families of course come here and join in our programmes but, after all, the men work a hard eight-hour day in the mines and then go home—and that is the end of their day as far as they are concerned.

Spontaneous Activities

There are close links between informal recreation and formal associations. Respondents report that, periodically and quite spontaneously, they decide that it would be most enjoyable to spend the evening bowling or curling. They are not able to do this on the spur of the moment, because the facilities are taken up by bowling and curling leagues. In order to participate the player must join a team and follow the playing schedule, which means playing regularly whether he feels like it or not. If he drops out too often, he incurs the anger of his team mates.

In much the same way, several middle-aged male respondents reported smelling autumn in the air and wishing to "toss a football around" and have a "real workout," or, on a soft spring evening, having an urge to "get out and play a bit of baseball" and recapture the rapture of youth. Team companions, preoccupied with daily chores, were hard to come by. One respondent reported that in a burst of enthusiasm, they made up a baseball team, and entered a local league. He described the disenchantment of having to play on schedule, whether in the mood or not. He then described the end of the season when the team played every night of the week, all day Saturday and Sunday to make up games that had been rained out during the schedule. He ended the long recital with the words: "We'll never try that again!"

Whether urban or small community, it is more and more difficult for an adult to participate in sports (other than solitary hobbies or sports) without becoming a part of the structure and obligations of a formal association.

It may be said, in summary, that communities of single industry have a large number of associations, clubs and special interest groups, so many that they cannot all be supported all the time—this lack of support is called "apathy" by the club leaders. The facilities required for some activities are extensive, and it was noted that the sponsor of the activity and the owner of the facilities made a considerable difference to the interaction patterns in the community. If all recreation is centred in a community—or company-owned recreation centre, the resulting interaction is quite different from that of a community where recreation is sponsored by various denominations.

One distinctive quality of all recreation in communities of single industry is that it is active and participatory rather than inactive, spectator—or appreciation-oriented. There is little commercial recreation; these are communities in which "you make your own fun." This type of activity, however, raises the problems of skills and leadership. Pottery-making groups, theatre groups, and sports teams need active and skilled voluntary leaders. The quality and quantity of leadership at any given time has a great influence upon the amount of activity in itself as well as on the area in which this activity is directed. The age cycle of the community and changing recreation fads also influence the amount of activity in particular areas of recreation. The smaller the community the more likely it is to have informal recreation; a very small community may be organizationally dormant.

It is just as impossible to satisfy a spontaneous urge to go bowling or curling in a small community of single industry as it is in the urban areas. A great many activities have become institutionalized into league, club and team structures requiring schedule discipline.

To the extent that there is active participation, recreation activities are effective agents of social control. The sponsors of the activities and available facilities affect the degree of social integration that takes place. Church sponsorship and church facilities limit accessibility to the programmes, incorporate, by implication, symbolic ideological aspects, and reinforce shared values. The lack of criss-crossing of memberships limits the integrative qualities of these activities. In general, although the recreation activities imply social control, the extent of the reaffirmation of parochial group values limits the reinforcement of shared community values.

Recreational activities described and discussed by the respondents in this chapter are characteristic of half the population of Canada. The major variable affecting the activities is the size of community. The sponsorship offered by some industries is an additional bonus of liability, depending on how one wishes to evaluate it.

NOTES:

1. Burnet's paper illustrates the moral indignation and action in urban areas.
2. See the discussion of this point of view in Rossides (1968), especially part V. Rossides links the idea of leisure to the early Greeks. "Leisure to them meant a richly stimulating but congruent social and moral order. Implicit throughout their conception of leisure (or the good life) is the idea of aretê or versatility combined with excellence," (Rossides, 1968:287).
3. See also Derbyshire (1960:63-75) and the Institute of Local Government, Queen's University, *Single Enterprise Communities in Canada* (Ottawa, 1953) Chapters XI and XII.
4. See the Institute of Local Government, Queen's University, *Single Enterprise Communities in Canada* (1953: 169-176).
5. Other studies relevant to the subject are Babchuk and Booth (1969); Caplow and Forman (1950); Kuper et al. (1953); Reissman (1954); White (1955) and Young and Willmott (1957). The implications of recreation are discussed in Center for Settlement Studies, University of Manitoba. *Proceedings—Symposium on Reserve Frontier Communities,* (Winnipeg, 1968).
6. *The Globe and Mail* (Toronto, May 23, 1968). See also the discussion in Institute for Local Government, Queen's University, *Single-Enterprise Communities in Canada* (1953:140-142).
7. For an example see Carlton (1967).
8. See Michelson's (1969) systematic analysis of seasonal differences in activities in suburban Toronto, as well as the discussion in *Single Enterprise Communities in Canada* (1953:140-142).

REFERENCES

Andrew, Alick R.
1967   "Social Crisis and Labour Mobility. A Study of Economic and Social Change in a New Brunswick Railway Community." Unpublished MA thesis, University of New Brunswick.

Babchuk, N. and Booth, A.
1969   "Voluntary Association Membership. A Longitudinal Analysis." American Sociological Review, 34, Feb.

and Edwards, J. N.
1965   "Voluntary Associations and the Integration Hypothesis." Sociological Inquiry, Spring.

Burnet, Jean R.
1961   "The Urban Community and Changing Moral Standards." In S. D. Clark (ed.), Urbanism and the Changing Canadian Society. Toronto: University of Toronto Press.

Caplow, T. and Forman, R.
1950   "Neighbourhood Interaction in a Homogeneous Community." American Sociological Review, 15, June.

Carlton, Richard A.
1967   "Differential Educational Achievement in a Bilingual Community." Unpublished doctoral dissertation, University of Toronto.

Center for Settlement Studies, University of Manitoba
1968   Proceedings, Symposium on Resource Frontier Communities. December 16, Winnipeg.

Clark, S. D.
1942   The Social Development of Canada. Toronto: University of Toronto Press.

Derbyshire, Edward
1960   "Notes on the Social Structure of a Canadian Pioneer Town." Sociological Review, 8 (1).

Gordon, C. S. and Babchuk, N.
1959   "A Typology of Voluntary Organizations." The American Sociological Review, 24, February.

Hausknecht, M.
1962   The Joiners. New York: Bedminster Press.

Institute of Local Government, Queen's University
1953   "Single- Enterprise Communities in Canada." Kingston.

Kuper, L. et. al.
1953   Living in Towns. London: Cressett Press.

Lundberg, G. A., Komarovsky, M., and McInerny, M.A.
1934   Leisure, A Suburban Study. New York; Columbia University Press.

Michelson, W.
1969   "Space as a Variable in Sociological Inquiry: Serendipitous Findings on Macro-Environment." Paper presented at American Sociological Association Meeting.

Reissman, L.
1954   "Class, Leisure, and Social Participation." American Sociological Review, 19, February.

Robinson, Ira M.
1962   New Industrial Towns on Canada's Resource Frontier. Programme of Education and Research in Planning, Research paper no. 73, Dept. of Geography, University of Chicago.

Rose, A.
1965　　*Sociology: The Study of Human Relations.* New York: Knopf.

Rossides, D. W.
1968　　*Sociology as a Functional Process, An Introduction to Sociology.* Toronto: McGraw Hill.

Smith, D. H.
1966　　"The Importance of Formal Voluntary Organizations for Society." *Sociology and Social Research*, July.

Warriner, C. K. and Prather, J. E.
1965　　"Four Types of Voluntary Association." *Sociological Inquiry*, Spring.

White, R. C.
1955　　"Social Class Differences in Uses of Leisure." *American Journal of Sociology*, 1, September.

Young, M. and Willmott, P.
1957　　*Family and Kinship in East London.* London: Routledge and Kegan Paul.

SPORTS AND THE CAREER IN CRESTWOOD HEIGHTS

John R. Seeley, R. Alexander Sim, Elizabeth W. Looseley

To the people of Crestwood Heights, the career is of all concerns the most momentous. It may be called "success," or "getting ahead," or "doing well." Whatever its name, it is thematic to the mythology of the Western world. Cinderella, Dick Whittington, Abraham Lincoln, or the Jack of numberless stories—Jack who killed the giant after taking his lyre and his gold, Jack who met and won the King's daughter (Chase:1943): these are stories that antedate capitalism and the expanding industrial technology of North America. Yet they have been so absorbed into the Western ethos that they continue to nourish the spirit and implant conceptions in the minds of children in Crestwood Heights.

The Social Setting

The Crestwood child's environment includes the very criteria by which the success of the career is measured. The conditions which make for comfort are in themselves the hallmarks of success in the career: harmonious surroundings keyed to the latest conceptions of beauty and elegance; the opportunity to consume food which is rich, yet approved by nutritionists as nourishing; the house, and the privilege of living, in a select area; superior opportunities for travel, education, entertainment, and training in special skills. These are the rewards of the father's capacity to earn, which is thus a major measure of a successful career.

The connections between the career and the symbols of success and the attendant attitudes and values are obvious. The child, who in more static social situations might be permitted to take certain aspects of the common life for granted, is in Crestwood Heights made to "appreciate" the close connection between effort and achievement: where there has been rapid personal mobility (and will be more) one cannot take anything for granted. The past has been outmoded too recently. The present social and economic status of the parent is too precarious. The goals ahead, higher up the ladder of achievement, beckon too invitingly for complacency. It seems that personal mobility develops a momentum of its own, which, until it is spent, carries the individual and his family from status to status. Yet it is inevitable that the child for whom so much is being done should also tend to "take everything for granted," including the inevitability of his own success. At the same time there is much uncertainty in Crestwood Heights as to whether the person who does not receive such a good start (like many of the adults who voice these doubts) does not really have the advantage; is he not more strongly oriented towards struggle and competition—and therefore more likely to achieve?[1]

Various social interests have a stake in the development of career-oriented persons. The complex contemporary division of labor requires certain components at the professional and managerial level which become essential to the smooth operation of an industrial society. The maintenance of this group is, in turn, assured, it seems, by three conditions: mobility in space and in social class; occupational opportunity with commensurate rewards in material objects and class position; and finally, personal flexibility and adaptability within fairly well defined limits respecting attitude, behavior, and occupational techniques. These are the prerequisites of the successful career.

Mobility is, as we see it here, the highly developed pattern[2] of movement from one job to another, from one place of residence to another, from one city to another, from one class position to another. To the individual, therefore, moving must not only hold the promise of material reward and added prestige, but, in spite of cost and labor, it should itself be "exciting". The chance to meet new friends, the known but as yet untried amenities in the distant city, together with the exhilaration of leaving behind the frustrations and jealousies of office, clique, and neighborhood, help to make moving more than tolerable. The man and woman of the Heights have few bonds[3] that cannot be broken at the promise of a "promotion". They have been prepared for this from the cradle.[4]

Mobility must be matched by opportunity: opportunity for training, employment, and advancement. Training must be available if the mobile person, bent upon a career, is to acquire the expected and necessary technical skills and social graces. He must have, of course, at least a minimum standard of intelligence, energy, and poise; but, more importantly, he must be drawn towards the enterprise around which skill, grace, intelligence, energy, and poise will play, and out of which his own career will develop. He must wish to manage or cure—and be prepared to learn to cure or manage.

The web of occupational opportunity for the executive and the professional which extends outward from Crestwood Heights to other upper middle class communities is an essential part of the career orientation of the individual. There must be posts to fill. It is best if there are more opportunities than men, but even if the opposite is the case, the satisfactions which come from keen or even ruthless competition can be stressed. In either case, whether there is a buyers' market or a sellers', the experience is rationalized and justified.

The third prerequisite calls for a readiness in the professional and executive to abandon cherished usages and techniques as new ones arise. Of course the desire for change must not be so strong as to impair the individual's performance at the level presently occupied; the costs and risks of moving may help to bridle his ambition, but the job itself has its own satisfactions. Nevertheless, he must be willing to acquire new conceptions of life and organization, and revise constantly in later life his procedures within his chosen field. The differences between the career of the person who has risen by his own effort and the person who has been placed in Crestwood Heights by the parent, have a relation to the flexibility which is so essential to the professional and executive person in a rapidly changing society. Since the individual who "gets a good start" is more likely to accept current techniques and practices than the individual who is struggling upward, the latter must challenge the very arrangements which give advantage to the former. Personal flexibility is a valued characteristic, whereas rigidity is generally condemned. "Flexibility" allows the person to accept innovation, to manoeuvre in difficult situations where precedent gives little guidance, and to seek by his own efforts new solutions to social and technological problems.

Careers are made within a structure of relationships, some of the elements of which have already been mentioned: incentives, checks and limitations to ambition, compensation for failure, and a delicate balancing between opposites. These elements and others are caught up in the notion of competition as it is understood and played out in the daily rounds of work and play in Crestwood Heights.[5] In the Heights one encounters competition everywhere: in sport, in the classroom, at the dinner table ("Now let's see who will finish his vegetables first"), at the traffic light, in raising money for charity, in the mission of the church.

Competition, it seems, like duelling or mating, requires the pairing of opposites, the pitting against one another for mutual gratification of (usually) two persons or groups, alike in all respects save one: the quality at issue.

Hockey and Canadian football, two typically male, typically North American games, seem to represent symbolically the structure of competition. More than any other game, football would appear to be the property of the upper middle class and is particularly associated with the university, where it is firmly established as an autumn ceremonial. By analogy, the structure of the relationships within which the person bent on a career plays out his roles may be illuminated by looking at the game.[6]

The game is played by two competing teams.[7] The teams are evenly matched in number, in ascribed roles and, if possible, in strength—for the odds for winning should be as even as possible. Equal strength depends on player ability, coaching and management skill, the eye appeal of the playing grounds, uniforms, equipment, and drum majorettes. The two teams are members of a league, and the league is tied in a series of relationships to other leagues devoted to the promotion of the game. In a single game, therefore, the issue at stake is not simply the final score of the game but actually the interlocking interests of all the teams in the league, of all the leagues, officials, players, coaches, and subsidiary parties to the game—of distributors of sporting equipment, news and radio commentators, and so on.

The teams play together in highly combative style. In essence, the play centers around a violent contention for possession of the ball. Possession gives the possessor nothing more than the right or initiative in the aggressive policy of gaining ground from the opposition. The play which ranges back and forth upon the territorial limits of the "field", is governed by a set of rules which are commonly accepted. They are administered by neutral officials whose prominent function it is to act as mobile judiciary as the game proceeds. The existence of a common body of codified usages emphasizes that what appears as competition between two groups takes place within a large scale cooperative effort of a single group, which besides those immediately engaged ultimately involves the public as represented by the spectators present and at home. Time, place, apparatus, rules and behavior, are largely agreed. What takes place is not so much competition as cooperation within a competitive setting.

Simultaneously, competition takes place within a cooperative setting. Like baseball (and unlike "soccer") the game is so structured that the "star" is prominent in the enterprise. To him the burden and glory of heroic behavior are assigned. The possibilities of stardom are not equal for all members of the team, since the quarterback and back-field players are more visible, and are more often given the possession of the ball. For the men in the line, nevertheless, there are situations where any member of the team can win stardom. The game in its basic structure lies somewhere between a status or fixed arrangement, where only one member of the team, by virtue of his assigned role, is permitted a star's part, and a much more fluid situation where anyone might be the star—or none. The members of a team cooperate to defeat the opposition, but this is usually accomplished when one (or more) of the players on the team has outshone his comrades on the playing field. Their purpose, it seems, can best be accomplished when they are set against other members of their own team in a sharply competitive relation. However, the will to win usually keeps in check what might engender hostility between team-mates, revealing only the fighting spirit of each player bent on team victory.

A more detailed analysis of the game cannot be pursued, though a study of changes in it, of field rules, the foul, the fumble, and the stratagems of secrecy, suspense, and surprise are all relevant to the present argument and would illuminate more fully the basic competitive structure within which careers in Crestwood Heights are made and validated. The points of analogy are many. The career is also a device for permitting a degree of personal achievement and recognition for the individual. His "careerdom" is earned within a given context of action, partly with the help of colleagues and friends, and partly at their expense. The competitors oppose one another in pairs of groups; in either case, the classification that puts certain ones "in the same league" draws them together co-operatively against all others whether of higher or lower qualifications, and at the same time sets them against each other in earning the fruits of achievement. The context of action includes the prevailing legal and moral understandings in which the industrial system operates, as well as codes of professional or business ethics which regulate the activities of special groups.

Pairs are also counterposed in the game—passer and receiver, outfield peg and infield catch. So too we find in Crestwood Heights—in a setting where monogamy is the rule, where there is high mobility, and where an urban massing of the population creates a need for compensation—special emphasis upon the continual linking of pairs: in modern dancing, in the family where a third child is expected to create problems of adjustment, and in various work situations.[8]

The emergence of a dominant one in a pair, and the dissolution of the pair as its members move into solo efforts or into larger groupings, parallel the behavior of the star who is a *sine qua non* of sport and drama in North America. The career is the vehicle which permits the enactment of the star's role in a highly complex, hierarchical division of labor. In the characteristic breakdown into smaller groupings within the large corporation or the great hospital, individuals can excel in competition with others of like status. There is a place for a top sales man, a proficient nurse, and an efficient foreman, within the larger grouping at a given place and level in the hierarchy. Rewards appropriate to the level give satisfaction, despite the knowledge that there are other and higher levels in the hierarchy or in the community.

There is an endless constraint, however, against "over-doing".[9] The star in Crestwood Heights must constantly practise "modesty," and pass the honor of victory on to the coach, his team-mates, or even his mother who has fed him so well. He must strive to establish the record, but once it is established he can be confident it will not be forgotten provided he properly disclaims credit for the victory. He can quickly submerge himself in the group, the team, or the firm.[10]

The fact that a star who excels too well puts himself out of his own league is a deterrent to over-performance; it helps a man to relate himself more co-operatively to the team. In careers (as in baseball, hockey, and horse racing) if the performer is constantly superior to his fellows within the class or group, he is forced to compete in another class where his chances of starring are reduced. In the pursuit of the career, there is thus a system of checks and balances where the good is blunted by the bad, incentive offset by deterrent, and ambition bridled by the fear of excess.

NOTES

1. Such an interpretation of the career could only be checked by watching one generation through all the stages of the career, rather than observing, as in this study, different generations in all the stages of the career.
2. Mobility has a somewhat different pattern among professional and executive people, but only in the sense that the executive is sent and the professional is "called". The

executive operates within the orbit of "the firm"; his moves are in response to its needs. The professional senses in a new location an opportunity to serve or advance and seeks to establish himself in the new environment.

3. It should be noted that "bond" is the most popular term to describe meaningful social linkage, and this sociological terminology unconsciously reflects the contemporary notion that intimate social relationship implies constraint; so do such alternative words as "ties," "links", etc.

4. Emotionally, they are gypsies. It is perhaps a pity that their way of life calls for the accumulation of so much furniture. It is interesting to note that E. M. Forster, writing in 1910, made this comment in *Howard's End* about "moving":

   The Age of Property holds bitter moments even for a proprietor. When a move is imminent, furniture becomes ridiculous . . . . It was absurd, if you came to think of it . . . . The feudal ownership of land did bring dignity, whereas the modern ownership of movables is reducing us again to a nomadic horde. We are reverting to the civilization of luggage, and historians of the future will note how the middle classes accreted possessions without taking root in the earth, and may find in this the secret of their imaginative poverty.

5. Competition as a form of behavior is found in all cultures, but in each it appears in a form peculiar to the group under observation.

6. Canadian Rugby football is derived from English Rugby football. Football was imported into the United States from McGill University by Harvard and Yale, the first game being played in 1874. Since this importation, an American game has developed with little resemblance to the original; from it Canadian Rugby football has recently adopted many rules and play formations. For an early history of football see Camp and Deland: (1896); and for a suggestive treatment of football with the thought that it may yet be used as a means of acculturation as the world seeks the explanation of American military and financial successes on the playing fields of Notre Dame, see Riesman and Denney (1951).

7. Note also the frequent identification of the moiety as one of two mutually exclusive divisions of a group which is made in the social organization of primitive societies. They are frequently concerned with ritual and games. See Chapple and Coon, (1942: 321-322); and, for a discussion of symbols and techniques of competition, (614-628).

8. The pair is, of course, a universal social form, for as Simmel says, "The fact that male and female strive after their mutual union is the foremost example or primordial image of a dualism which stamps our life-contents generally" (Wolff, 1950: 128).

9. Such restraint is found even in the vastly more expressive culture of the Kwakiutl. (See Benedict, 1934: 173-222).

10. The boxer, on the other hand shakes hands with himself after the victory; but then boxing is not a Crestwood game.

REFERENCES

Benedict, R. F.
1934   *Patterns of Culture*. Boston and New York: Houghton Mifflin.

Camp, W. C. and L. F. Deland
1896   *Football*. Boston and New York: Houghton Mifflin.

Chapple, E. D. and C. S. Coon
1942   *Principles of Anthropology*. New York: Henry Holt.

Chase, R. (ed)
1943   *The Jack Tales*. Boston: Houghton Mifflin.

Riesman, D. and R. Denny
1951   "Football in America". A study in Culture Diffusion. *American Quarterly* 3. Also in
        J. W. Loy and G. S. Kenyon (eds.), *Sport, Culture and Society*. Toronto: Collier-
        Macmillan, 1969.
Wolff, K. H. (ed. and trans.)
1950   *The Sociology of Georg Simmel*. Glencoe III: Free Press.

ACADEMIC-ATHLETIC-POPULARITY SYNDROME IN THE CANADIAN HIGH SCHOOL SOCIETY (1967)

David Friesen

One of the most readily accepted generalizations regarding adolescent society is that boys prefer athletics over academics, and girls prefer popularity. Proof of this statement has been found in a number of studies. James S. Coleman, in his large-scale study of ten mid-western high schools in the United States, found evidence to this effect (Coleman, 1963: 30).

About 31 per cent of the boys wanted to be remembered as "brilliant students", compared with 45 per cent of those who wished to be remembered as "athletic stars". For the girls, 28 per cent preferred to be remembered as "brilliant students", with about 72 per cent who chose to be remembered as "leader in activities", or "most popular". On the basis of these findings, Coleman concluded that "the image of the athletic star is most attractive for boys, and the image of activities leader and most popular are more attractive to girls than brilliant student" (Coleman, 1963:30).

Coleman proceeded to probe for an explanation of this priority in values by high school students. He found evidence that the athlete who gained much status in his school did so because he had accomplished something for the school and the community in leading his team to victory. "The outstanding student, by contrast, has few ways—if any—to bring glory to his school" (Coleman, 1963: 309).

Thus the failure of the academic image to achieve top priority in the adolescent subculture may be the result of the organization of the school itself. As a "social system" the school may not provide for the realizations of the "personality needs" of the adolescent. Does the school permit the outstanding student to bring honor to his school and his community, and, more important, to his own informal peer group?

Coleman's approach may suffer limitations because of semantics. Using "high grades", "honor roll", "outstanding student", and "brilliant student" at various times to refer to the boy who represents the scholar may introduce sources of bias. Furthermore, the student who chooses to be remembered as a "brilliant student" may actually be spending most of his energy in athletics. Similarly, the one who wishes to be remembered as a "star" athlete may be spending his energy in academic work. There is at least the possibility that the outstanding student, taking his achievement for granted, may long to add another feather to his cap—and this could be in athletics. If outstanding students have never been granted much recognition for their achievement, it is entirely logical for them to aspire to recognition in some other field.

But it is not in this area that this research wishes to examine the problem. The assumption is that the students value athletics, popularity, and academic achievement in differing proportions. Why? Several reasons will be advanced.

First of all, the adolescent wishes for recognition in his own society; he wants to be accepted, respected, and applauded for his activities. This source of gratification, which is near to him and meaningful in his own terms is also immediate. How does he receive this immediate gratification? Obviously, he will derive this from activities with the high school group itself. Those who wish to be popular will be encouraged to adopt behavior leading to popularity. This could be athletics, cheerleading, dating or even under some conditions drinking, smoking, or "demonstrating". Such behaviour depends strongly on the value held in the peer group with which the individual identifies himself.

Immediate gratification could also come out of parent-student relationship. If parents want their children to be successful in the things that count in school, and permit the peer group complete independence in determining what counts (e.g. making the basketball team), the value structure of the peer group will simply be reinforced. However, if the parents genuinely reward academic achievement with recognition, the peer group influence will be subdued or negated.

Immediate gratification can also stem from the school and society. The school, chief educating agent of society, needs to develop an organization or structure that will reward those activities most closely aligned to its major function, and use the peripheral activities to channel the energies of youth toward learning. If schools do not plan for effective education, the short-term goals of adolescents can submerge the real goals of the school.

The Academic-Athletic-Popularity Syndrome

Before stating the hypothesis of this study, it may be advisable to briefly review the currently accepted position regarding the academic-athletic-popularity syndrome of the Canadian adolescent society. This belief originates mainly from American research, especially Coleman's, but also in part from that of Gordon (1957), Hollingshead (1949), Tannenbaum cited in Coleman (1963: 309-310), Goodman (1960), Riesman (1961), and Erikson (1963). Simply stated, the belief is that adolescents value athletics, popularity, and academics in that order. Lawrence W. Downey states this clearly:

> If one is to comprehend the ways of our adolescents, one must look for partial explanations of their behaviour in the value system which is their own—not in the value system which characterizes the broader culture. One important question, then, is what do adolescents value?
> (1) Adolescent boys appear to value athletics and adolescent girls appear to value social success much more than they value academic achievement.
> (2) Popularity, especially with the opposite sex, is such an impelling value among adolescents that it leads to a fetish for attractiveness (Downey, 1965: 140-141).

The Hypothesis

The hypothesis, then, for this study, is as follows: The priority of values of Canadian adolescents is in the order of athletics, popularity, and academic achievement.

The Sample

The responses to questions in the area of athletics, popularity, and academics of 10,019 high school students (in grades 10 to 12) in a large western Canadian city will be used to examine the hypothesis (Friesen, 1967). This study will also draw on previous research of a similar nature in an Eastern Canadian city where two urban high schools, with a total population of 2,425 students, were studied (Friesen, 1966a). Finally, it will draw evidence from a mid-western Canadian urban and rural high school study where eight schools of diverse nature, each with a random sample of 200 students, were examined (Friesen, 1966b). All the research, now in its third year, was conducted under the same researcher and with practically the same instruments. In each case, except the mid-western Canadian study, the sample included the total available school population present on the day of the survey. In all, nineteen schools and 15,000 students were involved.

Statistical Treatment of Data

Procedures similar to those used in previous sociological studies on values and attitudes of high school students were employed. Frequency distributions, percentage distributions, and chi-square analyses were used in the examination of student responses to forced-choice items. The items were constructed on the basis of the literature and recognized research in the area of the adolescent society. They were refined during three years of research. Because of the large sample size, it was found unnecessary to dwell on the statistical significance of the difference.

The Problem Examined

Table I illustrates that the public high school students chose friendliness, good looks, money, and athletics as values which would precede academic excellence as a means of gaining membership in the leading crowd. The same order of preference, with very little variation, was observed in the eastern, and mid-western studies.

Table II illustrates that students chose leading crowd membership, being an athletic star, and even having a nice car as values more instrumental in gaining popularity than high grades or being on the honor roll. The variation in choices between different studies was significant, though not extensive. Rural students placed more value on cars and high grades, urban students placed more emphasis on being in the leading crowd.

Table III indicates what the students considered most important for success in life. Personality took precedence over academic achievement, which was preferred only slightly to friendliness. The hierarchy, though, was in the order of personality, academic achievement, friendliness, money, and last, athletics. Very slight variations occurred between the responses of students in the three regions.

TABLE I

MAJOR CHARACTERISTICS CONSIDERED NECESSARY FOR MEMBERSHIP IN LEADING CROWD

	Per Cent Responding (N = 10,019)
Friendliness	51.3
Good looks	25.4
Money	13.8
Athletic ability	7.0
Academic excellence	2.5

TABLE II

ITEMS CONSIDERED MOST IMPORTANT FOR POPULARITY

	Per Cent Responding (N = 10,109)
Being in the leading crowd	64.3
Being an athletic star	18.7
Having a nice car	12.7
High grades, honor roll	4.2

TABLE III

CHARACTERISTICS CONSIDERED MOST IMPORTANT FOR SUCCESS IN LIFE

	Per Cent Responding (N = 10,109)
Personality	57.4
Academic Achievement	17.7
Friendliness	15.6
Money	8.8
Athletics	0.5

These findings *suggest* that academic achievement is relegated to a very minor position in the hierarchy of values in the samples of Canadian high school students studied. In the eyes of the adolescent, academic achievement does not help him appreciably in attaining a position in the leading crowd of the high school; it does not help him in his quest for popularity—which, as we shall see, emerges as a powerful element in the adolescent society—and it does not seem to merit the highest position for the attainment of success in life.

It is relatively easy to conclude that the thesis which holds that adolescents value athletics higher than academic work because it leads to recognition in the peer group and brings satisfaction is essentially correct. But a more careful look at the findings will reveal that athletic prowess is not the most important value; it was chosen fourth as contributing towards leading crowd status, and second as leading to popularity. When viewed in its contribution to success in life, it was chosen last and by less than one per cent of the students in all three regions.

The rather nebulous concepts of "friendliness", "leading crowd membership", and "personality" were chosen as contributing most to the three goals specified. The strength of the social factors in the adolescent subculture is indicated.

What, then, about the place of athletics and academic ability? Where do they fit in the complex structure of the adolescent value system? To gain an insight into their place in the students' value system, three additional items will be analyzed briefly.

The Problem Investigated

Table IV presents the student responses to the question similar to that pursued in Coleman's study. In all three Canadian studies, the students preferred to be remembered as outstanding students, with the strongest such desire expressed by the mid-western student and the weakest by the western urban students. Very little difference existed between the three studies in regard to the percentage of students who desired to be remembered as athletic stars. However, the desire for popularity took second place in the triad for the western urban students. For the total group, the order was significant. The choices for outstanding student were far ahead of those for athletic star, which were slightly ahead of those for being most popular.

Table V presents a summary of the findings for the western urban study by total and by sex. Popularity was perceived as the most satisfying for school life by the majority of these students. It was chosen slightly over academic achievement, largely on the strength of the girls' choice for popularity. Boys chose academic achievement as most important for a satisfying school life.

Table VI presents the summary of student responses to the question "Which one of the following do you regard as most important for your future: academic achievement, popularity, or athletics and cheerleading?" The choices for athletics were almost negligible; but the choices for academic achievement were preponderant.

TABLE IV

PER CENT OF STUDENTS CHOOSING TO BE REMEMBERED BY THREE CHARACTERISTICS

	Outstanding Student	Athletic Star	Most Popular	No Response	N
Western Urban	43.5	26.0	30.5	0.0	(10,019)
Eastern Urban	54.0	25.4	17.3	3.3	(2,425)
Midwest Urban and Rural	60.8	22.6	15.1	1.5	(1,600)

TABLE V

PER CENT OF STUDENTS CHOOSING CHARACTERISTICS AS MOST SATISFYING FOR SCHOOL LIFE (N = 10,109)

	Academic Achievement	Athletics	Popularity
Western urban total	43.0	12.5	44.5
Boys	42.9	16.8	40.3
Girls	43.1	8.5	48.4

TABLE VI

PER CENT OF STUDENTS CHOOSING CHARACTERISTICS SEEN AS MOST IMPORTANT FOR THEIR FUTURE (N = 10,019)

	Academic Achievement	Athletics Cheerleading	Popularity
Western urban total	81.7	2.3	16.0
Boys	82.8	2.8	14.4
Girls	80.5	1.7	17.8

By examining each of these three characteristics in turn, it can be seen that the high school student seems quite aware of what he is doing when he chooses athletic stardom as something for which he wishes to be remembered. He acknowledges that it is not the most satisfying characteristic in his school life and, furthermore, that it holds little value for his future; yet it holds strong immediate value for him, especially through his referent peer group.

The responses to the two alternatives to athletics are more ambivalent. To be remembered as an outstanding student has high priority in all centers, especially in the rural schools. Several explanations could be advanced for this unexpected phenomenon. One is the emergence of alternate courses in urban areas. Here the vocational area may receive more emphasis than the academic. The rural high schools of the mid-western study, even though fairly large, did not offer much beyond the matriculation program.

There also may be a psychological explanation. Having achieved a respectable academic performance without much reward or recognition students may desire achievement in more visible areas, and thus turn to athletic or social competencies. A third explanation is derived from viewing the school as a social system. The"organization" student in the urban setting may be reacting against the bureaucracy of the school, or he may be suffering from a dearth of social or personal satisfactions, and thus turn to the "popularity" goal as something out of his reach. It is interesting to note that 49.3 per cent (4,774) of the western urban high school students claimed that they did not participate in a single extracurricular activity in school.

No wonder that 44.5 per cent (4,261) of the students claimed that they "strive most in school to be accepted and liked by other students." Schools may have neglected to look at the adolescent society for the purpose of discovering the motivations inherent in it. The social system of the school may have to come to grips with the needs of teen-agers and provide the structure for them to perform satisfactorily in school.

What is most satisfying for the adolescent? Two patterns emerged strongly. Almost 43 per cent found most satisfaction in academic work, as compared with 44.5 per cent who found popularity in social interaction. Surprisingly, boys found the academic area slightly more satisfying than girls; the difference can be attributed to the girls' greater interest in popularity.

How do these values appear to the adolescent when he views his own future? The athletic interest collapses, the interest in popularity declines, and the academic value increases greatly. Almost 82 per cent of the students claimed that academic achievement is most important for their future. Boys exceeded girls only slightly in this value area.

A broad aim of the school is to effect socially acceptable behavior in the student. Presumably this is accomplished through the activities and practices the student experiences in school. The school, as a social system, has expectations for each student as it is laid down by its bureaucratic imperatives. However, if the student achieves the desired behavior, he will also have to satisfy his major personality needs. These needs have been somewhat delineated in this brief report.

Most students need social and athletic participation beyond the academic role prescribed. A number of students seem to derive satisfaction from their academic role alone. Others need greater social and athletic satisfactions to make them function effectively in the social system. The schools have failed to provide ample satisfactions in all three areas.

(1) The academic area does not receive full support from the adolescent subculture. High marks do not substantially contribute to popularity, or to leading crowd membership. The school's visible honors are awarded mostly to top athletes. Academic honors are reserved only for narrowly defined matriculation students.

(2) The athletic area is reserved only for a small group, especially in the large urban school. Half the students have no involvement in any extracurricular activities; they receive no satisfactions from this vital, adolescent "need" zone.

(3) Popularity, which occupies a high place in the eyes of the adolescent, is desired by the majority of students. Yet only 25.7 per cent claimed to be in the leading crowd. Only 22.6 per cent had been elected to any kind of position during their last two years of school. About 28 per cent worried most about being accepted and liked by friends. Against this, about 28 per cent never went out with friends.

Conclusions

The commonly accepted position that adolescent boys value athletics, and girls social success much more than academic achievement, is not tenable in the light of the evidence.

The pattern for "enduring" values for boys emerged in the order of:

Academic > athletics > popularity

For girls it was:

Academic > popularity > athletics

The pattern for a most satisfying value in school for boys emerged in the order of:

Academic > popularity > athletics

For girls it was:

Popularity > academic > athletics

As a value of greatest importance for the future, academic achievement was chosen overwhelmingly by both boys and girls. The pattern was in the order of:

Academic > popularity > athletics

This research started with the hypothesis that the Canadian adolescent society has developed a hierarchy of values in the order of athletics > popularity > academic. The research has shown that the hypothesis must be rejected.

However, the data reveal that for the satisfaction of the needs of the students in the high school social system, the athletic and popularity areas are prominent, though not as overpowering as was hypothesized. Furthermore, they do not seem inexorably at variance with the goals of the school; in fact, they may provide avenues leading to the satisfaction that is needed by the students.

The research has also demonstrated the relative similarities existing in the adolescent society which indicate the presence of a subculture. Friendliness, good looks, popularity, personality, and athletics are prime values in the youth society that makes its habitat in the long corridors of our schools and on the miles of pavement in our modern cities.

These are the criteria by which youngsters judge each other and their teachers, and in turn by which they will groom their appearance and behavior. Can the school channel the energy in our adolescent subculture to make it functional in terms of the broad aims held for the school?

REFERENCES

Coleman, James S.
1963   The Adolescent Society. New York: The Free Press.

Downey, Lawrence W.
1965   The Secondary Phase of Education. New York: Blaisdell.

Erikson, Erik H.
1963   The Challenge of Youth. New York: Doubleday.

Friesen, David
1966a   "The Ottawa Study." Unpublished papers.
1966b   "A study of the subculture of students in eight selected western Canadian high schools." Unpublished doctoral dissertation, University of North Dakota.

and Knill, W. D., and Ratsoy, Euguene
1967   "The Edmonton Study: Adolescent Values and Attitudes," Edmonton, Faculty of Education.

Goodman, Paul
1960   *Growing Up Absurd*. New York: Vintage

Gordon, Wayne C.
1957   *The Social System of the High School*. New York: The Free Press.

Hollingshead, August B.
1949   *Elmtown's Youth*. New York: John Wiley.

Reisman, David
1961   *The Lonely Crowd*. New Haven: Yale University Press.

PART SIX

Sport and Moral Order

Introduction[1]

The three contributions included in this final section are concerned with the interaction between sport and the dominant values, beliefs, and ideologies[2]—the "moral order" (cf., Geertz, 1972; Henricks, 1974)—of Canadian society. As an introduction to this topic, we want to make two points. *First*, the relationship between sport and contemporary value systems is a *reactive* one. That is, sport is both a reflection of the dominant values and ideologies stemming from the complex interplay between individual personalities and the contemporary system of productive relationships, and an agency of socialization which legitimates these values and ideologies. However, as a *second* point, it should be emphasized that sport is not a consistent socializer. Indeed, sport often tends to develop its own patterns and styles of behaviour, which while nonetheless rooted to the material order, often come into apparent conflict with the so-called "core values" of modern life. This multi-sided, and seemingly paradoxical, relationship to "moral order", is one of sport's most striking and sociologically interesting features.

In the first paper, Albinson presents the results of a sample survey of minor hockey coaches. Asked about their likes and dislikes in coaching, and rated on their "orientations" to the game, coaches' responses suggested that it is the teaching of individual skills and the development of efficient team play that are used as the standard for measuring the quality of the coaching experience. This emphasis on technique, Albinson notes, is similar to findings presented by Harry Webb (1969) in a more general study of the "professionalization" of play attitudes. Webb proposed that when "skill" (technique) came to define the *prime function* of ludic activities, the activities could be depicted as professionalized. This tendency toward professionalization reflects a central organizing principle of contemporary life—the belief in the *necessity* for achievement, progress, and technical mastery (see Gruneau's discussion of socio-historical themes in Part One of this volume). Thus, as Jacques Ellul (1964:384) has argued, in sport one increasingly "finds the same spirit, criteria, morality, action and objectives . . . which he encounters in the office or factory".[3]

The problem here, is whether the belief in the *necessity* for skill mastery and progress, is becoming the main standard for evaluating involvement in sport. If we assume that people's work settings are frequently rationalized to the point where people can only find true satisfaction in their leisure pursuits (ie. they work to play), the rationalization and professionalization of the play world may have serious implications

374 Sport and moral order

for the overall quality of human life. Certainly, the belief that in order to have "fun" one must become progressively "better", may fulfill Huizinga's worst fears (1955) and extinguish any similarities that *sport* may have to *play*. But, as Albinson concludes, it already seems to be the case that the rationalized logic of our adult work world is passed on to children through the socialization experiences they undergo in organized sports.[4]

However, as we suggested above, sometimes that same adult logic leads to situations in the sport world that on the surface seem incompatible with prevailing value standards. What is defined as "deviant behaviour" outside the sporting situation becomes legitimated within the context of the sporting milieux. It is this process of the legitimation of violent behavior in hockey that Mike Smith examines. Smith develops an analysis of assaultive behavior in hockey as a specific "normative action" and seeks to determine how individuals performing this "action" receive "authorization" for performing an act which appears to be breaching the "moral" conduct of society at large. Smith concludes that the authorization, or legitimation, is received from the perception the actor has of how such action is sanctioned by "significant others". The moral referents provided by people most closely associated with the hockey sub-culture (ie. father, team-mates, coaches and male non-playing friends) tend to define assaultive behavior under specific game situations as an expected and legitimate part of the game. At the same time, the moral referents provided by those less closely associated with the game (ie. mothers) are less approving. Smith also notes that coaches approval of assaultive action is dampened by disapproval if the violence leads to penalties which might affect the game's outcome.

The point of Smith's paper is simply to reaffirm that however problematic violence in hockey may be from the standpoint of mainstream moral values, it is legitimated by the games own idiosyncratic morality; a morality which many suspect has been greatly contoured by the professionalized model of the N.H.L. (cf., McMurty, 1974 and Levasseur's paper in Part One of this volume).

In the final paper in this section Alan Listiak elevates the notion of "legitimate deviance" to the level of political economy. To begin, Listiak evaluates the impact of behaviors associated with "Grey Cup Week" on the value systems of different social classes in Canadian society. Participant observation of a sample of bars during the week's festivities (enjoyable no-doubt) revealed that the festive atmosphere was largely restricted to middle-class bars and lounges. In lower class bars business continued as usual.

On the basis of such findings Listiak infers that festivals like Grey Cup Week tend to become middle class binges. As "time-outs" from the normative constraints on expected public behavior, they allow for a certain amount of accepted deviation from the prevailing standards affecting sexual morality, drunkenness and aggressive behavior. He argues that festivals like Grey Cup Week do not serve integrative "functions" as is commonly believed, but instead reinforce the distinctions between the dominant and subordinant classes in Canadian society. Somewhat tongue in cheek, Listiak concludes by hypothesizing that the dynamics of this process are readily discernable by an historical analysis of the development of Canadian monopoly capitalism. The legitimate deviant behavior experienced during Grey Cup Week is depicted as functioning as an outlet for the "expression of aggressive and sexual frustrations which stem from the oppressive aspects of urban life and the alienated and oppressive nature of work, leisure and sex in Canadian society." There are, of course, alternative plausible interpretations, but Listiak's paper, written from the conflict perspective, provides a provocative and occasionally humourous assessment of the social and cultural "meaning" of the Grey Cup Festival.

NOTES

1. The expression "moral order" must not be construed as suggesting the existence of normative consensus. We use the expression here only to refer to those *mainstream* values associated with the dominant institutional structure. The fact that many people appear to comply with such standards does not, as Mann (1970) suggests, necessarily mean they wholeheartedly support them (cf., Parkin, 1972; Chapters 2 and 3).
2. Clement (1975:270) argues that "Ideologies are frameworks of assumptions, ideas and values incorporated into the perspective of an individual or collective used to guide analyses, interests and commitments into a system of meaning." That sport has become an institution whose prime function appears to be increasingly ideological, has been a notable fact of the last few decades.
3. Or, as Georges Magnane notes (1964:66): "Like the worker, the athlete must effect a total transformation upon himself, upon his nervous and muscular system, and subject himself to an apprenticeship which demands concentration and perserverance. Sports is an activity which puts the accent on the intensity of the effort, the sureness and efficiency of the action, speed combined with regularity, to the total exclusion of hesitation, merely standard performances, or moments of inactivity which were tolerated or even encouraged by many fields in patriarchal civilizations." For other readings on these issues see Brohm (1972) and Ingham (1975).
4. However it should be noted that in a similar study of hockey coaches, McPherson (1974) utilized the professionalism scale and reports less extreme results than Albinson.

REFERENCES

Brohm, Jean-Marie
1972   "Sociologie politique du sport." In *Sport, culture et répression*. Paris: petite maspero.

Clement, Wallace
1975   *The Canadian Corporate Elite*. Toronto: McClelland Stewart.

Ellul, Jacques
1967   *The Technological Society*. New York: Alfred A. Knapp.

Henricks, Thomas
1974   "Professional Wrestling as Moral Order." *Sociological Inquiry* 44(33).

Huizinga, Johan
1955   *Homo Ludens*. Boston: Beacon Press.

Faulkner, Robert R.
1974   "Making Violence by Doing Work". *Sociology of Work and Occupations*, 1(3)

Geertz, Clifford
1972   "Deep Play: Notes on the Balinese Cockfight." *Daedalus* (Winter).

Ingham, Alan
1975   "Occupational Subcultures in the Work World of Sport." In D. Ball and J. W. Loy (eds.), *Sport, and Social Order*. Reading: Addison-Wesley.

Magnane, George
1964   *Sociologie du Sport*. Paris: N. R. F. Gallimard

Mann, Michael
1970   "The Social Cohesion of Liberal Democracy." *American Sociological Review*, 35 (June).

McMurtry, William
1974   *Investigation and Inquiry into Violence in Amateur Hockey*. Toronto: Queen's Printer.

McPherson, Barry
1974   "Career Patterns of a Voluntary Role: The Minor Hockey Coach". Paper presented at the 9th Annual Meeting of Canadian Sociological and Anthropological Association, Toronto, August.

Parkin, Frank
1972   *Class Inequality and Political Order*, London: Paladin Books.

Vaz, Edmond
1974   "What Price Victory? An Analysis of Minor Hockey League Players' Attitudes Towards Winning." *International Review of Sport Sociology*, 9 (2) 33-56.

Webb, Harry
1969   *"Professionalization of Attitudes Toward Play Among Adolescents."* In G. S. Kenyon (ed.), *Aspects of Contemporary Sport Sociology*. Chicago: The Athletic Institute.

THE "PROFESSIONAL ORIENTATION" OF THE AMATEUR HOCKEY COACH[1]

John G. Albinson

Introduction

Canadians are involved with hockey for at least six months of the year. For some, this involvement takes the *passive, secondary* form, which may involve conversations about the game, and exposure through the media. For others, the involvement takes an *active, secondary* form (e.g. attendance at games), and for still others, the involvement is *active* and *primary* through actual play.[2] The C.A.H.A. and associated organizations provide the structure for the greatest amount of active primary involvement. The organization of minor hockey in Canada necessitates the interaction of many groups including players, coaches, officials, organization executives, parents, peers, sponsors, media people, and government.[3] The research reported in this paper focusses on one of these interacting groups—the coach.

Coaches hold a central position in the minor hockey program and because of this they are able to exert considerable influence on the players. This influence extends from the level of development of the technical skills, to the attitudes the players hold for the game itself. It is these attitudes that come to define the "morality" of the game.

Recently, organized hockey has been cited as being too "professional" and its supposed positive influence on children questioned.[4] The coach because of his centrality and visibility, has been accused of being the promoter of such orientations. Such accusations stem from the observation of individual cases and not from any systematic analysis. The purpose of this paper is to provide some preliminary systematic data which may clarify why some individuals coach minor hockey and the degree to which they hold a "professional" orientation toward the sport.

Professionalization

Harry Webb (1969) has emphasized that the play of young children is a situation in which "equity" or "fairness" is paramount. Anyone can play, the rules are minimal, there are no referees, the rewards are few, and admission is based on factors other than skill. One becomes a member because he or she lives in the neighbourhood, goes to the same school, is the same age, is friendly, etc. As a child gets older, he or she becomes involved in more formalized play. The transition from play, to games, to sports, is parallelled by an increasing importance of achievement. During the transition, the role of player becomes one which has to be achieved rather than one which is ascribed (as in young children's play). Accordingly, Webb maintains that "fairness" or "equity" may in fact decrease the possibility of success. On the other hand, "skill" increasingly enhances the opportunity for "success" or "victory" and therefore, replaces "fairness" as the paramount value in children's play. It is this substitute of "skill" for "equity" that Webb (1969) identifies as the shift from a "play orientation" to a "professional orientation". Why does this occur? Webb suggests that the reason lies in the rationalization of play itself, and the fact that this simply mirrors the realities of North American industrial society. From the perspective of mainstream liberal ideology "individual differences in ability, training, and desire, and their consequences for influencing excellence (are) presumably rewarded in a free competitive atmosphere" (Webb, 1969:161).

Ideally, by being more skillful than others under conditions which are equal for all, an individual receives success as measured by status or position.[5] This, according to Webb, functions to some degree in sport, but remains ideology in the business and political worlds. Yet, the fact that organized sport reflects an ideal rather than the reality of economic and political behaviour does not affect its role in the process of socialization. Sport clearly emphasizes the legitimacy of achievement values. However, as Webb sees it, an overemphasis on skill and performance is frequently at odds with the values of play and the definition of good sportsmanship.

> Thus, play experience in play institutions prepare the young for later participation in an "achievement" economy and a "democratic" polity, but its contribution may be at odds with that originally asserted, and asserted in terms of the components of "sportsmanship" whose major constituent, it should be emphasized, is fairness (Webb, 1969: 163).

While Webb did not discuss the role of the coach in the process of the "professionalization" of play attitudes, Vaz (1974) made this a focal concern in his study of house league and "All star" teams at all levels of the minor hockey system. Vaz concentrated on the significance of winning, and the attitude towards the use of methods outside the rules as a means of controlling opposing players. Players were asked for their perceptions of their coaches' attitudes in these areas and for their own attitudes. Interpreting the data, Vaz (1974:51-52), concluded that the importance of team success in itself (meaning winning games), decreased both for players, and players' perceptions of their coaches' attitudes, as the players advanced through the league (i.e. increased in age). The importance was increasingly placed on the techniques required in the game.[6] As Vaz did not assess the "equity" factor, he identified the shift as one from the importance of "success" to an importance of "skill". The primacy of either "skill" or "success" would, by Webb's hypothesis, be a "professional orientation". Since all the subjects in Vaz' study were members of organized sport leagues, this would be consistent with the work of Mantel and Vander Velden (1971), and Maloney and Petrie (1974), who have observed that boys involved in *organized sport* tend to have a "professional orientation" to play. In both these studies, the researchers also noted that boys who were not involved in sport or who were involved only in house league—intramural type sport, placed greater emphasis on "equity".

A major difference between the sport environment of the house league —intramural, and that of the highly organized minor sport and interschool leagues, is the presence or absence of a "coach". Vaz' (1974) argument that the coach is a primary socializing agent in the professionalization of players' attitudes seems to be relevant here, but Vaz only assessed the players' perceptions of the coaches' attitudes, while Mantel and Vander Velden (1974), and Maloney and Petrie (1974) made no attempt to assess coaches' orientations at all. By contrast, the data presented in this paper represent a specific attempt to assess the coaches' attitudes toward play and their motivations for coaching.

The Sample

The study reported here was part of a larger study conducted on a sample of 178 minor league ice hockey coaches who were involved in five organizations in the same community. A mailed questionnaire was

TABLE I

DEMOGRAPHIC DATA ON A SPECIFIC SAMPLE OF MINOR LEAGUE HOCKEY COACHES

Education	
Elementary	2.5%
Some High School	41.2
Completed High School	25.2
Some College	12.6
Completed College	17.6
N.R.	0.8
Income	
Under $5,000	2.5%
5,000—6,999	10.9
7,000—9,999	37.8
10,000—14,999	29.4
15,000—19,999	7.6
20,000 +	6.7
N.R.	5.0
Years Coached	
1	25.2%
2	20.2
3	13.6
4	5.9
5	8.4
6-9	13.5
10 +	11.8
N.R.	1.9
N = 119	

used to collect the data; 119 useable questionnaires were returned which represented a 67% return.

The demographic data on the sample are reported in Table 1.

Instruments

Responses from seven questions on the original questionnaire were used in the analysis at hand. Three questions dealt with variables[7] thought to influence coaches' decisions to begin and to continue coaching. Coaches were asked to respond to each variable by suggesting the level of influence it exerted on their decisions. Two other questions were designed to probe what coaches liked and disliked about coaching, and the last two questions utilized Webb's (1969) "Professionalization Scale" in an attempt to classify coaches' orientations toward playing the game.

TABLE II
COACHES' EXPRESSION OF LEVEL OF INFLUENCE OF FACTORS ON DECISION TO COACH ICE HOCKEY

Response Categories	Level of Influence (% given in brackets)						
	Low		Moderate	High			
	1	2	3	4	5	N.R.	Rank
My Son is Playing	21 (17.6)	27 (22.7)	7 (5.9)	25 (21.0)	5 (4.2)	34 (33.6)	5
Hockey Has Always Been Part of my Life	7 (5.9)	14 (11.8)	13 (10.9)	59 (49.6)	14 (11.8)	12 (10.1)	2
I Enjoy Coaching Most Sports	14 (11.8)	27 (22.7)	14 (11.8)	38 (31.9)	10 (8.4)	16 (13.4)	3
I Enjoy Opportunity to Meet Other Adults	15 (12.6)	35 (29.4)	11 (9.2)	27 (22.7)	8 (6.7)	23 (19.3)	4
I Enjoy Working With Kids	1 (0.8)	1 (0.8)	9 (7.6)	70 (58.8)	26 (21.8)	12 (10.1)	1
I am Getting Too Old to Play Hockey	26 (21.8)	39 (32.8)	5 (4.2)	16 (13.4)	2 (1.7)	31 (26.1)	6
Hockey Provides an Opportunity to Get Out of the House	27 (22.7)	50 (42.0)	1 (0.8)	5 (4.2)	3 (2.5)	33 (27.7)	7
Other	2 (1.7)	2 (1.7)	2 (1.7)	2 (1.7)	11 (9.2)	100 (84.0)	

N = 119

Results

Why They Coach

Data on coaches' ratings of the factors influencing a person to begin coaching are presented in Table II. The most significant factor appears to be the enjoyment of working with children. Over 80% of the coaches designated this as exerting a high influence on the decision to begin coaching. The second most influential factor, was the degree to which hockey has always been a part of the coach's life. The third most important factor was enjoyment of coaching in general, and that hockey is an available sport to coach during the winter (40.3% indicated this as a significant influence). According to coaches' responses, the least important factors were "hockey as a means of getting out of the house" (8%), and being "too old to play" (5%). Coaching as an opportunity to meet other adults was perceived as a moderately important factor. Approximately 29% indicated that it had a high degree of influence in the decision to begin coaching. Twenty-five percent indicated that having a son(s) playing, greatly influenced their decision to begin coaching hockey.

Table III presents data on the factors influencing coaches *to continue their* coaching. Coaches who had coached for at least one season prior to the season in which the study was conducted, were asked to rate the degree of influence of selected factors in a manner similar to the previous question. Of the 119 coaches who returned completed questionnaires, 89 (75%) had coached one or more years. Again, it was enjoyment of working with children that appears as the dominant factor in maintaining involvement in coaching. Ninety-two percent of the coaches listed this as exerting a high influence on their decisions to continue. Coaches also claimed that the last year's won-lost record had little influence on their continued involvement. This low ranking was also true for hockey as "a chance to get out of the house". Finally, Table III reveals that coaches differentially evaluated the influence of having a son still playing. Nearly 43% indicated that this factor exerted a low influence, while nearly 36% indicated that it exerted a high influence. Sixty-five percent of the sample did have sons playing, but about half of these coaches claimed that this factor was not a prime influence in their desires to continue coaching.

In a further attempt to assess the coaches' motives for coaching, a more indirect method was utilized. This method was used on the assumption that an individual's personal motives would influence their response. The coaches were then asked to indicate why they thought that other people coached hockey. The coach was asked to check off one of eight alternatives.

TABLE III

COACHES' EXPRESSION OF LEVEL OF INFLUENCE OF FACTORS ON DECISION TO CONTINUE COACHING ICE HOCKEY

Level of Influence (% given in brackets)

Response Categories	Low		Moderate	High		N.R.	Rank
	1	2	3	4	5		
Record of Last Year's Team	20 (22.5)	45 (50.6)	2 (2.2)	10 (11.2)	2 (2.2)	10 (11.2)	4
Friends I Made	11 (12.4)	13 (14.6)	10 (11.2)	37 (41.6)	10 (11.2)	8 (9.0)	2
Enjoyed Working With Kids	1 (1.1)	0 (0.0)	5 (5.6)	62 (69.7)	20 (22.5)	1 (1.1)	1
My Son is Still Participating	15 (16.9)	23 (25.8)	4 (4.5)	24 (27.0)	7 (7.9)	16 (18.0)	3
A Chance to Get Out of the House	27 (30.3)	33 (37.0)	1 (1.1)	1 (1.1)	2 (2.2)	25 (28.0)	5
Other	1 (1.1)	2 (2.2)	0 (0.0)	18 (20.0)	5 (5.6)	63 (70.8)	

N = 89

TABLE IV

COACHES' PERCEPTIONS OF WHY PEOPLE COACH ICE HOCKEY

Response Catagories	Number of Responses	Responses as Percent of Sample
Social Recognition	3	2.5
Competition	31	26.1
Companionship	0	0.0
Self Realization	7	5.9
Self Satisfaction	35	29.4
Relaxation	3	2.5
To Have Fun	23	19.3
To Blow Off Steam	0	0.0
To Be Aggressive	1	0.8
N.R.	16	13.4
N	119	100

The most frequent choices were "for the competition" (26.1%), "for the self-satisfaction" (29.4%), and "to have fun" (19.3%). If, as these responses indicate, self-satisfaction and having fun are significant motives prompting an individual to become a coach, it would be important to know what it is about coaching that is fun and self-satisfying. Responses in Tables II and III suggest that working with kids and being associated with sport generally, were prime personal motives. This would seem consistent with the results shown in Table IV. Working with kids and being associated with sport may be the means of gaining self-satisfaction and of having fun. Wanting to be associated with a *sport* is also consistent with the high number of responses to 'competition' as being a reason for being a coach.

Coaches' Likes and Dislikes

In an attempt to clarify coaches' motives, we went one step further. On the assumption that the things a person will like best about coaching will be those things that fulfill his motives for being there, and the things that he likes least will be those which thwart his fulfilling his motives, the coaches were asked to list three things that they enjoyed about coaching and in another question to list three things that they did not enjoy about coaching. Responses to these questions are categorized in Table V.

From the responses to what the coaches enjoy about coaching, we are able to better hypothesize about where the self-satisfaction and fun is

TABLE V

FACTORS ENJOYED MOST BY COACHES OF ICE HOCKEY

	Number of Coaches Responding	Percent of Coaches Responding in each Category N = 119	Percent of Total Responses N = 357[a]
Winning, Competition, Excitement of Games	45	37.8	12.6
Hockey—Being Involved With It	24	20.2	6.7
Working with Boys, Teaching Skills	97	81.5	27.2
Seeing Boys Develop and Improve Hockey Skills	69	57.9	19.3
Seeing Team Develop	30	25.2	8.4
Seeing Boys Enjoy Themselves	21	17.6	5.9
Respect, Responsibility, Helping Community	20	16.8	5.9
Meeting Other Adults	11	9.2	3.1
Other	29	24.4	8.2
N.R.	11	9.2	3.1

[a]Each coach was asked to give three (3) responses, therefore, the total of possible responses is 3 x 119 = 357.

achieved. From these data it would seem that the coaches satisfy their motives from working with the boys, but in a specific way. It is working with them in terms of the instruction of technical aspects of the game, rather than working with boys per se. If the latter were the case, one would expect a greater percent of responses in the categories of 'seeing boys enjoy themselves' and one would have expected references to things that might be categorized as seeing boys mature, develop character, etc. To the 27.2% of the responses reflecting the enjoyment of working with boys in terms of hockey, we added other game-related responses indicating enjoyment from winning, being involved in the game, individual improvement of players, and team development. Seventy-four percent of the responses indicate that the enjoyment of coaching comes from the game, thereby suggesting that the coach receives his personalized reward for coaching from the game itself and its inherent components (skills, team play, competition, excitement).

Response frequencies in catagories reflecting factors enjoyed *least* about coaching are presented in Table VI. The distribution of responses is not as clear cut as those related to *most* enjoyed factors.[8] While 26.3% of the possible responses might be classified as "game-oriented" (losing, officials, environment, indifference, interference) another 21.9% of the possible responses reflect a "player-orientation" (uninerested parents, cutting

TABLE VI

FACTORS ENJOYED LEAST BY COACHES OF ICE HOCKEY

	Number of Coaches Responding	Percent of Coaches Responding in Each Category N = 119	Percent of Total Possible Responses N = 357
Losing: Especially When it Involves Lack of Effort	11	9.2	3.1
Poor Officials: Bad Rules	21	17.6	5.9
Environmental Conditions: Cold Rinks, Practice Times, Lack of Time and Money	35	29.4	9.8
Indifferent Attitude of Players	13	10.9	3.6
Interference of Players	14	11.8	3.9
Uninterested Parents	41	34.5	11.5
Cutting Boys	37	31.1	10.4
Winning at all Costs	24	20.2	6.7
Poor Sportsmanship; Dirty Play	60	50.4	16.8
Other	39	32.8	10.9
N.R.	62	52.1[a]	17.4

[a] Coaches were to list three items; therefore this represents the percent of coaches who did not list three items.

players). The response categories labelled "winning at all costs" and "poor sportsmanship" are not as easily categorized as it may be that they reflect detractions from the ideal technical game or that they reflect a dissatisfaction with the "moral" quality of the individuals involved in such behaviour. These two categories represent 23.5% of the possible responses.

Coaches' Professional Orientation

Webb's three-item scale[9] was presented to the respondents with two different instructions. They were first instructed to respond with reference to their own feelings while the second set of instructions asked that they respond in terms of how they felt other coaches in their league would answer. The scale was included under the second condition because coaches may perceive their personal attitude toward play to be different from other coaches in the league. A coach may take the position that his coaching behaviour does not reflect his personal attitude but reflects the attitude of the other coaches. He adopts the perceived prevailing standard in order 'to be fair' to the players he is coaching. Since the coach's actual behaviour (i.e. emphasis on 'equity", 'victory' or 'skill') would be exposed to a greater degree than his personally held attitude, it was necessary to assess the perceptions coaches had of the "generally held" attitude in the league.

As reflected in the data in Tables VII and VIII, the paramount value expressed by the coaches under both response conditions was that of "skill".[10] Only one coach placed 'equity' (to play fair) first as a personal attitude and only 8% of the sample perceived it as a value commonly held by other coaches.

Webb (1969) contends that the replacement of 'equity' as the paramount value in play signifies the shift to a "professional orientation". Applying this conceptualization to the data presented, some empirical evidence is found to support the contention that amateur hockey coaches do in fact approach the game with a "professional orientation".

TABLE VII

RANKING BY VOLUNTEER COACHES OF: TO PLAY FAIRLY; TO BEAT YOUR OPPONENT; AND TO PLAY IT AS WELL AS YOU ARE ABLE (in %)

	Rank		
	1	2	3
Play Fairly	0.8	84.6	14.5
Beat Opponent	27.4	12.8	59.8
Play Well	71.8	2.5	25.6

N = 117

TABLE VIII

PERCEPTION OF HOW OTHER COACHES WOULD RANK; TO PLAY IT FAIRLY; TO BEAT YOUR OPPONENT; AND TO PLAY IT AS WELL AS YOU ARE ABLE (in %)

	Rank		
	1	2	3
Play Fairly	7.7	62.4	29.9
Beat Opponent	35.9	11.1	53.0
Play Well	56.4	26.5	17.1

N = 117

Discussion

Based on responses to two measures, the Webb scale and the question regarding what they like about coaching, coaches in this sample emphasized their commitment to the technical aspects of the coaching role. This finding is compatible with Vaz' (1974) conclusions about the orientations of players. As noted earlier in this paper, Vaz indicated that players progressively emphasize "skill" as years of exposure to the hockey environment (including coaches) increases. Given that the research reported here reveals the importance coaches seem to attach to the mastery of technique, it seems only logical to infer that this concern is passed on to the players through secondary socialization. However, it should be recognized that the data presented are descriptive and preliminary. The Webb scale for example, is not a sophisticated index of "professionalization" and its use leaves certain ambiguities unresolved. Most important of these is that a specific referent for what "playing well" entails and why it is important are not given. Indeed, if "playing well" encompasses a concern for the mastery of technique, then the functional consequences of this, or the motivations underlying it, are not clear. However, three hypotheses are possible:

(a) "Skill" is most important because skill is needed to gain victory
(b) "Skill" is most important because it is seen as an end in itself
(c) "Skill" is most important because of personal interest in the technical aspects of the game but that "equity" or "fairness" is important for the players.

(a) "Skill" for victory.
Organized minor hockey leagues pattern themselves after the professional leagues, keeping records of wins, losses, individual goals and assists, minutes in penalties, etc. By doing this, the emphasis is put on the 'product' of the participation, not on the participation per se, thereby making it an *"ends-oriented"* system as opposed to a *"means-oriented"* system.

The leagues advertise their ends orientations through such means as the publishing of standings and the public presentation of trophies for successful production. This public statement would tend to attract the type of individual to coaching who has an interest in producing the products which receive the awards. The coach then would be interested in the development of skills, because the payoff is in the result, and the results are the things that show at the end of the year in terms of won-loss record, league standing, who gets the trophies and who doesn't.

On the surface, this interpretation would seem to be in conflict with the data presented, since of the eighty-four coaches who listed "skill" as the paramount value, only 14 (17%) selected victory as second most important. Furthermore only 9.2% (Table VI) of the total sample indicated that "losing" was one of the things that they disliked about coaching. Although 37.8% (Table V) of the sample listed "winning, competition, excitement of games" as something enjoyable about coaching, it is not clear from that data what percent actually listed just "winning".

The "skill as a means to victory" hypothesis also would not be supported by Vaz' (1974) data since he indicated a decreasing emphasis on the importance of winning. Yet if coaches were socializing the players with respect to the importance of skill, would it not be logical to expect that winning in some form would be a natural concomitant?

The above argument is based on Webb's (1969) interpretation of "success" to mean "beating your opponent". However, it is possible that "success" for coaches is achieved in other ways such as "his" players making "All Star" teams, "his" player scoring the most goals, having the most assists, etc. or even having one of "his" players drafted by a Junior professional team. The coach's status may come from making the machine (the player) work efficiently and effectively (skillful). Although the data presented in Table V do not allow for definitive analysis of these conjectures, the high response indicating that coaches' enjoyment comes from "teaching skills", "seeing boys develop and improve hockey skills", and "seeing the team develop" (54.9% of all responses) lends some credibility to the hypothesis.

(b) "Skill" as an end in itself.

If this hypothesis were to be supported, the importance of "equity" and "victory" would be expected to be about equal. This was not the case. It was clearly exhibited from the response to the Webb Scale, that "beating your opponent" was supported to a lesser degree than was "playing fairly" (Table VII and Table VIII). The responses of the coaches about the enjoyable and unenjoyable aspects of coaching (Table V and Table VI) did not reveal any data that would support or reject this hypothesis.

(c) "Skill" for personal interest and "equity" for players.

The responses to the Webb Scale might be interpreted as supporting this to a limited extent. Of the eighty-four coaches who saw skill as the paramount factor, 70 (83%) indicated that equity was placed second. Caution must be used because of problems associated with social desirability and the forced-choice nature of the question. Some support for the results of the Webb Scale data may be interpreted as coming from the responses coded in the categories of "winning at all costs", "poor officials; bad rules", "poor sportsmanship" (Table VI) which indicate things enjoyed least about coaching. The responses related to enjoyable things about coaching did not suggest data which supported this hypothesis.

Conclusion

Mantel and Vander Velden (1974) and Maloney and Petrie (1974) concluded that those participating in organized sport had "professional"
attitudes toward play. Vaz' (1974) data suggest that players in minor
league hockey and junior professional league hockey possesss "professional" attitudes toward play and that they perceive their coaches as
possessing similar attitudes. The data presented in this paper show that
minor league ice hockey coaches do tend to have a "professional orientation" toward the game. They see the technological aspect as the paramount value of the coaching situation. Whether the importance of skill
is an end in itself, or is a means to gain success in some form, is not clear
from these data. But, if Webb's (1969) arguments are at all accurate,
then the values emphasized in the rationalized play world of organized
sports, are structurally similar to those ideological premises which
underly the liberal ideal of a market society. From this perspective, it is
expertise which stands clearly at the core of the reward structure. To see
amateur hockey in Canada as emphasizing personal growth, honour,
generosity, tolerance or just plain fun, may simply be to overlook the
degree to which the logic of our adult world structures minor league
hockey organizations, and the values of the coaches who work within
them.

NOTES

1. The data presented in this paper is a synthesis and reanalysis of two earlier works by
   the author (Albinson, 1973; Albinson, 1974).
2. For a discussion on the categorization of involvement in sport see Kenyon (1969).
3. Hockey is only one of many sports which are highly organized in Canada. Others such
   as swimming, gymnastics, lacrosse, etc., together with hockey involve an enormous
   section of the Canadian population, old and young. Despite the numbers involved and
   the impact sport has on family and community life, social scientists have been reluctant to legitimize the study of sport.
4. For examples see Orlick (1974); Orlick and Botterill (1975); and Hansen (1972).
5. Webb (1969) bases his scale on the belief that as a society moves from communal-
   agrarian to urban-industrial, "achievement" becomes the basis for the assigning of
   rewards and roles rather than ascription. The qualifications based on ability, education,
   training, etc. rather than family or group membership became the necessary means for
   the "distribution of roles, at least in the economic and political institutions" (p. 16) of a
   society based on technological knowledge and division of labour. Webb maintains that
   the analogy between sport and the real world has validity because, while it is primarily
   ideology in the policical and economic world, does function to some extent in these
   domains. For a fuller explanation of the basis of the "professional" analogy the author
   recommends the reading of Webb's (1969) original article.
6. Vaz (1974:51) argues that players' perceptions of their coaches' attitudes toward
   winning were reflected in the players' own attitudes. These attitudes manifested
   themselves in players' willingness to use "any" tactics in the course of the game.
   These relationships were strongest in the "All Star" levels.

7. These categories were constructed based on data obtained from open ended questions in a pilot study in another community.
8. The high percentage of coaches (52.9%) who did not respond fully to the question, together with the higher 'other' (10.9%) response rate, may have affected the results. The high no response rate also may reflect the fact that the level of expertise of the coaches does not permit an accurate analysis of those factors which are in fact thwarting their motives.
9. The scale is constructed from the responses to the following question:
   What do you think is MOST important in playing a game?
   Place a "1" next to the one you think is MOST important.
   Now place a "3" next to the one you think is LEAST important.
   _____to play as well as you can
   _____to beat the other player or team
   _____to play the game fairly
10. When these results are placed on the Webb Professionalism Index, the results are as presented in the table below. From these results it is apparent that the coaches perceive their peers as having a more "professional orientation" than they maintain for themselves. If this perception of others affects their own behaviour, then players may be exposed to a more "professional" atmosphere than would be expected from obtaining only coaches' personally held attitudes.

Professionalism of Amateur Hockey Coaches (in %)
Professional Orientation

	Low		Moderate		High	
	1	2	3	4	5	6
Personal Ranking	0.0	0.8	60.0	12.0	24.2	2.6
Ranking of Others	5.1	2.6	47.9	8.5	14.5	21.4

N = 117

REFERENCES

Albinson, J. G.
1973   "Professionalized Attitudes of Volunteer Coaches Toward Playing a Game." *International Review of Sport Sociology*, 8(2).
1974   "Motives of Volunteer Ice Hockey Coaches to Coach." Paper presented to First Canadian Interdisciplinary Conference on Sport Sciences, Montreal.
Hansen, H. C. J.
1972   "Plea to Save Thousands of Hockey Players Who Want to Enjoy the Sport." *Canadian Coach*, 7 July.
Kenyon, Gerald
1969   "Sport Involvement: A Conceptual Go and Some Consequences Thereof." In G. Kenyon (ed.), *Aspects of Contemporary Sport Sociology*. Chicago: The Athletic Institute.
Maloney, T. L. and B. M. Petrie
1974   "Professionalization of Attitudes Towards Play Among Canadian School Pupils as a Function of Sex, Grade and Athletic Participation." *Journal of Leisure Research*, 4.

Mantel, R. C. and L. Vander Velden
1974   "The Relationship Between the Professionalization of Attitudes Toward Play of Preadolescent Boys and Participation in Organized Sport." In George H. Sage (ed.), *Sport and American Society*. Reading: Addison-Wesley.

Orlick, Terry
1974   "The Athletic Drop-out—A High Price for Inefficiency." *CAHPER Journal*, September/October.

and Cal. Botterill
1975   *Every Kid Can Win*. Chicago: Nelson-Hall.

Webb, H.
1969   "Professionalization of Attitudes Toward Play Among Adolescents." In G. Kenyon (ed.), *Aspects of Contemporary Sport Sociology*. Chicago: The Athletic Institute.

Vaz, E. W. and D. Thomas
1974   "What Price Victory?" *International Review of Sport Sociology*, 9(2).

THE LEGITIMATION OF VIOLENCE:
Hockey Players' Perceptions of Their Reference Groups' Sanctions for Assault*

Michael D. Smith

Much research in the last decade has been aimed at uncovering the causes, processes, and consequences of individual and collective violence in society. Yet, although few better natural laboratories than sport appear to exist for the testing of propositions and theories of human aggression, relatively little serious attention has been paid to this behaviour in the sport context. One reason for this may be that violence in sport, whether legal or illegal, traditionally has been invested with an aura of legitimacy: qualities of 'righteousness,' 'goodness,' or 'justifiability' have by collective judgment been attributed to it, and a system of formal and informal sanctions has enforced this judgment (Ball-Rokeach, 1972:101).

Social theorists since the time of Aristotle have concerned themselves with the concept of legitimacy, chiefly with respect to certain types of

---

* This is a greatly modified version of a paper presented at the Scientific Congress of the Twentieth Olympiad, Munich, August, 1972.

political authority. Max Weber, however, was the first to discover the universal applicability of the notion and to use the term for classifying and comparing a wide array of sociopolitical phenomena (Weber, 1957; Sternberger, 1968). He noted, in particular, the state's virtual monopoly on the legitimate use of violence. Since then, social scientists have examined further ramifications of legitimate violence: the processes of legitimating and delegitimating a given act (Ball-Rokeach, 1972), values as sources of the justification of violent means (Ball-Rokeach, 1974, Blumenthal et al., 1972; Gerson, 1968; Wolfgang and Ferracutti, 1967), the legitimation of violence as a product of the salient social characteristics of assailant and victim (Baker and Ball, 1969; Ball-Rokeach, 1972; Fanon, 1963; Garfinkel, 1949), the strange interplay between legitimacy and legality (Graham and Gurr, 1969:xxxi, 808; Wheeler, 1967:202-3), and so on. By paying attention to the idea of legitimation, it becomes easier to understand why most individuals appear to perceive no equivalence between assault, say, in an alley and on the playing field. The former is deviance; the latter is taken for granted as 'part of the game.' In the institutionalization of the game, 'A way of doing' has become '*The* way of doing' (Ingham and Loy, 1973:4; Berger and Luckmann, 1966).

Questions of legality and illegality often have little to do with the legitimacy status of an act of violence. In the sport of ice-hockey, for example, widely held informal norms about how performers should behave appear to buttress many actions which violate official rules. Although formal negative sanctions in the form of official penalties may be meted out, such actions, if widely approved, are in balance rewarded, not punished. A great deal of the officially proscribed violence in the National Hockey League is, in fact, normal behaviour. Yearly, the per game penalty average is over twenty minutes, mostly the result of assault of some sort (NHL Guide, 1971). One NHL general manager observes that 'A home team playing aggressive, pleasing hockey has to pick up at least five penalties' (*Toronto Star* 21 Nov. 1972:16).

If there is as broad a consensus on the legitimacy of much of the violence in hockey as penalty statistics, research (Faulkner, 1971, 1973; Smith, forthcoming; Vaz, 1972; Vaz and Thomas, 1974), and everyday observation suggest, performers likely perceive others as supportive of such conduct. As Ball-Rokeach (1972:108) notes: 'Overt evaluative reactions, such as approval or disapproval, are . . . the most direct indicators of the legitimacy status of violent actions.' Following this line of argument, the writer sought, first, to ascertain players' perceptions of their parents', peers', and coach's sanctions for certain violent behaviours (physical assaults against others) in hockey and, second, to determine by means of factor analysis whether the sanctions formed independent dimensions.

Theory

Reference groups have been shown to be important mechanisms in the articulation of individual social processes in society, especially that of socialization. Reference groups, in general, help to orient the actor in a course of action or in attitude; normative reference groups, in particular, provide the actor with a guide to action by setting norms and espousing values (Kemper, 1969). One way in which this is accomplished is through the expression of approval and disapproval. The actor's perceptions of his normative groups' sanctions for various acts should have a significant impact on his behaviour.

Although there is much yet to be learned about what determines a specific person's choice of normative group, the literature suggests that parents, peers, and teachers most often serve this purpose (Elkin and Handel, 1972; Inkeles, 1968). Given the pervasiveness of violent sport, it should not be surprising to find widespread positive sanctioning by these groups of certain assaultive behaviours in the sport setting. Theory and data suggest, however, that sanctions are not uniform. Because father, mother, teammates, non-playing peers, and coach are subject to varying cultural expectations, have different role relationships with the actor, and presumably have different stakes in the outcome of the contests in which he is performing, their sanctions for assault may take somewhat divergent patterns. There is some research evidence – albeit peripheral – to support this proposition.

Of all the social roles an individual plays, perhaps most salient is his sex role. Part of the male sex role adopted by fathers is the overt expression of aggression, especially when 'attacked, threatened, or dominated by another male' (Kagan, 1964:139). Fathers, too, of course, are charged with teaching male values and norms to their young. Aberle and Naegele (1952) reported that middle class fathers freely stated that they would be concerned if their sons showed insufficient aggression. These fathers presumably punished their sons for insufficient aggression and rewarded them for the opposite behaviour (Mussen, 1971). Similarly, Bandura and Walters (1959), in their study of aggressive adolescents, noted that the boys' fathers were inclined to encourage their sons' aggression when directed toward peers. It may be inferred, moreover, from descriptions of 'subcultures' (Wolfgang and Ferracutti, 1967) and 'regional cultures' (Gastil, 1971) of violence that fathers play a part in transmitting to their sons the ethos of violence central to such groups. Despite the fact that the above investigations were considerably removed from the context of sport, it is reasonable to suggest that fathers may approve of some forms of athletic assault perpetrated by their offspring.

Mothers, themselves constrained by sex role norms requiring the inhibition of verbal and physical aggression (Bardwick, 1971; Kagan, 1964), may take a more positive view of their sons' assaultive conduct. The Bandura and Walters' (1959) study revealed that mothers rewarded their sons' aggression when it was aimed at other boys. It has been observed, too, that punitive (as opposed to non-punitive) mothers are likely to insist that their sons fight for their rights (Becker, 1964). Journalistic descriptions of 'little league mothers' support the notion that mothers may look favourably upon their sons' assaultive behaviour in sport. The secretary of the Metropolitan Toronto Hockey League reported at least a dozen cases in the 1972-3 season where referees were 'bodily assaulted' by spectators, some of whom were women. In one game, a 'woman punched the referee who . . . had broken up a fight between her son and another player' (*Toronto Star* 26 April 1973:190). An official of a minor lacrosse association writes in a similar vein: 'I have seen young mothers at tyke and novice games [six to ten years old] screaming at their sons to "kill" the opposing player' (*Toronto Star II* June 1973:7). Despite such lurid accounts, it seems unlikely that most mothers legitimate violence to the same degree as fathers. A *Canadian Magazine* readers' poll (Grescoe, 1972) on several national issues (nearly thirty thousand questionnaires were returned) asked the question: 'Should National Hockey League players be given automatic game penalties for fighting?' The responses were: male 61 per cent yes, 38 per cent no; female 73 per cent yes, 25 per cent no. It would be interesting to know how many of the respondents were or had been associated with the game. Perhaps in Canada, players and supporters of hockey form a subculture sharing values supportive of violence, while those more remote from the sport tend to look askance upon such conduct.

Data is both abundant and consistent regarding peer support of violence in 'subcultures' and 'regional cultures' of violence (Gastil, 1971; Wolfgang and Ferracutti, 1967), and the conferring of prestige for violence in certain types of delinquent gangs has been well verified (Wheeler, 1967). Miller (1958) has identified 'toughness' (including skill in physical combat) as one of several 'focal concerns' of lower class culture from which delinquent gangs often spring. But boys (Sexton, 1969) and men not belonging to deviant groups also gain peer approval for aggression in certain situations. Several recent "inside' glimpses of the occupational world of the athlete have illuminated the 'machismo' codes undergirding sport violence (Shaw, 1972). Faulkner (1971, 1973) reports, after interviewing American Hockey League professionals, that players regard violence as essential in gaining and maintaining the respect of opponents and teammates who see violent encounters as 'character contests.' In a study of minor hockey in a Canadian city, Vaz (1972) and Vaz and Thomas (1974) observed that violence is an integral part of the occupational culture shared by players and others associated with the game. It is important to note, however, that although violence is an important occupational tool, players who 'run amok' are as much reviled as those who fail in 'character contests.' These codes, Faulkner (1973) notes, are reminiscent of honour, revenge, and retribution in 'primitive' societies. Because hockey violence, then, is not random but rule-governed, its use is sometimes negatively sanctioned – as when it interferes with winning.

Coach-sanctioned intimidation by violence, or the threat of it, as an aid to winning in some sports seems established practice. Some hockey coaches, among others, keep 'statistics' on the number of 'hits' – legal and illegal – made by their players, often attributing losses to insufficient 'hitting,' and vice versa. American Hockey League players perceive toughness and fighting ability as important in impressing coaches and management (Faulkner, 1973); and in minor hockey, particularly at the midget level, 'illegal tactics and "tricks" of the game are both encouraged and taught; rough play and physically aggressive performance are strongly encouraged, and sometimes players are taught the techniques of fighting' (Vaz, 1972). Sixty-two per cent of Vaz's (1974) fifteen- to sixteen-year-olds (compared to 26 per cent of the seven- to nine-year-olds) reported that one of the most important qualities a coach looks for is 'being aggressive at all times.' Presumably, coaches reward their pupils for learning their lessons well. But the coaches' enthusiasm for violence is likely tempered by the detrimental effects it sometimes has on game outcomes.

As suggested, players' normative groups' sanctions for assault are contingent upon a host of circumstances, many of which have to do with winning and losing. Violence is commonly seen as justified if it is a means to a desired end: and winning in athletics is one terminal value that underpins the use of violent tactics. For instance, when illegal violence enhances victory, as often appears to be the case, then the greater the importance of winning, the greater the legitimation of violent means. But when official penalties for fighting and other illegal acts of assault are severe enough that victory is jeopardized, athletes may receive negative sanctions, especially from coaches and colleagues, who, it can be assumed, have the greatest stakes in team success. Indeed, hockey players learn early that there are 'good' and 'bad' penalties; the former are encouraged, the latter deplored (Vaz, 1972).

In summary, research, journalism, and everyday observation suggest the existence in hockey of a value-climate which fosters the legitimation of legal and illegal violence. A player's perceptions of his parents', peers', and coach's sanctions for assault, however, may form distinctive patterns because they have been differentially shaped by the norms which accompany each group's role relationships with the actor. In addition, sanctions probably vary with the nature of the act and the situation in which it occurs.

Method

Subjects from whom data were collected in the present study came from a population of male adolescents who play interscholastic hockey in Toronto. In general, these players represent the second echelon of talent in their age range (the most promising players tend to play Junior B or Junior A hockey). Most are too old to participate in the highly competitive, professionally oriented community and city-wide leagues; but all are products of these organizations and are therefore similar to young hockey players throughout the country. The sample comprised eighty-three players, all the regular members of seven teams selected to reflect a wide range of socioeconomic status.[1] The teams were chosen from among the seventeen high schools which entered hockey teams in the Toronto Secondary Schools Athletic Association for 1970-1.

Data were generated from the responses to interviews conducted with the players and their coaches during the spring of 1971. Frequencies of responses were tabulated regarding players' perceptions of their normative reference groups' sanctions for several assaultive behaviours in hockey.[2] The intercorrelation matrix of the items was then subjected to orthogonal, principal component factor analysis, rotated to simple structure through the varimax routine, to determine whether or not the sanctions formed separate dimensions.

Results

Table I shows that the players' views of their normative group sanctions for violence were a function both of the reference group in question and the type of act.

Examination of parental sanctions for assault reveals that 96 per cent of the fathers were seen by players as either approving or strongly approving of hard but legal bodychecking. The majority of fathers also positively sanctioned 'fighting, but because the other guy started it'; only 23 per cent disapproved of this conduct, 2 per cent strongly so. Although most fathers disapproved of starting fights and other penalty-getting rough play, roughly one-third approved of the latter acts. Sixty-seven per cent of mothers were perceived as approving of or strongly approving of bodychecking, but over 50 per cent, contrary to the literature cited, were against fighting back when attacked. Mothers overwhelmingly negatively sanctioned the other dimensions of violence.

Players tended to view their teammates as strongly encouraging bodychecking and somewhat less in favour of fighting back. Team members were evenly divided, however, regarding penalty-sanctioned assaultive conduct such as boarding and crosschecking. With regard to being the aggressor in a fight, the majority of teammates disapproved (55 per cent) or strongly disapproved (11 per cent). Non-playing peers, in contrast to the other reference groups, were perceived as approving of or highly approving of all four aspects of violence.

TABLE I

FREQUENCIES OF RESPONSES TO ITEMS REGARDING PLAYERS' PERCEPTIONS OF NORMATIVE REFERENCE GROUP SANCTIONS FOR VIOLENCE

Variables	Strongly disapprove		Disapprove		Approve		Strongly approve	
	N	%	N	%	N	%	N	c
Father's sanctions for								
Bodychecking	0	(0)	3	(4)	41	(49)	39	(4
Fighting back	2	(2)	19	(23)	45	(54)	17	(2
Starting Fight	17	(21)	51	(61)	11	(13)	4	(
Boarding, crosschecking, etc.	5	(6)	47	(56)	28	(34)	3	(
Mother's sanctions for								
Bodychecking	4	(5)	22	(26)	41	(49)	15	(1
Fighting back	13	(16)	31	(37)	31	(37)	8	(1
Starting fight	39	(48)	41	(49)	2	(2)	1	(
Boarding, crosschecking, etc.	24	(29)	52	(63)	7	(8)	0	
Teammates' sanctions for								
Bodychecking	0	(0)	0	(0)	25	(30)	58	(7
Fighting back	1	(1)	11	(13)	37	(45)	34	(4
Starting fight	10	(11)	45	(55)	25	(30)	3	
Boarding, crosschecking, etc.	5	(6)	36	(44)	33	(40)	9	(1
Peers' sanctions for								
Bodychecking	0	(0)	0	(0)	27	(33)	56	(6
Fighting back	9	(0)	3	(4)	45	(53)	35	(4
Starting fight	5	(6)	24	(29)	39	(47)	15	(1
Boarding, crosschecking, etc.	0	(0)	16	(20)	45	(54)	22	(2
Coach's sanctions for								
Bodychecking	0	(0)	1	(1)	43	(52)	39	(4
Fighting back	10	(11)	28	(34)	30	(36)	15	(1
Starting fight	28	(34)	47	(57)	7	(8)	1	
Boarding, crosschecking, etc.	8	(10)	45	(54)	24	(29)	6	

TABLE II

INTERCORRELATIONS AMONG VARIABLES ASSOCIATED WITH NORMATIVE REFERENCE GROUP SANCTIONS FOR VIOLENCE

Sanctions	1	2	3	4	5	6	7	8	9	10	11	12	13	14	15	16	17	18	19	20
For boarding, crosschecking, etc.																				
1/Father's	1.00																			
2/Mother's	0.10	1.00																		
3/Peers'	-0.01	0.06	1.00																	
4/Teammates'	0.00	0.20	0.48	1.00																
5/Coach's	-0.04	0.18	0.50	0.66	1.00															
For starting fight																				
6/Father's	0.92	0.02	-0.05	-0.06	-0.09	1.00														
7/Mother's	0.17	0.46	-0.02	0.00	-0.04	0.19	1.00													
8/Peers'	0.22	0.18	0.51	0.24	0.16	0.19	0.22	1.00												
9/Teammates'	-0.03	-0.03	0.23	0.42	0.25	-0.03	0.05	0.34	1.00											
10/Coach's	-0.10	0.19	0.37	0.40	0.50	-0.09	0.01	0.15	0.42	1.00										
For bodychecking																				
11/Father's	0.90	-0.01	-0.07	-0.05	-0.07	0.90	0.05	0.16	-0.11	-0.14	1.00									
12/Mother's	0.09	0.18	0.02	-0.01	-0.11	0.11	0.25	0.09	0.00	0.04	0.11	1.00								
13/Peers'	0.05	0.05	0.27	0.13	-0.09	0.08	-0.07	0.27	0.00	-0.19	0.19	0.07	1.00							
14/Teammates'	-0.06	0.11	-0.02	0.09	-0.03	-0.05	0.12	-0.02	0.07	0.07	0.01	0.05	0.28	1.00						
15/Coach's	0.08	0.21	0.29	0.19	0.32	0.10	0.06	0.24	-0.04	0.04	0.13	0.01	0.40	-0.01	1.00					
For fighting back																				
16/Father's	0.86	0.05	-0.06	-0.02	-0.02	0.92	0.12	0.21	-0.05	-0.06	0.91	0.05	0.05	-0.08	0.10	1.00				
17/Mother's	0.15	0.36	0.05	0.03	0.00	0.22	0.48	0.39	0.15	0.10	0.11	0.50	-0.07	0.00	0.03	0.25	1.00			
18/Peers'	0.16	0.13	0.37	0.29	0.27	0.17	0.14	0.53	0.27	0.18	0.14	-0.01	0.23	-0.01	0.22	0.28	0.38	1.00		
19/Teammates'	0.09	0.16	0.17	0.40	0.28	0.11	0.08	0.31	0.36	0.26	0.09	0.05	0.05	0.00	0.14	0.23	0.38	0.68	1.00	
20/Coach's	-0.13	0.18	0.28	0.29	0.40	-0.06	0.07	0.31	0.18	0.49	-0.09	-0.01	0.04	-0.05	0.19	0.04	0.31	0.34	0.59	1.0

NOTE: Coefficient of 0.21 required for significance at .05 level.

The coaches' sanctions for assault, perhaps not surprisingly, were seen by players as corresponding closely to the sanctions of their teammates. Coaches were perceived as having positive attitudes toward bodychecking. But only slightly more than half approved of (31 per cent) or strongly approved of (18 per cent) retaliating when attacked. More than 90 per cent of the coaches were opposed to starting a fight, and 70 per cent disapproved of other illegal acts of hockey violence.

In short, players tended to regard their fathers, teammates, and coaches as favourably disposed toward the legal and defensive aspects of assault but as against illegal acts, including initiating fights. It is noteworthy that in the latter instances there were relatively few strong disapprovals and many approvals. Mothers and non-playing peers present a contrast: the former were seen as generally disapproving and the latter approving of violence.

Table I may be viewed in two ways: by reference group or type of act; thus, a factor analysis was performed to determine what independent conceptual dimensions might underlie the data. When the intercorrelations of the twenty variables measuring reference group sanctions were factor analysed, four factors emerged representing the sanctions of 1/ father, 2/mother, 3/non-playing peers, and 4/teammates and coach. Table II gives the intercorrelation matrix for the twenty items. Table III shows the factor loadings. The factors representing father's and mother's sanctions were clear cut (no loading less than 0.65); the factors for non-playing peers', and teammates' and coach's sanctions somewhat less so.

Conclusion

The results indicate that players' perceptions of their normative reference groups' sanctions for assault were a function mainly of the particular group in question, and each group's sanctions were somewhat contingent upon the nature of the assault. Sex role standards, first of all, probably accounted for the divergence between mothers' and the male groups' sanctions, and for the general approval among the latter of 'bodychecking' and 'fighting back' when assailed. The culture of the game, too, without question supports these kinds of actions. It may be assumed that females are generally more remote than males from this culture.

More significantly, players' responses to unstructured questions revealed that they perceived their coach's and, to a lesser degree, teammates' sanctions as turning on the apparent importance to each of the team's success. These perceptions were borne out in interviews with coaches who made it clear that any disapproval of potential penalty-

TABLE III

FACTOR LOADINGS FOR VARIABLES ASSOCIATED WITH NORMATIVE REFERENCE GROUP SANCTIONS FOR ASSAULT

	Factors			
Sanctions	*Father's sanctions*	*Teammates and coach's sanctions*	*Mother's sanctions*	*Non-playing peers' sanctions*
For boarding, crosschecking, etc.				
1/Father's	0.96	0.00	0.10	0.05
2/Mother's	0.00	0.28	0.66	−0.23
3/Peers'	−0.07	0.52	−0.01	0.64
4/Teammates'	0.00	0.75	−0.02	0.21
5/Coach's	−0.03	0.81	−0.08	0.06
For starting fight				
6/Father's	0.96	−0.05	0.10	0.04
7/Mother's	0.09	0.00	0.77	−0.03
8/Peers'	0.15	0.11	0.24	0.72
9/Teammates'	−0.04	0.42	0.00	0.44
10/Coach's	−0.08	0.77	0.10	−0.01
For bodychecking				
11/Father's	0.95	−0.08	0.00	0.03
12/Mother's	0.04	−0.08	0.65	0.22
13/Peers'	0.06	−0.11	−0.11	0.41
14/Teammates'	−0.04	0.05	0.11	−0.07
15/Coach's	0.07	0.18	0.04	0.14
For fighting back				
16/Father's	0.95	−0.03	−0.05	0.00
17/Mother's	0.11	−0.07	0.74	0.19
18/Peers'	0.16	0.09	0.06	0.42
19/Teammates'	0.10	0.20	0.06	0.09
20/Coach's	−0.10	0.37	0.09	−0.04

getting behaviour was because penalties in school hockey hindered winning, their chief concern. Since the high school games are of relatively short duration, owing to lack of ice time, playing short-handed can be costly for the penalized team. What is more, referees are probably quicker to impose penalties in school-sponsored sport than in other leagues. And penalties tend to be more severe; for example, fighting entails two game suspensions for the offenders. The relatively more widespread approval of illegal violence by team members, compared to coaches, may reflect a greater concern among players with personal status via assault, as opposed to coaches' overriding emphasis on team victory.

Players regarded their non-playing peers as eager to see violence in any form. A typical response to unstructured questions about friends was, 'Most of them come to the games just to see somebody get killed.' Although there are few reliable data regarding the influence of spectators' sanctions on performers' conduct, there is an element of credibility in the belief – even at the level of schoolboy sport – that some of the violence is a response to the demands of onlookers. In professional hockey it is believed by some, that 'brawling helps sell hockey' (*Toronto Star* 15 Dec. 1971:19).

In conclusion, it can be stated with some equivocation that high school hockey players tend to view their normative reference groups as approving of a variety of assaultive acts in hockey. This approval is dampened to the extent that each group is concerned about the potential negative effects of penalties on game outcomes. It may not be dampened in hockey leagues where the special constraints peculiar to school-sponsored sport are absent. Seen in light of the concept of legitimation, much of the legal and illegal violence in sport is in no way aberrant; rather, it is socially acquired normative behaviour.

NOTES

1. Owing to the substantial agreement on the linkages among lower SES parents, physically punitive child-rearing practices, and subsequent children's agression (Becker, 1964), and the tendency of lower SES athletes to gravitate toward combative sports (Loy, 1969), SES was controlled. Neither school SES nor family SES, however, had an impact on players' perceptions of their reference group sanctions.
2. Responses to questions pertaining to: 1/'hard but legal bodychecking'; 2/'fighting, but because the other guy started it'; 3/'rough play like boarding or crosschecking which results in penalties'; and 4/'starting a fistfight.'

REFERENCES

Aberle, D. F. and K. D. Naegele
1952   'Middle Class Fathers Occupational Roles and Attitudes Toward Children.' *American Journal of Orthopsychiatry*, 22.

Baker, R. and S. J. Ball
1969   *Violence and the Media*. Washington DC: United States Government Printing Office.

Ball-Rokeach, S.J.
1972   'The Legitimation of Violence.' In J. F. Short Jr, and M. E. Wolfgang (eds.), *Collective Violence*. Chicago: Aldine-Atherton.
1974   "Values and Violence: A Test of the Subculture of Violence Thesis.' *American Sociological Review*, 38.

Bandura, A. K. and R. H. Walters
1959   *Adolescent Aggression*. New York: Ronald Press.

Bardwick, J. M.
1971   *Psychology of Women: A Study of Bio-Cultural Conflicts*. New York: Harper and Row.

Becker, W. C.
1964   'Consequences of Different Kinds of Parental Discipline.' In M. L. Hoffman and L. W. Hoffman (eds.), *Review of Child Development Research*, Vol. I. New York: Russel Sage Foundation.

Berger, P. L. and T. Luckmann
1966   *The Social Construction of Reality*. Garden City, New York: Anchor Doubleday.

Blumenthal, M. R. Kahn, F. Andrews, and K. Head
1972   *Justifying Violence: Attitudes of American Men*. Ann Arbor: Institute for Social Research, University of Michigan.

Elkin, F. and G. Handel
1972   *The Child and Society*. New York: Random House.

Fanon, F.
1963   *The Wretched of the Earth*. New York: Grove Press.

Faulkner, R. R.
1971   'Violence, Comaraderie and Occupational Character in Hockey.' Paper presented at the Conference on Sport and Social Deviancy, New York State University at Brockport.

1973   'On Respect and Retribution: Toward an Ethnography of Violence.' *Sociological Symposium*, 9.

Garfinkel, H.
1949   'Research Note on Inter- and Intra-Racial Homocides.' *Social Forces*, 27.

Gastil, R. D.
1971   'Homocide and a Regional Culture of Violence.' *American Sociological Review*, 36.

Gerson, W. M.
1968   'Violence as an American Value Theme.' In O. N. Larsen (ed.), *Violence and the Mass Media*. New York: Harper and Row.

Graham, H. D. and T. R. Gurr
1969   *The History of Violence in America*. New York: Bantam.

Grescoe, P.
1972   'We Asked You Six Questions.' *Canadian Magazine*, January 29.

Ingham, A. G. and J. W. Loy Jr.
1973   'The Social System of Sport: A Humanistic Perspective.' *Quest*, 19.

Inkeles, A.
1968   'Society, Social Structure and Child Socialization.' In J. A. Clausen (ed.), *Socialization and Society*. Boston: Little, Brown.

Kagan, J.
1964   'Acquisition and Significance of Sex Typing and Sex Role Identity.' In M. L. Hoffman and L. W. Hoffman (eds.), *Review of Child Development Research*. Vol. 2. New York: Russell Sage Foundation.

Kemper, T. D.
1969   "Reference Groups, Socialization and Achievement." In E. F. Borgatta (ed.), *Social Psychology: Readings and Perspective*. Chicago: Rand McNally.

Loy, J. W.
1969   'The Study of Sport and Social Mobility.' In G. S. Kenyon (ed.), *Aspects of Contemporary Sport Sociology*. Chicago: The Athletic Institute.

Miller, W. B.
1958   'Lower Class Culture as a Generating Milieu of Gang Delinquency.' *Journal of Social Issues*, 14.

Mussen, P. H.
1971   'Early Sex-Role Development.' In N. Reeves (ed.), *Womankind: Beyond the Stereotypes*. Chicago: Aldine-Atherton.

National Hockey League Guide
1971   '1971-72 Schedule and 1970–1971 Final Statistics.' Montreal: National Hockey League Information and Statistics Bureau.

Sexton, P.C.
1969   *The Feminized Male.* New York: Vintage.

Shaw, G.
1972   *Meat on the Hoof.* New York: St. Martin's Press.

Smith, M. D.
1975   'Significant Others' Influence on the Assaultive Behaviour of Young Hockey Players.' *International Review of Sport Sociology,* 10.

Sternberger, D.
1968   'Legitimacy.' *International Encyclopedia of the Social Sciences,* Vol. 9. New York: Macmillan and the Free Press.

Vaz, E. W.
1972   'The Culture of Young Hockey Players: Some Initial Observations.' In A. W. Taylor (ed.), *Training: Scientific Basis and Application.* Springfield: Charles C. Thomas.

and D. Thomas
1974   'What Price Victory: An Analysis of Minor Hockey League Players' Attitudes Toward Winning.' *International Review of Sport Sociology,* 9(2).

Weber, M.
1957   *The Theory of Social and Economic Organization.* New York: The Free Press.

Wheeler, S.
1967   'Delinquency and Crime.' In H. S. Becker (ed.), *Social Problems: a Modern Approach,* New York: John Wiley.

Wolfgang, M. E. and F. Ferracutti (eds.)
1967   *The Subculture of Violence.* London: Tavistock Press.

"LEGITIMATE DEVIANCE" AND SOCIAL CLASS: Bar Behavior During Grey Cup Week*

Alan Listiak

Studies of deviant behaviour have focused on many forms of rule-breaking behaviour, from "major" violations such as crime, drug addiction, mental illness, sexual deviations, suicide, alcoholism and excessive

* Mr. John Woodard assisted in the research for this paper and made useful comments on it. His contribution and support are deeply appreciated.

drinking, etc., to "minor" breaches such as pool hustling (Polsky, 1967) swearing (Hartogs, 1967; Sagarin, 1962), smelling bad (Largey and Watson, 1972), being obese (Cahnman, 1969), and work-related infractions (Bensman and Gerver, 1963; Harper and Emmert, 1963; Stoddard, 1968). These works are predicated on the assumption that deviant behaviour is misbehaviour which is not socially sanctioned or highly tolerated especially if it is widespread. Yet, it is commonly known that there are times when and places where widespread deviant behaviour is socially sanctioned and highly tolerated, when, it may be said, deviant behaviour is legitimate.

During periods of legitimate deviance a "Time Out" is "called" from the demands of accountability and conformity, social control is relaxed, and almost anything goes. Such Time Outs are often called by ceremonial arrangement and take the form of ritualistic festivals, fiestas, celebrations, parties, and the like.[1] For example, MacAndrew and Edgerton (1969) summarize a great deal of anthropological research illustrating the universality and frequency of the ceremonial Time Out among Indians and other native peoples. These Time Outs are characterized by a great amount of aggression, violence, debauchery, generally wild behaviour, and, in many cases, extreme drunkenness—behaviour which is not tolerated in everyday life.[2]

The ceremonial Time Outs are not restricted to "primitive" societies. Modern, urbanized, so-called developed societies also have a multitude of such rituals. There are countless thousands of festivals, celebrations, and spectacles at the community and other levels in North America and Western Europe. Among the best known of these are the Oktober-Fest in Germany, the Mardi-Gras in New Orleans, the Winter Carnivals in St. Paul and Quebec, the Calgary Stampede in Alberta, the Grey Cup, etc. These urban festivals are characterized by a state of loosened social control which permits and even encourages, within-limits, boisterous and aggressive behaviour, property destruction, illicit sexual behaviour, excessive drinking and drunkennness, frenzied commercial activity, etc. Unfortunately, these rituals have received scant scrutiny from social scientists.

This lack of attention is especially strange in light of the imputed importance of these Time Out rituals in maintaining order and stability in society. Periods of legitimate deviance are believed to function in much the same manner as "deviant" deviance, i.e., as "safety-valves," to maintain system equilibrium, to contribute to solidarity and integration, to demark normative boundaries. (On the functions of "deviant" deviance, see, for e.g., Coser, 1967; Davis, 1966; Dentler and Erickson, 1959; Erickson, 1964, 1966.) For example, the liberated atmosphere of these periods allows the expression of "tension release" behaviours which derive from the strain and frustration of living within the confines of the social norms.

> ... societies have provided traditional, conventional situations in which people could to some degree "let themselves go," abandoning themselves to relatively unrestricted following of impulses that are ordinarily inhibited and limited in expression ...
>
> Such occasions provide a satisfying, yet legitimate, escape from the restrictions of the usual social norms. Particularly in modern society, the maintenance of reserve and dignity is inculcated in the person as an important value from childhood. It is not easy for the individual to drop this decorous posture and most of the time, the norms do not permit him to do so. At times, the norms of propriety may seem confining and frustrating (Turner and Killian, 1957:153-154).

If people save the expression of their frustrations and tensions for "occasions that fall under the purview of one or another form of sanctioned Time Out, not only are the adverse repercussions that would normally ensue either eliminated or significantly reduced, so too is the likelihood that such disruptions will occur at other times" (MacAndrew and Edgerton, 1969:169). By allowing such deviance to occur legitimately during the safety-valve of a "controlled" setting, the society supposedly drains off tensions and strains which could accumulate and eventually "explode" into more "destructive" forms of deviance with a minimum of adverse consequences.

Periods of legitimate deviance also perform an integrative function through their role "in facilitating the resolution of cultural conflict" (Turner and Killian, 1957:155) and thus restoring temporarily community integration and solidarity. This may be accomplished by the symbolic reaffirmation of the basic moral values of the system, as, for example, in the English Coronation. Shils and Young (1953:67, 72), drawing upon Drukheim, argue that "The Coronation is a ceremony in which the society reaffirms the moral values which constitute it as a society and renews its devotion to those values by an act of communion ... The fact that the experience is communal means that one of the values, the virtue of social unity or solidarity, is acknowledged and strengthened in the very act of communion."

The integrative function may also be accomplished by allowing the expression of values which are normally suppressed, implicit, unofficial, or illegal. Turner and Killian (1957:155-157) and Smith (1968) discuss how certain values such as "keeping the Negro in his place," "showing a horse thief no mercy," etc. "cannot always be attained through due process," and thus find expression in a conventionalized pattern of crowd behaviour such as lynching. The contribution to solidarity is noted by

Turner and Killian (1957:161): "Even when lynchings were relatively frequent in the South it was observed by the Southern Commission for the Study of Lynchings that a lynching often seemed to give a community a period of immunity from the repetition of such behaviour."

An underlying assumption of both the safety-valve and integrative functions is that social norms and their related institutional goals are uniformly distributed and valued throughout the society. From this it follows that the lower-class by virtue of its structural position has the least access to the legitimate means of realizing the norms and goals of the society. As such, it suffers the greatest strain and frustration from conformity.[3] Consequently, it would benefit the most from such rituals wherein social control is relaxed, and therefore would be expected to have a high rate of participation in them.

The hypothesis of high lower-class participation, generalized as full community participation, has been incorporated into sociological writings with little or no empirical support for either the hypothesis itself or the underlying assumptions. A typical example of such incorporation is the following statement by Quinn (1955:23):

> Generally, the institutions found within the city become functionally integrated in such a manner that most residents obtain locally the satisfactions of their basic needs. Citizens also participate in carrying on local governments and schools; they read the same newspapers, *patronize the same local recreational facilities, and enjoy the same celebrations.* Together they share a common social life that reflects much of the general social-cultural complex of the larger society. (Emphasis added.)

It may be true that community life "reflects much of the general social-cultural complex of the larger society." However, some would disagree with the functionalist perceptions of this larger complex and, consequently, disagree with the functionalist portrait of community life and participation. Birnbaum (1953) addressed himself to these issues as they are contained in Shils and Young's (1953) interpretation of the meaning of the Coronation. He notes that the ritual had little effect on the working classes other than the provision of a holiday. He (1953:13) argues that "to speak of the assimilation of the working class into the consensus of British society is to define that consensus by exclusive reference to middle and upperclass groups . . . The national moral community is defined in terms of the propertied classes and their servitors." Birnbaum (1953:18) goes on to counter Shils and Young's "claim that the family was the social unit 'recognized' as the most appropriate for entry into the Coronation celebration. Since most people were home from work, it is difficult to see what other units they could have formed. But the note on the family contradicts the claim that the Coronation atmosphere overcame the 'customary barriers' between people. The customary barriers of social distance are strongest, by general agreement, where the boundaries of the family begin." Shils and Young claim that the ritual of the Coronation and participation in it *decreases* the social distance between the classes. Birnbaum argues that the ritual serves as an *affirmation* of social distance and is even fundamentally divisive.

The one study presently available of a conventionalized urban Time Out ritual indicates that Birnbaum's critique is well taken. Ossenberg (1969) investigated bar behaviour in a sample of upper-middle-class, middle-class, and lower-class public drinking establishments in Calgary, Alberta during the Calgary Stampede. The Stampede is well-known for its wild and free-for-all Time Out atmosphere. Ossenberg found that participation in the Stampede as indexed by bar behaviour was limited mainly to the middle-class, the lower-class and upper-middle-class choosing to remain outside the festivities. He (1969:34) concluded that the Stampede was "a middle-class binge, suggesting that even socially approved deviant behaviour is endogamous." These results do not support the functionalist hypothesis of high lower-class participation in community sponsored conventionalized Time Out periods of legitimate deviance.

To make sense of such a contradictory finding, one is driven to re-examine the assumptions from which the high participation hypothesis is drawn. It is found that the assumption of an inverse relationship between frustration (status-type) and social class is questioned by (1) the many studies which reveal little or no relationship between deviance (especially crime and delinquency) and class (see, for e.g., Akers, 1964, 1968; Empey and Erickson, 1966; Hirschi, 1969; Mizruchi, 1967, Spiller, 1965; Vaz, 1967; Voss, 1966; Winslow, 1968); (2) the studies which show that the lower-class is characterized by lower success aspirations and success pressures than the middle and upper-classes (see, for e.g., Empey, 1956; Hyman, 1953; Spiller, 1965; Wilson, 1959; the references cited in Roach and Gursslin, 1965); (3) the contradictory findings of class differentials in perceived opportunities (Elliot (1963), Hyman (1953). Short, Rivera and Tennyson (1965) find that lower-class youth perceive their opportunities to be lower than middle and upper-class youth, whereas Mizruchi (1964) and Winslow (1968) find that lower-class youth perceive equal opportunities or anticipate future opportunities on a par with middle-class and upper-class youth; (4) the nonsocial conditions of lower-class life, especially the economic deprivation and lack of satisfaction of physical needs (Roach and Gursslin, 1965, 1967; Roach, 1965, 1967).

The assumption that norms and values and goals are evenly distributed and held in society is also questioned by a good deal of research. These studies indicate that the various social classes are distinguished by different interests, values, life-styles, child-rearing and socialization patterns, etc. (see, for e.g., Berger, 1960; Gans, 1962; Green, 1946; Kohn, 1969; Miller, 1958, 1959; Rainwater, 1960; Roach, 1965, 1967; Sewell, 1961; Shostak, 1969; Shostak and Gomberg, 1964; Spiller, 1965). The chief differentiating factors between social classes for the purposes of this discussion are the presence of values and actions associated with the material conditions of affluence and the Protestant Ethic in the middle-class and their absence in the lower-class. The middle-class is classically characterized as so future oriented that the present is almost an obsession, i.e., in order to assure the "good life" in the future, the daily round must be productive in terms of status enhancement and the attainment of success. Thus, there is great concern for conformity and meeting the expectations of others; deviant and aggressive behaviour are strongly prohibited. Those in the lower-class, in contrast, are noted for their lack of inhibition and their hedonistic propensity to immediate gratification, especially with respect to physical and sexual impulses. Violative behaviour, inhibition release, and aggression and violence are the keynotes of the lower-class.

Given these considerations, it seems reasonable to hypothesize, as Ossenberg (1969:30) did, that if the middle-class "is more sensitive to legal and other restrictive norms," then it may also be "more responsive to the relaxation of social controls represented by the relatively lax enforcement of those norms during community festivals." Consequently, it would be expected that the middle-class would be the main exhibitor of legitimate deviant behaviour during conventionalized urban Time Out rituals (if, in conjunction, the class structure in the community is relatively "open" and formal social control is not heavily used to prevent the other classes from expressing their frustrations).

To further test these hypotheses and to assess the functionality of the conventionalized Time Out ritual (and in the process generate needed knowledge of both the ritual and the nature of legitimate deviant behaviour expressed during such rituals), a replication of Ossenberg's (1969) study of bar behaviour during the Calgary Stampede was performed during Grey Cup Week 1972 in Hamilton, Ontario, November 27-December 3, 1972. It was hypothesized that during Grey Cup Week 1972 in Hamilton, a high level of legitimate deviant behaviour in the form of festival-related aggressive expressive behaviour would be found in middle-class drinking places and a lower level of such behaviour would be found in lower-class drinking places.[4]

The Grey Cup

The Grey Cup is emblematic of the Canadian Football League championship. Each year the Western and Eastern Conference winners meet in the final game of the season to determine the league champion. Each year this final game alternates between various cities in Eastern and Western Canada. The Cup itself was donated to the league in 1909 by Earl Grey, then the presiding Governor-General of Canada. Around this game has grown up an urban Time Out festival of clamorous proportions known as Grey Cup Week, which is (obviously) a week long in duration and culminates in the Grey Cup Game itself. (On the history and development of the Grey Cup, see Cosentino, 1969; Currie, 1968; Sullivan, 1970). Grey Cup Week is traditionally associated with forms of legitimate deviant behaviour otherwise known as merriment and hoopla, and many observers feel it has become a Canadian nativistic ritual. Fans of the representative teams and interested observers from all across Canada descend upon the particular city chosen that year for a week of unrestrained festivity and celebration. The host city, in conjunction with the Grey Cup Committee, gears itself for the role by putting on all types of activities, (for example, dinners, dances, ceremonies, beauty pageants, special shows, revues, parades, concerts, parties, gigantic sales, etc.), thereby creating an atmosphere of spontaneity and gaiety. This atmosphere is further enhanced by various businesses which decorate themselves in Grey Cup related themes, erect elaborate displays in their windows, and put up signs welcoming visitors and cheering on the respective teams. Obviously, the role of host is most profitable for the city (or at least certain segments of it) in terms of business and publicity. Hotels and motels are booked to capacity, often for miles around the city, and the main business section does a booming business.

The local and national media, especially newspapers and television, give detailed coverage of the week's events, reporting daily highlights and devoting full coverage to both the Grey Cup Parade and the Grey Cup Game—the 1972 Game reached a Canadian television audience of approximately 6 million.

As in most ceremonial Time Outs, alcohol plays an important part in the proceedings: copious quantities of alcohol are such an integral aspect of Grey Cup Week that it is often referred to as "The Grand National Drunk." Many events are marked by a high degree of drunken and boisterous behaviour, often erupting into fights and brawls. Excessive drinking, illegal drinking, fighting, sexual looseness, and generally impulsive behaviour are among the forms of deviance which are legitimated by the attitude of tolerance and constraint shown by the police and other social control agencies. Yet, behaviour during Grey Cup Week cannot be said to be totally uninhibited—there are limits beyond which the type and degree of legitimate deviant behaviour rarely goes. The only time these limits were seriously transgressed was in the 1966 festivities in Vancouver, when the ritual became a riot:

> The police haul was 689 persons in four hours of rioting. They broke store windows, ripped street decorations, lit fires in ornamental trash cans, indulged in a wild bottle-throwing melee, engaged in beer bottle attacks. When order was restored the count was 159 charged with unlawful assembly, another 115 were in jail charged with drunkenness and malicious damage and hundreds others were booked on a variety of counts (Sullivan, 1970:167).

The Grey Cup is said to be an integrating device on two levels. At the national level it is said to operate to unite Canada as a nation and to develop Canadian identity. For example, Sam Berger, the owner of the Montreal Alouettes of the C.F.L. has said, "The Grey Cup and the league are Canadian institutions that make us conscious of staying a nation." Donald McNaughton, president of Schenley's (the liquor company which sponsors the annual awards to outstanding players in the league) notes, " . . . Football is . . . the one thing that gets us thinking east-to-west in this country instead of north-to-south. When I travel across Canada during Grey Cup Week that thinking hits a terrific peak. It keeps us conscious of being Canadians" (both cited in Batten, 1972:90).

At the community level, the Grey Cup is said to operate to promote civic pride in the inhabitants both by the favourable publicity of the city generated and the process of "showing the visitors a good time," etc. Hamilton's Mayor, Mr. Vic Copps, said that the Grey Cup "has been a great unifying force for the city," and that the Grey Cup "has made us a first class big city" and would attract business and hotels to the city (*Hamilton Spectator*, December 4, 1972, p. 7). Jack MacDonald, Chairman of the Grey Cup Committee, and a local businessman, found "people saying now that they are proud to be Hamiltonians." Columnist Stan McNeill, the day after the game wrote, "It was impossible to watch yesterday's show . . . not just the game itself, but the whole package . . . without a sudden feeling of pride in being a part of Hamilton" (*Hamilton Spectator*, December 4, 1972, p. 63).

The Grey Cup is said also to operate to promote peace and order within the community by the generalized participation of the inhabitants in legitimate deviance or "tension-release" behaviours. The safety-valve function is noted in an editorial from the *Ottawa Journal* reprinted in the *Hamilton Spectator* on December 5, 1972: "In a climatic national sports contest, such as the Grey Cup, with attendent socializing, parades and fun, we can get that oft needed release from everyday cares."

It was fortunate, for the purposes of this study, that Grey Cup Week 1972 took place in Hamilton, Ontario. Hamilton is a traditional "hotbed" of football enthusiasm, despite being financially overshadowed by its large neighbor, Toronto. Hamilton has always maintained its own football teams in top level leagues (both professional and amateur), and has hosted the Grey Cup seven times before 1972 (the years being 1910, 1912, 1913, 1928, 1935, 1944. For a history of Hamilton's involvement with football, see *Hamilton Spectator*, Grey Cup Edition, November 28, 1972). It was fortunate also in that the hometown Tiger-Cats were scheduled to play in the big game against the Western representative, the Saskatchewan Roughriders. These two facts resulted in a high degree of interest and participation in Grey Cup Week in Hamilton.

Indeed the week's activities certainly lived up to the finest Grey Cup tradition. Legitimate deviant behaviour abounded as social control was relaxed and tensions were released. King Street, Hamilton's main street, was filled to overflowing by thousands of people who danced, drank, cheered, sang, rang cowbells, and fought their way up and down the main business section of the street until at least 4 a.m. on each of the last three nights of the festivities. While people flowed in all directions on both sides of the street, the hard-core revellers moved continuously up and down King Street within a 6-block limit, moving West up King on the North side, crossing over and returning East down King on the South side, crossing over and starting the trip again.

Just as the throngs of people on foot moved up and down King Street whooping it up, so the traffic, jammed up for over half a mile, circled the downtown area to contribute its share to the intensity of the merriment already taking place in the main business section. As the jam moved along, honking all the way, drivers and passengers would jump out of their cars to dance, shout, pass drinks among each other, etc. Several pedestrians were moving in and out of the traffic passing out drinks to the motorists. Cars were painted in Tiger-Cat and Roughrider colours; people were hanging over the outside of the vehicles, and also on the hood, roof, and trunk. Convertibles had their tops down and were filled with people; pick-up trucks were similarly loaded up with celebrants. When traffic moved ahead a few feet, the revellers would hang their heads out of the windows and renew their shouting and cheering.

The legitimacy of most deviance was respected by the police. For example, one obviously ineibriated Westerner, resplendent in Saskatchewan colours, was passing out cans of beer from a loaded case tucked under his arm to appreciative passers-by, in full view of nearby police officers. In another instance, several young men standing in a doorway passing a bottle of whiskey among themselves received only a warning from a policeman to "keep the bar moving." The limits of legitimacy were tested on occasion: celebrations in the massive (1,500 seat) Junior Chamber of Commerce hospitality tent got so out of hand, that the bar had to be closed before 9:30 p.m. on the night before the game. The Reception Centre at Jackson Square, a favorite meeting place of teenagers, closed shortly thereafter because of a large brawl in which several temporary walls were knocked down. Yet relatively few persons were arrested either that night or during the entire week of the festival.

Method

The method employed to measure participation in Grey Cup festivities and exhibition of legitimate deviant behaviour is a participant observation of behaviour in a sample of public drinking establishments in the festival area. The utilization of bar behaviour as the index of participation and exhibition is justified for the following reasons:

1. As indicated earlier, drinking and drinking-related behaviour is an integral aspect of the Grey Cup. Yet, excessive drinking is a taboo in normal life (Jessor, *et al.*, 1968). As such, "excessive drinking represents a form of deviant behaviour which becomes 'normal' and even goal-directed" during the festival (Ossenberg, 1969:31); that is, it becomes a form of legitimate deviance as well as a rationale for explaining away other acts of deviance engaged in (on this point see MacAndrew and Edgerton, 1969).

2. Thus, bars are an important "arena" of Grey Cup action (see Fisher, 1972 for an elaboration of this concept).

3. Bars present a much more stable picture of the situation and are more amenable to participant observation than the street with its fast flowing pace or various activities of relatively short duration.

4. "It is reasonable to assume that inhibitions concerning cross-class interaction are more easily dissolved with the aid of alcoholic beverages" (Ossenberg, 1969:30).

5. "Bars are an effective informal index of the social structure in which they exist" (Ossenberg, 1969:30; Clinard, 1962, 1965; Hunter, 1969).

6. Cavan's (1966) study revealed little difference in the degree of "social licentiousness" in middle-class and lower-class bars, even though behaviour in middle-class bars was expected to be more constrained and respectful than in lower-class bars. If it is reasonable to hypothesize that this finding is applicable to the Hamilton drinking scene, and limited observation indicates that it is, then any differences in licentiousness which are found become that much

more significant.[5] However, a difference does exist in the event of physical aggressiveness in lower and middle-class bars. Fights and verbal violence are more common to the lower-class bar. Thus, there are some aspects in which behaviour in middle-class bars is more restrained than lower-class bars, and any observed deviation from this pattern is significant.

7.   Like Professor Ossenberg, and maybe even more so, we enjoy drinking beer.

For the study sample, eleven beer parlours and lounges were selected, all of which were within or very close to the core area of the festival site (downtown Hamilton). Of the eleven, six establishments were classified as middle-class and five as lower or working class. In Hamilton, beer parlours are licensed to serve only beer, while lounges are able to serve beer, wine and liquor. As in most Canadian cities, beer parlours traditionally cater to the lower-class (blue-collar workers, Canadian Forces personnel, the unemployed, welfare recipients, old age pensioners, Indians, and other ethnic and immigrant groups). Lounges are usually identified with a middle-class clientele (general office and white-collar workers, middle-level professional and executive types and university and senior high school students, especially since the legal age was lowered to 18).

Upper or upper-middle-class bars are omitted from the sample simply because there were none to be found in Hamilton's core area. This is most likely a reflection of (1) the close proximity to Toronto, (2) the relative lack of "first class" accomodation, and (3) the basic class structure of the city – Hamilton is basically an industrial city and is often called a "lunch bucket" town; in fact, one of the symbols of the city (in great evidence during Grey Cup Week) is a construction worker's hard hat.[6]

Unlike Professor Ossenberg, the present researchers had little prior knowledge of the drinking scene in Hamilton. Bars were included in the sample on the basis of advice from long-term residents. Subsequently, the eleven bars in question were returned to several times in order to gauge behaviour in them on more normal evenings.

Each drinking place was visited on two evenings at the end of Grey Cup Week – a Friday and Saturday. It is reasonable to assume that these two evenings would have the most intense "search for collective gratification" by virtue of their being the last two evenings before the *raison d'etre* of the festival, the Grey Cup itself, as well as being the end of the normal work week.

Within the bars the same aspects were observed as in Ossenberg's (1969:31) research, namely:

1.   "The apparent social class comparison of patrons."

2. The wearing of costumes and/or paraphernalia indicitive of team support.
3. "The noise level (including the spontaneity and intent of expressive vocalization): and
4. Physical and social interaction, including evidences of aggression and general themes of conversation." (These last two aspects were observed as to their conformity or deviation from the usual standing patterns of behaviour found in the particular bars).

Findings

MIDDLE-CLASS DRINKING PLACES

A complicating factor in this study is the fact that the legal drinking age in Ontario was recently lowered from 21 to 18 years of age. This has enlarged the entire drinking population considerably, especially the middle-class drinking population: so much so that line-ups are very common on normal weekends and often on weeknights at any middle-class drinking places. During Grey Cup Week long line-ups were the order of the day at all of the middle-class establishments in the sample. At several lounges, people waited as long as 2 hours to gain entrance. However, because many bars had to be investigated, time could not be wasted standing in line-ups. Therefore, certain forms of circumvention were employed, such as utilizing some prior knowledge of the bouncer (for example, "Bill sent me"), the wearing of Saskatchewan buttons and ribbons as a means of facilitating "hospitable" responses,[7] cutting into the line close to the front, and sneaking past the bouncer at the door.

Five of the six middle-class drinking places in the sample were lounges. The sixth was a youth-oriented beer parlour. All of the places had entertainment in the form of various types of live musical presentation: trios, folk groups, rock bands, etc. Observation of those in the line-ups and in the places themselves revealed that the middle-class composition of the patrons was somewhat higher than on more normal days, when a small number of blue-collar and working-class types could usually be found. It was to these places that most of the out-of-towners came, as evidenced by the many patrons wearing Saskatchewan colours. Moreover, when advice was sought from locals as to "where the action was," the answers were to frequent middle-class bars (some of which were in the sample).

Approximately three-fourths of the patrons wore some type of Grey Cup paraphernalia, ranging from team-buttons, ribbons, festive hats of many types (especially stetsons and hard-hats), to full costumes of various types (for example, green and white cowboy suits for Saskatchewan fans and tiger outfits for Hamilton fans). In five out of the six places, the bar personnel were also attired in Grey Cup costumes.

In the middle-class drinking places the "standing patterns of behaviour" were somewhat upset, especially with respect to the range of "permissible behaviour" and "normal trouble."[8] The atmosphere of these establishments was supercharged with a high degree of gregarious behaviour and boisterous conduct, and the level of this legitimate deviance continued to rise as the evening and the drinks flowed on. Spontaneous shouts and yells and horn-blowing emanated from various parts of the bar, competing with each other in terms of volume and also in terms of Eastern Canada versus Western Canada. For example, one group of Westerners would shout, "Yeah, Saskatchewan!" or would go through the ritual, "Gimme an 'S,' gimme an 'A,'" etc. In reply, a group of Easterners would attempt to drown out this call with a louder "Yeah, Hamilton!" or "Gimme an 'H,' gimme an 'A,'" etc. Every two or three minutes the Hamilton Tiger-Cat fight song would ring through the entire place:

> Oskee wee wee
> Whiskey wa wa
> Holy Mackinaw
> Tigers,
> Eat 'em raw!

Football was a main topic of conversation, with animated discussions of how the Tiger-Cats would handle the 'Riders, and vice versa. As the evening wore on, the conversations became more expressively pleasure-seeking, turning to themes of how and where to get a sexual partner, where the party was later, retaliation to some "son-of-a-bitch" for a perceived put-down of self, and so forth.

The supercharged effect was not only verbal but physical as well. Males engaged in spirited camaraderie and backslapping types of behaviour. Sporadically spirited fights would break out; upon which the special football-player-type bouncers (hired for the occasion) would eventually descend to "clean up" the premises. Ladies did not engage in such activities. However, they did involve themselves with males in such practices as indiscriminate necking and sexually charged dancing. In one instance, a young woman was sitting on the lap of a male partner surrounded by other men. She was the center of attraction and was obviously enjoying the attention she was receiving in the form of four pairs of hands roaming all over her body.

One establishment, as a measure of economy and precaution, served drinks only in cheap plastic cups. Such a move proved to be a wise one. Several other lounges which served beer in bottles and liquor in glasses, found these objects being used as missles which were hurled at the walls, at other patrons, and even at the entertainers. It did not take long for the floors of these places to resemble a veritable sea of broken glass. However, the plastic cups were also put to good use. One group of 10 or 12 people, who it seemed all worked in the same office, were sitting at one long table. They began to build a huge pyramid of cups, the base as long as the table, the height up to the ceiling. After a number of futile attempts, which were downed both by missles thrown at the pyramid and/or the instability of the pyramid itself (much to the chagrin of the builders and the amusement of everyone else), the deed was finally accomplished and rewarded with a great cheer from all—and the demolition received an even greater cheer.

The effect of the prolonged fast and heavy drinking began to take its effects as early as suppertime. In one bar, shortly after 5 p.m., one young gentleman evidently had moved his chair into an area between several tables so as not to disturb his friends, and quietly passed out. Sometime later he awoke, joined his friends, and picked up his drinking where he left off. When his friends decided to leave to get something to eat, he joined our table, introduced himself and bought a round for the table, telling us that he had been going at it for 3 straight days and nights.

The buying of rounds was a common means of facilitating and sustaining interaction between visitors and Hamiltonians, and also between males and females.[9] Westerners were spotted by locals and invited to join their table. Upon entering a lounge, a local gentleman saw us and shouted, "Hey, Saskatchewan!" and offered us a round of beer. He asked about the Saskatchewan football team. Interwoven in the football talk was an exchange of descriptions of life in the West and the East and the spinning of biographies.[10]

Although the majority of patrons were grouped in terms of friendship circles and office-affiliations, table-hopping was common, especially on the part of males "moving in" on females, with round-buying the entrance ticket. In fact, sexual availability was a keynote of the middle-class drinking place, especially once the entertainment and the dancing began.[11] However, unlike Ossenberg's (1969) study, few prostitutes of any type were observed. This is most likely because there were few of them in these establishments; the presence of a large number of young, eligible women who were willing to "give it away," and, in fact, who often sought out sexual contacts, most likely obviated the demand for a prostitute's services. Young women, recently liberated by both ideology and law, travelled the pub circuit in groups of two, three or more, usually splitting up when suitable partners were "found." In some cases, to make a "find," these ladies were not adverse to initiating the contact themselves by starting up a conversation, by requesting a dance, or by buying a drink for the potential partner (thereby establishing the same mutual obligations and potential relationship as when the male treats the female; Cavan, 1966:112-132, 184-186).

LOWER CLASS DRINKING PLACES

The sample of lower-class drinking places consisted of four beer parlours and one lounge. The lounge and two of the beer parlours provided live entertainment, the other two beer parlours had only juke boxes. The lounge and three of the beer parlours had provisions for dancing.

Line-ups at the lower-class bars were conspicuous by their absence. Closely related to this was the absence of the "youth" or student trade. Relatively few university types were to be found in these bars, nor were the groups of young single women found making the rounds of the middle-class bars present. The young people who were present were working types: construction or industrial workers, truck drivers, wait-resses, hairdressers, and so forth, who were normally present in these bars.

In fact, most of those who regularly patronized these bars were pre-sent along with the usual smattering of drifters. The whole lower-class bar scene could be described as "business as usual." In most cases the premises were just over three-quarters full.

Also conspicuous by their absence were the "Oskee wee wee's" and competing yells which characterized the middle-class bars. The standing patterns of behaviour were as usual; Grey Cup related expressive behav-iour was at a minimum. Only about one in ten customers wore any Grey Cup paraphernalia, and this was limited mostly to stetson, or hard-hats, ribbons and buttons; very few patrons were "fully" costumed. Those who were identified in some manner with the Grey Cup sat in groups of three or four or more, and if there was more than one group, they were scattered throughout the place. They did not interact with the other patrons in any meaningful way; it would be fair to say that the regular customers basically ignored them, except in several instances, when one of the regulars took a dislike to one of the Cuppers and started a fight with them. They did not exhibit the same degree of legitimate deviant behaviour as those in middle-class bars. They were very subdued by comparison, sitting quietly drinking their beer, talking about the game and its players, the problems of locating easy sex (if not accompanied by female companions), checking over their financial resources, where to go next, etc. On the whole the Grey Cuppers did not stay much over two or three beers before moving on.

The regular patrons behaved in their normal fashion. While there was some interest in the Grey Cup Game on the part of these patrons (mainly the younger men), it did not dominate conversations and was soon dropped as the beer kept coming. Topics shifted to problems associated with work and family, the fight with "the old lady," the great "lay" of last night, drinking exploits, the virtues, power and speed of their cars and of other makes, etc. Two of the beer parlours were distinguished by the sexual segregation of "ladies and escorts" and "men only" beverage rooms. The only apparent effects of this distinction were the "toning down" of sexually-oriented conversations and the limitation of hustling by both males and females to the ladies side.

The animation of the conversations and the noise level also rose as the beer poured on until the dull roar was shattered every so often by the sound of breaking glasses, upturning tables, cries of "You cocksucker!" and fists striking jaws. Fights broke out every hour or so, over a number of things, and often over nothing at all. In one case, four gentlemen were sitting arguing over whose turn it was to buy the round when suddenly one of them threw a roundhouse right which landed on another's face. As the second gentleman went over backward in his chair, he took the table and the beer on it with him, to the dismay of the others.

It was not possible to gauge, in concrete terms, the number of prostitutes working these bars, even though a higher proportion of women than usual was present. Certainly they were present, often making no pretensions as to their business. However, even with follow-up visits, no conclusions can be drawn regarding Ossenberg's observations that more hookers may be found in lower-class bars during a festival.

As the evening wore on and the music and dancing started, hustling became a prime activity on the ladies side. Women, on the whole, were older and less aggressive than in the middle-class bars, but just as available, often giving the old "come on" (i.e. big eyes but shy, stare and look away, smile coyly), especially if they were hookers (whereupon if accepted they would leave with the "john" and return within the hour).

Summary and Conclusions

Despite the continued debate over the definition of deviance (e.g., Akers, 1968; DeLamater, 1968; Gibbons and Jones, 1971; Gibbs, 1966), there appears to be agreement on some aspects. Among them are the assumptions that deviant behaviour is negatively sanctioned in some manner and not highly tolerated, especially if it is widespread. Yet, there are times when certain forms of deviance receive social sanction and are highly tolerated even though they are widespread; that is, when deviant behaviour is legitimate. These periods of legitimate deviance are manifested in conventionalized Time Out rituals such as urban festivals.

It is believed that members from all class and status groups participate in these Time Outs. Moreover, the legitimate deviant behaviour expressed during these periods is said to function to restore community solidarity and integration and also as a community safety-valve. The results of a participant observation of bar behaviour in a sample of public drinking places during Grey Cup Week 1972 in Hamilton, Ontario support the hypothesis that more legitimate deviant behaviour would be exhibited by the middle-class than the lower-class. Middle-class patrons were found to exhibit a much higher level of festival-related aggressive expressive behaviour than lower-class patrons. The spontaneity of the middle-class was contrasted with the disinterest of the lower-class in Grey Cup festivities. On this basis, it would appear that Grey Cup Week is more "functional" for members of the middle-class; that is, it is the middle-class which takes advantage of the temporary relaxation of social control to achieve "release from everyday cares" and in the process becomes more unified and integrated. The main forms of deviant behaviour which were legitimated during this period were excessive drinking and drunkenness, sexual immoralities, minor forms of violence and aggression, and loud and boisterous conduct.

These findings suggest that important differences exist in the nature and degree of the tension and frustration suffered by the social classes and/or in the paths by which they vent these frustrations.

Grey Cup Week, like other conventionalized urban Time Out periods of legitimate deviant behaviour, is said to contribute to the solidarity and integration of the host city by involving its citizens in various promotional and recreational activities and by attracting favorable attention to the city. Grey Cup Week is also said to be a safety-valve in that participation in legitimate deviance provides the citizens with the chance to escape the pressures and tensions of everyday life.

It is true that the methodology employed is somewhat subjective and limited (inherent problems in participant observations, especially of large crowds, but not damaging; see Fisher, 1972). It is also true that the definitions of social class employed are broad and unrefined. However, it cannot be denied that despite the physical proximity of the festivities taking place on the street and at various near-by locations, the lower-class was reluctant to become involved in such activities, preferring to remain enclosed in its habitat. In conjunction, the middle-class seldom entered into that habitat; people preferred to stand in line for long periods of time in order to get into middle-class bars rather than go around the corner to a lower-class bar where they would be seated immediately, and where they could conceivably create their own atmosphere of gaiety by simply "taking over" the place.

It is hard to imagine how such behaviour functions to restore community integration and solidarity. Social distance cannot be said to have decreased significantly during Grey Cup Week 1972 in Hamilton, except within the middle-class. If anything was solidified, it was the existing social distance between the classes. The classes remained pretty well endogamous in their behaviour, the middle-class engaging in celebrations and legitimate deviant behaviour, developing feelings of solidarity among themselves as well as feelings of civic pride; the lower-class simply going about its normal routine. Moreover, it was only middle-class business establishments in the downtown business core which involved themselves in "putting on a show" by dressing up windows in Grey Cup themes, putting up signs such as "Welcome Visitors," "Go Tigers Go," etc., and by selling Grey Cup souvenirs and paraphernalia.

In reality, Grey Cup Week 1972 was found to be basically a middle-class "binge" sponsored, promoted, and profited from mostly by businessmen and politicians. As such, Grey Cup Week 1972 functioned both as an integrative device and a safety-valve for the middle-class. It functioned to provide a shot-in-the-arm in terms of immediate economic gain for middle-class businesses by stimulating local consumers and attracting eager tourists. It functioned to promote an image of the city's administration (many of whom are local businessmen) as effective, efficient, and working towards the city's best interests. And it functioned to reinforce the major class boundary existing in the city.[12]

The existence of important class differences and the functional reality of Grey Cup Week are obscured by the somewhat misguided and idealistic functionalist formulations and assumptions. Obviously, a more realistic and penetrating theoretical framework is necessary to handle the reality of Grey Cup festivities and other Time Out periods of legitimate deviance. The findings of this study may be added to the plethora of others which reveal the great gap which exists between theory and research and the in-operation of the dialectic between the theoretical and the observable so necessary to the development of adequate scientific sociological theory (Lachenmeyer, 1971; Listiak, 1971). This lack of empirical content in sociological theory has long been known and criticized (Blumer, 1954; Mills, 1959; Filstead, 1970), and is thought by some to stem from the fact that such theory is ultimately unfalsifiable and untestable in terms of the criteria of scientific logico-deductive models (e.g., Homans, 1964; Douglas, 1970; Park, 1969; Stinchcombe, 1968; Willer, 1967; Zetterberg, 1965; Lachenmeyer, 1971). While this seems to be a plausible explanation of why research showing the existence of class differences in interests, material conditions, values, life-styles, etc., has not been incorporated into theoretical formulations, it seems likely that the problem goes deeper than this.

The growing documentation of the real problems of lower-class work and life (e.g., Romano, 1970; Christoffel, *et al.*, 1970; Beneson and Lessinger, 1970) and the evidence that no substantial structural change or redistribution of wealth or power have taken place in North American society despite the many liberal reform efforts and claims to the contrary (Kolko, 1962; Nossiter, 1964; Christoffel, *et al.*, 1970), does not sit well with the liberal ideology with which sociological functionalism has aligned itself. This ideological commitment together with the static, ahistorical, idealistic, quasiholistic nature of this version of functionalism (e.g., Frank, 1966, 1967; Listiak, 1971) leads to the promotion of a consensus image of society through its attempt to incorporate the lower classes into the mainstream of social life, as defined by middle-class standards, regardless of the reality of the situation. According to Smith (1971), functionalists have identified with the middle class and view its vast growth as the achievement of an efficient and benevolent society. For example, Lipset (1963:440) argues that in such a society "the fundamental political problems of the industrial revolution have been solved; the workers have achieved industrial and political citizenship." As such, lower-class and working people are viewed as typical Canadians with the only difference between them and other Canadians being the social situation in which they happen to live.

In such a view, problems like widespread inequalities in social condition *are not indicative of fundamental contradictions in society*, but are *minor operating problems* which can be resolved on a non-ideological basis by providing more and better opportunities for citizens to participate fully in society (see Gruneau's discussion of "order" and "conflict" perspectives in Part One of this volume). There is no need to totally dismantle or reorganize the society; there is no reason to stop participating. To believe, or do so, is not only illigitimate but an indication that one's grasp of reality is "disturbed". Thus, sociologists who study those who rebel or attack the existing structure of social and political arrangements, or do not participate "fully" in the mainstream of "middle-class" life, show a great deal of concern for the "irrationality" of such actions. Sociological studies of the lower class for example, focus on misanthropy, authoritarianism, anomie, frustrated desires, etc. Lower-class culture is

depicted as authoritarian, unsophisticated, anti-intellectual, undemo-
cratic, intolerant, less stable, etc. (Lipset, 1963:114, 113, 121, 91, 94, 110,
108); it is a culture based on stretched or shadow values—values derived
from and subordinate to those upheld in the common (read dominant)
culture. The unfortunate (read oppressive) socio-cultural conditions in
which the lower-class live, engender an inability to live up to the inter-
nalized values of the common culture. To cope with these failures and
the guilt thus produced, surface rationalizations are developed, but on a
posthoc and independent basis. Such reactive values have little or no
validity in themselves (since they do not reflect how lower-class people
really feel) and obviously cannot form a distinct and autonomous culture.
Consequently, the lower-class has little it can call its own, culturally, and
nothing to contribute to the common culture: the lower-class is "culturally deprived" (Hodges, 1970) and should be aided in entering the Great
Cultural Mainstream.

However, it is a gross distortion to argue that lower-class culture is not
operative and self-sustaining. Even a shadow culture once created, has a
life of its own. Moreover, a culture does not have to be strong and well
developed, i.e. effective in determining behavior, to serve as a source of
identity and support which could have important social consequences
at future dates. It is also a distortion to argue that lower-class culture has
few, if any, useful and distinctive values, survival techniques, rituals, etc.,
of its own.[13] Further, the confinement of attention to socio-cultural
factors ignores the significance of the nonsocial environment, in particular, the material conditions in which the social class lives. In the lower-
class, economic and material deprivation or the threat of it leads to a
preoccupation with physical needs which often are insufficiently satisfied.
This deprivation can and does have important effects upon behaviour and
culture (e.g., Roach, 1965: Kohn, 1969, 1972).

The expression of legitimate deviant behaviour during a conventionalized Time Out ritual like Grey Cup Week cannot be understood by
ignoring such considerations. Nor can the functions of Time Out periods
such as Grey Cup Week be understood in terms of the still-life photogra-
phy of an ideologically blinded functionalism. A proper analysis must
investigate the meanings of legitimate deviant behaviour during Time
Out periods to various classes and groups as determined by their respective material cultural conditions in conjunction with an holistic consideration of the historical and structural context within which the Time Out
has developed and operates. Moreover, this analysis must be developed
with continual reference to the reality it represents.

At this stage, only several hypotheses as to the beginning of such an analysis of legitimate deviant behaviour and the functions of Grey Cup Week can be presented.

1. The origin and development of Grey Cup Week in the late 1940's and early 1950's may be depicted as stemming from the monopoly capitalistic nature of Canadian society. Specifically, it appears to have originated from the hinterland-metropolis nature of West-East relations, the reflection of this relation in the development of Canadian professional football, and the political and personal motives of a Western politician in 1948. Grey Cup Week developed through the expansion and commercialization of the pre-game activities by the Toronto Junior Board of Trade and then by other business and political interests. (Note: Toronto was the host city of every Grey Cup from 1941 to 1957 except two, and of every Grey Cup from 1941 to 1965 except five).

Grey Cup Week functions to provide immediate economic gain and to reduce the effects of competition for business interests. It effectively performs these functions by virtue of the expression of legitimate deviant behaviour allowed by its festival atmosphere and relaxation of social control which attracts many visitors and locals and reduces their "practical" inhibitions. Thus, Grey Cup Week functions at once as both a generator and an absorber of surplus value and is an important aspect of the capitalistic sales effort.

2. a. The continued growth of Grey Cup Week (and the continued growth of commercialized professional football in Canada) is a product of the continued growth of monopoly capitalism in Canada. The legitimate deviant behaviour expressed during Grey Cup Week functions as an outlet for the expression of aggressive and sexual frustrations which stem from the oppressive aspects of urban life and the alienated and oppressive nature of work, leisure and sex in Canadian society. The commercial and sensate consumptive aspects of Grey Cup Week also function to satisfy these needs.

   However, the degree of oppression in society varies by class. Those in the middle of the social structure are unable to express openly their aggression and sexuality and find satisfaction in a short-lived period of commercialized, impersonal, aggressive, and overindulgent legitimate deviant behaviour.

   Those in the bottom of the social structure are relatively more oppressed and have a lower ability to consume and have a different history than those above them. Hence, they tend to utilize structures more suited to the satisfaction of their needs, e.g., mental disorders, relatively unconstrained physical and sexual expression, consumption of flagrantly "violent" and "sexual" sports (like wrestling, boxing, certain forms of automobile racing, etc.).

b. Grey Cup Week as a Time Out Within-limits allows participants to engage legitimately in "tension-release" behaviour which, while deviant, neither exceeds certain culturally determined limits, nor challenges the basic values of the society, in effect reinforcing capitalistic values (sexism, sensate consumption, etc.). As such, it also functions to promote a degree of solidarity among those who participate in it.

c. As a fragmented conglomerate of parades, contests, special events, special sales, parties, visiting politicians, legitimate deviance, etc., Grey Cup Week is a spectacle which functions to mystify the nature of Canadian society, that is, to present an image of society as so complex and overwhelming that it is impossible to understand, change, or escape.

d. Grey Cup Week thus functions as a mechanism of social control over a limited but important segment of the population. Those who are found not to participate in Grey Cup Week will either have functional equivalents more suited to their needs or will be unimportant to the maintenance of the system (except by virtue of their structural position, i.e., poverty is functional.)

These considerations are, of course, only a preliminary outline of what an adequate analysis must entail. They are certainly not a complete outline, but must be added to and more fully developed in the light of the theoretical framework from which they are drawn. They must be subjected to empirical test at every level by whatever and as many methods as are appropriate.

This empirical verification would involve:

1. Historical analysis of the development of the festival with particular attention to the class interests operative (also to be determined historically).

2. Quantitative analysis (longitudinal if possible) of the absorption and generation of surplus value by examining the increase in business spending on sales efforts, the consumer response, the total amount of resources absorbed, etc.

3. Investigation into the nature of alienation and oppression and its varying degrees by class; into the mechanisms utilized by the classes to relieve themselves; into the place of Grey Cup Week in the total class structure. Participant observation, ethnomethodological and survey investigation into the meanings attached to both the festival

and the legitimate deviance expressed during it, and how and why one participates in it or does not participate in it.

4. Participant observations of behaviours indicative of feelings of solidarity (e.g., extending friendship, cross-class interaction, manifestations of civic pride, etc.). Pre- and post-festival surveys as to the degree of solidarity felt by participants as compared to nonparticipants before, during, and after Grey Cup Week, and also to determine if any significant differences exist in the background characteristics, perceptions of society, feelings of alienation, frustration, etc. between those who participate and those who do not.

NOTES

1. Ceremonial arrangement is not the only way by which Time Outs may be called. MacAndrew and Edgerton (1969:168) note that people may call a Time Out "by temporarily assuming one or another alternation in their social positions. (In the New Guinea highlands, for example, one can escape burdensome economic responsibilities by exhibiting 'wild men' behaviour [Newman, 1964], and in Hindu India this escape can be accomplished by donning the orange robes of the *sanyasi* [Dumont, 1960].) In other societies, conduct can come under the heading of Time Out by virtue either of the willful action of another (as in the case, for example, of witchcraft, sorcery, and the like) or by the action of a supernatural agent who might briefly take possession of one's will for alien purposes . . . in many societes persons have available to them the option of calling Time Out by producing an altered state of consciousness in themselves."

2. The deviant behaviour legitimated during Time Outs is not totally uninhibited in its expression but almost always stays within certain culturally determined limits. See MacAndrew and Edgerton, 1969: Ch.4.

    Moreover, alcohol is not necessarily an ingredient of Time Outs. In those societies where alcohol is believed to produce an altered state of consciousness rendering one unresponsible for one's actions, drunkenness is considered as a Time Out. However, in North American society excessive drinking and drunkenness are themselves forms of deviant behaviour (Jessor, *et al.*, 1969). Thus, during ceremonially arranged Time Outs like urban festivals, the state of drunkenness not only serves to legitimate one's deviance, but itself becomes a form of legitimate deviance.

3. This strain and frustration is primarily of the "status" type—the only type theoretically possible because man is conceived as *homo sociologicus* in sociological theory. That is to say, sociological theory is built on an image of man who is a role player, whose existence is determined entirely by social norms and institutions; man is a social actor whose behaviour is normatively regulated and "oriented to anticipated states of affairs such as goals, ends or objectives" (Roach, 1965:70; Dahrendorf, 1961; Hornosty, 1970; Rich, 1966; Wrong, 1961).

    Thus, within the confines of sociological theory it is virtually impossible to deal with frustrations and strains which arise from nonsocial sources, such as overcrowding, malnutrition, etc.

4. The concept of "lower-class" as used in this discussion shall encompass both the lower-lower-class (those below the poverty level) and the upper-lower-class (or working class). It is understood that there are important differences between these two classes, especially with regard to the influence of economic and material conditions and to the relative strength of their respective cultural elements (Gans, 1962; Roach, 1965,

1967; Roach and Gursslin, 1965, 1967). However, the focus of this discussion is upon certain behavioural aspects common to both sub-classes.

The lower-class in this discussion is defined in terms of the patrons of public drinking places which are frequented by blue collar and construction workers, Canadian Forces personnel, the unemployed, welfare recipients, old-age pensioners. Canadian Indians and other ethnic and immigrant groups.

Similarly, the concept of "middle-class" used in this discussion shall include both the lower-middle-class and the upper-middle-class (and/or the "old" and the "new" middle classes, depending upon definition: see Mills, 1951; Kahl, 1957; Nelson, 1968; Boskoff, 1970), as it is only certain behavioural characteristics shared by both sub-classes which are under scrutiny here.

The middle-class in this discussion is defined in terms of the patrons of public drinking places which are frequented by general office and white-collar workers, middle-level professional and executive types, and university and senior high school students.

5. Licentious behaviour refers to behaviour which, by usual puritanical middle-class mores, would be regarded as sexually loose or unrestrained, such as overt sexual gestures in public, indiscriminate fondling and necking, connotations which denote sexual availability, etc. This is the normal meaning of the concept and this is the way Cavan (1966) uses it.

6. One particular lounge, located in the city's oldest and poshest hotel, was normally characterized by an upper-middle-class clientele. For the Grey Cup, however, the hotel was the "festival headquarters," thus attracting great crowds to its facilities, and thus diversifying the usual class composition of the lounge.

7. The wearing of Saskatchewan colours was not adopted totally out of devious designs, for the researchers were from the West (Manitoba and Saskatchewan) and were hoping the Roughriders would defeat the Tiger-Cats. Unfortunately, our hopes were not realized. The Tiger-Cats won the game on a last second field-goal.

8. These concepts are taken from Sherri Cavan's classic, ethnography of bar behaviour, *Liquor License*. Standing patterns of behaviour "define for the actor what activity can take place as a matter of course and without question, and for what conduct those present will be held accountable. They may further delimit who is or is not eligible to enter a given setting, the ways the routine tasks are to be distributed, the varieties of reputations that can be accorded to those entering, the kinds of fates that can be alloted to those present and the like" (Cavan, 1966:3).

   Her study illustrates that public drinking places, even though they have a Time Out atmosphere, have standing patterns of behaviour which are "both routinely expected within the setting and treated as fitting and proper for the time and place" (Cavan, 1966:7). Because such establishments are Time Out settings in which the usual formality and repression of social life is somewhat relaxed, the range of permissable behaviour and "normal trouble" (that is, "improper activities which are frequent enough to be simply shrugged off or ignored" Cavan, 1966:18) is of greater latitude than in other public settings. The concepts of normal trouble and permissible behaviour are equivalent to our concept of legitimate deviance. The deviance legitimated in bars is not of the same magnitude as during conventionalized Time Out rituals.

9. Cavan (1966:112-113) refers to round-buying as "treating," and elaborates a number of functions to this ritual. Those functions relevant to this discussion at this point are the "binding together temporarily patrons in an ongoing encounter by establishing a set of mutual obligations between them," and "Formalizing the change in relationship between two patrons from interactants to ephemeral acquaintances" (1966: 113, see also pp. 184-186).

10. Because of the openness of patrons and the limited nature of encounters in bar settings, it is possible for an individual to pass himself off to others as almost anything he wants with little fear of exposure either in the present or in the future. See Cavan, (1966: 79-87.)

11. In those places which had no provision for dancing, that is, which had no dance floor, patrons danced in the aisles and between tables, and sometimes on the tables.

12. Although it was not possible to test the functions of the Grey Cup on the national level, it is possible to say a few things. The Grey Cup is said to unite Canada by making Canadians think in terms of East-West and to stir up nationalistic cultural sentiments. To some extent it does do this via the great media exposure and the people travelling to the host city. However, it is a strange nationalism that is fostered, for it is based on a game that is English in origin and American in development and commercialization, and whose stars and heroes and coaches are imported from the United States. Top players are continually playing out the option clause in their contract in order to move "up" to the American professional leagues. Even the commitment of the Canadian Football League itself to Canada is questionable considering the recent debate over expansion into the United States and the relative lack of programs to develop Canadian talent.

13. Those who recognize the existence of an operative cultural system in the lower-class use it as an explanatory device, e.g., the "culture of poverty" group (e.g., Harrington, 1962; Riessman, 1962; Will and Vatter, 1965) and the subcultural delinquency school (e.g. Cohen, 1955; Cloward and Ohlin, 1960). However, they deal only with the upper-lower or working-class and ignore the differences between the working-class and the lower-lower class. The lower-lower-class is characterized by physical frustrations rather than status frustration and a weak normative system which is determined by the harsh economic and material conditions in which it exists (Roach and Gursslin, 1965, 1967).

The working-class, because of its relatively less oppressive economic and material conditions, is able to develop more status concern, to focus more of its frustration, and thus, to develop a stronger cultural system through interaction in subcultures. Yet, to treat working-class culture as reactive or as a shadow or as value-stretched is also a distortion which ignores the physical conditions of the working-class and the fact that the culture itself has been interpreted as a traditional cultural system with a unique set of values developed over many generations (e.g., Miller, 1958, 1959).

REFERENCES

Akers, Ronald L.
1964   "Socio-economic status and delinquent behaviour: a retest." *Journal of Research on Crime and Delinquency*, 1 (January).
1968   "Problems in the sociology of deviance: social definitions and behaviour." *Social Forces*, 46, (June).

Batten, Jack
1972   "Will the Canadian Football League survive?" *Maclean's*, 86 (October).

Beneson, Harold and Eric Lessinger
1970   "Are workers becoming middle-class?" In Tom Christoffel, *et al.* (eds.), *Up Against the American Myth.* New York: Holt, Rinehart, Winston.

Bensman, Joseph and Israel Gerver
1963   "Crime and punishment in the factory: the function of deviance in maintaining the social system." *American Sociological Review*, 28 (August).

Berger, Bennett
1960   *Working Class Suburb: A Study of Auto Workers in Suburbia.* Berkeley: University of California Press.

Birnbaum, Norman
1953   "Monarchs and sociologists." *Sociological Review*, 2.

Blumer, Herbert
1954   "What is wrong with social theory?" *American Sociological Review*, 19 (February). ary).

Boskoff, Alvin
1970   The Sociology of Urban Regions. 2nd ed. New York: Appleton-Century-Crofts.

Cahnman, Werner
1969   "The stigma of obesity." Sociological Quarterly, 9 (Summer).

Cavan. Sherri
1966   Liquor License: An Ethnography of Bar Behaviour. Chicago: Aldine.

Christoffel, Tom, David Finkelhor, and Dan Gilbarg (eds.)
1970   Up Against the American Myth. New York: Holt, Rinehart, Winston.

Clinard, Marshall B.
1962   "The public drinking house in society." In D. J. Pitman and C. R. Synder (eds.),
        Alcohol, Culture and Drinking Patterns. New York: John Wiley.
1965   The Sociology of Deviant Behaviour. New York: Holt, Rinehart, Winston.

Cloward, Richard A. and Lloyd L. Ohlin
1960   Delinquency and Opportunity. New York: Free Press.

Cohen, Albert K.
1955   Delinquent Boys. New York: Free Press.

Cosentino, Frank
1969   Canadian Football: The Grey Cup Years. Toronto: Musson.

Coser, Lewis A.
1967   "Some functions of deviant behaviour and normative flexibility." In Lewis A.
        Coser. Continuities in the Study of Social Conflict. New York: Free Press.

Currie, Gordon
1968   100 Years of Canadian Football. Toronto: Pagurian Press.

Dahrendorf, Ralf
1961   "Democracy without liberty." In Seymour M. Lipset and Leo Lowenthal (eds.),
        Culture and Social Character: The Work of David Riesman Revisited. New York:
        Free Press.

Davis, Kingsley
1966   "Sexual behaviour." In Robert K. Merton and Robert A. Nisbet (eds.), Contempo-
        rary Social Problems. New York: Harcourt, Brace & World.

DeLamater, John
1968   "On the nature of deviance." Social Forces, 46 (June).

Dentler, Robert A. and Kai T. Erickson
1959   "The functions of deviance in groups." Social Problems, 7 (Fall).

Douglas, Jack D.
1970   "Deviance and order in a pluralistic society." In John C. McKinney and Edward A.
        Tiryakian (eds.), Theoretical Sociology: Perspectives and Developments. New York:
        Appleton-Century-Crofts.

Dumont, L.
1960   "World renunciations in Indian religions." Contributions to Indian Sociology, 4.

Elliot, Delbert S.
1962   "Delinquency and perceived opportunity." Sociological Inquiry, 32 (Spring).

Empey, LaMar T.
1956   "Social class and occupational aspiration: a comparison of absolute and relative
        measurement." American Sociological Review, 21 (December).

Empey, LaMar T. and Maynard L. Erickson
1966   "Hidden delinquency and social status." Social Forces, 44 (June).

Erickson, Kai T.
1964   "Notes on the sociology of deviance." In Howard S. Becker (ed.), The Other Side:
        Perspectives on Deviance. New York: Free Press.
1966   Wayward Puritans. New York: John Wiley.

Filstead, William (ed.).
1970   Qualitative Methodology: Firsthand Involvement with the Social World. Chicago: Markham.

Fisher, Charles S.
1972   "Observing a crowd: the structure and description of protest demonstrations." In Jack D. Douglas (ed.), Research on Deviance. New York: Random House.

Frank, Andre Gunder
1966   "Functionalism, dialects and synthesis." Science and Society, 30 (Spring).
1967   "Sociology of development and the underdevelopment of sociology." Catalyst, 3 (Summer).

Gans, Herbert J.
1962   The Urban Villagers. New York: Free Press.

Gibbons, Don C. and Joseph F. Jones
1971   "Some critical notes on current definitions of deviance." Pacific Sociological Review, 14 (January).

Gibbs, Jack
1966   "Conceptions of deviant behaviour: the old and the new." Pacific Sociological Review, 9 (Spring).

Green, Arnold W.
1946   "The middle-class male child and neurosis." American Sociological Review, 11.

Harper, Dean and Frederick Emmert
1963   "Work behaviour in a service industry." Social Forces, 42 (December).

Harrington, Michael
1962   The Other America. New York: Macmillan.

Hartogs, Renatus with Hans Fantel
1967   Four-Letter Word Games: The Psychology of Obscenity. New York: Dell.

Hirschi, Travis
1969   Causes of Delinquency. Berkeley: University of California Press.

Hodges, Harold M. Jr.
1970   "Peninsula people: social stratification in a metropolitan complex." In Robert Gutman and David Popenoe (eds.), Neighborhood, City, and Metropolis. New York: Random House.

Homans, George D.
1964   "Contemporary theory in sociology." In Robert E. L. Faris (ed.), Handbook in Modern Sociology. Chicago: Rand McNally.

Horonosty, Roy W.
1970   "The development of sociological theory and the delinquencies of man." Paper presented at the sixth annual meetings of the Canadian Sociology and Anthropology Association, Winnipeg, Manitoba.

Hunter, V. Dianne
1969   "The Semi-Legal Drinking Place: Its Characteristics and Functions as a Reflection of the Social Structure." Unpublished M.A. thesis, University of Calgary, Calgary.

Hyman, Herbert H.
1953   "The value system of different classes: a social psychological contribution to the analysis of stratification." In Reinhard Bendix and Seymour M. Lipset (eds.), Class, Status and Power. New York: Free Press.

Jessor, Richard, Theodore D. Graves, Robert C. Hanson, and Shirley L. Jessor
1968   Society, Personality and Deviant Behaviour. New York: Holt, Rinehart, Winston.

Kahl, Joseph A.
1957   The American Class Structure. New York: Holt, Rinehart, Winston.

Kohn, Melvin L.
1969   Class and Conformity: A Study in Values. Homewood, Ill.: Dorsey Press.
1972   "Class, family, and schizophrenia: a reformulation." Social Forces, 50 (March).

Kolko, Gabriel
1962   Wealth and Power in America: An Analysis of Social Class and Income Distribution. New York: Praeger.

Lachenmeyer, Charles
1971   The Language of Sociology. New York: Columbia University Press.

Largey, Gale Peter and David Rodney Watson
1972   "The sociology of odors." American Journal of Sociology, 77 (May).

Lipset, Seymour M.
1963   Political Man. Garden City, N.Y.: Doubleday.

Listiak, Alan
1971   "Alienation: the failure of a concept and the failure of positivistic sociology." Paper presented at the thirteenth annual meetings of the Western Association of Sociology and Anthropology, Calgary, Alberta.

MacAndrew, Craig and Robert B. Edgerton
1969   Drunken Comportment: A Social Explanation. Don Mills, Ont.: Thomas Nelson.

Miller, Walter B.
1958   "Lower-class culture as a generating milieu of gang delinquency." Journal of Social Issues, 14.
1959   "Implications of urban lower-class culture for social work." Social Service Review, 33 (September).

Mills, C. Wright
1951   White Collar. New York. Oxford University Press.
1959   The Sociological Imagination. New York: Oxford University Press.

Mizruchi, Ephraim Harold
1964   Success and Opportunity. New York: Free Press.
1967   "Aspiration and poverty: a neglected aspect of Merton's anomie." Sociological Quarterly, 8 (Autumn).

Nelson, Joel I.
1968   "Anomie: comparisons between the old and new middle-class." American Journal of Sociology, 74 (September).

Newman, P. L.
1964   "Wild man behaviour in a New Guinea highlands community." American Anthropologist, 66.

Nossiter, Bernard D.
1964   The Mythmakers. New York: Houghton Mifflin.

Ossenberg, Richard J.
1969   "Social class and bar behaviour during an urban festival." Human Organization, 28 (Spring).

Park, Peter
1969   Sociology Tomorrow. New York: Pegasus.

Polsky, Ned
1967   Hustlers, Beats and Others. Chicago: Aldine.

Quinn, James A.
1955   Urban Sociology. New York: American Book Co.

Rainwater, Lee
1960   And the Poor Get Children. Chicago: Quadrangle Books.

Reissman, Frank
1962   The Culturally Deprived Child. New York: Harper & Bros.

Rich, Harvey
1966   "Homo Sociologic and personality theory." Canadian Review of Sociology and Anthropology, 3 (August).

Roach, Jack L.
1965   "Sociological analysis and poverty." American Journal of Sociology, 71 (July).

1967   "Toward a theory of lower-class culture." In Llewellyn Gross (ed.), *Sociological Theory: Inquiries and Paradigms*. New York Harper and Row.

Roach, Jack L. and Orville R. Gursslin
1965   "The lower-class, status frustration, and social disorganization." *Social Forces*, 43 (May).
1967   "An evaluation of the concept culture of poverty." *Social Forces*, 45 (March).

Romano, Paul
1970   "Life on the job." In Tom Christoffel, *et. al.* (eds.), *Up Against the American Myth*. New York: Holt Rinehart, Winston.

Sagarin, Edward
1962   *The Anatomy of Dirty Words*. New York: Lyle Stuart.

Sewell, William H.
1961   "Social class and childhood personality." *Sociometry*, 24 (December).

Shils, Edward and Michael Young
1953   "The meaning of the coronation." *Sociological Review*, 1 (December).

Short, James F., Jr., Ramon Rivera, and Ray A. Tennyson
1965   "Perceived opportunities, gang membership and delinquency." *American Sociological Review*, 30 (February).

Shostak, Arthur B.
1969   *Blue-Collar Life*. New York: Random House.

Shostak, Arthur B. and William Gomberg (eds.).
1964   *Blue-Collar World*. Englewood Cliffs, N.J.: Prentice-Hall.

Smith, Dusky Lee
1971   "The Sunshine Boys: toward a sociology of happiness." In J. David Colfax and Jack L. Roach (eds.), *Radical Sociology*, New York: Basic Books.

Smith, Thomas S.
1968   "Conventionalization and control: an examination of adolescent crowds." *American Journal of Sociology*, 74 (September).

Spiller, Bertram
1965   "Delinquency and middle-class goals." *Journal of Criminal Law, Criminology and Police Science*, 56.

Stinchcombe, Arthur L.
1968   *Constructing Social Theories*. New York: Harcourt, Brace & World

Stoddard, Ellwyn R.
1968   "The 'informal code' of police deviance: a group approach to 'blue-coat crime'." *Journal of Criminal Law, Criminology and Police Science*, 59 (June).

Sullivan, Jack
1970   *The Grey Cup Story*. Toronto: Pagurian Press.

Turner, Ralph H. and Lewis M. Killian
1957   *Collective Behaviour*. Englewood Cliffs, N.J.: Prentice-Hall.

Vaz, Edmund W. (ed.)
1967   *Middle-Class Juvenile Delinquency*. New York: Harper and Row.

Voss, Harwin L.
1966   "Socio-economic status and reported delinquent behaviour." *Social Problems*, 13 (Winter).

Will, Robert E. and Harold G. Vatter (eds.)
1965   *Poverty in Affluence*. New York: Harcourt, Brace & World.

Willer, David
1967   *Scientific Sociology*. Englewood Cliffs, N.J.: Prentice-Hall.

Wilson, Alan B.
1959   "Residential segregation of social classes and aspirations of high school boys." *American Sociological Review*, 24 (December).

Winslow, Robert W.
1968   "Anomie and its alternatives: a self-report study of delinquency." *Sociological Quarterly,* (Fall).

Wrong, Dennis
1961   "The oversocialized conception of man in modern sociology." *American Sociological Review*, 26 (April).

Zetterberg, Hans L.
1965   *On Theory and Verification in Sociology*. Totowa, N.J.: Bedminster Press.